해설로 짜는 전략의 적용,

해설주의 토익
실전 모의고사 RC

해설주의 토익 실전 모의고사 RC 5회분

지은이 김병기
초판 1쇄 인쇄 2018년 3월 9일
초판 1쇄 발행 2018년 3월 23일

발행인 박효상 **총괄이사** 이종선 **편집장** 김현 **기획 · 편집** 김효정, 김설아 **디자인** 김보연
표지디자인 물질과비물질 **조판** 조영라
마케팅 이태호, 이전희 **관리** 김태옥

종이 월드페이퍼 **인쇄 · 제본** 현문자현

출판등록 제10-1835호 **발행처** 사람in **주소** 121-839 서울시 마포구 양화로 11길 14-10 (서교동) 4F
전화 02) 338-3555(代) **팩스** 02) 338-3545
E-mail saramin@netsgo.com **Homepage** www.saramin.com

책값은 뒤표지에 있습니다.
파본은 바꾸어 드립니다.

ISBN
978-89-6049-659-0 14740
978-89-6049-658-3 (세트)

사람이 중심이 되는 세상, 세상과 소통하는 책 **사람in**

해설주의 토익
실전 모의고사 RC

김병기 저

사람In
saram
in.com

그리스 신화 속에 등장하는 이카루스는 아버지인 다이달로스가 발명한 날개를 달고 하늘을 날았지만 태양을 향해 너무 높이 날아 오른 탓에 날개를 붙인 밀랍이 녹아 안타깝게 추락하고 만다.

이카루스의 모습에서 TOEIC 고득점에 실패하는 자들의 모습이 반영된다면 지나친 억측일까. 누구나 처음 TOEIC 수험서를 구매할 때의 결심과 열정은 경외심이 들 만큼 순수하고 대단하다. 하지만 얼마 지나지 않아 마치 태양빛에 녹아 사라지는 눈과 같은 그 순수한 열정은 마치 이카루스의 날개를 이어 붙인 밀랍과도 같다. 언제 추락할지 모른다.

노력과 성실함이 뒷받침되지 않은 열정만 가지고서는 결코 높이 도약할 수 없다. 나의 밀랍이 얼마 가지 못하는 열정만으로 구성되었다면 나의 추락은 예정된 것이다.

TOEIC 고득점이란 쇠는 자고로 탄탄한 기본기라는 불구덩이에서 달궈지고, 최신 TOEIC의 경향이 제대로 반영된 문제라는 망치로 두들겨 맞고, 노력과 성실함이란 물에 푸욱 빠져봐야 비로소 제법 여물어 나오는 쇠붙이와 같은 존재다.

TOEIC에서 고득점에 번번이 실패하는 이유, 혹은 내가 원하는, 현재의 내 실력보다는 조금 높은 듯한 바로 그 목표 점수에 도달하지 못하는 이유, 각자가 원하는 선에서 TOEIC을 정복하지 못하는 이유는 바로 이러한 TOEIC 장인의 생산 과정을 거치지 못하는 데 있지 않았던가?

필자의 모의토익 RC 5세트는 신토익으로 바뀐 이후 출제 경향을 치밀하게 분석한 땀과 고민의 산물이다. 신내림을 받아 작두를 타는 것처럼 이 안에서 여러분은 한 해의 TOEIC이 어떻게 출제되고 바뀌는지 그 흐름을 익힐 수 있을 것임을 자부한다.

본서는 여러분의 기본기로 달궈진 TOEIC을 힘차게 두들기며 다듬는 풀무질의 역할을 할 것이며, 그 와중에 여러분도 마치 격렬한 노역을 하듯 맑고 정직한 땀으로 범벅이 된 스스로의 모습에 놀라게 될 것이다. 그러다보면 어느새 인가 자신의 노력과 성실함 속에서 잘 벼려진 쇠붙이와 같은 여러분만의 TOEIC 고득점을 비로소 볼 수 있지 않겠는가.

쉽지는 않을 수 있겠지만 원하는 점수는 결코 편안하게 만들어지지 않는다. 여러분이 TOEIC에 대해 느끼는 답답함과 자괴감이 일요일 늦은 오후에 술잔을 비운다고 가뭇없이 사라질까.

다가올 정기 TOEIC에서 여러분의 건승을 기원하며.

김병기

문제지

Actual Test 1

Actual Test 2

Actual Test 3

Actual Test 4

Actual Test 5

해설지

Actual Test 1

Actual Test 2

Actual Test 3

Actual Test 4

Actual Test 5

PART 1

	신토익	구토익
유형	사진 묘사	사진 묘사
문항수	총 6문항	총 10문항

사진을 묘사하는 4개의 보기가 등장하는 유형 유지

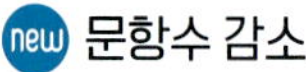 문항수 감소

PART 2

	신토익	구토익
유형	질의 응답	질의 응답
문항수	총 25문항	총 30문항

질문에 대한 적절한 응답을 찾는 유형은 유지

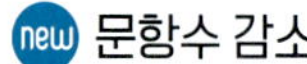 문항수 감소

PART 3

	신토익	구토익
유형	짧은 대화	짧은 대화
문항수	13개 대화(대화당 3문항) 총 39문항	10개 대화(대화당 3문항) 총 30문항

new 3명의 화자가 대화를 나누는 신유형 추가

new 대화와 문항수 증가

PART 4

	신토익	구토익
유형	설명문	설명문
문항수	10개 설명문(설명문당 3문항) 총 30문항	10개 설명문(설명문당 3문항) 총 30문항

new 제시된 정보를 참고하는 신유형 추가

PART 5

	신토익	구토익
유형	단문 공란 채우기	단문 공란 채우기
문항수	총 30문항	총 40문항

단문에 있는 공란에 적절한 단어/표현을 채우는 유형 유지

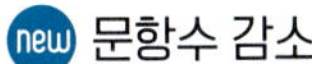 문항수 감소

PART 6

	신토익	구토익
유형	장문 공란 채우기	장문 공란 채우기
문항수	총 16문항	총 12문항

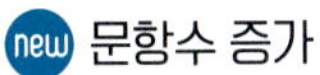 문제 형태 변화

문항수 증가

PART 7

	신토익	구토익
유형	단일 지문	단일 지문
문항수	10개 단일 지문 지문당 2–4문항 총 29문항	9개 단일 지문 지문당 2–5문항 총 28문항
유형	이중 지문	이중 지문
문항수	2개 세트 지문 세트당 5문항 총 10문항	4개 세트 지문 세트당 5문항 총 20문항
유형	삼중 지문	
문항수	3개 세트 지문 세트당 5문항 총 15문항	
문항수	총 54문항	총 48문항

신유형인 삼중 지문 유형 추가

기존 독해 문제 풀이 방식 유지

문항수 증가

Questions 131-134 refer to the following information.

The Haru Battery you have purchased was designed to last for approximately three years or about 30,000 miles. When your battery finally dies, you should dispose of it ------- **131.** Please do not just throw it in a trash can. Most municipalities currently recommend users not ------- **132.** their dead batteries away with trash.

Most experts say discarded batteries can cause fires and explosions if they ------- **133.** loose in boxes or bags with metal items. That's why our company offers a quick and easy disposal method to customers. ------- **134.** When you turn them over to us, our recycling specialists take care of them in the proper fashion at no additional charge.

131. (A) immediately
(B) properly
(C) confidentially
(D) respectively

132. (A) throw
(B) to throw
(C) throwing
(D) thrown

133. (A) stores
(B) are stored
(C) stored
(D) will be stored

134. (A) Some batteries left in your garage can cause several safety concerns.
(B) Please do not combine old and new batteries or different types or makes of batteries.
(C) New small-size batteries are used in mobile phones and motor-driven electric tools.
(D) All you have to do is return your dead battery to one of our recycling centers in your area.

기출 난이도를 반영한 신토익
최신 경향 반영 문제

To: Nancy Palosi <npalosi@millerco.com>
From: David Thornbush <guestservice@grandritz.com>
Date: September 11
Subject: Your requests for Ms. Falcone and Mr. Stern

[183] This is a confirmation of the reservation you made over the phone last week for Ms. Carmina Falcone and Mr. Daniel Stern at the Grand Ritz Hotel. [185A/C] Two single rooms have been booked on the executive floor. All their business needs will be met inside their rooms. [185B] Each room is equipped with a computer with Internet access, a printer, and a fax machine. I received the package that was sent by courier from your company in Seattle. It will be placed in Ms. Falcone's room when she arrives.

[184] As Mr. Stern is arriving around 10 A.M., I have arranged an early check-in time of 10:30 A.M. free of charge. [185] Mr. Stern and Ms. Falcone will have full use of conference room C at 2 P.M. on the day of their arrival. Conference room C is located on basement level one. [185] We have also reserved a special dinner for our two guests at our hotel restaurant, The Olive. The meals will be charged to the guests' account. If you have any other questions at all about their stay, please contact us before their arrival, and I am sure we can assist you with any request you might have. Thank you.

Mina Sohn
Service Manager
Grand Ritz Hotel, El Paso

수신: Nancy Palosi <npalosi@millerco.com>
발신: David Thornbush <guestservice@grandritz.com>
날짜: 9월 11일
제목: Falcone 씨와 Stern 씨에 대한 요청사항

[183] 지난 주 Grand Ritz 호텔에 유선상으로 하신 Carmina Falcone 씨와 Daniel Stern 씨의 예약 건에 대한 확인 메일입니다. [185A/C] 두 개의 1인실이 귀빈층에 예약되어 있을 것입니다. 모든 사무용 집기들이 객실 안에 있을 것입니다. [185B] 각 객실들은 인터넷 사용이 가능한 컴퓨터, 프린터, 그리고 팩스기기를 갖추고 있습니다. 저는 시애틀에 있는 귀사에서 택배 회사를 통해 보내신 소포를 받았습니다. 그것을 팔콘 씨가 도착하면 받으실 수 있도록 객실에 가져다 두겠습니다.

[184] Stern 씨가 거의 오전 10시에 도착하시기 때문에, 입실시간을 10시 30분으로 추가비용이 없이 정해놓았습니다. [185] Stern 씨와 Falcone 씨는 도착 당일 오후 2시부터 C 회의실을 단독으로 사용하실 수 있습니다. C 회의실은 지하 1층에 위치해 있습니다. [185] 저희는 또한 두 분을 위해 호텔식당인 The Olive에 특별 저녁식사를 준비해놓았습니다. 식사비는 두 분의 객실 요금에 청구될 것입니다. 두 분의 숙박에 대해 문의가 있으시면, 두 분이 도착하시기 전에 미리 연락을 주시면 어떠한 요청사항에 대해서도 도와드릴 것을 약속드립니다. 감사합니다.

Mina Sohn
서비스 담당자
Grand Ritz Hotel, El Paso

1. 스크립트 해석 및 단서 확인

해당 스크립트 해석 및 문제의
단서를 통하여 지문을 분석한다.

2. 문제 해설

해당 문제에 대한 깊이 있고
적확한 해설을 통해 출제 의도를
이해한다.

3. 문제 분석

문제의 구조적 분석을 통한
방향성 있는 접근을 제시한다.

4. 토익 분석

해당 문제의 출제 경향을 포함한
전반적인 신토익 문제 경향 및
풀이법을 파악한다.

NEW TOEIC READING 부분의 출제 경향을 반영한 대비책을 간결하게 정리하여 제시하자면, 파트 5와 파트 6에서는 '자잘한 실수를 범하지 않도록 주의하자'와 '빈출 어휘와 서로 짝을 이루는 어휘에 집중하자', 그리고 파트 7은 '어려운 독해를 위해 많은 시간을 투자하자'라고 할 수 있겠다.

그렇다면 과연 이러한 제안이 구체적으로 의미하는 바와 NEW TOEIC 고득점 대비에 유의해야 할 주요 내용들에 어떤 것들이 있을지 체계적으로 정리하고자 하니, 여러분이 이를 추후 정기토익 READING 분야에서 약진을 위한 초석으로 삼아준다면 강사로써 이만한 보람된 일도 없을 것이라 생각한다.

Part 5

파트 5에서의 기본 유형은 여전히 1) 품사 및 어형 2) 어법 3) 어휘 부분으로 나뉘어서 출제가 되고 있으며, 이전 토익에 비해 문항 수가 10문항이 감소했지만 출제 비율을 보자면 여전히 이 세 가지 분야는 비교적 균등하게 다뤄지고 있다고 할 수 있다. 물론 어법(40%)에 비해 품사 및 어형 문제와 어휘 부분(60%)에 대한 출제 비중이 상대적으로 약간 높은 편이라 할 수 있다. 품사와 어형을 다루는 문제는 매회 평균 10문항이 출제되고 있는데, 처음 파트 5의 학습을 시작할 때 영어 문장이 구성되는 어순 및 품사별 전개 방식을 열심히 공부해 두면 품사와 어형 문제에 있어 지속적인 만점이 가능하며 아울러 문법 학습과 빠른 독해에도 큰 도움이 된다는 점 잊지 말았으면 한다.

신토익 파트 5도 예년에 비해 큰 변화 없이 주로 반복적으로 출제되는 소재들이 계속해서 등장한다. 구체적으로 동사의 수 / 태 / 시제 문제부터 소유격 대명사를 포함한 인칭 대명사, 상관접속사, 명사절 / 형용사절 / 부사절 접속사, 부정사, 동명사, 동명사가 아닌 Ing 명사, 부정대명사, 수량사, 비교구문에 이르는 내용과 연관된 어법 문제들이 출제되는 상황이라 할 수 있다. 다시 말해, 출제 경향이 주로 반복 출제되는 어법 아이템 중심으로 굳혀져있는 만큼, 해당 부분의 기본 어법 개념 정리를 꼼꼼하게 익힌 후, 기출 유형의 문제를 최대한 많이 풀어가며, 문제가 묻는 요지가 어법의 어느 부분을 집중적으로 테스팅하려는지, 빠른 시간 내에 문제를 파악하는 혜안을 넓힘과 동시에 자잘하고도 생각이 없는 실수를 최대한 줄이는 방향으로 대비하는 것이 가장 바람직하다고 본다. 즉, 난이도가 크게 높아졌다고 할 수 없는 상황에서 문항 수는 감소되었기 때문에 완전 고득점을 노리지 않는다면 기본에 충실한 학습을 통해 소위 말하는 '반복되는 실수(?)'를 줄이는 것이 매우 중요하게 되었다는 것이다.

어휘 부문에서도 출제비중에 있어서는 기존의 출제방식, 즉 기출 어휘 정답 90% 새로운 어휘 정답 10%의 비율도 비슷하게 지켜졌다. 이를테면 이전 구 토익에서도 단적으로 sequence나 excursion처럼 예년에 자주 출제되지 않았던 새로운 어휘가 소개되면서 많은 토익 응시생들의 감점 폭을 대폭 키워준 바 있으며, 뿐만 아니라 compromise나 deteriorating과 같이 이전 토익에서 자주 접하지 못했던 어휘들이 등장하여 토익 응시생들이 당황했던 적도 있지만, 그렇다고 해도 여전히 기존 어휘의 출제 비중이 새로운 어휘의 출제 비중을 압도하고 있는 경향에는 변화가 없다.

신토익에서도 shortcomings, exhaustive와 같이 새로운 어휘가 출제되었으며 이를 처음 접하게 되는 경우 당연히 한 번 정도 틀릴 순 있지만 어차피 한 번 제대로 야무지게 익히고 나면 그 이후에는 해당 어휘가 출제될 때 틀릴 일이 거의 없는 어휘 문제 풀이의 속성상 정기토익을 한 번만 볼 것이 아니라면 처음 제시되는 어휘에 대해 지나치게 우려하는 것은 기우에 가깝다. 따라서 기존 기출 어휘를 중심으로 학습하되 어휘는 항상 같이 뭉쳐서 사용되는 연어들을 묻는 경우도 빈번하므로 이에 대해 대비하는 것이 기존 어휘 문제에서 좋은 성적을 거둘 수 있는 지름길임을 알아두자. 예컨대 동사 recommend, qualified, responsible은 부사 highly와 같이 가고, 동사 assort, organize는 부사 alphabetically와 함께 가고, 명사 information은 형용사 confidential, sensitive 또는 useful과 함께 쓰이며, 명사 survey, research, data, report 등은 그 내용을 suggest, show, indicate하며, 동사 inspect, examine은 부사 thoroughly를, 명사 variety, collection, selection, range, array, diversity는 선택 범위가 넓거나 다양하다는 의미를 구성할 수 있는 형용사 wide와 함께 한다는 방식으로 공부하는 것이 실전 어휘 문제에서 강세를 보일 수 있는 효율적이고 현명한 학습법임을 알아두도록 한다. 그리고 토익은 부사 어휘를 매달 평균 3-4문제씩 출제할 정도로, 다른 품사의 어휘보다 유독 부사 어휘를 광적으로 선호한다는 성향도 알아두면 품사별 어휘 공부에 보탬이 되지 않을까 싶다. 다시 한 번 강조하지만 아무리 많이 익혀도 지나침 없는 분야가 어휘라는 점을 기억하자.

이론적으로 보자면 파트 6도 출제영역이 구조/문법/어휘가 되는데 실제로는 6-8문항 정도의 어휘유형과 1-2개 정도의 구조유형, 3-4개의 문법문제로 구성된다. 여기서 주목해야 할 점은 문법 유형의 문제 중 시제 문제가 거의 대부분이라는 점이다. 이는 신토익으로 바뀐 이후에도 여전히 지속적으로 유지되고 있는 기조이다. 그렇다면 관건은 '어휘와 시제' 이 두 가지인데 어휘야 시간 투자가 필요한 분야지만 시제는 단기간에도 성취가 가능한 영역이므로 기출 유형의 문제를 중심으로, 어떤 식의 시제문제가 출제되고 있는지 확실히 공부를 해 두어야 할 필요가 있다.

파트 6의 시제 문제는 해당 문장에서 시제 단서를 제시하지 않고 문맥을 통한 시점 파악을 토대로 시제 문제를 풀이하는 것이 특징이다. 아울러 신토익으로 바뀌며 새롭게 추가된 빈칸 삽입 유형 문제는 전반적인 지문의 내용적 흐름을 파악해야만 수월하게 풀이할 수 있다. 더군다나 파트 6 지문의 길이가 그다지 긴 편은 아니므로 파트 6은 지문의 내용을 정독하며 주어진 문제를 풀이하고 마지막으로 빈 칸에 적합한 문장의 내용을 선택하는 문제를 해결하는 것이 시간 관리 면에서 효율적이며 관련 문제를 상대적으로 수월하게 풀이할 수 있다.

시제 문제의 정답은 미래 시제(현재 / 현재 진행 포함) – 현재 완료 시제 – 과거 시제 순으로 출제되는 경향이 있음을 알아두면 파트 6의 시제 문제를 풀이할 때 유용하게 활용할 수 있을 것이다. 아마도 미래의 행사 및 회의 혹은 전시회 따위가 편지 및 이메일의 내용으로 자주 등장하기 때문일 것이다. 파트 6에서의 어휘도 크게 다를 것이 없다. 전반적으로 앞서 언급한 파트 5 부분에서의 어휘 학습법에 대한 조언을 참조하도록 하자. 다만 파트 6에서는 접속 부사에 대해서 자주 묻는 경향이 있으므로 평소 인과, 대조, 상반, 역접, 순접, 첨가 등 여러 논리적 연결고리의 역할을 담당하는 접속 부사를 촘촘하게 익혀둘 것을 권고한다.

파트 7의 비중이 예전에 비해 매우 높아졌다. 과거 2008년부터 현재에 이르기까지 난이도 높은 파트 5와 파트 6 문제 출제 비중이 점차 감소해왔으며 심지어 신토익에서는 파트 5와 파트 6의 문항 수가 52문항에서 46문항으로 무려 10문항이나 줄어들었다. 파트 5와 파트 6의 문항수가 대폭 감소한 대신 독해 비중이 현저하게 증가하였으며 결국 독해의 변별력이 토익 응시생들의 최종 점수에 결정적인 영향을 미치는 중요한 요소가 되었다. 물론 문제풀이 순서에는 개인적 선호도로 인한 차이가 존재할 수 있지만, 일반적으로 파트 5와 파트 6을 풀고 남은 제한된 시간에 단일 지문과 이중 지문을 얼마나 많이 풀어내는가, 그리고 신토익과 함께 등장한 삼중지문에 대한 화두와 여기서의 정답 비중이 얼마만큼 되는지가 800점 중반을 넘어서는, 소위 고득점의 핵심이라고 이야기할 수 있게 된 것이다. 그런 까닭에 800점 중반 이후 900점 후반에 이르는 고득점을 목표로 한다면 파트 7에서 상대적으로 배점 비중이 높은 이중 지문과 삼중 지문을 먼저 풀고 나서 단일 지문을 풀이하는 방식을 연습하는 것도 하나의 현명한 방법이라 할 수 있다.

Part 7이란 영역이 어려운 이유를 생각해보면 의외로 그 맥락은 간단하다. 난이도가 전반적으로 평이한 듯 보이는 달은 일부 난이도가 높은 지문으로 인해 시간이 많이 소요되며, 그로 인해 평이한 난이도를 지녔다는 다른 일부 지문들은 손도 제대로 대보지 못하고 접어야 하는 경우가 다반사이기 때문이고, 그렇지 않은 경우라면 출제 지문들의 전체적인 난이도가 동반 상승하면서 토익 응시생들의 리딩 속도 조절, 전체적인 시간 관리, 그리고 문제 풀이 요령/방식에 있어 큰 부담을 안겨주는 속성들을 지니고 있기 때문이다.

신토익 파트 7도 그러한 흐름에서 크게 벗어나지 않는다. 전체적으로 이중 지문과 삼중 지문의 난이도가 상승하는 경향을 보였을 뿐만 아니라 단일 지문의 난이도도 종종 높아졌으며, 이에 덧붙여 살짝 꼬아서 출제되는 문제들까지 등장하게 되면서, 정답을 빨리 찾지 못해 당황한 나머지 시간을 많이 허비하는 경우도 있었다. 그 뿐만 아니다. 추론 문제나 시간을 많이 요구하는 사실 여부를 확인하는 진위 문제(TRUE/NOT TRUE)들도 적잖이 출제되었고 덧붙여 신토익에서 새로 등장한 지문과 문제 유형들은 이래저래 토익 응시생들에게 크나큰 부담으로 다가왔다고 해도 과언이 아니다. 더 안타까운 것은 이러한 고난이도 파트 7이란 경향, 이제 토익 RC의 최종 점수를 결정하는 파트 7이라는 흐름은 일시적인 현상이나 난이도 조절에서 초래된 현상이 아니라 신토익의 정석적인 추세로 자리를 굳힌 상황이라는 점에 있다.

이렇게 어려운 파트 7의 시대를 살아가는 우리에게 있어 지나친 잡설과 스킬에 대한 선호는 철 지난 우상에 불과하며, 굳이 필요하다면 이는 기본적인 독해력을 탄탄하게 갖춘 이후에, 정답율 향상을 위한 약간의 보조적인 도움으로 활용하는 선에서 만족해야 한다. 리딩과 문법 이해에 대한 기본기가 부실한데 파트 7에서 잡설과 스킬을 제대로 활용할 수 있을 것 같은가? 도리어 잡설과 스킬 내용을 익히다가 날이 새고 만다. 잡설과 스킬도 이를 실제 지문 내용 파악과 문제 풀이에 응용시키고 적용시키는 힘이 필요하다.

이제 고득점의 핵심은 파트 7이다. 파트 7 독해 영역이라는 분야가 파트 5과 파트 6처럼 문제를 예상하는 것이 가능하지도 않을뿐더러, 단순하게 강의나 교재에만 의존해서는 단기간에 고득점의 성취를 쉽게 이뤄낼 수 있는 영역이 결코 아니기 때문이다. 더군다나 지문을 읽고 이해를 할 수 있더라도 시간이 오래 걸리면 무용지물이기 때문에 제한된 시간에 지문을 빨리 읽고 정리할 수 있는 능력도 길러내야 한다. 결국 다양한 글을 많이 읽고 내공을 쌓는 것이 유일한 방법인데, 본서에 등장하는 지문들은 실제 기출의 경향과 자주 언급되는 어휘 / 표현을 익히기에 최적화되어 있는 자료라는 점에 주목해 보자. 이를 잘 활용하는 것은 고난도 파트 7의 시대를 살아가는 토익 응시생들에게 있어 선택이 아니라 필수라는 점은 재삼재사 강조해도 지나침이 없겠다.

물론 여기서 독해에 시간을 많이 투자하라는 제안은 단순하게 문제를 많이 풀어보자는 수준이 아니다. 문제를 풀었으면 복습할 때는 몰랐던 단어와 표현 혹은 문장들이 있었을 테니 그 부분을 완전 암기 혹은 이해할 수 있을 때까지 학습을 하라는 것이다. 수박의 겉을 핥아서 어찌 그 단물을 먹을 수 있겠는가? 또한 지문을 읽을 때는 너무 빠른 속도로 정리 없이 "그냥" 읽어 내리는 것을 경계해야 한다. 영어건 한글이건 어떤 글을 읽었을 때는 최소한 단락별로 어떤 전개가 되고 있는지 정도는 정리를 하면서 읽어야 질문에 대해 답을 할 수가 있는데 시간에 쫓겨 빠르게 글을 읽게 되면 내용 정리가 되지 않으니 어차피 지문을 재삼재사 반복해서 읽어야 한다. 시간이 부족한 것은 학습량이 부족해서 그러한 것이니 본서의 지문들을 한 회씩 소화할 때마다 그에 따른 어휘와 표현을 잘 숙지하고, 문제 유형에 따른 풀이 방식을 반복 연습하며, 각 지문의 주제와 문단별 핵심 내용, 그리고 문제에서 묻는 세부적인 사항을 빠르게 파악하고자 노력하는 자세가 추가된다면, 회차를 거듭할수록 점차 빨라지는 본인의 독해 및 문제풀이 속도, 그리고 정답율의 향상을 직접 체험하게 될 것임을 확신한다.

정기토익을 맞이하는 여러분의 건투와 건승을 기원한다.

정릉 4동 연구실에서

김병기

READING TEST

In the Reading test, you will read a variety of texts and answer several different types of reading comprehension questions. The entire Reading test will last 75 minutes. There are three parts, and directions are given for each part. You are encouraged to answer as many questions as possible within the time allowed.

You must mark your answers on the separate answer sheet. Do not write your answers in your test book.

PART 5

Directions: A word or phrase is missing in each of the sentences below. Four answer choices are given below each sentence. Select the best answer to complete the sentence. Then mark the letter (A), (B), (C), or (D) on your answer sheet.

101. Ms. McGowan has been ------- recommended by some of her former employers.
(A) high　　　　(B) higher
(C) highest　　　(D) highly

102. Mr. Chandler said during ------- press briefing that the market deserves freedom, but should respect its responsibility as well.
(A) he
(B) his
(C) him
(D) himself

103. Our stocks usually benefit ------- the so–called January effect that causes the price of these stocks to rise between December and January.
(A) of
(B) since
(C) from
(D) within

104. BK Technology's new accounting software makes it ------- than before for companies to create their financial statements.
(A) easy　　　　(B) easier
(C) ease　　　　(D) more easily

105. KS Electronics has overcome the economic depression by ------- some of their manufacturing plants in Eastern European countries.
(A) close
(B) closing
(C) closed
(D) closes

106. ------- we have to travel to Seoul for business, we will need to consult with our travel agent as quickly as possible.
(A) Whether
(B) But
(C) Even though
(D) If

107. When ------- moved into the new apartment last year, it was not fully completed.
(A) they
(B) them
(C) their
(D) themselves

108. Next month, the government ------- a set of measures to stimulate the sluggish economy and create jobs in the short term.
(A) announcing
(B) will announce
(C) announced
(D) is announced

109. Employees who want to get reimbursed for their travel ------- should submit original receipts to the accounting department by Tuesday.
(A) plans
(B) budgets
(C) expenses
(D) occasions

110. The Wimbledon Creek Apartment is very popular among people because of its ------- to several city parks.
(A) route
(B) distance
(C) proximity
(D) similarity

111. The new study indicated that men are more ------- to be addicted to online games than women.
(A) clear
(B) probable
(C) likely
(D) necessary

112. Fortunately, there were no reports of injuries ------- damages from the earthquake that occurred yesterday.
(A) except
(B) when
(C) or
(D) yet

113. The spokesperson announced that the London Symphony Orchestra is ------- holding some additional concerts for the enthusiastic American fans.
(A) consider
(B) considering
(C) considered
(D) considers

114. The ------- of our warehouse has significantly increased its storage capacity for imported goods.
(A) expand
(B) expanding
(C) expanded
(D) expansion

115. Please be aware ------- before employees begin to operate a new printing machine, it is essential that they thoroughly review the operating manual.
(A) of
(B) whether
(C) that
(D) from

116. Some domestic analysts said the recent increase in oil prices in the Middle East is a key ------- that will determine the future economic growth of the country.
(A) series
(B) factor
(C) system
(D) basis

117. To improve the quality of our customer service, every customer inquiry should be ------- at all times.
(A) monitor
(B) monitored
(C) monitors
(D) monitoring

118. Our restaurant franchises are expanding quickly in California and they are handling a high ------- of customers every day.
(A) size
(B) section
(C) volume
(D) total

119. Many people have ------- become very accustomed to shopping at large department stores in big cities.
(A) concisely
(B) recently
(C) severely
(D) diligently

120. The expected recovery in corporate investment and private spending has been ------- in the economic outlook for next year.
(A) reflected
(B) reflecting
(C) reflection
(D) reflect

121. The water supply was very inadequate for supporting a ------- population due to the serious drought problem.
(A) sizable
(B) numerous
(C) wide
(D) plenty

122. ------- his experience in South America, Mr. Murphy understands Mexican's working style better than other employees in his company.
(A) Owing to
(B) In spite of
(C) Regardless of
(D) Nevertheless

123. Every employee must follow security procedures when sending ------- documents or files electronically to clients.

(A) confident
(B) confidentiality
(C) confidential
(D) confidentially

124. The income tax rate was originally set at 4% of the employee's income and has been ------- increased by the state government.

(A) shortly
(B) intensely
(C) arguably
(D) incrementally

125. ------- completion of any of the business courses offered by Monroe College, diplomas will be issued to the participants.

(A) As
(B) Within
(C) Until
(D) Upon

126. Private and museum art collectors responded ------- to the works of Ms. Isabella Choi, one of the world's foremost surrealism painters.

(A) enthusiasm
(B) enthusiast
(C) enthusiastic
(D) enthusiastically

127. According to the data released yesterday by the government, the official unemployment rate has been on the decline for the fifth ------- year.

(A) consecutive
(B) successful
(C) significant
(D) separate

128. The infectious disease is prevailing throughout the country, but there is no ------- vaccination method for patients.

(A) competitive
(B) extensive
(C) adequate
(D) inexpensive

129. All the passengers of our express bus are ------- to wear their seat belts to prevent injuries or death in road traffic accidents.

(A) advise
(B) advisory
(C) advised
(D) advisable

130. Bella Computer, the country's largest laptop computer maker, ------- a new manufacturing plant in Slovenia last month.

(A) developed
(B) established
(C) acquired
(D) specialized

Directions: Read the texts that follow. A word, phrase, or sentence is missing in parts of each text. Four answer choices for each question are given below the text. Select the best answer to complete the text. Then mark the letter (A), (B), (C), or (D) on your answer sheet.

Questions 131-134 refer to the following notice.

Last month, our company Lamtech announced the retirement of former CEO Charles Iverson. Affectionately called "Big Charlie" by fellow colleagues, Mr. Iverson -------- himself
131.
to the company for thirty years. -------- he joined the company in 1982, Lamtech has tripled
132.
the number of employees on payroll and quadrupled its revenue. He has been a personal mentor for numerous employees as well. --------.
133.

To honor his dedication and contribution to the -------- of Lamtech, the company will hold a
134.
farewell reception on Friday, December 12, at the Hilltop Hotel ballroom. Please RSVP by contacting our secretary Emma Lyons at elyons@lamtech.com or (134) 421-6891.

131. (A) was dedicated
(B) has dedicated
(C) is dedicating
(D) dedicate

132. (A) How
(B) Meanwhile
(C) Since
(D) Before

133. (A) His leadership has enabled Lamtech to grow into the international company it is today.
(B) We have high hopes that he will be a great leader for the future of Lamtech.
(C) The company will complete the construction of a new hotel in the city by December 12.
(D) Last month's farewell reception for Mr. Iverson was incredibly successful.

134. (A) value
(B) relocation
(C) foundation
(D) expansion

Questions 135-138 refer to the following article.

The international phone company Techno announced the development of their new smart phone, T-700. This is an upgraded version of T-500, ------- was a worldwide success **135.** last year. While keeping the convenient features of the previous model, the new model ------- with various new features, such as a 32-megapixel camera, 1.5 GHz CPU, and a **136.** shatterproof screen. Techno stated that consumers will be able to test the T-700 at the upcoming Technology Convention on June 20. -------. It is speculated that the new model **137.** has been produced to ------- to rival company Mandoo, which recently released its new **138.** phone, the GX-8, in parts of Asia.

135. (A) who
(B) which
(C) what
(D) when

136. (A) equipment
(B) is equipping
(C) is equipped
(D) equipped

137. (A) The T-700 sales have not yet exceeded that of the GX-8.
(B) The release date for T-700 is July 10 for Asia and July 21 for Europe.
(C) About 70 percent of the customers said they use mobile phones and tablet computers.
(D) The T-700 is currently receiving positive reviews and getting popular among customers.

138. (A) respond
(B) precede
(C) introduce
(D) oppose

Questions 139-142 refer to the following webpage.

Wildlife Conservatory is a nonprofit organization that aims to promote research in and conservation of endangered wildlife. By using scientific methods and advanced technological equipment, we try ------- the cause of wildlife decline in Asian countries. **139.** Since our ------- in 2003, we have helped numerous animals, including the endangered **140.** Sumatran tiger, spring back from the brink of extinction. However, as a nonprofit organization, we ------- heavily on the support of our members and donors. As of now, we **141.** have over four thousand supporters, but we are always on the lookout for more. We invite you to join our cause. -------. Members receive a subscription to our bimonthly and get **142.** regular updates on our research results.

139. (A) study
(B) studying
(C) to study
(D) have studied

140. (A) extension
(B) founding
(C) intermission
(D) resignation

141. (A) decline
(B) respond
(C) assist
(D) depend

142. (A) As a supporter, you can help research and preserve wildlife.
(B) Thank you for joining our organization and helping the preservation of wildlife.
(C) The Sumatran tiger is no longer considered endangered.
(D) Our job opening will close next month.

Questions 143-146 refer to the following email.

From: email@globalhealth.org
To: julie_newman@gotmail.com
Date: July 23
Subject: Thank you for supporting Global Health

Dear Ms. Julie Newman,

On behalf of Global Health, I would like to thank you for your monthly commitment of $25.00. Your ------- will help underprivileged communities in developing communities gain
143.
better access to health care and sanitation.

With help like yours, we were able to ------- 4,500 vaccinations and 7,000 health checkups
144.
last year. This year, we hope to increase the amount of vaccines administered to 6,000 and health checkups to 10,000. In addition, we plan to build infrastructures that ------- the
145.
livelihoods of local communities. -------.
146.

For more information on donations and our organization, please take a look at our Web site. If you have any questions or concerns, please contact us at (892) 332-7777 or e-mail email@globalhealth.org.

We thank you again for your donation.

Sincerely,
Kyle Patterson
Director of Funds
Global Health

---

143. (A) labor
(B) employment
(C) generosity
(D) appointment

144. (A) provide
(B) provided
(C) providing
(D) have provided

145. (A) improved
(B) can improve
(C) have improved
(D) improving

146. (A) We have already built numerous facilities that can help poor communities.
(B) For example, we are going to install 200 water pumps throughout Ghana this year.
(C) Also, they will offer advanced health care to infants and children.
(D) Please let us know if you would like to change the amount of your monthly donations.

PART 7

Directions: In this part you will read a selection of texts, such as magazine and newspaper articles, e-mails, and instant messages. Each text or set of texts is followed by several questions. Select the best answer for each question and mark the letter (A), (B), (C), or (D) on your answer sheet.

Questions 147-148 refer to the following message.

For the attention of: Peter Jones

Date: Friday, April 20 2:35 P.M.

Caller: Adam Johnson

Business: The Woolshed Clothing Store

Phone number: 925-7399

Message:

Mr. Johnson from the Woolshed Clothing Store called to inquire about the location of his order. He claims that he ordered 500 sweaters from our company last Monday, but they have not yet been delivered to his store. He would like you to email the order tracking number to him so that he can contact the delivery company. His e-mail address is A.Johnson@ woolshed.net

Message taken by: *Barbara Lewis*

147. Why did Mr. Johnson telephone Mr. Jones?

(A) To schedule a meeting
(B) To pay an invoice
(C) To make an inquiry about an order
(D) To check whether some sweaters are available

148. What did Mr. Johnson ask Mr. Jones to do?

(A) Send him some information by e-mail
(B) Fax him a copy of a contract
(C) Phone him at his home
(D) Send him a catalogue by post

Get away from it all on one of our luxury cruises!

Caribbean Cruises Ltd. offers luxury family-oriented cruises
at affordable prices for large families.

Our cruise packages include:
* A visit to 3 different Caribbean islands
* 7 days aboard our luxury cruise ship *The Princess*
* Free rental of scuba and snorkeling equipment
* Three hot meals served daily at our exclusive 4-star restaurant
Don't delay. Book your vacation today!

To make a reservation, please call 1-800-2992. Our sales staff is available to
take your call from 9 A.M. to 5 P.M. from Monday to Saturday.

Earn a 10% special discount with our "Refer a Friend" program. You will receive
a discount if your friend mentions your name when making a reservation!

149. What is NOT included in the cruise package?
(A) Seven days aboard a ship
(B) A free pass to the ship's movie theater
(C) Free use of diving equipment
(D) Free meals in the restaurant

150. What special offer does the advertisement mention?
(A) A $100 discount for booking online
(B) Free hotel pickup if a reservation is made before October 1
(C) A discount if a friend also makes a reservation
(D) A free souvenir T-shirt for every child on board the ship

151. On what day does the booking staff NOT take calls?
(A) Monday
(B) Tuesday
(C) Wednesday
(D) Sunday

Questions 152-155 refer to the following text message chain.

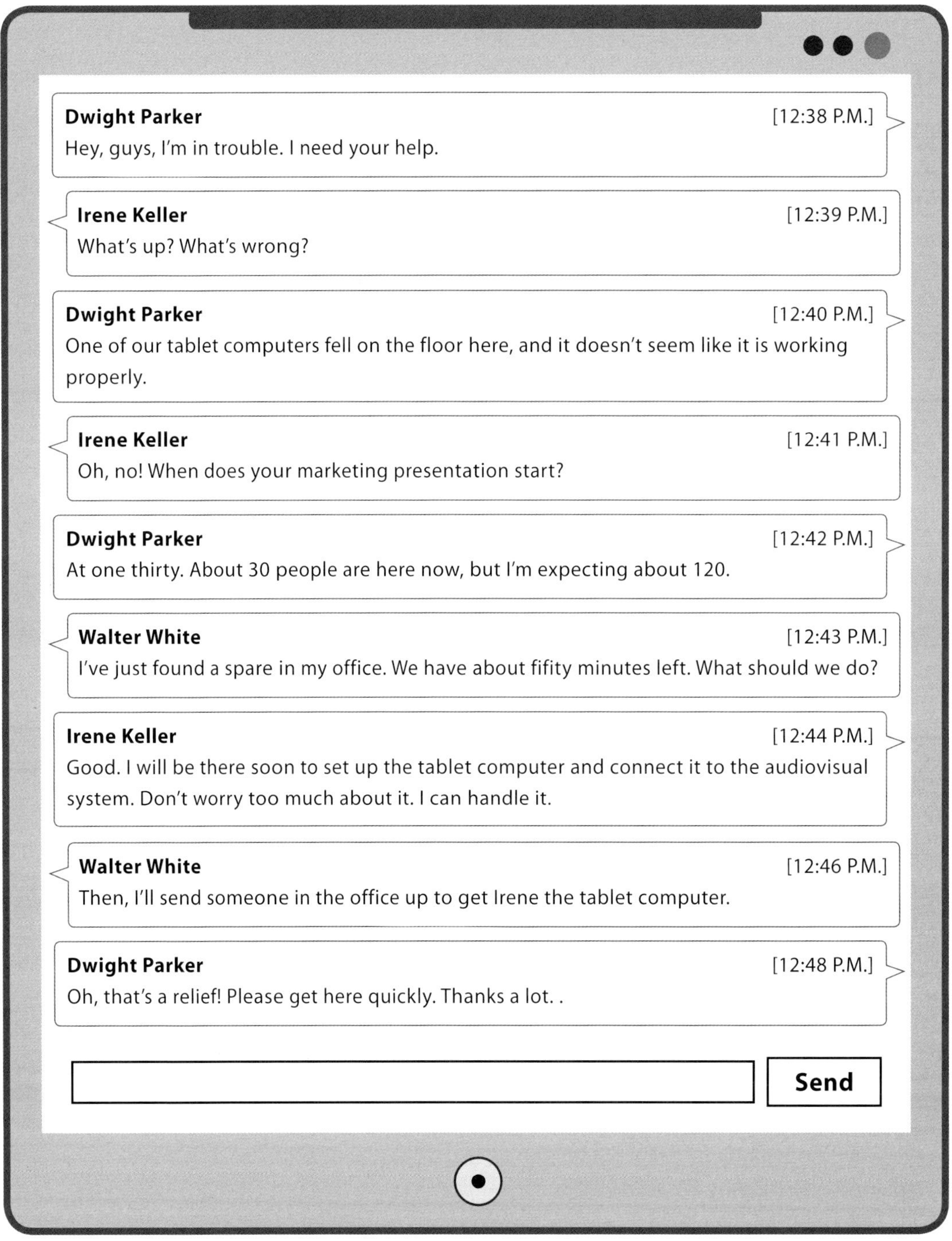

152. Where most likely is Mr. Parker?

(A) In a conference room

(B) In an electronics store

(C) At a movie theater

(D) In his office

153. At 12:41 P.M., why does Ms. Keller say, "Oh, no"?

(A) An event has been canceled.

(B) Some people have not arrived.

(C) An employee called in sick this morning.

(D) A piece of equipment is damaged.

154. What is implied about Ms. Keller?

(A) She is a marketing manager.

(B) She is Mr. Parker's supervisor.

(C) She is good at handling machines.

(D) She is one of the big clients.

155. What will Mr. White most likely do next?

(A) Give a marketing presentation

(B) Buy a new tablet computer

(C) Have someone bring a machine up

(D) Install a machine with Mr. Parker

Gaby Motor Co. expects record sales and profits for the second straight year. Spurred by a sales growth in North America and South Korea, along with the sales recovery in Europe, Gaby Motor Co. is the fastest growing automobile manufacturer in the world. In this fiscal year, which started April 1, Gaby expects minimum support from the weak dollar, but is confident in increasing sales volume, especially in its line of sports utility vehicles.

---

156. What does the article discuss?
(A) The expansion of the sports utility vehicle market
(B) The financial status of Gaby Motors Co.
(C) The advertising strategies of Gaby Motors Co.
(D) The sales prediction of Gaby Motors Co.

157. Which is NOT a factor that contributed to the increase of the sales volume of Gaby Motors Co.?
(A) The revival of European markets
(B) The depreciation of the dollar
(C) The growing customer demand in South Korea
(D) The increased sales performance in North America

Questions 158-159 refer to the advertisement.

Summer Promotion

Starling Leisure Center

47 Bell Street

Miami, Florida

Phone: 404-466-0278

Take advantage of our discounted prices this summer.

Swimming and mini-golf: 50% off in July!

Enjoy lunch in our cafeteria, served from 1 P.M.

Opening Hours

Monday to Friday: 09:30 A.M.—6:00 P.M.

Saturday and Sunday: 10:00 A.M.—09:00 P.M.

Closed on public holidays.

158. What is the announcement for?

(A) A summer promotion at a leisure center

(B) Changes to a lunch menu

(C) The reopening of a store

(D) The dates of a public holiday

159. What is indicated about the Starling Leisure Center?

(A) It is famous throughout Florida.

(B) It opens later on weekends.

(C) Lunch is served all day.

(D) Its prices have recently increased.

New College Dormitory Complex For Hayward State University by Alicia Adams, Beat Reporter

June 27—The new plans were finalized and the appropriate personnel put into place. Construction has started for the new college dormitory complex. A ceremony took place last Thursday at the intersection of Brompton Avenue and Route 20, where Hayward State University is building its new dormitory complex, Pioneers Lofts. Delilah Sorcarro, President of Hayward State University, turned over the first shovelful of dirt at the site, located three miles north of the main campus. — [1] —.

Pioneers Lofts is a joint venture between the college (a public institution) and the Weingarten Group (a local property-development firm). It will consist of three large mixed-use buildings. — [2] —. The Weingarten Group will develop the site and manage the retail operations. "Until recently, most of our students have been commuters," Ms. Sorcarro said. "Now we are seeing a sharp increase in the number of applicants who request campus housing — [3] —. The high-rise dormitory we built last spring has helped to some extent. But when this project is completed, we will be in a much better position to serve our students".

Daniel Ho, the Weingarten Group's city planner, has told the university board that several retailers have already expressed interest in leasing space in the complex, including a number of clothing stores and health food outlets, and he has invited a large supermarket chain in the area. — [4] —. The complex and the campus will be connected by a scenic footpath.

160. Who most likely is Ms. Sorcarro?
(A) A resident
(B) A property developer
(C) A college administrator
(D) A store owner

161. What business has the Weingarten Group invited to the new establishment?
(A) A construction firm
(B) A travel agency
(C) A private education institute
(D) A grocery store

162. In which of the positions marked [1], [2], [3], and [4] does the following sentence best belong?

"Each will have retail space at ground level and just above that, student apartments."
(A) [1]
(B) [2]
(C) [3]
(D) [4]

Questions 163-166 refer to the following article.

HARTVILLE (September 3)—The Hartville Transit Board would like to update residents on the current status of various infrastructure improvements that are taking place throughout the city, and their impact on commuting and foot traffic. "Please especially take note of the effect that many of these projects will have on the main commuter routes," says Gary Rondell, chairman of the transit board.

Two lanes of the Dayton Valley Bridge have been closed for urgent repaving since August 29. Due to this closure, it is common for motorists to face delays of up to one hour during morning and evening rush hour. Additionally, the underground tunnel that crosses under 14th Avenue downtown is inaccessible due to construction work that will continue until mid-September. The Carson Avenue Bridge, just 100 meters further down 14th Avenue, serve as an alternative, safe pedestrian crossing point until the tunnel construction is finished.

University lecturer Harold Blackley reported delays of at least 45 minutes during his daily commute between New Haven and Angler University in downtown Hartville. "Traffic on Wells Boulevard is often at a complete standstill," Mr. Blackley said. "These days, if I want to make it on time for my first class, I have no choice but to leave one hour earlier than I normally would." Chet Landry, a motorbike courier, has also encountered many problems. "In my job, things have to run smoothly so that my packages are delivered on time. Clients depend on me to deliver packages promptly, but that is increasingly difficult with all the street maintenance that is going on."

Mr. Rondell warns drivers to take increased care when traveling through busy road maintenance areas. "Motorists should try to remain patient and stay vigilant of the environment. There are many obstacles and a large number of road crew workers on the streets, and we don't want any unnecessary accidents to occur."

163. What is the purpose of the article?
(A) To encourage residents to make use of public transportation
(B) To outline a proposal for a citywide urban development project
(C) To describe the construction of a new commuter route to New Haven
(D) To inform local people of the effects of ongoing maintenance

164. According to the article, where can pedestrians walk while the underground tunnel is closed?
(A) On the Dayton Valley Bridge
(B) On 14th Avenue
(C) On the Carson Avenue Bridge
(D) On Wells Boulevard

165. In paragraph 3, line 11, the word "run" is closest in meaning to
(A) send
(B) operate
(C) drive
(D) improve

166. What does the chairman of the transit board advise people to do?
(A) Leave for work earlier than usual
(B) Try to carpool with other people
(C) Exercise caution when driving
(D) Avoid using cars whenever possible

167. What type of business does Mr. Mitchell work in?

(A) A shipping company
(B) A moving company
(C) A laundry service
(D) A law firm

168. At 2:31 P.M., what does Ms. Morgan most likely mean when he writes, "They need the delivery by 3 P.M."?

(A) He has plans for his golf game today.
(B) There are more deliveries to be done.
(D) He is angry about the car accident.
(D) The client needs the job done on time.

Questions 169-171 refer to the following advertisement.

Special Announcement

To: The Editor, Bradford University's Student Magazine

From: Kelly Francis, Keepsafe Insurance

Marketing Manager

Keepsafe Insurance

These days, it can often be difficult for young people to find affordable travel insurance to cover them for vacations or trips abroad. That is why we at Keepsafe Insurance are launching our new Backpacker Insurance package, which is aimed specifically at people aged eighteen to twenty-five.

When traveling, there are a number of dangers and risks that travelers need to be protected from. Our Backpacker Insurance package will allow you to claim compensation in the event of theft or loss of luggage. It will also allow you to claim a refund if your flight is cancelled. The policy covers you in the event of a medical emergency as Keepsafe Insurance will pay all hospital bills up to $10,000.

To find out more information about our Backpacker Insurance package, you are invited to attend my twenty-minute presentation in the student auditorium at 4 P.M. on Thursday, March 18. If this is not convenient for you, you can email me with any questions at kellyfrancis@ keepsafe.com or phone the office at 1-800-3020-5939 and ask for Kelly.

169. What age group is the Backpacker Insurance package designed for?
(A) 30- to 40-year-olds
(B) 10- to 15-year-olds
(C) 18- to 25-year-olds
(D) 60- to 75-year-olds

170. What is NOT stated as being covered by this insurance package?
(A) The cancellation of a flight
(B) Medical expenses
(C) The theft of luggage
(D) Legal bills

171. Which of these is NOT mentioned as a way to learn more about the Backpacker Insurance package?
(A) Telephoning Kelly at the office
(B) Sending an email to Kelly
(C) Sending a letter to Kelly at her private address
(D) Attending a presentation given by Kelly

Nagasaki (June 14)—Artist Akemi Kitagawa, who specializes in landscape watercolors, has been traveling the more rural parts of her country for the past 5 years and painting the entire time. — [1] —. She takes photos of her pieces and posts them almost daily on her blog, which can be viewed at www.travelandpaint.com.

— [2] —. She describes individuals she meets as well as different cultures and dialects she encounters, and she shares her thoughts while on long, lonely stretches of road.

Ms. Kitagawa's site has drawn a large following as her blog statistics report an average of 3.2 thousand hits each day. For those blog readers who agree to take a brief survey, the top demographic for these readers is female college graduates in their mid-twenties and early-thirties. — [3] —. One anonymous reader commented on the blog, "I visit here every day because Akemi is living the life I feel I missed out on — one of adventure and self-discovery."

When asked what inspired her to start her blog, Ms. Kitagawa explained, "Honestly, it first started out simply as a digital journal — a way to record my thoughts while on this journey. Only after my readership kept increasing did I realize that others would be interested in what I had to say. I'm happy to share my thoughts, however personal or simple, with the world." — [4] —.

172. What is the subject of the article?

(A) A painter's personal experiences

(B) New trends in photography

(C) Different cultures in Japan

(D) Traveling rural roads in Japan

173. In the article, the word "drawn" in paragraph 3, line 1, is closest in meaning to

(A) described

(B) illustrated

(C) attracted

(D) labeled

174. What is NOT featured on Akemi Kitagawa's blog?

(A) Descriptions of her surroundings

(B) The cost of her artwork

(C) Her personal feelings

(D) Tales of her adventures

175. In which of the positions marked [1], [2], [3] and [4] does the following sentence best belong?

"Also on her blog are diary-like entries recording her adventures on her travels."

(A) [1]

(B) [2]

(C) [3]

(D) [4]

ARTHOUSE.COM
the leading online art supply retailer

Art House has everything the modern artist needs to create their next great masterpiece. For the next five days only, we are offering deep discounts on...

- 12 pack assorted clipart stencils $7
- Brandt easel-carrying case $27
- Art House brand 24 color charcoal set $9

Also, with purchases of $75 or more, customers receive a 4 pack of dry erase markers.

If you need any assistance with your purchases, let one of our online customer service representatives assist you. Just click the customer service tab at the top left of our main page.

Art Today
Your place for the latest on everything for art

An art guide: Featured store of the month

Art House is a great place to find good deals and is different from the well-known art supply stores that often have higher prices and lower quality products. Art House actually produces some of its own products and sells them along with other popular brands. They have a growing selection of items on their site ranging from brushes to plaster and pencils. The quality of their products is not as high as some of the more popular brands, but for artists that need more affordable supplies, this is the place to go.

Also, Art House offers discounts on shipping with purchases over $80. However, since they do most of their shipping themselves, it takes a lot longer for customers to get their items. But the lower prices are worth the wait. Visit their Web site at www.arthouse.com for hundreds of great deals.

176. What special offer is being advertised?

(A) Canvases for half price

(B) A gift with the purchase of $75

(C) Free shipping on all purchases

(D) A discount on all coloring supplies

177. What is suggested about Art House?

(A) It is attractive to artists who need to save.

(B) It does not advertise in newspapers and magazines.

(C) It has more than one store location.

(D) It allows only a certain number of purchases each day.

178. Which of the advertised products is produced by Art House?

(A) The stencils

(B) The easel case

(C) The charcoal set

(D) The markers

179. What does the reviewer consider a disadvantage of Art House?

(A) The low quality of its customer service

(B) The high cost of many of its products

(C) The time it takes to receive its products

(D) The smaller selection of brushes

180. In the review, the word "deals" in paragraph 1, line 2, is closest in meaning to

(A) quantities

(B) bargains

(C) contracts

(D) compromises

To:	Dearan Reagan <dreagan@CMT/Intl.com>
From:	Rebecca Dawson <rebecca.moore@CMT/Intl.com>
Date:	October 18
Subject:	Recommendations

Dearan,

I just learned that you went on a trip to Ho Chi Minh a few months ago. I hope you don't mind my e-mailing to ask a few questions. I was hoping for a little bit of advice about conducting business there. From what I understand, a lot of your business takes you all over East and Central Asia. Any tips you can give me would be a huge help. This is my first trip as section director, and I'm eager to make a good first impression.

Thanks for everything, and good luck with your sales meeting this Friday. Hope to hear back from you soon.

Sincerely,
Rebecca Dawson

To:	Rebecca Dawson <rebecca.moore@CMT/Intl.com>
From:	Dearan Moore <dmoore@CMT/Intl.com>
Date:	October 19
Subject: Re:	Recommendations

Rebecca,

I'd be happy to help you in any way that I can. Well, I can gather that you will most likely do a bit of research about Ho Chi Minh before you depart. I would suggest seeing a few cultural sites or something of historical significance right when you arrive. This will give you a few topics of conversation with the business contacts you will be meeting there.

Also, remember that the traffic laws there are very different from back at home, and people don't pay as much attention to pedestrians as in other places I've been to. Be sure to leave plenty of time in advance to get to meetings and appointments. The traffic is out-of-control and a little bit unnerving to maneuver around.

If you have any other questions, let me know. I'm trying to deliver a great presentation this

Friday. I feel confident, but I'm not counting on anything yet. I still have some more things to prepare for it. I hope to wrap it up by the end of the day

Have a safe trip and enjoy yourself. Vietnam, it's a beautiful country.

Dearan

181. What is the main reason of Ms. Dawson's e-mail?
(A) To ask about an upcoming sales meeting
(B) To inquire about tourist attractions in Ho Chi Minh
(C) To ask a colleague about a business meeting
(D) To request advice about a business trip to Ho Chi Minh

182. What is suggested about Ms. Dawson?
(A) She will move to another country in Asia next month.
(B) She just started a new position.
(C) She has visited Vietnam several times.
(D) She has just been introduced to Mr. Reagan.

183. Why does Mr. Reagan mention his business dealings in his e-mail?
(A) To address a comment made by Ms. Dawson
(B) To celebrate the closing of a deal
(C) To invite Ms. Dawson to be a part of the meeting
(D) To emphasize the importance of advance research

184. What is NOT one of Mr. Reagan's suggestions?
(A) Visit some cultural and historical sites
(B) Be on time for business meetings
(C) Have a good time
(D) Be difficult with clients to earn respect

185. In the second e-mail, the phrase "counting on" in paragraph 3, line 2, is closest in meaning to
(A) being certain of
(B) coming up with
(C) measuring up to
(D) keeping records of

The City of Banshee
Local Lifelong Education Classes - August

A variety of education classes are now open to all residents of Banshee ages eighteen or over. Classes will be held at the Banshee Community College campus unless otherwise noted. For more information on enrollment, fees, and payment methods, please go to the next page.

How to Get a Real Estate License
Mondays, 6 P.M.—9 P.M.
Main Hall, Room 112
Instructor: Judy Elena, from National Real Estate Association

Running a Small Business
Mondays, 7 P.M.—9 P.M.
General Library, Room 306
Instructor: Kelly Hamilton, Small Business Developer

Photography Techniques
Tuesdays, 7 P.M.—9 P.M.
Main Hall, Room 112
Instructor: Britney Hannah, Freelance photographer

Vehicle Care
August 22 and 24, 9 A.M.—1 P.M.
Banshee Vocational High School
Instructor: Robert Juilan, from Juilan Brothers Auto Repair

To: Williams Hutchson <whutchson@hauzenmail.com>
From: Jammy Oscar <Joscar@banshee.gov>
Subject: Class postponed
Date: August 23

To Mr. Hutchson

Ms. Elena told me to contact everyone to let them know that the class has been postponed because of an event she must participate in. It will be rescheduled soon. As soon as we find out the rescheduled date, we will contact you via e-mail and send a new parking permit, because the one you have now will expire soon. Sorry for the inconvenience.

Regards,

Jammy Oscar
Department of Local Lifelong Education
City Government of Banshee

Banshee Community Parking Permit
ALTERNATIVE PASS FOR TODAY ONLY

LOT A

Valid: August 27

Time Stamp: 6:45 P.M.

* This must be displayed on the front side of your vehicle window and
be visible from the outside.

186. Who most likely is Robert Juilan?

(A) A college professor

(B) A city official

(C) A high school teacher

(D) A local entrepreneur

187. What is NOT indicated about participants
in the Continuing Education Classes?

(A) They must be at least eighteen years
old.

(B) They are required to pay a registration
fee.

(C) They should be residents of Banshee.

(D) They are graduates from Banshee
Community College.

188. What is Ms. Hutchson most likely
interested in?

(A) Real estate

(B) Management

(C) Photography

(D) Car care

189. In the e-mail, the word "participate"
in paragraph 1, in line 2, is closest in
meaning to

(A) listen to

(B) wait on

(C) take care of

(D) be present at

190. On what date did the rescheduled class
take place?

(A) August 22

(B) August 23

(C) August 24

(D) August 27

Facility care

At the townhall meeting on Tuesday, the Cass Town mayor looked for more options for work to be done on town facilities. According to Gamily Cruise, town clerk, the expenditure for renovation of the Cass Community Center was lower than the amount that was designated for the project. Therefore, the mayor decided to come up with other smaller projects that can be done with the rest of the funds.

Some suggested projects are a paved road to the entrance of the Cass Public Library, more lights in the Public Sports Park, and new tiles in the train station. Mr. Cruise has announced that the mayor will acquire some other ideas from residents. Anyone interested may contribute ideas at the council's meeting on Tuesday, June 20, at 4 P.M. or send an e-mail to the mayor's office before June 31. After reviewing public comments, the planning council will put forth a final proposal for the mayor to discuss, with a decision expected by July 15.

From:	hyulius@citymail.com.au
To:	cassmayor@cass.org.au
Date:	25 June
Subject:	extra projects

Dear Mayor and Council Members,

I heard that you are looking for suggestions for the usage of leftover money from the community center's renovation. I was not able to participate in the council meeting due to an appointment, but I'd like to suggest placing more lights in the park. This plan would be more affordable than others, and it will raise the number of visitors to the Public Sports Park, especially during the winter term, which will be certainly beneficial to everyone. The park is a good place for everyone, and it will be much better after being renovated. I would appreciate it if you would consider this.

Hanamori Yulius

From: mlinderman@hgnetwok.co.au
To: gcruise@cass.org.au
Date: 27 June
Subject: town development

Dear Mr. Cruise,

I was happy to hear that the final renovation was successfully completed with the leftover money. The community center provides activities for residents such as adolescents, parents, and children. Therefore, I would like to suggest a new project for the elderly and infirm.

The public library is the most common place for adults to gather, and the new way to the entrance can provide visitors with a nice atmosphere for them to have a conversation or wait for transportation. It would be a remarkable improvement that would be admired by everyone in Cass. In July, when the discussion for the new plan begins, please consider my suggestion so everyone can be more interested in using Cass's public facilities.

Thank you,
Michael Linderman

191. Why does the town of Cass have funds available?
(A) The mayor has canceled a project.
(B) The city has raised tax rates.
(C) Its citizens have donated money.
(D) Its previous project cost less than expected.

192. In the article, the phrase "put forth" in paragraph 2, line 10, is the closest in meaning to,
(A) grow
(B) exert
(C) propose
(D) request

193. When did Ms. Yulius have an appointment?
(A) On June 20
(B) On June 25
(C) On June 30
(D) On July 15

194. What does Mr. Linderman mention in his e-mail about the Cass Community Center?
(A) It is located near public transportation.
(B) It is used mainly by residents.
(C) It previously served another purpose.
(D) Its programs will run year-round.

195. On what point would Mr. Linderman and Ms. Yulius most likely agree?
(A) The chosen project should be beneficial to the entire community.
(B) The city should spend as little money as possible on its next project.
(C) The mayor should extend the deadline for community comments.
(D) Patrons of the library and the park should work together to raise money.

Questions 196-200 refer to the following e-mail, notice, and order form.

From: John Delaffe <jd@naturalgreenfield.com>
To: Joel Stevenson <js@greenworld.com>
Subject: Delivering company
Date: August 1

Hello Mr. Stevenson,

We are very happy that you have registered for deliveries of our products, including vegetables, fruits, flowers, and herbs, which are all harvested from our family-owned farm. I'm confident that our items will be better than those of our competitors. You and your customers will be satisfied with the products we provide.
Your store is located in an area that is not familiar to us, but we are excited to expand our business to North Shore. We appreciate your business.

Sincerely yours,
John Delaffe

STORE GREEN WORLD

NEW THIS WEEK!

August 26

Produce from Natural Greens Field

Dear Customers,
We have many new products in our produce section. You will find fresh, local fruits and vegetables that have just been harvested and are in great condition. All of the items on the list below come straight from a beautiful farm in the Pateon area.

√ Sweet potato   √ Chili
√ Potato   √ Onions
√ Rosemary, basil, thyme, and oregano

In the fall, we will be bringing products from Aeron Cycle Orchard in Rosemary. If you want to learn more about them, please contact us.

Natural Greens Field Order Form

Customer: Store Green World

Order date: August 30

Delivery date: September 3

Delivery details:

Same as last order except for the following:

- No herbs are needed. I still have a lot left.

- For onions, please send them in burlap bags.

  (like the photo sample you've posted on the Web site)

- Add two pumpkins to the order.

Comments: Honestly, I don't have any problems or complaints about the overall service. The delivery is punctual, and the driver is polite. Above all, the products are always in the best condition.

Name: Joel Stevenson, Manager

Signature: *Joel Stevenson*

---

196. Why did Ms. Delaffe send the e-mail?
(A) To advertise new products
(B) To welcome a new customer
(C) To request a delivery estimate
(D) To complain about a policy change

197. Where is Store Green World probably located?
(A) In Auckland
(B) In North Shore
(C) In Pateon
(D) In Yerorn

198. In the notice, what is indicated about Natural Greens Field's produce?
(A) It is grown in the Pateon area.
(B) It is more healthful than other products.
(C) It will be in stock starting next month.
(D) It will be discounted for one week.

199. What does Store Green World NOT request to receive on September 3?
(A) Potatoes
(B) Onions
(C) Pumpkins
(D) Rosemary

200. What does Mr. Stevenson indicate in the order form?
(A) He has a preference for how items are packaged.
(B) Pumpkin sold particularly well last week.
(C) He was disappointed by the delivery service.
(D) The herbs delivered last week were not fresh.

Stop! This is the end of the test. If you finish before time is called, you may go back to Parts 5, 6, and 7 and check your work.

101. D	121. A	141. D	161. D	181. D
102. B	122. A	142. A	162. B	182. B
103. C	123. C	143. C	163. D	183. A
104. B	124. D	144. A	164. C	184. D
105. B	125. D	145. B	165. B	185. A
106. D	126. D	146. B	166. C	186. D
107. A	127. A	147. C	167. C	187. D
108. B	128. C	148. A	168. D	188. A
109. C	129. C	149. B	169. C	189. D
110. C	130. B	150. C	170. D	190. D
111. C	131. B	151. D	171. C	191. D
112. C	132. C	152. A	172. A	192. C
113. B	133. A	153. D	173. C	193. A
114. D	134. D	154. C	174. B	194. B
115. C	135. B	155. C	175. B	195. A
116. B	136. C	156. D	176. B	196. B
117. B	137. B	157. B	177. A	197. B
118. C	138. A	158. A	178. C	198. A
119. B	139. C	159. B	179. C	199. D
120. A	140. B	160. C	180. B	200. A

ACTUAL TEST

2

READING TEST

In the Reading test, you will read a variety of texts and answer several different types of reading comprehension questions. The entire Reading test will last 75 minutes. There are three parts, and directions are given for each part. You are encouraged to answer as many questions as possible within the time allowed.

You must mark your answers on the separate answer sheet. Do not write your answers in your test book.

PART 5

Directions: A word or phrase is missing in each of the sentences below. Four answer choices are given below each sentence. Select the best answer to complete the sentence. Then mark the letter (A), (B), (C), or (D) on your answer sheet.

101. The new research center was constructed to provide information ------- weather, earthquakes, and the environment.
(A) regarding   (B) besides
(C) along   (D) pending

102. Due to her busy schedule, Ms. Wilson delegated some of her work to her colleagues instead of completing it -------.
(A) she
(B) her
(C) hers
(D) herself

103. According to the local history record, the Manor of Southstead was constructed ------- 420 years ago.
(A) approximate
(B) approximation
(C) approximately
(D) approximated

104. ------- submitting all of your related documents, please check all of your information and be sure that it is correct.
(A) Since   (B) Unless
(C) Despite   (D) Prior to

105. The British Petrochemicals built the first ------- facility to commercially produce gas near the North Sea.
(A) local
(B) locals
(C) locally
(D) localize

106. The Philippines is one of the last countries to ------- its ban on our company's mobile phones and tablet computers.
(A) face
(B) attract
(C) damage
(D) lift

107. Mr. Davis was trying to move to another company after he failed to ------- his employment contract with his former company.
(A) expand
(B) proceed
(C) terminate
(D) renew

108. To increase next year's sales, the design department for Kamon Cosmetics is currently ------- a package redesign.
(A) consider
(B) considered
(C) considering
(D) consideration

109. All of the job ------- for our company are responsible for providing accurate personal information before the first round of job interviews.
(A) applicants
(B) experts
(C) openings
(D) employees

110. According to the sales report, our ------- of automobiles and of cosmetics to China have been growing for the last five years.
(A) shipment
(B) shipping
(C) shipments
(D) shipped

111. ------- of our analysts predicts the size of the global advertising industry will explode as social commerce companies grow rapidly.
(A) Every
(B) Most
(C) Each
(D) Plenty

112. Ms. McKenzie attributes her success as a novelist to dedicating herself to her work and ------- what makes a best seller.
(A) understand
(B) understanding
(C) was understanding
(D) understood

113. The government plans to get 35% of its electricity production from wind so that it ------- leave the coal in the ground.
(A) be
(B) should
(C) has to
(D) can

114. The annual winter festival of our city ------- skiing, winter swimming, sledging, and many other fun events.
(A) include
(B) including
(C) includes
(D) is included

115. The federal government will improve the investment environment by ------- removing regulations for the new few years.
(A) continue
(B) continuation
(C) continuous
(D) continuously

116. The lease with the local shopping mall ------- if the renovation works are completed successfully next week.
(A) will be continued
(B) was continuing
(C) have continued
(D) had been continued

117. The chairman of BK Financial Group planned his congratulatory speech at a reception ------- the event.
(A) following
(B) behind
(C) prior
(D) until

118. The company has recently changed all the lights in some of the branch offices for ------- efficient LED lights.
(A) heavily
(B) almost
(C) nearly
(D) highly

119. Andrew Accounting has become one of the famous accounting companies in America ------- its exceptional services.
(A) in spite of
(B) thanks to
(C) except for
(D) as well as

120. With ------- demand for various crops, water usage will most likely double over the next thirty years.
(A) reserved
(B) leading
(C) increased
(D) partial

121. People should learn the new safety procedures to protect ------- from serious dangers caused by earthquakes below or near the sea.
(A) they
(B) themselves
(C) their
(D) theirs

122. For a fixed monthly charge, callers can make ------- telephone calls as they wish in their immediate area.
(A) a lot of
(B) as many
(C) various
(D) unlimited

123. In recognition of her ------- talent, Ms. Scofield became the first woman to be named board director since our company's founding in 1974.
(A) academic
(B) exceptional
(C) previous
(D) economical

124. The new treaty was adopted last year with the ------- of fighting global warming and environmental destruction in the future.
(A) solution
(B) factor
(C) aim
(D) prevention

125. ------- of the companies is committed to expanding business activities in the United States, which is a strategic core area.
(A) Every
(B) Each
(C) Other
(D) Them

126. The government cannot sustain the national economy ------- it makes efforts to create more businesses and jobs.
(A) who
(B) that
(C) unless
(D) therefore

127. Energy companies should develop different forms of ------- energy that can reduce pollution and conserve the scarce resources.
(A) possible
(B) collaborative
(C) satisfactory
(D) alternative

128. It is illegal to build new agricultural farms and orchards if ------- is not granted by the minister of environment.
(A) application
(B) inspection
(C) permission
(D) expense

129. KB Heavy Industries has been placing a strong ------- on the research and development sectors to compete in the increasingly fierce industry environment.
(A) emphasize
(B) emphasis
(C) emphatic
(D) emphasized

130. Commercial flight testing is usually conducted to ------- that the airplane meets all safety and performance requirements of the government agency.
(A) certify
(B) resolve
(C) grant
(D) enable

Questions 131-134 refer to the following advertisement.

San Francisco Real Estate Apartment for lease

701 Trinity Street Apt. 12

A clean, spacious two-bedroom, one-bathroom apartment is ------- on Trinity Street. The
131.
unit comes with basic kitchen appliances, a dishwasher, and in-unit laundry machine. The
apartment ------- conveniently in the heart of town. The nearest subway station is only
132.
a five-minute walk away, and the nearest bus station is at a ten-minute walk. There is a
convenience store in the apartment complex. The rent is $750 a month, which includes
gas, electricity, and water. -------. Pets are strictly prohibited. Please contact Ms. Isabella
133.
Choi at (452) 321-3955 for more information or to ------- an appointment for showing.
134.

131. (A) applicable
(B) capable
(C) affordable
(D) available

132. (A) locating
(B) has located
(C) is located
(D) is locating

133. (A) Note that rent does not cover Internet.
(B) There is also a supermarket that sells kitchen supplies.
(C) Please visit our office to sign a lease.
(D) There is a monthly charge of $10 for electricity.

134. (A) arrangement
(B) arrange
(C) arranged
(D) arranging

Questions 135-138 refer to the following article.

Palo Lagota's Mayor, Ms. Betty Hwang, signed a new ------- that mandates the gradual **135.** increase of the minimum wage to $13 an hour next year. The current minimum wage of Palo Lagota is $11 an hour, making it one of the highest in the country. -------, Palo Alto also has **136.** one of the highest living costs in the country. Last year, the Golden State was declared the fifth ------- state with an average home price of about $1,550,000. The new bill is receiving **137.** mixed reviews by economists and market analysts. -------. Nevertheless, some of the city **138.** council members believe that the new minimum wage in Palo Lagota is the continuation of a logical economic policy.

135. (A) contract
(B) receipt
(C) legislation
(D) treaty

136. (A) Consequently
(B) Apparently
(C) Therefore
(D) However

137. (A) expensive
(B) expensively
(C) more expensive
(D) most expensive

138. (A) While a higher wage can aid full-time workers, it may negatively impact employment rates.
(B) Various political debates will continue until the city council passes the bill.
(C) The mayor still hasn't decided whether she will sign the bill or not.
(D) All of the irregular workers in California will be making $13 an hour next year.

Questions 139-142 refer to the following Web page.

Gold membership for Xpress Shop

Tired of waiting for your package to arrive? Desperate for a little bit of shopping therapy? Hate paying for expedited shipping? Become a gold member today and ------- those **139.** problems. Gold members ------- free same-day shipping for an unlimited amount of **140.** deliveries. -------, members receive a $30 electronic gift certificate every year. -------. For **141.** **142.** an annual fee of just $39, become a gold member today. Take advantage of this golden opportunity! You will not regret it!

139. (A) avoid
    (B) embrace
    (C) allow
    (D) delay

140. (A) enjoyment
    (B) enjoying
    (C) enjoy
    (D) enjoyed

141. (A) In spite of
    (B) Simultaneously
    (C) In addition
    (D) Therefore

142. (A) We sincerely thank for your interest in becoming a gold member.
    (B) Our store also provides gold members with additional discounts on purchases.
    (C) We are surprised that you did not receive your shipment and apologize for the delay.
    (D) By spending over $150, you will qualify for discounts and free same-day shipping.

Questions 143-146 refer to the following article.

Starting next Wednesday, the Metropolitan Art Museum will be holding an exhibit on the works of photographer Ms. Sally Murphy. Ms. Murphy's photos ------- many international **143.** awards. The rising artist is renowned for her black and white photos that feature the socially oppressed. She was the sole apprentice of the late Nola Kozlowski, a prominent photographer who focused on capturing the lives of indigenous peoples. Based on ------- **144.** she learned from Ms. Kozlowski, Ms. Murphy went on to take photos of homeless people, beggars, child workers, and other socially ignored citizens. "Like the indigenous people that are not being fully recognized globally, there are people within our own cities that are being ignored," stated Ms. Murphy. "I wanted to capture their lives through photography ------- **145.** my audience can see and reconnect with their forgotten neighbors." The photographer hopes to contribute to society through her works. -------. The exhibit will last for four **146.** months.

143. (A) receives
(B) were received
(C) have received
(D) will receive

144. (A) that
(B) which
(C) what
(D) how

145. (A) so
(B) therefore
(C) however
(D) although

146. (A) She plans to donate all of the exhibition's profits to charity organizations.
(B) The exhibition will be based on Ms. Kozlowski 's photos of indigenous people.
(C) The photographer mentioned future plans of taking photos of homeless people.
(D) Several magazines and publications will contact her to use her pictures soon.

PART 7

Directions: In this part you will read a selection of texts, such as magazine and newspaper articles, letters, and advertisements. Each text is followed by several questions. Select the best answer for each question and mark the letter (A), (B), (C), or (D) on your answer sheet.

Questions 147-148 refer to the following receipt.

CASH ALLOWANCE RECEIPT

DATE 23 November

NAME (IN BLOCK LETTERS) HANK SHREDDER

DETAILED INFORMATION	AMOUNT
Business travel and meal expenses associated with the accounting conference I will attend in Manhattan, New York from 25 to 26 November	$1,974

I confirm receipt of the above sum.

Signature *Hank Shredder*

147. What will Mr. Shredder do in New York in November?
(A) Sign a new contract
(B) Go on vacation
(C) Hire some accountants
(D) Participate in an event

148. What does Mr. Shredder confirm?
(A) Purchasing new accounting software
(B) Submitting original receipts
(C) Paying hotel costs
(D) Receiving some funds

New Line Office Supply Warehouse

25200 Carlos Bee Blvd, Hayward, CA 94542 510-212-6313

Delivery Invoice

Date: Jan 10

Invoice No: 941796

Purchased by: Anna Gunn

Delivery Address: 540 Pine Street, Daly City, CA 94015

Prima Silver Work Desk / Workstation $209.95

Support System 10 Desk Chair $109.95

Samson 19-inch Monitor $149.95

Samson Computer (Model #: Andromeda X110) $909.90

Subtotal $1,559.75

Frequent Shopper Discount $100.00

Tax $86.99

Total $1,546.74

Thank you for shopping at New Line Office Supply Warehouse.

149. What is suggested about Ms. Gunn?
- (A) She will pick up her items from the store.
- (B) She works for an office supplies company.
- (C) She often shops at New Line Office Supply Warehouse.
- (D) She will purchase a desk next week.

150. What is the total amount paid on this invoice?
- (A) $1,559.75
- (B) $1,546.74
- (C) $909.90
- (D) $86.99

Bangkok, Thailand

Bangkok is a thrilling, vibrant city that has many attractions to excite the modern traveler. Whether you are here to sample Thai culture, taste the delicious food, or simply to shop, Bangkok has something for you.

Things to see:
The Grand Palace is one of the main attractions, and most visitors to the city head there first. This palace was built in the eighteenth century and features many precious Buddha statues.

The market in Chinatown draws huge crowds of tourists on weekends. You can find some fantastic bargains that will make great gifts for people at home. Don't be afraid to bargain, but be polite. Watch out for pickpockets, who operate in this area.

Accommodations:
There are many great budget hotels around the city. Try the Royal Thai Hotel for reasonably priced rooms in a central location (single rooms $10, double $18). The Bangkok Inn is also popular with tourists. It offers rooms with TVs and hot showers in the heart of the tourist district (single rooms $12, double $20).

151. In what type of publication would the article mostly likely be found?
(A) An economic report
(B) A business journal
(C) A hotel magazine
(D) A travel guidebook

152. Why must tourists be cautious when visiting the market in Chinatown?
(A) There is a lot of traffic on the roads.
(B) There are some thieves in the market.
(C) Taxis charge high prices to go to the market.
(D) Lots of pirated goods are sold at the market.

153. What is indicated about the Royal Thai Hotel?
(A) It is located in a central area.
(B) Its rooms are spacious and clean.
(C) The restaurant serves fantastic Thai cuisine.
(D) The hotel has a swimming pool for guests to use.

Roseville Community Center

Located just a short 10-minute drive from downtown Roseville in a scenic mountain setting, the Roseville Community Center (RCC) is the community's new center for leisure, exercise, and relaxation. The RCC is a great place for families and singles to get a massage, play sports, go swimming, and even take a nap in our sunroom.

With a variety of things to keep you busy and a variety of ways to relax, the RCC is an ideal place for family get-togethers and short business meetings, and a comfortable spot to meet other singles. Our on-site coordinator will help you create the perfect plan for your day. For an additional charge, we provide a personal bath accessory package.

For memberships, please call the front desk at 404-555-3242, or send us an e-mail at members@rcc.com. To contact our on-site coordinator, please call 404-575-4331. For more information, photos, directions, and feedback from other members, please visit us at www.rcc.org.

154. What is indicated about the Roseville Community Center?
(A) It is located in the heart of town.
(B) It offers massages.
(C) It provides catering service.
(D) It has a café in the building.

155. What is available for an extra charge?
(A) Transportation from downtown
(B) A large meeting room
(C) Use of the exercise facilities
(D) Bath accessories

156. According to the advertisement, how can people get directions to the Roseville Community Center?
(A) By visiting the center's Web site
(B) By calling the coordinator
(C) By contacting the front desk
(D) By e-mailing the manager

Superfit Sportswear

490 Over Street
London
England

November 23

Jeremiah Osterland
490 Rinke Strata
Vienna, Austria

Dear Mr. Osterland,

Thank you for your e-mail inquiring about our sportswear products. We are a dynamic, growing company, and we are excited about the prospect of supplying our sportswear to your stores all over Austria.

Superfit Sportswear is a family business established in 1992. Currently, our company has over thirty stores serving the needs of over one million customers throughout England every year. We manufacture and sell a range of products from footwear to sports therapy products.

Please find enclosed our trade catalogue for you to look at. This catalogue contains a list and descriptions of all of our current products.

I have arranged for our sales director, Mr. Rhodes, to fly to Vienna to meet with you on December 12. He will be able to negotiate the terms and conditions of the sales contract with you to create a deal profitable for both parties.

We look forward to doing business with you.

Sincerely,

Paul Goodman

Paul Goodman
Superfit Sportswear

157. To what kind of communication is Mr. Goodman replying?
(A) A magazine article
(B) A shareholder's letter
(C) An e-mail inquiry
(D) A telephone message

158. What does Mr. Goodman send along with his letter?
(A) A flight ticket
(B) A trade catalogue
(C) A booklet of discount vouchers
(D) A list of business contacts

159. Why is Mr. Rhodes going to fly to Vienna?
(A) To examine one of Mr. Osterland's stores
(B) To take a vacation with Mr. Osterland
(C) To discuss the details of a contract
(D) To establish a branch of the company

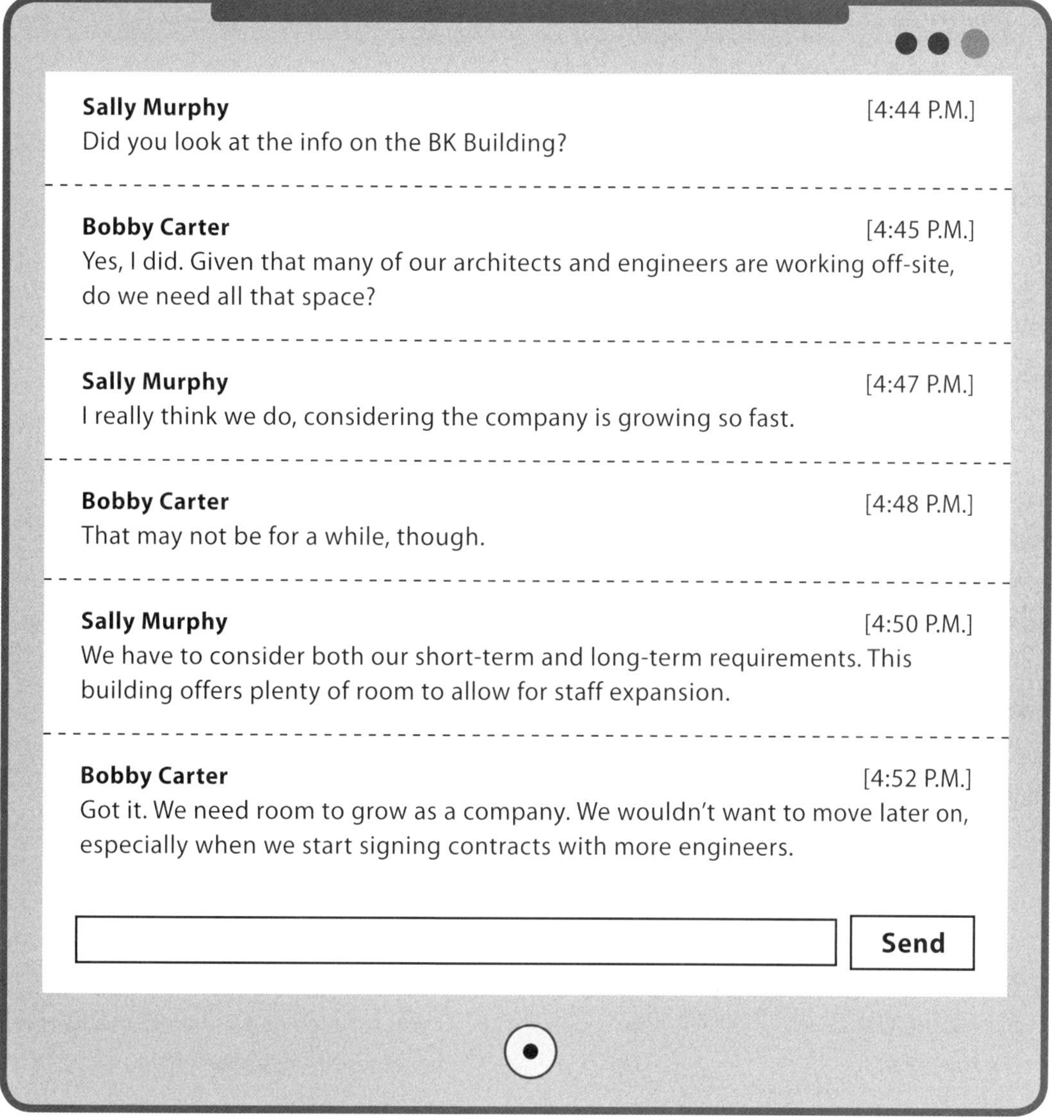

160. Where do Ms. Murphy and Mr. Carter work?

(A) An architectural firm
(B) A moving company
(C) A real estate agency
(D) A local interior design firm

161. At 4:52 P.M., what does Mr. Carter most likely mean when he writes, "Got it"?

(A) They need to improve their existing office space.
(B) A new space will be too expensive.
(C) The building may accommodate plans for future growth.
(D) The property needs structural improvements.

To: Bandar@bestmail.com
From: ClaireSaturna@ipi.org

Dear Mr. Bandar

I'm writing to thank you for your considerable support for the International Petroleum Institute. As a reminder, registration for the annual IPI Conference in Sao Paulo is October 15. — [1] —. There are exciting things in store for this conference, including over 200 vendors, displays, and lectures, all in a state-of-the-art convention facility right in the heart of town. — [2] —.

As a preferred contributor to the programs at the International Petroleum Institute, we are offering you a voucher for 20% off your hotel and complimentary shuttle service to the convention hall. — [3] —. Visit our Web site to register online. — [4] —. You may reach us by phone at 512-555-8760. Please have your membership number ready.

Sincerely,
Anna Bondell
Membership Coordinator

162. Who most likely is Mr. Bandar?
(A) An oil company executive
(B) A conference organizer
(C) A journalist
(D) A teacher

163. What is NOT a benefit being offered?
(A) A reduced hotel rate
(B) A hotel room upgrade
(C) Access to hundreds of vendors' booths
(D) Complimentary transportation to the event

164. In which of the positions marked [1], [2], [3], and [4] does the following sentence best belong?

"You will also find a detailed conference program there, as well as a map of the vendor booths."
(A) [1]
(B) [2]
(C) [3]
(D) [4]

President Hotel to Reopen in Santa Fe
By Darren Pinkman – Santa Fe Weekly

Santa Fe—After being closed for six months while much-needed renovations were carried out, President Hotel reopened for business Monday at 9 A.M.

The manager of the hotel, Janice Ha, claims that the hotel is better than ever before. "Everybody loved the old hotel," she claimed, "but this building work was essential in allowing us to keep up with modern trends. We were experiencing a lot of demand from tourists that we couldn't cope with before. As such, we have installed a state-of-the-art swimming pool and gym, upgraded our restaurant, and added a movie theater for our guests to enjoy. Everybody here is excited about the reopening and can't wait to get back to work."

Designer and owner Chan Hong spoke of his inspiration for the new design. "I wanted to create a memorable experience for our guests," he said. "I wanted people of all ages to be able to enjoy the hotel, whether it be for business or pleasure." When asked if he believed the new hotel is equipped to meet the needs of the ever-demanding travel community, Mr. Hong said that he was "extremely confident that it would be able to cater to even the most discriminating of tastes."

One of the first to sample the delights of the new hotel was Jim Gomez, who works out four times a week. "The new gym is great," said Mr. Gomez. "It has everything you need to keep yourself in shape on your vacation. I loved the swimming pool and restaurant, too. I would definitely stay here again."

President Hotel certainly looks regal, both inside and out. Each room is now equipped with a wide-screen TV, a king-sized bed, and wireless Internet access. And if you're feeling like you want to splurge, the luxurious Emperor Suite offers exceptional value for money. Priced at $220, these exclusive rooms are certainly fit for royalty.

165. What is the purpose of the article?
   (A) To publicize the reopening of a hotel
   (B) To compare several different hotels
   (C) To offer free use of facilities to the local community
   (D) To advertise job vacancies for staff at a hotel

166. What is NOT mentioned about President Hotel?
   (A) It will be open on Christmas Day.
   (B) It has a swimming pool.
   (C) It was closed for six months.
   (D) It is owned by Mr. Hong.

167. What is suggested about Jim Gomez?
   (A) He stayed at the hotel with his wife and children.
   (B) He works in the hotel industry.
   (C) He is passionate about exercising.
   (D) He helped plan the improvements to the fitness center.

Questions 168-171 refer to the following online chat discussion.

Molly Vernon [12:08 P.M.]
Mike, would you mind taking a look at the company Web site? I can't see the pictures of our products on my computer. Do you see them on yours?

Mike Snow [12:13 P.M.]
No, I sure don't. Has this been going on long?

Molly Vernon [12:14 P.M.]
Probably no more than a few hours. I was just contacted by a potential customer who wanted to review the item she'd purchased but couldn't see it anymore. There were no complaints earlier today or yesterday. Would you let the IT team know?

Mike Snow [12:15 A.M.]
Larry, something happened to the image files on the online store section of our Web site.

Larry McKee [12: 18 P.M.]
That's strange... Looks like they've been removed.

Mike Snow [12:19 P.M.]
I hope we've kept backup files.

Larry McKee [12:20 P.M.]
We always do, just in case. I'll upload them again now.

Mike Snow [12:21 P.M.]
Good. And we'll need to send a short explanation online and tell everyone that it is fixed.

Molly Vernon [12:22 P.M.]
I'll take care of that.

168. What problem does Ms. Vernon report?

(A) Online purchases are not processing.

(B) Incorrect information is listed on the company's Web site.

(C) The company's Web site appears to have been hacked.

(D) Product photos cannot be viewed in the online store section.

169. From whom did Ms. Vernon learn about the problem?

(A) An accountant

(B) An IT coworker

(C) A customer

(D) The company president

170. At 12:19 P.M., what does Mr. Snow mean when he writes, "I hope we've kept backup files"?

(A) He is afraid that the company has lost a lot of money.

(B) He wants his coworker to explain the procedures for handling files.

(C) He is looking for clients' financial transaction records.

(D) He hopes all of the pictures are still available.

171. What will Ms. Vernon most likely do next?

(A) Update her personal profile

(B) Contact the safety office

(C) Contact the IT team.

(D) Post a note online

Sweetwater Lake State Park

Things to Do

At Sweetwater Lake State Park, you can fish, paddle, hike, picnic, camp or stay in a cabin, and go boating.

Rent our group hall for your next reunion!

Alligators live in the park; read our alligator safety tips before your visit. — [1] —.

Fish: Sweetwater Lake State Park is 26,810-acres, and the lake itself harbors more than 70 species of fish.

We have a fishing pier and a boat ramp. You do not need a fishing license to fish from shore in a state

park. — [2] —. Ask about borrowing fishing equipment to use in the park.

Paddle: Explore Sweetwater Lake's twists and turns. Rent a canoe in the park or bring your own canoe or

kayak.— [3] —.

Stay:

• Choose from 46 campsites, ranging from water only to full hookup sites.

• Stay at a screened shelter.

• Rent one of our historic cabins. These range from two- to six-person cabins, and

　several are accessible to the handicapped.

Hike: Explore the forest afoot. One-quarter mile of the Sweetwater Forest Trail is handicapped accessible.

Learn more on our Interactive Map page. — [4] —.

Volunteers: Visit our Volunteer page to see how you can help.

172. What is indicated about the Sweetwater Lake State Park?

(A) It is difficult to get to from the highway.

(B) It is a man-made lake and relatively new.

(C) A variety of activities are provided.

(D) The fee for entry is very affordable.

173. What is indicated about camping at the park?

(A) There are many options available.

(B) There is no electricity at any of the campsites.

(C) There is no camping allowed this year.

(D) Many additional campsites are being constructed.

174. What is NOT suggested about Sweetwater Lake State Park?

(A) It is only for in-state residents.

(B) It has options for the handicapped.

(C) It has many forms of wildlife.

(D) It opened with many initial problems.

175. In which of the positions marked [1], [2], [3], and [4] does the following sentence best belong?

"Click on the link for the Handicapped Trail."

(A) [1]

(B) [2]

(C) [3]

(D) [4]

To: Eric Woodhouse, AZA Medical Supplies
From: Ryan Taylor, Manager, Ivy Hote
Date: November 29
Subject: Your stay at the Ivy Hotel
Attachment: AZAinvoice.txt

Dear Mr. Woodhouse,

We were pleased that you and your colleagues chose to stay at the Ivy Hotel during your visit to Montreal for the medical conference. We hope that you enjoyed your stay on November 26. Your credit card payment has just cleared. I have attached your receipt to this email. Thank you for your prompt payment

As the Ivy Hotel is quite new, we are always keen to receive feedback from our customers on ways that we can improve our services. If you or your staff have any comments about any aspect of your stay, please let us know so that we can better serve you in the future.

It was a pleasure to have you stay with us. If you choose the Ivy Hotel again for the next conference, we will offer you a 20% discount.

Sincerely,

Ryan Taylor
General Manager
The Ivy Hotel

To: Ryan Taylor, Manager, Ivy Hotel
From: Eric Woodhouse, AZA Medical Supplies
Date: December 1
Subject: Re: Your stay at the Ivy Hotel

Dear Mr. Taylor,

Thank you for your e-mail. My staff and I thoroughly enjoyed our stay at your hotel. The staff was very helpful, and the rooms were spacious and a pleasure to stay in. You made us feel very welcome.

My staff and I are actually returning to Montreal to attend a sales workshop next month. We would like to book four rooms to stay at your hotel if possible. Would it be possible to stay in the same rooms as the last time? They were all fantastic although the bathroom in the Oak Room was a little dirty.

We would really like to hold our next conference on March 1 in your hotel.

Sincerely,

Eric Woodhouse
Sales Consultant
AZA Medical Supplies

176. What is one purpose of the first email?
(A) To advertise a job opening at a hotel
(B) To promote the opening of a new hotel
(C) To request customer comments on a hotel stay
(D) To place an order for medical supplies

177. In the first email, the word "prompt" in paragraph 1, line 4, is closest in meaning to
(A) delayed
(B) late
(C) financial
(D) punctual

178. How did Mr. Woodhouse pay Mr. Taylor?
(A) With cash
(B) By credit card
(C) By check
(D) By bank transfer

179. What comment does Mr. Woodhouse make about the Oak Room?
(A) The toilet was not functioning.
(B) The window was broken.
(C) The bathroom was messy.
(D) The room was fantastic.

180. When will Mr. Woodhouse most likely receive a special discount?
(A) November 26
(B) November 29
(C) December 1
(D) March 1

The Daily News

December 1

For a "Pick-me-up"

Aaron Milton's days revolve around coffee beans, sugary syrups, and cream, with a variety of unique flavors added. His recently opened shop, the Daily Perk, serves a nice selection of deli sandwiches and sugary sweets, but it is the custom coffee drinks that really stand out. By combining his home-grown and roasted coffee beans with a creative flair for flavor combinations, Aaron Milton has become famous as "Mr. Coffee" among store patrons. Mr. Milton, a former school teacher, now produces the best caffeinated beverages in town. Because his drink concoctions are often inspired by the seasons (for example, pumpkin spiced pie during the fall and candy cane delight during the winter holidays), the selection of flavors changes frequently. Even the staff is encouraged to put their own personal touches to the menu and have created several staple items available year-round.

Mr. Milton started the Daily Perk with a loan from his parents, which he was able to repay just after his first year of business.

If you haven't been there yet, The Daily Perk is conveniently located at the corner of Weems Lane and Elm Street. It opens every morning at 6:30 A.M. For more information, visit their Web site at www.perkup.com.

To: Aaron Milton <amilton@mail.com>
From: Peter Vickers <Pvickers@mail.com>
Subject: Article
Date: December 3

Dear Aaron,

I saw the newspaper story about you in The Daily News, and it reminded me that I haven't been to your coffee shop yet. It sounds great, and I hope to stop by soon. We miss you at Crown Pointe Academy. Several students still ask about you. Things are going well here. We're renovating the science lab this summer, which I know you had been begging for years! You'll have to come see it when all the work is done.

I'll be seeing you soon!
Peter

181. What is suggested about Mr. Milton?
(A) He joined the family business.
(B) He owes his parents money.
(C) He farms some of his ingredients himself.
(D) He plans to change careers.

182. In the article, the word "revolve" in paragraph 1, line 1, is closet in meaning to
(A) resign
(B) design
(C) involve
(D) postpone

183. What is NOT indicated about the Daily Perk?
(A) It only has evening hours.
(B) Its menu changes often.
(C) It has experienced quick success.
(D) It offers a variety of products.

184. Why did Mr. Vickers send the e-mail?
(A) To ask Mr. Milton to come to his party
(B) To ask Mr. Milton for a job
(C) To ascertain his interest in an investment opportunity
(D) To tell Mr. Milton he read an article about his business

185. Where most likely did Mr. Vickers and Mr. Milton work together?
(A) At a coffee shop
(B) At a school
(C) At an advertising agency
(D) At a charity event

Sponsor decided for the upcoming Barrington Children's Hospital Marathon • May 5

It has been confirmed that the Pueblo Corporation will be the biggest sponsor for the upcoming Barrington Children's Hospital Marathon. Details regarding the sponsorship are to be announced in the near future. The corporation is ranked as the third largest pharmaceutical company in the country.

The Barrington Children's Hospital Marathon has been held annually for the past fifteen years. Over the years, more than $15 million have been raised to help children suffering from rare diseases. The event consists of a marathon (26 miles) and a half marathon (13 miles). All profits and contributions will be donated to the Barrington Children's Hospital. Participants are encouraged to make their own fundraising efforts.

The event will commence next month on Saturday, June 16. The Barrington Children's Hospital Marathon is the twentieth largest marathon in the nation, with over 10,000 participants for the half marathon and about 5,000 participants for the full marathon.

From:	Teresa Martinez <teresamartinez@pueblo.net>
To:	Jim Douglas <jimdouglas@pueblo.net>
Date:	May 10
Subject:	Interview with Social Interests News

Dear Mr. Douglas,

Following the recent press release on the Barrington Children's Hospital Marathon, multiple news media agencies have requested an interview. They want to hear our public relations department's opinion on the sponsorship decision. Out of them, I picked out the most reputable agency, Social Interests News. A writer from Social Interests News will contact you soon to schedule an interview. Considering your schedule, it seems like you will be free on May 12th, 14th, 15th, and 20th. I hope one of these days will work.

From: Matthew Stokes <mstokes12@socialinterestnews.com>
To: Jim Douglas <jimdouglas@pueblo.net>
Date: May 10
Subject: Interview Request to Pueblo Corporation

Dear Mr. Jim Douglas,

My name is Matthew and I am a writer at Social Interests News. I already contacted your secretary Teresa Martinez regarding an interview. I have heard about your company's decision to become a sponsor of the upcoming Barrington Children's Hospital Marathon. Our newspaper thought it would be a great opportunity for us to introduce a major sponsor to the public. We have no doubts that the interview will also be beneficial for your company's publicity. Will you be available on any of the following dates: 13, 14, or 16? If not, I can try to accommodate a better time for you.

186. What is NOT indicated about the Barrington Children's Hospital Marathon?
(A) It has been held every year for fifteen years.
(B) It is a fundraising event for children with illnesses.
(C) It consists of only a 26-mile marathon.
(D) It will be held mid-June this year.

187. Who most likely is Mr. Douglas?
(A) A director of Pueblo Corporation's public relations
(B) A secretary at Pueblo Corporation
(C) A chief editor at Social Interests News
(D) A representative of Barrington Children's Hospital

188. What is suggested about Pueblo Corporation?
(A) Its employees are participating in the marathon.
(B) It has always been a sponsor for the marathon.
(C) It is the biggest pharmaceutical company in the country.
(D) It specializes in producing medicinal drugs.

189. In the third email, the word "beneficial" in the paragraph 1, line 5, is closest in meaning to
(A) helpful
(B) useless
(C) critical
(D) alternative

190. When will the interview be most likely held?
(A) May 13
(B) May 14
(C) May 16
(D) June 16

Questions 191-195 refer to the following advertisements and e-mail.

http://www.allhousinglondon.uk

Visiting Professor Seeking Downtown Apartment

Topic: Six-Month Sublease
Date: September 12
Posted by: Reed McMahon

I will be in London from January to June on a teaching assignment at Coleridge College. I am looking for a six-month lease (or sublease) for the upcoming year.

I am not looking for anything luxurious. I'm in the market for a nice, clean one- or two-bedroom apartment with the basic amenities, including a stove and refrigerator. Anything else would be an added bonus. A patio or open balcony would be ideal, as I like to entertain friends and colleagues. I am looking to live near the college, however, as I will not be bringing my car from the United States. My budget is 1,600 American dollars per month, including water, gas, and electricity. I am a non-smoker.

http://www.allhousinglondon.uk

Apartment for Rent in London

Topic: Real Estate and Housing
Date: September 13

Enjoy this great one-bedroom apartment after a thorough renovation of the property. This clean and simple, yet modern apartment will be move-in ready on December 15. It will feature a lovely balcony, new floors throughout, and all new appliances. The apartment is just outside of downtown London, but close to major public transportation hubs. It is an ideal option for students and staff at Coleridge College, as well as the post office and other government buildings. It is less than a kilometer from a major municipal park. £1,000 per month pays for water, sewer, garbage pickups, and general upkeep of the property. The electricity and natural gas will be the responsibility of the tenant. Non-smokers only. A one-time security deposit equal to one month's rent should be paid upon signing the rental agreement.
Please feel free to call me at 926-7399 or e-mail me at turnerproperties@hmail.net.

<table>
<tr><td>To</td><td>Martha Turner<turnerproperties@hmail.net></td></tr>
<tr><td>From</td><td>Dr. Reed McMahon <reed.mc@talkmail.com></td></tr>
<tr><td>Subject</td><td>Apartment</td></tr>
<tr><td>Date</td><td>September 14</td></tr>
</table>

Dear Ms. Turner,

I am responding to your listing for the newly renovated one-bedroom apartment just outside of downtown. It sounds very appealing to me and definitely fits in my budget. Unfortunately, I won't be able to see the apartment firsthand, as I won't be in London until December 18. Could you send some pictures of the property? Obviously, it is still being renovated, but I'm sure I can fill in the blanks. Please use this e-mail address to respond or if you wish, feel free to call me anytime.

Thank you.

Dr. Reed McMahon
512.578.6090

191. Why is Dr. McMahon moving?

(A) To teach students

(B) To relocate a laboratory.

(C) To get close to a company

(D) To coach professional athletes

192. What aspect of the property does NOT match Dr. Reed's preferences?

(A) The monthly cost

(B) The size

(C) The location

(D) The smoking rules

193. What will happen on December 15?

(A) Ms. Turner's apartment will be sold.

(B) Dr. McMahon will travel to London.

(C) Ms. Turner's apartment will become available.

(D) Dr. McMahon will pay a deposit.

194. What does Dr. McMahon request?

(A) Dates of apartment availability

(B) A discount on the monthly rent

(C) Renovation staff contact information

(D) Photos of the apartment

195. What can be inferred the rent at Ms. Turner's property?

(A) It must be paid at the beginning of each month.

(B) It is less than 1,600 American dollars.

(C) It includes gas and electricity.

(D) It can be paid using a different currency.

Questions 196-200 refer to the following form, e-mail, and Web page.

BELLA AIR
Late Arrival Baggage Form

Dear Bella Air Customers,

We are sorry to inform you about the late arrival of your luggage. Please write down the details below to help us track your belongings and return them to you as soon as possible. A Bella Air clerk will inform you by phone as soon as we find your luggage. Any luggage that can't be found for more than a day should be reported on our company's Web site so instructions can be given.

Date: November 16
Name: Raymond Walker
Local Address: Hotel Quet, Downtown, 984-2 Auckland, New Zealand
Tel: +62 185 0253
Flight No.: K53GC6

Delayed Luggage Information

	Quantity	Descriptions
*Suitcase	1	Small red suitcase with 2 wheels; "Raymond Walker" on the name tag
Backpack		
Handbag		
*Box	1	Small plastic box with "Raymond Walker, Samion Foods" written on it
Other		

From:	Harry Homez <hhomez@samionfoods.com>
To:	Raymond Walker <rwalker@samionfoods.com>
Subject:	Re: Food Samples
Date:	November 16, 5:23 P.M.

Dear Mr. Walker

Since we cannot be sure when your luggage will be found and returned, I've sent sauce samples by night shipping. That way, you'll have goods to show the clients at tomorrow's meeting. It's really important that we get feedback about them. There are five flavors packed discretely as well as two small sauce bottles with labels. I sent the items with TWS Shipping to your lodging. The package will arrive by 9:30 A.M., so you can bring sauces and packages to the meeting and show them when you speak at the meeting at eleven.

Sincerely,

Harry Homez
Samion Foods

https://www.twsshipping.co.au/overnight

TWS SHIPPING
The Expedited and Reliable Shipping Company

- Your Shipment Information
Ship from:
  Samion Foods, 27 Earot Street, Archeis 1, 1UE, AU

Ship to:
  HOTEL QUET, Downtown, 984-2 Auckland, New Zealand

Weight: 0.68 kg

( ) Enclosed   (X) Box   ( ) Custom packaging

- Your Overnight Shipment Options

TWS Early morning; Deliver by 9:30 A.M. tomorrow [$62 Ship Now]
TWS morning; Deliver by 11:30 A.M. tomorrow [$49 Ship Now]
TWS afternoon; Deliver by 3:00 P.M. tomorrow [$31 Ship Now]
TWS evening; Deliver by 8:30 P.M. tomorrow [$35 Ship Now]

196. What is indicated about Bella Air?

(A) It requires customers to include name tags on all pieces of luggage.

(B) It guarantees that missing luggage will be returned in three days.

(C) It will notify Ms. Walker when her luggage is found.

(D) It will reimburse Mr. Walker for her lost luggage.

197. Where did Mr. Walker most likely pack his samples?

(A) In a box

(B) In a refrigerator

(C) In a briefcase

(D) In a backpack

198. What is implied about Mr. Homez?

(A) He is meeting with clients in New Zealand.

(B) He travels frequently for Samion Foods.

(C) He is a Bella Air customer service agent.

(D) He wants clients to .review some products.

199. According to the e-mail, what will Mr. Walker do tomorrow at 11 A.M.?

(A) Accept a delivery

(B) Give a presentation

(C) Check out of the hotel

(D) Confirm his return flight

200. How much was Mr. Homez most likely charged for shipping?

(A) $35.00

(B) $31.00

(C) $49.00

(D) $62.00

Stop! This is the end of the test. If you finish before time is called, you may go back to Parts 5, 6, and 7 and check your work.

101. A	121. B	141. C	161. C	181. C
102. D	122. B	142. B	162. A	182. C
103. C	123. B	143. C	163. B	183. A
104. D	124. C	144. C	164. D	184. D
105. A	125. B	145. A	165. A	185. B
106. D	126. C	146. A	166. A	186. C
107. D	127. D	147. D	167. C	187. A
108. C	128. C	148. D	168. D	188. D
109. A	129. B	149. C	169. C	189. A
110. C	130. A	150. B	170. D	190. B
111. C	131. D	151. D	171. D	191. A
112. B	132. C	152. B	172. C	192. C
113. D	133. A	153. A	173. A	193. C
114. C	134. B	154. B	174. A	194. D
115. D	135. C	155. D	175. D	195. B
116. A	136. D	156. A	176. C	196. C
117. A	137. D	157. C	177. D	197. A
118. D	138. A	158. B	178. B	198. D
119. B	139. A	159. C	179. C	199. B
120. C	140. C	160. A	180. D	200. D

ACTUAL TEST

3

READING TEST

In the Reading test, you will read a variety of texts and answer several different types of reading comprehension questions. The entire Reading test will last 75 minutes. There are three parts, and directions are given for each part. You are encouraged to answer as many questions as possible within the time allowed.

You must mark your answers on the separate answer sheet. Do not write your answers in your test book.

PART 5

Directions: A word or phrase is missing in each of the sentences below. Four answer choices are given below each sentence. Select the best answer to complete the sentence. Then mark the letter (A), (B), (C), or (D) on your answer sheet.

101. The recent economic report shows that many small companies are financially ------- in the early stages of their business.
(A) cause
(B) cautious
(C) caution
(D) cautiously

102. West Sea Bridge was recently chosen as the ------- construction structure in Asia by young professionals in architecture.
(A) fine
(B) finer
(C) finest
(D) fineness

103. Most frozen foods are neither healthy ------- nutritious, so people should avoid eating them regularly.
(A) but
(B) nor
(C) yet
(D) and

104. ------- high profits, most pharmaceutical companies are unable to conduct research to improve public health care.
(A) From
(B) Without
(C) Inside
(D) Along with

105. Bella's Bistro, the best restaurant in Cupertino, is conveniently ------- near the financial area of the city.
(A) locate
(B) locating
(C) located
(D) location

106. Almost all of the ------- in the local job fair are considering finding jobs in information technology.
(A) participants
(B) participating
(C) participation
(D) participate

107. If your application meets the criteria of our company, you will receive written ------- that you have been hired.
(A) notify
(B) notifying
(C) notification
(D) notifies

108. Municipal boards of education in each city in California need time ------- for the new school system.
(A) to prepare
(B) preparing
(C) prepared
(D) prepare

109. When researchers handle the flammable chemicals in the research laboratory, they must be ------- and follow the safety instructions.
(A) tentative
(B) careful
(C) operational
(D) reliable

110. Domestic construction activities fell about 15% last year, ------- by a prolonged slump in the housing construction sector.
(A) led
(B) lead
(C) leading
(D) be led

111. There are retail shops, beauty shops, restaurants, and art galleries ------- walking distance for most residents in the city.
(A) inside
(B) within
(C) until
(D) from

112. ------- our company is growing in terms of revenue, we are not yet strong enough to compete with other foreign companies.
(A) When
(B) Even though
(C) In case
(D) Nonetheless

113. Lisa Jones has proved ------- a successful singer as well as an outstanding songwriter in North America.
(A) she
(B) her
(C) hers
(D) herself

114. Any foreigner who wants to work at our new factory for over a month must apply for a ------- work permit.
(A) relevance
(B) relevancies
(C) relevant
(D) relevantly

115. ------- discourage wasteful use, the newly revised law will raise the cost of water and electricity next year.
(A) In order to
(B) Thanks to
(C) Due to
(D) With regard to

116. According to the report, construction for the new stadium complex in Oakland is ------- 80 percent complete.
(A) currently
(B) frequently
(C) so far
(D) once

117. Mandoo Heavy Machines was able to introduce itself on international markets with ------- huge success in South Korea.
(A) whose
(B) whom
(C) those
(D) its

118. The process of creating the TV commercial for Bella Cosmetics was ------- complete when the client asked for some changes.
(A) nearer
(B) nearest
(C) nearby
(D) nearly

119. Based on their resumes and recommendation letters, the final two candidates seem ------- qualified for our sales director position.
(A) high
(B) successfully
(C) equally
(D) punctually

120. The cost of gasoline has become ------- high that many people commuting to work are unable to pay for their commute without a pay raise.
(A) so
(B) very
(C) too
(D) such

121. About 200 flights to the southern resort island of Cayo Costa ------- due to the pilots' partial strike.
(A) canceling
(B) cancels
(C) will be canceled
(D) have canceled

122. The board of directors is going to reward some ------- employees who have been with the company for over ten years.
(A) dedicated
(B) satisfied
(C) temporary
(D) promotional

123. Ms. Whitman established her own post-impressionism style after she was ------- by many impressionist artists in Europe.
(A) presented
(B) reminded
(C) influenced
(D) determined

124. The institute ------- the brand power of major foreign companies based on their global market shares and export volumes.
(A) built
(B) evaluated
(C) nominated
(D) attracted

125. Our board members ------- planned to set out for New York on Wednesday but were held up by the inclement weather.
(A) inadvertently
(B) precisely
(C) knowingly
(D) initially

126. According to famed British music magazine Classic, Mr. McDonald can play any song on the guitar after hearing it just -------.
(A) once
(B) again
(C) now
(D) yet

127. The customer service manager requested that all questions from customers ------- answered quickly and courteously.
(A) are
(B) were
(C) will be
(D) be

128. Some city officials said that factory ------- will be introduced to improve Beijing's air quality and the health of citizens.
(A) close
(B) closed
(C) closely
(D) closure

129. Some analysts often avoid sharing information ------- may damage their company's revenue streams.
(A) who
(B) which
(C) whose
(D) what

130. The city government must ban plastic bags in markets ------- people want to live on a landfill sooner or later.
(A) whether
(B) where
(C) unless
(D) how

PART 6

Directions: Read the texts that follow. A word, phrase, or sentence is missing in parts of each text. Four answer choices for each question are given below the text. Select the best answer to complete the text. Then mark the letter (A), (B), (C), or (D) on your answer sheet.

Questions 131-134 refer to the following information.

The Haru Battery you have purchased was designed to last for approximately three years or about 30,000 miles. When your battery finally dies, you should dispose of it -------.
131.
Please do not just throw it in a trash can. Most municipalities currently recommend users not ------- their dead batteries away with trash.
132.

Most experts say discarded batteries can cause fires and explosions if they ------- loose in
133.
boxes or bags with metal items. That's why our company offers a quick and easy disposal method to customers. -------. When you turn them over to us, our recycling specialists take
134.
care of them in the proper fashion at no additional charge.

131. (A) immediately
(B) properly
(C) confidentially
(D) respectively

132. (A) throw
(B) to throw
(C) throwing
(D) thrown

133. (A) stores
(B) are stored
(C) stored
(D) will be stored

134. (A) Some batteries left in your garage can cause several safety concerns.
(B) Please do not combine old and new batteries or different types or makes of batteries.
(C) New small-size batteries are used in mobile phones and motor-driven electric tools.
(D) All you have to do is return your dead battery to one of our recycling centers in your area.

Questions 135-138 refer to the following e-mail.

From: customerservice@diamondcinemas.com

To: rwillis12@bizwiz.com

Date: October 11

Subject: Emerald Member Status

Dear Rochelle Willis,

Congratulations! Our records ------- that your recent purchase qualifies you as an emerald **135.** member. The emerald membership can be attained by purchasing over $250 worth of movie tickets within a year. As thanks, we are sending you five free movie tickets and eight coupons for free popcorn. This status also gives you special ------- to our exclusive movie **136.** premieres. The next level, which is the ruby membership, can be acquired by spending over $400 on movie tickets within a year. -------. **137.**

We thank you again for your ------- and we look forward to seeing you at our movie **138.** theaters nationwide.

Sincerely,

Diamond Cinemas Customer Service

---

135. (A) indicate
(B) indication
(C) indicating
(D) has indicated

136. (A) excess
(B) access
(C) advice
(D) assess

137. (A) If you are a first-time customer, please join our Diamond Cinemas membership program.
(B) Ruby members receive 8 free movie tickets and 12 free popcorn coupons.
(C) Movie tickets are non-refundable and non-exchangeable.
(D) Please do not bring outside food or drinks into the movie theater.

138. (A) honesty
(B) assistance
(C) loyalty
(D) improvement

To: Melina Ramos Sandoval<mrs@watchmedia.com>

From: Customer Service <welcome@nationwidejobs.com>

Date: 25 October

Subject: About Your Registration

Dear Ms. Sandoval,

Welcome to the Nationwide Jobs Network, one of the leading online profession matchmakers in the country. Your personal information, ------- **139.** your address and work experience, will be securely kept only in our database if you allow us to do so.

The collected information will be used to analyze your job preferences, and we will provide it to employers who are ------- **140.** a job applicant just like -------. **141.** Regular e-mail notifications about job openings in your area will be sent after you subscribe to our service.

-------. **142.** Therefore, we handle your personal information very carefully. If you want to join us, please visit our Web site at www.njn.com or call 1-888-926-7677.

Thank you.

Truly yours,

Nationwide Jobs Network

Customer Service

---

139. (A) and
(B) such as
(C) as well as
(D) now that

140. (A) looking into
(B) laying off
(C) relying upon
(D) searching for

141. (A) me
(B) you
(C) ours
(D) us

142. (A) We know anyone can be a victim of identity theft.
(B) Customer satisfaction has always been our top priority.
(C) Our job database is usually updated monthly.
(D) Your résumé has recently been reviewed by the board members.

Questions 143-146 refer to the following letter.

April 5

Dr. Nina Lee
5th Avenue #310
Phoenix, AZ 50505

Dr. Michael Westen
25200 Carlos Bee Blvd #302
Hayward, CA 94542

Dear Dr. Michael Westen:

Thank you for your invitation to Hayward for the urban economy conference ------- by **143.** California State University. It was ------- an honor to receive the invitation. **144.**

Unfortunately, I am already committed during the period of your event. -------. **145.**

I am working on getting an equally qualified faculty member from Arizona State University that would be willing to come. If you think this person is qualified, he or she could go in my -------. If you have any further questions, please do not hesitate to get in touch with me. **146.**

Best regards,

Dr. Nina Lee
Professor
The Department of Economics
Arizona State University

143. (A) interested
(B) specialized
(C) scheduled
(D) organized

144. (A) very
(B) so
(C) quite
(D) much

145. (A) I am very sorry that I will not be able to participate in the conference.
(B) Please consider making time to commit yourself to this great opportunity.
(C) The registration fee before May 1 is $250 for a member, and $350 for a non-member.
(D) Thank you in advance for agreeing to participate in this important event.

146. (A) place
(B) expertise
(C) perspective
(D) presentation

Questions 147-148 refer to the following e-mail.

From: Office King Customer Service <infor@officeking.com>
To: Isabella Choi <ischoi@kamongcorp.com>
Subject: Order #1123
Date: 11 September

Dear Isabella Choi,

Your order has been cancelled as you requested. For your reference, here is a summary of your September 9 order.

Order #1123 Apple 110 BK Printer
Status: Cancelled

According to our policy, you will get a full refund within three business days.

If you need some further information, please visit us at www.officeking.com, or call us at 1-800-692-9815.

We always appreciate your business.

Office King

147. Why was the e-mail sent?
(A) To inquire about a refund policy
(B) To inform a customer of a sales promotion
(C) To confirm an order cancellation
(D) To correct a mistake

148. What is suggested about Ms. Choi?
(A) She has already paid for the item.
(B) She will get a full refund in one week.
(C) She will receive a printer in three days.
(D) She has been offered a special discount.

Attention Creative Writing Students!

The annual Sandstone Short Story Writing Contest has begun.

Entries are being accepted from now the deadline of October 30. All short stories should be between 1,000 and 4,000 words in length and can be on any topic. A panel of noted authors—horror novelist Samuel J. Kingston, mystery writer Janice Bonderman and essayist Diana Jacobi—will judge the entries.

There will be numerous prizes awarded in two different age categories:

— Ages 16 and under

— Ages 17-19

The winner of the major prize of Most Promising Writer will receive a $1,000 university scholarship, a three-day all-expenses-paid trip to New York to visit two major publishing houses and publication of his or her short story in the Sandstone Beacon Gazette.

Registration forms are available from English teachers at all local area schools. Send the forms by mail to:

Sandstone Short Story Writing Contest

P.O.Box 50

Sandstone, VA 65455

Best of luck to all budding writers out there!

149. What date must all entries be received by?

    (A) October 3

    (B) October 16

    (C) October 19

    (D) October 30

150. Where should registration forms be sent?

    (A) To Samuel J. Kingston

    (B) To the local newspaper

    (C) To a special Post Office Box number

    (D) To the local community center

151. What will the top prize winner get?

    (A) A full four-year university scholarship

    (B) A week's stay in New York with all expenses paid

    (C) A chance to meet top publishers

    (D) An internship at a popular magazine company

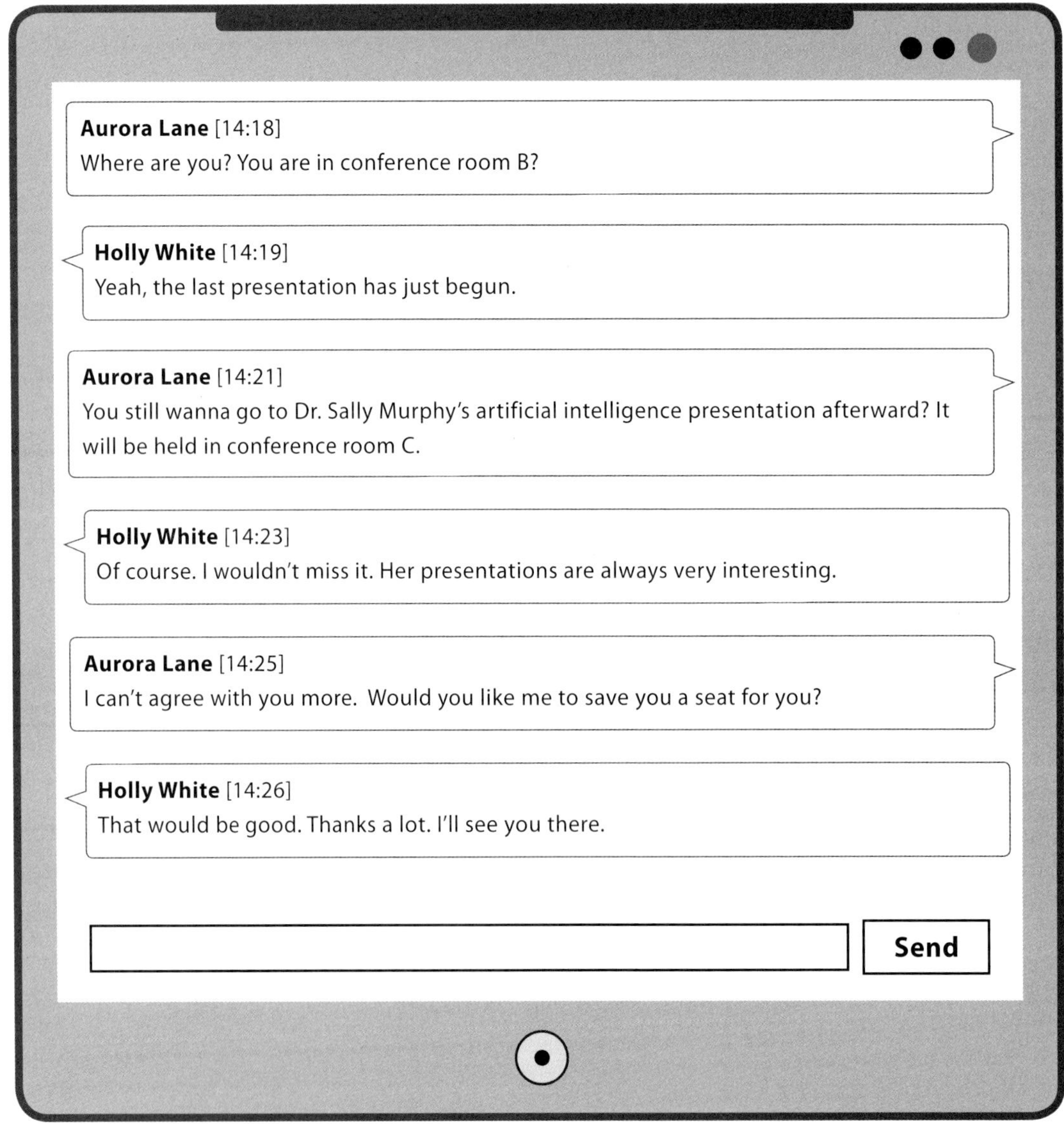

152. At 14:25, what does Ms. Lane most likely mean when she writes, "I can't agree with you more"?
(A) She thinks there is no evidence to support Dr. Murphy's theory.
(B) She is certain Ms. White is mistaken in his speech.
(C) She was very impressed with Ms. White's presentation.
(D) She agrees with Ms. White's opinion of Dr. Murphy's speech.

153. What is probably true about Ms. Lane?
(A) She will go to conference room C before Ms. White.
(B) She will give a presentation after Dr. Murphy.
(C) She has already reserved a conference room for an event.
(D) She wants to write a thesis on artificial intelligence with Ms. White.

The World Economy Leader
Business News

September 13, Los Angeles—Lance Merrier, Vice President of Apple Republic Corporation, released a statement on Tuesday stating that the company is going through with plans to open stores in Chicago, Atlanta, New York, and New Orleans within the next year.

Mr. Merrier admitted mistake on his part last year, when the company first tried to expand. He confessed that the main problem with the unsuccessful expansion was that the company was not yet strong enough financially to make that kind of move. He acknowledged that the company had misjudged its value. With a strong marketing campaign and a revitalized mission, the company maintains that the expansion will be far easier this time.

Los Angeles-based Apple Republic Corporation was founded by Christopher Lee and maintained a clean and classic style marketed at middle-aged adults. The company will begin adding a younger line of clothing in the spring in its new stores. The company will keep a close watch on how well its first foray into children's clothing starts out. Early projections have the four new stores bringing in record numbers, but no one at the company is going to believe it until they see it.

154. What is suggested about Apple Republic Corporation?
(A) It moved its main office to Los Angeles.
(B) It recently closed half its stores.
(C) It carries children's clothing.
(D) Its merchandise is currently limited to adults.

155. Where is Apple Republic Corporation currently located?
(A) In Chicago
(B) In New York
(C) In Los Angeles
(D) In New Orleans

To: Dr. Harvey Davis, Chief Resident

From: Dr. Dana Kamon, Head of Pediatrics

Subject: Nursing shortages

As you know from the buzz around the wards, the staff shortages are becoming too much of a distraction. We all know we need more nurses, but the budget is tight. I wanted to propose more job sharing, which might be at least a temporary solution to the crisis.

Of course, in the long term, we need to hire full-time nurses but here in Pediatrics where we have had job sharing for over a year, we feel it works well. I'm not saying it's a perfect solution, but to cover shortages of staff, it has worked.

156. What is the issue being discussed?
(A) A shortage of hospital beds
(B) Doctors working too many long shifts
(C) Patient care in the pediatric ward
(D) A nurse staffing problem

157. What is the solution being suggested by Dr. Kamon?
(A) Job sharing by the nurses
(B) Hiring more full-time doctors
(C) Cutting the nursing staff
(D) Rotating doctors from ward to ward

Questions 158-160 refer to the following advertisement.

The Sea World
The Pacific Ocean Hotel

Good day to you, and welcome to the Pacific Ocean Hotel. We hope you will thoroughly enjoy your stay. If you are looking for a restaurant with delicious food and the best view in town, look no further than the Sea World, our hotel restaurant located on the first floor. Chef Albert Condoza will be serving up some of the freshest catch of the day all evening long, and there is a table waiting just for you.

The Sea World is open Tuesday through Sunday from 11:00 A.M. to 11:30 P.M. If you are in your room and would like to order room service, we have a room service menu posted in every room. You can order anything from the Sea World menu during regular restaurant hours.

Come and visit this Sunday between 1:00 P.M. and 3:00 P.M. You can enjoy the shrimp and crab feast. All you need to do is bring this advertisement with you to the restaurant, and you can enjoy unlimited amount of succulent crab meat and giant shrimp.

158. At what time does the restaurant open on Wednesdays?
(A) 11:00 A.M.
(B) 11:30 A.M.
(C) 1:00 P.M.
(D) 3:00 P.M.

159. What is NOT indicated about the room service?
(A) It includes the full menu.
(B) If offers many items at low prices.
(C) It is available during business hours.
(D) Its food is from the Sea World.

160. What will the Pacific Ocean Hotel offer some of its clients?
(A) A discount coupon for the restaurant
(B) Complimentary room service
(C) Free seafood meals
(D) Special water ballet shows

From: Wesley Kim, Personnel Manager

To: All employees

Date: 13 September

Subject: Maintenance Work

Dear colleagues:

Please be advised that our underground parking lot will be unavailable from October 2 through October 5 due to maintenance work. — [1] —. It is scheduled to reopen on Monday, October 6. Employees who drive to work are encouraged to use nearby parking lots such as the downtown public parking lot, and the company will reimburse any parking costs. — [2] —. Also, employees can discuss with their department heads the possibility of working from home if they have a long commute. — [3] —.

We will have ten additional parking spaces once the maintenance work has been completed. — [4] —. If you are a full-time employee and have worked over three years, you can get one of them via lottery. Please call me at ext. 1123 to enter the lottery.

Thank you for your understanding and cooperation in advance.

Wesley Kim

Personnel Manager

Hayward Accounting Firm

161. What can employees discuss with their supervisors?

(A) Transition to permanent employment

(B) A lottery drawing for a parking space

(C) The possibility of telecommuting

(D) Reimbursement for their travel expenses

162. What is probably true of the downtown public parking lot?

(A) It will reopen on October 6.

(B) It charges for parking.

(C) It is far from Hayward Accounting Firm.

(D) It was recently expanded.

163. In which of the positions marked [1], [2], [3], and [4] does the following sentence best belong?

"We have decided to expand the underground parking lot to provide room for more vehicles."

(A) [1]

(B) [2]

(C) [3]

(D) [4]

To: Chris Bundy <cbundy@dahmercorp.com>
From: Yuliana Lim <ylim@trentonhotel.com>
Subject: Trenton Hotel Reservation Inquiry
Date: August 19

Dear Mr. Bundy,

I just received your e-mail regarding your upcoming reservations at our hotel. You are correct that your September stay will be eligible for our reward points plan for frequent guests. — [1] —.

In your e-mail, you mentioned that you would like to check in early on September 1. As you are probably aware, our normal check-in time is not until 2 P.M., but we will do our best to have your room ready by noon. — [2] —. You may call the front desk in advance to ask about this. If you choose to turn up early and your assigned room is still being prepared, you may leave your luggage with the front desk staff, and they will store it securely while you relax or walk around town.

You are also correct about the issue regarding your July reservation at our hotel. Due to a computer error, we failed to refund the $100 security deposit after you checked out. I have now personally made sure that the amount was deposited back into your account this morning. — [3] —. To make amends for this mistake, I have arranged for you to receive a gift certificate that can be exchanged for two tickets to see any film at the nearby Odeon Cinema.

If you have any further questions, please contact me directly at 555-5674. — [4] —.

Regards,

Yuliana Lim
Trenton Hotel Reservations Manager

164. What is the purpose of the e-mail?

    (A) To inform a guest that a check-out time has been changed

    (B) To request that a guest send an advance payment

    (C) To notify a guest that a room is unavailable on a certain date

    (D) To confirm that a guest is eligible for a special program

165. What is mentioned about the Trenton Hotel?

    (A) It is situated next to a fitness center.

    (B) It has recently renovated some of its rooms.

    (C) It allows guests to store their bags.

    (D) It has notified Mr. Bundy about reduced room rates.

166. What problem did Mr. Bundy experience when he last stayed at the Trenton Hotel?

    (A) He was overcharged for room service.

    (B) He did not receive his security deposit.

    (C) He lost some of his personal belongings.

    (D) He was unable to check in at the standard time.

167. In which of the positions marked [1], [2], [3], and [4] does the following sentence best belong?

"I apologize for this oversight and any inconvenience it may have caused you."

    (A) [1]

    (B) [2]

    (C) [3]

    (D) [4]

Calvert City News
A Chance to Escape the City

By Kelly McGowan

MAY 23—Rather than focusing on activities and restaurants based here in Calvert City, I decided to make this week's column a little different by discussing the beautiful town of Grey Bridge, just 20 kilometers north of the city limits. Grey Bridge is a quaint, peaceful little town that offers everyone a chance to escape the noise and chaos of the city. It also boasts a surprising number of things to do and places to eat. Below, you can read my suggestions for planning an enjoyable day-trip to Grey Bridge.

(8:30 A.M.) When you arrive, you should head straight for Dale Bakery. Although it is primarily a bakery, selling various breads and pastries to customers, it also has a dining area and boasts a limited, yet delicious menu. It has been a long-time fixture in Grey Bridge, and it has become particularly well-known for its delicious breakfast offerings. Try the full English breakfast with some freshly brewed coffee.

(9:45 A.M.) After gaining energy from your delicious breakfast, I recommend taking a walk along nearby Glenford River. Not only is the entire river area picturesque, but it contains several sites of interest. During your walk, stop to check out the many sculptures and murals at the Balgay Art Park, and don't miss the Alton Farm Petting Zoo, which will be of particular interest to young children.

(1:30 P.M.) Once you've worked up an appetite walking along the river, head back into town and visit Alma's Country Kitchen for lunch. Although it has not been open long, it has already established itself as one of the town's premier eateries. Alma's serves dishes that are made using only produce from nearby farms and suppliers, and I would specifically single out its expertly-cooked grilled salmon and chopped salad for special praise. Its menu can be viewed online at www.almascountrykitchen.co.uk. Be warned, however, that you may face a long wait if you go there on the weekend. Also, it's possible to take out certain foods, such as baguettes and baked potatoes, which means you can enjoy them in nearby Meadow Park if you choose. This is a great choice when the weather is nice

(3:00 P.M.) For the remainder of your day in Grey Bridge, try taking a guided tour of Grey Bridge Cathedral. This stunning building was built in the late-fifteenth century and is preserved and maintained by the Grey Bridge Cultural Heritage Society. One wing of the cathedral has been converted into an art gallery, which features various artworks from local painters and sculptors. Admission to both the cathedral and its gallery is free from Monday to Thursday. At all other times, a ticket must be purchased at the main entrance. Check www.greybridgecathedral.org for current rates.

Do you have any of your own suggestions regarding what to do during daytrips to Grey Bridge? If so, please send your thoughts to ggilford@calvertnews.org.

168. The word "boasts" in paragraph 1, line 8, is closest in meaning to

(A) awards

(B) announces

(C) equips

(D) offers

169. What is suggested about Ms. McGowan's column?

(A) It often focuses on Grey Bridge.

(B) It ordinarily includes interviews.

(C) It is a weekly feature in a publication.

(D) It is the publication's newest column.

170. According to the article, what is true about Alma's Country Kitchen?

(A) It offers a wide variety of baked goods.

(B) It opens for business at 1:30 P.M. every day.

(C) It uses only locally-sourced ingredients.

(D) It is generally less busy on weekends.

171. What is NOT a recommendation made by Mr. Gilford?

(A) Purchasing a ticket for the cathedral in advance

(B) Taking restaurant food to a local park

(C) Visiting an exhibition of paintings

(D) Submitting ideas for things to do in Grey Bridge

Neil Webster [09:34 A.M.]: Hey Lora, do you know what's happening to the refund on order #3920? The customer wants to know the progress.

Lora McDaniel [09:35 A.M.]: Wasn't that the order containing the yoga mat and dumbbells? I thought they were already processed.

Neil Webster [09:36 A.M.]: The customer said that he hasn't received the payment yet. It has already been two weeks since he returned the products and requested a refund.

Lora McDaniel [09:37 A.M.]: I'm not sure what's going on then. Let me check with customer services.

Lora McDaniel [09:39 A.M.]: Max, can you look up the refund process on order #3920? The customer still hasn't received the payment.

Max Francis [09:42 A.M.]: It looks like there was a mistake in the processing. I can work on it immediately, but it will still take a week for the customer to receive the payment. Is that alright?

Neil Webster [09:43 A.M.]: I guess we don't have a choice. Thanks for taking care of it though.

172. What type of business do the writers work for?
(A) A real estate agency
(B) An exercise equipment store
(C) An accounting firm
(D) A fitness center

173. What did the customer ask for?
(A) A refund on a previous order
(B) A change in shipping address
(C) An addition to an order
(D) An update on the order delivery

174. Why does Ms. McDaniel contact Mr. Francis?
(A) To ask for advice on product delivery
(B) To look up where the returned package is
(C) To find out if she can get a refund for her order
(D) To know why a refund has not been processed yet

175. At 9:43 A.M., what does Mr. Webster most likely mean when he writes, "I guess we don't have a choice."?
(A) He wants Mr. Francis to process the problem immediately.
(B) He is accepting the fact that it will inevitably take time to fix the problem.
(C) He does not understand why the processing takes so long.
(D) He is asking for additional help from customer services.

Simmons Heat & Air

September 2
Ms. Jessie Spano
Dunder Miflin Corp.
9923 Swanson Street
Nashville, TN 92929

Dear Ms. Spano,

We were going through our records in the past few days and found that the heating unit you installed at your company was purchased almost a year ago. This message is a recommendation to have your system examined. As noted in your contract, your purchase comes with a five-year warranty, so you can have any defective parts replaced for free. Just send us an e-mail to schedule a convenient time for us to come by and check the unit.

Even if you think the unit is working fine right now, it is never a bad thing to have an overall check up and make sure nothing is close to wearing out or breaking. It will save you lots of money in the long run. Now is the best time to schedule a service check because the winter months can get very busy with requests, house calls, and service repairs.

Get in touch with us as soon as you can to ensure that you are cozy and warm throughout the winter months. You can call us at 606-555-0994 or e-mail at customerservice@simmonshna.com.

Sincerely,

J. K. Simmons

J. K. Simmons

President
Simmons Heat & Air

To: customerservice@simmonshna.com
From: jspano@dundermif.com
Date: September 5
Subject: Heating Unit Inspection

Dear Mr. Simmons,

I received your letter about inspecting my current heating system. You are correct: our unit has not been examined since we purchased it. I do think it is time we should get a proper inspection to ensure that it is running efficiently. Would it be possible to send someone out next week?

I also would like the service technician to check our current air conditioning system. We are looking into getting a new one because our current one is getting old and unreliable. We are in the office from 9 A.M. until 6 P.M., so you can send a service technician any time we are here. Just e-mail and inform me when your technician will be coming by.

Thank you.

Jessie Spano
Director of Operations
Dunder Miflin Corp.

176. What is the purpose of the letter?
(A) To recommend a service
(B) To report test retake days
(C) To cancel an appointment
(D) To inquire about a replacement part

177. According to Mr. Simmons, why should an inspection be scheduled promptly?
(A) Winter weather has damaged some components.
(B) A manufacturing error has been detected.
(C) The warranty will expire at the end of the fall.
(D) It will be difficult to schedule an inspection in winter.

178. When was the heating system at Dunder Miflin Corp. inspected?
(A) One week ago
(B) One month ago
(C) One year ago
(D) Two years ago

179. What is suggested about Dunder Miflin Corp.'s air-conditioning system?
(A) It is broken.
(B) It is not in good working order.
(C) It has never been inspected.
(D) It was installed just recently.

180. In the e-mail, the phrase "looking into" in paragraph 2, line 2, is closest in meaning to
(A) expecting
(B) investigating
(C) observing
(D) researching

Questions 181-185 refer to following memo and e-mail.

MEMO

From: Nancy Palosi, Executive Assistant, Office of the Vice President
To: Carmina Falcone, Chief Financial Officer
Date: September 13
Subject: Bixby Inc. Tour

The itinerary has unfortunately been changed for the Bixby Inc. facilities tour next month starting in El Paso and ending in San Antonio. I have listed the new dates and times of your new flights from Seattle to El Paso as well as from El Paso to San Antonio below. Your flight from San Antonio returning to Seattle has not been determined yet. I will give that information to you as soon as I have it.

Flight E443 departing Seattle 10:00 A.M. September 19
Arrive El Paso 12:50 P.M. September 19
Flight F559 departing El Paso 2:40 P.M. September 21
Arrive San Antonio 4:30 P.M. September 21

Mr. Stern's flight arrives in El Paso a few hours before you, so he has asked if you could contact him once you have landed. The two of you will then proceed to Bixby Inc.'s El Paso plant and commence the tour. Because of the arrival time of your flight, the meeting was moved back to 2 P.M.

To: Nancy Palosi <npalosi@millerco.com>
From: David Thornbush <guestservice@grandritz.com>
Date: September 11
Subject: Your requests for Ms. Falcone and Mr. Stern

This is a confirmation of the reservation you made over the phone last week for Ms. Carmina Falcone and Mr. Daniel Stern at the Grand Ritz Hotel. Two single rooms have been booked on the executive floor. All their business needs will be met inside their rooms. Each room is equipped with a computer with Internet access, a printer, and a fax machine. I received the package that was sent by courier from your company in Seattle. It will be placed in Ms. Falcone's room when she arrives.

As Mr. Stern is arriving around 10 A.M., I have arranged an early check-in time of 10:30 A.M. free of charge. Mr. Stern and Ms. Falcone will have full use of conference room C at 2 P.M. on the day of their arrival. Conference room C is located on basement level one. We have also reserved a special dinner for our two guests at our hotel restaurant, The Olive. The meals will be charged to the guests' account. If you have any other questions at all about their stay, please contact us before their arrival, and I am sure we can assist you with any request you might have. Thank you.

Mina Sohn
Service Manager
Grand Ritz Hotel, El Paso

181. What is the main purpose of Ms. Palosi's memo?

(A) To request a new date for the trip
(B) To determine who will go on the trip
(C) To confirm a change in travel plan
(D) To cancel a planned meeting

182. Where will the facilities tour take place?

(A) In El Paso
(B) In San Antonio
(C) In Seattle and El Paso
(D) In El Paso and San Antonio

183. Where will the two guests hold their meeting?

(A) In a hotel conference room
(B) In the San Antonio office
(C) At the El Paso facilities
(D) In Ms. Falcone's office

184. What is mentioned about Mr. Stern's arrival?

(A) It will be delayed because his flight was canceled.
(B) It will take place before the documents from the office arrive.
(C) It will be earlier than standard hotel check-in time.
(D) It will be after Ms. Falcone has arrived.

185. What is NOT mentioned about the guest rooms that have been reserved?

(A) They are single rooms.
(B) They have office equipment.
(C) They are on the same floor.
(D) They are adjacent to the dining room.

Flywheel Knife Sharpener

Are you a determined home kitchen cook or a seasoned knife-wielding chef? Well, the Flywheel Knife Sharpener is the ideal kitchen-counter appliance that sharpens all bladed kitchen tools in a snap. Best of all, it is rugged, lightweight, and built for performance!

Features: The enclosed diamond-tipped sharpening wheels provide superior performance and safety, as well as reliability and endurance. Its waterproof gears allow for knife sharpening in all environments you can sharpen your knives in the toughest kitchen conditions.

Warranty: We include a ten-year warranty on all parts and labor—a standard not met by any other brand on the market. This is our guarantee that the product will provide years of hard use.

Regular purchase price: $250.00 / Flywheel Products Loyalty members price: $199.00

---

www.flywheelcountertopappliances.uk/2345/mn

| HOME | PRODUCTS | REVIEW | FAQ |

Rating : ★ ★ ★ ★ ★

I've never been more impressed by a knife sharpener! I am not a chef and my wife does all the cooking, but I am a professional knife maker. I make custom knives for a living. I make all kinds of knives kitchen knives, tactical knives, and hunting knives. I regularly travel to trade shows, so the weight of the Flywheel Sharpener is ideal for me. I need to move it from place to place constantly. It is a mainstay on my travelling van. I am particularly impressed by its various features from the different speeds to the adjustable bevel angles. Well done. Highly recommended!

Posted by *David Baker*
August 29

www.flywheelcountertopappliances.uk/2345/mn/response

HOME	PRODUCTS	**REVIEW**	FAQ

Thank you for your kind comments, Mr. Baker. At Flywheel, we are committed to serving customers—particularly customers who need a reliable, powerful tool in order to get the job done. You said you travel for work, but what about the wife? Couldn't she use a Flywheel Sharpener on her kitchen countertop? We'd like to recommend a lighter version of your sharpener: the Flywheel Knife Sharpener Express. It has all of the features of your sharpener, but in a slightly lighter package. It also comes in a variety of colors, so your wife can match her appliances for a clean, coherent look in the kitchen. See it on our Web site at : www.flywheelcountertopappliances/sharpeners/express

Again, thanks for your vote of confidence, and keep on sharpening!

Posted by Flywheel Customer Service on August 29.

186. What is NOT mentioned in the product description as a feature of the knife sharpener?
(A) It is very reliable.
(B) It is suitable for professional chefs.
(C) It is larger than competitors' knife sharpeners.
(D) It is great for the home kitchen.

187. What is indicated in the customer review?
(A) The sharpener comes with detailed instructions.
(B) Mr. Baker is not a chef.
(C) Flywheel products come in a variety of colors.
(D) The sharpener is very heavy.

188. What is suggested in the manufacturer's response?
(A) They want Mr. Baker to purchase another model for cooking.
(B) They want Mr. Baker to extend a warranty.
(C) They want to offer Mr. Baker a discount on his next purchase.
(D) They want Mr. Baker to be their new head researcher.

189. Why would the Flywheel Knife Sharpener Express be recommended for Ms. Baker?
(A) It is inexpensive.
(B) It is dishwasher proof.
(C) It is easy to assemble.
(D) It is lightweight.

190. What is suggested by the date of the manufacturer's response?
(A) They respond very quickly.
(B) They take their time.
(C) They are interested in marketing.
(D) They are outselling their competitors.

Questions 191-195 refer to the following letters and invoice.

Jack Stanford
1123 Pine St.
Queen City, CA 92152

Snape's Second-Hand Books
45 Capon St.
Los Angeles, CA 94721

Dear Mr. Snape,

I visited Snape's Second-hand Books at the Antiquarian Book Fair in California last year. I noticed that you have a variety of products in reliable condition, so I ordered some books through your Web site. As I take great care of my books and am not interested in collecting any damaged books, I always check the descriptions to learn about the condition of a book before I place an order. I expected the products I ordered not to have any defects but when I inspected the products upon arrival, I found that the cover of *Timmy's Voyage as a a Captain* had not been attached properly and looks like it has been rebound several times. However, given your store policy, I cannot send the book back.
Please reply to me as soon as possible to solve this frustrating situation.

Sincerely,

Jack Stanford

INVOICE

Snape's Second-Hand Books
45 Capon St.
Los Angeles, CA 94721

Jack Stanford
1123 Pine St.
Queen City, CA 92152

Item Number	Book Title	Price
BK 1123	Timmy's Voyage as a Captain	$94.25
BC 6030	New Line of the World	$58.00
CJ 7399	How Should I Live	$86.00
KS 9013	Behind the History	$131.00
	Total	$369.25

Snape's Second-Hand Books
'We Offer You Every Book You Want'
45 Capon St.
Los Angeles, CA 94721

Jack Stanford
1123 Pine St.
Queen City, CA 92152

Dear Mr. Stanford,

I can tell you that I carefully check all our books myself and write the descriptions of their conditions on our Web site. When I received your letter, I remembered that the book was rebound by the original owner over six decades years ago. Therefore, the book has been in its original condition since I received the book.

I understand you are disappointed, so to try to make it up to you, your payment for the least expensive book your purchased will be paid back.

On behalf of our company, I apologize for any inconvenience we may have caused you.

Thank you for your understanding and cooperation in advance.

Sean Snape
Sean Snape
Chief Executive Officer

191. Why did Mr. Stanford write to Mr. Snape?
(A) To dispute an inaccurate bill
(B) To cancel recently placed orders
(C) To object to an item's condition
(D) To inquire about a missing item

192. How much did Mr. Stanford most likely pay for a book with a cover problem?
(A) $94.25
(B) $58.00
(C) $86.00
(D) $131.00

193. What is suggested about Snape's Second-Hand Books?
(A) It does not have an online store.
(B) It does not have much inventory.
(C) It does not sell illustrated books.
(D) It does not allow product returns.

194. Which of the books will Mr. Stanford receive a refund for?
(A) Timmy's Voyage as a Captain
(B) New Line of the World
(C) How Should I Live
(D) Golden Island

195. What is stated in the second letter?
(A) Mr. Snape inspected the products himself.
(B) Mr. Snape's item has not been mailed yet.
(C) Mr. Snape will mail a replacement soon.
(D) Mr. Snape will send a book to an expert for evaluation.

Questions 196-200 refer to the following the e-mail, Web page, and article.

To	Shurred Nuhans <shurrednuhans@nexusgarage.com>
From	Nathan Phillips<nphillips@nexusgarage.com>
Subject	Request
Date	13 January

Dear Mr. Nuhans

I carefully ask that our company consider entering the PATC Virtual Business Tournament. The contest, established by the Portugal& American Trade Cooperation (PATC), asks participants to improve and conduct business plans that make an imaginary company stable and continuous.

Participation in this contest would bring high benefits to our company. We know that some of the participants are in non-decision-making positions in their groups, but the contest will demand a wide range of leadership practices from them. In the process, some of them can find out about the realities and complexities of an entrepreneur's work. Furthermore, they are likely to use the skills obtained or improved from the competition such as team work, research, and problem solving when they do their actual work. Moreover, participating in the competition can serve as a promotion to the public. Approximately seven months after the last tournament, about more than a half of the eighty-five companies that participated in the event reported an improvement in business results.

Information about the participation is on the PATC Website, www.patc.org.

Sincerely,

Nathan Phillips
Nexus Garage Corporation

---

http//www.PATC.org/events/tournament_information

PATC Virtual Business Tournament

Entry Information

Registration for this year's tournament is from 12 May to 12 June whereas the tournament starts on 8 October. More than two teams from a same company cannot be enrolled. A rank for each team will be posted on 14 October and will receive an honor during a ceremony on 19 November at Hotel Hilltop, Sydney, Australia.

A Virtual Breakthrough For Nexus

(October 15)—The PATC Virtual Business Tournament required teams from many companies to find out how to operate a virtual business successfully. Many teams from England joined the event before but had never won until now. Indeed, the team representing Nexus Garage Corp. took third rank in a field consisting of 109 teams from over ninety companies. The victorious team was led by Mr. Nathan Phillips. The team will be honored at the PATC Virtual Business Awards.

196. What is the goal of participants in the PATC tournament?
(A) To secure an international agreement
(B) To create materials for training prospective managers
(C) To run a nonexistent company
(D) To design a business Web site

197. What does Mr. Phillips NOT say is a benefit of participating in the PATC tournament?
(A) Better understanding of the tasks that managers perform
(B) Increased opportunities to invest in regional companies
(C) Greater public awareness of a company's offerings
(D) Improved cooperation among employees

198. What most likely is true about Mr. Phillips?
(A) He will be invited to a celebratory event.
(B) He is being considered for a managerial position.
(C) He has taken part in interactive online competitions before.
(D) He recommends implementing new management practices.

199. What is suggested about Nexus Garage Corporation?
(A) Its services are in great demand.
(B) It does business in England.
(C) It will formulate new business strategies in October.
(D) It registered two teams for the PATC tournament.

200. What is indicated about the most recent PATC tournament?
(A) It was sponsored by a Brazilian hotel chain.
(B) It saw the introduction of a set of new criteria.
(C) It drew participation from more companies than last year's event.
(D) It received more press coverage than last year's tournament.

Stop! This is the end of the test. If you finish before time is called, you may go back to Parts 5, 6, and 7 and check your work.

101. B	121. C	141. B	161. C	181. C
102. C	122. A	142. A	162. B	182. D
103. B	123. C	143. D	163. A	183. A
104. B	124. B	144. C	164. D	184. C
105. C	125. D	145. A	165. C	185. D
106. A	126. A	146. A	166. B	186. C
107. C	127. D	147. C	167. C	187. B
108. A	128. D	148. A	168. D	188. A
109. B	129. B	149. D	169. C	189. D
110. A	130. C	150. C	170. C	190. A
111. B	131. B	151. C	171. A	191. C
112. B	132. B	152. D	172. B	192. A
113. D	133. B	153. A	173. A	193. D
114. C	134. D	154. D	174. D	194. B
115. A	135. A	155. C	175. B	195. A
116. A	136. B	156. D	176. A	196. C
117. D	137. B	157. A	177. D	197. B
118. D	138. C	158. A	178. C	198. A
119. C	139. B	159. B	179. B	199. B
120. A	140. D	160. C	180. B	200. C

ACTUAL TEST

4

READING TEST

In the Reading test, you will read a variety of texts and answer several different types of reading comprehension questions. The entire Reading test will last 75 minutes. There are three parts, and directions are given for each part. You are encouraged to answer as many questions as possible within the time allowed.

You must mark your answers on the separate answer sheet. Do not write your answers in your test book.

PART 5

Directions: A word or phrase is missing in each of the sentences below. Four answer choices are given below each sentence. Select the best answer to complete the sentence. Then mark the letter (A), (B), (C), or (D) on your answer sheet.

101. The 74 Star brand was registered in 1950 and has been in operation ------- almost 70 years.
(A) for
(B) since
(C) within
(D) after

102. For all his knowledge and abilities, Mr. Washington is very not ------- of other colleagues and clients.
(A) consider
(B) considerable
(C) consideration
(D) considerate

103. Presently, the government is trying hard to find ------- ways to carry out more effective residential welfare policies.
(A) practice
(B) practical
(C) practicing
(D) practically

104. The new battery charger is ------- with almost all types of mobile phones on the domestic market.
(A) popular
(B) compatible
(C) innovative
(D) concerned

105. The company gave assurance that consumer profiles will be recorded and kept for a limited ------- of time.
(A) part
(B) amount
(C) value
(D) ahead

106. Safety ------- must be taken before handling the flammable chemicals in the research laboratory.
(A) speculation
(B) manuals
(C) precautions
(D) inspectors

107. Mr. Kiesling will work at the company's Moscow branch office, ------- three of his colleagues will work in Seoul.
(A) while
(B) in case
(C) during
(D) that

108. According to marketing experts, customers usually make purchasing decision ------- two minutes.
(A) towards
(B) within
(C) about
(D) up to

109. As high technologies have been ------- developing, cars are equipped with more electronic features than ever in order to enhance their driving stability.
(A) continue
(B) continues
(C) continual
(D) continually

110. The vice president asked one of his employees to ------- the press conference for November 23.
(A) host
(B) reschedule
(C) postpone
(D) prolong

111. Ace Electronics has recently launched a ------- of innovative and high-performance computers.
(A) length
(B) portion
(C) series
(D) shortage

112. As a token of our apology, ------- is a $50 gift certificate we hope you will accept as a gesture of good will.
(A) attach
(B) attachment
(C) attached
(D) attaching

113. BK Corporation offers special language courses to teach employees the proper way ------- foreign languages.
(A) speak
(B) to speak
(C) speaking
(D) spoken

114. The government will increase the volume of crude oil and natural gas imported ------- some countries of the Middle East.
(A) within
(B) from
(C) after
(D) throughout

115. ------- takes the chief executive officer job, the business situation facing our company is too difficult to expect a quick and sharp improvement.
(A) Whichever
(B) Whoever
(C) Since
(D) Even though

116. Entrepreneurs usually read newspapers and business magazines in order to obtain ------- information about the recent consumer trends.
(A) assigned
(B) obscure
(C) sensitive
(D) accurate

117. Godong Landscaping Service was chosen to supervise the construction of a new company garden given that it can do the project at a ------- price.
(A) compact
(B) considerable
(C) sharp
(D) reasonable

118. New apartments are usually so profitable ------- reconstruction projects often pop up for the next several years.
(A) such as
(B) that
(C) which
(D) therefore

119. Our hotel suites feel like your own private paradise since the hotel is located on the island of Borneo and it is ------- only by boat.
(A) transported
(B) accessible
(C) operated
(D) adjacent

120. Rhode Island was one of the ------- gateways to the city of New York for the Scot-Irish, who moved to the United States in the early nineteenth century.
(A) principal
(B) outgoing
(C) eligible
(D) constant

121. According to the data, the productivity of our employees was ------- higher than that of rival companies.
(A) significance
(B) significant
(C) more significant
(D) significantly

122. ------- of the world famous paintings in our municipal gallery is over 500 years old, and we receive millions of visitors each year.
(A) They
(B) All
(C) Each one
(D) Other

123. Domestic steel production rose ------- this year maintaining our company in second position after Haru Steel.
(A) mostly
(B) conspicuously
(C) technically
(D) marginally

124. We can't improve our competitiveness in the global market ------- we develop innovative technologies to commercialize.
(A) because
(B) neither
(C) when
(D) unless

125. Many salespeople are consistently using social network services and various online blogs to ------- young consumers.
(A) call out
(B) manage
(C) advertise
(D) appeal to

126. If customers want more ------- information, they should make their questions more detailed.
(A) specify
(B) specific
(C) specifics
(D) specifically

127. According to the market analysis report, Gaby Technologies' price ------- will not bring any changes to the domestic market.
(A) reductions
(B) anticipations
(C) exchanges
(D) sensations

128. Some economists predict that the pace of economic recovery will slow down without a ------- improvement in the fourth quarter.
(A) marked
(B) broad
(C) intensive
(D) respective

129. The mayor plans ------- our city into a cultural, tourist, and economic hub for people living in the cities around us.
(A) to transform
(B) transforming
(C) transformed
(D) transformation

130. Due to an unexpected audiovisual system malfunction, our marketing workshop ------- until further notice.
(A) will postpone
(B) has been postponed
(C) to postpone
(D) have postponed

PART 6

Directions: Read the texts that follow. A word, phrase, or sentence is missing in parts of each text. Four answer choices for each question are given below the text. Select the best answer to complete the text. Then mark the letter (A), (B), (C), or (D) on your answer sheet.

Questions 131-134 refer to the following article.

Luke's Ice Cream was ------- in 2004 when Ms. Luke, a German immigrant to the United
131.
States of America, bought an old clothing plant on Pine Street. This plant had gone out of
business and was put up for sale at a knockdown price. Ms. Luke spent all of her savings
to buy it and hired several ------- employees to start her ice cream company.
132.

------- new ice cream flavors, she used some of her family's favorite traditional recipes.
133.
Then, she enhanced the flavors with a wide variety of produce, including strawberries,
plums, apples, and even nuts. -------. They quickly became highly popular, and there are
134.
now seven Luke's Ice Cream store locations in Boston.

131. (A) find
    (B) found
    (C) founding
    (D) founded

132. (A) experiences
    (B) experience
    (C) experiencing
    (D) experienced

133. (A) To invent
    (B) Invents
    (C) Had invented
    (D) Invention

134. (A) In fact, it is widely known that ice cream has a lot of sugar and fat in it.
    (B) Some fruits are slightly more expensive than other ingredients.
    (C) The new ice cream flavors have been described as rich, buttery and delicate.
    (D) Some ice cream products will be declining in popularity because of the rising cost of milk.

Questions 135-138 refer to the following e-mail.

From: Jennifer Lawrence <jlawrence@powerelectric.com>
To: John Morrison <johnm@bellastore.com>
Date: September 9
Subject: Price Changes

Dear Mr. Morrison:

Please accept this e-mail as notification of a slight rate adjustment, ------- October 1. The
135.
adjustment is a result of increased transportation costs ------- the last twelve months.
136.

A summary of rate changes is located at the bottom of this e-mail. We anticipate no
additional rate adjustments for the next full year.

Should you have any further questions regarding our services, please contact our company
at 692-9815. -------.
137.

Thank you for understanding that this price increase means that we can ------- superior
138.
quality standards for our products and services in the coming year.

Very truly yours,

Jennifer Lawrence
Chief Executive Officer
Power Electro, Inc.

135. (A) acute
(B) good
(C) effective
(D) entitled

136. (A) with
(B) until
(C) over
(D) following

137. (A) We have great difficulty
communicating with overseas clients.
(B) Marketing is concerned with customer
needs and customer satisfaction.
(C) Our customer service representatives
will be happy to assist you.
(D) Better service for all customers
should be a priority for every store
and restaurant.

138. (A) examine
(B) maintain
(C) organize
(D) accomplish

Questions 139-142 refer to the following letter.

Homestead Corporation
51 Benson Street
Bronx, New York 10465

May 10

Aura Lane Manufacturing, Inc.
7401 Fifth Avenue
New York, New York 10055

To whom it may concern:

We intend ------- a new office copier before the end of the fiscal year. We would like to
139.
consider one of your copies and wonder if you have a model that would suit our needs.

Our company is a little small, and the copier would be shared by twenty employees. We
make ------- 7,800 copies a month and prefer a machine that uses regular paper. -------.
140. **141.**

Since our fiscal year ------- on June 30, we hope to hear from you before then.
142.

Sincerely yours,

Jim Preston
Personnel Manager
Homestead Corporation

139. (A) purchase
(B) purchasing
(C) having purchased
(D) to purchase

140. (A) approximate
(B) approximating
(C) approximately
(D) approximation

141. (A) We would also like to know about
your warranty and repair service.
(B) A printer which is combined with a
scanner can function as a kind of
photocopier.
(C) We are happy to supply you with the
estimate you requested.
(D) The company expressed
disappointment at the deadline being
missed.

142. (A) end
(B) ends
(C) has ended
(D) ended

Questions 143-146 refer to the following e-mail.

From: David Kiesling <dkiesling@samsonelectronics.com>
To: Linda Kim <lindakim@businessworld.com>
Date: November 23
Subject: Investment Opportunity

Dear Ms. Kim:

I obtained your name from Ms. Betty Hwang, one of your board members.

We ------- in manufacturing liquid displays utilized for car navigation systems, computers,
143.
and various control panels for home appliances.

Because of the superior quality of our semiconductors, and because of the increasing
popularity of our products in the industry, we want to seize the opportunity -------
144.
immediately; however, in order to do so, we are asking for the help of outside investors.

I believe this is a great opportunity for a profitable investment. ------- are our pamphlets
145.
explaining our services and the expansion plans.

-------. Please let me know when I should call to make an appointment.
146.
Thank you.

Very truly yours,

David Kiesling
Finance Director
Samson Electronics

---

143. (A) make
(B) enroll
(C) specialize
(D) participate

144. (A) expand
(B) expanding
(C) expanded
(D) to expand

145. (A) Attach
(B) Attached
(C) Attaching
(D) Attachment

146. (A) Once the updates are made, please review your contract carefully.
(B) We have failed to provide sufficient funds for developing key technologies.
(C) I would like to discuss this exciting offer with you early next week.
(D) Our investment will increase job opportunities and improve living standards.

PART 7

Directions: In this part you will read a selection of texts, such as magazine and newspaper articles, letters, and advertisements. Each text is followed by several questions. Select the best answer for each question and mark the letter (A), (B), (C), or (D) on your answer sheet.

Questions 147-148 refer to the following text message.

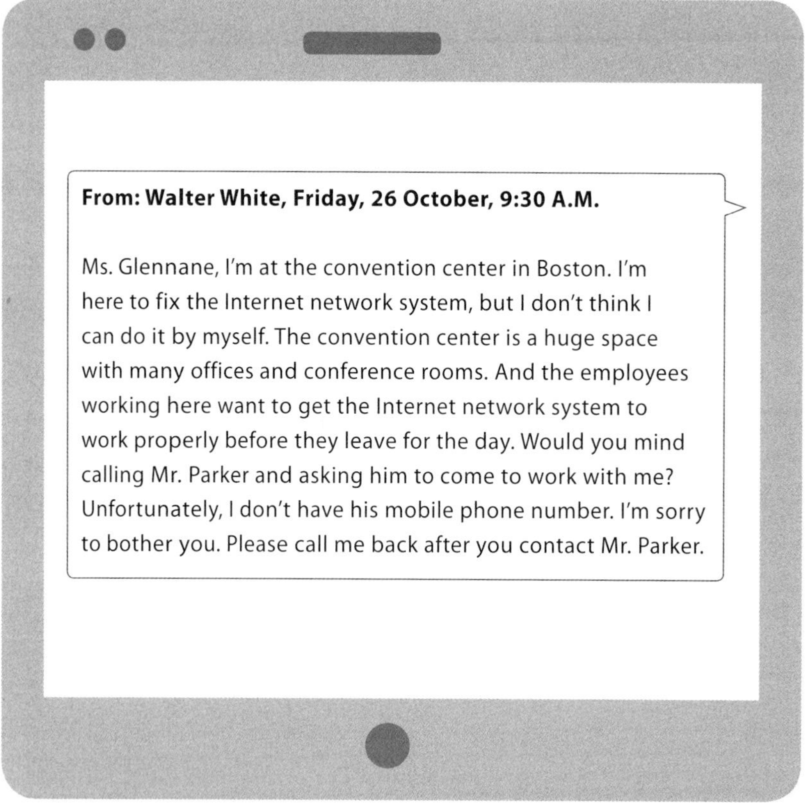

147. What problem does Mr. White mention?

(A) Mr. Parker called in sick this morning.

(B) He has some repair work he can't do alone.

(C) A colleague is not answering the phone.

(D) He doesn't know the exact location of a convention center.

148. What does Mr. White want Ms. Glennane to do?

(A) Install audiovisual equipment

(B) Contact a coworker

(C) Cancel a corporate event

(D) Reschedule a conference at a hotel

INVOICE

Starz Service LTD

"We Always Get You What You Need"

From: Starz Service LTD.
1188 Mission Blvd, San Francisco, CA 94712

To: Dr. Ash Williams
Ash Williams Hospital
310 Harder Road, Hayward, CA 94542

Order Date: June25
Delivery Date: June 29

Item Code	Item	Unit Price	Quantity
44BK	Absorbent Cotton Box	$25.00	15 / $375.00
73KG	Disinfectant Box	$78.00	10 / $780.00
*49GS	Medical Mask	$3.25	10 / $32.50
42SK	Sanitary Gloves	$2.50	20 / $50.00

TOTAL AMOUNT : $1,237.50

Starz Service LTD is one of the largest suppliers in the western part of the United States. We thank you for your business.

* We will deliver 49GS next Tuesday because they are currently out of stock.

149. What type of business is Starz Service LTD?
(A) A pharmaceutical company
(B) A general hospital
(C) A medical supplies company
(D) A shipping company

150. According to the invoice, what will probably happen on June 29?
(A) Mr. William's order will be shipped.
(B) A payment will be made to the hospital.
(C) A regular inventory check will be taken.
(D) New medical products will be released.

151. What is suggested about the masks?
(A) They will be delivered on June 29.
(B) They will come in a variety of colors.
(C) They won't be manufactured any more.
(D) They are currently unavailable.

Receipt Number: 7374-1123

DO NOT lose this number. You will need it if you want to get help from our customer service representatives.

Received from Chuck Finley: $44 payment to Khandar Theater

Charged to the credit card ending in XXXX-0909 on November 23, 6:15 P.M.

* Your ticket is non-refundable.

• This receipt is for Mr. Chuck Finley for the music festival on December 12, 7:00 P.M.

• Please print this receipt and bring it with you to the theater. Please arrive one hour before the concert begins so that we can check your name and seat number at the ticket counter.

152. What will Mr. Finley do on December 12?
(A) Purchase a ticket
(B) Attend a musical event
(C) Receive a new credit card
(D) Organize a local festival

153. What is Mr. Finley asked to do?
(A) Make a reservation
(B) Fill out an application form
(C) Present his identification card
(D) Bring a receipt with him

Elk Wood Cabins

Elk Wood Park Service is pleased to announce a project to build 25 beautiful log cabins by Raccoon Lake in Elk Wood National Park. Work is expected to begin in approximately two weeks. If all goes according to plan, we hope to have the site prepared and the main structural foundations in place within a month. That may seem like quite a huge task, but we are desperate to have everything finished before the summer season begins. The new cabins at Raccoon Lake should be completed by June this year.

There will be two types of cabins available: standard cabins that have two floors and sleep up to 5 people and group cabins that have three floors and sleep up to 10 people. Both kinds of cabins will be fully air conditioned and will have modern bathrooms, including hot tubs. The kitchens in both cabin types will be equipped with a full range of appliances, including a refrigerator, microwave, washing machine, and gas range.

The Elk Wood cabins will be conveniently located beside beautiful Raccoon Lake. This will make them perfect for anyone who wishes to escape the city heat and enjoy some fishing, swimming, and water sports in the national park. Contact an agent from the Elk Wood Park Service today to make an advance booking for one of the cabins.

Most cabins will be available to rent starting June 4.

Contact us at 555-6892 for further details.

154. What is stated about the cabins?
(A) Construction began two weeks ago.
(B) Kitchen appliances are included.
(C) The bedrooms are very spacious.
(D) They cannot accommodate large groups.

155. What information is NOT included in the advertisement?
(A) The date the first cabins open
(B) The cabin styles available
(C) The cost of a cabin rental
(D) The location of the cabins

Questions 156-157 refer to the following online chat discussion.

Anna Gunn 2:11 P.M.

Hey, I don't know how to open the meeting invitation in my e-mail. Actually, it's my first time attending an online business course for employees. Can you help me?

Harrison Morgan 2:13 P.M.

It's a piece of cake. All you have to do is enter the access code from the e-mail. It's GS6929815.

Anna Gunn 2:15 P.M.

It says, "Your access code is not right. Please try again." Something's wrong with the access code.

Harrison Morgan 2:16 P.M.

Hold on. Let me check that for you.

Anna Gunn2:17 P.M.

There might be a problem with the e-mail invitation I received.

Harrison Morgan 2:19 P.M.

Oh, I'm sorry. I gave you the wrong access code. It's my mistake. Please enter the access code JA870603.

Anna Gunn 2:20 P.M.

Yeah, it's working!

Harrison Morgan 2:23 P.M.

Okay. Let me tell you one more thing. You see the mute button at the bottom of the monitor screen? You don't need to use your microphone, so you should click it.

156. At 2:19 P.M., what does Ms. Morgan most likely mean when she writes, "Oh, I'm sorry"?

(A) She needs to start a business workshop without Ms. Gunn.

(B) She has given Ms. Gunn wrong information.

(C) She hasn't found the cause of a problem yet.

(D) She will not register for the business course.

157. What is probably true about Ms.Gunn?

(A) She has recently bought a new headset.

(B) She will lead a business seminar tomorrow.

(C) She doesn't need to speak during the online course.

(D) She hasn't received an e-mail invitation.

Questions 158-160 refer to the following article.

Spotlight on real-world business

September 15—Industry leading executive Brian McCallister began teaching at St. Olaf Industrial Institute a few years ago and regularly invites guest speakers who are engaged in real-world business activities to speak in his classes. — [1] —.

These business leaders share their experiences with the students enrolled in introductory marketing and economics courses at St. Olaf. — [2] —. The professor's objective is to help students to make connections between the theories they study in the classroom and their practical applications in their future careers.

The visitors show them that the lessons in everyday life can be just as important as anything they read in their computer and printed literature. — [3] —. He lets students propose and invite their own classroom guests, including relatives, friends, and acquaintances, to share their experiences in the real world particularly when it comes to problem solving, collaboration, and execution.

Mr. McCallister's students are encouraged to ask people associated with business they are curious about to come to speak, as well. McCallister's students all agree that the speakers are interesting. Although the class includes a few weeks in which students work as interns in various local companies, the guest speakers provide a very different perspective of the world of business. — [4] —.

158. What does the article discuss?

(A) How future industry leaders can plan their retirement

(B) A student's unusual opportunity to study abroad

(C) A way for students to plan their homework time

(D) An instructor's classroom practice

159. According to the article, what is Mr. McCallister's goal?

(A) To expand students' exposure to real-world industry practices

(B) To find ways businesses can work more efficiently

(C) To create literature that is better suited to students' needs

(D) To teach students to make better public presentations

160. In which of the positions marked [1],[2],[3], and [4] does the following sentence best belong?

"The focus is on organization and strategies to overcome obstacles in the industrial business world."

(A) [1]

(B) [2]

(C) [3]

(D) [4]

From:	Rebecca Jenington<rjenington@goodtravel.com>
To:	Michael Wilson <michaelw@heymail.net>
Subject:	Vacation
Date:	May 9, 15:46

Hi. This is Rebecca Jenington, your travel agent. I want to check on the details of your vacation with you. — [1] —. You told me on the phone that you wanted to fly to Italy on July 2. This is possible, but the flight will cost $620 per person. — [2] —. If you were to delay your vacation and fly one week later on July 9, the cost would be much cheaper at $450 per person. Let me know what you want to do about this.

I also have some questions about the hotel that you would like to book. — [3] —. You mentioned that there are four people going on vacation: two adults and two children. Would you like one large family room or two smaller rooms? If you would like a family room, I would recommend the Prince Hotel as it represents excellent value for the price. The rooms in this hotel come with a hot tub, a TV, and a computer and have wireless Wi-Fi access for connection to the Internet for free. — [4] —.

Please call me as soon as possible at 1-800-7767-3232 to let me know your preferences.

Regards,

Rebecca Jenington

161. What is the purpose of the e-mail?

(A) To offer Mr. Wilson a discounted vacation package to Italy

(B) To inform Mr. Wilson that his vacation has been cancelled

(C) To promote a travel insurance package to Mr. Wilson

(D) To ask Mr. Wilson some questions about his vacation arrangements

162. What is suggested about Mr. Wilson?

(A) He manages a big hotel chain.

(B) He is a celebrated travel writer.

(C) He has spoken with Ms. Jenington.

(D) He will lead a workshop in July.

163. In which of the positions marked [1],[2],[3], and [4] does the following sentence best belong?

"Could you be more flexible with your vacation dates?"

(A) [1]

(B) [2]

(C) [3]

(D) [4]

164. What does Ms. Jenington NOT mention about the Prince Hotel?

(A) It represents excellent value for the price.

(B) Each of its rooms is fitted with a hot tub.

(C) Family suites are available at the hotel.

(D) Every room provides free Internet access.

Safebet Insurance

193 Lake Street

Austin, TX 49302

(800) 2020-5830

July 4

Dear Ms. Charlotte Henderson,

I am writing with regard to our telephone conversation held on July 1, during which you requested further information on our insurance packages. Please find enclosed a company brochure.

In the brochure, the various types of insurance that are currently being offered are outlined. I would like to take this opportunity to recommend our Total Cover policy, which would cover both you and your husband in the event of an accident or emergency. This policy is priced at just $1,200 per year (or $100 per month) and is our most popular program with our clients in your region.

I understand that choosing an appropriate insurance policy can often be a stressful and overwhelming business. That is why we at Safebet Insurance have recently set up some insurance seminars. These are held one Saturday a month at the Austin town hall and last for approximately one hour. These seminars are designed to help you decide just which insurance package is right for you. At these sessions, you can also take the chance to speak to one of our dedicated advisers about your own personal situation.

For further information on our insurance seminars and for detailed information on our terms and conditions, please visit our website at www.safebetinsurance.com.

Thank you for choosing Safebet. I wish you a pleasant day.

Sincerely,

Judy Pennington

Insurance Development Head

Safebet Insurance

165. What is the purpose of the letter?

(A) To outline the terms and conditions of an insurance policy

(B) To provide further product information as requested by a client

(C) To offer the reader a position within the company

(D) To announce the opening of a new store

166. What is the purpose of the seminar sessions?

(A) To train new employees in sales techniques

(B) To provide education in the area of Website design

(C) To discuss the company's sales figures with board members

(D) To help customers choose the appropriate insurance policy

167. What is NOT mentioned about the Total Cover policy?

(A) It costs twelve hundred dollars a year.

(B) The policy would be valid for both Mrs. Henderson and her spouse.

(C) Ms. Henderson's children would be covered by the policy.

(D) It is the company's best-liked insurance program in the local area.

May 10—Scolan Construction's president, Lyle Vines, stated at a press conference that the company would donate 1.5 million dollars to the Canton Parks Restoration Initiative over the next year.

With the initiative's financial support having decreased over the last two years, the funding is greatly needed.

"Our organization couldn't be happier with Scolan's generous donation," said Canton Parks commissioner Betty Judge. "It will certainly help us in our objective of maintaining and improving the parks in Canton."

The Canton Parks Restoration Initiative was established five years ago by the Canton Parks Commission (CPC) to help improve park and playground facilities around Canton. When it was first started, the local government provided funding for the initiative, but two years ago, the Canton City Council voted to use the revenue for CPC to fund a new commercial district. The initiative has had difficulties finding funding since then.

Finally, CPC began asking for donations from companies in the area six months ago. "We sent out letters to many companies with a pamphlet showing the beauty of our parks," Ms. Judge stated. The photographs in the pamphlets showed the parks throughout the years, and many had children playing in them. "We had no idea that Mr. Vines is a former resident, until he called and asked about making a contribution to the initiative," Ms. Judge said.

Citizens and community leaders of Canton are pleased about the increased funding the initiative will receive. Councilman Carl Nesmith lauded Mr. Vines for his company's donation. The city council has talked about placing honorary plaques in the parks. "Canton has a number of beautiful parks that are very beneficial to everyone in the community," said Mr. Vines when announcing the donation, "My fascination with building actually began when I would play at these parks. If it weren't for the time I spent making little cities in the sandboxes at playgrounds, I may have chosen a different career. I just hope this donation helps the community continue to enjoy the parks."

Michael Pyke, Local Reporter

168. When was the Canton Parks Restoration Initiative started?
(A) Six months ago
(B) One year ago
(C) Two years ago
(D) Five years ago

169. According to the article, why was the initiative losing financial support?
(A) The funding from the local government was redistributed.
(B) The cost of maintenance increased too much.
(C) Residents of Canton were moving away from the city.
(D) Further maintenance work was no longer needed.

170. Who is NOT a current resident of Canton?
(A) Lyle Vines
(B) Betty Judge
(C) Carl Nesmith
(D) Michael Pyke

171. What does Mr. Vines mention about the parks in Canton?
(A) They are not used by members of the community.
(B) They led him to his career in construction.
(C) Companies in the area should provide support for them.
(D) All parks should have a plaque giving information about donors.

Questions 172-175 refer to the following online chat discussion.

Jim Preston (4:10 P.M.)	Valentina and I are going to stop for an early dinner at 6 P.M. Anyone care to join us?
April Armstrong (4:11 P.M.)	Maybe. Where are you thinking of going?
Jim Preston (4:12 P.M.)	We can try the Chinese restaurant on Fifth Avenue. It's called The Great Wall. I heard their food is exceptional.
Mary Barnes (4:13 P.M.)	Oh, man! You are out of luck. John and I stopped by there last week. Unfortunately, it has already closed for business.
Jim Preston (4:14 P.M.)	I didn't know that. That's too bad. The reviews were pretty good on the Internet.
Mary Barnes (4:16 P.M.)	Why don't we go to the Korean restaurant, Chosun Dynasty, on Pine Street? Have you ever tried Korean barbeque?
Jim Preston (4:18 P.M.)	That would be great. I had Korean barbeque several months ago when I went on a business trip to Los Angeles. It was really good. You guys want to go there?
April Armstrong (4:19 P.M.)	Yeah, I like Korean cuisine, too. count me in.
Jim Preston (4:20 P.M.)	All righty. Meet me in the lobby at 6:30 P.M. Is that okay?
Mary Barnes (4:20 P.M.)	Yes, that works. I'll see you at 6:30 P.M.
April Armstrong (4:22 P.M.)	Um… I won't get out of the office until 6:30 P.M., though. Jim, I have to finish the designs for our new products, which will be released next month. But I'll get there by 7:30 P.M.

172. What are the writers talking about?
(A) Where to host a corporate event
(B) Who to invite a meal
(C) Where to go for dinner
(D) When to meet with clients in Los Angeles

173. What is indicated about the Chinese restaurant?
(A) It has moved to a new location.
(B) It received very poor reviews.
(C) It is no longer in business.
(D) It offers a special menu after 6:30 P.M.

174. At 4:14 P.M., what does Mr. Preston mean when he writes "That's too bad"?
(A) He has a prior engagement.
(B) He cannot meet a deadline for his project.
(C) He wanted to try Chinese food.
(D) He thinks a new restaurant is too far away.

175. What will Ms. Armstrong do next?
(A) Work on a project design
(B) Meet her colleagues in the lobby.
(C) Go to a new restaurant
(D) Leave for a business trip

Hotel Santa Maria

Touted as the Jewel of Tuscany, Hotel Santa Maria is nestled in the rolling landscape and fruitful vineyards of Italy. Our 50-room establishment has received 4-diamond recognition by the Worldwide Chamber of Hotels and Lodging (WCHL) and enjoys the patronage of many elite guests. While guests can enjoy Italy's "Old World," our amenities are anything but that. Our rooms are equipped with high-speed wireless Internet, flat-screen televisions, and premium cable channels, and our facility includes an elite pool and hot tub, fitness facility, business center, and complimentary European breakfast.

Hotel Santa Maria offers three types of rooms:

- **Platinum** Intended for up to two guests, this room features a king-sized bed with premium linens, vineyard views from a private balcony, complimentary morning room service, and a jetted tub and steam shower. €372 per night, including taxes and fees.

- **Gold** Intended for up to 4 guests, this room has courtyard views from your own balcony, free breakfast, a kingsized bed and a couch pullout bed or 2 queen-sized beds, and a steam shower. €285 per night for 2 guests + €30 for each additional guest, including taxes and fees.

- **Silver** These rooms can be connected to make a joint suite rooming up to 8 guests or kept separate for up to 4 guests. Situated on our garden level, you will have easy access to all the hotel's amenities. Rooms include a king-sized bed and a couch pullout bed or 2 queen-sized beds. €250 per night per room (up to four guests each), including taxes and fees.

To check our availability, please visit our website at www.smhotel.it or call us at 510-445-4331.

To:	reservations@smhotelfrontdesk.it
From:	smcgowan@bkmail.uk
Date:	9 Oct.
Subject:	Change to Reservation

I just tried logging into my online reservation to make a change, but the username and password I had set up are not working. I do not know if I did not write it down correctly or if your system is not working. Either way, I need to make a change to my reservation, reference #110074.

Originally, my daughter and her husband were going to join my husband and me on our trip to Tuscany, and we decided to go spend five nights and six days there. So I booked a 2-room Silver Suite. However, my husband just learned that he would go on a business trip to at that point. (He would be in London by that time.) Thus, I need to change our reservation from two rooms to one. But while we're making that change, I would also like to upgrade from a Silver to a Platinum room.

This will be our first trip to Tuscany, so we are very excited. If you could direct me to a reputable tourist firm, I would appreciate your assistance. Please also reply to confirm the above changes in my reservation.

Thank you.
Silvia McGowan

176. What is mentioned about the hotel?

(A) It sits on a historic site.

(B) It is centrally located.

(C) It was recently remodeled.

(D) It has scenic views.

177. In the advertisement, the word "establishment" in paragraph 1, line 2, is closest in meaning to

(A) expansion

(B) foundation

(C) accommodation

(D) corporation

178. What does Ms. McGowan inquire about in the e-mail?

(A) Check-in time

(B) Famous travel agency

(C) Public safety in Tuscany

(D) The price of upgrade

179. What reason does Ms. McGowan give for changing his reservation?

(A) The budget for his trip has changed.

(B) His travel dates have changed.

(C) His travel destination has changed.

(D) The number of guests has changed.

180. How much will Ms. McGowan most likely pay for the hotel charges?

(A) €1,250

(B) €1,425

(C) €1,860

(D) €2,232

To: Carson Center Building Tenants

From: Ms. Natalie Mills, Colbert Management Company

Date: May 22

Colbert Management Company will assume the management of the Carson Center building starting June 1. We will be committed to complete satisfaction of all the tenants.

Below is a list of contacts you should know.

On-Site Maintenance

Maintenance Manager, Mr. Jung Ah Choi<jachoi@colbert.com>

All maintenance issues are to be directed to Ms. Choi.

Legal Department

Administrative Assistant, Mr. Matthew Perry

<mperry@colbert.com>

General Management

Office Manager, Ms. Rebecca Hales <rhales@colbert.com>

Colbert Management Company

1-303-555-1276

From: Natasha Dawson <ndawson@brownfinance.com>
To: Jung Ah Choi <jachoi@colbert.com>
Date: June 5
Subject: Security Code

My name is Natasha Dawson. I work at Brownstone Finance. Our offices are located on the third floor at the Carson Center building. We need to reset the code for our security system. The system lost power over the weekend and has since been turned back on. Unfortunately, the security code was reset, and we need a new one. Could you please send someone over to assist us with this problem immediately? We do not want our offices unprotected over the weekend.

Sincerely,
Natasha Dawson

181. What kind of business is Colbert Management Company?
(A) A property management company
(B) A construction company
(C) A housing development company
(D) A security company

182. In the memo, the word "assume" in paragraph 1, line 1, is closes in meaning to
(A) hire
(B) suppose
(C) undertake
(D) deliberate

183. What is indicated in the memo?
(A) The Carson Center building is seeking new tenants.
(B) Internet connections are being repaired.
(C) Colbert Management Company will fire some staff.
(D) Various individuals may be contacted for assistance.

184. What is the purpose of Ms. Dawson's e-mail?
(A) To report lost building keys
(B) To check the cost of installing a lock
(C) To receive assistance with a security system
(D) To request information about the management office

185. To what office did Ms. Dawson send the e-mail?
(A) On-Site Maintenance
(B) Technical Support
(C) Legal Department
(D) General Management

| Interior Design | Painting | Receive an Estimate | Contact |

http://phreshpaint.com

Save money with Phresh Paint!

Our company specializes in interior design painting services for your home. Our painters are friendly and experienced. We want you to be pleased with every step of the process from selecting the paint and the painting job to rearranging the items in the room after the paint dries.

Our price depends on the number of rooms and their sizes. We have base rates for the number of rooms, and an additional fee is paid depending on the colors chosen and the size of the rooms.

Our base rates are:

1 room = $200, 2 rooms = $400, and 3 rooms = $800.

For a full custom estimate, complete the order form with details about the work you need done.

* Fall Phresh Paint Pass: From September through November, we are reducing the additional fees for orders scheduled on Mondays & Tuesdays by up to 30%!!!

Phresh Paint **Job Order Form**	
Submission Date	Monday, May 29
Name	Brooklyn Oliver
E-mail address	a_mail to:bkoliver@dogmail.com
Telephone	832-713-5555
Address	7530 Rugsby, Las Vegas, NV 10104
Request Service Date	June 17
What Is Needed	My kitchen and living room need to be painted. I have not decided on the colors yet. I will need assistance picking out two colors, one for each room.
Comments	The kitchen is very small. The living room is twice the size of the kitchen. I need an estimate of the cost for the service. Also, I would like the job to be done next Tuesday, if possible.

To:	Brooklyn Oliver
From:	Brandon McDonald
Date:	June 1
Subject:	Service Estimate
Attachment:	Service #: 12345098AFC

Hello Brooklyn,

Thanks for contacting Phresh Paint.

We would be happy to provide an estimate for completing both rooms and suggest some colors. We have staff on-hand to help! In regard to picking out colors, please feel free to call our office at 832-456-8202. Our interior design specialist is willing to talk over suggestions based on your favorite colors. As for the price quote, we will need to measure your rooms and it will also depend on the colors you end up choosing.

I have noted your name on our calendar for next Tuesday, so we hope to talk to you soon about your colors!

Sincerely,
Phresh Paint
Natasha Dawson

186. In the Web page, the word "pleased" in paragraph 1, line 2, is closest in meaning to
(A) confused
(B) satisfied
(C) thoughtful
(D) offered

187. What can be inferred about Mr. Oliver?
(A) He will receive a discount.
(B) He recently moved into a new house.
(C) He has already chosen the colors for his kitchen.
(D) His schedule is very flexible.

188. How much will Mr. Oliver most likely pay as a base rate?
(A) $100
(B) $200
(C) $400
(D) $800

189. What is NOT true about Mr. Olive?
(A) His kitchen is smaller than his living room.
(B) He is a regular customer of Phresh Paint.
(C) He has not yet chosen paint colors for the rooms.
(D) He plans on having two rooms repainted.

190. According to Mr. McDonald, what can Phresh Paint do?
(A) Paint the entire home
(B) Clean the kitchen and the living room after the job
(C) Expand the size of the kitchen
(D) Offer color choices over the phone

Http://www.whatshot.ca

THIS MONTH

Event Name: Summer Sand Sculpture Contest
Location:Teriland Beach, Helson Tribon
Dates: 20-22 September
Level:Professional and amateur
Contact:Skyla Bonnie: sbonnie@eosandssculpture.ca

This event has been held annually for the past three years. This year, over 78 professional and amateur participants were invited from around the world. Participants can decide whether to work solo or as a team. The contest is very popular and recorded about 10,000 spectators last year, which was the highest attendance among the beach events held in Helson Tribon. Teriland Beach is a long beach covered in white sand. Helson Tribon is in the vicinity of Rabitory. Moreover, during the event, there will be live music for three days, a wide selection of food and beverages, craft vendors, and sand art lessons for visitors. No entry fee for anyone, but those who use the parking lot will be charged $7.

Winners of the Third Annual Summer Sand Sculpture Contest

* For Solo Contestants *

	Name	**Nationality**	**Work Title**
First Prize	Henry Tyson	Australia	Blue Mermaid
Second Prize	William McGowan	Canada	Pod of Dolphin
Third Prize	Angus Truman	U.S.	Hearst Castle
Fourth Prize	Pitution Queset	Brazil	Safari Jungle
Fifth Prize	James McQueen	U.K.	Sea Creatures

What's new in Rabitory?

By Ophelia Parker

This year's Summer Sand Sculpture Contest ended last weekend, and it was a great way to end the summer. Thanks to nice weather, the number of visitors doubled compared to that of the previous event.

The contest drew numerous solo and team contestants. They made masterpieces by using local sand and water. Shells, seaweed, driftwood, and other materials from nature were used in the sculptures as well.

Henry Tyson from Australia took first place again by beating William McGowan from Canada with his *Blue Mermaid* sculpture, which was decorated with sea weed and seashells. All the sculptures were beautiful, but I personally liked *Safari Jungle* best. The lower part of the sculpture was filled with driftwood, something I had never seen before.

I'm sure all the spectators also enjoy themselves. Some professional sculptors volunteered to help participants create better artworks during the event. With music and artisans, the event gave us all unforgettable memories.

191. What is indicated about the contestants?
(A) They are all amateurs.
(B) They are from a variety of countries.
(C) They are acquainted with Ms. Bonnie.
(D) They are requested to register in advance.

192. In the article, the word "drew" in the paragraph 2, line 1, is closest in meaning to
(A) won
(B) pictured
(C) moved
(D) attracted

193. What most likely is true of this year's event?
(A) It had more than 10,000 visitors.
(B) It cost $5 per person to attend.
(C) It was held in Teriland Beach for the first time.
(D) It was longer than last year's event.

194. What is implied about Mr. Tyson?
(A) He has won the competition previously.
(B) He has given sand sculpting lessons.
(C) He used driftwood in his sculpture.
(D) He recently moved to Canada.

195. Whose sculpture did Ms. Parker like the most?
(A) Tyson's
(B) McGowan's
(C) Truman's
(D) Queset's

Griphin Hotels Get New Family

BEIJING (10 March)—Griphin Inc. merged with President Hotel Group. Griphin Inc. is a small company compared to President Hotel Group. It owns a hotel chain in the local area. By acquiring Griphin properties, President Hotel Group currently owns 11 hotels and more than 1,800 guest rooms in Beijing.

Before the acquisition, President was widely known for its President Travel Suites, which were designed specifically for business travelers.

Griphin's four branches include the deluxe Foxy Hotel, built in 1924, and the Wales Inn, an upscale hotel that was launched just last year. "President Hotel Group welcomed Griphin Inc. to be a part of them," said President spokesperson Brian Parkman. "Griphin is reputable in Beijing, and they will be a perfect complement to President's existing hotels."

President's loyal members are now able to earn points and apply vouchers when they stay at Griphin Hotels.

Beijing City Center
Visiting Beijing? Want to stay in the city center? Then stay at one of the President's hotels. Below are our most popular hotels in the downtown area.

Atlanta Hotel
Our amenities include wireless Internet service, double beds, 55-inch TVs, and an inside swimming pool. This hotel is ready to provide everything for everyone. Great for Families!

Heart Grand
Try our newly decorated guest rooms and enjoy quiet dining at our recently renovated eatery. You can also visit nearby theaters, shopping malls, and other city attractions.

Hotel Polish
With no fee for transportation to the airport and a perfectly remodeled business center, this is the best hotel for business travelers. It has conference rooms and complimentary wireless Internet service.

Tradition D. Inn
This old-fashioned but convenient inn includes double beds, flat TVs, and wireless Internet service in each room, like a modern hotel. It features a charming decor, appetizing free breakfast, and nearby public transportation. This is a beautiful place to stay during your holiday in Beijing.

Or have a look at our other hotels in Beijing. Choosing President is choosing the best.

Heart Grand
☆☆☆☆

I really enjoyed my stay at the Heart Grand. My room was quite relaxing, and all my meals at the hotel restaurant were delightful. The hotel provided me with excellent service as well, but I would have liked transportation, such as a shuttle service, to the airport. Since it was my first visit, catching a taxi to the airport was difficult, and it wasn't cheap. Other than this problem, I enjoyed my stay at Heart Grand.

Andrew Kim

196. What does the article suggest about President Hotel Group?
(A) It is relocating its headquarters.
(B) It has discontinued its loyalty club.
(C) It specializes in luxury hotels.
(D) It wants to appeal to a wider variety of customers.

197. What do the four hotels mentioned in the advertisement have in common?
(A) They all have swimming pools.
(B) They were all built a long time ago.
(C) They are all located in downtown Beijing.
(D) They all offer discounts to business travelers.

198. Which hotel is most likely NOT Griphin's property?
(A) Atlanta Hotel
(B) Hotel Polish
(C) Heart Grand
(D) Tradition D. Inn

199. What disappointed Mr. Kim about his stay?
(A) The unfriendly staff
(B) The high price of the room
(C) The low quality of the restaurant
(D) The lack of affordable transportation

200. What information is provided about the hotel in which Mr.Kim has stayed?
(A) Its restaurant has been redone.
(B) It provides free Internet service.
(C) It is available for conference.
(D) It includes a gift shop.

Stop! This is the end of the test. If you finish before time is called, you may go back to Parts 5, 6, and 7 and check your work.

101. A	121. D	141. A	161. D	181. A
102. D	122. C	142. B	162. C	182. C
103. B	123. D	143. C	163. B	183. D
104. B	124. D	144. D	164. D	184. C
105. B	125. D	145. B	165. B	185. A
106. C	126. B	146. C	166. D	186. B
107. A	127. A	147. B	167. C	187. A
108. B	128. A	148. B	168. D	188. C
109. D	129. A	149. C	169. A	189. B
110. B	130. B	150. A	170. A	190. D
111. C	131. D	151. D	171. B	191. B
112. C	132. D	152. B	172. C	192. D
113. B	133. A	153. D	173. C	193. A
114. B	134. C	154. B	174. C	194. A
115. B	135. C	155. C	175. A	195. D
116. D	136. C	156. B	176. D	196. D
117. D	137. C	157. C	177. C	197. C
118. B	138. B	158. D	178. B	198. B
119. B	139. D	159. A	179. D	199. D
120. A	140. C	160. D	180. C	200. A

ACTUAL TEST

5

READING TEST

In the Reading test, you will read a variety of texts and answer several different types of reading comprehension questions. The entire Reading test will last 75 minutes. There are three parts, and directions are given for each part. You are encouraged to answer as many questions as possible within the time allowed.

You must mark your answers on the separate answer sheet. Do not write your answers in your test book.

PART 5

Directions: A word or phrase is missing in each of the sentences below. Four answer choices are given below each sentence. Select the best answer to complete the sentence. Then mark the letter (A), (B), (C), or (D) on your answer sheet.

101. The ------- retail price of a pair of new blue jeans, $43, is about $7 less than it was a week ago.
(A) suggested
(B) suggest
(C) suggests
(D) suggesting

102. A local business magazine says lawyers from both companies are currently reviewing ------- options.
(A) they
(B) their
(C) them
(D) themselves

103. The film *"The Twenty Cats"*, which was modestly budgeted, ------- expectations at the box-office last year.
(A) believed
(B) expressed
(C) exceeded
(D) accomplished

104. Some employees are very self-centered and greedy, so they are ------- of other colleagues in the company.
(A) impossible
(B) unaware
(C) inconsiderate
(D) uncourteous

105. Corporate investment in plant and machinery rose 3 percent in the second quarter compared to the same period a year -------.
(A) ago
(B) now
(C) past
(D) away

106. After the board meeting tomorrow, our president ------- whether we will expand our business into the pharmaceutical industry.
(A) deciding
(B) is decided
(C) have decided
(D) will decide

107. Newly developed subway cars have ------- seats as large-sized commercial buses with sixty seats.
(A) as many
(B) as much
(C) so many
(D) so much

108. The local newspaper reported that Countryside& Mills and Kamon Farming will consolidate through a ------- merger next week.
(A) strategy
(B) strategic
(C) strategize
(D) strategically

109. Our company outing has been rescheduled ------- the day after tomorrow due to the inclement weather.
(A) for
(B) during
(C) until
(D) on

110. Many customers come back time and time again to Mimi's Department Store because of the special guarantee on ------- items purchased.
(A) all
(B) each
(C) every
(D) plenty

111. The World Economy is the second ------- distributed magazine in the United States and Canada.
(A) wide
(B) wider
(C) more widely
(D) most widely

112. Dr. Andrew Lee, one of the most prominent economists in California, ------- a new labor economics theory last year.
(A) terminated
(B) supervised
(C) interpreted
(D) invented

113. According to the quarterly sales report, Last Ship Merchant Marine's revenue showed a ------- improvement at the end of the second quarter.
(A) wealthy
(B) drastic
(C) comparing
(D) worsening

114. The chief executive officer ------- took care of pending business issues important to our company before going on vacation.
(A) accurately
(B) increasingly
(C) meticulously
(D) correctly

115. Many scholars offered their -------
to Dr. McDonald for his remarkable
accomplishments.
(A) congratulate
(B) congratulations
(C) congratulating
(D) congratulatory

116. When there is a problem with our
database system, you should -------
contact the technology support
department as quickly as possible.
(A) ever
(B) always
(C) precisely
(D) efficiently

117. Global warming and water pollution
threaten to ------- the extinction of all life
on earth, including fish species.
(A) lead
(B) prevent
(C) survive
(D) cause

118. Different jobs require different skilled
employees, and should ------- have
various mandatory retirement ages.
(A) however
(B) furthermore
(C) therefore
(D) often

119. The economic crisis of a nation usually
develops ------- a global phenomenon
that must be solved by international
efforts.
(A) for
(B) into
(C) from
(D) with

120. The company spokesperson said board
members are ------- to have an influential
entrepreneur, Mr. Simpson, as their CEO.
(A) thrill
(B) thrilling
(C) thriller
(D) thrilled

121. Our city's tour bus routes are operated
------- for the north of the river and south
of the river areas.
(A) separate
(B) separating
(C) separation
(D) separately

122. Major companies must carry out the
social ------- of a business by sponsoring
various activities for public interests.
(A) ties
(B) responsibilities
(C) developments
(D) promotions

123. ------- the new business plan is not cost effective and environmentally friendly, there will be problems approving it.
(A) Since
(B) While
(C) Although
(D) Unless

124. The plant manager could not find replacement parts for some of the broken conveyor belts because the component suppliers have ------- in stock.
(A) none
(B) every
(C) them
(D) little

125. Ms. Sarah Scofield launched her company with an ------- investment of twenty-five thousand dollars last year.
(A) attentive
(B) initial
(C) instant
(D) appealing

126. The foreign company expressed its intention last week to ------- with the laws and regulations of South Korea to do new business.
(A) accomplish
(B) comply
(C) authorize
(D) designate

127. Most of the meat processing companies will need more farmlands to raise more cows, ------- the beef consumption increases.
(A) unless
(B) provided that
(C) although
(D) now that

128. According to the recent market analyst report, our company's G7 ------- BK's X10 for the last three years.
(A) were outsold
(B) will outsell
(C) has been outselling
(D) would have been outsold

129. Brilliant artistry is one of the ------- reasons why various Asian cultures have recently been identified as unique.
(A) chief
(B) straight
(C) reliable
(D) adept

130. The state government recently decided ------- companies will build a new highway between Spokane and Seattle, one of the largest infrastructure projects in the area.
(A) which
(B) each
(C) where
(D) those

Directions: Read the texts that follow. A word, phrase, or sentence is missing in parts of each text. Four answer choices for each question are given below the text. Select the best answer to complete the text. Then mark the letter (A), (B), (C), or (D) on your answer sheet.

Questions 131-134 refer to the following e-mail.

To: Emily Brunt <ebrunt@brightwing.co.nz>
From: Alicia Morgan <amorgan@bluedot.org.nz>
Date: June 12
Subject: About Your Interview

Dear Ms. Blunt,

We have received your application for the job ------- as a caterer at Blue Dot Catering
                                          131.
Services. We have been searching for job candidates who have an immense amount of experience in the catering industry. After reviewing your resume and references, we have found you have a long and ------- career in the business. -------.
                                 132.   **133.**
We would like to invite you in for a job interview. We are scheduling a ------- interview time
                                                                    134.
for June 25 at 10 A.M. This schedule may be altered according to circumstances. If you want to change the time or date the time or date, please feel free to call me at 924-7332.

Thank you. Have a good day.

Alicia Morgan
Head of Personnel
Blue Dot Catering Services

---

131. (A) training
(B) responsibility
(C) opening
(D) description

132. (A) respect
(B) respected
(C) respecting
(D) respects

133. (A) Now you're wondering how to make the interview go really well.
(B) You are one of the most qualified candidates for our company.
(C) This cooking contest is a popular international culinary competition.
(D) Our company is interested in learning about your new recipes and cooking techniques.

134. (A) joint
(B) exclusive
(C) tentative
(D) preliminary

Questions 135-138 refer to the following letter.

May 21

Ms. Sarah Fox
8248 Central Avenue
Houston, TX 77025

Dear Ms. Fox,

We are very pleased to inform you that the Waco Recycling Program will commence in your area on April 5. Residents who would like to participate in the ------- **135.** will be issued a green wheeled-container. To ------- **136.** a container, please call 1-800-575-4331.

Curbside recycling will take place twice a month, rather than once a week, as initially proposed. -------, **137.** trips to neighborhoods will be less frequent, which will lower fuel costs and emissions.

A list of recyclable materials can be found in the enclosed brochure. For more information on schedules of citywide recycling programs, visit www.wacorecycling.org. -------. **138.**

Sincerely yours,

Thomas Lee
Thomas Lee
Manager of Waco Recycling Program

135. (A) initiative
(B) hearing
(C) competition
(D) exhibition

136. (A) prepare
(B) return
(C) repair
(D) request

137. (A) After all
(B) Furthermore
(C) As a result
(D) In fact

138. (A) We hope that you will take part in this important program.
(B) Your container will arrive at your door within seven days.
(C) Please make sure not to put broken glass into the container.
(D) The city has invested an enormous sum in this project.

MEMORANDUM

From: Anna Hopewell, Personnel Director

To: All employees

Date: June 8

Subject: The Resignation of Ms. Lisa Evans

Ms. Lisa Evans announced yesterday that she will ------- as President of Blue Jet Airlines
139.
next Monday to start her own aviation business. She was very instrumental in shaping our growth and direction as the nation's leading low-cost airliner. She made a considerable contribution to the expansion of our company. -------.
140.

We have undertaken formal organizational changes within the company. Ms. Isabella Choi, our vice president, will take over the duties of Ms. Evans. We expect Ms. Choi to bring her ------- experience in airline planning, finance, marketing, and leadership to this new
141.
position. We are confident that our new president ------- our company to new levels of
142.
excellence with your support.

Thank you for all your efforts to keep us strong.

---

139. (A) serve
(B) assume
(C) lay off
(D) step down

140. (A) She will bring passion and
professionalism to our airline
company in the future.
(B) The former president has used
innovative ideas and methods to
increase our sales.
(C) Our company is recognized as one of
the leading companies thanks to your
dedications.
(D) We would like to express our
appreciation for her hard work and
leadership over the years.

141. (A) to extend
(B) extend
(C) extended
(D) extensive

142. (A) lead
(B) will lead
(C) is led
(D) has led

Questions 143-146 refer to the following article.

BK Petrochemical announced Thursday that it ------- **143.** Won International in a deal valued at 120 million dollars.

Mr. Andrew Kim, the spokesperson of BK Petrochemical, said this morning the company purchased Won International to bolster its overseas operations and increase its global -------. **144.** He also said BK Petrochemical aims to double its global sales by the end of next year.

-------. **145.** Therefore, many industry experts strongly believe this acquisition will make BK Petrochemical the top leading producer and vendor of petrochemical goods since Won International is expected to offset its weakest point.

BK Petrochemical plans ------- **146.** Won International's current workforce and to hire additional staff over the next two years.

143. (A) sold
(B) acquired
(C) organized
(D) merged

144. (A) compete
(B) competition
(C) competitor
(D) competitiveness

145. (A) Won International is known for its strong sales network and sales power.
(B) It is regarded as one of the best managed large corporations in North America.
(C) The board of BK Petrochemical made the big decision to recruit foreign talent next year.
(D) We will accomplish this goal by making use of BK Petrochemical's recently updated production facilities.

146. (A) maintain
(B) seek
(C) offer
(D) encourage

Questions 147-148 refer to the following flyer.

Broughton MegaBowl

is offering a selection of special discounts to our customers:

Wednesday – Receive a coupon for a free cold drink for every game played!

Thursday – Buy two games of bowling and get one free!

Friday – Half-priced bowling for groups of over six people!

Saturday – A 50% discount for bowlers on all food and beverages purchased!

Thank you for your custom.

147. What is the purpose of the flyer?
(A) To promote a series of discounts
(B) To publicize new opening times
(C) To advertise job vacancies at a bowling alley
(D) To inform customers of changes to the drinks menu

148. What will bowling customers receive on Wednesday?
(A) Discounts on food and drink products
(B) Discounts on the price of bowling games
(C) Free bowling games
(D) Complimentary beverages

For: April Wilson

Date: Monday, November 2

Time: 2:25 P.M.

Caller: Jim Mathers

Of: Custom Kitchen Renovations

Phone: 434-555-0214

Message: Mr. Mathers has requested a postponement of your meeting with him, which was to be held on Wednesday at 9 A.M., as the tile samples you requested have been delayed. They should arrive by Thursday. He is available on Friday between 10 A.M. and 2 P.M. Please call him to reschedule. In addition, he is still waiting on the sketch of your kitchen dimensions you were to send him.

Taken by: Debra Morgan

149. Why did Mr. Mathers call Ms. Wilson?
- (A) To make some changes to her tile order
- (B) To request a company brochure from her
- (C) To arrange a new time for a meeting
- (D) To request a job interview

150. What does Mr. Mathers want Ms. Wilson to do?
- (A) Give him some information about the size of her office
- (B) Arrange for the delivery of a new desk
- (C) Submit the measurements he requested
- (D) Purchase some living room furniture

Lynn Jacobs [3:11 P.M.]

Hey Cedric, can I ask you how the product design is getting along? Our client wants to check our progress this week.

Cedric Clark [3:13 P.M.]

I'm working on the colors right now. I don't know whether to use bright colors or dark colors.

Lynn Jacobs [3:15 P.M.]

Can you send me a sample of both? I'll let you know how I feel.

Cedric Clark [3:16 P.M.]

Thanks! I just sent them to your e-mail.

Lynn Jacobs [3:18 P.M.]

Are you sure? My inbox is still empty.

Cedric Clark [3:20 P.M.]

Sorry. I accidentally sent it to your old e-mail account. Do you mind checking again?

Lynn Jacobs [3:21 P.M.]

I got it. I like the brightly colored version better.

151. What type of business does Mr. Clark most likely work for?

(A) An art college
(B) An auto manufacturer
(C) An accounting firm
(D) A design agency

152. At. 3:18 P.M. what does Ms. Jacobs most likely mean when she writes, "Are you sure"?

(A) She is questioning Mr. Clark's color choice.
(B) She is asking if Mr. Clark sent the e-mail.
(C) She is wondering if Mr. Clark could start the product design project.
(D) She is surprised by the progress Mr. Clark has made.

My Account

Welcome to Prototype Shopping, Ms. Chastain! Now you can access your online grocery shopping account and reach our customized shopping for you more easily than ever! Please take time to view our newly improved shopping Web site. Among the features you will discover are:

- Easier navigation of the Website
- Better pictures of products with more detailed descriptions
- Heightened encryption that ensures our customers' sensitive financial data is more secure than ever before
- Increased online customer service tools, including the ability to chat live for your personalized shopping.

153. Who most likely is Ms. Chastain?

(A) An online shopper
(B) A grocery store manager
(C) A bank consultant
(D) A Web site designer

154. What is NOT mentioned as a new feature of the Web site?

(A) Pictures with higher resolution
(B) Greater information security
(C) A listing of all service fees
(D) Chatting service for customized shopping

Questions 155-157 refer to the following e-mail.

To: Employees at Daily Best Corporation
From: Michael Moore<mm@dbc.com>
Date: June 15
RE: Save the Date!

You are invited to a dinner honoring Richard Hutchson's 45 years of hard work and dedication. Richard started working for Daily Best Corporation at the age of 16, when he worked as a temporary office boy. As the years passed, Richard slowly worked his way up the chain. By the age of 26, he had both earned his master's in Accounting from California State University and been established as the head accountant in the bookkeeping department. Finally, at age 45, Richard joined our corporate staff as vice president of Financial Affairs, where he spent the remainder of his career. Richard will be retiring at the end of the month and is looking forward to spending his days relaxing with his wife of 38 years, his 4 children, and his 9 grandchildren, all of whom live in the area.

If you would like to speak at Richard's retirement dinner, please e-mail Ms. Bakinsale with your intention by June 20. Each employee is permitted to bring one guest to the event. Please RSVP to Ms. Bakinsale to let her know if you will be attending by June 20.

We hope to see you there.

Sincerely,

Michael Moore
President and CEO
Daily Best Corporation

155. What was Mr. Hutchson's position when he started working at Daily Best Corporation?
(A) Accountant
(B) Office Assistant
(C) Finance Officer
(D) Vice President

156. When will Mr. Hutchson retire?
(A) June 15
(B) June 20
(C) June 30
(D) July 1

157. What are employees asked to do if they want to give a speech?
(A) E-mail Mr. Hutchson
(B) Submit the contents of the speech
(C) Complete an application
(D) Contact Ms. Bakinsale

New Restaurant Set to Open Soon

By John Wilson – New Jersey Daily Telegraph

Jersey City—Soul Food Café will be opening its doors this Friday for breakfast at 8:00 A.M. Soul Food Café is the welcome addition to the area's main street restaurants.

The owner of Soul Food Café, Linda Hamilton, says, "Soul Food Café will specialize in down-home country style meals. We are different from other restaurants in that we offer a lower calorie, healthier version of good country cooking by using healthier oils and cooking practices. We want our customers to enjoy high-quality entrées that are not high in fat and cholesterol. Our goal is to make the customers want to come back and maybe even become a little healthier in the meantime."

Ms. Hamilton, the former head chef at Creole's Home Cooking, started her plans for her own restaurant over two years ago. After looking at several spaces around the city for her restaurant, she bought the former carpet store on the main street location and had it fully restored and renovated. She explains, "I worked with the designers personally to get this place looking exactly like some of the southern restaurants I went to as a kid in Alabama."

Soul Food Café is beautiful both inside and outside. We will soon see if many residents will patronize the restaurant like Linda and her eager staff hope. Soul Food Café will be open daily from 8:00 A.M. to 9:00 P.M. except for Sundays, when it will open for brunch starting at 10:00 A.M.

158. What is the purpose of the article?
(A) To explain food preparation techniques
(B) To review local restaurants
(C) To describe an entrepreneur's business strategy
(D) To publicize the opening of a new restaurant

159. What is NOT mentioned about Soul Food Café?
(A) It is owned by Creole's Home Cooking.
(B) It serves low-calorie meals.
(C) It is close to downtown.
(D) It will open at 8:00 A.M. almost every day.

160. What is suggested about Ms. Hamilton?
(A) She enjoys all cuisine.
(B) She is new to the industry.
(C) She helped design the interior.
(D) She specializes in architecture.

We thank you for choosing to purchase a Pegasus Electronics mobile phone. If you made your purchase between July 1 and July 31, you are entitled to a gift pack containing Pegasus Electronics accessories, including a case, a set of earphones, and a protective screen cover.

Once you have completed this form by entering the requested details below, send it, along with an original proof of purchase, to Pegasus Electronics Head Office, Johnson Technology Park, Edmonton, Alberta T5A 0FH. Should you have any questions, please do not hesitate to contact Pegasus Electronics' customer service department at customerservice@pegasus.ca.

I confirm that I would like to be sent a free set of Pegasus Electronics mobile phone accessories. X

Name: Brendan Baker
Address: 55 Joseph Street
City/Province/Postal code: Bracebridge, ON P1L 5JY
Phone number: 555-9231
E-mail address:
Purchased mobile phone model: S350   S400   X S450

Delivery of your items may take up to two weeks. This offer is a limited-time offer that ends on August 30. The offer does not extend to purchases made outside of Canada, or purchases made on our Web site. Also, persons currently employed by Pegasus Electronics are not permitted to take advantage of this offer.

By supplying your e-mail address, you indicate that you wish to receive Pegasus Electronics' monthly newsletter, which contains information about forthcoming phone models and special discounts.

161. What is suggested about Pegasus
Electronics?
(A) It is headquartered in Edmonton.
(B) It will discontinue production of
mobile phones on August 30.
(C) It has created a store membership
plan for customers.
(D) It has recently launched a new model
of mobile phone.

162. Why did Mr. Baker fill out the form?
(A) To ask that a product be exchanged
(B) To give feedback about a service
(C) To request a refund on a product
(D) To receive complimentary items

163. What is implied about Mr. Baker?
(A) He is a former employee of Pegasus
Electronics.
(B) He ordered a mobile phone from
Pegasus Electronics' Web site.
(C) He would like to receive Pegasus
Electronics' monthly newsletter.
(D) He bought a Pegasus Electronics
mobile phone in July.

August 10

Professor Jim Moore

Gentech Enterprises, 290 Swallow Court, Hackney, London, UK, E15 6PP

Dear Professor Moore,

—[1]—. We have strived to assemble a team of the most experienced professionals from the fields of stem cell engineering and gene therapy.

We meet with all of our contributing experts annually at the International Genetics Conference in January. —[2]—. Next year's event will be held at the Wilshire Hotel in Los Angeles. All experts are expected to attend this event, in addition to monthly meetings with our editorial team via teleconference. Our editorial team handles the bulk of the writing for the journal, but our contributing experts provide their invaluable knowledge, expertise, and advice on all issues and developments related to the field. —[3]—. As a contributing expert, you will be expected to fulfill the following duties:

- Report recent developments in stem cell research
- Recommend leading figures for interviews
- Write occasional columns about your field of research
- Answer letters from readers that our staff cannot adequately answer

Within the next two weeks, we will contact you with more details, including contact information for our other contributing experts, in case you would like to confer with them on any topics. During this time, we suggest that you familiarize yourself with our journal by reading through the three issues we previously mailed to you. —[4]—. This will help you get a good idea of our style and content.

All of us here look forward to working with you!

Warm regards,

Beatrice Hopper
Chief Editor
Stem Cell Monthly

164. What is the purpose of the letter?

(A) To invite Professor Moore to speak at a conference

(B) To announce the release of a new science journal

(C) To describe guidelines for submitting articles

(D) To outline the responsibilities of a position

165. With whom is Professor Moore expected to stay in regular contact?

(A) London-based scientists

(B) Government officials

(C) Stem Cell Monthly subscribers

(D) Editorial team members

166. In which of the positions marked [1],[2],[3], and [4] does the following sentence best belong?

"We truly appreciate your decision to join our pool of contributing experts here at Stem Cell Monthly."

(A) [1]

(B) [2]

(C) [3]

(D) [4]

167. What is Professor Moore encouraged to do within the next two weeks?

(A) Forward his contact details

(B) Organize a meeting with other contributors

(C) Register for an upcoming conference

(D) Review some publications

Transit Council Approves Walkways Construction

CASTRO VALLEY(July 14)—The Transit Council of Castro Valley has voted in approval of a using $300,000 to build pedestrian walkways over ten of the busiest streets in the city. — [1] —. The approval comes after the city conducted a safety audit following complaints from pedestrians living in Castro Valley about dangerous traffic conditions and long waiting times at pedestrian crosswalks. The conductors of the audit agreed that the issues brought up by pedestrians should be addressed within the next year. — [2] —. The walkways will allow pedestrians to cross roads without hindering the flow of traffic, which will also make drivers happy, especially during the tourist season, when traffic around the riverside district can be very congested.

Mr. Simon Livingston, Mayor of Castro Valley, suggested the construction of the walkways to the transit council on March 12. Mr. Livingston related the outcome of a study of residents of Castro Valley that was conducted in November. — [3] —. The study shows that only 10 percent of the population in Castro Valley enjoyed jogging or walking in the city. Based on happenings when similar walkways were constructed in surrounding cities, Mr. Livingston believes that the amount of people who walk or jog recreationally or for exercise could triple.

The initial phase for the construction will include temporarily closing down lanes on the road when necessary. Detours will be marked at these times. After the initial construction, the walkways will be painted and have lights added to make them accessible to residents at night. — [4] —.

168. What is a purpose of the article?

(A) To report some plans to attract tourists

(B) To give details about a new commuter expressway

(C) To explain a project that caters to pedestrian

(D) To recruit workers to renovate council offices

169. What is indicated about Castro Valley?

(A) There are many problems year-round with traffic near the riverside district.

(B) More than 10,000 people enjoy walking recreationally in the city.

(C) The number of residents has tripled over the last few years.

(D) The riverside district is popular among tourists.

170. What is scheduled to be done as part of the construction?

(A) The streetlights on roads will be replaced.

(B) New roads for car only will be added.

(C) The walkways will be painted to be more noticeable to pedestrians.

(D) Lanes for walking and jogging will be separated.

171. In which of the positions marked [1],[2],[3], and [4] does the following sentence best belong?

"Construction on the first walkway will begin on August 3, and all ten will be completed within 4 months."

(A) [1]

(B) [2]

(C) [3]

(D) [4]

Kelly Han 1:25 P.M.

Hey guys, I'm in trouble. I need some help.

Isabella Choi 1:26 P.M.

What's up? Something's wrong?

Kelly Han 1:28 P.M.

Where are you? Are you in the office, or are you on your way back?

William Smith 1:29 P.M.

I'm still at lunch. I'll be back at the office in fifteen minutes.

Isabella Choi 1:30 P.M.

I've just walked in. Do you need my help?

Kelly Han 1:31 P.M.

I've left some important documents on my desk. I need them for my presentation in about half an hour.

Isabella Choi 1:32 P.M.

Hold on. I'll check it out.

William Smith 1:33 P.M.

Wasn't your presentation scheduled on Thursday?

Kelly Han 1:35 P.M.

Yes, it was. But it has been moved forward because the CEO is going on a business trip to South Korea on Thursday.

Isabella Choi 1:36 P.M.

You mean the VIP Sports presentation file?

Kelly Han 1:37 P.M.

Right. Could you get it to me ASAP? I'm in the conference room on the eighth floor.

Isabella Choi 1:39 P.M.

Okay. On my way.

Kelly Han 1:40 P.M.

What a relief! Thanks a lot. I owe you one.

172. What is Ms. Han's problem?

(A) She cannot find a ride to work.

(B) She has broken her laptop computer..

(C) She hasn't brought some documents.

(D) She may not be able to meet a
deadline.

173. At 1:29 P.M., what does Mr. Smith mean
when he writes, "I'm still at lunch"?

(A) He can't help Ms. Han.

(B) He will not give a presentation today.

(C) He can't start working right now.

(D) He is currently enjoying his food.

174. What is suggested about Mr. Smith?

(A) He will be giving a presentation on
Thursday.

(B) He currently works at VIP Sports
Corporation.

(C) He will meet with an important client
this afternoon.

(D) He hasn't been informed of the
presentation schedule change.

175. What will Ms. Choi most likely do next?

(A) Leave for a business travel

(B) Bring important papers to Ms. Han

(C) Prepare for some research

(D) Send an e-mail to Mr. Smith

Questions 176-180 refer to the following poster and e-mail.

★ ★ ★ ★ ★ ★ ★ ★ ★ ★

Miguel's Mexican Restaurant
Help us celebrate our 20th birthday!

This year, Miguel's Mexican Restaurant is celebrating its twentieth year of serving the Phoenix community. To honor this event and to say thank you to all of our loyal customers, Miguel's is hosting a month of special promotions and events!

Take advantage of these great upcoming promotions at designated times throughout July:

- July 5 – 50% off all starters and main dishes!
- July 10 to July 15 – A free bowl of nachos with any order over $10!
- July 20 – Receive two free Mexican beers with any main dish!
- July 30 – A free taco for every guest!

In addition, do not miss the chance to take part in these fantastic events:

- July 3 – Dance around the Mexican hat – Live music provided by guitarist Fernando Chavez
- July 8 – Quiz night – Win great prizes: Mexican hats, T-shirts, and many more
- July 16 – Fancy dress evening – Prizes awarded to anyone in a fancy Mexican dress
- July 21 – Karaoke contest – $10 entry per person: Winner will receive $100!
- July 28 – Mexican culture evening – Readings from Mexican poet Maria Osolitos

Join the fiesta at Miguel's Mexican Restaurant.

140 Main Street – opposite the HB Bank

www.miguelsmexican.com

★ ★ ★ ★ ★ ★ ★ ★ ★

To:　　　Miguel Sanchez <miguelsanchez@miguelsmexican.com>
From:　　Tony Simpson <T.Simpson@yaho.com>
Date:　　June 29
Subject:　Anniversary Event

Dear Miguel,

My wife and I read your advertisement for the birthday celebrations at your restaurant. Congratulations to everybody at Miguel's! The restaurant has been a huge success, and I know how much people love it.

We have been regulars at your restaurant ever since it opened twenty years ago. Both my wife Irene and I love Mexican cuisine, and we believe that Miguel's serves the best food outside Mexico. We will definitely try to attend as many events as possible. I am especially looking forward to the one on July 16. It sounds like it will be great fun!

As you may remember, I work for the local newspaper The Phoenix Express. Would it be okay to interview you for the paper sometime this week? I'm sure a picture of you and the article appearing in our publication would increase publicity for the great promotions and events that you are hosting. Please let me know when you are available, and I will stop by the restaurant.

Many thanks. Keep up the good work!

Tony Simpson

176. What is the restaurant announcing in the poster?
(A) Changes to its menu
(B) Adjustments to its opening times
(C) Its anniversary celebrations
(D) Its reopening of a restaurant

177. Which of these promotions is NOT being offered in July?
(A) Free tacos
(B) Half-price starters and main dishes
(C) Free dessert
(D) Complimentary bowls of nachos

178. On which date will musician Fernando Chavez perform at the restaurant?
(A) July 3
(B) July 8
(C) July 16
(D) July 21

179. According to the email, which event is Tony Simpson looking forward to?
(A) The quiz night
(B) The fancy dress evening
(C) The music contest
(D) The Mexican culture evening

180. Who most likely is Tony Simpson?
(A) A restaurant owner
(B) A musician
(C) A fashion designer
(D) A journalist

To: Faulker and Pennyworth Accounting
From: Dina Wilks, General Manager
Subject: May Painting Plans
Date: April 25
Attachment: Office Packing and Moving Schedule

All Staff:

We are all aware of the interior design changes that will begin in May. Many rooms will need to be emptied in order to accommodate painters, designers, and electricians. Staff members will need to pack up their personal items and office supplies by 6 P.M. the day BEFORE their scheduled move. PLEASE LEAVE YOUR DESKTOP COMPUTERS (the schedule is attached).

Three separate teams will be working simultaneously so that we experience the least amount of lost productivity, so more than one office will be moving at a time. Note that rooms due for work on Monday, May 2 must be packed up and vacated by Friday afternoon, April 30.

Boxes and tape will be provided. Please do not lift a box that you cannot carry yourself— ask for help! Unfortunately for some, sharing offices can be a bit cramped. You can use one of our conference rooms, copy rooms, or the employee lounge to work. Please make sure you have your files and laptops handy. Telecommuting for your assigned moving day will be allowed, but please see your supervisor for permission.

Again, we apologize for the temporary inconvenience this may cause. Just know that when the entire project is complete, we will have a modern and innovative workplace that will facilitate our continued excellence.

Work Schedule May 2 to May 6

Monday, May 2 / Tuesday, May 3	Office 502 (Meeting Room) / Room 506 (Stephen Blass & Jarvis Embry)
Wednesday, May 4 / Thursday, May 5	Office 503 (Courtney Goodroad & Cynthia de la Cruz) / Office 507 (Meeting Room)
Friday, May 6	Office 504 (Oliver Tran) / Office 508 (Yejin Hwang & Trisha Wang)

181. Why was the memo sent to employees?
(A) To announce cutbacks in schedules
(B) To announce a design contest in the office
(C) To alert them of upcoming renovations
(D) To explain recent additions to computer software

182. What are employees instructed to do?
(A) Take two days of paid vacation between May 2 and May 6
(B) Call to reschedule any client appointments
(C) Box their own personal items and supplies
(D) Update their contact information online

183. What option is available to the affected employees?
(A) Telecommuting
(B) Schedule adjustment
(C) Additional parking
(D) Commuting fees refund

184. When should Ms. Hwang have her supplies boxed up?
(A) On May 5
(B) On May 6
(C) On May 7
(D) On May 8

185. What is suggested about workflow for affected employees?
(A) They can choose where they will be working.
(B) They are not required to leave their offices.
(C) They may not share offices with others.
(D) They must remain in the copy rooms.

Opening of Crescent River •
City Magazine • April Edition

Last year, city officials announced that the Crescent River transformation project was finished, and the river was open to the public. Ever since the opening, the river and its scenic walkway have been crowded with visitors from around the country.

Contrasting with the bustling city that surrounds it, the Crescent River is full of greenery and resting areas. The visitors—picnicking families, couples on dates, playing children and workers on breaks—all seem to be attracted to the peaceful setting the river offers.

However, the project had some major drawbacks. For starters, it cost the city over $200 million. Also, the restoration project of Crescent River required careful planning and intensive construction that lasted for over 18 months. During that period, commuters had to deal with high traffic volume and increased commuting time.

Regardless of its costs, the Crescent River is considered a tremendous success by many. The once smelly, dirty river that shamed the city is now one of its most popular tourist attractions. Citizens are now looking forward to the summer as there will be public pools opening in various parts of the river.

City Magazine would like to hear about our readers' personal experiences at Crescent River. Please send us your own Crescent River story, and we will select the most heartwarming stories to be shared in our next edition. Winners will receive gift cards.

From:	carmellafischer@biznet.com
To:	editor@citymagazine.org
Date:	April 19
Subject:	My story

Dear editor,

When I was young, I would spend countless hours by Crescent River. My home was only five minutes away, so I would always go to the river to play in the water, catch crayfish, and hang out with the neighborhood kids. I got along with one in particular, Charlie. We became dear friends, and we met every single day. When I turned nine, my parents moved to the countryside and I lost touch with him. I didn't know that Crescent River had changed so much over the last twenty years until I returned to the city last year. Last month, I heard that the construction finished, so I decided to visit. As I was strolling along the walkway, someone called my name. I looked back and could not believe my eyes. It was Charlie, just twenty years older than when I last saw him. Now we are engaged. I owe my love story to the Crescent River. I have attached a photo of us now and when we were nine years old.

Carmella Fischer

From: editor@citymagazine.org
To: carmellafischer@biznet.com
Date: April 23
Subject: Congratulations

Dear Carmella Fischer,

Thank you for sending your story to us. I was instantly hooked by it. It is such an incredible love story. I would like to share your tale with all our readers. Would it be alright if I added the two photos as well? I'm sure I can write a very interesting article about strange and wonderful ties, and it will get a lot of attention from our readers in the May issue. Also, can you send me your address so that I can send you your gift card?

Congratulations on your engagement.

Sincerely,
Zack Cruse
Chief Editor

186. In the article, what is indicated about Crescent River?
(A) It is not yet open to the public.
(B) Its restoration project cost $200 million.
(C) Its construction lasted for 20 years.
(D) It currently has public pools.

187. What is NOT implied about Ms. Fischer?
(A) She used to play by the river as a child.
(B) She used to live near the river.
(C) She was involved in the restoration project.
(D) She used to live in the countryside.

188. Why will Ms. Fisher most likely receive a gift certificate?
(A) She helped with the opening of Crescent River.
(B) She won an award at a photo competition.
(C) She attracted many advertisements from large corporations.
(D) She was chosen as a winner of the *City Magazine* contest.

189. In the article, the word "contrasting" in paragraph 2, line 1, in closest in meaning to
(A) differing
(B) monitoring
(C) comparing
(D) describing

190. What is suggested about *City Magazine*?
(A) It was involved in the construction of Crescent River.
(B) It published an article on Crescent River one year ago.
(C) Its editor is getting engaged.
(D) It is a monthly magazine.

Questions 191-195 refer to the following schedule, e-mail and letter.

Modern Art Gallery of Austin
Scheduled Exhibitions

Dates	Exhibition Titles	Descriptions
7 May-5 October	*The Moon and Sea*	This outstanding collection of drawings and photographs from various regions, including several Caribbean nations, how the moon and the sea have inspired humankind for many centuries.
28 May-5 October	*Furniture is Art*	We think that furniture is just functional, but it is also artful. This collection shows an array of distinctive antiques and modern furniture from across Europe.
3 July-18 December	*Dance: Art by Movement*	Through sculpture, paintings, photographs, and digital recordings, this exhibition portrays performing arts from several African countries.
24 July-22 August	*The Photography of Animals*	This exhibition is a collection of fascinating photographs of a variety of wild animals in the world.

For more information about tickets, visit our Web site or send an e-mail to cedlecon@magob.org. We will provide two free tickets to all members. To become a member, visit the membership page.

From: Molly Hudson<mhudson@mason.inet>
To: Sharon De Leon<Sharondl@maga.org>
Subject: Tickets
Date: May 1

I have complimentary tickets for the *Dance:Art by Movement* exhibition, but I wish to purchase two more tickets. I'm sure my credit card information is in your database. So, could you make a payment with my credit card and send the tickets via mail? I'd like to see *Furniture is Art*, although I'd be happy to see any of the others. Thank you for these gorgeous exhibits.

Molly Hudson

3 May

Molly Hudson
P.O Box N-123
NASSAU N.P

Dear Ms. Hudson,

Thank you for being as a patron of the Modern Art Gallery of Austin. I regret to inform you that the exhibition you requested has been cancelled and replaced with *Indigenous Cultures of the Americas.*

I have enclosed the two additional tickets you paid for. These may be used for this new exhibit, which will run in our gallery until 18 December. Your JPax credit card has been charged $24.

Sincerely,
Sharon De Leon
Modern Art Gallery of Austin
Enclosures

191. According to the Web site, what do all of the exhibitions have in common?
(A) They include photographs.
(B) They include live performances.
(C) They feature works by artists from the Caribbean.
(D) They feature works from multiple countries.

192. What is implied about Ms. Hudson?
(A) She is requesting a refund.
(B) She has a membership to the museum.
(C) She is a contemporary artist.
(D) She has already seen all of the exhibits.

193. In the letter, the word "run" in paragraph 1, line 5, is closest in meaning to
(A) last
(B) manage
(C) move
(D) cover

194. Which exhibit has been cancelled?
(A) Moon and Sea
(B) Furniture is Art
(C) Dance: Art in Movement
(D) The Photography of Animals

195. What did Ms. De Leon do for Ms. Hudson?
(A) Mailed a list of upcoming events
(B) Changed the date of an exhibition
(C) Waived a membership fee
(D) Charged her credit card

Question 196-200 refer to the following e-mails and the attachment.

To:	Mary Benson; Ramina Taylor; James Porter
From:	Tim Rolland
Date:	June 12, 7:54 A.M.
Subject:	Office Space
Attachment:	Properties

Hi all,

I thoroughly enjoyed our luncheon at Manke Grill last Monday. As an AHG Consultants employee, I am excited to be a part of the first branch in Alamo. I look forward to giving advice to clients in Alamo about using information technology to help them with their startups.

I would appreciate it if you could give me your opinions about the type of office space that would be suitable. I have explored syeogain.ca to find well-conditioned ones that can fit our basic criteria and budget and have summarized the information to make a short list. Please read the attached document and let me know your opinion.

Tim Rolland
AHG Consultants

3874 Thunderland Hilltop

Open concept office/retail space in a well-developed rural area of Alamo with a lot of pedestrians. The building has a remarkable appearance and enough space for a signboard for your company use. High energy-efficient heating system will keep your winter expenditure low.
Monthly lease: $1,000

29485 Clearance Path

First-floor office. Elegantly decorated. Surrounded on-site parking with security fence. Located near Union Park, in the vicinity of the train station, 30 minutes from downtown. Union Park's path is very popular with exercisers. Vodafone phone system is already installed for your use.
Monthly lease: $950

4991 Commercial Park Lot

Non-communal, one-story building. Equipped with furniture made by famous designers. Safe parking lot near the street and a discount for renters. Fast Internet access can be installed. Located west of the city, in the suburbs.

Monthly lease: $875

1432 Timothy Street

Fourth-floor office suite. Covered garage for vehicles with security system and guards. Located right in the heart of Alamo. Business equipment, including a color copier, a scanner, a printer and a fax machine ready for use. A video conferencing studio renovated with the latest technology and free high-speed wireless Internet.

Monthly lease: $1,000

To:	Mary Benson; Tim Rolland; Ramina Taylor
From:	James Porter
Date:	June 15, 4:39 P.M.
Subject:	Re: Office Space

Dear all,

Thank you Tim for narrowing down the options for us. I heard last Monday's meeting went very well. I would have loved to be there, but my trip to Toronto made it impossible. It looks like I am the latest person to provide comments through e-mail. Thank you for your patience.

Ramina, I like the office with a lot of space, but I feel it'd be better to be located in the middle of downtown. Is anyone familiar with Alamo public transit systems? It would be helpful to know if we will be using them to commute.

I also agree with Tim's opinion that we should attend the technology fair in Alamo. I'm going to visit it next weekend while I look at housing options. Also, I will be having lunch with an Alamo delegate who used to work for AHG Consultants. I will let you know when I have any news.

James Porter
AHG Consultants

196. Who most likely is Mr. Rolland?

(A) A technology expert

(B) A small business owner

(C) A conference organizer

(D) A real estate agent

197. What is one property feature mentioned in the attachment?

(A) A break room for employees

(B) A popular fitness club

(C) An electricity bill paid by its owner

(D) A location close to exercise trail

198. What is suggested about Mr. Porter?

(A) He missed the gathering at Manke Grill.

(B) He is currently living in Alamo.

(C) He plans to attend a performance.

(D) He prefers not to use public transportation.

199. What most likely is true about Ms. Taylor?

(A) She just relocated to a new home.

(B) She will meet her former client.

(C) She sent an e-mail to her colleagues.

(D) She used to live in Alamo.

200. Which property does Mr. Porter most likely favor?

(A) 3874 Thunderland Hilltop

(B) 29485 Clearance Path

(C) 4991 Commercial Park Lot

(D) 1432 Timothy Street

Stop! This is the end of the test. If you finish before time is called, you may go back to Parts 5, 6, and 7 and check your work.

101. A	121. D	141. D	161. A	181. C
102. B	122. B	142. B	162. D	182. C
103. C	123. A	143. B	163. D	183. A
104. C	124. A	144. D	164. D	184. A
105. A	125. B	145. A	165. D	185. A
106. D	126. B	146. A	166. A	186. B
107. A	127. B	147. A	167. D	187. C
108. B	128. C	148. D	168. C	188. D
109. A	129. A	149. C	169. D	189. A
110. A	130. A	150. C	170. C	190. D
111. D	131. C	151. D	171. D	191. D
112. D	132. B	152. B	172. C	192. B
113. B	133. B	153. A	173. A	193. A
114. C	134. C	154. C	174. D	194. B
115. B	135. A	155. B	175. B	195. D
116. B	136. D	156. C	176. C	196. A
117. D	137. C	157. D	177. C	197. D
118. C	138. A	158. D	178. A	198. A
119. B	139. D	159. A	179. B	199. C
120. D	140. D	160. C	180. D	200. D

ACTUAL TEST

1

해설서

101 준동사의 수식은 부사

★★ 어형 / 부사어휘 + 혼동부사

McGowan 씨는 그녀의 몇몇 전 고용주들에 의해 강력히 추천을 받았다.

문제 분석

high 높은/높게(형/부)
highly 매우/가장/크게(부)

어휘 former 전임의, 전자의 employer 고용주

Ms. McGowan has been ------- recommended by some of her former employers.

(A) high
(B) higher
(C) highest
(D) highly

문제 해설

빈칸이 has been과 과거분사인 recommended 사이에 위치하고 있으므로 빈칸에는 과거분사인 recommended를 수식하는 부사가 와야 한다. 다만 high와 highly는 모두 부사로 high는 '높게'란 뜻을, highly는 '매우, 가장, 강력하게'란 뜻을 지니고 있음을 고려할 때 빈칸에는 전 고용주들에 의해 강력하게 추천을 받고 있다는 문맥을 구성할 수 있는 highly가 적합하다. 각 부사마다 달리 쓰이는 각 부사의 의미를 정확하게 이해하지 않으면 빈칸이 단순히 부사가 위치해야 한다는 점만 파악한 것만으로 문제를 풀이할 수 없다.

토익 분석

토익에서는 과거분사를 비롯하여 현재분사, 동명사, To 부정사와 같은 준동사들을 수식하는 어형을 묻는 문제들이 출제되며 이 때 준동사들이 어떠한 품사의 역할을 하더라도 기본적으로 동사이므로 수식은 부사가 해야 한다는 특징을 간과하지 않도록 한다.

102 한정사 문제는 대부분 소유격 대명사로 출제

★ 한정사 / 소유격 대명사

Chandler 씨는 기자 회견을 하는 동안 시장은 자유를 보장받아야 하지만 그에 따른 책임 또한 존중해야 한다고 이야기했다.

어휘 press briefing 기자 회견, 기자 대상 발표 deserve ~을 할 만하다, ~을 할 자격이 되다 respect 존중, 존경, ~을 존경하다 responsibility 책임, 담당 as well 또한, 역시

Mr. Chandler said during ------- press briefing that the market deserves freedom, but should respect its responsibility as well.

(A) he
(B) his
(C) him
(D) himself

문제 해설

빈칸에 적합한 인칭 대명사를 묻는 문제로 빈칸이 기자 회견을 뜻하는 복합명사인 press briefing 앞에 위치하고 있다. 따라서 빈칸에는 명사와 함께 쓰일 수 있는 유일한 인칭 대명사인 소유격 대명사 his가 와야 한다.

토익 분석

매달 정기 토익에서는 명사의 범위를 좁혀주는 한정사를 묻는 문제가 출제된다. 대표적인 한정사로는 관사, 소유격 대명사, 수량을 나타내는 수량사가 있으나 한정사 문제는 대부분 소유격 대명사와 관련되어 출제되고 있으며 간간히 적합한 수량 표현을 묻는 문제가 출제되고 있다. 특히 소유격 대명사를 묻는 한정사 문제는 주로 101번에서 110번 사이에서 등장하는 경향이 있다.

103

Our stocks usually benefit ------- the so-called January effect that causes the price of these stocks to rise between December and January.

(A) of
(B) since
(C) from
(D) within

문제 해설

빈칸에 적절한 전치사를 묻는 문제로 빈칸이 benefit이란 동사 뒤에 위치하고 있다. 무엇보다 benefit이 형성할 수 있는 의미는 '~에게 혜택을 주다'라는 의미 또는 '~로부터 혜택을 보다'란 의미를 형성할 수 있는 것이 전부이다. 즉, 혜택을 주거나 혜택을 보거나 받는다는 의미 외에는 없다는 것이다. 다만 benefit이란 동사가 '~에게 혜택을 주다'란 뜻으로 쓰일 때는 목적어를 직접 취하는 타동사이므로 빈칸에는 '~로부터 혜택을 보다'란 뜻을 형성할 수 있도록 출처를 의미하는 전치사인 from이 와야 한다.

토익 분석

문제 유형이라 함은 반복적으로 출제되는 고정된 형태만 제시되는 것이 아니라 이를 역으로 변형하여 출제되기도 한다. 출제동사 benefit은 전치사 from과의 연결 관계뿐만 아니라 전치사 from을 통해 동사 benefit을 선택하는 문제 또한 출제된 바 있으므로 이 두 가지 출제 방식을 모두 숙지하도록 한다.

★★ 어휘 / 전치사

우리 주식들은 12월과 1월 사이에 주가 상승을 촉진시키는 소위 1월 효과로 인해 주가 상승의 혜택을 보고 있다.

문제 분석

benefit from sth ~로부터 혜택을 보다/~의 도움을 받다
benefit sth ~에게 혜택을 주다 / ~에게 득이 되다.

어휘 stock 주식, 재고 benefit from ~로부터 혜택을 보다, ~로부터 이익을 얻다 effect 효과 cause ~을 초래하다, ~을 야기하다 rise ~이 상승하다, ~이 솟아 오르다

104

BK Technology's new accounting software makes it ------- than before for companies to create their financial statements.

(A) easy
(B) easier
(C) ease
(D) more easily

문제 해설

빈칸이 비교급 전치사 than 앞에 위치하고 있으므로 빈칸에는 비교급 어형이 가능한 형용사나 부사가 와야 하며 또한 빈칸이 동사 makes와 가목적어 it 뒤에 자리잡고 있으므로 빈칸은 목적격 보어가 적합한 자리임을 파악할 수 있다. 따라서 목적격 보어는 부사가 아닌 형용사만 가능하다는 점을 고려할 때 빈칸에는 비교급 형용사 어형인 easier이 와야 한다.

토익 분석

주격/목적격 보어의 어형을 묻는 문제는 대부분 형용사 보어를 중심으로 출제가 되고 있으며 목적격 보어에 비해 주격 보어의 출제 비중이 크다. 다만 주격 보어의 난이도에 비해 목적격 보어를 묻는 난이도가 상대적으로 높기 때문에 난이도가 높은 보어 어형을 묻고자 한다면 해당 문제처럼 목적격 보어와 연관된 문제가 출제된다. 이 경우 목적격 보어를 취하는 5형식 구조의 절을 구성하는 동사로는 make / keep / find / consider이 주된 출제 대상임을 알아두도록 한다.

★★ 어형 / 비교급 형용사

BK Technology 사의 새로운 회계 소프트웨어는 회사들이 재무제표를 이전보다 손쉽게 작성할 수 있도록 한다.

문제 분석

make + 목적어 + 목적격 보어 (형용사 보어) // 목적어가 ~한 상태가 되도록 하다

어휘 accounting 회계 financial statement 재무제표

★ 어형 / 전치사 + 동명사

KS Electronics 사는 동유럽 국가들에 위치한 일부 제조공장들을 폐쇄함으로써 불경기를 극복했다.

문제 분석

by + V-ing ~을 함으로써

어휘 overcome ~을 극복하다 economic depression 불경기 | manufacturing plant 제조 공장

KS Electronics has overcome the economic depression by ------- some of their manufacturing plants in Eastern European countries.

(A) close
(B) closing
(C) closed
(D) closes

문제 해설

빈칸이 전치사 by 뒤에 위치하고 있으므로 빈칸에는 전치사의 목적어 역할을 할 수 있는 명사가 와야 한다. 다만 이 명사는 빈칸 뒤 some이란 대명사를 목적어를 취할 수 있는 명사여야 하므로 빈칸에는 동명사인 closing이 위치해야 한다.

토익 분석

전치사 뒤 빈칸 자리는 전치사의 목적어인 명사가 위치해야 한다. 하지만 빈칸 뒤에 또 다른 명사/대명사가 자리하고 있다면 빈칸에는 또 다른 명사/대명사를 목적어로 취할 수 있는 명사 어형이 와야 한다. 명사가 또 다른 명사를 목적어로 대동할 수 없다는 점을 고려하면 전치사 + ____ + 명사/대명사 구조에서는 동명사 어형이 와야 한다. 이는 빈칸에 명사 어형과 동명사 어형 중 무엇이 와야 하는지 묻는 혼동 어형 문제로 정기 토익에서 거의 매달 출제되고 있으므로 이를 구분할 수 있는 원리를 꼭 숙지하도록 한다.

★★ 어휘 / 부사절 접속사

만약 우리가 사업차 서울로 가야 한다면, 우리는 최대한 빨리 여행사 직원과 논의해야 할 필요가 있다.

문제 분석

If 조건 부사절 접속사: 만약 ~라면, 명사절 접속사: ~인지 아닌지 (=whether)

어휘 travel to ~로 여행하다, ~로 이동하다 consult with ~와 협의하다, ~와 논의하다 travel agent 여행사 직원

------- we have to travel to Seoul for business, we will need to consult with our travel agent as quickly as possible.

(A) Whether
(B) But
(C) Even though
(D) If

문제 해설

빈칸은 부사절을 이끄는 부사절 접속사가 와야 하는 자리이다. 빈칸 뒤에 사업차 서울로 가야 한다는 내용이, 빈칸 이후에는 최대한 빨리 여행사 직원과 논의해야 할 필요가 있다는 내용이 등장하고 있다. 따라서 여행사 직원과의 빠른 논의의 전제 조건은 사업차 서울로 가야 한다는 것이므로 빈칸에는 조건 부사절 접속사인 if가 적절하다.

토익 분석

정기 토익에서는 조건 부사절 접속사로서의 If를 묻는 문제의 출제 비중이 높지만 '~인지 아닌지'란 뜻을 지닌 명사절 접속사로서 출제되기도 하므로 두 가지 접속사로서의 기능을 모두 알아두어야 한다. 특히 동사 뒤에 If가 온다면 이는 명사절 접속사로서 쓰인 것이니 이를 조건 부사절 접속사로 오해하지 않도록 한다.

107

When ------- moved into the new apartment last year, it was not fully completed.

(A) they
(B) them
(C) their
(D) themselves

★ 어형 / 주격 대명사

그들이 작년에 새로운 아파트로 입주했을 때, 그 아파트는 완공된 상태가 아니었다.

문제 분석

complete 완전한, 완비된, 철저한(형용사)
completed 완료된, 종료된(과거분사)

어휘 move into ~로 입주하다, ~로 들어가다 fully 완전히, 전적으로

문제 해설

빈칸에 적합한 인칭대명사를 묻는 문제이다. 빈칸이 부사절 접속사인 When과 시간 부사절의 동사인 moved 사이에 위치하고 있으므로 빈칸에는 주어 역할을 할 수 있는 대명사가 필요하다. 따라서 빈칸에는 주격 대명사인 they가 와야 한다.

토익 분석

정기 토익에서는 생각보다 다양한 인칭대명사를 묻는다. 한정사 문제로서는 소유격 대명사가 자주 출제되고 있지만 이 외에도 주어나 목적어 자리에 위치해야 할 주격 인칭대명사/목적격 인칭대명사를 묻는 문제도 빠짐없이 꾸준하게 출제되고 있다.

108

Next month, the government ------- a set of measures to stimulate the sluggish economy and create jobs in the short term.

(A) announcing
(B) will announce
(C) announced
(D) is announced

★ 어형 / 동사 어형 + 동사 시제

다음 달에, 정부는 단기간에 부진한 경제를 회생시키고 일자리를 창출할 수 있는 일련의 조치들을 발표할 것이다.

문제 분석

a set of + 가산 복수명사 / 불가산명사
a set of measures 일련의 조치들

어휘 a set of 일련의, 종합적인 measure 조치 stimulate ~을 자극하다, ~을 활성화하다, ~을 부양하다 sluggish 부진한 in the short term 단기간에

문제 해설

빈칸에 적절한 동사의 어형을 묻는 문제이므로 우선적으로 announcing이란 준동사 형태는 오답으로 소거해야 한다. 아울러 문두에 위치한 Next month를 통해 미래 시제임을 파악할 수 있으며 빈칸 이후에 a set이란 목적어가 위치하고 있으므로 능동태가 필요함을 알 수 있다. 따라서 빈칸에는 미래시제이며 능동태를 구성하는 will announce란 동사 어형이 적합하다.

토익 분석

동사 어형을 묻는 문제는 매달 출제되는 대표적인 문제 유형이다. 우선 선택지에서 절을 구성할 수 없는 준동사 어형, 즉 V-ing / Vp.p(과거분사) 형태를 먼저 소거하고 이어서 주어/동사 수일치 – 목적어 유무를 통한 능동태/수동태 선택 – 시제 순으로 어형을 파악하는 것이 효율적인 문제풀이 방법이다. 다만 문두나 문미에 바로 시제를 파악할 수 있는 시제 통제부사가 등장하는 경우 시제가 반영된 어형부터 살펴봐도 무방하다.

109

★★ 어휘 / 복합 명사

출장비 환급을 원하는 직원들은 화요일까지 경리부로 영수증 원본을 제출해야 한다.

문제 분석

• get reimbursed for ~에 대한 환급/보상을 받다
• receipt 영수증(가산명사), 수취/수령(불가산명사)

어휘 get reimbursed for ~에 대한 환급을 받다 submit ~을 제출하다 original receipt 영수증 원본 accounting department 경리부 budget 예산 occasion 때, 경우, 계기

Employees who want to get reimbursed for their travel ------- should submit original receipts to the accounting department by Tuesday.

(A) plans
(B) budgets
(C) expenses
(D) occasions

문제 해설

빈칸에는 travel과 함께 쓰여 복합명사를 구성할 수 있는 명사가 필요하다. 무엇보다 get reimbursed, 즉 환급을 받는다는 내용이 등장하고 있으므로 빈칸에는 환급이 가능한 대상을 지칭하는 명사가 와야 한다. 따라서 빈칸에는 비용을 뜻하는 expenses가 적합하다.

토익 분석

명사와 명사가 합쳐 새로운 의미의 명사 어휘를 구성하는 것을 복합명사라 한다. 정기 토익에서는 비즈니스와 관련된 복합명사를 반복적으로 묻는 경우가 많다. 따라서 빈출 복합명사들을 사전에 익혀두는 것이 빠른 문제풀이에 도움이 된다.

---

110 출제자가 의도하는 어휘

★★★ 어휘 / 명사 어휘

Wimbledon Creek 아파트는 몇몇 시립 공원들과의 근접성으로 인해 사람들 사이에서 선호도가 매우 높다.

문제 분석

(be) in proximity to ~에 근접한

어휘 among ~중에서, ~사이에서 several 몇몇 route 길, 도로 distance 거리 proximity 근접성, 인접성 similarity 유사성

The Wimbledon Creek Apartment is very popular among people because of its ------- to several city parks.

(A) route
(B) distance
(C) proximity
(D) similarity

문제 해설

빈칸에 적절한 명사 어휘를 묻는 문제이다. 빈칸이 포함된 내용은 빈칸에 앞서 사람들 사이에서 Wimbledon Creek 아파트의 인기가 높다는 결과에 따른 이유가 제시되어야 한다. 아울러 빈칸 뒤에 몇몇 시립 공원들이 언급되고 있으므로 빈칸에는 이를 Wimbledon Creek 아파트가 구가하는 인기와 결부시킬 수 있는 명사 어휘가 와야 함을 알 수 있다. 따라서 Wimbledon Creek 아파트가 몇몇 시립 공원들과의 근접성으로 인해 인기가 높다는 문맥이 타당하므로 빈칸에는 '근접성'을 뜻하는 명사 proximity가 적합하다.

토익 분석

정기 토익에서 출제되는 어휘 문제를 풀이할 때 항상 염두에 두어야 하는 가이드라인으로 제시하고 싶은 것은 단순히 선택지에 나온 4개의 어휘를 무작정 해석하며 해석을 근간으로 풀이하는 방식은 지양하라는 것이다. 다시 말해서 어휘 문제 풀이에 있어 가장 중요한 점은 문제를 풀이하는 자의 관점에서 적합한 어휘를 선택해야 하는 것이 아니라 출제자가 의도하는 어휘가 무엇인지 파악하는 방식으로 문제 풀이에 접근해야 한다는 것이다. 따라서 빈칸 주변의 내용을 해석하며 빈칸에 어떠한 어휘가 적합한지 가늠할 수 있는 단서로 활용이 가능한 어휘나 표현을 파악하는 방식으로 문제를 풀이해야 한다. 그래야 어휘 문제의 정답율을 높일 수 있을 뿐만 아니라 문제풀이에 소요되는 시간도 절약할 수 있다.

111

The new study indicated that men are more ------- to be addicted to online games than women.

(A) clear
(B) probable
(C) likely
(D) necessary

문제 해설

빈칸에 적합한 형용사 어휘를 묻는 문제이다. 빈칸을 전후하여 남자가 여자에 비해 인터넷 게임에 더욱 중독된다는 내용이 제시되고 있으므로 빈칸에는 남자가 여자보다 인터넷 게임에 더욱 중독된다는 성향이나 가능성 또는 개연성의 의미를 부여하는 '~할 것 같은'이란 뜻을 지닌 형용사 likely가 적합하다.

토익 분석

정기 토익에서 출제되는 어휘 문제는 앞서 언급한 어휘 문제 풀이 방식을 통해 효율적으로 문제를 풀이할 수도 있다. 하지만 'be likely to + 동사원형'이란 표현은 형용사 likely를 묻는 형용사 어휘 문제로 자주 출제되는 편이므로 사전에 미리 해당 표현 자체를 익혀두는 것이 현명하다.

★★ 어휘 / 형용사 어휘

새로운 연구는 남자가 여자에 비해 인터넷 게임에 더욱 중독되는 경향이 있음을 밝히고 있다.

문제 분석

indicate that S + V / ~라는 점을 밝히다/지적하다/가리키다/나타내다

어휘 indicate ~을 나타내다, ~을 가리키다, ~을 지적하다 be addicted to ~에 중독되다 probable 그럴듯한, 가능성 있는 necessary 필요한

112

Fortunately, there were no reports of injuries ------- damages from the earthquake that occurred yesterday.

(A) except
(B) when
(C) or
(D) yet

문제 해설

빈칸에 적합한 전치사 혹은 접속사를 묻는 문제이다. 빈칸 뒤 damages from the earthquake가 절이 되려면 빈칸에는 주어가 위치해야 하나 빈칸 앞에는 이미 there were no reports of injuries란 절이 등장하고 있으므로 빈칸에는 주어의 역할을 할 수 있는 접속사가 와야 한다. 하지만 when이란 접속사는 주어나 목적어가 빠진 불완전한 구조의 절이 아닌 완전한 구조의 절과 함께 쓰여야 하므로 이는 오답이다. 그러므로 damages는 동사가 아닌 복수명사이며 궁극적으로 damages from the earthquake는 절이 아닌 구의 형태임을 알 수 있다. 원론적으론 빈칸에 전치사인 except가 올 수 있지만 except가 오는 경우 문맥상 부자연스럽기 때문에 이 또한 오답으로 처리해야 한다. 무엇보다 문제를 풀이할 수 있는 결정적인 단서는 빈칸을 사이에 두고 injuries란 복수명사와 damages란 복수명사가 등장하고 있다는 점이다. 빈칸을 사이에 두고 동일한 품사의 어휘가 제시되고 있다는 점을 고려할 때 빈칸에는 등위 접속사가 와야 함을 알 수 있으며 어제 발생한 지진으로 인한 부상이나 피해에 관한 보고가 없다는 문맥을 형성하는 것이 논리적으로 타당하므로 빈칸에는 등위 접속사 or이 적절하다.

토익 분석

등위접속사는 정기 토익에서 꾸준하게 출제되고 있는 영역이다. 등위접속사로는 and, but, or, yet, for, nor, so이 있으나 단어/구/절을 모두 앞뒤로 대등하게 연결시켜줄 수 있는 등위접속사로는 and, but, or, yet 뿐이며 등위접속사는 대부분 and, but, or을 중심으로 출제되는 경향이 있다.

★★★ 접속사 / 등위 접속사

다행스럽게도, 어제 발생한 지진으로 인한 부상이나 피해에 관한 보고가 없었다.

문제 분석

A or B A 또는 B

어휘 fortunately 운 좋게도, 다행스럽게도 injury 부상 earthquake 지진 occur ~이 발생하다

113

★★ 어형 / 현재분사

대변인은 London Symphony Orchestra가 열정적인 미주 팬들을 위해 콘서트를 추가로 개최할 것을 고려 중에 있다고 밝혔다.

문제 분석

announce that S+V ~라는 점을 발표하다
be considering + O ~라는 점을 고려하다

어휘 spokesperson 대변인 announce ~을 발표하다 consider ~를 고려하다, ~라고 여기다 additional 추가적인 enthusiastic 열정적인

The spokesperson announced that the London Symphony Orchestra is ------- holding some additional concerts for the enthusiastic American fans.

(A) consider

(B) considering

(C) considered

(D) considers

문제 해설

빈칸이 주격 보어를 취하는 2형식 동사인 be 동사 이후에 등장하고 있으므로 빈칸에는 주격 보어의 역할을 할 수 있는 명사나 형용사가 와야 하나 선택지에는 consider의 명사 어형이 등장하지 않고 있을 뿐만 아니라 토익에서 보어 관련 문제는 대부분 형용사 중심으로 출제되는 경향이 있다. 따라서 현재분사인 considering과 과거분사인 considered 중 정답을 택일해야 하며 빈칸 뒤에 holding some additional concerts라는 동명사구 목적어가 위치하고 있음을 고려할 때 빈칸에는 현재분사인 considering이 적합하다.

토익 분석

정기 토익에서 매달 출제되는 유형의 문제 중 하나가 바로 be 동사 뒤에 위치해야 할 분사어형을 묻는 문제로 능동태/수동태를 구분하는 문제라 할 수 있는데 정기 토익에서는 대부분 타동사의 분사 어형을 묻기 때문에 명사인 목적어의 유무를 통해 능동태/수동태를 선택하도록 한다. 목적어가 있다면 현재분사, 목적어가 없다면 과거분사라 여기고 문제를 풀이한다면 90% 이상은 정답을 맞춰낼 수 있다. 만약 자동사가 나와서 틀렸다면 이는 팔자소관이고 해당 정기 토익의 시험 운이 없었을 뿐이다. 세상의 모든 자/타동사를 다 기억할 순 없는 터 그 다음 정기 토익에서는 다시 정답을 맞춰낼 수 있으니 너무 심려하지 말자.

114

★★ 어형 / 명사

우리 창고의 확장은 수입품을 위한 저장 공간을 상당히 증가시켰다.

문제 분석

significantly(=considerably/substantially) increase 상당히 증가하다

어휘 expansion 확장 warehouse 창고 significantly 상당하게, 꽤 storage 저장 capacity 용량 imported goods 수입품

The ------- of our warehouse has significantly increased its storage capacity for imported goods.

(A) expand

(B) expanding

(C) expanded

(D) expansion

문제 해설

빈칸이 한정사인 정관사 the 뒤에 위치하고 있으므로 빈칸에는 명사 어형이 필요하다. 따라서 빈칸에는 expansion이 와야 한다. 혹자는 expanding을 동명사로 보고 명사를 요구하는 빈칸에 위치할 수 있다고 생각할 수 있으나 무엇보다 동명사는 관사와 같은 한정사를 취하지 않으므로 이는 오답으로 소거해야 함이 옳다.

토익 분석

명사와 동명사는 명사의 역할을 할 수 있다는 공통점이 있지만 엄연히 서로 다른 존재라는 점을 간과해서는 안 된다. 동명사 어형인 V-ing 형태는 기본적으로 준동사 어형이다. 다시 말해서 절을 만들어낼 수 없을 뿐, 동사인 V-ing 형태가 명사 역할을 하는 것이기 때문에 또 다른 명사를 목적어로 취하는 것도 가능하다. 하지만 명사는 또 다른 명사를 목적어로 취하는 것이 불가하다. 아울러 동명사는 썩어도 준치라고, 준동사이기 때문에 순수하게 명사의 범위만을 제한하는 한정사와는 상극이란 점을 알아두도록 한다.

115

Please be aware ------- before employees begin to operate a new printing machine, it is essential that they thoroughly review the operating manual.

(A) of
(B) whether
(C) that
(D) from

문제 해설

빈칸에 적합한 전치사 혹은 접속사 중 택일해야 하는 문제이다. 대개 접속사 문제는 의미상 적합한 접속사를 묻는 문제 유형과 구조만 파악하여 전치사와 접속사 중 한 가지를 택일해야 하는 문제가 출제되고 있다. 접속사는 겹쳐서 사용하지 않으나 접속사가 필요한 자리 이후에 두 개의 절이 등장하는 경우라면 이야기가 달라진다. 즉, [S+V+접속사+접속사+S+V, S+V]와 같은 구조이다. 더군다나 절이 두 개일 때 하나의 접속사가 필요하므로 주어진 문제처럼 문장이 세 개의 절로 구성된 경우라면 두 개의 접속사가 필요하므로 빈칸에는 접속사가 와야 함을 알 수 있다. 형용사 aware은 전치사 with가 아닌 of와 결합하지만 빈칸 다음 이어지는 before ~ printing machine이 부사절이므로 이를 제거하면 it is essential~이 나오므로 전치사 of를 사용할 수 없다. 따라서 빈칸에는 aware이 취하는 명사절 접속사 that이 와야 한다.

토익 분석

형용사 aware은 형용사 어휘 문제로도 자주 출제되고 있을 뿐만 아니라 뒤이은 전치사 혹은 명사절 접속사를 묻는 문제로도 출제되고 있다. 따라서 전치사는 of, 명사절 접속사는 that과 함께 쓰인다는 점을 꼭 숙지하도록 한다.

★★★ 접속사 / 명사절 접속사

직원들이 새로운 윤전기를 가동시키기 전에 직원들이 설명서를 완전하게 검토하는 것이 필수이다.

문제 분석
be aware of + 명사구
be aware that S+V [명사절] – ~라는 점을 알다/~라는 점을 인식하다

어휘 aware 인식하는, 아는 operate ~을 가동시키다 essential 필수의 thoroughly 철저하게, 완전하게, 철두철미하게 review ~을 검토하다 operating manual 설명서

116

Some domestic analysts said the recent increase in oil prices in the Middle East is a key ------- that will determine the future economic growth of the country.

(A) series
(B) factor
(C) system
(D) basis

문제 해설

빈칸에는 핵심을 뜻하는 key라는 명사와 결합하여 문맥에 적합한 의미를 구성할 수 있는 명사 어휘가 필요하다. 중동지역의 최근 유가 상승은 국가의 향후 경제 성장을 결정짓는 요인이라 할 수 있으므로 빈칸에는 '요소, 요인'을 뜻하는 factor이 적절하다.

토익 분석

명사 key를 포함한 복합명사로서 key factor(핵심 요인) / key element(핵심 요인)을 함께 기억해 두도록 한다.

★★ 어휘 / 명사 어휘

몇몇 국내 분석가들은 중동지역에서의 최근 유가 상승은 국가의 향후 경제 성장을 결정짓게 될 핵심 요인이라 언급했다

문제 분석
key factor 핵심 요인

어휘 domestic 국내의 analyst 분석가 recent 최근의 increase 증가, ~이 증가하다, ~을 증가시키다 factor 요인, 요소 determine ~을 결정하다 economic growth 경제 성장 basis 근간, 토대, 기초

★ 어형 / 과거분사

고객 서비스의 수준을 향상시키기 위해서 고객의 모든 문의는 항상 기록되어야 한다.

어휘 improve ~을 개선하다, ~을 향상시키다 quality 품질, 특성 inquiry 문의 monitor ~을 관리하다, ~을 기록하다, ~을 감독하다 at all times 항상

To improve the quality of our customer service, every customer inquiry should be ------- at all times.

(A) monitor
(B) monitored
(C) monitors
(D) monitoring

문제 해설

빈칸이 주격 보어를 취하는 2형식 동사인 be 동사 이후에 등장하고 있으므로 빈칸에는 주격 보어의 역할을 할 수 있는 명사나 형용사가 와야 한다. 만약 monitor가 명사라면 주어인 every inquiry와 동격일 수 없으므로 명사 monitor/monitors는 오답이다. 반면에 monitor가 동사라면 be 동사 뒤에선 현재분사 혹은 과거분사의 형태만 가능하므로 이 중 한 가지를 택일해야 한다. 빈칸 뒤에 명사인 목적어가 위치하지 않으므로 빈칸에는 과거분사 형태인 monitored가 적합하다.

토익 분석

정기 토익에서 매달 출제되는 유형의 문제 중 하나가 바로 be 동사 뒤에 위치해야 할 분사어형을 묻는 문제로 능동태/수동태를 구분하는 문제라 할 수 있는데 정기 토익에서는 대부분 타동사의 분사어형을 묻기 때문에 명사인 목적어의 유무를 통해 능동태/수동태를 선택하도록 한다. 목적어가 있다면 현재분사, 목적어가 없다면 과거분사라 여기고 문제를 풀이한다면 90% 이상은 정답을 맞춰낼 수 있다.

★★★ 어휘 / 명사 어휘

California 지역에서의 우리 레스토랑 프랜차이즈의 규모는 빠르게 확장하고 있으며, 그들은 매일같이 많은 고객들을 다루고 있다.

문제 분석

a high volume of + 가산 복수명사 / 불가산명사 다량의, 다수의

어휘 expand ~을 확대하다, ~을 확장하다 handle ~을 다루다 volume 부피, 용량, 체적, 크기 size 크기, 규모 section 부분, 구역, 부문 total 총, 전체, 합계

Our restaurant franchises are expanding quickly in California and they are handling a high ------- of customers every day.

(A) size
(B) section
(C) volume
(D) total

문제 해설

빈칸에 적합한 명사 어휘를 묻는 문제로 빈칸이 high라는 형용사와 of customers란 전치사구 사이에 위치하고 있다. 그러므로 빈칸에는 고객들의 수나 규모가 높은 수치임을 나타낼 수 있는 명사가 필요하다. 그러므로 빈칸에는 '용량, 규모, 총계' 등의 뜻을 지닌 volume이란 명사가 와서 '다량의' '다수의'란 의미를 형성하는 a volume of란 표현을 구성할 수 있어야 하며 궁극적으론 a high volume of customers를 통해 고객이 다수임을 언급할 수 있어야 한다.

토익 분석

정기 토익에서 자주 접할 수 있는 수량 표현은 사전에 미리 익혀두는 것이 좋다. a size of는 of 이하에 등장하는 명사의 크기란 뜻을 형성하며 이를테면 a size of 5 meter, '5미터의 크기'나 a size of the new facility, '새로운 시설의 크기'처럼 쓰인다. 그리고 a total of 역시 'of 이하에 등장하는 명사의 총계'란 뜻으로 쓰이며 예컨대 a total of 200 people, '총 200명'처럼 쓰인다는 점에서 a (high) volume of와는 큰 차이가 발생한다.

119

Many people have ------- become very accustomed to shopping at large department stores in big cities.

(A) concisely
(B) recently
(C) severely
(D) diligently

★★ 어휘 / 부사 어휘

최근에 많은 사람들은 대도시에 위치한 대형 백화점에서 쇼핑하는 것에 매우 익숙하다.

문제 분석

be/become accustomed to V-ing ~에 익숙하다

어휘 accustomed 익숙한 concisely 간소하게, 간결하게 severely 심하게, 엄하게 diligently 부지런하게

문제 해설

빈칸에 알맞은 부사 어휘를 묻는 문제이다. 빈칸을 중심으로 많은 사람들이 대도시에 위치한 대형 백화점에서 쇼핑하는 것에 매우 익숙한 상태라는 내용이 등장하고 있다. 그러므로 빈칸에는 많은 사람들이 대도시에 위치한 대형 백화점에서 쇼핑하는 것에 매우 익숙해진 상태와 직접적으로 연계하여 사용할 수 있는 부사 어휘가 와야 한다. 우선 (A) concisely는 양/정도가 간결한 상태를, (C) severely는 정도가 심한 상태를, (D) diligently는 부지런한 상태를 뜻하나 사실상 이들은 모두 많은 사람들이 대도시에 위치한 대형 백화점에서 쇼핑하는 것에 매우 익숙해진 상태와 무관하다. 따라서 빈칸에는 대형 백화점에서 쇼핑하는 것에 익숙해진 시기가 '최근'임을 언급할 수 있도록 부사 어휘인 recently가 와야 한다.

토익 분석

무엇보다 '최근에'란 뜻을 지닌 recently/lately란 부사 어휘는 주로 현재완료 시제나 과거시제와 쓰인다는 시제적 특징을 기억해두면 부사 어휘 문제를 풀이하거나 또는 동사의 시제를 파악하는 문제 풀이에 도움이 된다.

120

The expected recovery in corporate investment and private spending has been ------- in the economic outlook for next year.

(A) reflected   (B) reflecting
(C) reflection   (D) reflect

★★ 어형 / 과거분사

기업 투자와 개인 소비 부문에서의 예상되는 회복은 내년도 경제 전망에 반영되어 있다.

문제 분석

be reflected in ~가 ~에 반영되다

어휘 recovery 회복, 복원 corporate investment 기업 투자 private spending 개인 소비 reflect ~을 반영하다 economic outlook 경제 전망

문제 해설

빈칸에 적합한 어형을 묻는 문제로 빈칸이 has been 뒤에 위치하고 있으므로 빈칸에는 보어의 역할을 행할 수 있는 명사나 형용사가 와야 하며 대부분 보어 관련 문제에서는 명사가 아닌 형용사와 관련하여 출제되고 있다. 주어인 The expected recovery, 즉 예상되는 회복이 곧 반영이라는 reflection이란 명사와 동격이라 할 수 없으므로 형용사 보어의 역할을 할 수 있는 현재분사 reflecting과 과거분사 reflected 중 정답을 택일해야 한다. 아울러 빈칸 뒤에 명사 목적어가 등장하지 않으므로 빈칸에는 과거분사인 reflected가 와야 한다.

토익 분석

정기 토익에서 매달 출제되는 유형의 문제 중 하나가 바로 be 동사 뒤에 명사/현재분사/과거분사 중 어떠한 어형이 와야 하는지 묻는 문제라 할 수 있다. 우선 be 동사 뒤에 명사가 오기 위해서는 앞선 주어와 동일인 또는 동일 대상이어야 한다. 하지만 정기 토익에서는 be 동사 뒤에 명사 어형이 오는 경우보다는 현재분사 혹은 과거분사가 오는 경우가 압도적으로 많다. 아울러 대부분 타동사의 분사 어형을 묻기 때문에 명사인 목적어의 유무를 통해 능동태/수동태를 선택하도록 한다. 목적어가 있다면 현재분사, 목적어가 없다면 과거분사라 여기고 문제를 풀이한다면 90% 이상은 정답을 맞춰낼 수 있다.

★★★ 어휘 / 형용사 어휘

심각한 가뭄으로 인해 물이 충분하지 않아 상당한 규모의 지역 주민들에게 수도를 제공하기엔 무리가 있었다.

문제 분석

a sizable population 상당한 규모

어휘 inadequate 불충분한 support ~을 지지하다, ~을 지원하다 sizable 상당한 크기의, 꽤 큰 population 인구, (일정 지역의) 전체 거주민, 사람들 serious 심각한 drought 가뭄 numerous 많은 plenty 충분하게, 많은

The water supply was very inadequate for supporting a ------- population due to the serious drought problem.

(A) sizable
(B) numerous
(C) wide
(D) plenty

문제 해설

빈칸에 적합한 형용사를 묻는 문제이며 빈칸을 중심으로 가뭄으로 인해 지역 인구에 제공할 수도에 필요한 물이 충분하지 않다는 내용이 언급되고 있다. 무엇보다 빈칸 뒤에 '인구'를 뜻하는 population이 위치하고 있으므로 빈칸에는 population과 전체 문맥에 적합한 의미의 형용사가 와야 한다. 인구의 규모가 상당하니 물의 공급이 원활하지 않다는 문맥이 적절하므로 빈칸에는 '상당한 크기의, 꽤 큰'이란 뜻을 지닌 형용사 sizable이 와야 한다.

토익 분석

정기 토익에서 자주 접할 수 있는 수량 표현은 사전에 꼼꼼히 숙지돼둬야 한다. 우선 numerous는 수 자체가 많다는 뜻의 형용사로 가산 복수명사와 함께 쓰여야 하며 plenty는 가산 복수명사와 불가산명사와 모두 쓰여 수나 양이 많음을 나타낼 수 있지만 무엇보다 a plenty of라는 형태로 사용해야 한다. 그리고 wide는 '넓은'이란 뜻의 형용사로 선택/종류/범위의 폭이 넓다는 의미로 쓰이게 된다.

★★ 어휘 / 전치사

남미에서의 그의 경력 덕분에, Murphy 씨는 멕시코 사람들의 작업 방식을 회사 내 그 누구보다도 잘 이해하고 있다.

문제 분석

owing to = due to = because of = on account of = thanks to ~로 인해, ~덕분에

어휘 experience 경력 working style 작업 방식, 근무 방식 in spite of ~임에도 불구하고 regardless of ~와 무관하게 nevertheless 그럼에도 불구하고

------- his experience in South America, Mr. Murphy understands Mexican's working style better than other employees in his company.

(A) Owing to
(B) In spite of
(C) Regardless of
(D) Nevertheless

문제 해설

빈칸 뒤에 his experience in South America란 구가 등장하고 있으므로 빈칸에는 Nevertheless와 같은 접속부사가 아닌 전치사가 위치해야 한다. 남미에서의 경력은 Murphy 씨가 멕시코 사람들의 작업 방식을 회사 내 다른 직원들보다 더욱 잘 이해하게 되는 근거가 되므로 빈칸에는 이유/원인을 뜻하는 전치사가 와야 한다. 그러므로 빈칸에는 Owing to가 적합하다.

토익 분석

전치사 문제는 매달 정기 토익에서 접할 수 있는 문제 유형으로 이유 관계를 나타내는 전치사와 역접 관계를 나타내는 전치사는 출제 비중이 상당히 높은 편이다. 이유 관계를 나타내는 전치사는 owing to / due to / because of / on account of / thanks to가 있으며 이유 관계를 뜻하는 접속부사인 so / therefore / thus / as a result와 혼동하지 않도록 한다. 아울러 역접 관계를 의미하는 전치사 in spite of / despite / notwithstanding와 접속부사 but / however / nonetheless / nevertheless를 구분할 수 있도록 한다.

123

Every employee must follow security procedures when sending ------- documents or files electronically to clients.

(A) confident

(B) confidentiality

(C) confidential

(D) confidentially

문제 해설

빈칸이 명사 documents 앞에 위치하고 있으므로 빈칸에는 명사를 수식할 수 있는 형용사 어형이 와야 한다. 그러나 confident와 confidential이 모두 형용사이므로 이 중 문맥에 적합한 의미를 지닌 형용사를 구분해야 한다. 수식하는 명사가 '서류'를 뜻하는 documents임을 고려할 때 정답으로는 '비밀의, 기밀의'란 뜻을 지닌 confidential을 선택해야 한다.

토익 분석

정기 토익에서는 혼동 어휘와 관련된 문제가 출제될 수도 있기 때문에 유사한 어휘와 뜻을 사전에 숙지하여 혼동하지 않도록 해야 한다. 형용사 confident는 '자신이 있는, 확신이 있는'이란 뜻을, 형용사 confidential은 '비밀스런, 기밀의'란 뜻을 지니고 있으므로 이를 헷갈리지 않도록 주의해야 한다. 아울러 아래에 언급한 혼동어휘들은 정리해서 꼭 숙지하도록 한다.

argumentative 논쟁적인	arguable 논쟁의 여지가 있는
considerable 꽤, 상당히	considerate 사려 깊은
economic 경제의	economical 경제적인
extensive 범위가 넓은	extended 연장된
favorable 호의적인, 찬성하는	favorite 아주 좋아하는
confident 자신감이 있는	confidential 기밀의, 비밀의
reliable 믿을 수 있는	reliant 의지하는
responsible 책임이 있는	responsive 응답하는, 대응하는
successful 성공적인	successive 연속적인

★★ 어형 / 형용사 + 혼동 형용사 어휘

직원들이 인터넷을 통해 기밀서류나 파일들을 고객들에게 발송할 때는 보안 절차를 필히 따라야 한다.

문제 분석

confidential 비밀스런, 기밀의
confident 자신감이 있는, 확신에 찬

어휘 follow ~을 따르다, ~를 이해하다 security procedures 보안 절차 confidential 기밀의, 비밀의 electronically 전자적으로, 인터넷으로 client 고객 confident 자신이 있는, 확신이 있는 confidentiality 기밀성 confidentially 은밀하게

124

증감의 동사와 함께 쓰이는 부사

The income tax rate was originally set at 4% of the employee's income and has been ------- increased by the state government.

(A) shortly

(B) intensely

(C) arguably

(D) incrementally

문제 해설

빈칸에 적합한 부사 어휘를 묻는 문제이다. 빈칸이 increased 앞에 위치하고 있으며 주정부에 의해 세율이 증가해오고 있다는 문맥이 등장하고 있으므로 빈칸에는 증가의 정도를 표현할 수 있는 의미의 부사 어휘가 필요하다. 따라서 빈칸에는 '점차, 끊임없이'란 뜻을 지닌 부사 incrementally가 적절하다.

토익 분석

정기 토익에서는 증감/변화를 뜻하는 동사(increase/rise/decrease/drop/decline/change)와 함께 쓰이는 부사 어휘를 자주 묻는 경향이 있다. 특히 증감/변화의 폭이 크거나 작다는 의미를 지닌 considerably/significantly/substantially/sharply/dramatically/markedly/rapidly/slightly와 같은 부사 어휘들은 기본적으로 꿰차고 있어야 한다.

★★★ 어휘 / 부사 어휘

소득세율은 본래 직원 급여의 4%로 정해졌었지만 주정부에 의해 점차 증가해왔다.

문제 분석

incrementally increase 점차 증가하다

어휘 income 소득 tax rate 세율 originally 본래 state government 주 정부 shortly 곧, 조만간 intensely 격렬하게, 치열하게, 강력하게 extensively 광범위하게, 널리 arguably 아마 틀림없이, 분명히, 논증할 수 있지만 incrementally 점차, 끊임없이

★★★ 어휘 / 전치사

Monroe 대학에 의해 제공되는 어떠한 경영학 과정이라도 수료를 하면 과정 참석자들에게 학위가 발급될 것이다.

문제 분석

On(Upon) + 명사 / V-ing ~하자마자, ~하면

어휘 completion 종료, 완료 offer ~을 제공하다 diploma 학위 be issued to ~에게 발급되다 participant 참석자

------- completion of any of the business courses offered by Monroe College, diplomas will be issued to the participants.

(A) As
(B) Within
(C) Until
(D) Upon

문제 해설

빈칸 뒤에 completion of any of the business courses라는 구가 등장하고 있으므로 빈칸에는 전치사가 위치해야 한다. 무엇보다 학위가 발급되려면 과정의 수료가 우선되어야 하므로 '과정을 수료하자마자 내지는 과정을 수료하면'이란 문맥을 구성할 수 있도록 빈칸에는 '~하자마자, ~하면'이란 뜻을 지닌 전치사 upon이 와야 한다.

토익 분석

정기 토익에서 전치사 On/Upon에 관한 질문으로 제일 자주 출제되는 것은 바로 '~하자마자, ~하면'이란 뜻을 지닌 On(Upon) + 명사 / V-ing이다.

---

126 부사가 포함된 토익 빈출 어순 구조

★★ 어형 / 부사

개인 및 박물관 미술품 수집가들은 전 세계에서 가장 유명한 초현실주의 화가인 Isabella Choi 씨의 작품에 열광적으로 반응하고 있다.

문제 분석

respond to - ~에 답변하다 / ~에 응답하다

어휘 private 개인적인 art collector 예술품 수집가 respond to ~에 대응하다, ~에 응답하다, ~에 답변하다 works 작품 foremost 으뜸가는, 일류의, 선두의, 가장 중요한, 주요한 surrealism 초현실주의 enthusiasm 열정 enthusiast 애호가 enthusiastic 열정적인 enthusiastically 열정적으로

Private and museum art collectors responded ------- to the works of Ms. Isabella Choi, one of the world's foremost surrealism painters.

(A) enthusiasm
(B) enthusiast
(C) enthusiastic
(D) enthusiastically

문제 해설

빈칸에 적합한 어형을 묻는 문제로 빈칸이 자동사인 responded와 전치사구 to the works 사이에 위치하고 있을 뿐만 아니라 절 전체의 구조 역시 자동사와 전치사구가 등장하고 있는 완전한 구조의 절임을 알 수 있다. 따라서 빈칸에는 자동사인 responded를 수식할 수 있는 부사 어형인 enthusiastically가 자리해야 한다.

토익 분석

정기 토익에서 가장 많이 출제되는 어형 문제 중 하나가 바로 부사 어형 문제로 매달 평균 3문항 이상의 부사 어형 문제가 출제된다. 따라서 아래 부사 어휘가 포함된 어순의 구조를 숙지하여 부사 어형을 묻는 문제를 최단 시간에 풀이할 수 있도록 사전에 대비하도록 한다.

1. 동사 + 목적어 + 부사, 부사 + 동사 + 목적어
2. 자동사 + 부사 + 전치사구
3. Has/Have + 부사 + 과거분사, Has/Have + 과거분사 + 부사
4. 조동사 + 동사원형 + 부사
5. (조동사) + be + 부사 + 현재/과거분사

127

According to the data released yesterday by the government, the official unemployment rate has been on the decline for the fifth ------- year.

(A) consecutive
(B) successful
(C) significant
(D) separate

문제 해설

빈칸에 적합한 형용사를 묻는 문제이며 빈칸 앞에는 the official unemployment rate has been on the decline, 즉 공식적인 실업률이 지속적으로 하락세에 있음을 언급하고 있으며 빈칸을 중심으로 기간을 나타내는 전치사인 for과 다섯 번째라는 서수 the fifth 그리고 빈칸 뒤에는 해를 뜻하는 year 이 등장하고 있다. 무엇보다 공식적인 실업률이 지속적으로 하락세인 상황이므로 이를 통해 빈칸에 는 다섯 번째 해까지 계속/연속이란 의미를 구성할 수 있는 형용사가 필요함을 알 수 있다. 그러므 로 빈칸에는 '연속적인'이란 뜻을 지닌 형용사 consecutive가 와야 한다.

토익 분석

정기 토익에서는 '연속적인'이란 뜻을 지닌 형용사로 consecutive 외에도 successive, 그리고 전치사 구인 in a row가 있음을 함께 묶어서 숙지하도록 한다.

★★★ 어휘 / 형용사 어휘

어제 정부에 의해 발간된 자료에 의하면, 공식적인 실업 률은 5년 연속으로 하락세에 있다.

문제 분석

for the fifth successive/consecutive year = for five successive/consecutive years = for five years in a row 5년 연속으로

어휘 release ~을 출시하다 official 공무원, 공식적 인 unemployment rate 실업률 be on the decline 하 락세이다 consecutive 연속적인 successful 성공적인 significant 상당한, 꽤 separate 분리하는, 따로, 별개로

128

The infectious disease is prevailing throughout the country, but there is no ------- vaccination method for patients.

(A) competitive
(B) extensive
(C) adequate
(D) inexpensive

문제 해설

빈칸에 적합한 형용사를 요구하는 문제로 앞서 전체적으로 전국에 전염병이 만연하고 있지만 환자 를 위한 접종 수단이 없다는 내용이 제시되고 있다. 빈칸 앞에는 no가, 빈칸 뒤에는 '접종'을 뜻하는 vaccination이란 명사가 등장하고 있으므로 빈칸에는 환자들을 위한 충분한 접종 수단이 없다는 내 용을 구성할 수 있도록 '충분한'이란 뜻을 지닌 형용사 adequate가 와야 한다.

토익 분석

정기 토익에 대비하여 '충분한'이란 뜻을 지닌 어휘로는 enough, sufficient, adequate가 출제되고 있으므로 이들을 모두 숙지하도록 한다.

★★★ 어휘 / 형용사 어휘

전국에 전염병이 만연하고 있지만, 환자들을 위한 충분한 접종 수단이 없다.

어휘 infectious 전염성의, 감염성의 prevail ~이 만연하 다 throughout 전역에 걸쳐 vaccination method 접종 수 단 patient 환자 competitive 경쟁적인, 경쟁력이 있는 extensive 포괄적인, 종합적인 adequate 충분한

★★★ 어형 / 형용사 + 혼동 형용사 어휘

우리 고속버스의 모든 탑승객들은 도로 교통사고에서의 부상이나 사망을 미연에 방지하기 위해 안전벨트를 착용하도록 권유를 받고 있다.

문제 분석

사람주어 + be advised to V / that S+V ~를 ~하도록 권고하다
It is advisable that S+V ~를 권고할 만하다

어휘 passenger 탑승객 prevent ~을 예방하다, ~을 방지하다 injury 부상 traffic accident 교통사고 advise ~을 권고하다 advisory 조언의, 권고의, 자문의 advisable 권할만한, 타당한

All the passengers of our express bus are ------- to wear their seat belts to prevent injuries or death in road traffic accidents.

(A) advise
(B) advisory
(C) advised
(D) advisable

문제 해설

빈칸이 주격 보어를 취하는 2형식 동사인 be 동사 뒤에 위치하고 있으며 선택지에는 명사 어형이 등장하지 않고 있으므로 빈칸에는 주격 보어의 역할을 행할 수 있는 형용사 어형이 와야 한다. 그러나 advisory, advised, advisable이 모두 형용사이므로 이들 중 문맥에 적합한 의미를 지닌 형용사 하나를 선택해야 한다. 형용사 advisory는 '조언의, 권고의, 자문의', 형용사 advised는 '권고를 받는' 그리고 형용사 advisable은 '권할 만한, 타당한'이란 뜻이며 안전벨트 착용은 모든 탑승객들이 권고되는 것이므로 빈칸에는 advised가 위치해야 한다.

토익 분석

토익에서는 advisory, advised, advisable이란 형용사를 모두 선택지를 통해 접할 수 있으나 advisory는 명사를 수식하는 한정 형용사로만 쓰이고 be 동사 뒤 서술 형용사로는 쓰이지 않는다는 점을 고려해야 한다. 아울러 형용사 advised는 주어가 사람 명사일 때 쓰이며 형용사 advisable은 가주어 it과 함께 쓰이는 진주어의 내용이 사람에게 권고할 만한 내용일 때 쓰이는 용례를 숙지하도록 한다.

★★ 어휘 / 동사 어휘

국내에서 가장 큰 규모의 노트북 컴퓨터 제조사인 Bella Computer 사는 지난 달 Slovenia에 새로운 제조 공장을 설립하였다.

어휘 maker 제조사 manufacturing plant 제조공장 establish ~을 설립하다 acquire ~을 획득하다 specialize ~을 특화하다, ~을 전문화하다

Bella Computer, the country's largest laptop computer maker, ------- a new manufacturing plant in Slovenia last month.

(A) developed
(B) established
(C) acquired
(D) specialized

문제 해설

빈칸에 적합한 과거시제 형태의 동사 어휘를 묻는 문제이다. 빈칸 앞에는 Bella Computer라는 회사의 이름이, 빈칸 뒤에는 a new manufacturing plant, 즉 새로운 제조공장이 등장하고 있으므로 빈칸에는 새로운 제조공장과 연관이 있는 의미의 동사가 필요하다. 따라서 빈칸에는 '설립하다'란 뜻을 지닌 동사 established가 와야 한다.

토익 분석

정기 토익에서 establish는 동사 및 과거분사가 출제된 전력이 있다. 특히 토익에서 establish는 establish a company (회사를 창립하다), establish customer base (고객층을 확보하다), establish a new policy (새로운 방침을 세우다), establish a goal (목표를 세우다), establish a law (법을 제정하다)와 같은 establish의 쓰임새를 숙지하도록 한다.

Questions 131-134 refer to the following notice.

Last month, our company Lamtech announced the retirement of former CEO Charles Iverson. Affectionately called "Big Charlie" by fellow colleagues, Mr. Iverson ------- **131.** himself to the company for thirty years. ------- **132.** he joined the company in 1982, Lamtech has tripled the number of employees on payroll and quadrupled its revenue. He has been a personal mentor for numerous employees as well. ------- **133.**.

To honor his dedication and contribution to the ------- **134.** of Lamtech, the company will hold a farewell reception on Friday, December 12, at the Hilltop Hotel ballroom. Please RSVP by contacting our secretary Emma Lyons at elyons@lamtech.com or (134) 421-6891.

지난 달 우리 회사 Lamtech는 전직 최고 경영자인 Charles Iverson 씨의 정년 퇴직을 발표했습니다. 직장 동료들로부터 애정이 담긴 "Big Charile"란 별명으로 불리기도 했던 Iverson 씨는 30년 간 근속해왔습니다. 1982년도에 입사한 이후로 Lamtech 사는 유급 직원의 수가 세 배 증가했고 회사의 수익은 네 배 늘었습니다. 그는 많은 직원들의 정신적인 지주이기도 했습니다. 그의 지도력으로 Lamtech 사는 오늘날과 같이 국제적인 회사로 성장하는 것이 가능했습니다.

Lamtech 사의 발전에 대한 그의 헌신과 기여를 기리고자, 회사에서는 12월 12일 금요일 Hilltop 호텔에서 환송 파티를 개최합니다. 제 비서인 Emma Lyons에게 elyons@lamtech.com로 이메일을 보내시거나 또는 (134) 421-6891로 연락을 하셔서 참석이 가능한지 여부를 최대한 빨리 알려 주십시오.

어휘 retirement 은퇴 former 전직의 affectionately 애정을 담아서 fellow colleague 직장 동료 join ~에 합류하다, ~에 입사하다 triple 세 배로 늘다 payroll 급여, 급여명부 quadruple 네 배로 늘다 amount 양, 액수 revenue 수익 personal 개인적인, 사적인 mentor 스승, 조언자 numerous 많은 as well 역시, 또한 dedication 헌신, 전념 contribution 기여, 기부, 기고 hold ~을 개최하다 farewell 이별, 환송 RSVP (=Répondez s'il vous plait) 회답을 하다 contact ~에게 연락하다

131

(A) was dedicated
(B) has dedicated
(C) is dedicating
(D) dedicate

★★★ 어형 / 동사 어형 + 동사 시제

문제 분석

S + dedicate oneself to + N/V-ing 주어는 자신을 ~에 전념/헌신/집중하게 하다
= S' (oneself) + be dedicated to + N/V-ing 주어 ~에 전념/헌신/집중하다

토익 분석

토익에서 동사의 어형을 묻는 문제는 파트5와 파트6에서 매달 출제되는 문제 유형이다. 이 경우 선택지에서 절을 구성할 수 없는 준동사 어형(To + 동사원형/V-ing)부터 소거한 후 주어/동사 수 일치 – 목적어 유무를 통한 능동태/수동태 선택 – 시제[수-태-시] 순으로 어형을 파악하는 것이 동사 어형 문제를 가장 효율적으로 풀이할 수 있다는 점을 숙지한다.

문제 해설

빈칸에 적합한 동사 어형을 묻는 문제이다. 빈칸 앞 주어가 Iverson 씨라는 단수 주어이므로 단수 동사 형태이어야 하며, 빈칸 뒤에는 himself라는 재귀대명사가 목적어로 제시되고 있으므로 수동태가 아닌 능동태 구조여야 한다. 아울러 빈칸에 앞서 전직 최고 경영자인 Charles Iverson 씨가 퇴직하게 되었음을 밝히고 있으며 빈칸 이후에는 30년 간이라는 기간이 제시되고 있다. 그러므로 빈칸에는 지난 달에 퇴사할 때까지 30년이 넘도록 회사에서 근속했다는 의미를 형성할 수 있는 현재완료시제가 적절하다. 따라서 빈칸에는 단수동사이자 능동태, 그리고 현재완료시제 형태를 지닌 동사 어형인 has dedicated가 와야 한다.

132

(A) How
(B) Meanwhile
(C) Since
(D) Before

★★ 부사절 접속사

문제 분석

Since + S + V-ed(과거시제), S+ has/have Vp.p(과거분사) ~ 이후로, ~가 ~하다
Since + 과거시점, S+ has/have Vp.p(과거분사) ~ 이후로 ~가 ~하다

토익 분석

토익에선 부사절 접속사나 부사구를 형성하는 전치사로서 '~ 이후로'란 뜻의 since와 주절의 현재완료시제가 상관 관계를 갖는 부분에 관해 묻는 문제가 자주 출제되는 경향이 있음을 알아두도록 한다.

문제 해설

빈칸이 부사절 앞에 위치하고 있으므로 빈칸에는 적합한 부사절 접속사가 와야 한다. 빈칸 뒤 부사절은 그가 1982년이라는 과거에 회사에 입사했음을 나타내고 있으며, 주절은 현재까지 유급 직원의 수가 세 배 증가하고 회사의 수익이 네 배로 늘어났음을 밝히는 현재완료시제가 등장하고 있다. 따라서 빈칸에는 그가 입사한 지난 1982년을 기준으로 지금까지 직원의 수가 세 배 증가하고 회사의 수익이 네 배로 늘어났다는 문맥을 구성할 수 있도록 '~ 이후로'란 뜻을 지닌 부사절 접속사 Since가 와야 한다.

★★ 빈칸 문장론

(A) 그의 지도력으로 Lamtech 사는 오늘날과 같이 국제적인 회사로 성장하는 것이 가능했습니다.
(B) 우리는 그가 Lamtech 사의 미래를 책임질 훌륭한 리더가 될 것이라 크게 기대하고 있습니다.
(C) 회사는 그 도시에 건설하는 새로운 호텔을 12월 12일까지 완공할 것입니다.
(D) Iverson 씨를 위한 지난 달 환송 파티는 엄청나게 성공적이었습니다.

문제 분석

S + enable + O + to Vr 주어는 목적어가 ~하는 것을 가능하게 하다

토익 분석

빈칸 문장 추론 문제는 전체 지문의 내용 흐름을 파악한 상태에서 풀어야 하므로 맨 마지막에 풀이하는 것이 효율적이다.

(A) His leadership has enabled Lamtech to grow into the international company it is today.
(B) We have high hopes that he will be a great leader for the future of Lamtech.
(C) The company will complete the construction of a new hotel in the city by December 12.
(D) Last month's farewell reception for Mr. Iverson was incredibly successful.

문제 해설

빈칸에 적절한 내용을 묻는 문제이다. 빈칸 앞에는 Since he joined the company in 1982, Lamtech has tripled the number of employees on payroll and quadrupled the amount of revenue이라며 그가 1982년도에 입사한 이후로 Lamtech 사는 유급 직원의 수가 세 배 증가했고 회사의 수익은 네 배 늘어났다는 내용과 He has been a personal mentor for numerous employees as well이라며 그는 많은 직원들의 정신적인 지주이기도 했다는 내용이 언급되고 있다. 그러므로 빈칸에는 그가 많은 직원들의 마음을 보듬어주며 사세를 증가시켜 직원의 수가 세 배 증가했고 회사의 수식이 네 배가 늘 수 있었던 능력의 소유자임을 밝히는 내용인 His leadership has enabled Lamtech to grow to the international it is today이 적합하다.

★★ 명사 어휘

문제 분석

To honor his dedication and contribution to ~ ~에 대한 그의 성실함과 공헌을 기리고자

토익 분석

정기 토익에서는 규모의 증가/확장을 뜻하는 expansion과 시간이나 길이의 연장을 의미하는 extension이 자주 언급되고 있다. 물론 범위가 넓은 상태, 즉 '종합적인'이란 뜻을 지닌 extensive와 시간이나 길이가 연장된 상태를 뜻하는 extended도 같은 어휘에서 파생된 혼동어휘들이므로 함께 묶어서 익혀두도록 한다.

(A) value
(B) relocation
(C) foundation
(D) expansion

문제 해설

빈칸에 적절한 명사 어휘를 묻는 문제로 빈칸을 중심으로 회사의 무엇인가에 대한 그의 헌신과 기여를 기리고자 한다는 내용이 등장하고 있다. 이에 앞서 Since he joined the company in 1982, Lamtech has tripled the number of employees on payroll and quadrupled the amount of revenue이라며 그가 1982년도에 입사한 이후로 Lamtech 사는 유급 직원의 수가 세 배 증가했고 회사의 수익은 네 배 늘어났다는 내용이 제시되고 있으므로 빈칸에는 회사의 발전에 대한 그의 헌신과 기여를 기린다는 내용을 형성할 수 있도록 '확장'이란 뜻을 지닌 expansion이란 명사가 와야 한다.

Questions 135-138 refer to the following article.

The international phone company Techno announced the development of their new smart phone, T-700. This is an upgraded version of T-500, ------- was a worldwide success last year. While keeping the convenient features of the previous model, the new model ------- with various new features, such as a 32-megapixel camera, 1.5 GHz CPU, and a shatterproof screen. Techno stated that consumers will be able to test the T-700 at the upcoming Technology Convention on June 20. -------. It is speculated that the new model has been produced to ------- to rival company Mandoo, which recently released its new phone, the GX-8, in parts of Asia.

135. **136.** **137.** **138.**

국제 전화 회사인 **Techno** 사는 새로운 스마트 전화기 T-700의 개발을 발표했다. 이 제품은 작년에 전 세계적으로 성공을 거두었던 **T-500**이 개선된 제품이다. 새로운 모델은 이전 모델의 편리한 기능은 유지하면서 32 메가픽셀 카메라, 1.5 **GHz** 중앙 처리 장치, 그리고 비산 방지 스크린과 같은 다양한 신기능이 추가되었다. **Techno** 사는 소비자들이 6월 20일에 있을 **Technology Convention** 에서 T-700를 시험적으로 사용해보는 것이 가능할 것이라 언급했다. T-700은 아시아 지역에선 7월 10일, 유럽에서는 7월 21일에 출시될 예정이다. T-700은 **Techno** 사의 경쟁사인 **Mandoo** 사가 아시아 일부 지역에 출시한 새로운 전화기인 **GX-8**의 대항마로서 생산된 것이라 추정되고 있다.

어휘 upgraded 개선된, 개정된 convenient 편리한 feature 기능, 특징 while ~하는 동안에, ~인 반면에 various 다양한 previous 이전에 such as 이를테면 shatterproof 분쇄 방지의 state ~을 진술하다, ~을 언급하다 consumer 소비자 upcoming 다가 올 speculate ~을 추측하다, ~을 분석하다, ~을 예상하다 respond to ~에 응답하다, ~에 대응하다, ~에 답변하다 release ~을 출시하다

135

(A) who
(B) which
(C) what
(D) when

문제 해설

빈칸이 두 절 사이에 위치하고 있으므로 빈칸에 적절한 접속사를 묻는 문제이다. 빈칸 앞은 T-500 이란 이전 전화기 제품이 선행사로 제시되고 있으며 빈칸 이후에는 주어가 빠지고 be동사인 was부터 등장하는 불완전한 구조의 절이 이어지고 있다. 따라서 빈칸에는 사물을 선행사로 취하며 불완전한 구조의 절과 함께 쓰일 수 있는 접속사인 which가 와야 함을 알 수 있다.

★★ 접속사

문제 분석

사물 선행사 + which + (주어) + 동사 + (목적어)

토익 분석

정기 토익에서는 who/whose/which란 접속사를 유독 자주 묻는 편이므로 각 접속사의 특징에 대해 사전에 확실하게 숙지해야 한다. 앞서 언급했듯이 접속사 which는 주어나 목적어가 빠진 불완전한 절의 구조와 함께 쓰이며 사물 선행사를 취하며 주격과 목적격의 형태가 동일하기 때문에 격을 구분할 필요가 없다. 접속사 who역시 불완전한 구조의 절과 함께 쓰이며 선행사로는 사람명사만을 취한다. 접속사 whose는 주어나 목적어가 빠지지 않은 완전한 구조의 절과 함께 쓰이며 사람/사물을 모두 선행사로 취하는 것이 가능하다. 아울러 접속사 what은 선행사를 취하지 않는다. 또한 when은 시간명사를 선행사로 취하며 이 역시 완전한 구조의 절과 함께 쓰인다는 선행사/구조와 관련된 특징을 숙지하도록 한다.

136

(A) equipment
(B) is equipping
(C) is equipped
(D) equipped

문제 해설

빈칸이 분사구문 While keeping the convenient features of the previous model의 수식을 받는 주절의 주어인 the new model 뒤에 위치하고 있으므로 주절에 적합한 동사의 어형을 묻는 문제가 되겠다. 빈칸 앞 주어가 the new model로 단수 주어이며, 빈칸 뒤에는 '~을 구비하다'란 뜻을 지닌 동사 equip의 목적어가 존재하지 않으므로 능동태가 아닌 수동태 구조여야 한다. 따라서 빈칸에는 is equipped가 와야 한다.

★★ 동사 어형 / 동사의 시제

문제 분석

be equipped with ~가 구비된 상태이다

토익 분석

정기토익에서 동사의 분사 어형을 묻는 문제는 거의 매달 출제된다고 해도 과언이 아니다. 대부분 타동사에 대한 분사 어형을 묻기 때문에 명사 목적어의 유무를 통해 분사 어형을 선택하는 것이 효율적이다. 목적어가 존재하는 경우 능동태가 되어 현재분사(V-ing) 형태가, 목적어가 없는 경우에는 수동태가 되어 과거분사(Vp.p)가 정답이란 점을 숙지하도록 한다.

★★ 빈칸 추론

(A) T-700의 매출은 아직 GX-8의 매출을 초과하지 못했다.
(B) T-700은 아시아 지역에선 7월 10일, 유럽에서는 7월 21일에 출시될 예정이다.
(C) 그 고객들의 대략 70%는 그들이 휴대전화와 태블릿 컴퓨터들을 사용하고 있다고 밝혔다.
(D) T-700는 현재 호평을 받고 있으며 고객들 사이에서 점차 유명해지고 있다.

토익 분석

빈칸 문장 추론 문제는 전체 지문의 내용 흐름을 파악한 상태에서 풀어야 하므로 맨 마지막에 풀이하는 것이 효율적이다.

(A) The T-700 sales have not yet exceeded that of the GX-8.
(B) The release date for T-700 is July 10 for Asia and July 21 for Europe.
(C) About 70 percent of the customers said they use mobile phones and tablet computers.
(D) The T-700 is currently receiving positive reviews and getting popular among customers.

문제 해설

빈칸에 적합한 내용의 문장을 묻는 빈칸 추론 유형의 문제이다. 빈칸에 앞서 Techno stated that consumers will be able to test the T-700 at the upcoming Technology Convention on June 20th, 즉 Techno 사는 소비자들이 6월 20일에 있을 Technology Convention에서 T-700를 시험적으로 사용해보는 것이 가능할 것이라 언급했다는 내용이 제시되고 있다. 시험 사용은 제품이 상용화되기 직전 단계를 의미하고 시험 사용이 끝나면 실제로 시장에 판매가 되어 상용화가 된다는 점을 고려할 때 빈칸에는 The release date for T-700 is July 10th for Asia and July 21st for Europe, 즉 T-700의 아시아 지역과 유럽에서의 출시일에 대해 언급하고 있는 내용이 와야 한다.

★★ 동사 어휘

문제 분석

respond to ~에 대답하다/~에 응답하다/~에 반응을 보이다

토익 분석

동사 respond와 명사 response는 모두 전치사 to와 함께 쓰인다는 점을 숙지하도록 한다. 정기 토익에서는 동사 혹은 명사 어휘 문제로 respond나 response가 출제될 때 전치사 to로 인해 상대적으로 쉽게 풀이할 수 있는 경우가 빈번하다.

(A) respond
(B) precede
(C) introduce
(D) oppose

문제 해설

빈칸에 알맞은 동사 어휘를 묻는 문제로 빈칸이 전치사 to 앞에 위치하고 있으므로 문맥에 적합해야 할 뿐만 아니라 전치사 to와 같이 쓰일 수 있는 동사 어휘가 필요하다. 빈칸에 앞서 새로운 제품이 생산되었다는 내용이, 빈칸 이후에는 경쟁사인 Mandoo 사가 아시아 일부 지역에 출시한 새로운 전화기인 GX-8에 대해 언급하고 있다. 따라서 빈칸에는 새로운 T-700 제품이 생산된 것은 아시아 일부 지역에 출시한 새로운 전화기인 GX-8에 대응하고자 생산된 제품이란 의미를 형성할 수 있으며 전치사 to를 수반하는 동사 어휘인 respond가 적절하다.

Questions 139-142 refer to the following webpage.

Wildlife Conservatory is a nonprofit organization that aims to promote research in and conservation of endangered wildlife. By using scientific methods and advanced technological equipment, we try ------- the cause of wildlife decline in Asian countries. Since our ------- in 2003, we have helped numerous animals, including the endangered Sumatran tiger, spring back from the brink of extinction. However, as a nonprofit organization, we ------- heavily on the support of our members and donors. As of now, we have over four thousand supporters, but we are always on the lookout for more. We invite you to join our cause. -------. Members receive a subscription to our bimonthly and get regular updates on our research results.

139.
140.
141.
142.

Wildlife Conservatory는 멸종 위기에 빠진 야생동물들에 대한 연구와 보존을 촉진시키는 비영리 단체입니다. 과학적인 방법과 첨단 기술 장비를 사용하여, 저희는 아시아 지역에서 야생동물들의 개체 수가 줄어드는 이유에 대해 연구하려고 노력합니다. 저희 단체는 2003년도에 설립된 이후로 수마트라 호랑이를 포함하여 많은 동물들이 멸종 위기에서 되살아날 수 있도록 도왔습니다. 그러나 저희는 비영리단체로서 회원들의 지원과 기부금에 상당히 많이 의지하고 있습니다. 현재로선, 4천 명이 넘는 후원자들을 지니고 있습니다만 더 많은 지원자들을 찾고 있습니다. 저희는 귀하도 저희의 대의에 참여하도록 권고하고 싶습니다. 귀하는 후원자로서 야생동물의 연구와 보존을 도울 수 있습니다. 회원들은 저희가 격월로 발간하는 야생동물 잡지를 받아보시게 되며 연구 결과를 정기적으로 접하실 수 있습니다.

어휘 nonprofit organization 비영리 단체 aim to Vr ~하는 것이 목적이다 promote ~을 승진시키다, ~을 판촉하다, ~을 증진시키다 endangered 위험에 빠진, 멸종 위기의 wildlife 야생동물 cause 원인, 대의 decline 하락, 감소 numerous 많은 include ~을 포함하다 spring back from ~로부터 도약하다 brink 직전, 위기 extinction 멸종 heavily 과도하게, 과중하게 support 지원, 지지, 후원, ~을 지원하다, ~을 후원하다 as of now 현재로서는 lookout 경계, 감시, 장래성, 전망 subscription 구독 bimonthly 격월의 up-to-date 최신의

139

(A) study
(B) studying
(C) to study
(D) have studied

문제 해설

빈칸에 적합한 어형을 묻는 문제이다. 빈칸이 동사 try 뒤에 위치하고 있으므로 동사 try가 목적어로 취하는 준동사 어형을 선택해야 하나 동사 try는 To 부정사 형태와 동명사인 V-ing 형태를 모두 취하는 것이 가능하다는 점이 문제이다. 무엇보다 동사 try가 목적어로 To 부정사 어형을 취할 때는 '~을 하고자 노력하다'란 뜻이 되지만, 동명사인 V-ing 형태를 취하는 경우 '한 번 ~해보다'란 뜻을 형성한다. 따라서 해당 문장은 아시아 지역에서 야생동물들의 개체 수가 줄어드는 이유에 대해 연구하고자 노력한다는 내용이 바람직하므로 빈칸에는 to study가 적절하다.

★★ To 부정사 어형

문제 분석

try + N/V-ing ~를 한 번 해보다 / try to Vr ~를 하기 위해 노력하다

토익 분석

동사의 목적어로 To Vr / V-ing 형태를 모두 취하는 대표적인 동사로서는 try / stop / remember / regret / forget/ propose 등이 있다.

140

(A) extension
(B) founding
(C) intermission
(D) resignation

문제 해설

빈칸에 알맞은 명사 어휘를 묻는 문제이다. 빈칸이 전치사 since로 시작하는 부사구에서 2003년이란 해 앞에 위치하고 있으며 빈칸 이후 주절은 we have helped numerous animals, 즉 현재완료 시제와 함께 많은 동물들에게 도움을 지속적으로 제공해 왔다는 내용이 등장하고 있다. 그렇다면 많은 동물들에게 도움을 지속적으로 제공해온 행위의 시작은 바로 Wildlife Conservatory라는 비영리 단체의 설립 이후에 가능한 것임을 알 수 있으므로 빈칸에 '설립, 창립'이란 뜻을 지닌 명사 어휘 founding이 와야 한다.

★★ 명사 어휘

문제 분석

founding 설립
foundation 근간, 기초, 재단

토익 분석

정기 토익에서 명사 어형을 묻는 문제는 평이한 수준인 경우 선택지에 명사 어형이 하나만 제시되지만 약간의 난이도 상승이 이뤄지는 경우 선택지에는 명사 어형이 두 개 이상 등장하며 정답 선택의 어려움을 초래한다. 대개 사람인 명사와 사람이 아닌 명사 혹은 –tion/ment로 끝나는 일반적인 명사의 형태와 V-ing로 끝나는 명사(여기선 동명사가 아닌 building이나 meeting과 같은 보통 명사를 지칭)를 구분하게끔 만드는 경우가 대부분이다. 따라서 해당 문제와 같은 유형의 문제는 풀이하면서 각 명사들을 명확하게 숙지하고 정리하는 편이 바람직하다.

★★ 동사 어휘

문제 분석

depend heavily on/upon = be dependent heavily on/upon
~에 상당히 의존하다

토익 분석

정기 토익에선 오랫동안 동사 **depend** 또는 형용사 **dependent**와 함께 쓰이는 전치사 **on/upon** 또는 이들과 함께 쓰여 '~에 의존하다'란 뜻을 만들어낼 수 있는 **depend/dependent**를 묻는 문제가 출제되어 왔다. 특히 형용사 **dependent**를 묻는 경우 선택지에 **dependable**이란 혼동 형용사가 등장하기도 하는데 **dependable**은 '신뢰할 만한'이란 뜻을 지니므로 이를 선택하지 않도록 주의한다.

(A) decline
(B) respond
(C) assist
(D) depend

문제 해설

빈칸에 적절한 동사 어휘를 묻는 문제로 빈칸 이후에 전치사 on이 등장하고 있으므로 빈칸에는 전치사 on과 함께 쓰이며 전반적인 문맥에 부합하는 뜻의 동사 어휘가 와야 한다. 빈칸에 앞서 as a nonprofit organization라며 자신들이 단체인 Wildlife Conservatory가 비영리 단체임을 밝히고 있으며 빈칸 이후에는 회원들과 기부자들의 후원이 언급되고 있다. 그러므로 빈칸에는 이들의 후원에 상당히 의존을 하고 있다는 내용을 형성할 수 있도록 빈칸에는 '~에 의지하다, ~를 의존하다'란 뜻을 지닌 동사 depend가 적합하다.

★★★ 빈칸 문장 추론

문제 분석

빈칸 문장 추론 문제는 전체 지문의 내용 흐름을 파악한 상태에서 풀어야 하므로 맨 마지막에 풀이하는 것이 효율적이다

토익 분석

동사 **respond**와 명사 **response**는 모두 전치사 **to**와 함께 쓰인다는 점을 숙지하도록 한다. 정기 토익에서는 동사 혹은 명사 어휘 문제로 **respond**나 **response**가 출제될 때 전치사 **to**로 인해 상대적으로 쉽게 풀이할 수 있는 경우가 빈번하다.

(A) As a supporter, you can help research and preserve wildlife.
(B) Thank you for joining our organization and helping the preservation of wildlife.
(C) The Sumatran tiger is no longer considered endangered.
(D) Our job opening will close next month.

문제 해설

빈칸 추론 문제로 빈칸에 적합한 내용의 문장을 묻는 문제이다. 빈칸에 앞서 We invite you to join our cause라며 귀하도 저희의 대의에 참여하도록 권고하고 싶다는 내용이 언급되고 있으며 빈칸 이후에는 Members receive a subscription to our bimonthly and get regular updates on our research results라며 회원들은 격월로 발간하는 야생동물 잡지를 받아보시게 되며 최신 연구 결과를 정기적으로 접할 수 있다는 회원들의 혜택이 소개되고 있다. 그러므로 빈칸에는 Wildlife Conservatory이 대의, 즉 멸종 위기에 빠진 야생동물들에 대한 연구와 보존에 대해 도움을 줄 수 있다는 내용을 지닌 As a supporter, you can help research and preserve wildlife가 와야 한다.

Questions 143-146 refer to the following email.

From: email@globalhealth.org
To: julie_newman@gotmail.com
Date: July 23
Subject: Thank you for supporting Global Health

Dear Ms. Julie Newman,

On behalf of Global Health, I would like to thank you for your monthly commitment of $25.00. Your ------- **143.** will help underprivileged communities in developing communities gain better access to health care and sanitation.

With help like yours, we were able to ------- **144.** 4,500 vaccinations and 7,000 health checkups last year. This year, we hope to increase the amount of vaccines administered to 6,000 and health checkups to 10,000. In addition, we plan to build infrastructures that ------- **145.** the livelihoods of local communities. ------- **146.** .

For more information on donations and our organization, please take a look at our Web site. If you have any questions or concerns, please contact us at (892) 332-7777 or e-mail email@globalhealth.org.

We thank you again for your donation.

Sincerely,
Kyle Patterson
Director of Funds
Global Health

발신: email@globalhealth.org
수신: julie_newman@gotmail.com
일자: 7월 23일
제목: Global Health를 후원해주셔서 감사합니다.

Julie Newman 씨에게

Global Health 사를 대표하여, 귀하의 25달러의 월 기부금에 대해 감사를 드립니다. 귀하의 너그러움은 개발 도상국의 저소득 계층이 더 나은 공중 보건과 위생을 이용하는데 도움을 줄 것입니다.

귀하의 기부금과 같은 도움으로 인해, 작년 4천 5백 개의 백신과 7천 명에게 건강 검진 혜택을 제공할 수 있었습니다. 올해 저희는 6천 명에게 백신을 투여하고 만 명에게 건강 검진의 혜택을 제공할 수 있길 희망합니다. 아울러 저희는 지역 사회의 생활 수준을 향상시킬 수 있는 기반 시설을 건설할 계획입니다. 일례로, 저희는 Ghana 전 지역에 걸쳐 200개의 양수 펌프를 설치하고자 합니다.

기부와 저희 단체에 관한 더 많은 정보를 원하시면, 저희 홈페이지를 확인해주십시오. 만약 질문이 있으시면, (892) 332-7777으로 저희에게 연락을 주시거나 email@globalhealth.org로 이메일을 주십시오.

다시 한 번 귀하의 기부에 감사 드립니다.

어휘 on behalf of ~를 대신하여 commitment 위임, 수감, 범행, 약속, 의무, 전념, 금전 사용 underprivileged 저소득 계층의, 혜택을 받지 못하는 gain better access to ~에 쉽게 접근하다, ~을 쉽게 이용하다 sanitation 위생 vaccination 백신 check-up 검진 amount 양, 금액 administer to ~에 주사하다, ~에 투입하다 in addition 추가로, 덧붙여 infrastructure 기간/기반 시설 livelihood 생계, 생활, 살림 donation 기부

143

(A) labor
(B) employment
(C) generosity
(D) appointment

★★ 명사 어휘

문제 분석

access (명사) to + N/V-ing // access (타동사) + 목적어

토익 분석

정기 토익에서는 기부(donation/contribution) 또는 기부 행사(charity)와 연계된 어휘 문제로 '관대'를 뜻하는 명사 generosity, '관대한'이란 뜻을 지닌 형용사 generous가 출제되고 있다.

문제 해설

빈칸에 적절한 명사 어휘를 묻는 문제이다. 빈칸 앞에는 I would like to thank you for your monthly commitment of $25.00라며 귀하의 월간 기부금 25달러에 대해 감사를 드린다는 내용이 등장하고 있으며 빈칸 이후에는 will help underprivileged communities in developing communities gain better access to health and sanitation, 즉 월간 기부금 25달러가 개발 도상국의 저소득 계층이 더 나은 공중 보건과 위생적인 환경을 누릴 수 있도록 도움을 줄 것이란 내용이 언급되고 있으므로 빈칸에는 월간 기부금 25달러를 달리 표현할 수 있는 또 다른 명사 어휘가 와야 한다. 따라서 빈칸에는 월간 기부금 25달러를 기부자의 '너그러움'으로 표현하는 명사 어휘 generosity가 적합하다.

144

★ 동사 어형

문제 분석

be able to Vr / ~하는 것이 가능하다

토익 분석

정기 토익에서는 be able to Vr (~하는 것이 가능하다) /
be ready to Vr (~할 준비가 되다) / be willing to Vr (~할
의지/의도가 있다) / be eligible to Vr (~할 자격이 되다) /
be reluctant to Vr (마지못해 ~하다) / be likely to Vr (~할
것 같다)와 같은 표현들이 어휘 문제 또는 to 부정사 어형
연계 문제로 자주 출제되고 있다.

(A) provide
(B) provided
(C) providing
(D) have provided

문제 해설

빈칸에 적절한 동사의 어형을 묻는 문제이다. 무엇보다 형용사 able 뒤에는 전치사 to가 아닌 To 부
정사가 위치하므로 빈칸에는 To 부정사 형태를 유지할 수 있도록 동사원형이 와야 한다. 그러므로
빈칸에는 provide가 적합하다.

145

★★ 동사 어형 / 동사의 시제

문제 분석

improve [향상/개선시키다] + quality (품질) / working
conditions (근무 환경) / efficiency (효율성) / productivity
(생산성)

토익 분석

파트6에서 시제가 반영된 동사의 어형 문제는 주로 조동
사(can/shoud/will…)과 동사원형이 결합된 미래 시제 형
태 – 현재/현재 진행 형태 – 현재 완료 형태에 대해 집
중적으로 묻는 경향이 있다.

(A) improved
(B) can improve
(C) have improved
(D) improving

문제 해설

빈칸이 접속사인 that 뒤에 위치하고 있으므로 빈칸에 알맞은 동사 어형을 묻는 문제로 빈칸에 앞
서 we plan to build infrastructures라며 향후에 기반 시설을 건설할 계획임을 밝히고 있다. 아울러
접속사 that은 infrastructures라는 가산 복수명사를 선행사로 취하며 주어 역할까지 겸하는 접속사
(관계대명사/형용사절 접속사)이자 빈칸 뒤에는 the livelihoods라는 명사 목적어가 제시되고 있다.
따라서 복수동사, 능동태 구조이자 미래시제를 지닌 형태의 동사가 필요하나 조동사를 선행하는 미
래 시제의 동사 형태는 단/복수 여부를 구분할 수 없다는 점을 고려할 때 빈칸에는 능동태 구조/미
래시제를 지닌 동사 어형 can improve가 적절하다.

146

★★ 빈칸 문장 추론

(A) 저희는 이미 가난한 지역사회를 도울 수 있는 많은 시
설들을 건설했습니다.
(B) 예컨대, 저희는 올해 Ghana 전 지역에 걸쳐 200개의
급수 펌프를 설치할 예정입니다.
(C) 또한, 그들은 향상된 보건 진료 혜택을 소아와 아동들
에게 제공할 것입니다.
(D) 만약 귀하의 월 기부금 액수를 바꾸고 싶으시면 저희
에게 알려주시기 바랍니다.

토익 분석

빈칸 문장 추론 문제는 전체 지문의 내용 흐름을 파악한
상태에서 풀어야 하므로 맨 마지막에 풀이하는 것이 효율
적이다

(A) We have already built numerous facilities that can help poor communities.
**(B) For example, we are going to install 200 water pumps throughout
Ghana this year.**
(C) Also, they will offer advanced health care to infants and children.
(D) Please let us know if you would like to change the amount of your monthly
donations.

문제 해설

빈칸에 적합한 내용의 문장을 묻는 문제이다. 빈칸에 앞서 we plan to build infrastructures that
can improve the livelihoods of local communities라며 지역 사회의 생활 수준을 향상시키는 기반
시설을 건설할 계획을 밝히고 있으므로 빈칸에는 기반 시설 건설 계획에 대한 구체적인 내용이나
추가 정보가 위치해야 함을 알 수 있다. 따라서 빈칸에는 For example, we are going to install 200
water pumps throughout Ghana this year, 즉 올해 Ghana 전 지역에 걸쳐 200개의 급수 펌프를
설치할 예정이라며 지역 사회의 생활 수준을 개선시킬 기반 시설을 어떻게 건설할 것인지 건설 계
획의 구체적인 실례를 제시하고 있는 내용이 와야 한다.

Questions 147-148 refer to the following message.

For the attention of: Peter Jones
Date: Friday, April 20 2:35 P.M.
Caller: Adam Johnson
Business: The Woolshed Clothing Store
Phone number: 925-7399

Message:

[147] Mr. Johnson from the Woolshed Clothing Store called to inquire about the location of his order. He claims that he ordered 500 sweaters from our company last Monday, but they have not yet been delivered to his store. [148] He would like you to email the order tracking number to him so that he can contact the delivery company. His e-mail address is A.Johnson@woolshed.net

Message taken by: Barbara Lewis

147-148 다음 메시지를 참조하시오.

Peter Jones 앞
날짜: 4월 20일 금요일 오후 2:35
발신자: Adam Johnson
사업체: Woolshed 의류점
연락처: 925-7399

메시지:
[147] Woolshed 옷 가게의 Johnson 씨가 주문품의 위치 문의로 전화 했습니다. 그는 지난 주 월요일 우리 회사에 500벌의 스웨터를 주문했는데 아직 가게로 배송되지 않았다고 합니다. [148] Johnson 씨는 주문 송장번호를 이메일로 보내주길 원했으며 그 번호로 배송회사에 연락을 취하겠다고 했습니다. 이메일 주소는 A.Johnson@woolshed.net 입니다.

메시지 수신자: Barbara Lewis

어휘 For the attention of: ~앞(업무용 서한 · 팩스 앞머리에 수신자를 명시할 때) tracking number 송장번호 have not yet 아직 ~하지 않았다 make an inquiry 문의하다 by post 우편으로

147

Why did Mr. Johnson telephone Mr. Jones?

(A) To schedule a meeting
(B) To pay an invoice
(C) To make an inquiry about an order
(D) To check whether some sweaters are available

★ 전화를 건 이유

Johnson 씨가 Jones 씨에게 전화를 한 이유는 무엇인가?
(A) 회의 일정을 잡기 위해서
(B) 운송장 지불을 위해서
(C) 주문품에 대해 문의하기 위해서
(D) 스웨터가 주문 가능한지 확인하기 위해서

토익 분석

전화를 건 이유는 지문에서 인사말/자기소개를 제외한 초반 2-3문장 중심으로 파악해라.

문제 해설

메시지 초반 Mr. Johnson from the Woolshed Clothing Store called to inquire about the location of his order를 통해 Johnson 씨는 주문품의 위치와 관련하여 문의를 하고자 연락했었음을 알 수가 있다. 그러므로 정답은 (C)가 되겠다.

148

What did Mr. Johnson ask Mr. Jones to do?

(A) Send him some information by e-mail
(B) Fax him a copy of a contract
(C) Phone him at his home
(D) Send him a catalogue by post

요청사항 ★

Johnson 씨가 Jones 씨에게 요청한 것은 무엇인가?
(A) 그에게 관련 정보를 이메일로 보낼 것
(B) 그에게 계약서 사본을 팩스로 보낼 것
(C) 그의 집으로 전화를 해줄 것
(D) 그에게 우편을 통해 카탈로그를 보낼 것

토익 분석

요청/요구/제안/권고 내용은 지문 종료 직전 2-3문장 부분에 집중해라.

문제 해설

메시지 후반 He would like you to email the order tracking number to him so that he can contact the delivery company라고 언급된 내용에서 Johnson 씨는 Jones 씨가 이메일로 자신이 주문한 물품의 추적 번호를 알려줄 것을 요청하고 있음을 알 수 있다. 다만 질문의 order tracking number이란 단서가 선택지에서는 정보, 즉 information이란 유사표현으로 바뀌어 제시되고 있음에 유의하도록 한다.

149-151 다음 광고를 참조하시오.

Questions 149-151 refer to the following advertisement.

Get away from it all on one of our luxury cruises!

Caribbean Cruises Ltd. offers luxury family-oriented cruises
at affordable prices for large families.

Our cruise packages include:
* A visit to 3 different Caribbean islands
[149] * 7 days aboard our luxury cruise ship *The Princess*
[149] * Free rental of scuba and snorkeling equipment
[149] * Three hot meals served daily at our exclusive 4-star restaurant
Don't delay. Book your vacation today!

To make a reservation, please call 1-800-2992. [151] Our sales staff is available to
take your call from 9 A.M. to 5 P.M. from Monday to Saturday.

[150] Earn a 10% special discount with our "Refer a Friend" program. You
will receive a discount if your friend mentions your name when making a
reservation!

럭셔리 크루즈로 모든 것을 떨쳐버리세요!

Caribbean Cruises 사는 대가족을 대상으로 적절한 가격
으로 럭셔리 가족 맞춤형 크루즈 상품을 제공합니다.

당사의 크루즈 상품은 다음 내용을 포함하고 있습니다:

* 세 곳의 **Caribbean** 섬 방문
[149] *7일간의 럭셔리 크루즈 'The Princess 호' 탑승
[149] * 스쿠버와 스노쿨 장비 무료 대여
[149] *타의 추종을 불허하는 4성급 레스토랑에서 매일
따뜻한 세 끼 식사 제공

늦지 마세요! – 오늘 당신의 휴가를 예약하세요!!!

예약하시려면 1-800-2992로 전화하세요. [151] 저희 직
원이 월요일부터 토요일, 오전 9시~5시까지 전화 상담해
드립니다.

[150] "친구 추천" 프로그램으로 10% 특별 할인을 받으세
요. 친구분이 예약 시에 고객님의 이름을 말하면 할인 혜
택을 받을 수 있습니다.

어휘 get away from ~에서 떠나다, 빠져 나가다 **family-
oriented** 가족적인, 가족지향의 **affordable** (가격이) 알
맞은, 입수 가능한 **abroad** (배, 기차 등에) 탄; 배 안에서
exclusive 유일한, 독점적인 **book** 예약하다 **take one's
call** ~의 전화를 받다 **refer** 언급하다, 보내다

149

What is NOT included in the cruise package?

(A) Seven days aboard a ship
(B) A free pass to the ship's movie theater
(C) Free use of diving equipment
(D) Free meals in the restaurant

★★ 진위

크루즈 상품에 포함되지 않는 것은 무엇인가?
(A) 7일간의 승선
(B) 선내 극장의 무료티켓
(C) 다이빙 장비의 무료 이용권
(D) 레스토랑 무료 식사권

토익 분석

세부사항/진위를 문제는 질문에서 빠른 키워드(핵심어)
파악이 관건이다.

1. 인명 / 직책 / 사물 지칭 명사
2. 숫자 / 시간 / 장소
3. 성질/감정 상태
4. 동사
5. If로 시작하는 절

문제 해설

크루즈 상품에 포함되지 않는 것을 묻는 진위 문제이므로 키워드인 cruise package가 등장하
는 부분을 중심으로 제시되는 정보를 통해 단서를 파악해야 한다. 광고문 두 번째 단락 초반
cruise packages가 제시되면서 크루즈 상품의 내역이 자세하게 언급되고 있다. 무엇보다 7 days
aboard our luxury cruise ship *The Princess*을 통해 7일간 승선하게 됨을, Free rental of scuba and
snorkeling equipment을 통해 다이빙 장비의 무료 이용을, 마지막으로 Three hot meals served
daily at our exclusive 4-star restaurant을 통해 고급 식당에서의 무료 식사를 제공받을 수 있게 됨
을 알 수 있다. 따라서 정답은 (B)가 되겠다.

150

What special offer does the advertisement mention?

(A) A $100 discount for booking online
(B) Free hotel pickup if a reservation is made before October 1
(C) A discount if a friend also makes a reservation
(D) A free souvenir T-shirt for every child on board the ship

★★ 세부사항

광고에서 언급하고 있는 특별 혜택은 무엇인가?
(A) 인터넷 예약을 통한 100달러 할인
(B) 10월 1일 이전 예약에 한해 제공받는 무료 호텔 픽업 서비스
(C) 친구가 예약을 하게 되면 받는 할인
(D) 승선하는 모든 아동들에게 무료 기념 티셔츠 제공

토익 분석

• 세부사항을 묻는 문제는 질문에서 빠른 키워드(핵심어) 파악이 중요하다. 다만 질문에서의 키워드는 지문에서 유사 어휘나 표현으로 바뀔 수 있다.
• special offer = special discount

문제 해설

질문에서 special offer이 키워드이므로 광고문에서 특별한 혜택에 관한 정보가 제공되는 부분에 집중해야 한다. 광고문 말미에서 Earn a 10% special discount with our "Refer a Friend" program. You will receive a discount if your friend mentions your name when making a reservation라고 언급하는 내용을 통해 친구에게 해당 상품을 추천하여 친구가 예약을 하게 되는 경우 본인이 10%의 할인 혜택을 받을 수 있다는 점을 알 수 있다. 따라서 정답은 (C)가 되겠다.

151

On what day does the booking staff NOT take calls?

(A) Monday
(B) Tuesday
(C) Wednesday
(D) Sunday

★ 세부사항

예약 담당 직원이 전화를 받지 않는 날은 언제인가?
(A) 월요일
(B) 화요일
(C) 수요일
(D) 일요일

토익 분석

시간/시점/요일을 묻는 문제에선 지문에서 시간/시점/요일이 언급되는 부분에만 빠르게 찾아 집중하라.

문제 해설

예약 담당 직원이 전화를 받지 못하는 날은 예약 관련 정보를 제공하는 부분에서 제시될 것임이 분명하다. 광고문의 세 번째 단락에서 Our sales staff is available to take your call from 9 A.M. to 5 P.M. from Monday to Saturday라고 언급하며 예약 제반 사항에 대한 내용을 전달하고 있다. 월요일부터 토요일까지 오전 9시부터 오후 5시까지 예약을 받으므로 직원이 예약전화를 받지 못하는 날은 일요일임을 알 수 있다. 따라서 정답은 (D)이다.

152-155 다음 문자 메시지를 참조하시오.

Dwight Parker [12:38 P.M.] 여러분, 제가 좀 곤란한 상황인데 도움을 주실 수 있나요?

Irene Keller [12:39 P.M.] 무슨 일인가요? 뭔가 잘못되었나요?

Dwight Parker [12:40 P.M.] [152, 153] 태블릿 컴퓨터 하나가 이 곳 바닥에 떨어졌어요. 제대로 작동하지 않는 것 같아요.

Irene Keller [12:41 P.M.] [153] 오, 어떡하지요! [152] 발표는 언제 시작하나요?

Dwight Parker [12:42 P.M.] 오후 1시 30분이에요. 현재는 대략 30분이 오셨는데, 약 120분 정도가 오실 겁니다.

Walter White [12:43 P.M.] 사무실에서 방금 여분의 태블릿 컴퓨터를 찾았어요. 한 50분 정도 시간이 남았지요. 어떻게 할까요?

Irene Keller [12:44 P.M.] 좋아요. [154] 제가 곧 그리로 가서 태블릿 컴퓨터를 설치하고 시청각 시스템에 연결시켜 놓을게요. 너무 걱정하지 마세요. 제가 알아서 처리할게요.

Walter White [12:46 P.M.] 그러면, [155] 저는 사무실에 있는 사람을 시켜 Irene에게 태블릿 컴퓨터를 가져다 주도록 할게요.

Dwight Parker [12:48 P.M.] 정말 안심이 되네요. 얼른 서둘러서 와주세요. 정말 고마워요.

어휘 be in trouble 곤란한 상황에 빠지다 fall on the floor 바닥에 떨어지다 properly 알맞게, 적절하게 spare 여분의 것, 여분으로 남기다 set up ~을 설치하다, ~을 정하다 audiovisual system 시청각 시스템 handle ~을 다루다, ~을 취급하다 relief 안도, 안심하게 하다 real quick 정말 빠르게

Questions 152-155 refer to the following text message chain.

Dwight Parker [12:38 P.M.] Hey, guys, I'm in trouble. I need your help.

Irene Keller [12:39 P.M.] What's up? What's wrong?

Dwight Parker [12:40 P.M.] [152, 153] One of our tablet computers fell on the floor here, and it doesn't seem like it is working properly.

Irene Keller [12:41 P.M.] [153] Oh, no! [152] When does your marketing presentation start?

Dwight Parker [12:42 P.M.] At one thirty. About 30 people are here now, but I'm expecting about 120.

Walter White [12:43 P.M.] I've just found a spare in my office. We have about fifity minutes left. What should we do?

Irene Keller [12:44 P.M.] Good. [154] I will be there soon to set up the tablet computer and connect it to the audiovisual system. Don't worry too much about it. I can handle it.

Walter White [12:46 P.M.] Then, [155] I'll send someone in the office up to get Irene the tablet computer.

Dwight Parker [12:48 P.M.] Oh, that's a relief! Please get here quickly. Thanks a lot.

152

★ 장소 유추

Parker 씨는 어느 곳에 있을 것 같은가?
(A) 회의실
(B) 전자제품 매장
(C) 영화관
(D) 그의 사무실

토익 분석

장소 유추는 지문에서 장소를 추측할 수 있는 관련 어휘를 파악해라.

Where most likely is Mr. Parker?

(A) In a conference room
(B) In an electronics store
(C) At a movie theater
(D) In his office

문제 해설

문자 메시지를 통한 대화가 발생하고 있는 곳을 유추하는 문제이므로 장소를 추측할 수 있을만한 관련 어휘나 표현이 제시되는 부분에 집중해야 한다. Parker 씨는 오후 12시 40분에 One of our tablet computers fell on the floor here, and it doesn't seem like it is working properly라며 태블릿 컴퓨터 하나가 이 곳 바닥에 떨어져서 제대로 작동하는 것처럼 보이질 않는다는 문제점을 제기하고 있으며 이어서 Keller 씨는 When does your marketing presentation start?라며 마케팅 발표가 언제인지를 묻고 있다. 따라서 이를 통해 Parker 씨는 마케팅 발표를 준비하고 있음을 가늠할 수 있으므로 정답은 회의실, 즉 (A)임을 알 수 있다.

153

At 12:41 P.M., why does Ms. Keller say, "Oh, no"?

(A) An event has been canceled.

(B) Some people have not arrived.

(C) An employee called in sick this morning.

(D) A piece of equipment is damaged.

문제 해설

오후 12시 41분에 Keller 씨가 "Oh, no"라고 말한 화자의 의도를 묻는 문제이다. 이에 앞서 Parker 씨는 One of our tablet computers fell on the floor here, and it doesn't seem like it is working properly라며 태블릿 컴퓨터 하나가 이 곳 바닥에 떨어져서 제대로 작동하는 것처럼 보이질 않는다는 문제점을 제기한 부분에 대해 Keller 씨가 Oh, no라고 말하고 있다. 따라서 Keller 씨가 Oh, no라고 이야기한 것은 장비의 파손으로 인한 놀라움이 반영된 표현임을 알 수 있으므로 정답은 (D)가 되겠다.

154

What is implied about Ms. Keller?

(A) She is a marketing manager.

(B) She is Mr. Parker's supervisor.

(C) She is good at handling machines.

(D) She is one of the big clients.

문제 해설

Keller 씨에 대해 유추할 수 있는 내용을 묻는 문제이므로 Keller 씨에 대한 정보가 제시되는 부분에 집중해야 한다. Keller씨는 오후 12시 44분에 I will be there soon to set up the tablet computer and connect it to the audiovisual system. Don't worry too much about it. I can handle it이라며 Keller 씨는 자신이 가서 태블릿 컴퓨터를 설치하고 이를 시청각 시스템과 연결시켜줄 것이고 자신이 잘 처리할 테니 염려하지 말라며 자신 있게 언급하고 있다. 따라서 이를 통해 Keller 씨는 컴퓨터나 시청각 시스템을 능숙하게 다루는 사람임을 유추할 수 있으므로 정답은 (C)가 되겠다.

155

What will Mr. White most likely do next?

(A) Give a marketing presentation

(B) Buy a new tablet computer

(C) Have someone bring a machine up

(D) Install a machine with Mr. Parker

문제 해설

White 씨가 이후에 무엇을 할 것인지 묻는 마지막 유추 문제이므로 문자 메시지를 통한 대화 후반부에서 White 씨에 관한 언급되는 정보에 집중해야 한다. White 씨는 오후 12시 46분에 I'll send someone in the office up to get Irene the tablet computer라며 누군가를 시켜 태블릿 컴퓨터를 Irene에게 가져다 주도록 할 것임을 언급하고 있다. 그러므로 정답은 (C)가 되겠다.

156-157 다음 기사문을 참조하시오.

[156] Gaby Motor 사는 2년 연속으로 기록적인 영업과 이윤을 기대하고 있다. 유럽에서의 판매 회복과 함께 북미 지역의 판매 증가에 힘입어 Gaby Motor 사는 세계에서 가장 빠른 성장을 보이는 자동차 제조업체가 되었다. 4월 1일로 시작된 이번 회계연도에서 [157] Gaby Motor 사는 달러 약세에서 비롯되는 혜택은 기대하지 않고 있는 반면, SUV 차량의 판매량 증가를 확신하고 있다.

어휘 fiscal year 회계연도 spur 박차를 가하다, 고무하다 along with ~와 더불어, ~와 함께 confident 확신하는 sales volume 판매량 expansion 확장 financial status 재정상태 revival 부활, 회복 depreciation 가치하락

Questions 156-157 refer to the article.

[156] Gaby Motor Co. expects record sales and profits for the second straight year. Spurred by a sales growth in North America and South Korea, along with the sales recovery in Europe, Gaby Motor Co is the fastest growing automobile manufacturer in the world. In this fiscal year, which started April 1, [157] Gaby expects minimum support from the weak dollar, but is confident in increasing sales volume, especially in its line of sports utility vehicles.

156

★★ 뉴스의 주제 난이도

뉴스가 보도하고 있는 내용은 무엇인가?
(A) SUV 차량 시장의 확대
(B) Gaby Motors 사의 재정 상태
(C) Gaby Motors 사의 기록적인 판매 실적
(D) Gaby Motors 사의 판매 예상

토익 분석

단락 구분이 없는 기사문의 주제는 주로 지문 초반 2-3 문장에서 제시된다.

What does the article discuss?

(A) The expansion of the sports utility vehicle market
(B) The financial status of Gaby Motors Co.
(C) The advertising strategies of Gaby Motors Co.
(D) The sales prediction of Gaby Motors Co.

문제 해설

뉴스의 주제에 대해 묻는 문제이다. 뉴스 초반 Gaby Motor Co. expects record sales and profits for the second straight year을 통해 뉴스는 Gaby Motor 사는 2년 연속으로 기록적인 영업과 이윤을 기대하고 있다는 내용을 보도하고 있음을 알 수 있다. 따라서 뉴스의 주제는 바로 Gaby Motors 사의 판매 실적 예상에 관한 것임을 알 수 있으므로 정답은 (D)이다.

157

★★ 부정 내용 난이도

Gaby Motors 사의 판매량 증가에 기여하는 요소가 아닌 것은 무엇인가?
(A) 유럽 시장의 부활
(B) 달러화 가치의 하락
(C) 한국에서의 소비자 수요 증가
(D) 북미 지역에서의 판매 증가

토익 분석

사실이 아닌 한 가지 내용을 묻는 문제[NOT TRUE]는 선택지를 키워드로 삼아 각 선택지의 내용이 지문에서 언급되는지 여부를 파악하는 방식으로 풀이하는 것이 효율적이다.

Which is NOT a factor that contributed to the increase of the sales volume of Gaby Motors Co.?

(A) The revival of European markets
(B) The depreciation of the dollar
(C) The growing customer demand in South Korea
(D) The increased sales performance in North America

문제 해설

Gaby Motors 사의 판매량 증가에 기여하는 요소가 아닌 것을 묻는 마지막 문제이다. 따라서 기사문 후반부에서 주어진 선택지의 내용이 제시되는지 여부만 빠르게 확인하는 방식으로 문제를 풀이하는 것이 효율적이다. 기사문 후반 Gaby expects minimum support from the weak dollar을 통해 Gaby Motors 사는 달러화 가치 하락으로 인한 혜택은 기대하지 않고 있음을 알 수 있다. 그러므로 정답은 (B)이다.

Questions 158-159 refer to the advertisement.

[158] Summer Promotion
Starling Leisure Center
47 Bell Street
Miami, Florida
Phone: 404-466-0278

[158] Take advantage of our discounted prices this summer.
Swimming and mini-golf: 50% off in July!
Enjoy lunch in our cafeteria, served from 1 P.M.

Opening Hours
[159] Monday to Friday: 09:30 A.M. – 6:00 P.M.
Saturday and Sunday: 10.00 A.M. – 09:00 P.M.
Closed on public holidays.

158-159 다음 광고를 참조하시오.

[158] 하계 판촉 행사
Starling Leisure Center
47 Bell Street
Miami, Florida
전화: 404-466-0278

[158] 올 여름 저희가 제공하는 할인 특가를 활용하세요.
수영과 미니 골프: 7월에는 50% 할인
1시부터 제공되는 점심을 카페테리아에서 즐기세요!

영업시간
[159] 월요일에서 금요일: 오전 9:30 ~ 오후 6:00
토요일과 일요일: 오전 10:00 ~ 오후 9:00
공휴일은 휴무

어휘 take advantage of ~을 이용하다 opening hours 영업시간 public holiday 공휴일

158

What is the announcement for?

(A) A summer promotion at a leisure center
(B) Changes to a lunch menu
(C) The reopening of a store
(D) The dates of a public holiday

문제 해설

광고문 제목 Summer Promotion에서 여름 판촉 행사에 대한 광고임을 알 수 있으며, 아울러 이어지는 Take advantage of our discounted prices this summer. Swimming and mini-golf: 50% off in July! Enjoy lunch in our cafeteria, served from 1 P.M.을 통해 특가 제공 내역이나 카페테리아에서의 점심식사와 같은 여름 판촉 행사에 대한 구체적인 사항들 파악할 수 있다. 따라서 정답은 (A)이다.

★ **지문의 목적**

이 공지의 목적은 무엇인가?
(A) 레저 센터의 여름 판촉
(B) 점심메뉴의 변경사항
(C) 가게의 재개장
(D) 공휴일 날짜

토익 분석

광고의 목적은 광고문 제목과 광고문 초반 2문장 내용을 통해 파악해라.

159

What is indicated about the Starling Leisure Center?

(A) It is famous throughout Florida.
(B) It opens later on weekends.
(C) Lunch is served all day.
(D) Its prices have recently increased.

문제 해설

Starling Leisure Center에 대해 언급된 내용을 묻는 진위 문제로 Starling Leisure Center가 키워드라 할 수 있다. 그러나 광고문 전반에 걸쳐 Starling Leisure Center가 소개되고 있으므로 지문에서 키워드인 Starling Leisure Center가 언급되는 부분을 찾아 단서를 파악하기 어렵다. 그러므로 선택지에 제시된 내용을 키워드로 삼아 지문에서 해당 선택지의 내용이 등장하는지 여부만 빠르게 파악하는 방식으로 문제풀이에 접근해야 한다. 따라서 지문 후반부 개장시간을 소개하는 부분, Monday to Friday: 09:30 A.M. – 6:00 P.M. Saturday and Sunday 10:00 A.M. – 09:00 P.M.을 통해 주중 개장시간 9시 30분과 주말 개장시간 10시를 비교하면 주말의 개장이 더 늦어진다는 점을 알 수 있다. 그러므로 정답은 (B)가 되겠다.

★ **진위 문제**

Starling Leisure Center에 대해 언급되는 것은 무엇인가?
(A) Florida 전역에서 유명하다.
(B) 주말에는 늦게 연다.
(C) 점심은 온종일 제공된다.
(D) 가격이 최근에 올랐다.

토익 분석

사실 내용을 묻는 문제[TRUE]의 키워드가 지문 전반에 걸쳐 언급되는 경우 선택지의 내용을 키워드로 삼아 지문에서 해당 내용이 언급되는지 여부를 빠르게 파악한다.

160-162 다음 기사를 참조하시오.

Hayward State University의 새로운 기숙사
Alicia Adams, Beat Reporter

6월 27일-새로운 계획이 확정되었고 적절한 인원이 배치되었다. 새로운 기숙사 복합 시설의 공사가 시작되었다. 기공식은 지난 목요일 Brompton Avenue와 Route 20 교차로에서 열렸으며 이 곳은 주립학교에서 새로운 주택 단지인 Pioneers Lofts를 건설하게 될 지역이다. ¹⁶⁰ 대학 총장인 Delilah Sorcarro 씨는 본교에서 북쪽으로 3마일 떨어진 이 곳에서 공사의 첫 삽을 떴다.

Pioneers Lofts는 대학 (공공 기관)과 Weingarten Group (지역 부동산 개발 회사) 간의 합작 투자 회사이다. ¹⁶² 기숙사 복합 시설은 3개의 대형 혼합 건물로 구성된다. ¹⁶² 각 건물의 1층에는 소매업을 할 수 있는 공간을 보유하게 되며 바로 그 위에는 기숙사가 위치하게 될 것이다. Weingarten Group은 부지를 개발하고 소매업 운영을 관리한다. "최근까지 대부분의 학생들은 통학을 했습니다." 라고 대학 총장인 Sorcarro 씨는 말했으며 이어서 "현재 캠퍼스 내 기숙사 거주를 신청하는 지원자의 수가 증가하고 있습니다. "지난 봄에 우리가 지은 고층 기숙사는 어느 정도 도움이 되었습니다. 그러나 이 공사가 완공되면 우리는 학생들에게 보다 더 잘 지원할 수 있게 될 겁니다." 라고 언급했다.

Weingarten Group의 도시 계획가인 Daniel Ho는 주민들에게 몇몇 소매상은 많은 의류 매장과 건강 식품 매장을 포함하여 단지를 임대하는 것에 이미 관심을 표명하고 있으며 ¹⁶¹ 이 지역에 대형 슈퍼마켓 체인을 유치했다고 말했다. 복합 단지와 캠퍼스는 경치가 좋은 산책로로 연결된다.

어휘 finalize ~을 마무리하다 appropriate 알맞은, 타당한, 적절한 personnel 직원, 인력 put into place 제 자리에 위치하다, ~이 정상적으로 가동하다 dormitory 기숙사 ceremony 기념 행사 take place ~이 발생하다 intersection 교차로 complex 단지, 시설, 복잡한 turn over ~을 뒤집다 shovelful 한 삽 가득 dirt 흙, 먼지 site 장소, 위치 joint venture 합작 사업 consist of ~로 구성되다 mixed-use 다목적의, 다용도의, 주상복합의 retail space 소매 사업을 할 수 있는 공간 commuter 통근자 sharp increase 급작스러운 증가 request ~을 요청하다 high-rise 고층 to some extent 다소, 어느 정도 complete ~을 끝내다, ~을 마무리하다 in a much better position 더 좋은 위치에 있다 retailer 소매업자, 소매업체 lease ~을 임대하다 outlet 배출구, 출구, 대형 할인점 connect ~을 연결하다 scenic 경치가 좋은 foot path 산책로

Questions 160-162 refer to the following article.

New College Dormitory Complex
For Hayward State University
by Alicia Adams, Beat Reporter

June 27—The new plans were finalized and the appropriate personnel put into place. Construction has started for the new college dormitory complex. A ceremony took place last Thursday at the intersection of Brompton Avenue and Route 20, where Hayward State University is building its new dormitory complex, Pioneers Lofts. ¹⁶⁰ Delilah Sorcarro, President of Hayward State University, turned over the first shovelful of dirt at the site, located three miles north of the main campus. — [1] —.

Pioneers Lofts is a joint venture between the college (a public institution) and the Weingarten Group (a local property-development firm). ¹⁶² It will consist of three large mixed-use buildings. ¹⁶² — [2] —. Each will have retail space at ground level and just above that, student apartments. The Weingarten Group will develop the site and manage the retail operations. "Until recently, most of our students have been commuters," Ms. Sorcarro said. "Now we are seeing a sharp increase in the number of applicants who request campus housing — [3] —. The high-rise dormitory we built last spring has helped to some extent. But when this project is completed, we will be in a much better position to serve our students".

Daniel Ho, the Weingarten Group's city planner, has told the university board that several retailers have already expressed interest in leasing space in the complex, including a number of clothing stores and health food outlets, and ¹⁶¹ he has invited a large supermarket chain in the area. — [4] —. The complex and the campus will be connected by a scenic footpath.

160

★ Sorcarro 씨의 정체

Sorcarro 씨는 누구일 것 같은가?
(A) 거주민
(B) 부동사 개발업자
(C) 대학 관리자
(D) 점주

토익 분석

인명은 중요한 키워드로 지문에서 인명이 제시되는 부분에서 단서를 파악해라.

Who most likely is Ms. Sorcarro?

(A) A resident
(B) A property developer
(C) A college administrator
(D) A store owner

문제 해설

Sorcarro 씨의 신분에 대해 묻는 문제이므로 지문에서 Sorcarro라는 이름이 제시되는 부분에서 단서를 파악해야 한다. 지문의 첫 번째 단락 말미에서 Delilah Sorcarro, President of Hayward State University라고 언급된 부분을 통해 Delilah Sorcarro 씨는 Hayward 주립대학교 총장임을 알 수 있다. 그러므로 정답은 college administrator, 즉 학교 관리자를 뜻하는 (D)가 되겠다.

161

What business has the Weingarten Group invited to the new establishment?

(A) A construction firm
(B) A travel agency
(C) A private education institute
(D) A grocery store

문제 해설

Weingarten Group이 새로운 시설에 유치한 회사의 업종이 무엇인지 세부적인 내용을 묻는 문제이므로 지문에서 Weingarten Group이 유치하는 회사의 업종이 언급되는 부분에 집중해야 한다. 지문의 마지막 세 번째 단락 말미에서 he has invited large supermarket chain in the area라며 도시 계획가인 Daniel Ho는 이 지역에 대형 슈퍼마켓 체인을 유치했음을 밝히고 있다. 그러므로 정답은 식료품점을 뜻하는 (D)가 되겠다.

★★ 세부사항

Weingarten Group이 새로운 시설에 유치한 회사의 업종은 무엇인가?
(A) 건설사
(B) 여행사
(C) 사교육 기관
(D) 식료품점

토익 분석

업종/직장을 묻는 질문은 지문에서 업종/직장과 관련된 어휘나 표현을 파악하는 것이 관건이다.

162

In which of the positions marked [1], [2], [3], and [4] does the following sentence best belong?

"Each will have retail space at ground level and just above that, student apartments."

(A) [1]
(B) [2]
(C) [3]
(D) [4]

문제 해설

주어진 문장이 위치해야 하는 곳을 묻는 문제이므로 주어진 문장의 의미를 이해한 후 이와 내용적 연계성을 지닌 적절한 위치를 파악해야 한다. 주어진 문장은 각 건물의 1층에는 소매업을 할 수 있는 공간을 보유하게 되며 바로 그 위에는 기숙사가 위치하게 될 것이란 뜻을 지닌다. 그러므로 이 앞에는 각 건물이 어떠한 건물인지 설명하고 있는 내용이 위치해야 함을 가늠할 수 있다. 두 번째 단락 초반에는 It will consist of three large mixed-use buildings라며 기숙사 복합 시설은 3개의 대형 혼합 건물로 구성된다는 점을 밝히고 있으므로 해당 문장의 내용은 바로 [2]에 위치해야 함을 알 수 있다. 따라서 정답은 (B)가 되겠다.

★★★ 문장 위치 파악

아래 문장은 [1], [2], [3], 그리고 [4]번 중 어디에 위치해야 하는가?
"각 건물의 1층에는 소매업을 할 수 있는 공간을 보유하게 되며 바로 그 위에는 기숙사가 위치하게 될 것이다."
(A) [1]
(B) [2]
(C) [3]
(D) [4]

토익 분석

• 문장 위치는 주어진 문장 내용과 앞선 문장 내용과의 연결고리로 활용할 수 있는 접속사, 접속부사, 고유명사, 대명사를 파악해라.
• 강사로서 문제풀이 시간을 단축시킬 수 있는 방법으로는 [3] – [4] – [1] – [2] 순서로 정답 비중이 높기 때문에 주어진 문장 내용을 순차적으로 해당 위치에 삽입해보며 내용 연결성을 비교하는 것이다.

163-166 다음 기사를 참조하시오.

HARTVILLE (9월 3일) – [163] Hartville 교통위원회가 현재 도시 전역에 일어나고 있는 각종 인프라 개선 현황 및 통근과 왕래에 미치는 영향에 관한 최신 소식을 전한다. "여러 프로젝트들이 주요 통근 노선에 미치는 영향에 주의해 들어주시길 바랍니다." 라고 교통 이사회의 회장인 **Gary Rondell** 씨가 말했다.

8월 29일부터 **Dayton Valley Bridge**의 두 차선이 긴급 재포장 공사를 위해 폐쇄되었다. 이 폐쇄 탓에, 운전자들은 아침과 저녁 출퇴근 시간이 최대 1시간 지연될 수 있다. [164] 또한 9월 중순까지 진행되는 건설 공사로 인해 시내 14번가 밑으로 가로질러 가는 지하 터널 접근이 불가하다. 대신 14번가를 따라 100미터를 내려가면 있는 **Carson Avenue Bridge**가 터널 공사가 완성되기 전까지 보행자들을 위해 안전한 우회 횡단 도로로 지정된다.

대학 강사인 **Harold Blackley** 씨는 **New Haven**에서 시내 **Hartville**에 있는 **Angler** 대학교까지의 통근거리가 최소 45분 이상 지연되었다고 보고했다. "**Wells** 가는 자꾸 교통이 완전한 정체 상태가 되곤 합니다. 요즘 첫 수업 시간에 늦지 않으려면 원래 출근하던 것보다 한 시간 일찍 나가는 수밖에 없어요." 라고 **Blackley** 씨는 말했다. 오토바이 택배원인 **Chet Landry** 씨 또한 많은 문제에 직면해 있다. "직업 특성상 소포가 제시간에 배달되려면 모든 게 원활히 [165] 진행되어야 합니다. 고객들은 제가 제시간에 소포를 배달할 것이라고 믿고 있는데, 이렇게 많은 도로 보수로 제시간에 배송하는 것이 점점 어려워지고 있습니다."

[166] **Rondell** 씨는 바쁜 도로 보수 지역들을 지나갈 때 운전자들에게 더 많이 주의할 것을 경고하고 있다. "운전자들은 인내심을 갖고 주변 환경을 확인해야 합니다. 도로에 장애물도 많고 도로 작업단도 많이 있기에, 불필요한 사고가 발생하는 것을 원하지 않습니다."

어휘 impact ~에 영향을 미치다 commute 통근하다 take note of ~에 유의하다 commuter 통근자 route 길 transit board 교통 위원회 urgent 긴급한 up to 최대 rush hour 출퇴근 혼잡 시간대 additionally 추가적으로 inaccessible 접근이 불가한, 이용이 불가한 due to ~ 이기 때문에 alternative 대체, 대안 pedestrian 보행자 lecturer 강연자 standstill 정지한, 움직임이 없는 make it on time 시간에 맞춰 도착하다 have no choice but to ~ 할 수 밖에 없다 courier 택배 encounter ~과 마주치다 vigilant of ~에 대해 경계하는

Questions 163-166 refer to the following article.

HARTVILLE (September 3)— [163] The Hartville Transit Board would like to update residents on the current status of various infrastructure improvements that are taking place throughout the city, and their impact on commuting and foot traffic. "Please especially take note of the effect that many of these projects will have on the main commuter routes," says Gary Rondell, chairman of the transit board.

Two lanes of the Dayton Valley Bridge have been closed for urgent repaving since August 29. Due to this closure, it is common for motorists to face delays of up to one hour during morning and evening rush hour. [164] Additionally, the underground tunnel that crosses under 14th Avenue downtown is inaccessible due to construction work that will continue until mid-September. The Carson Avenue Bridge, just 100 meters further down 14th Avenue, serve as an alternative, safe pedestrian crossing point until the tunnel construction is finished.

University lecturer Harold Blackley reported delays of at least 45 minutes during his daily commute between New Haven and Angler University in downtown Hartville. "Traffic on Wells Boulevard is often at a complete standstill," Mr. Blackley said. "These days, if I want to make it on time for my first class, I have no choice but to leave one hour earlier than I normally would." Chet Landry, a motorbike courier, has also encountered many problems. "In my job, things have to [165] run smoothly so that my packages are delivered on time. Clients depend on me to deliver packages promptly, but that is increasingly difficult with all the street maintenance that is going on."

[166] Mr. Rondell warns drivers to take increased care when traveling through busy road maintenance areas. "Motorists should try to remain patient and stay vigilant of the environment. There are many obstacles and a large number of road crew workers on the streets, and we don't want any unnecessary accidents to occur."

163

★★ 지문의 목적

이 기사의 목적은 무엇인가?
(A) 지역 주민들에게 대중 교통 사용을 장려하기 위해서
(B) 도시 전역에 걸친 도시 개발 프로젝트에 관한 제안서를 설명하기 위해서
(C) New Haven으로 이어지는 새로운 통근 경로 건설을 설명하기 위해서
(D) 진행 중인 보수공사의 영향을 지역 사람들에게 알려 주기 위해서

토익 분석

기사문의 주제/목적은 단락 구분이 있는 경우 첫 번째 단락 초반 2-3문장에서 제시된다. 다만 주제/목적 문제의 난이도가 높아지는 경우 주제/목적은 두 번째 단락의 초반 2-3문장에서 다뤄진다.

What is the purpose of the article?

(A) To encourage residents to make use of public transportation
(B) To outline a proposal for a citywide urban development project
(C) To describe the construction of a new commuter route to New Haven
(D) To inform local people of the effects of ongoing maintenance

문제 해설

기사문의 목적은 대개 기사문의 첫 번째 단락 초반부에서 드러난다. 기사문 초반 The Hartville Transit Board would like to update residents on the current status of various infrastructure improvements that are taking place throughout the city, and their impact on commuting and foot traffic을 통해 Hartville 교통위원회에서 현재 전 도시에 걸쳐 진행 중인 다양한 인프라 개선 공사의 현황과 이러한 공사가 교통에 미치는 파급효과에 대해 시민들에게 알리고자 함을 다루는 기사문임을 알 수 있다. 따라서 정답은 (D)이다.

164

According to the article, where can pedestrians walk while the underground tunnel is closed?

(A) On the Dayton Valley Bridge
(B) On 14th Avenue
(C) On the Carson Avenue Bridge
(D) On Wells Boulevard

문제 해설

지하 터널이 막혀있을 동안 보행자들이 이용해야 하는 것을 묻고 있으므로 기사문에서 지하 터널에 대해 집중적으로 언급하고 있는 부분을 중심으로 단서를 찾아야 할 필요가 있다. 기사문 두 번째 단락 중단과 하단 Additionally, the underground tunnel that crosses under 14th Avenue downtown is inaccessible due to construction work that will continue until mid-September. The Carson Avenue Bridge, just 100 meters further down 14th Avenue, will serve as an alternative, safe pedestrian crossing point until the tunnel construction is finished에서 지하터 널이 공사로 인해 폐쇄된 동안에는 14번가를 100미터 정도 따라가면 나오는 카슨 애비뉴 다리를 이용해야 한다는 내용을 언급하고 있으므로 정답은 (C)라고 할 수 있다.

165

In paragraph 3, line 11, the word "run" is closest in meaning to

(A) send
(B) operate
(C) drive
(D) improve

문제 해설

주어진 문장 내에서 run은 배달이 제 시간에 이뤄지려면 모든 것이 어긋나는 것 없이 원활하게 진행되어야 한다는 뜻으로 사용되었으므로 이에 대한 동의어로는 operate가 적절하다. 따라서 정답은 (B)가 되겠다.

166

What does the chairman of the transit board advise people to do?

(A) Leave for work earlier than usual
(B) Try to carpool with other people
(C) Exercise caution when driving
(D) Avoid using cars whenever possible

문제 해설

교통 위원회 회장이 사람들에게 어떠한 조언을 하고 있는지 묻고 있으므로 교통 위원회 회장인 Rondell 씨가 등장하는 부분을 중심으로 단서를 찾아야 할 필요가 있다. 기사문의 마지막 단락 초반 Mr. Rondell warns drivers to take increased care when traveling through busy road maintenance areas을 통해 Rondell 씨가 바쁜 공사현장을 운전해 갈 때는 평소보다 더 많은 주의를 기울여야 할 것임을 권고하고 있음을 알 수 있으므로 정답은 (C)가 되겠다.

167-168 다음 문자 메시지를 참조하시오.

Debra Morgan [2:20 p.m.]
[167] 세탁한 옷을 Memorial 하우스로 배달했나요?

Arther Mitchell [2:30p.m.]
가고 있는 길이에요. 이 쪽 동네 교통 정체 현상이 심하네요.

Debra Morgan [2:31p.m.]
[168] 고객이 연락을 했었어요. 세탁한 옷이 오후 3시까지 필요하다고 하네요.

Arther Mitchell [2:32p.m.]
[168] 제시간에 도착할 겁니다. 염려 마세요.

Debra Morgan [2:33p.m.]
다른 길로 가는 것이 어때요?

Arther Mitchell [2:33p.m.]
모르겠어요. 좋은 루트를 휴대전화로 검색해볼게요. 지금 가고 있는 이 도로에선 차 사고가 발생한 것이 아닐까 싶어요.

Debra Morgan [2:34P.M.]
좋아요. 조심해서 빨리 가 주세요. 배송 마치면 문자메시지 보내주시고요.

어휘 laundry 빨래, 세탁 on one's way ~로 가는 길이다 route 도로, 길, 경로 safely 안전하게 quickly 빠르게 text message 문자 메시지

Questions 167-168 refer to the following text message chain.

Debra Morgan [2:28 P.M.]
[167] Did you get the laundry delivery to the Memorial house?

Arther Mitchell [2:30 P.M.]
I'm on the way now. Traffic is bad on this side of town.

Debra Morgan [2:31 P.M.]
The client called. [168] They need the delivery by 3 P.M.

Arther Mitchell [2:32 P.M.]
[168] I am sure that it will be there on time. Don't worry.

Debra Morgan [2:33 P.M.]
Can you take a different route?

Arther Mitchell [2:33 P.M.]
No idea. I will check on my phone for the best route. I think there was a car accident.

Debra Morgan [2:34 P.M.]
Yes. Get there safely and quickly. And send a text message after you're done with the delivery.

167

★ Mitchell 씨의 직장 유추

Mitchell 씨는 어느 회사에서 근무하고 있는가?
(A) 배송 회사
(B) 이삿짐 회사
(C) 세탁 서비스 제공 회사
(D) 법률 회사

토익 분석

업종/직장을 묻는 질문은 지문에서 업종/직장과 관련된 어휘나 표현을 파악하는 것이 관건이다.

What type of business does Mr. Mitchell work in?

(A) A shipping company
(B) A moving company
(C) A laundry service
(D) A law firm

문제 해설

Mitchell 씨의 직장을 유추하는 문제이므로 문자 메시지들에서 Mitchell 씨의 직장을 추측할 수 있을 만한 관련 어휘나 표현을 파악해야 한다. Debra Morgan 씨는 오후 2시 28분 Arther Mitchell 씨에게 Did you get the laundry delivery to the Memorial house?이라며 세탁한 옷을 Memorial 하우스로 배달했는지 여부를 묻고 있다. 따라서 이를 통해 Mitchell 씨는 세탁 서비스 제공 회사에서 근무함을 알 수 있으므로 정답은 (C)가 되겠다.

At 2:31 P.M., what does Ms. Morgan most likely mean when he writes, "They need the delivery by 3 P.M."?

(A) He has plans for his golf game today.

(B) There are more deliveries to be done

(D) He is angry about the car accident

(D) The client needs the job done on time

문제 해설

화자의 의도를 묻는 문제이므로 주어진 표현이 제시되는 부분을 전후하여 제시되는 문맥에 집중해야 한다. 오후 2시 31분에 모건 씨는 고객이 연락했으며 세탁된 빨래가 오후 3시까지 이루어지길 바라고 있음을 언급하고 있다. 그리고 오후 2시 32분에 Mitchell 씨는 시간에 맞춰 배송이 될 것이니 걱정하지 말라고 당부하고 있다. 이를 통해 오후 2시 31분에 Morgan 씨가 "They need the delivery by 3 P.M."이라고 쓴 것은 고객이 시간에 맞춰 세탁물이 배달되길 바라고 있음을 전달하고자 하는 의도가 있음을 가늠할 수 있다. 그러므로 정답은 (D)가 되겠다.

★★ 화자의 의도

오후 2시 31분에 Morgan 씨가 "They need the delivery by 3 P.M."이라고 쓴 것이 의미하는 바는 무엇인가?

(A) 그는 오늘 골프를 할 계획이 있다.

(B) 처리해야 할 더 많은 배송들이 있다.

(D) 자동차 사고로 인해 화가 났다.

(D) 그 고객은 시간에 맞춰 배달이 이뤄지길 바라고 있다.

토익 분석

특정 표현에 담긴 화자의 의도에 대한 이해하기 위해서는 주어진 특정 표현 전후의 내용 파악이 선행되어야 한다. 난이도가 높아지는 경우에는 전체 지문의 내용을 다 파악해야만 풀 수 있는 경우도 발생한다.

169-171 다음 광고를 참조하시오.

특별 공지
수신: Bradford 대학교내 학생잡지사, 편집장
발신: Kelly Francis, Keepsafe Insurance
마케팅 부장
Keepsafe Insurance

오늘날, 젊은이들이 방학이나 해외여행에 대해 보상받을 수 있는 적절한 여행보험을 찾는 것은 종종 어려운 일일 수 있습니다. [169] 이것이 Keepsafe Insurance가 특별히 18살~25살의 젊은이들만을 대상으로 한 Backpacker Insurance 상품을 출시하는 이유입니다.

여행 시에, 여행자가 보호받아야 마땅한 많은 어려움과 위험이 있습니다. [170] Backpacker Insurance 상품은 수화물 분실이나 강도의 경우에도 보상 요구를 받아 들일 것입니다. 또한 항공권이 취소되는 경우에도 환불을 요청하실 수 있습니다. Keepsafe Insurance는 만 불까지 의료비를 지원하기 때문에 응급의료의 경우에도 보장받으실 수 있습니다.

[171] Backpacker Insurance 상품에 대해 더 자세한 내용을 원하시면, 3월 18일 목요일 오후 4시 학생 대강당에서 개최되는 20분짜리 설명회에 참석하세요. 참석이 어려우시다면, 이메일 kellyfrancis@keepsafe.com를 통해 문의하시거나 1-800-3020-5939 번으로 사무실로 전화하셔서 켈리를 찾아주세요.

어휘 cover (보험)보장하다 trip abroad 해외여행 aim at ~를 표적으로 두다. specifically 특히, 한정하여 claim (보상금을) 청구하다 compensation 보상(금) theft 절도 policy 보험증권 in the event of ~의 경우에 convenient 편리한

Questions 169-171 refer to the following advertisement.

Special Announcement
To: The Editor, Bradford University's Student Magazine
From: Kelly Francis, Keepsafe Insurance
Marketing Manager
Keepsafe Insurance

These days, it can often be difficult for young people to find affordable travel insurance to cover them for vacations or trips abroad. [169] That is why we at Keepsafe Insurance are launching our new Backpacker Insurance package, which is aimed specifically at people aged eighteen to twenty-five.

When traveling, there are a number of dangers and risks that travelers need to be protected from. [170] Our Backpacker Insurance package will allow you to claim compensation in the event of theft or loss of luggage. It will also allow you to claim a refund if your flight is cancelled. The policy covers you in the event of a medical emergency as Keepsafe Insurance will pay all hospital bills up to $10,000.

[171] To find out more information about our Backpacker Insurance package, you are invited to attend my twenty-minute presentation in the student auditorium at 4 P.M. on Thursday, March 18. If this is not convenient for you, you can e-mail me with any questions at kellyfrancis@keepsafe.com or phone the office at 1-800-3020-5939 and ask for Kelly.

169

★ 세부사항

Backpacker Insurance 상품이 대상으로 하는 고객의 연령대는 어떻게 되는가?
(A) 30~40살
(B) 10~15살
(C) 18~25살
(D) 60~75살

토익 분석

고객의 연령대란 세부사항을 묻는 문제이므로 지문에서 연령대가 언급되는 부분만 빠르게 찾아 그 내용을 확인하는 것이 관건이다.

What age group is the Backpacker Insurance package designed for?
(A) 30- to 40-year-olds
(B) 10- to 15-year-olds
(C) 18- to 25-year-olds
(D) 60- to 75-year-olds

문제 해설

상품이 대상으로 하는 고객의 연령대를 묻고 있으므로 지문에서 연령이 언급되는 부분에 집중해야 할 필요가 있다. 첫 번째 단락 후반 That is why we at Keepsafe Insurance are launching our new Backpacker Insurance package, which is aimed specifically at people aged eighteen to twenty-five를 통해 Backpacker 보험상품은 18세에서 25세 사이의 고객을 대상으로 함을 알 수 있다. 따라서 정답은 (C)이다.

170

What is NOT stated as being covered by this insurance package?

(A) The cancellation of a flight
(B) Medical expenses
(C) The theft of luggage
(D) Legal bills

★★ 진위 문제

이 보험 상품으로 보상받지 못하는 것은 무엇인가?
(A) 비행편의 취소
(B) 의료 경비
(C) 수하물 도난
(D) 법정 비용

토익 분석

사실이 아닌 내용을 묻는 문제[NOT TRUE]는 선택지를 키워드로 삼아 지문에서 선택지의 내용이 언급되는지 여부만 빠르게 확인하는 방식으로 문제를 풀이하는 것이 효율적이다.

문제 해설

보험 상품이 보상하지 못하는 부분에 대한 질문이므로 보험 상품이 보장해주는 범위에 대해 구체적으로 소개하는 부분에 초점을 맞춰야 한다. 두 번째 단락에서 Our Backpacker Insurance package will allow you to claim compensation in the event of theft or loss of luggage. It will also allow you to claim a refund if your flight is cancelled. The policy covers you in the event of a medical emergency as Keepsafe Insurance will pay all hospital bills up to $10,000라고 언급하며 구체적인 보험의 보장 범위를 설명하고 있다. 이를 통해 이 보험 상품은 비행편이 취소되는 상황, 의학적 긴급한 상태가 발생하는 경우, 그리고 수화물의 도난이나 분실되는 경우까지 모두 처리해주고 있음을 알 수 있다. 그러므로 정답은 (D)가 되겠다.

171

Which of these is NOT mentioned as a way to learn more about the Backpacker Insurance package?

(A) Telephoning Kelly at the office
(B) Sending an email to Kelly
(C) Sending a letter to Kelly at her private address
(D) Attending a presentation given by Kelly

★★ 진위 문제

Backpacker Insurance상품에 대한 정보를 얻을 수 있는 방법으로 언급되지 않은 것은 무엇인가?
(A) 사무실에 있는 켈리에게 전화할 것.
(B) 켈리에게 이메일을 전송할 것.
(C) 켈리의 개인 주소로 편지를 발송한 것.
(D) 켈리가 주최하는 세미나에 참석할 것.

토익 분석

사실이 아닌 내용을 묻는 문제[NOT TRUE]는 선택지를 키워드로 삼아 지문에서 선택지의 내용이 언급되는지 여부만 빠르게 확인하는 방식으로 문제를 풀이하는 것이 효율적이다.

문제 해설

백패커 보험상품에 대한 추가 정보를 얻을 수 있는 방법으로 언급되지 않은 것을 묻고 있으므로 지문에서 백패커 보험상품에 대한 추가 정보를 얻을 수 있는 방법을 제시하고 있는 부분에 집중해야 할 필요가 있다. 맨 마지막 단락에서 you are invited to attend my twenty-minute presentation in the student auditorium at 4 P.M. on Thursday, March 18라고 언급하는 부분에서 보험 상품에 대한 발표회에 참석하는 방법, you can e-mail me with any questions at kellyfrancis@keepsafe.com에서 켈리 씨에게 이메일을 보내는 방법, 마지막으로 phone the office at 1-800-3020-5939 and ask for Kelly을 통해 직접 켈리 씨에게 전화를 거는 방법이 있음을 파악할 수 있다. 그러므로 정답은 (C)가 되겠다.

172-175 다음 기사문을 참조하시오.

Nagasaki(6월 14일) – [172] 풍경 수채화를 전문으로 하는 아티스트 **Akemi Kitagawa**는 지난 5년 동안 국내의 많은 시골 지역을 여행하면서 그림을 그려왔다. 그녀는 자신의 작품을 사진으로 촬영해 거의 매일 자신의 블로그에 올리고 있는데, www.travelandpaint.com에서 볼 수 있다.

[175] 그녀의 블로그에는 또한 여행 중에 있었던 모험들을 기록한 일기와도 같은 작품들도 있다. 그녀는 자신이 만나는 사람들, 다양한 문화 또는 마주치는 방언들을 서술하기도 하며, 길 위에서의 외로운 발걸음을 재촉하면서 느끼는 자기만의 은밀한 생각들도 공유해 나간다.

Kitagawa 씨의 사이트는 엄청난 팔로잉을 [173] 모으고 있는데, 그녀의 블로그 통계치가 하루 평균 3천 2백회의 조회 수를 보여주고 있기 때문이다. 간단한 설문조사에 응한 블로그 독자들을 보면, 이들의 최대 인구집단은 20대 중반이나 30대 초반의 여성 대졸자이다. 어느 익명의 독자가 블로그에 남긴 말이 있다, "내가 매일 여기 들르는 이유는, **Akemi**가 내가 잃어버렸다고 생각한 일종의 모험과 자기 발견의 삶을 살고 있기 때문입니다."

무엇이 자신의 블로그를 시작하게 영향을 주었냐는 질문을 받았을 때, **Kitagawa** 씨는 "솔직히 말해, 처음에는 단순히 하나의 디지털 저널로 시작된 것이에요 – 여행을 하는 동안 내 생각들을 기록하는 하나의 방법일 뿐이었죠. 제 독자들이 계속 늘어나기 시작한 후에야 저는 다른 사람들이 내가 말하는 것에 관심을 가질 수도 있다는 점을 깨달았습니다. 내 생각을 세상과 공유하는 것이 행복합니다. 그것이 아무리 개인적인 것이고 단순한 것이든 말이죠."라고 설명했다.

어휘 specialize in ~을 전문으로 하다 landscape watercolor 풍경 수채화 take photos of her pieces 자신의 작품들을 사진으로 찍다 post 게재하다 diary-like entries 일기와 유사한 글들 describe 기술하다, 설명하다 dialect 방언, 사투리 encounter 마주치다, 직면하다 while (she is) on long, lonely stretches of road 길고 외롭게 펼쳐진 길 위에 있는 동안 draw a large following 많은 팔로잉을 모으다

Questions 172-175 refer to the following article.

Nagasaki (June 14)— [172] Artist Akemi Kitagawa, who specializes in landscape watercolors, has been traveling the more rural parts of her country for the past 5 years and painting the entire time. — [1] —. She takes photos of her pieces and posts them almost daily on her blog, which can be viewed at www.travelandpaint.com.

[175] — [2] —. Also on her blog are diary-like entries recording her adventures on her travels. She describes individuals she meets as well as different cultures and dialects she encounters, and she shares her thoughts while on long, lonely stretches of road.

Ms. Kitagawa's site has [173] drawn a large following as her blog statistics report an average of 3.2 thousand hits each day. For those blog readers who agree to take a brief survey, the top demographic for these readers is female college graduates in their mid-twenties and early-thirties. — [3] —. One anonymous reader commented on the blog, "I visit here every day because Akemi is living the life I feel I missed out on — one of adventure and self-discovery."

When asked what inspired her to start her blog, Ms. Kitagawa explained, "Honestly, it first started out simply as a digital journal — a way to record my thoughts while on this journey. Only after my readership kept increasing did I realize that others would be interested in what I had to say. I'm happy to share my thoughts, however personal or simple, with the world." — [4] —.

172

★★ 주제 문제

기사의 주제는 무엇인가?
(A) 어느 화가의 개인적 경험
(B) 사진의 새로운 트렌드
(C) 일본의 다양한 문화들
(D) 일본의 시골길 여행

토익 분석

기사문의 주제/목적은 단락 구분이 있는 경우 첫 번째 단락 초반 2-3문장에서 제시된다. 다만 주제/목적 문제의 난이도가 높아지는 경우 주제/목적은 두 번째 단락의 초반 2-3문장에서 다뤄진다.

What is the subject of the article?

(A) A painter's personal experiences
(B) New trends in photography
(C) Different cultures in Japan
(D) Traveling rural roads in Japan

문제 해설

기사문(article)의 경우 주제는 보통 첫 단락에 제시되는 경우가 많다. 첫 단락의 Artist Akemi Kitagawa, who specializes in landscape watercolors, has been traveling the more rural parts of her country for the past 5 years and painting the entire time에서 풍경 수채화 화가인 Akemi Kitagawa가 5년 동안 일본을 여행했고, 여행하면서 촬영한 사진들을 블로그에 올린다는 내용을 통해 기사문의 주제는 화가의 개인적인 경험을 통한 작품 활동임을 파악할 수 있으므로 정답은 (A)가 되겠다.

173

In the article, the word "drawn" in paragraph 3, line 1, is closest in meaning to

(A) described   (B) illustrated

(C) attracted   (D) labeled

문제 해설

주어진 문장인 Ms. Kitagawa's site has drawn a large following as her blog statistics report an average of 3.2 thousand hits each day은 기타가와 씨의 사이트는 엄청난 팔로잉을 보유하고 있으며 그녀의 블로그 통계치가 하루 평균 3천 2백회의 조회 수를 보여주고 있다는 내용을 언급하고 있다. 여기서 has drawn은 많은 팔로잉을 끌어들였다는 뜻으로 쓰인 것이므로 선택지에서는 '~을 끌어들이다, ~을 모으다'란 의미를 지닌 attracted가 유사어로 적합하다. 그러므로 정답은 (C)가 되겠다.

174

What is NOT featured on Akemi Kitagawa's blog?

(A) Descriptions of her surroundings

(B) The cost of her artwork

(C) Her personal feelings

(D) Tales of her adventures

문제 해설

Akemi Kitagawa 씨의 블로그에 포함되지 않은 것을 묻는 진위 문제이나 지문 전반에 걸쳐 해당 블로그에 대한 내용이 다뤄지고 있으므로 블로그란 키워드만 파악해서는 단서를 쉽게 파악할 수 없다. 따라서 문제 풀이 시간을 줄이고자 한다면 선택지의 내용을 키워드로 활용해야 한다. 다시 말해서 선택지의 내용을 살펴본 후 지문에서 선택지의 내용이 제시되는 부분이 있는지 여부에만 집중하며 정답을 파악해야 한다. 자신 주변의 서술을 뜻하는 (A)와 그녀 개인의 감정을 뜻하는 (C)는 두 번째 단락 She describes individuals she meets as well as different cultures and dialects she encounters, and she shares her thoughts에서 다뤄지고 있으며, 자신의 모험에 대한 이야기를 뜻하는 (D)는 Also on her blog are diary-like entries recording her adventures on her travels에서 등장하고 있다. 그러므로 Akemi Kitagawa 씨의 블로그에 포함되지 않은 내용은 바로 (B)가 되겠다.

175

In which of the positions marked [1], [2], [3] and [4] does the following sentence best belong?

"Also on her blog are diary-like entries recording her adventures on her travels."

(A) [1]   **(B) [2]**

(C) [3]   (D) [4]

문제 해설

주어진 문장은 그녀의 블로그에는 또한 여행 중에 있었던 모험들을 기록한 일기와도 같은 작품들도 있다는 내용을 지니고 있다. 무엇보다 또한, 즉 also에서 이 내용은 그녀의 블로그에 담긴 또 다른 추가적인 내용을 다루고 있으므로 그녀의 블로그에 담긴 첫 번째 내용을 언급한 이후에 제시되어야 함을 파악할 수 있다. 첫 번째 단락 후반부에서 She takes photos of her pieces and posts them almost daily on her blog, which can be viewed at www.travelandpaint.com이라며 그녀는 자신의 작품을 사진으로 촬영해 거의 매일 자신의 블로그에 올리고 있는데, www.travelandpaint.com에서 볼 수 있음을 언급하며 그녀의 블로그와 블로그에 담긴 첫 번째 내용에 대해 다루고 있다. 따라서 주어진 문장은 이 문장 바로 이후에 위치해야 함을 알 수 있다. 따라서 정답은 (B)가 되겠다.

176-180 다음 광고 및 리뷰를 참조하시오.

ARTHOUSE.COM
선두적인 온라인 미술용품 소매업체

Art House는 현대 미술가가 다음 명작을 창조하는 데 필요로 하는 모든 것을 갖추고 있습니다. 다음 5일 동안만, 다음 제품을 대상으로 대폭 할인을 해드립니다.

- 여러 가지 종류의 클립아트 스텐실 12통 $7
- 브란트 이젤 가방 $27
- [178] Art House 상표의 24색 목탄 세트 $9

또한, [176] $75 이상 구매 시, 마커 세트 4통을 드립니다.

구매 물품에 대해 도움이 필요하시면, 저희 온라인 고객 서비스 직원이 도와드리겠습니다. 홈페이지 메인 화면 왼쪽 상단에 있는 고객 서비스 탭을 클릭하세요.

Art Today
미술에 필요한 모든 최신품들이 있는 곳

미술 가이드: 이달의 우수 상점

Art House는 [180] 저렴한 가격으로 물건을 살 수 있는 곳이며, 품질이 낮은 제품을 비싼 가격에 판매하는 유명한 미술용품점과는 다릅니다. Art House는 실제로 Art House만의 제품을 생산하고 있으며, 다른 인기 있는 브랜드와 함께 판매합니다. 붓에서 회반죽과 연필에 이르기까지 보다 더 다양한 제품을 사이트에서 취급합니다. [177] 보유 제품의 품질이 더 유명한 브랜드의 품질만큼 좋진 않지만, 적절한 가격의 미술용품을 필요로 하는 예술가들에게는 좋은 곳입니다.

또한, Art House는 $80 이상 구매시 배송비 할인을 해드립니다. [179] 하지만 Art House가 대부분 직접 배송을 하기 때문에, 고객에게 배송 완료되기까지 시간이 훨씬 더 오래 걸릴 것입니다. 하지만 저렴한 가격은 기다릴 만한 가치가 있습니다. 홈페이지인 www.arthouse.com을 방문하셔서 다양한 좋은 제품들을 확인하세요.

어휘 leading ~을 선도하는 art supply retailer 미술용품 판매업체 masterpiece 명작 deep discounts 큰 할인 혜택 assorted 다양한 charcoal 석탄 erase ~을 지우다 assistance 도움 customer service representative 고객 상담원 assist ~를 돕다 at the top left of ~이 상단 좌측에 deal 거래 be different from ~과 다른 well-known 유명한 art supply store 미술용품 상점 quality products 좋은 품질의 제품 produce ~을 생산하다 along with ~과 함께 popular brand 유명한 브랜드 a growing selection of 선택의 폭이 넓은, 점차 다양해지는 range from A to B A에서 B에 이르는 범위 affordable 적절한 가격의, 저렴한 가격의 ship ~을 배송하다 lower 더 낮은, ~을 낮추다, ~을 인하하다 be worth ~가 가치가 있다 hundreds of 수백 개의

Questions 176-180 refer to the following advertisement and review.

ARTHOUSE.COM
the leading online art supply retailer

Art House has everything the modern artist needs to create their next great masterpiece. For the next five days only, we are offering deep discounts on...

- 12 pack assorted clipart stencils $7
- Brandt easel-carrying case $27
- [178] Art House brand 24 color charcoal set $9

Also, [176] with purchases of $75 or more, customers receive a 4 pack of dry erase markers.

If you need any assistance with your purchases, let one of our online customer service representatives assist you. Just click the customer service tab at the top left of our main page.

Art Today
Your place for the latest on everything for art

An art guide: Featured store of the month

Art House is a great place to find good [180] deals and is different from the well-known art supply stores that often have higher prices and lower quality products. Art House actually produces some of its own products and sells them along with other popular brands. They have a growing selection of items on their site ranging from brushes to plaster and pencils. [177] The quality of their products is not as high as some of the more popular brands, but for artists that need more affordable supplies, this is the place to go.

Also, Art House offers discounts on shipping with purchases over $80. [179] However, since they do most of their shipping themselves, it takes a lot longer for customers to get their items. But the lower prices are worth the wait. Visit their Web site at www.arthouse.com for hundreds of great deals.

176

What special offer is being advertised?

(A) Canvases for half price
(B) A gift with the purchase of $75
(C) Free shipping on all purchases
(D) A discount on all coloring supplies

문제 해설

광고의 주제를 묻는 문제이므로 광고문 초반에서 제시되는 광고 대상에 집중해야 한다. 광고 초반 with purchases of $75 or more, customers receive a 4 pack dry erase board markers라고 언급한 부분을 통해 75 달러 이상 구매 시에 사은품으로 보드마커를 제공하는 특별 할인이 포함된 광고임을 알 수 있으므로 정답은 (B)가 되겠다.

★ 광고 주제

어떠한 특별 할인이 광고되고 있는가?
(A) 반값의 캔버스
(B) $75 구매시 사은품
(C) 모든 구매품의 무료 배송
(D) 모든 채색용품의 할인

토익 분석

광고의 주제/목적은 광고문 제목과 광고문 초반 2문장 내용을 통해 파악해라.

177

What is suggested about Art House?

(A) It is attractive to artists who need to save.
(B) It does not advertise in newspapers and magazines.
(C) It has more than one store location.
(D) It allows only a certain number of purchases each day.

문제 해설

Art House에 대해 유추할 수 있는 내용을 묻고 있으므로 이를 위해서는 Art House에 관한 직접적인 정보를 파악하는 것이 선행되어야 한다. 그러나 지문 전반에 걸친 내용이 Art House에 관한 내용이므로 이를 모두 파악한 후 유추를 하게 된다면 상당한 시간이 소요될 것임이 분명하다. 따라서 이 경우 선택지에 나온 내용을 먼저 파악한 후 선택지의 내용을 추론할 수 있는 근거가 지문에 제시되는지 여부를 역으로 확인하는 방식으로 문제를 풀이하는 것이 바람직하다.

두 번째 지문인 평론의 첫 번째 단락 하단에서 The quality of their products is not as high as some of the more popular brands, but for artists that need more affordable supplies, this is the place to go라고 언급하면서 저렴한 가격의 미술용품을 원하는 미술가들이 좋아할 만한 장소라고 설명하고 있으므로, 이를 토대로 돈을 절약해야 하거나 궁핍한 미술가들이 선호할 만한 장소임을 유추할 수 있다. 따라서 정답은 (A)임을 알 수 있다.

★★★ 유추

Art House에 대해 유추할 수 있는 것은 무엇인가?
(A) 절약해야 하는 미술가들에게 매력적이다.
(B) 신문이나 잡지에는 광고되지 않는다.
(C) 한 곳 이상의 상점이 있다.
(D) 매일 특정한 구매 횟수가 정해져 있다.

토익 분석

유추 문제의 키워드가 지문 전반에 걸쳐 언급되고 있는 상태에서 적절한 유추 내용을 파악해야 한다면 선택지에 나온 내용을 먼저 파악한 후 선택지의 내용을 유추할 수 있는 근거가 지문에 제시되는지 여부를 역으로 확인하는 방식으로 문제를 풀이해라.

178

★ 세부사항

광고된 제품 중 어떠한 제품이 **Art House**가 제작한 것인가?

(A) 스텐실
(B) 이젤 가방
(C) 목탄 세트
(D) 보드 마커

토익 분석

선택지에 나온 네 가지 제품을 먼저 살펴 본 후 지문에서 해당 제품이 등장하고 있는지 여부를 빠르게 확인하는 방식으로 문제를 풀이하라.

Which of the advertised products is produced by Art House?

(A) The stencils
(B) The easel case
(C) The charcoal set
(D) The markers

문제 해설

광고 중인 제품 중에서 Art House가 제작한 제품이 무엇인지 묻는 문제이다. Art House 광고문의 제품 목록에 Art House brand 24 color charcoal set가 등장하고 있으므로 Art House가 제작한 제품은 바로 목탄 세트임을 알 수 있다. 그러므로 정답은 (C)이다.

179

★★ 세부사항

평론가가 **Art House**의 단점으로 언급한 것은 무엇인가?
(A) 낮은 수준의 고객 서비스
(B) 많은 제품의 비싼 가격
(C) 제품을 수령하기까지의 소요 시간
(D) 덜 다양한 붓의 종류

토익 분석

선택지에 나온 네 가지 단점을 먼저 살펴 본 후 지문에서 해당 단점이 언급되는 부분이 있는지 여부를 빠르게 확인하는 방식으로 문제를 풀이해라.

What does the reviewer consider a disadvantage of Art House?

(A) The low quality of its customer service
(B) The high cost of many of its products
(C) The time it takes to receive its products
(D) The smaller selection of brushes

문제 해설

평론가가 Art House의 단점으로 지적한 사항에 대해 묻고 있으므로 평론을 중심으로 Art House에 대한 부정적 내용이 제시되는 부분을 신속하게 찾아야 한다. 논평의 두 번째 단락 초반 However, since they do most of their shipping themselves, it takes a lot longer for customers to get their items에서 Art House가 배송을 직접 하기 때문에 배송시간이 유독 길다는 점을 밝히고 있으므로 정답은 (C)라고 할 수 있다.

180

★★★ 유사어

논평에서, 첫 번째 단락 첫 번째 줄의 "deals"와 의미상 가장 유사한 단어는 무엇인가?
(A) 다량
(B) 염가 판매
(C) 계약
(D) 타협

토익 분석

유사어 문제는 해당 어휘가 포함된 문장을 비롯하여 그 전후 문장 내용을 파악한 후 해당 어휘와 유사한 의미를 지닌 어휘를 선택해라. 유사어 문제는 다른 문제보다 먼저 풀이하는 것도 가능하다.

In the review, the word "deals" in paragraph 1, line 2, is closest in meaning to

(A) quantities
(B) bargains
(C) contracts
(D) compromises

문제 해설

주어진 문장 내에서 deals는 저렴한 가격으로 좋은 제품을 구매하는 거래란 뜻으로 등장하고 있으므로 이에 대한 동의어로는 bargains가 적절하다고 할 수 있다. 그러므로 정답은 (B)이다.

Questions 181-185 refer to the following e-mails.

To: Dearan Reagan <dreagan@CMT/Intl.com>
From: Rebecca Dawson <rebecca.moore@CMT/Intl.com>
Date: October 18
Subject: Recommendations

Dearan,

[181] I just learned that you went on a trip to Ho Chi Minh a few months ago. I hope you don't mind my e-mailing to ask a few questions. I was hoping for a little bit of advice about conducting business there. From what I understand, a lot of your business takes you all over East and Central Asia. Any tips you can give me would be a huge help. [182] This is my first trip as section director, and I'm eager to make a good first impression.

Thanks for everything, and [183] good luck with your sales meeting this Friday Hope to hear back from you soon.

Sincerely,
Rebecca Dawson

To: Rebecca Dawson <rebecca.moore@CMT/Intl.com>
From: Dearan Moore <dmoore@CMT/Intl.com>
Date: October 19
Subject: Re: Recommendations

Rebecca,

I'd be happy to help you in any way that I can. Well, I can gather that you will most likely do a bit of research about Ho Chi Minh before you depart. [184] I would suggest seeing a few cultural sites or something of historical significance right when you arrive. This will give you a few topics of conversation with the business contacts you will be meeting there.

Also, remember that the traffic laws there are very different from back at home, and people don't pay as much attention to pedestrians as in other places I've been to. [184] Be sure to leave plenty of time in advance to get to meetings and appointments. The traffic is out-of-control and a little bit unnerving to maneuver around.

If you have any other questions, let me know. [183] I'm trying to deliver a great presentation this Friday. I feel confident, but I'm not [185] counting on anything yet. I still have some more things to prepare for it. I hope to wrap it up by the end of the day

[184] Have a safe trip and enjoy yourself. Vietnam, it's a beautiful country.

Dearan

181-185 다음 이메일을 참조하시오.

수신: Dearan Reagan <dreagan@CMT/Intl.com>
발신: Rebecca Dawson <rebecca.moore@CMT/Intl.com>
날짜: 10월 18일
제목: 추천

Dearan,

[181] 당신이 몇 달 전 호치민 출장을 다녀왔다는 사실을 이제 막 알게 되었습니다. 문의차 이렇게 보내드리는 메일에 양해 부탁드립니다. 저는 그 곳에서 사업을 펼치는 것에 대해 약간의 조언을 듣고자 합니다. 제가 이해한 바로는, 당신이 동아시아에서 중앙아시아까지 사업차 곳곳을 다니신다고 들었습니다. 해주실 만한 조언이 있다면 저에게 큰 도움이 될 수 있을 것입니다. [182] 이번에 제가 지역 담당 이사로써 처음으로 출장하는 것이라 좋은 첫 인상을 만들 수 있기를 바랍니다.

감사드리며, [183] 이번 주 금요일에 있을 영업회의에서 좋은 성과를 거두시길 바랍니다. 그럼 회신 기다리겠습니다.

진심을 담아,
Rebecca Dawson

어휘 go on a trip to ~로 여행가다 mind -ing ~을 꺼리다 a little bit of 약간의 conduct business 사업을 하다 East Asia 동아시아 Central Asia 중앙아시아 be eager to ~하기를 열망하다 first impression 첫인상 hear back from ~로부터 답을 듣다

수신: Rebecca Dawson <rebecca.moore@CMT/Intl.com>
발신: Dearan Moore <dreagan@CMT/Intl.com>
날짜: 10월 19일
제목: 답장: 추천

Rebecca,

제가 어떤 방법으로든 도와드릴 수 있다면 기꺼이 도와드리겠습니다. 출발 전에 호치민에 대해 어느 정도 조사를 해 보시리라 생각합니다. [184] 도착하시면 몇몇 문화 유적이나 역사적으로 중요한 장소 등을 방문해 보시길 권해 드립니다. 현지에서 만날 사업 관계자들과 대화하실 때 대화의 화제로 사용하실 수 있을 것입니다.

또한, 현지의 교통법이 우리나라와 많이 다르다는 것을 잊지 마시기 바랍니다. 사람들이 다녀 본 다른 곳만큼 보행자들에게 주의를 기울이지 않습니다. [184] 회의나 약속에 가실 때 충분한 시간을 가지고 출발하십시오. 교통 체증이 상당히 심각하며 이동하는 것이 뜻대로 잘 되지 않습니다.

다른 질문이 있으시면 알려 주십시오. [183] 이번 금요일에 중요한 프리젠테이션을 할 예정이며 회의에 대해 상당히 자신감이 있습니다. 하지만 아직은 아무것도 [185] 확신하지는 않습니다. 아직 준비할 것들이 좀 남아 있습니다. 오늘 퇴근 전에 마무리할 예정입니다.

[184] 안전한 여행 하시고 즐거운 시간 보내십시오. 베트남, 아름다운 나라입니다.

Dearan

어휘 gather 이해하다 most likely 아마도 depart 출발하다 cultural site 문화 유적지 of significance 중요한 business contacts 사업상 인맥 traffic law 교통법 pay attention to ~에 주의를 기울이다 as much ~ as … … 만큼 ~한 pedestrian 보행자 be sure to 반드시 ~하다 out-of-hand 감당할 수 없는 unnerving 무기력하게 하는 maneuver 잘 처리하다 deliver a presentation 발표하다 wrap up 마무리짓다

★★ 지문의 목적/주제

Dawson 씨가 이메일을 발송한 주된 이유는 무엇인가?
(A) 다가오는 영업 회의에 대해 물어보기 위해서
(B) 호치민의 관광 명소에 대해 물어보기 위해서
(C) 사업 회의에 대해 동료에게 물어보기 위해서
(D) 호치민 시로 출장 가는 것에 대한 조언을 구하기 위해서

토익 분석

이메일의 주제/목적은 이메일 초반 2~3문장의 내용을 통해 파악할 수 있으며 주제/목적 문제의 선택지들은 굳이 먼저 읽어볼 필요가 없다.

What is the main reason of Ms. Dawson's e-mail?

(A) To ask about an upcoming sales meeting

(B) To inquire about tourist attractions in Ho Chi Minh

(C) To ask a colleague about a business meeting

(D) To request advice about a business trip to Ho Chi Minh

문제 해설

첫 번째 이메일의 첫 번째 단락 초반 I just learned that you went on a trip to Ho Chi Minh a few months ago. I hope you don't mind my e-mailing to ask a few questions. I was hoping for a little bit of advice about conducting business there을 통해 Dawson 씨는 호치민 시로 출장을 가기에 앞서 먼저 다녀온 Reagan 씨에게 호치민 시에 대해 미리 알아보고자 이메일을 보냈음을 알 수 있으며 덧붙여 사업 회의에 대한 문의가 아님에 혼동하지 않도록 한다. 그러므로 정답은 (D)가 되겠다.

182

★★★ 유추

Dawson 씨에 대해 암시되는 것은 무엇인가?
(A) 그녀는 다음 달에 아시아의 다른 도시로 이사할 것이다.
(B) 그녀는 막 새로운 직책을 맡았다.
(C) 그녀는 베트남을 여러 번 방문한 적이 있다.
(D) 그녀는 최근 Reagan 씨와 알게 되었다.

토익 분석

유추 문제의 키워드가 지문 전반에 걸쳐 언급되고 있는 상태에서 적절한 유추 내용을 파악해야 한다면 선택지에 나온 내용을 먼저 파악한 후 선택지의 내용을 유추할 수 있는 근거가 지문에 제시되는지 여부를 역으로 확인하는 방식으로 문제를 풀이해라.

What is suggested about Ms. Dawson?

(A) She will move to another country in Asia next month.

(B) She just started a new position.

(C) She has visited Vietnam several times.

(D) She has just been introduced to Mr. Reagan.

문제 해설

Dawson 씨는 첫 번째 이메일의 첫 번째 단락 하단에서 This is my first trip as section director, and I'm eager to make a good first impression라고 말하며 그 곳으로의 출장이 구역 담당 이사로서 처음이기 때문에 첫 인상을 잘 남겨야 한다는 바람을 언급하고 있다. 따라서 이를 토대로 Dawson 씨는 이 직책을 맡게 된 지 얼마 되지 않았음을 추론할 수 있으므로 정답은 (B)가 되겠다.

183

★★★ 두 지문 연계 문제

Reagan 씨가 이메일에서 그의 사업 거래에 대해 언급한 이유는 무엇인가?
(A) Dawson 씨가 한 언급에 대답하기 위해서
(B) 거래의 성사를 축하하기 위해서
(C) Dawson 씨가 회의의 일원이 되는 것을 허락하기 위해서
(D) 사전 조사의 중요성을 강조하기 위해서

토익 분석

• 이중지문에서는 이메일 + 이메일, 즉 편지류 + 편지류 형태의 구성의 출제 비중이 가장 높다.
• 이메일을 포함한 편지류의 경우, 수신자 / 발신자를 비롯, 날짜와 제목까지 모두 읽도록 한다.
• 두 지문 연계 유형의 문제는 대부분 4번째 문제나 5번째 문제로 출제되고 있으므로 이들을 풀이할 때는 두 번째 지문을 먼저 살펴본 후 첫 번째 지문으로 접근하며 단서를 파악하는 것이 효율적이다.

Why does Mr. Reagan mention his business dealings in his e-mail?

(A) To address a comment made by Ms. Dawson

(B) To celebrate the closing of a deal

(C) To invite Ms. Dawson to be a part of the meeting

(D) To emphasize the importance of advance research

문제 해설

두 번째 이메일 세 번째 단락 초반 I'm trying to deliver a great presentation this Friday. I feel confident, but I'm not counting on anything yet. I still have some more things to prepare for it. I hope to wrap it up by the end of the day라고 이야기하는 부분을 통해 Reagan 씨는 본인의 영업회의에 대한 사업 상의 업무를 언급하고 있음을 알 수 있으며, 그 이유는 첫 번째 이메일 말미에서 Dawson 씨가 good luck with your sales meeting this Friday라고 말하며 금요일에 있을 레이건 씨의 영업 회의가 잘되길 바란다는 바람을 밝혔기 때문이므로 정답은 (A)라고 할 수 있다.

184

What is NOT one of Mr. Reagan's suggestions?

(A) Visit some cultural and historical sites
(B) Be on time for business meetings
(C) Have a good time
(D) Be difficult with clients to earn respect

문제 해설

두 번째 이메일의 두 번째 단락 중단 I would suggest seeing a few cultural sites or something of historical significance right when you arrive에서 문화 유적지를 방문하도록 제안하고 있으며 세 번째 단락 중단 Be sure to leave plenty of time in advance to get to meetings and appointments 에선 교통 사정이 좋지 않으니 일찍 출발하여 약속시간에 맞춰 정시에 도착하도록 조언하고 있다. 아울러 마지막 단락에선 Have a safe trip and enjoy yourself라고 언급하며 즐거운 시간을 보내도 록 하라고 제안하고 있다. 따라서 정답은 (D)임을 알 수 있다.

★★★ 진위

Reagan 씨의 제안 사항이 아닌 것은 무엇인가?
(A) 문화 및 역사 유적지에 방문할 것
(B) 사업 회의에 정시에 도착할 것
(C) 좋은 시간을 보낼 것
(D) 존경을 받기 위해 고객에게 까다롭게 굴 것

토익 분석

사실이 아닌 내용[NOT TRUE]을 묻는 문제는 선택지 내용 을 파악한 후 지문의 내용과 대조하며 사실 가능성이 적 은 선택지를 오답으로 소거하며 정답을 찾아내는 방식으 로 풀이하라.

185

In the second e-mail, the phrase "counting on" in paragraph 3, line 2, is closest in meaning to

(A) being certain of
(B) coming up with
(C) measuring up to
(D) keeping records of

문제 해설

주어진 문장에서 counting on은 확신한다는 의미로 사용되었으므로 이와 유사한 표현으로는 being certain of가 무난하다고 할 수 있다. 따라서 정답은 (A)가 되겠다.

★★ 동의어

두 번째 이메일에서, 두 번째 단락 두 번째 줄의 "counting on"과 의미상 가장 유사한 표현은 무엇인가?
(A) 확신하는
(B) 고안하는
(C) 달하는
(D) 기록하는

토익 분석

유사어 문제는 해당 어휘가 포함된 문장을 비롯하여 그 전후 문장 내용을 파악한 후 해당 어휘와 유사한 의미를 지닌 어휘를 선택해라.

Banshee 시
평생 교육 강좌 – 8월

다양한 교육 강좌들이 현재 [187(C)] Banshee 지역 내 [187(A)] 18세 이상의 모든 주민들께 공개되어 있습니다. 수업은 별도의 공지가 있지 않는 한 Banshee 전문 대학교의 캠퍼스에서 시작될 것입니다. 등록과 [187(B)] 수강료, 그리고 지불 방식과 관련된 추가 정보를 보시려면, 다음 페이지로 가시기 바랍니다.

[188] 부동산 관련 허가증 취득 방법
월요일, 오후 6시~9시
본관, 112호실
[188] 강사: Judy Elena, 전국 부동산 협회

소기업 경영
월요일, 오후 7시~9시
일반 도서관, 306호실
강사: Kelly Hamilton, 소기업 개발 전문가

사진 촬영 기술
화요일, 오후 7시~9시
본관, 112호실
강사: Britney Hannah, 프리랜서 사진가

차량 관리
9월 22일과 24일, 오전 9시~오후 1시
Banshee 직업 고등학교
강사: [186] Robert Juilan, Juilan Brothers 자동차 정비소

어휘 continuing education 평생 교육 a variety of 다양한 resident 주민 tuition 수업 unless otherwise noted 별도의 공지가 없는 한 enrollment 등록 fee 수업료, 요금 method 방법 how to do ~하는 법 real estate 부동산 run ~을 운영하다 small business 소기업 photography 사진 촬영(술) vehicle 차량 care 관리, 돌봄

---

[188] 수신: Williams Hutchson ⟨whutchson@hauzenmail.com⟩
발신: Jammy Osar ⟨Joscar@banshee.gov⟩
제목: 수업 일정 연기
날짜: 8월 23일

Hutchson 씨께:

[188, 189] Elena 씨가 꼭 참여해야 하는 행사로 인해 수업이 연기되었다는 사실을 모든 분께 연락드릴 것을 말씀하셨는데요, 곧 일정이 재조정될 것입니다. [190] 재조정된 날짜를 알게 되는 대로, 이메일로 여러분께 연락드리고 새 주차증을 보내 드릴 예정인데, 이는 현재 소유하고 계신 것이 곧 만료되기 때문입니다. 불편을 끼쳐 드려 사과 드립니다.

안녕히 계십시오.

Jammy Oscar
평생 교육과
Banshee 시청

어휘 postpone ~을 연기하다 contact ~에게 연락하다 let A know that A에게 ~라고 알리다 because of ~ 때문에 urgent 긴급한 participate in ~에 참여하다 reschedule ~의 일정을 재조정하다 parking permit 주차증 possess ~을 소유하다 expire 만료되다 inconvenience 불편함

The City of Banshee
Local Lifelong Education Classes - August

A variety of education classes are now [187(C)] open to all residents of Banshee [187(A)] ages eighteen or over. Classes will be held at the Banshee Community College campus unless otherwise noted. [187(B)] For more information on enrollment, fees, and payment methods, please go to the next page.

[188] How to Get a Real Estate License
Mondays, 6 P.M.—9 P.M.
Main Hall, Room 112
[188] Instructor: Judy Elena, from National Real Estate Association

Running a Small Business
Mondays, 7 P.M.—9 P.M.
General Library, Room 306
Instructor: Kelly Hamilton, Small Business Developer

Photography Techniques
Tuesdays, 7 P.M.—9 P.M.
Main Hall, Room 112
Instructor: Britney Hannah, Freelance photographer

Vehicle Care
August 22 and 24, 9 A.M.—1 P.M.
Banshee Vocational High School
Instructor: [186] Robert Juilan, from Juilan Brothers Auto Repair

---

[188] To: Williams Hutchson <whutchson@hauzenmail.com>
From: Jammy Oscar <Joscar@banshee.gov>
Subject: Class postponed
Date: August 23

To Mr. Hutchson

[188, 189] Ms. Elena told me to contact everyone to let them know that the class has been postponed because of an event she must participate in. It will be rescheduled soon. [190] As soon as we find out the rescheduled date, we will contact you via e-mail and send a new parking permit, because the one you have now will expire soon. Sorry for the inconvenience.

Regards,

Jammy Oscar
Department of Local Lifelong Education
City Government of Banshee

Banshee Community Parking Permit
ALTERNATIVE PASS FOR TODAY ONLY

LOT A
[190] Valid: August 27
Time Stamp: 6:45 P.M.

*This must be displayed on the front side of your vehicle window and be visible from the outside.

Banshee Community 주차증
오늘 하루에 한하는 대체 출입증

주차장 A
[190] 유효일: 8월 27일
스탬프 시간: 오후 6:45

* 이 주차증은 반드시 차량 앞 유리 쪽에 게시되어 외부에서 보일 수 있도록 해야 합니다.

어휘 alternative 대체의 pass 출입증 lot 주차장 valid 유효한 display ~을 진열하다, 전시하다 visible 눈에 보이는, 알아볼 수 있는

186

Who most likely is Robert Juilan?

(A) A college professor
(B) A city official
(C) A high school teacher
(D) A local entrepreneur

문제 해설

Robert Juilan 씨의 이름은 첫 지문의 맨 마지막에 찾아 볼 수 있으며, '자동차 정비소의 Robert Juilan'이라는 표기를 통해 해당 업체의 소유주인 것으로 판단할 수 있다. 따라서 이와 같은 의미에 해당되는 것으로 '지역 기업가'를 의미하는 (D)가 정답이다.

★★ 유추 / Robert Julian 씨의 정체

Robert Julian 씨는 누구이겠는가?
(A) 대학 교수
(B) 시 당국자
(C) 고등학교 교사
(D) 지역 기업가

토익 분석

인물 유추는 인물의 정체를 유추할 수 있는 관련 어휘나 표현을 파악하는 것이 관건이다.

187

What is NOT indicated about participants in the Continuing Education Classes?

(A) They must be at least eighteen years old.
(B) They are required to pay a registration fee.
(C) They should be residents of Banshee.
(D) They are graduates from Banshee Community College.

문제 해설

첫 지문의 첫 단락에서 (A)에 제시된 '최소 18세'라는 나이 기준은 ages eighteen or over 부분에, 같은 단락의 (B)에서 말하는 등록비 지불은 For information on enrollment, fees, and payment methods ~ 부분에서 확인할 수 있다. 그리고 Banshee 지역의 주민이어야 한다는 조건이 제시된 (C)의 내용도 같은 단락의 open to all residents of Banshee에 나타나 있다. 하지만 Banshee 전문 대학교는 해당 강좌들이 열리는 장소로만 언급되어 있으므로 (D)가 정답이다.

★★★ 진위

평생 교육 강좌 참가자들에 관해 알 수 있는 내용이 아닌 것은 무엇인가?
(A) 반드시 최소 18세여야 한다.
(B) 등록비를 지불해야 한다.
(C) Banshee의 시민이어야 한다.
(D) Banshee 전문 대학교의 졸업생이어야 한다.

토익 분석

사실이 아닌 한 가지 내용을 묻는 진위 문제[NOT TRUE]는 선택지를 키워드로 삼아 각 선택지의 내용이 지문에서 언급되는지 여부를 파악하는 방식으로 풀이하는 것이 효율적이다.

★★★ 두 지문 연계 문제

Hutchson 씨는 무엇에 관심이 있는가?
(A) 부동산
(B) 경영
(C) 사진 촬영
(D) 차량 관리

토익 분석

• 해당 문제의 단서가 나와야 할 지문에 단서가 불충분하게 언급된다면 이는 두 지문 연계 문제이다.
• 삼중 지문의 두 지문 연계 문제는 대개 두 번째 문제와 네 번째 문제(2-4) 또는 세 번째 문제와 다섯 번째 문제(3-5)로 짝지어 출제되는 경향이 있다.
• 삼중 지문에 따른 문제에서 특정인에 대한 세부정보를 묻거나, **probably, most likely, imply**를 대동하는 유추 문제가 출제된다면 이 역시 두 지문 연계 문제이다.

What is Ms. Hutchson most likely interested in?

(A) Real estate
(B) Management
(C) Photography
(D) Car care

문제 해설

Hutchson 씨가 유일하게 등장하는 지문이 이메일이나 이메일에서 Hutchson 씨의 관심 분야가 직접적으로 언급되지 않고 있으므로 이는 두 지문 연계 문제임을 알 수 있다. 그러므로 해당 이메일에서 Hutchson 씨의 관심 분야를 파악할 수 있는 단서가 제공되는 다른 지문과의 연결 고리를 찾는 것에 집중해야 한다. 이메일에서는 Elena 씨의 수업이 연기되었다며 Ms. Elena told me to contact everyone to let them know that the class has been postponed이라고 언급하고 있으며, 첫 지문에서 이 사람의 이름이 쓰여 있는 강좌가 How to Get a Real Estate License, 즉 부동산 관련 허가증 취득 방법이므로 정답은 (A)가 되겠다.

★ 유사어

이메일에서, 1번째 단락의 2번째 줄에 있는 단어 **"participate"**과 의미가 가장 가까운 어휘는 무엇인가?
(A) 듣다
(B) 기다리다
(C) 처리하다
(D) 출석하다

토익 분석

유사어 문제는 해당 어휘가 포함된 문장을 비롯하여 그 전후 문장 내용을 파악한 후 해당 어휘와 유사한 의미를 지닌 어휘를 선택해라

In the e-mail, the word "participate" in paragraph 1, in line 2, is closest in meaning to

(A) listen to
(B) wait on
(C) take care of
(D) be present at

문제 해설

주어진 문장 내에서 participate은 긴급한 행사와 관련해 '참여하다'라는 의미를 나타낸다는 것을 알 수 있다. 따라서 '~에 출석하다'라는 의미로 쓰이는 (D)가 정답이다.

★★★ 두 지문 연계 문제

일정이 재조정된 수업은 언제 열렸는가?
(A) 8월 22일
(B) 8월 23일
(C) 8월 24일
(D) 8월 27일

토익 분석

삼중 지문 중 하나가 양식서라면 해당 양식서와 관련된 두 지문 연계 문제는 필히 출제되며 이 경우 문제를 풀이할 수 있는 가장 결정적인 단서는 양식서를 통해 제시된다.

On what date did the rescheduled class take place?

(A) August 22
(B) August 23
(C) August 24
(D) August 27

문제 해설

일정이 재조정된 수업은 언제 열렸는지 구체적인 날짜를 묻고 있으며 수업 일정 재조정과 관련된 내용은 두 번째 지문에서 제시되고 있다. 하지만 막상 수업 일정 부분에서 재조정된 날짜를 알게 되는 대로 이메일로 연락하여 새 주차증을 보내 준다며 we will contact you via e-mail and send a new parking permit라고 언급하는 내용만 등장할 뿐 일정이 재조정된 수업의 날짜가 언제인지는 등장하지 않고 있다. 따라서 두 지문 연계 문제임을 가늠할 수 있으며 나머지 절반의 단서를 파악하기 위해서는 주차증을 살펴봐야 한다. 주차증의 유효 날짜가 Valid: August 27, 즉 8월 27일로 되어 있으므로 이를 토대로 일정이 재조정된 수업은 8월 27일에 열렸음을 알 수 있다. 따라서 (D)가 정답이다.

Questions 191-195 refer to the following article and e-mails.

Facility care

At the townhall meeting on Tuesday, the Cass Town mayor looked for more options for work to be done on town facilities. According to Gamily Cruise, town clerk, [191] the expenditure for renovation of the Cass Community Center was lower than the amount that was designated for the project. Therefore, the mayor decided to come up with other smaller projects that can be done with the rest of the funds.

Some suggested projects are a paved road to the entrance of the Cass Public Library, more lights in the Public Sports Park, and new tiles in the train station. Mr. Cruise has announced that the mayor will acquire some other ideas from residents. [193] Anyone interested may contribute ideas at the council's meeting on Tuesday, June 20, at 4 P.M. or send an e-mail to the mayor's office before June 31. After reviewing public comments, the planning council will [192] put forth a final proposal for the mayor to discuss, with a decision expected by July 15.

From : hyulius@citymail.com.au
To : cassmayor@cass.org.au
Date : 25 June
Subject : extra projects

Dear Mayor and Council Members,

I heard that you are looking for suggestions for the usage of leftover money from the community center's renovation. [193] I was not able to participate in the council meeting due to an appointment, but I'd like to suggest placing more lights in the park. This plan would be more affordable than others, and it will raise the number of visitors to the Public Sports Park, especially during the winter term, [195] which will be certainly beneficial to everyone. The park is a good place for everyone, and it will be much better after being renovated. I would appreciate it if you would consider this.

Hanamori Yulius

191-195 다음 기사와 두 이메일을 참조하시오.

시설 관리

화요일에 있었던 논의에서, Cass Town의 시장은 시의 시설물에 대해 추가로 완료되어야 하는 작업에 관한 더 많은 선택사항들을 물색했다. Gamily Cruise 서기관의 말에 따르면, [191] Cass Community Center의 보수 공사에 사용된 지출 비용이 프로젝트에 지정된 것보다 더 낮았다. 따라서, 시장은 나머지 자금으로 할 수 있는 다른 소규모 계획들을 내놓기로 결정했다.

제안된 몇몇 프로젝트에는 Cass Public Library으로 들어가는 입구에 도로 포장 작업을 하는 것과 Public Sports Park에 더 많은 전등을 설치하는 것, 그리고 기차 역에 타일을 교체하는 것이 포함되어 있다. Cruise 씨는 시장이 주민들로부터 다른 의견들도 얻을 것이라고 알렸다. [193] 관심 있는 사람은 누구나 6월 20일 화요일, 오후 4시에 시 의회 회의에서 의견을 전달하거나 6월 31일 이전에 시장 집무실로 편지를 보낼 수 있다. 주민들의 의견을 검토한 후에, 기획 위원회가 시장에게 최종 제안서를 [192] 제출해 논의할 것이며, 최종 결정은 7월 15일까지 이뤄질 것으로 예상된다.

어휘 mayor 시장 decide to do ~하기로 결정하다 look for ~을 찾다 extra 추가의 according to ~에 따르면 expenditure 지출 renovation 보수, 개조 than designated 지정된 것보다 come up with ~을 내놓다, 생각해 내다 the rest of ~의 나머지 fund 자금 suggested 제안된 include ~을 포함하다 paved road 포장된 도로 place ~을 놓다, 두다 announce that ~라고 알리다, 발표하다 acquire ~을 얻다 resident 주민 council 의회 review ~을 검토하다 put forth ~을 제시하다, 제출하다 proposal 제안(서)

발신: hyulius@citymail.com.au
수신: cassmayor@cass.org.au
날짜: 6월 25일
제목: 추가 프로젝트

시장님과 의원님들께,

Community Center의 보수 공사에서 남은 자금의 활용 방안에 대한 의견을 구하고 계신다고 들었습니다. [193] 저는 선약으로 인해 시의회 회의에 참석할 수 없었지만, 공원에 더 많은 전등을 설치하는 작업을 제안하고자 합니다. 이 작업은 다른 계획들에 비해 저렴할 것이고, 특히 겨울 동안 Public Sports Park를 찾는 방문객들의 수를 늘려 줄 것이며, [195] 이는 분명히 모든 사람들에게 유익할 것입니다. 이 공원은 모든 사람들에게 좋은 장소이며, 보수된 후에는 훨씬 더 나아질 것입니다. 이 의견을 고려해 주신다면 감사하겠습니다.

Hanamori Yulius

어휘 leftover 남은 것, 나머지 participate in ~에 참여하다 due to ~로 인해 scheduled 예정된 appointment 약속, 예약 affordable (가격이) 저렴한 compared to ~와 비교해 raise ~을 늘리다, 증가시키다 the number of ~의 수, 숫자 especially 특히 certainly 분명히 beneficial 이로운, 이득이 되는 much better 훨씬 더 나은 appreciate ~에 대해 감사하다 consider ~을 고려하다

From: mlinderman@hgnetwok.co.au
To: gcruise@cass.org.au
Date: 27 June
Subject: town development

Dear Mr. Cruise,

I was happy to hear that the final renovation was successfully completed with the leftover money. [194] The community center provides activities for residents such as adolescents, parents, and children. Therefore, I would like to suggest a new project for the elderly and infirm.

The public library is the most common place for adults to gather, and the new way to the entrance can provide visitors with a nice atmosphere for them to have a conversation or wait for transportation. It would be a remarkable improvement that would be admired by everyone in Cass.
In July, when the discussion for the new plan begins, please consider my suggestion so [195] everyone can be more interested in using Cass's public facilities.

Thank you,

Michael Linderman

191

★★★ 세부사항

Cass 시가 이용 가능한 자금을 보유한 이유는 무엇인가?
(A) 시장이 한 가지 프로젝트를 취소했다.
(B) 시에서 세율을 높였다.
(C) 시민들이 돈을 기부했다.
(D) 이전의 프로젝트에 예상보다 적은 비용이 들었다.

토익 분석

- 세부사항을 묻는 문제는 질문에서 빠른 키워드(핵심
  어) 파악이 중요하다.
- Cass 시가 이용 가능한 자금을 보유한 이유를 묻는 문
  제이므로 지문의 정독이 아니라 주요 단어들만 확인하
  면서 자금과 관련된 내용이 언급되는 부분인지 아닌
  지 여부만 대략적으로 빠르게 파악하는 요령 또한 필요
  하다.
- 질문에서의 키워드는 지문에서 유사 어휘나 표현으로
  바뀔 수 있다 [funds = expenditure]

Why does the town of Cass have funds available?

(A) The mayor has canceled a project.
(B) The city has raised tax rates.
(C) Its citizens have donated money.
(D) Its previous project cost less than expected.

문제 해설

Cass 시가 이용 가능한 자금을 보유한 이유에 대해 묻는 첫 번째 문제이므로 첫 지문 초반부에
서 Cass 시의 자금 여력에 관한 정보가 언급되는 부분에 집중해야 한다. 첫 지문의 첫 단락에 the
expenditure for renovation of the Cass Community Center was lower than the amount that
was designated for the project. Therefore, the mayor decided to come up with other smaller
projects that can be done with the rest of the funds라며 Cass Community Center의 보수 공사
에 소요된 지출 비용이 지정된 비용에 비해 더 낮았기 때문에 나머지 자금으로 할 수 있는 다른 계획
들을 내놓을 것임을 밝히고 있다. 따라서 한 프로젝트에 비용이 적게 들어간 사실을 언급한 (D)가
정답이다.

192

In the article, the phrase "put forth" in paragraph 2, line 10, is the closest in meaning to,

(A) grow
(B) exert
(C) propose
(D) request

문제 해설

이 문장에서 put forth의 목적어로 최종 제안서를 뜻하는 a final proposal가 쓰여 있으므로 제출 또는 제안의 의미로 쓰였음을 알 수 있다. 따라서 '제안하다'라는 뜻으로 쓰이는 (C)가 정답이다.

★★★ 유사어

기사에서, 두 번째 단락 12번째 줄의 표현 "put forth"와 의미가 가장 가까운 어휘는 무엇인가?
(A) 기르다
(B) 발휘하다
(C) 제안하다
(D) 요청하다

토익 분석

유사어 문제는 해당 어휘가 포함된 문장을 비롯하여 그 전후 문장 내용을 파악한 후 해당 어휘와 유사한 의미를 지닌 어휘를 선택해라.

193

When did Ms. Yulius have an appointment?

(A) On June 20
(B) On June 25
(C) On June 30
(D) On July 15

문제 해설

Yulius 씨가 쓴 이메일 초반부에서 I was not able to participate in the council meeting due to an appointment 라며 예정된 약속이 있어 시 의회 회의에 참석하지 못했음을 언급하고 있으며 무엇보다 Yulius 씨가 쓴 이메일임에도 불구하고 이메일에서 선약이 잡혀 있는 날짜가 언제인지 직접적으로 다뤄지고 있지 않으므로 두 지문 연계 문제임을 알 수 있다. 선약이 잡혀 있는 날이 시 의회에서 회의가 벌어진 날과 동일하므로 시 의회에서 회의가 열린 날이 제시되는 지문을 빠르게 찾아가야 한다. 따라서 첫 지문의 두 번째 단락에서 the council's meeting on Tuesday, 20 June이라며 해당 회의의 날짜가 6월 20일임을 알려주고 있으므로 (A)가 정답임을 알 수 있다.

★★★ 두 지문 연계 문제

Yulius 씨는 언제 약속이 있었는가?
(A) 6월 20일
(B) 6월 25일
(C) 6월 30일
(D) 7월 15일

토익 분석

• 삼중 지문에 따른 문제에서 특정인에 대한 세부정보를 묻거나, **probably**, **most likely**, **imply**를 대동하는 유추 문제가 출제된다면 이 역시 두 지문 연계 문제이다.
• 해당 문제의 단서가 나와야 할 지문에 단서가 불충분하게 언급된다면 이는 두 지문 연계 문제이다

★★ 세부사항

Linderman 씨는 자신의 이메일에서 Cass Community Center에 관해 무엇을 언급하는가?
(A) 대중 교통과 가까운 곳에 위치해 있다.
(B) 주로 주민층들에 의해 이용된다.
(C) 이전에 다른 목적을 위한 역할을 했다.
(D) 그곳의 프로그램들이 연중으로 운영될 것이다.

토익 분석

• 세부사항을 묻는 문제는 질문에서 빠른 키워드(핵심어) 파악이 중요하다.
  1. 인명 / 직책 / 사물 지칭 명사
  2. 숫자 / 시간 / 장소
  3. 성질/감정 상태
  4. 동사
  5. If로 시작하는 절

• 해당 문제는 주어진 Cass Community Center이란 키워드가 언급되는 부분을 중심으로 단서를 살펴야 한다.

What does Mr. Linderman mention in his e-mail about the Cass Community Center?

(A) It is located near public transportation.
(B) It is used mainly by residents.
(C) It previously served another purpose.
(D) Its programs will run year-round.

문제 해설

Linderman 씨가 쓴 이메일인 세 번째 지문의 첫 단락에서 The Community Center provides activities for residents such as adolescents, parents and children이라며 Community Center는 청소년과 학부모들, 그리고 아이들과 같은 주민들을 위한 활동을 제공하고 있음을 밝히고 있다. 그러므로 The Community Center는 주로 주민들에 의해 이용된다는 의미를 나타내는 (B)가 정답이다.

★★★ 두 지문 연계 문제

Linderman 씨와 Yulius 씨는 어떤 점에서 의견이 일치할 것 같은가?
(A) 선정된 프로젝트가 전체 지역 사회에 유익해야 한다.
(B) 시에서 다음 프로젝트에 대해 가능한 한 적은 비용을 소비해야 한다.
(C) 시장이 지역 사회 의견을 듣는 것에 대한 마감시한을 연장해야 한다.
(D) 도서관 및 공원을 찾는 손님들이 합심해서 자금을 마련해야 한다.

토익 분석

두 사람이 서로 다른 지문을 작성했으므로 두 사람이 동의하는 의견 또는 서로 동의하지 않는 의견을 묻는 문제는 두 지문 연계 문제임을 알 수 있다.

On what point would Mr. Linderman and Ms. Yulius most likely agree?

(A) The chosen project should be beneficial to the entire community.
(B) The city should spend as little money as possible on its next project.
(C) The mayor should extend the deadline for community comments.
(D) Patrons of the library and the park should work together to raise money.

문제 해설

Yulius 씨가 쓴 두 번째 지문인 이메일 하단에서 which will be certainly beneficial to everyone이라며 시설물이 모든 사람들에게 유익할 것이라 언급하고 있고, Oish 씨가 쓴 세 번째 지문인 이메일 후반부에도 everyone can be more interested in using Cass's public facilities라며 모든 사람들이 시설물에 관심을 가질 수 있도록 해 줄 것을 언급하고 있다. 그러므로 이들은 모든 사람들에게 이득이 되어야 한다는 공통점을 다루고 있으므로 이와 같은 부분을 언급한 (A)가 정답이 된다.

Questions 196-200 refer to the following e-mail, notice, and order form.

From: John Delaffe <jd@naturalgreenfield.com>
To: Joel Stevenson <js@greenworld.com>
Subject: Delivering company
Date: August 1

Hello Mr. Stevenson,

[196] We are very happy that you have registered for deliveries of our products, including vegetables, fruits, flowers, and herbs, which are all harvested from our family-owned farm. I'm confident that our items will be better than those of our competitors. You and your customers will be satisfied with the products we provide.

[196, 197] Your store is located in an area that is not familiar to us, but we are excited to expand our business to North Shore. We appreciate your business.

Sincerely yours,
John Delaffe

STORE GREEN WORLD

NEW THIS WEEK!

August 26

Produce from Natural Greens Field

Dear Customers,
We have many new products in our produce section. You will find fresh, local fruits and vegetables that have just been harvested and are in great condition. [198] All of the items on the list below come straight from a beautiful farm in the Pateon area.

∨ Sweet potato
∨ Chili
∨ Potato
∨ Onions
∨ Rosemary, basil, thyme, and oregano

In the fall, we will be bringing products from Aeron Cycle Orchard in Rosemary. If you want to learn more about them, please contact us.

196-200 다음 이메일과, 공지 그리고 주문 양식을 참조하시오.

발신: John Delaffe ⟨jd@naturalgreenfield.com⟩
수신: Joel Stevenson ⟨js@greenworld.com⟩
제목: 배송 회사
날짜: 8월 1일

안녕하세요, Stevenson 씨,

저희 가족 소유의 농장에서 거둬 들인 채소와 과일, 꽃, 그리고 허브 등과 같은 [196] 저희 제품에 대한 배송 등록을 해 주시어 대단히 기쁩니다. 저는 저희 제품이 경쟁사의 제품들보다 더 뛰어나다고 확신합니다. 귀하 및 귀하의 고객들께서는 저희가 제공해 드리는 제품에 만족하실 것입니다.

[196, 197] 귀하의 매장은 저희에게 익숙하지 않은 지역에 위치해 있지만, 저희는 North Shore까지 사업을 확장할 수 있다는 점에 대해 기쁘게 생각합니다. 귀사와의 거래에 감사드립니다.

안녕히 계십시오.
John Delaffe

어휘 register for ~에 등록하다, 등록해 신청하다 delivery 배송 such as ~와 같은 harvest ~을 수확하다, 거둬 들이다 be confident that ~라는 점을 확신하다 competitor 경쟁사 be satisfied with ~에 만족하다 be located in ~에 위치해 있다 be familiar with ~에 익숙하다, ~을 잘 알다 expand ~을 확장하다, 확대하다 prefer ~을 선호하다 based in ~을 기반으로 하는, ~에 본사가 있는 appreciate ~에 대해 감사하다 suggestion 제안, 의견

STORE GREEN WORLD
이번 주의 신제품!
8월 26일

Natural Greens Field에서 들여 온 농산물

고객 여러분,
저희 농산물 코너의 새로 들어온 제품에 주목해 주시기 바랍니다. 여러분께서는 좋은 상태로 갓 수확된 신선한 지역 과일 및 채소들을 보시게 될 겁니다. [198] 목록에 있는 저희 모든 상품들은 Pateon 지역에 위치한 아름다운 한 농장으로부터 공급받고 있습니다.

∨ 고구마
∨ 고추
∨ 감자
∨ 양파
∨ 로즈마리, 바질, 백리향, 오레가노

가을에, 저희는 Rosemary에 위치한 Aeron Cycle Orchard 로부터 저희 제품을 들여 올 예정입니다. 이 제품들에 관해 문의하기를 원하실 경우, 저희에게 연락 주십시오.

어휘 produce 농산물 pay attention to ~에 주목하다 seek for ~을 구하다, 찾다 local 지역의, 현지의 in a good condition 좋은 상태에 있는 located adjacent to ~와 인접한 곳에 위치한 bring ~을 들여 오다 inquire about ~에 관해 문의하다

Natural Greens Field 주문서

[197] 고객: Store Green World
주문 날짜: 8월 30일
[199] 배송 날짜: 9월 3일

배송 상세 정보:
[199] 아래의 물품들을 제외하고 지난 번 주문과 동일함.
– 허브는 불필요함. 아직 많이 남아 있음.
– [200] 양파의 경우, 마대 자루에 넣어서 보내 주세요. (귀
  사에서 홈페이지에 게시한 사진 견본처럼)
– 주문 사항에 두 개의 호박을 추가해 주세요.

의견: 솔직히, 저는 전반적인 서비스에 대해 어떠한 문제
점이나 불만도 없습니다. 배송은 제때 도착하고, 기사님
은 친절하십니다. 무엇보다도, 제품의 상태는 언제나 월
등합니다.

[197] 성명: Joel Stevenson, 매니저

서명: Joel Stevenson

어휘 order form 주문서 details 상세 정보, 세부 사항
same as ~와 동일한 addition 추가(되는 것) below 아
래에 burlap bag 마대 자루 post ~을 게시하다 add A to
B A를 B에 추가하다 comment 의견 honestly 솔직히
complaint 불만 overall 전반적인 punctual 제 시간의, 시
간을 엄수하는 polite 친절한, 공손한 above all 무엇보다
도

Natural Greens Field Order Form

[197] Customer: Store Green World
Order date: August 30
[199] Delivery date: September 3

Delivery details:
[199] Same as last order except for the following:
- No herbs are needed. I still have a lot left.
- [200] For onions, please send them in burlap bags.
  (like the photo sample you've posted on the Web site)
- Add two pumpkins to the order.

Comments: Honestly, I don't have any problems or complaints about the overall
service. The delivery is punctual, and the driver is polite. Above all, the products
are always in the best condition.

[197] Name: Joel Stevenson, Manager

Signature: Joel Stevenson

196

★★★ 이메일의 목적

Delaffe 씨가 이메일을 발송한 이유는 무엇인가?
(A) 신제품을 광고하기 위해
(B) 새로운 고객을 환영하기 위해
(C) 배송 비용 견적을 요청하기 위해
(D) 정책 변경에 관한 불만을 제기하기 위해

토익 분석

지문의 주제/목적은 단락 구분이 있는 경우 첫 번째 단락
초반 2–3문장에서 제시된다. 다만 주제/목적 문제의 난
이도가 높아지는 경우 주제/목적은 두 번째 단락의 초반
2–3문장에서 다뤄진다. 아울러 주제/목적 문제의 선택지
들은 굳이 먼저 읽어볼 필요가 없다.

Why did Ms. Delaffe send the e-mail?

(A) To advertise new products
(B) To welcome a new customer
(C) To request a delivery estimate
(D) To complain about a policy change

문제 해설

Delaffe 씨가 보낸 이메일 초반에서 We are very happy that you have registered for deliveries of
our products라며 자사 제품의 배송을 신청해줘서 감사하다는 내용이 등장하고 있다. 아울러 이
메일 후반에서는 Your store is located in an area that is not familiar to us, but we are excited to
expand our business to North Shore. We appreciate your business라며 귀하의 매장은 익숙하지
않은 지역에 위치해 있지만, 노스 쇼어 지역으로 사업을 확장할 수 있다는 점에 대해 기쁘게 생각하
며 귀사와의 거래에 감사한다는 내용을 밝히고 있다. 따라서 해당 이메일은 새로운 고객의 주문에
고마움을 전달하기 위해서 발송된 것임을 알 수 있으므로 정답은 (B)가 되겠다.

197

Where is Store Green World probably located?

(A) In Auckland
(B) In North Shore
(C) In Pateon
(D) In Yerorn

문제 해설

세 번째 지문인 주문서에서 상단의 고객명 항목과 하단의 성명 부분에서 Stevenson 씨가 Store Green World에 근무한다는 것을 알 수 있다. 하지만 주문서에서 Store Green World의 위치가 구체적으로 등장하지 않고 있으며 뿐만 아니라 Store Green World의 공지문인 두 번째 지문에서도 Store Green World의 위치가 드러나지 않고 있다. 그러므로 이 문제는 두 지문 연계 문제임을 알 수 있으며 나머지 절반의 단서는 첫 번째 지문을 통해 파악해야 함을 가늠할 수 있다. 첫 번째 이메일에서 Your store is located in an area that is not familiar to us, but we are excited to expand our business to North Shore이라며 귀하의 매장은 익숙하지 않은 지역에 위치해 있지만, North Shore 지역으로 사업을 확장할 수 있다는 점에 대해 기쁘게 생각하고 있음을 밝히고 있다. 따라서 이를 통해 Stevenson 씨가 근무하는 Store Green World가 North Shore에 위치해 있음을 가늠할 수 있으므로 정답은 (B)가 되겠다.

★★★ 두 지문 연계 문제

Store Green World는 어디에 위치해 있을 것 같은가?
(A) In Auckland
(B) In North Shore
(C) In Pateon
(D) In Yerorn

토익 분석

• 해당 문제의 단서가 나와야 할 지문에 단서가 불충분하게 언급된다면 이는 두 지문 연계 문제이다.
• 구체적인 장소나 지명을 묻는 두 지문 연계 문제의 경우 첫 번째 절반의 단서가 제시되고 있는 지문에서 등장하는 장소/지명은 정답을 유도하는 오답으로 이용된다는 점에 주의한다.

198

In the notice, what is indicated about Natural Greens Field's produce?

(A) It is grown in the Pateon area.
(B) It is more healthful than other products.
(C) It will be in stock starting next month.
(D) It will be discounted for one week.

문제 해설

Natural Greens Field의 농산물에 관해 묻는 내용이므로 지문에서 Natural Greens Field가 언급되며 이 곳에서 생산되는 농산물에 대한 정보를 제시하는 부분을 빠르게 찾아가야 한다. 공지에 해당되는 두 번째 지문의 중간에서 All of the items on the list below come straight from a beautiful farm in the Pateon area 에서 Pateon이라며 Pateon 지역의 한 농장에서 재배된 농산물들이 가게로 직송되고 있다는 사실을 밝히고 있다. 따라서 이를 통해 Natural Greens Field의 농산물은 시장과 가까운 곳에 위치해 있음을 알 수 있으므로 정답은 (A)가 되겠다.

★★ 세부사항

공지에서, Natural Greens Field의 농산물에 관해 언급하고 있는 것은 무엇인가?
(A) 파테온 지역에서 재배된다.
(B) 다른 제품들보다 건강에 더 좋다.
(C) 다음 달부터 재고가 갖춰지게 될 것이다.
(D) 일주일 동안 할인될 것이다.

토익 분석

• 삼중 지문에 따른 문제에서 특정인에 대한 세부정보를 묻거나, **probably, most likely, imply**를 대동하는 유추 문제가 출제된다면 이 역시 두 지문 연계 문제이다.
• 해당 문제의 단서가 나와야 할 지문에 단서가 불충분하게 언급된다면 이는 두 지문 연계 문제이다

★★ 세부사항

Store Green World는 9월 3일에 주문하지 않은 것은 무엇인가?
(A) 감자
(B) 양파
(C) 호박
(D) 로즈메리

토익 분석

세부사항을 묻는 문제는 질문에서 빠른 키워드(핵심어) 파악이 관건이다. 해당 문제에서는 9월 3일이란 날짜가 키워드이므로 지문에서 9월 3일이 등장하는 주문서에서 단서를 파악해야 한다.

What does Store Green World NOT request to receive on September 3?

(A) Potatoes
(B) Onions
(C) Pumpkins
(D) Rosemary

문제 해설

Store Green World가 9월 3일에 수령할 수 없는 대상이 무엇인지 묻고 있다. 주문서인 세 번째 지문에서 9월 3일이 배송 날짜로 되어 있고(Delivery date: September 3), 그리고 이어서 Same as last order except for the following: - No herbs are needed. I still have a lot left라며 허브는 재고가 충분하여 불필요하니 허브를 제외하고 나머지는 지난 번 주문과 동일하다고 언급하고 있다. 따라서 정답은 (D)가 되겠다.

★★ 진위

Stevenson 씨는 주문서에서 무엇을 보여주고 있는가?
(A) 제품이 포장되는 방식에 대해 선호하는 것이 있다.
(B) 호박이 지난 주에 특히 잘 판매되었다.
(C) 배송 서비스에 대해 실망했다.
(D) 지난 주에 배송된 허브가 신선하지 않았다.

토익 분석

• 사실 내용을 묻는 문제[TRUE]의 키워드가 지문 전반에 걸쳐 언급되는 경우 선택지의 내용을 키워드로 삼아 지문에서 해당 내용이 언급되는지 여부를 빠르게 파악한다.
• 대부분 문제의 순서와 단서가 제시되는 지문의 순서가 일치하므로 4-5번째 문제는 주로 마지막 지문에서 단서가 등장한다.

What does Mr. Stevenson indicate in the order form?

(A) He has a preference for how items are packaged.
(B) Pumpkin sold particularly well last week.
(C) He was disappointed by the delivery service.
(D) The herbs delivered last week were not fresh.

문제 해설

주문서인 세 번째 지문 중간에서 For onions, please send them in burlap bag like the photo sample you've posted on the Web site라며 양파를 마대 자루에 넣어서 보내 달라는 말과 함께 홈페이지의 사진 견본처럼 특정한 포장 방식으로 배송해줄 것을 요청하고 있다. 따라서 이와 같은 요청 사항을 언급한 (A)가 정답이다.

해설서

★★ 어휘 / 전치사

새로운 연구 센터는 날씨, 지진 및 환경에 관한 정보를 제공하고자 건설되었다.

문제 분석

provide sby (with sth) = provide sth (for/to sby) ~에게 ~을 제공하다

어휘 research center 연구센터 construct ~을 건설하다 provide ~을 제공하다 earthquake 지진 environment 환경 regarding ~에 관해 besides 게다가, 덧붙여 along ~을 따라 pending 미정의, 계류중인

The new research center was constructed to provide information ------- weather, earthquakes, and the environment.

(A) regarding
(B) besides
(C) along
(D) pending

문제 해설

빈칸에 적합한 전치사를 묻는 문제이다. 빈칸 앞에 정보를 뜻하는 information이란 명사가 등장하고 있고 빈칸 뒤에는 weather, earthquakes and the environment, 즉 날씨, 지진 및 환경이라는 소재가 등장하고 있으므로 빈칸에는 해당 정보가 무엇에 관한 정보인지 알려줄 수 있도록 '~에 관한'이란 뜻을 지닌 전치사인 regarding이 적절하다.

토익 분석

전치사를 비롯한 어휘 공부를 할 때 꼭 염두에 둬야 하는 것은 ETS라는 출제자가 바보가 아닐진대 가장 기본적인 어휘만 익히고 정기 토익을 보러 가는 것은 아무 의미도 없이 ETS에 로열티만 제공함으로써 국부 유출에 일조하는 것과 다를 것이 없다는 것이다. 무엇보다 '~에 관해'란 뜻을 지닌 전치사는 모든 전치사 중에서 지금까지 출제비중이 가장 높았던 전치사라는 점을 고려하며 기본적으로 about 외에도 동일한 의미를 지닌 regarding / concerning / as to / as for / pertaining to 까지 숙지하도록 한다.

★★★ 재귀대명사

Wilson 씨의 바쁜 일정으로 인해, 그녀는 자신의 업무 일부를 자신이 하는 대신 그녀의 직장동료들에게 위임하였다.

어휘 delegate 대표, 대표단, ~에게 위임하다 colleague 직장 동료

Due to her busy schedule, Ms. Wilson delegated some of her work to her colleagues instead of completing it -------.

(A) she
(B) her
(C) hers
(D) herself

문제 해설

빈칸에 적합한 대명사를 묻는 문제로 빈칸이 전치사구 instead of completing it 뒤에 위치하고 있다. 전치사구 뒤 동명사 completing의 주어는 Wilson 씨이며 it은 동명사 completing의 목적어이므로 빈칸에는 수식어인 부사 역할을 행할 수 있는 대명사가 필요하다. 따라서 빈칸에는 대명사 중 유일하게 부사 역할이 가능한 재귀대명사 herself가 와야 한다.

토익 분석

재귀대명사는 대명사임에도 불구하고 유일하게 수식어(부사)의 역할을 할 수 있으며 아울러 정기 토익에서는 S + V + O + oneself(oneselves) / to Vr + O + oneself(oneselves) / V-ing + O + oneself(oneselves) 구조에서 수식어로 쓰이는 재귀대명사의 용례를 묻는다는 점을 필히 기억하도록 한다.

103 ──

According to the local history record, the Manor of Southstead was constructed
------- 420 years ago.

(A) approximate
(B) approximation
(C) approximately
(D) approximated

문제 해설

빈칸에 적합한 어형을 묻는 문제이다. 빈칸에 앞서 등장하고 있는 the Manor of Southstead was
constructed은 수동태이며, 수동태는 완전한 구조의 절이므로 빈칸에는 완전한 구조의 절과 함께
쓰일 수 있는 수식어, 즉 부사가 필요하다. 따라서 빈칸에는 부사 어형인 approximately가 와야 한
다.

토익 분석

주어진 the Manor of Southstead was constructed가 완전한 구조라 할 수 있는 수동태이므로 빈칸
에는 수식어인 부사가 위치해야 함을 구조적으로 알 수 있다. 또는 숫자를 수식하는 것은 부사만 가
능하므로 숫자 420 앞에는 '대략, 약'이란 뜻을 지닌 approximately란 부사 어형이 와야 한다는 방
식으로 문제를 풀이할 수도 있다.

그 지역 역사 기록에 따르면, Southstead 장원은 420년
전에 건설되었다고 한다.

어휘 construct ~을 건설하다 approximate 대강의, 비슷
한, 가까운 approximation 어림짐작 approximately 대략,
약

104 ──

------- submitting all of your related documents, please check all of your
information and be sure that it is correct.

(A) Since
(B) Unless
(C) Despite
(D) Prior to

문제 해설

빈칸 뒤에 submitting all of your related documents라는 구가 등장하고 있으므로 빈칸에는 전치
사가 위치해야 한다. 서류에 기입한 정보를 확인하고 그 내용이 정확한지 살펴보는 것은 서류를 제
출하기에 앞서 이뤄져야 하는 과정이므로 빈칸에는 '이전에, 앞서'란 뜻을 지닌 전치사 prior to가 와
야 한다.

토익 분석

출제 빈도가 높은 전치사들은 역시 동일한 의미를 지니고 있는 다른 전치사들을 함께 묶어서 알아
둬야 한다. 이를테면 전후 시점을 나타내는 전치사의 경우 before/after만 익힌 상태에서 정기 토익
을 보게 될 경우 주어진 문제에 적절한 전치사가 before 혹은 after이란 걸 파악해도 막상 문제를 풀
지 못하게 되는 안타까운 상황에 직면할 수도 있다. 많은 분들이 before/after을 굉장히 쉽게만 여기
지만 평이하다고 무시하다가 맞게 되는 뒤통수가 제일 아프다는 점을 잊지 않도록 한다. 따라서 필
히 before = prior to / after = following을 함께 숙지하도록 한다.

귀하의 모든 관련 서류를 제출하기 전에, 귀하가 기입한
모든 정보를 확인하고 그 내용이 정확한지 명확하게 해야
합니다.

문제 분석
prior to = before – '~전에'

어휘 submit ~을 제출하다 related 관련된 completely 완
전하게, 전적으로 correct 정확한

105

★ 어형 / 형용사

British Petrochemicals 사는 북해 근처 지역에 상업적으로 가스를 생산할 수 있는 첫 번째 시설을 건설하였다.

어휘 petrochemical 석유 화학 facility 시설 commercially 상업적으로 produce ~을 생산하다 the North Sea 스코틀랜드 지역 북해

The British Petrochemicals built the first ------- facility to commercially produce gas near the North Sea.

(A) local
(B) locals
(C) locally
(D) localize

문제 해설

빈칸에 적합한 어형을 묻는 문제로 빈칸이 '시설'을 뜻하는 명사인 facility 앞에 위치하고 있으므로 빈칸에는 형용사 어형이 와야 한다. 따라서 빈칸에는 '지역의'란 뜻을 지닌 형용사 local이 적합하다.

토익 분석

그간 정기 토익에서 local과 관련된 어휘/어형 문제로 출제될 때는 대부분 형용사인 local이 주로 정답으로 등장했지만 간간히 해당 지역 사람을 뜻하는 명사로서의 local(s)이 정답으로 제시되기도 했다는 점을 함께 알아두도록 한다.

106

★★★ 어휘 / 동사 어휘

필리핀은 우리 회사의 휴대 전화와 태블릿 컴퓨터 제품에 대한 무역 금지 조치를 해제한 마지막 국가 중 하나이다.

어휘 ban 금지, 금지령, 반대, ~을 금지하다 face ~을 직시하다 damage 손상, 피해, 손해, ~에게 피해를 입히다 lift ~을 들어올리다, ~을 해제하다

The Philippines is one of the last countries to ------- its ban on our company's mobile phones and tablet computers.

(A) face
(B) attract
(C) damage
(D) lift

문제 해설

빈칸에 적합한 동사 어휘를 묻는 문제로 빈칸 뒤에 금수 조치를 뜻하는 ban이란 명사가 등장하고 있는데 이 ban이 문제를 풀이함에 있어 결정적인 키워드 역할을 한다. 조치는 취하거나 혹은 해제해야 하는 대상이므로 빈칸에는 금수 조치를 취하거나 또는 해제한다는 문맥을 구성할 수 있는 동사 어휘가 필요하다. 따라서 빈칸에는 조치를 들어 올린다, 즉 조치를 해제한다는 의미를 형성할 수 있도록 '들어 올리다'란 뜻을 지닌 동사 lift가 와야 한다.

토익 분석

어휘 문제 자체를 적당히 해석을 근간으로 풀이하는 것이라고 생각하는 분들이 많다. 이는 마치 밥이란 건 그저 물에 쌀을 넣어 불에 앉히기만 하면 되는 것이라 여기는 것만큼 단순하다 못해 측은하기까지 한 생각이다. 밥을 할 때는 사전에 물의 양을 측정하고 밥이 완성되기 전까지 불의 세기와 불을 가하는 시간 조절이 절대적이다. 어휘 문제 또한 그러하다. 어휘 문제는 여러 가지 형태가 존재한다. 나의 단순한 해석과 관점만 고집하기보단 빈칸 주변에서 어떠한 어휘를 원하는지 단서로 활용할 수 있는 어휘나 표현을 이해하며 문제를 풀이하기 전에 출제자의 출제 의도를 파악하는 것이 무엇보다 중요하다.

107

Mr. Davis was trying to move to another company after he failed to ------- his employment contract with his former company.

(A) expand
(B) proceed
(C) terminate
(D) renew

★★ 어휘 / 동사 어휘

Davis 씨는 전직 회사와의 근로 계약 갱신에 실패한 후 다른 회사로 이직하려는 시도를 하고 있었다.

어휘 fail to Vr ~을 못하게 되다 employment 고용, 채용 contract 계약 former 이전의, 전자의 expand ~을 확장하다, ~을 넓히다 proceed 가다, 진행하다, 계속 하다 terminate ~을 제거하다 renew ~을 갱신하다

문제 해설

빈칸에 적합한 동사 어휘를 묻는 문제이다. 빈칸 앞에는 Davis 씨가 실패했다는 내용이, 빈칸 이후에는 전직 회사와의 근로 계약이 언급되고 있다. 근로 계약과 실패를 연계시켜 생각해본다면 근로 계약 체결/갱신/해지 등의 의미를 구성할 수 있는 동사가 필요하다. 그러나 그가 타사로 이직하려고 시도했다는 내용을 고려한다면 근로 계약의 체결이나 해지가 아니라 근로 계약의 갱신이 적절함을 알 수 있으므로 빈칸에는 '갱신하다'란 뜻을 지닌 renew란 동사가 적절하다.

토익 분석

정기 토익에서는 '갱신하다'란 뜻을 지니고 있는 renew란 동사 외에도 '갱신'이란 의미의 명사 renewal도 출제된 바 있음을 함께 알아두도록 한다.

108

To increase next year's sales, the design department for Kamon Cosmetics is currently ------- a package redesign.

(A) consider
(B) considered
(C) considering
(D) consideration

★★ 어형 / 현재분사

내년도 매출을 증가시키기 위해서, Kamon 화장품 사의 디자인 부서는 현재 포장을 다시 디자인할 것을 고려 중에 있다.

어휘 design department 디자인 부서 cosmetics 화장품 currently 현재 consider ~을 고려하다, ~라고 여기다 consideration 고려

문제 해설

빈칸이 주격 보어를 취하는 2형식 동사인 be 동사 이후에 등장하고 있으므로 빈칸에는 주격 보어의 역할을 할 수 있는 명사 혹은 형용사가 위치해야 함을 알 수 있다. 다만 명사가 보어로 쓰이기 위해서는 주어와 동일 대상, 즉 동격 관계를 형성해야 한다는 전제조건을 충족시켜야 한다. 그러나 주어인 '디자인 부서'를 뜻하는 the design department가 '고려'를 뜻하는 명사 consideration과 동격 관계를 형성할 수 없으므로 이는 오답으로 소거해야 한다. 따라서 형용사 역할을 할 수 있는 현재분사인 considering과 과거분사인 considered 중 정답을 택일해야 하며 빈칸 뒤에 a package redesign이라는 복합명사 목적어가 위치하고 있으므로 빈칸에는 목적어를 취하는 것이 가능한 능동적 의미의 형용사인 현재분사 considering이 와야 한다.

토익 분석

정기 토익에서 보어와 관련된 어형 문제는 대부분 형용사를 중심으로 출제되는 경향이 있다는 점을 알아두도록 한다.

★★ 어휘 / 복합 명사

우리 회사의 모든 취업 지원자들은 1차 면접 이전에 정확한 개인 정보를 제공해야 할 책임이 있다.

어휘 be responsible for ~을 책임지다, ~을 담당하다 provide ~을 제공하다 accurate 정확한 personal information 개인 정보 applicant 지원자, 신청자 expert 전문가 opening 개장, 개회, 공석

All of the job ------- for our company are responsible for providing accurate personal information before the first round of job interviews.

(A) applicants
(B) experts
(C) openings
(D) employees

문제 해설

빈칸에 명사 job과 함께 쓰여 전체 문맥에 적합한 복합 명사를 구성할 수 있는 명사 어휘를 묻는 문제이다. 우선 빈칸 이후에 정확한 개인 정보를 제공해야 할 책임이 있다는 내용이 제시되고 있으므로 해당 명사는 사람을 지칭하는 명사이어야 한다. 또한 before their first round of job interviews, 즉 1차 취업 면접을 고려할 때 빈칸에는 전문가나 이미 일을 하고 있는 직원이 아닌 일자리를 구하기 위한 취업 지원자가 적절하다. 그러므로 빈칸에는 applicants가 와야 한다.

토익 분석

지금까지 정기 토익에서는 job과 함께 쓰여 복합명사를 구성할 수 있는 명사 어휘를 묻는 문제가 꾸준하게 출제되었다. '취업 지원자'를 뜻하는 job applicant 외에도 '일자리'의 job opening, '직무 소개'의 job description, '책무'의 job responsibility도 함께 숙지하도록 한다.

110

★★ 어형 / 명사 + 명사 단/복수 구분

영업 보고서에 따르면, 지난 5년 간 중국으로의 우리 자동차 및 화장품 수출 선적량이 지속적으로 성장하고 있다.

어휘 automobile 자동차 cosmetics 화장품 shipment 배송, 선적

According to the sales report, our ------- of automobiles and of cosmetics to China have been growing for the last five years.

(A) shipment
(B) shipping
(C) shipments
(D) shipped

문제 해설

빈칸에 적합한 어형을 묻는 문제로 빈칸이 명사의 범위를 제한시켜주는 한정사인 소유격 대명사 our 뒤에 위치하고 있으므로 빈칸에는 명사 어형이 와야 하지만 선택지에는 서로 다른 명사 어형이 세 개가 위치하고 있으므로 이 중 적절한 명사 어형을 선별해야 한다. 이 때 성급하게 문맥에 적합한 명사의 의미부터 파악하려고 덤벼들지 말고 우선 차분하게 동사의 형태부터 살펴보는 것이 바람직하다. 현재시제 완료상을 구성하는 have가 복수 형태라는 점을 고려할 때 이를 토대로 빈칸에 위치해야 하는 명사는 복수 어형이어야 함을 파악할 수 있다. 따라서 빈칸에는 유일한 복수명사 어형인 shipments가 와야 한다.

토익 분석

명사 어형을 묻는 문제가 평이한 난이도라면 선택지에서 명사 어형이 하나만 등장하겠지만 난이도가 상승하게 되면 선택지에는 명사 어형이 두 개 이상 제시된다. 이 때 두 개 이상 제시된 명사 어형 중에 동일한 명사 어휘임에도 불구하고 단/복수 어형이 동시에 등장하고 있다면 이 중 한 가지가 정답으로 제시될 가능성이 상당히 높다는 점을 알아두도록 한다.

111

------ of our analysts predicts the size of the global advertising industry will explode as social commerce companies grow rapidly.

(A) Every

(B) Most

(C) Each

(D) Plenty

문제 해설

빈칸에 적합한 어휘를 묻는 문제이다. 빈칸 뒤에는 수식어구인 전치사구 of our analysts와 동사 predicts가 등장하고 있으므로 빈칸에는 주어 역할을 할 수 있는 명사 또는 대명사가 와야 한다. 선택지에 제시된 Every는 가산 단수명사나 대명사와 함께 쓰이는 부정 형용사 역할은 가능하지만 단독적으로 쓰이는 부정 대명사로서는 쓰일 수 없으므로 오답이다. Plenty는 a plenty of라는 형태로 가산 복수명사나 불가산명사와 함께 쓰여 수나 양이 많음을 표현하며 부정 대명사로서는 사용이 불가하므로 이 역시 오답으로 소거해야 한다. 반면에 Most는 가산 복수명사나 불가산명사와 함께 쓰이는 부정 형용사로서의 용례뿐만 아니라 부정 대명사로 쓰이는 것이 가능하다. Each 또한 가산 단수명사나 대명사와 함께 쓰이는 부정 형용사로서의 용례뿐만 아니라 부정 대명사로서 쓰이는 것이 가능하다. 문제는 Most와 Each가 모두 부정 대명사로 쓰일 수 있으며 이들 중 어떠한 부정 대명사를 사용하더라도 모두 유사한 의미를 갖게 된다는 것이다. 무엇보다 빈칸 뒤 전치사구 of our analysts에서 가산 복수명사인 analysts가 결정적인 단서를 제공한다. Most가 가산 복수명사와 쓰이거나 가산 복수명사에 대한 부정 대명사로 쓰일 경우 복수동사와, 불가산명사와 쓰이거나 불가산명사에 대한 부정 대명사로 쓰일 경우 단수동사와 함께 쓰인다. 따라서 단수동사인 predicts를 취하려면 빈칸에는 단수로 여겨지는 부정대명사 Each가 적합하다.

토익 분석

토익에서 부정 대명사/부정 형용사와 관련된 문제는 주로 every / each / most가 출제되는 경향이 있음을 알아두도록 한다.

★★★ 어휘 / 부정 대명사

각 분석가는 인터넷 상업 회사들이 급속하게 성장함에 따라 전 세계적인 광고 산업의 규모도 폭발적으로 증가할 것이라 예측하고 있다.

문제 분석

Each of + 소유격 대명사/the + 가산복수명사 ~의 제각각
Most of + 소유격 대명사/the + 가산복수명사 ~의 대부분
Some of + 소유격 대명사/the + 가산복수명사 ~의 일부
All of + 소유격 대명사/the + 가산복수명사 ~ 모두

어휘 analyst 분석가 predict ~을 예측하다 explode 폭발하다 social commerce 인터넷 상업 grow ~이 성장하다, ~을 키우다 rapidly 급속하게, 빠르게

112

Ms. McKenzie attributes her success as a novelist to dedicating herself to her work and ------ what makes a best seller.

(A) understand

(B) understanding

(C) was understanding

(D) understood

문제 해설

빈칸에 적합한 어형을 묻는 문제로, 빈칸이 and란 등위접속사 뒤에 위치하고 있다. 아울러 '기인하다, 원인으로 돌리다'란 뜻을 지닌 동사 attribute는 전치사 to와 결합하여 attribute A to B의 형태로 쓰여 'A의 원인을 B에 두다'란 의미를 형성한다. 그러므로 전치사 to 이하에 등장하는 내용인 작업에 대한 전념과 and 이하의 내용인 베스트셀러를 만들어내는 요소는 모두 소설가로서 성공하게 된 이유에 해당되는 부분이다. 아울러 등위접속사 and가 단어/구/절을 모두 앞뒤로 대등하게 이어주는 구조를 취한다는 점을 고려할 때 궁극적으로 and 이하의 구 또한 전치사 to 이하의 동명사구 형태와 대등한 형태로 연결되어야 함을 알 수 있다. 따라서 빈칸에는 동명사 어형인 understanding이 적합하다.

토익 분석

토익에서의 전통적인 어형 문제로서 꼭 빠지지 않고 등장하는 문제 유형은 바로 To 부정사와 전치사 to를 구분하고 뒤이어 동사원형이 위치해야 할지 아니면 명사 혹은 동명사가 와야 할 것인지를 파악하는 문제이다. 이들은 사전에 대비하여 어느 정도 숙지해놓지 않으면 정답을 선택하기가 쉽지 않다. 따라서 be/become/get used(accustomed) to / look forward to / ascribe to / contribute to 와 같은 주요 표현들은 미리 알아두도록 한다.

★★★ 어형 / 동명사

McKenzie 씨는 소설가로서 성공한 이유로 작업에 대한 전념과 베스트셀러를 만드는 요소에 대한 이해를 들었다.

문제 분석

attribute A to + B(N/V-ing) A는 B에 기인한다

어휘 attribute A to B A는 B에 기인하다 novelist 소설가 dedicate ~에 바치다, ~에 전념하다, ~에 헌신하다

113

★★ 어휘 / 조동사 어휘

정부는 석탄을 채굴하지 않도록 전기 생산량의 35%를 풍력을 통해 조달할 계획이다.

어휘 electricity 전기 leave ~을 남겨두다, ~를 떠나다
in order that 주어 + can + Vr ~가 ~을 할 수 있도록 하기 위해

The government plans to get 35% of its electricity production from wind so that it ------- leave the coal in the ground.

(A) be
(B) should
(C) has to
(D) can

문제 해설

빈칸에 적합한 동사 또는 조동사를 묻는 문제로 빈칸이 so that이란 부사절 접속사에 이은 주어 it과 동사 원형인 leave 사이에 위치하고 있다. 무엇보다 so that은 목적/의도의 뜻을 지닌 부사절 접속사로 뒤이은 부사절은 주어 + can/may + 동사원형의 구조를 취한다는 점을 고려할 때 빈칸에는 leave라는 동사원형을 본동사로 취하는 조동사인 can이 와야 함을 알 수 있다.

토익 분석

부사절 접속사에는 목적/의도를 뜻하는 부사절 접속사인 'so that + 주어 + can/may + 동사원형~' 과 유사한 형태인 결과를 나타내는 '부사절 접속사 'so + 형용사/부사 + that + 주어 + 동사~'도 있다. 이 두 개의 부사절 접속사를 모두 정확하게 인식하고 이들을 서로 혼동하지 않도록 주의한다.

114

★ 어형 / 동사

우리 시의 그 연례 겨울 행사는 스키, 겨울 수영, 썰매 및 다른 많은 즐거운 행사들을 포함하고 있다.

어휘 festival 행사 sledging 썰매 many other 다른 많은
fun event 즐거운 행사 include ~을 포함하다

The annual winter festival of our city ------- skiing, winter swimming, sledging, and many other fun events.

(A) include
(B) including
(C) includes
(D) is included

문제 해설

빈칸에 적합한 어형을 묻는 문제로 빈칸이 주어인 The annual winter festival 뒤에 위치하고 있으므로 빈칸에는 절을 구성할 수 있는 동사 어형이 필요하다. 주어가 festival이 단수 주어이고 빈칸 뒤에는 skiing, winter swimming, sledging and many other fun events과 같은 여러 명사 목적어들이 등장하고 있으므로 빈칸에는 단수동사 형태이자 능동태를 형성하는 includes가 와야 한다.

토익 분석

동사 어형을 구분함에 있어 가장 기본적인 것은 절을 구성할 수 있는 정동사(동사)와 절을 구성하지 못하는 준동사를 분별하는 것부터 시작한다. To Vr / V-ing / Vp.p는 절을 구성하지 못하는 준동사 어형이므로 무조건 동사 어형 문제를 묻는 문제에서는 이들부터 오답으로 소거해야 한다. 이어서 주어 동사의 단/복수 형태 수 일치 – 능동태/수동태 구분 – 시제 확인 순으로 동사의 어형을 살펴보며 문제를 풀이하는 것이 동사 어형 문제를 가장 효율적으로 풀이할 수 있는 방식임을 알아두도록 한다.

115 부사의 수식을 받는 준동사

The federal government will improve the investment environment by -------
removing regulations for the new few years.

(A) continue
(B) continuation
(C) continuous
(D) continuously

★★ 어형 / 부사

연방 정부는 향후 몇 년 간 규제를 철폐함으로써 투자 환경을 개선하고자 한다.

어휘 federal government 연방 정부 improve ~을 향상시키다, ~을 개선시키다 investment 투자 environment 환경 remove ~을 제거하다, ~을 없애다 regulations 규정

문제 해설

빈칸에 적절한 어형을 묻는 문제이며 빈칸이 전치사 by와 동명사 removing 사이에 위치하고 있으므로 빈칸에는 동명사 removing을 수식할 수 있는 부사 어형이 와야 한다. 무엇보다 V-ing 형태의 동명사와 현재분사, 과거분사 그리고 To 부정사 형태와 같은 준동사 어형은 어떠한 품사의 역할을 하더라도 기본적으로 준동사인만큼 이들은 모두 부사의 수식을 받아야 한다는 점을 간과하지 않도록 한다. 따라서 빈칸에는 부사인 continuously가 적합하다.

토익 분석

준동사 어형은 다양한 품사의 역할을 할 수 있지만 어떠한 품사의 역할을 한다고 해도 기본적으로 준동사이므로 수식은 부사가 해야 한다는 점을 놓치지 않도록 주의한다. 특히 To Vr + O + 부사 / 부사 + to Vr + O / V-ing + O + 부사 / 부사 + V-ing + O / be + Vp.p + 부사 / be + 부사 + Vp.p 와 같이 모두 준동사 어형을 수식하는 부사를 요구하는 위치임을 숙지해 두도록 한다.

116

The lease with the local shopping mall ------- if the renovation works are
completed successfully next week.

(A) will be continued
(B) was continuing
(C) have continued
(D) had been continued

★★★ 어형 / 동사 + 시제

만약 보수공사가 다음 주에 성공적으로 마무리된다면 지역 쇼핑몰의 임대는 지속될 것이다.

어휘 lease 임대, ~을 임대하다 renovation works 보수공사 complete ~을 끝내다, ~을 마무리하다 successfully 성공적으로

문제 해설

빈칸이 '임대'를 뜻하는 주절의 주어 the lease와 수식어구인 with the local shopping mall 뒤에 위치하고 있으므로 빈칸에는 주절의 동사가 위치해야 한다. 무엇보다 주어인 the lease가 단수 주어이고 빈칸 뒤에 명사 목적어가 등장하지 않고 있으므로 빈칸에는 단수동사 형태이자 능동태를 구성할 수 있는 동사 어형이 필요하다. 아울러 조건 부사절이 다음 달로 예정된 보수 공사 완공이란 미래 의미를 현재시제인 are completed로 표현하고 있으므로 주절의 시제 또한 미래 시제여야 함을 가늠할 수 있다. 따라서 빈칸에는 will be continued가 적합하다.

토익 분석

동사 어형 문제는 주어/동사 수 일치 – 태 – 시제를 파악하는 과정을 통해 문제를 풀이하는 것이 적절하다. 하지만 만약 문두나 문미에 과거 또는 미래시제를 파악할 수 있는 시점 표현이 등장하고 있다면 그 형태만으로는 주어/동사의 수 일치 여부를 파악할 수 없다. 따라서 이 경우 주어/동사 수 일치는 건너뛰고 바로 시제 – 태 순서로 살펴보며 동사의 어형을 결정짓도록 한다.

★★ 어휘 / 전치사

BK Financial Group의 회장은 행사가 끝난 후 이어질 환영 만찬에서의 축하 연설을 계획했다.

문제 분석

전치사 following = 전치사 after ~이후에

어휘 chairman 의장, 회장 congratulatory speech 축하 연설 reception 환영식, 환영 만찬 following 이어지는, 이후에 prior ~전의, 앞서, 직전

The chairman of BK Financial Group planned his congratulatory speech at a reception ------- the event.

(A) following
(B) behind
(C) prior
(D) until

문제 해설

빈칸에 적합한 전치사를 묻는 문제이며 빈칸 뒤에는 '행사'를 뜻하는 the event란 명사가, 빈칸 앞에는 환영 만찬에서 계획된 축하 연설에 관한 내용이 등장하고 있다. 그러므로 축하 연설이 행사 이전 혹은 행사 이후에 이뤄지는지, 행사와 연설 사이의 선후 관계를 파악할 수 있는 전치사가 필요함을 알 수 있다. 따라서 빈칸에는 행사 이후란 시점이란 의미를 구성할 수 있는 전치사 following이 적합하다.

토익 분석

토익에서 after은 전치사와 접속사로서의 용례를 모두 묻고 있지만 출제 비중 면에서 살펴보면 접속사보다 전치사로서의 출제 비중이 높은 편이다. 아울러 전치사 after은 전치사 following으로 바뀌어 제시될 수도 있으므로 after = following을 꼭 기억해두도록 한다. 물론 following은 '이어지는, 뒤따라오는'이란 뜻도 지니고 있지만 이는 전치사가 아닌 형용사로 쓰일 때의 뜻이므로 전치사와 형용사로서의 의미를 혼동하지 않도록 주의한다. 아울러 한정사보다 앞에 쓰인 following은 전치사이며 한정사보다 뒤에 쓰인 following은 형용사이므로 어느 자리에 위치하고 있는지 확인하며 following의 구체적인 용례를 파악하도록 한다.

118

★★ 어휘 / 부사 어휘

그 회사는 최근 일부 지점 사무실들의 조명을 매우 효율적인 LED 등으로 교체했다.

문제 분석

high 높은/높게(형용사/부사)
highly 매우/가장/크게(부사)

어휘 recently 최근에 branch office 지점 사무실 efficient 효율적인

The company has recently changed all the lights in some of the branch offices for ------- efficient LED lights.

(A) heavily
(B) almost
(C) nearly
(D) highly

문제 해설

빈칸에 적합한 부사 어휘를 묻는 문제로 빈칸이 '효율적인'이란 뜻을 지닌 형용사 efficient 앞에 위치하고 있으므로 빈칸에 오는 부사 어휘는 효율적이란 의미와 쓰여 적절한 문맥을 구성할 수 있어야 한다. 따라서 그 효율이 어느 정도 상태인지 즉, 효율이 높은지 혹은 낮은지 이를 언급할 수 있는 형용사가 와야 함을 알 수 있다. 그러므로 빈칸에는 '매우'란 뜻을 지닌 부사 highly가 적합하다.

토익 분석

토익에 대비하여 highly가 포함된 주요 표현, 이를테면 (be) highly recommended '가장 권장되고 있는' / (be) highly competitive '매우 경쟁적인' / (be) highly profitable '매우 수익성이 높은' / (be) highly trained '고도로 훈련된' / (be) highly regarded for '~에 대해 높이 존경을 받는' / (be) highly sensitive '매우 민감한' / speak highly of '~를 매우 칭찬하는'과 같은 표현들은 미리 숙지해 두도록 한다.

119

Andrew Accounting has become one of the famous accounting companies in America ------- its exceptional services.

(A) in spite of
(B) thanks to
(C) except for
(D) as well as

문제 해설

빈칸 뒤에 its exceptional services란 구가 등장하고 있으므로 빈칸에는 전치사가 위치해야 한다. Andrew Accounting 사가 미국 내에서 가장 유명한 회계 회사들 중 한 곳이 될 수 있었던 원동력은 바로 뛰어난 서비스라 할 수 있으므로 빈칸에는 이유/원인을 의미하는 전치사로 '~덕분에'란 뜻을 지닌 thanks to가 와야 한다.

토익 분석

토익에서 thanks to와 유사 전치사로 쓰일 수 있는 because of / owing to / due to / on account of 를 함께 묶어서 익혀두도록 한다.

★★ 어휘 / 전치사

Andrew Accounting 사는 뛰어난 서비스 덕분에 미국 내에서 가장 유명한 회계 회사들 중 한 곳이 되었다.

어휘 exceptional 우수한, 뛰어난, 예외적인 in spite of ~임에도 불구하고 except for ~을 제외하곤 B as well as A A 뿐만 아니라 B도

120

With ------- demand for various crops, water usage will most likely double over the next thirty years.

(A) reserved
(B) leading
(C) increased
(D) partial

문제 해설

빈칸에 적절한 분사 형태의 형용사 어휘를 묻는 문제이다. 빈칸이 다양한 농작물에 대한 수요를 뜻하는 demands of various crops 앞에 위치하고 있으므로 수요의 구체적인 상태를 표현할 수 있는 형용사 어휘가 필요하다. 아무래도 수요의 상태란 '많거나 적거나, 증가하거나 감소하거나 또는 안정적인'이란 형용사와 밀접한 관련이 있을 수 밖에 없다. 따라서 빈칸에는 '증가된'이란 뜻을 지닌 increased가 적합하다.

토익 분석

유독 increased demand와 increasing demand 사이의 의미상 차이점을 정확하게 인식하지 못하는 경우가 많은데 increased demand는 이미 증가한 상태의 수요를 언급하고 있다면 increasing demand는 끊임없이 지속적으로 증가하고 있는 상태의 수요를 표현하는 것임을 알아두도록 한다.

★★ 어휘 / 형용사 어휘

다양한 농작물에 대한 수요의 증가로 인해, 물의 소비량이 향후 30년간 두 배로 늘어날 수 있다.

어휘 demand 요구, 증가, ~을 요구하다 various 다양한 crop 농작물 usage 사용, 용도, 소비 double 두 배, 두 배의, 두 배로 늘다 leading 선도하는

★★ 대명사 / 재귀 대명사

사람들은 해저 혹은 근처 해역에서 발생한 지진으로 인해 초래되는 심각한 위험으로부터 자신을 보호하기 위한 새로운 안전 절차를 배워야 한다.

어휘 safety procedures 안전 대책 serious 심각한 danger 위험 cause ~을 초래하다, ~을 야기하다 below ~의 아래에

People should learn the new safety procedures to protect ------- from serious dangers caused by earthquakes below or near the sea.

(A) they   **(B) themselves**
(C) their   (D) theirs

문제 해설

빈칸에 적합한 대명사를 묻는 문제로 빈칸이 준동사인 To 부정사 to protect 뒤에 위치하고 있으므로 목적어 역할을 할 수 있는 대명사가 필요하다. 하지만 빈칸은 주어 자리가 아닐뿐더러 빈칸 뒤에 명사가 등장하지 않으므로 주격 대명사인 they와 소유격 대명사 their은 모두 오답으로 처리해야 한다. 따라서 재귀대명사인 themselves와 소유대명사인 theirs 중 정답을 택일해야 하며 새로운 안전 절차는 사람들이 자신들을 보호하기 위해 익혀야 하는 대상이니만큼 빈칸에는 재귀대명사인 themselves가 와야 한다.

토익 분석

재귀대명사는 목적어로 쓰이는 용례와 부사로 쓰이는 용례, 이렇게 두 가지 용례를 지니고 있다. 목적어로 쓰이는 경우 재귀대명사는 주어와 동격 관계를 형성해야 하며, 부사로 쓰이는 경우 [주어 + (oneself/oneselves) + 동사 + 목적어 + (oneself/oneselves)]와 같이 완전한 절과 함께 쓰여 수식어 역할을 한다. 아울러 토익에서는 이 두 가지 용례에 관한 문제가 모두 출제되고 있다. 어떻게 쓰이더라도 보이는 형태야 oneself/oneselves로 늘 동일하지만 그 쓰임새와 의미가 다르므로 이에 유의한다. 재귀대명사는 생김새가 중요한 것이 아니라 자리와 기능이 중요하다.

122

★★★ 비교구문 / as – as 동등 비교구문

고정된 월간 비용을 지불함으로써, 전화 이용자들은 인접 지역에서 그들이 원하는 만큼 전화를 이용할 수 있다.

문제 분석

as many + 가산 복수명사 + as + S+V 주어가 ~하는 만큼의 ~을

어휘 fixed 고정된 monthly charge 월간 비용 wish ~을 바라다 immediate area 인접 지역

For a fixed monthly charge, callers can make ------- telephone calls as they wish in their immediate area.

(A) a lot of   **(B) as many**
(C) various   (D) unlimited

문제 해설

빈칸이 동사 make와 복합명사 목적어 telephone calls 사이에 위치하고 있으므로 빈칸에는 가산 복수명사인 telephone calls를 수식할 수 있는 형용사인 a lot of가 적절하다고 여길 수 있으나 뒤이어 등장하는 as they wish와 호응하지 못하기 때문에 오답이라 할 수 있다. 다른 형용사인 various와 unlimited 또한 가산 복수명사와 함께 쓰일 수 있지만 이들도 또한 같은 이유로 오답으로 처리해야 한다. 문제 풀이의 가장 결정적인 단서는 바로 as they wish로 빈칸에는 as they wish와 함께 연결될 수 있어야 할 뿐만 아니라 가산 복수명사도 취할 수 있어야 한다. 따라서 빈칸에는 as-as 동등 비교구문을 구성하며 as they wish와 동수를 의미하는 as many가 적절하다.

토익 분석

as-as 동등 비교구문의 경우 as만 별도로 물어보는 문제는 큰 어려움 없이 잘 풀지만 as many + 가산 복수명사 / as much + 불가산명사와 같이 확장된 형태를 묻는 경우 의외로 문제풀이에 어려움을 겪는 경우가 발생한다. 이 때 중요한 것은 복잡한 구조라 여겨질수록 이를 단순화시켜야 한다는 것이다. 다시 말해서 뒤에 가산 복수명사/불가산명사 + as 형태가 위치하고 있다면 앞에는 as many / as much가 자리하여 뒤이은 복수명사/불가산명사 + as와 형태 및 의미의 궤를 맞춰가야 한다고 정리하는 것이다. 안보고 있어도 '쩍'하고 떨어지면 수박이고 '픽'하고 떨어지면 호박이다. 항상 빈칸 전후에 as가 등장하면 동등 비교구문부터 의식하여 또 다른 빈칸에 적합한 정답으로 as를 먼저 떠올리도록 하자.

123

In recognition of her ------- talent, Ms. Scofield became the first woman to be named board director since our company's founding in 1974.

(A) academic
(B) exceptional
(C) previous
(D) economical

★★★ 어휘 / 형용사 어휘

그녀의 우수한 재능을 인정받아, Scofield 씨는 우리 회사가 1974년도에 설립된 이후 최고 경영자 직을 맡은 최초의 여성이 되었다.

문제 분석

exceptional 우수한, 뛰어난

어휘 recognition 인식 exceptional 우수한, 뛰어난, 예외적인 talent 재능 post 직책, 직위, 기둥, 게시물, ~을 게재하다 founding 설립 academic 학문적인 previous 이전에 economical 경제적인

문제 해설

빈칸에 알맞은 형용사 어휘를 묻는 문제이다. 빈칸이 소유격 대명사인 her과 '재능, 재주'를 뜻하는 talent 사이에 위치하고 있으며 뒤이은 주절에서 Scofield 씨가 회사 설립 후 최고 경영자 직을 맡은 최초의 여성임을 언급하고 있다. 따라서 Scofield 씨가 회사 설립 후 최초의 여성 최고 경영자인 것과 그녀의 재능의 인정을 고려하면 빈칸에는 그녀의 재능이 우수하다는 뜻을 구성할 수 있는 형용사 exceptional이 와야 함을 알 수 있다.

토익 분석

형용사 exceptional을 '예외적인'이란 뜻으로만 익히는 경우가 많은데, 물론 그러한 의미도 지니고 있지만 사실 토익에서 형용사 exceptional이 어휘/어형 문제로 출제될 땐 '예외적인'이란 뜻을 묻는 것이 아니라 '우수한, 뛰어난'이란 뜻으로 묻는다는 점을 꼭 숙지하도록 한다.

124

The new treaty was adopted last year with the ------- of fighting global warming and environmental destruction in the future.

(A) solution
(B) factor
(C) aim
(D) prevention

★★ 어휘 / 명사 어휘

새로운 조약은 미래에 있을 지구 온난화 현상과 환경 파괴에 대처하고자 하는 목적으로 작년에 채택되었다.

어휘 adopt ~을 선택하다, ~을 채택하다 global warming 지구 온난화 현상 environmental destruction 환경 파괴 solution 해결책 factor 요소, 요인 aim 목표, 목적 prevention 예방

문제 해설

빈칸에 적합한 명사 어휘를 묻는 문제로 빈칸에 앞서 작년에 새로운 조약이 채택되었다는 내용이 제시되고 있으며 빈칸 이후에는 향후에 있을 지구 온난화와 환경 파괴에 대처한다는 내용이 등장하고 있다. 이는 궁극적으로 새로운 조약이 채택된 배경이나 이유 또는 목적이라 할 수 있으므로 빈칸에는 이러한 의미를 지닌 명사가 와야 함을 파악할 수 있다. 따라서 빈칸에는 '목적'이란 뜻을 지닌 명사 aim이 적합하다.

토익 분석

토익에서 목적과 관련된 어휘 문제로는 aim / purpose / objective가 모두 출제된 바 있으므로 이들 모두 묶어서 숙지하도록 한다.

★★ 대명사/부정 대명사

각 회사들은 전략적 핵심 지역 중 한 곳인 미국에서의 사업 활동을 확장하는 것에 전념하고 있다.

문제 분석

Each of + 소유격 대명사/the + 가산복수명사 ~의 제각각
Most of + 소유격 대명사/the + 가산복수명사 ~의 대부분
Some of + 소유격 대명사/the + 가산복수명사 ~의 일부
All of + 소유격 대명사/the + 가산복수명사 ~ 모두

어휘 be committed to ~에 전념하다, ~에 집중하다 expand ~을 확장하다 business activity 사업 활동 strategic 전략적인 core area 핵심 지역

------- of the companies is committed to expanding business activities in the United States, which is a strategic core area.

(A) Every

(B) Each

(C) Other

(D) Them

문제 해설

빈칸이 전치사구 of the companies와 be 동사 is 앞에 위치하고 있으므로 빈칸에는 주어 역할을 할 수 있는 적절한 대명사가 필요하며 아울러 be 동사 is가 단수동사임을 고려할 때 빈칸에는 단수로 처리되는 대명사가 와야 함을 알 수 있다. 무엇보다 Every와 Other은 부정 대명사로서의 용례가 없으며 Them은 목적격 인칭 대명사이므로 이들은 모두 오답으로 소거해야 한다. 따라서 빈칸에는 부정 대명사로써 사용이 가능할 뿐만 아니라 단수로 취급 받는 Each가 적절하다.

토익 분석

Every는 뒤이어 대명사 혹은 명사를 취해야만 온전하게 쓰일 수 있으며 단독으로 쓰여 부정 대명사의 역할을 행할 수 없다. 아울러 other도 뒤이어 가산 복수명사 또는 불가산명사를 취해야 하며 이 역시 단독으로 쓰여 부정대명사가 될 수 없다. 따라서 Every (Other) of + the/소유격 대명사의 구조는 불가하다는 점을 꼭 기억해두도록 한다. 덧붙여 토익에서는 'other + 불가산명사'가 아니라 'other + 가산 복수명사'를 중점적으로 다룬다는 경향을 숙지하도록 한다.

★★ 접속사 / 부사절 접속사

정부가 더 많은 회사들과 일자리를 창출하고자 별도의 노력을 기울이지 않는다면 국가 경제를 유지하지 못할 것이다.

문제 분석

make efforts for ~를 위한 노력을 하다
make efforts to Vr ~하고자 노력을 하다

어휘 sustain ~을 유지하다, ~을 지탱하다 national economy 국가 경제 make extra efforts 별도의 노력을 기울이다 therefore 따라서, 고로, 그러므로

The government cannot sustain the national economy ------- it makes efforts to create more businesses and jobs.

(A) who

(B) that

(C) unless

(D) therefore

문제 해설

빈칸이 두 절 사이에 위치하고 있으므로 빈칸에는 접속사가 필요하다. 부사절 접속사 문제는 주절과 부사절 사이의 내용을 논리적으로 적절하게 연결시켜줄 수 있는 부사절 접속사를 선택해야 하며 명사절/형용사절 접속사의 경우 무엇보다 접속사 이후에 등장하는 절이 완전한 절의 구조인지 여부를 먼저 살펴봐야 할 필요가 있다. 빈칸 뒤 it makes extra efforts to create more businesses and jobs이란 절은 주어와 목적어 그리고 부사 역할의 to 부정사구까지 갖춘 완전한 구조의 절이므로 불완전한 구조의 절과 함께 쓰이는 who는 오답이 되겠다.

선행사가 없는 명사절 접속사로 쓰이는 that은 완전한 구조의 절과 함께 쓰이지만, 빈칸 자리가 주어나 목적어 또는 명사 보어의 역할을 하는 명사절 앞에 위치하고 있지 않으며 that이 선행사를 취하는 형용사절 접속사인 경우 불완전한 구조의 절과 함께 쓰인다는 점을 고려할 때 that 역시 오답으로 소거해야 한다. 아울러 therefore은 두 절 사이에 위치하지만 두 절을 이어주는 접속사의 역할을 할 수 없는 접속부사이므로 이 또한 오답이다. 따라서 빈칸에는 회사와 일자리 창출을 위해 별도로 노력하지 않으면 국가 경제를 지탱하지 못할 것이란 적절한 문맥을 구성하는 있도록 '~가 아니라면'이란 뜻을 지닌 조건 부사절 접속사 unless가 와야 한다.

토익 분석

주요 조건 부사절 접속사로는 If (만약~라면), Unless (만약 ~가 아니라면), Once (일단 ~하면)이 있으며 If의 경우 providing/provided that S+V / assuming that S+V / supposing that S+V와 같은 동일한 의미의 격식체 표현이 대체하여 정답으로 제시될 수도 있으므로 이들은 꼭 사전에 숙지하도록 한다.

127

Energy companies should develop different forms of ------- energy that can reduce pollution and conserve the scarce resources.

(A) possible
(B) collaborative
(C) satisfactory
(D) alternative

문제 해설

빈칸에 적합한 형용사 어휘를 묻는 문제로 빈칸이 energy라는 명사 앞에 위치하고 있으므로 명사 앞에는 different forms, 즉 다양한 형태라는 표현이 제시되고 있으므로 빈칸에는 다양한 형태의 에너지란 뜻에 문맥에 적절한 의미를 부가할 수 있는 형용사 어휘가 필요하다. 또한 빈칸 뒤에는 공해를 감소시키고 부족한 자원을 보존할 수 있다는 내용이 등장하고 있다. 따라서 빈칸에는 기존의 에너지처럼 공해를 많이 발생하지 않고 자원을 소비하지 않는 에너지란 의미를 형성할 수 있도록 '대체하는'이란 뜻을 지닌 형용사 alternative가 적절하다.

토익 분석

형용사 alternative/alternate은 모두 '대체의'란 뜻을 지닌 형용사인 것은 사실이나 일반적으로 '대체'는 alternate보다는 alternative이 쓰이는 비중이 더 크고 alternate은 '대체'보다는 '교대로/하나 거른(=격)'으로 사용되는 비중이 더 크다. 그러나 토익에선 '대체의'란 뜻을 지닌 형용사 어휘를 묻는 문제로서 alternative와 alternate이 모두 출제된 바 있다. 아울러 alternative는 '대체, 대안'이란 뜻을 지닌 명사로서도 쓰이는 것이 가능하며 역시 토익에서도 해당 의미를 묻는 어휘 문제로 여러 차례 출제된 바 있다. 토익에 대비해서는 alternative plan (대체 계획) / alternative approach (대체 방식) / alternative choice (양자 택일) / alternative route = alternate route (우회로, 대체 경로) 정도는 숙지하고 있어야 한다.

★★ 어휘 / 형용사 어휘

에너지 회사들은 공해를 감소시키고 부족한 자원을 보존할 수 있는 다양한 형태의 대체 에너지들을 개발해야만 한다.

어휘 form 형태 reduce ~을 감소시키다 pollution 오염, 공해 conserve ~을 보존하다 scarce 부족한, 희박한 resource 자원

128

It is illegal to build new agricultural farms and orchards if ------- is not granted by the minister of environment.

(A) application
(B) inspection
(C) permission
(D) expense

문제 해설

빈칸에 적합한 명사 어휘를 묻는 문제이다. 빈칸 앞에는 새로운 농장과 과수원을 건립하는 것이 불법이라는 내용이 등장하고 있으며 빈칸 뒤에는 만약 환경부에 의해 주어지지 않는다는 조건이 제시되고 있다. 그러므로 빈칸에는 환경부에 의해 부여되는 것이자 새로운 농장과 과수원을 합법적으로 건립하기 위해 필요한 것을 지칭하는 명사 어휘가 와야 한다. 따라서 새로운 농장과 과수원을 건립하려면 환경부에 의해 사전 허가 내지는 승인이 필요하다는 문맥이 논리적으로 타당하므로 빈칸에는 '허가'를 뜻하는 명사 어휘인 permission이 적합하다.

토익 분석

명사 permission은 '허가, 허락'을 뜻하며 동사 permit에서 파생된 명사 형태이다. 그러나 동사 permit은 그 자체로 명사 전환이 가능한데 이 경우 permit은 '허가증, 면허증, 인가서'를 의미하기 때문에 명사 permission과 의미 차이가 발생한다. 토익에서는 work permit (취업 허가증), parking permit (주차 허가증), building permit (건축 허가증)이 어휘 문제로 출제된 바 있으므로 이들도 함께 익혀두는 것이 바람직하다.

permission vs. permit

★★ 어휘 / 명사 어휘

환경부에 의해 허가되지 않은 새로운 농장과 과수원을 건립하는 것은 불법이다.

어휘 illegal 불법의 agricultural 농업의 orchard 과수원 grant ~을 ~에게 부여하다 inspection 검사 expense 비용

★ 어형 / 명사

KB Heavy Industries 사는 갈수록 치열해지는 산업 환경에서 경쟁하기 위해 연구 개발 분야를 무척이나 강조했다.

어휘 place A on B A를 B에 두다 research and development sector 연구 개발 분야 compete in ~에서 경쟁하다 increasingly 점차 늘어나는 fierce 치열한 environment 환경

KB Heavy Industries has been placing a strong ------- on the research and development sectors to compete in the increasingly fierce industry environment.

(A) emphasize
(B) emphasis
(C) emphatic
(D) emphasized

문제 해설

빈칸에 적합한 어형을 묻는 문제로 빈칸이 부정관사 a와 형용사인 strong 뒤에 위치하고 있으므로 빈칸에는 형용사 strong의 수식을 받는 명사 어형이 와야 한다. 따라서 '강조'를 뜻하는 명사 emphasis가 적합하다.

토익 분석

토익에서는 put/place a great/strong emphasis on sth 의 형태를 통해 명사 emphasis 를 묻기도 하지만 추가로 emphasize A for B, 즉 'B에 대한 A를 강조하다'란 표현을 통해 동사 emphasize를 묻는 어휘/어형 문제가 출제되기도 하므로 같이 학습해두도록 한다.

★★★ 어휘 / 동사 어휘

상업용 비행기 시험은 대개 해당 비행기가 정부 기관의 모든 안전 및 성능 조건을 충족시키고 있음을 보증하고자 실시된다.

어휘 commercial 상업 광고, 상업적인 usually 대개, 일반적으로 conduct ~을 행하다 certify ~을 보증하다, ~을 증명하다, ~을 확신시키다 performance 성능, 실적, 성과, 공연 requirement 요구, 요구조건 resolve ~을 해결하다 grant 보조금, 지원금, ~을 부여하다 enable ~을 가능하게 하다

Commercial flight testing is usually conducted to ------- that the airplane meets all safety and performance requirements of the government agency.

(A) certify
(B) resolve
(C) grant
(D) enable

문제 해설

빈칸에 적합한 동사 어휘를 묻는 문제이다. 빈칸에 앞서 상업용 비행기 시험이 시행된다는 내용이 등장하고 있으며 빈칸 이후에는 해당 비행기가 정부 기관의 모든 안전 및 성능 조건을 충족시키고 있음을 밝히고 있다. 그러므로 to 이하에 자리하는 동사 어휘는 상업용 비행기의 시험이 실시되는 목적/의도가 담긴 동사이어야 한다. 따라서 빈칸 이후 해당 비행기가 정부 기관의 모든 안전 및 성능 조건을 충족시킨다는 내용은 궁극적으로 상업용 비행기 시험을 통해 확인하거나 보증을 받기 위한 내용임을 알 수 있으므로 빈칸에는 '을 보증하다, ~을 증명하다'란 뜻을 지닌 동사인 certify가 적절하다.

토익 분석

토익에서는 동사 certify 외에도 certify에서 파생되는 두 개의 명사, 즉 certification과 certificate을 구분하여 명사를 선택하게끔 하거나 또는 두 개의 명사를 별도로 어휘/어형 문제로 출제한 바 있다. 우선 certification은 불가산명사로 '증명, 인가, 증명서 배부'를 뜻하며 certificate은 가산명사로 '증명서, 인증서'를 뜻한다. 만약 이를 구분해야 하는 문제가 출제되는 경우에는 부정관사의 등장 여부를 파악하여 부정관사가 있는 경우 certificate을, 그렇지 않으면 certification을 선택하도록 한다. 아울러 certificate은 gift certificate, 즉 상품권을 뜻하는 어휘 문제로도 출제되고 있음을 알아두도록 한다.

Questions 131-134 refer to the following advertisement.

San Francisco Real EstateApartment for lease
701 Trinity Street Apt. 12

A clean, spacious two-bedroom, one-bathroom apartment is ------- on Trinity
131.
Street. The unit comes with basic kitchen appliances, a dishwasher, and in-unit
laundry machine. The apartment ------- conveniently in the heart of town. The
132.
nearest subway station is only a five-minute walk away, and the nearest bus
station is at a ten-minute walk. There is a convenience store in the apartment
complex. The rent is $750 a month, which includes gas, electricity, and water.
-------. Pets are strictly prohibited. Please contact Ms. Isabella Choi at (452)
133.
321-3955 for more information or to ------- an appointment for showing.
134.

San Francisco 부동산 – 임대용 아파트
Trinity 가 701번지 12호

Trinity 가에 위치한 깨끗하고, 넓은 두 개의 침실과 한 개의 욕실을 지닌 아파트를 임대합니다. 이 아파트는 기본적인 주방 시설, 식기 세척기, 그리고 실내 세탁기가 구비되어 있습니다. 해당 아파트는 접근성이 좋은 시내에 위치하고 있습니다. 가장 가까운 지하철 역은 도보로 5분 거리에, 그리고 가장 가까운 버스 정류장은 도보로 10분 거리에 있습니다. 아파트 단지 안에는 편의점이 있습니다. 월 임대료는 가스, 전기, 그리고 수도 요금을 포함하여 750달러입니다. 월 임대료에 인터넷 사용 요금은 포함되지 않는다는 점에 유의해주시기 바랍니다. 애완동물을 키우는 것은 금지되어 있습니다. 더 많은 임대 정보를 원하시거나 아파트 구경을 위한 예약을 원하시면 Isabella Choi씨에게 (452) 321-3955로 연락을 주십시오.

어휘 spacious 넓은 kitchen appliances 주방 시설, 주방 기구 dishwasher 식기 세척기 in-unit 아파트 실내에 위치한 at the heart of downtown 도심의, 시내의 convenient store 편의점 apartment complex 아파트 단지 rent 지대, 임대료, ~을 빌리다 inclusive of ~을 포함하고 있는 strictly 엄격하게 prohibit ~을 금지하다 showing 전시, 상영

131

(A) applicable
(B) capable
(C) affordable
(D) available

★★ 어휘 / 형용사 어휘

토익 분석

available은 구체적으로 '구매가 가능한' '이용/사용이 가능한' 이란 뜻을 지니고 있지만 시간적 여력이 있는 상태/접촉(연락)이 가능한 상태를 의미하기도 한다. 특히 (be) available for '~에 이용이 가능한', (be) available to Vr '~하는 것이 가능하다, ~할 여력이 되다'과 같은 표현과 '가용성'을 뜻하는 명사 availability는 꼭 숙지하도록 한다.

문제 해설

빈칸에 적합한 형용사 어휘를 묻는 문제이다. 우선, 광고문에 San Francisco Real EstateApartment for lease, 즉 'San Francisco 부동산 – 임대용 아파트'라는 제목을 통해 해당 광고는 아파트 임대를 위한 것임을 알 수 있다. 빈칸 앞에는 A clean, spacious two bedroom, one bathroom apartment라며 깨끗하고, 넓은 두 개의 침실과 한 개의 욕실을 지닌 아파트가 등장하고 있으며 빈칸 뒤에는 on Trinity Street라며 Trinity 가에 있다는 위치에 대해 언급하고 있다. 따라서 빈칸에는 현재 해당 아파트가 임대가 가능하다는 의미를 형성할 수 있도록 '이용/사용이 가능한, 구매가 가능한'이란 뜻을 지닌 형용사 어휘 available이 와야 한다.

132

★★어형 / 동사 어형 + 동사의 시제

문제 분석

be located at / on / in ~에 위치하다

토익에선 locate의 어휘/어형을 묻는 문제들이 꾸준하게 출제되고 있다. 모두 (be) located라는 과거분사와 '장소/위치'를 뜻하는 location이란 명사를 묻는 문제들이라 할 수 있으며 이들 이외에 locate과 관련된 다른 어형들을 묻는 문제로 출제되는 경우는 없다. 아울러 located/location을 수식하는 형용사/부사인 current(ly) / convenient(ly) / strategical(ly) / envious(ly) 를 묻는 어휘/어형 문제도 지속적으로 출제되고 있으므로 이를 함께 연계하여 숙지하도록 한다.

(A) locating
(B) has located
(C) is located
(D) is locating

문제 해설

locate라는 동사의 어형을 묻는 문제로 동사의 어형을 묻는 문제는 주어/동사 수일치 – 태 – 시제 순으로 그 어형을 파악하는 것이 효율적이다. 주어가 the apartment로 단수 주어이고 빈칸 뒤에는 타동사인 locate의 목적어가 등장하지 않고 있으므로 능동태가 아닌 수동태 형태이어야 한다. 또한 '현재'라는 뜻을 지닌 currently라는 부사의 수식을 받고 있으므로 현재 시제가 적절하다. 따라서 빈칸에는 is located가 와야 한다.

133

★★ 빈칸 문장 추론

(A) 월 임대료에 인터넷 사용 요금은 포함되지 않는다는 점에 유의해주시기 바랍니다
(B) 주방 용품을 판매하는 슈퍼마켓이 있다.
(C) 임대 계약서를 서명하기 위해 저희 사무실을 방문해 주세요.
(D) 월 전기비인 10달러가 부과됩니다.

빈칸 문장 추론 문제는 몇 번째 문제로 출제가 되더라도 전체 지문의 내용 흐름을 파악한 상태에서 풀어야 하므로 가장 마지막에 풀이하는 것이 효율적이다.

(A) Note that rent does not cover Internet.
(B) There is also a supermarket that sells kitchen supplies.
(C) Please visit our office to sign a lease.
(D) There is a monthly charge of $10 for electricity.

문제 해설

빈칸에 적합한 내용의 문장을 묻는 문제로 빈칸에 앞서 The rent is $750 a month, which includes gas, electricity, and water라며 월 임대료는 가스, 전기, 그리고 수도를 포함하여 750달러임을 밝히고 있으며 빈칸 이후에는 Pets are strictly prohibited라며 애완동물을 키우는 것은 엄격히 금지되고 있음을 밝히고 있다. 그러므로 빈칸에 는 임대와 관련된 또 다른 정보가 등장해야 함을 가늠할 수 있으므로 Note that rent does not cover internet, 즉 월 임대료에 인터넷 사용 요금은 포함되지 않는다는 점에 유의해주길 바란다는 내용이 와야 한다.

134

★★ 어형 / 동사

To가 전치사인지 혹은 To 부정사인지 구분하여 뒤이은 어형이 명사 혹은 동명사(V–ing)인지 아니면 동사원형(Vr)인지를 구분하는 문제는 토익에서 오랫동안 출제된 전형적인 문제 유형이다. 이런 문제를 접할 때는 사전에 관련 표현들을 숙지한 상태에서 풀이하는 것이 가장 이상적이나 그렇지 못한 경우에는 to 이하의 구가 목적/의도의 부사로 쓰였는지 아니면 주어/목적어/보어 역할을 하는 명사로 쓰였는지 혹은 명사를 수식하는 형용사로 쓰였는지 그 의미를 먼저 파악한 후 이와 무관하면 전치사라 여기고 명사 혹은 동명사 어형을 정답으로 선택하도록 한다.

(A) arrangement
(B) arrange
(C) arranged
(D) arranging

문제 해설

빈칸에 알맞은 어형을 묻는 문제로 빈칸이 to 이하에 위치하고 있으므로 무엇보다 to가 부정사인지 아니면 전치사인지 여부를 파악하는 것이 우선이다. Isabella Choi 씨에게 전화를 거는 것은 더 많은 정보 또는 아파트 구경을 하기 위한 약속을 잡기 위한 목적이므로 to 이하는 목적/의도의 뜻을 지닌 부정사구를 구성할 수 있어야 함을 알 수 있다. 그러므로 빈칸에는 동사 원형인 arrange가 적합하다.

Questions 135-138 refer to the following article.

Palo Lagota's Mayor, Ms. Betty Hwang, signed a new ------ **135.** that mandates the gradual increase of the minimum wage to $13 an hour next year. The current minimum wage of Palo Lagota is $11 an hour, making it one of the highest in the country. ------ **136.**, Palo Alto also has one of the highest living costs in the country. Last year, the Golden State was declared the fifth ------ **137.** state with an average home price of about $1,550,000. The new bill is receiving mixed reviews by economists and market analysts. ------ **138.**. Nevertheless, some of the city council members believe that the new minimum wage in Palo Lagota is the continuation of a logical economic policy.

Palo Lagota 시장인 Betty Hwang 씨는 내년에 최소 임금을 점진적으로 시간당 13달러로 의무화하는 새로운 법안에 서명했다. 현재 Palo Alto 시의 최저 임금은 시간당 11달러이며, 이는 국내에서 가장 최저 임금이 높은 지역이기도 하다. 하지만 Palo Alto 시 또한 국내에서 생활비가 가장 비싼 지역 중 한 곳이기도 하다. 작년에 캘리포니아 주는 평균 주택가가 155만 달러에 달하여 국내에서 주택 구매 비용이 가장 비싼 5번째 주로 지명되었다. 새로운 법안은 경제학자들과 시장 분석가들의 엇갈린 반응을 얻고 있다. 높은 임금이 정규 직원들에겐 도움이 될 수 있지만, 이는 고용율에 부정적인 영향을 미칠 수도 있다고 한다. 그럼에도 불구하고, 일부 시 의원들은 최저 임금이 실제로 논리적 경제 정책의 지속이라 생각하고 있다.

어휘 mandate 의 통치를 위임하다, ~을 명령하다 gradual 점진적인 minimum wage 최저 임금 current 현재의 average 평균, 평균의 living costs 생활비 the Golden State 캘리포니아 주 mixed reviews 엇갈린 반응, 상반된 반응 economist 경제학자 market analyst 시장 분석가 nevertheless 그럼에도 불구하고 city council 시 의회 actually 사실은 logical 논리적인 economic policy 경제 정책

135

(A) contract
(B) receipt
(C) legislation
(D) treaty

★★★ 어휘 / 명사 어휘

토익 분석

명사 legislation의 유사어로는 '법안'을 뜻하는 bill이 있으며 최근 정기 토익에서도 bill이 어휘 문제로 출제된 바 있으므로 함께 묶어서 숙지하도록 한다.

문제 해설

빈칸에 알맞은 명사 어휘를 묻는 문제이다. 빈칸을 중심으로 Palo Lagota 시장인 Betty Hwang 씨가 내년에 최저 임금을 점진적으로 시간당 10달러로 의무화하는 무엇인가에 서명했다는 내용이 등장하고 있다. 무엇보다 시장이 서명한 것은 내년 최저 임금을 시간당 13달러로 의무화하는 내용에 해당되는 것임을 고려할 때 빈칸에는 법적인 강제력이 있는 '법안'이라는 뜻을 지닌 legislation이란 명사 어휘가 와야 한다.

136

(A) Consequently
(B) Apparently
(C) Therefore
(D) However

★★ 어휘 / 접속부사 어휘

문제 분석

역접 – however, nevertheless, nonetheless, but
인과 – so, therefore, thus, as a result
추가 – moreover, furthermore, besides, plus, in addition, additionally
예시 – for example, for instance
동시 – at the same time, simultaneously

토익 분석

접속부사는 접속사가 아니라 두 절의 내용을 논리적으로 자연스럽게 이어주는 연결어의 역할을 하는 부사 어휘이다. 특히 파트 6에서는 접속부사를 묻는 문제가 자주 출제되는 편이므로 아래에 언급된 주요 접속부사들을 사전에 꼼꼼하게 숙지하는 것이 바람직하다.

문제 해설

빈칸에 적절한 부사 어휘를 묻는 문제이다. 빈칸에 앞서 The current minimum wage of Palo Lagota is $11 an hour, making it one of the highest in the country 라며 현재 Palo Lagota 시의 최저 임금은 시간당 8달러로 이는 국내에서 최저 임금이 가장 높은 지역이라는 내용이, 빈칸 이후에는 Palo Alto also has one of the highest living costs in the country 라며 Palo Lagota 시 또한 국내에서 생활비가 가장 비싼 지역 중 한 곳이라는 내용이 언급되고 있다. 즉, 현재 Palo Lagota 시의 최저 임금이 11달러로 국내에서 가장 높긴 해도 그에 반해 Palo Lagota 시의 생활비 또한 전국에서 가장 비싼 지역 중 한 곳이라 높은 최저 임금의 효력이 반감되고 있다는 내용으로 두 절은 서로 상충되는 내용을 지니고 있음을 알 수 있다. 따라서 빈칸에는 '그러나'란 뜻으로 역접 관계를 나타내는 부사인 however이 와야 한다.

★★ 어형 / 최상급 형용사

문제 분석

one of the 서수 + 최상급 형용사 + 가산 복수명사 가장 ~
한 ~들 중에 하나

토익 분석

비교급 어형과 최상급 어형을 잘 구분하여 선택하기 위
해선 비교급 어형은 비교 대상이 둘인 경우에 가능하며
최상급 어형은 비교 대상이 최소 셋 이상인 경우에 발생
할 수 있다는 기본 개념을 명확하게 숙지해야 한다. 그리
고 최상급은 절대적이고 유일한 대상을 지칭하기 때문에
'정관사 the + 최상급 형용사 어형 (형용사 원급 + est /
most + 형용사 원급) + 명사'의 어순을 지니게 된다. 그리
고 절대적인 것이라도 상태에 따라 그 순서가 발생할 수
있다. 이를테면 30명의 사람들 중에서 가장 키가 큰 사람
은 하나겠지만, 두 번째, 세 번째, 네 번째…와 같이 가장
키가 큰 상태도 순서가 발생할 수 있기 때문에 최상급 앞
에는 정관사와 서수가 위치할 수 있다는 점을 이해하도록
한다.

(A) expensive
(B) expensively
(C) more expensive
(D) most expensive

문제 해설

서수는 기본적으로 수를 나타내는 것이 아니라 순서를 표현하므로 서수가 등장한다는 것은 결과적
으로 그 배경은 하나가 아닌 여럿이라는 것임을 의미하며 서수와 연계된 형용사는 둘 사이의 상대
적 비교를 나타내는 비교급 어형이 아니라 셋 이상의 대상에게서 쓰이는 최상급 어형을 지녀야 함
을 알 수 있다. 따라서 빈칸에는 most expensive가 와야 한다.

★★★ 빈칸 문장 추론

(A) 높은 임금이 정규 직원들에겐 도움이 될 수 있지만,
이는 고용율에 부정적인 영향을 미칠 수도 있다.
(B) 시 의회가 법안을 통과시킬 때까지 다양한 정치적 격
론이 지속될 것이다.
(C) 시장은 여전히 법안에 서명을 해야 할지 여부에 대해
결정하지 못하고 있다.
(D) California 주에 있는 모든 비정규 직원들은 내년부터
시간당 13달러를 받게 될 것이다.

토익 분석

지문의 전반적인 내용 흐름을 파악하고 빈칸 위치에 따라
제시되는 내용적 특징을 이해하며 내용적 연관성이 없는
어휘나 표현이 제시되는 선택지를 빠르게 오답으로 소거
해 나가며 정답을 택일하는 것이 가장 효율적인 풀이 방
법이다. 아울러 함께 출제된 다른 문제들을 먼저 풀이하
고 난 후 가장 마지막으로 풀이하는 것이 바람직하다.

(A) While a higher wage can aid full-time workers, it may negatively impact employment rates.
(B) Various political debates will continue until the city council passes the bill.
(C) The mayor still hasn't decided whether she will sign the bill or not.
(D) All of the irregular workers in California will be making $13 an hour next year.

문제 해설

빈칸에 적합한 내용의 문장을 묻는 문제이다. 빈칸에 앞서 The new bill is receiving mixed reviews
by economists and market analysts라며 새로운 법안은 경제학자들과 시장 분석가들의 엇갈린 반
응을 얻고 있다는 내용이, 빈칸 이후에는 Nevertheless, some of the city council members believe
that the new minimum wage in Palo Lagota is the continuation of a logical economic policy
라며 그럼에도 불구하고, 일부 시 의원들은 최저 임금이 실제로 논리적 경제 정책의 지속이라 생각
한다는 내용이 등장하고 있다. 또한 '~임에도 불구하고'란 뜻을 지닌 nevertheless란 접속부사가 두
절 사이에 위치하고 있음을 고려할 때 빈칸에는 새로운 법안이 경제학자들과 시장 분석가들의 엇갈
린 반응을 얻고 있다는 내용과 함께 일부 시 의원들은 최저 임금이 실제로 논리적 경제 정책의 지속
이라는 긍정적 평가에 상반되는 내용이 와야 함을 알 수 있다.

따라서 빈칸에는 높은 임금이 정규 직원들에겐 도움이 될 수 있지만, 이는 고용율에 부정적인 영향
을 미칠 수도 있다는 내용으로 최저 임금의 상승이 경제적으로 좋지 않은 영향을 미칠 수 있는 비
판적 문맥을 지닌 While a higher wage can aid full-time workers, it may negatively impact
employment rates이 와야 한다.

Questions 139-142 refer to the following Web page.

Gold membership for Xpress Shop

Tired of waiting for your package to arrive? Desperate for a little bit of shopping therapy? Hate paying for expedited shipping? Become a gold member today and ------- those problems. Gold members ------- free same-day shipping for an unlimited amount of deliveries. -------, members receive a $30 electronic gift certificate every year. -------. For an annual fee of just $39, become a gold member today. Take advantage of this golden opportunity! You will not regret it!
139. **140.** **141.** **142.**

Xpress 상점의 골드 회원

주문한 제품이 도착하는 걸 기다리기가 짜증나시나요? 약간의 쇼핑으로 위안을 얻고 싶으신가요? 특급 배송비를 지불하는 것이 싫으신가요? 오늘 골드 회원이 되셔서 이러한 문제점들을 피하세요. 골드 회원은 배달되는 제품의 양과 무관하게 무료 당일 배송의 혜택을 누릴 수 있습니다. 이에 추가로 골드 회원들은 해마다 30달러에 달하는 전자 상품권을 받으시게 됩니다. 저희 상점은 또한 골드 회원들에게 추가 할인 혜택을 제공합니다. 단 39달러에 해당하는 연간 회원비로 오늘 골드 회원이 되세요. 이 황금 같은 기회를 놓치지 마세요! 결코 후회하지 않으실 겁니다!

어휘 be tired of ~에 싫증나다, ~에 짜증이 나다 be desperate for ~를 간절히 원하다 expedite ~을 촉진시키다, ~을 촉진시키다 same-day shipping 당일 배송 unlimited 무제한의, 제약이 없는 amount 양, 금액 return 반품, ~을 반납하다 annual fee 연 회비 take an advantage of ~의 이점을 이용하다, ~의 혜택을 누리다 golden opportunity 아주 좋은 기회 regret ~을 후회하다, ~에 대해 유감으로 생각하다

139

(A) avoid
(B) embrace
(C) allow
(D) delay

★★ 어휘 / 동사 어휘

토익 분석

토익에서는 동사 avoid가 목적어로 명사뿐만 아니라 V-ing 형태의 동명사 어형을 취하는 것이 가능하다는 점을 묻는 문제도 오랫동안 출제된 바 있으므로 이 또한 알아두도록 한다.

문제 해설

빈칸에 적합한 동사 어휘를 묻는 문제이다. 빈칸에 앞서 Tired of waiting for your package to arrive? Desperate for a little bit of shopping therapy? Hate paying for expedited shipping?이라며 주문한 제품을 기다리는 것이 싫은지, 약간의 쇼핑을 통한 위안을 얻길 원하는지, 특급 배송비 지불이 싫은지 쇼핑할 때 겪을 수 있는 보통의 불편함에 대해 묻고 있다. 이어서 빈칸 앞에 골드 회원이 되라는 내용이, 빈칸 이후에는 앞서 언급된 문제점들 those problems이 등장하고 있다. 따라서 빈칸에는 이러한 문제점들을 겪을 필요가 없도록 자사의 골드 회원으로 가입하라는 문맥이 형성될 수 있도록 '피하다'란 뜻을 지닌 avoid가 와야 한다.

140

(A) enjoyment
(B) enjoying
(C) enjoy
(D) enjoyed

★ 어형 / 동사 어형 + 동사 시제

토익 분석

파트 6에서는 시제를 가늠할 수 있는 시제 통제 부사가 등장하지 않는 상태에서 동사 어형 문제가 출제되는 경우가 많다. 따라서 파트 6에서의 시제 문제는 미래 시제(현재 시제 - 현재 시제 진행상 포함) - 현재 시제 완료상 - 과거 시제 순으로 출제되는 경향이 있다는 점을 숙지하고 있으면 파트 6에서 동사의 시제가 반영된 어형 문제를 풀이할 때 상당한 도움이 된다.

문제 해설

빈칸에 적절한 어형을 묻는 문제로 빈칸이 주어인 Gold members와 목적어인 free same-day shipping 사이에 위치하고 있다. 그러므로 절을 구성할 수 있는 동사 어형인 enjoy와 enjoyed 중 정답을 택일해야 하며, 골드 회원이 누릴 수 있는 당일 무료 배송이란 혜택을 안내하고 있다는 점을 고려할 때 빈칸에는 일반적인 사실을 언급할 수 있는 현재 시제 형태인 enjoy가 적합함을 알 수 있다.

★★ 어휘 / 접속부사

문제 분석

- 역접
  접속부사 however, nevertheless, nonetheless, but
  전치사 in spite of, despite, notwithstanding
  접속사 although, though, even though
- 인과
  접속부사 so, therefore, thus, as a result
  전치사 as a result of
- 추가
  접속부사 moreover, furthermore, besides, in addition, additionally
  전치사 in addition to

토익 분석

접속부사 문제를 풀이할 때 유념해야 할 것은 선택지에는 접속부사뿐만 아니라 동일한 의미를 지닌 전치사나 접속사가 함께 등장시키며 혼동을 초래한다는 것이다. 따라서 각 접속부사마다 이와 유사한 뜻을 지닌 전치사나 접속사와 함께 묶어 학습하여 막상 접속부사 문제를 풀이할 때 어려움을 겪지 않도록 대비하도록 한다.

(A) In spite of
(B) Simultaneously
(C) In addition
(D) Therefore

문제 해설

빈칸이 두 개의 절 사이에 위치하고 있지만 두 개의 절이 서로 접속하여 하나의 문장으로 쓰이는 것이 아니라 두 절이 각각 단독적으로 쓰이고 있으므로 빈칸에는 두 절의 내용을 원활하게 이어주는 접속부사가 위치해야 한다. 빈칸 앞에는 free same-day shipping for an unlimited amount of deliveries라며 무료 당일 배송이 언급되고 있으며 빈칸 이후에는 members receive an 30$ electronic gift certificate every year라며 해마다 회원은 30달러에 달하는 상품권을 수령하게 된다는 내용이 등장하고 있다. 빈칸을 사이에 두고 골드 회원이 누릴 수 있는 혜택들이 연이어 제시되고 있으므로 빈칸에는 추가/첨가의 뜻을 지닌 In addition이 와야 함이 옳다.

★★ 빈칸 문장 추론

(A) 골드 회원 가입에 관심을 가져주셔서 진심으로 감사합니다.
(B) 또한 골드 회원에게는 구매 시 추가 할인을 제공합니다.
(C) 자연으로 인해 아직 수령받지 못하신 점 사과 말씀 드립니다.
(D) 150달러 이상을 구매하시면, 할인 및 당일 무료 배송 서비스를 받으실 수 있습니다.

토익 분석

지문의 전반적인 내용 흐름을 파악하고 빈칸 위치에 따라 제시되는 내용적 특징을 이해하며 내용적 연관성이 없는 어휘나 표현이 제시되는 선택지를 빠르게 오답으로 소거해 나가며 정답을 택일하는 것이 가장 효율적인 풀이 방법이다. 아울러 함께 출제된 다른 문제들을 먼저 풀이하고 난 후 가장 마지막으로 풀이하는 것이 바람직하다.

(A) We sincerely thank for your interest in becoming a gold member.
(B) Our store also provides gold members with additional discounts on purchases.
(C) We are surprised that you did not receive your shipment and apologize for the delay.
(D) By spending over $150, you will qualify for discounts and free same-day shipping.

문제 해설

빈칸에 적합한 내용의 문장을 묻는 문제이다. 빈칸에 앞서 members receive an $30 electronic gift certificate every year라며 골드 회원들은 해마다 30달러에 달하는 전자 상품권을 받게 된다는 내용이, 빈칸 이후에는 For an annual fee of just $39, become a gold member today라며 단지 39달러에 해당하는 연간 회원비로 오늘 골드 회원이 되길 바란다는 내용이 언급되고 있다. 따라서 빈칸에는 앞서 골드 회원들에겐 30달러에 달하는 전자 상품권이 주어진다는 한 가지 혜택에 이어 골드 회원들을 위한 추가 할인 혜택을 제공한다며 골드 회원으로서 얻게 될 또 다른 혜택에 대해 설명하고 있는 Our store also provides gold members with additional discounts on purchases이 와야 한다.

Questions 143-146 refer to the following article.

Starting next Wednesday, the Metropolitan Art Museum will be holding an exhibit on the works of photographer Ms. Sally Murphy. Ms. Murphy's photos ------- many international awards. The rising artist is renowned for her
143.
black and white photos that feature the socially oppressed. She was the sole apprentice of the late Nola Kozlowski, a prominent photographer who focused on capturing the lives of indigenous peoples. Based on ------- she learned
144.
from Ms. Kozlowski, Ms. Murphy went on to take photos of homeless people, beggars, child workers, and other socially ignored citizens. "Like the indigenous people that are not being fully recognized globally, there are people within our own cities that are being ignored," stated Ms. Murphy. "I wanted to capture their lives through photography ------- my audience can see and reconnect
145.
with their forgotten neighbors." The photographer hopes to contribute to society through her works. -------. The exhibit will last for four months.
146.

다음 주 수요일부터 Metropolitan 미술관에서는 사진작가 Sally Murphy의 작품전이 개최된다. Murphy 씨의 사진은 국제적으로 많은 상들을 수상했다. 이 떠오르는 신예 사진작가는 사회적으로 억압받는 사람들을 보여주는 흑백 사진으로 명성이 높다. 그녀는 원주민들의 삶을 포착하는 것에 집중한 저명한 사진작가로 지금은 고인이 되신 Nola Kozlowski 씨의 유일한 제자이다. 그녀는 Kozlowski 씨에게 배운 내용을 토대로, 지속적으로 노숙자, 거지, 아동 노동자 그리고 사회적으로 인정받지 못하는 시민들의 모습을 사진에 담았다. "전 세계적으로 잘 알려지지 않은 원주민들의 삶처럼, 우리가 살고 있는 도시 안에도 인정받지 못하는 사람들이 있습니다."라고 Murphy 씨는 이야기했으며, 또한 그녀는 "저는 그들이 살아가는 삶의 순간을 사진에 담아 제 사진을 보는 관람객들이 그 사진들을 보고 그들이 잊혀진 이웃들과 다시 연결될 수 있길 바랐습니다." 그 사진작가는 자신의 작품을 통해 사회에 기여할 수 있길 희망하고 있다. 그녀는 모든 전시회의 수익을 자선 단체에 기부할 계획이다. 그녀의 전시회는 넉 달 간 계속될 것이다.

어휘 hold ~을 잡다, ~을 쥐다, ~을 개최하다 photographer 사진사, 사진작가 award 상, 상을 수여하다 internationally 국제적으로 rising 떠오르는 be renowned for ~로 유명하다 black and white photos 흑백 사진 socially 사회적으로 oppress ~을 억누르다, ~을 압박하다, ~을 탄압하다 sole 홀로, 유일한, 단독의 apprentice 견습생, 도제, 제자 prominent 유명한 focus on ~에 집중하다 capture ~을 잡다, ~을 포착하나 indigenous 고유의, 토착의 be based on ~에 바탕을 두다, ~에 근간을 두다 go on to Vr 계속하여 ~를 하다 homeless people 노숙자 ignore ~을 무시하다 fully 완전히, 충분히 reconnect to ~에 다시 연결하다 forgotten 잊혀진 contribute to ~에 기여하다, ~에 기고하다, ~에 기부하다 last for ~만큼 지속되다

143

(A) receives
(B) were received
(C) have received
(D) will receive

★★ 어형 / 동사 어형 + 동사의 시제

문제 해설

빈칸에 적합한 동사의 어형을 묻는 문제로 빈칸 앞에는 Ms. Murphy's photos라는 복수 주어가 등장하고 있으며 복수 동사 어형이 필요하며 빈칸 이후에는 many international awards라는 목적어가 등장하고 있으므로 아울러 동사 어형은 수동태가 아닌 능동태 구조여야 한다. 이를 고려할 때 receives와 were received는 모두 오답으로 소거해야 하므로 have received와 will receive 중 정답을 택일해야 한다. 따라서 Sally Murphy 씨의 사진 전시회에 대한 소개를 하는 지문이므로 Sally Murphy 씨에 대한 홍보와 소개가 이뤄져야 하며 아울러 will receive가 위치해야 하는 경우 앞으로 국제적인 상들을 수상하게 될 것이라는 내용은 부적절하므로 지금까지 국제적인 상들을 수상했다는 내용을 형성할 수 있도록 have received가 와야 한다.

★★★ 접속사 / 명사절 접속사

토익 분석

접속사 중에서 who/whom/which/what과 선행사를 취하는 that만이 주어 혹은 목적어가 없는 불완전한 구조의 절과 함께 쓰이는 것이 가능하며 이들을 제외한 나머지 접속사들은 어떠한 접속사라 하더라도 완전한 절과 함께 쓰여야 한다는 점을 숙지하고 있어야 한다. 아울러 접속사 what은 선행사를 취하지 않는다는 특징을 지니고 있으므로 what/which 중에서 선행사가 보이지 않는다면 정답은 what이 되어야 한다.

(A) that   (B) which

(C) what   (D) how

문제 해설

빈칸에 적합한 접속사를 묻는 문제로 빈칸이 전치사 on과 she learned from Mr. Kozlowsk라는 절 사이에 위치하고 있다. 기본적으로 전치사는 구와 함께 쓰이지만, 전치사 뒤에 명사절 접속사가 오는 경우 명사절을 취하는 것이 가능하며 아울러 해당 접속사는 she learned from Mr. Kozlowsk란 전치사 from의 목적어가 빠진 불완전한 구조의 절과 함께 쓰여야 함을 알 수 있다. 선택지에 있는 접속사들 중 명사절 접속사 that과 how는 모두 완전한 구조의 절과 함께 쓰여야 하므로 이들은 오답으로 소거해야 한다. 따라서 빈칸에는 불완전한 구조의 절과 함께 쓰이는 which와 what 중에서 정답을 택일해야 하며, 그가 Kozlowsk 씨로부터 배운 것을 바탕으로 한다는 내용을 형성할 수 있으려면 빈칸에는 which가 아닌 what이 와야 한다.

★★ 접속사 / 목적 부사절 접속사

문제 분석

so that + 주어 + can / may + 동사원형 = in order that + 주어 + can / may + 동사원형 주어가 ~하는 것이 가능할 수 있도록 하고자

토익 분석

[목적 부사절 접속사 so that + 주어 + can / may + 동사원형]은 that이란 접속사를 묻거나 조동사 can / may 또는 that이 생략된 상태의 so를 묻는 형태로 출제된다. 아울러 so that에 비해 출제 빈도는 떨어지지만 so that을 in order that으로 바꾸어 쓸 수 있다는 점도 함께 알아두도록 한다.

(A) so   (B) therefore

(C) however   (D) although

문제 해설

빈칸이 두 절 사이에 위치하고 있으므로 빈칸에 알맞은 접속사를 묻는 문제임을 알 수 있다. 우선 therefore은 접속부사로 오답이며, however은 접속부사와 부사절 접속사로 쓰이는 경우가 모두 가능하나 접속부사로서의 however은 오답이며, 부사절 접속사로 쓰이는 however의 경우 however 뒤에 however이 수식하는 형용사나 부사가 와야 한다는 점을 고려할 때 부사절 접속사로서의 however 역시 오답으로 처리해야 한다. 아울러 although는 두 절의 내용이 서로 상반되어야 하므로 이 또한 오답이다. 무엇보다 신속한 문제풀이를 위해서는 빈칸 이후의 절 my audience can see and reconnect to their forgotten neighbors에서 can see를 간과하지 않도록 해야 한다. 따라서 빈칸에는 can see와 함께 쓰여 주절인 I wanted to capture their lives through photography, 즉 사진을 통해 그들의 삶을 촬영한 사진 촬영의 목적과 의도를 표현할 수 있는 목적 부사절 접속사를 구성할 수 있는 so (that)이 와야 한다.

★★★ 빈칸 문장 추론

(A) 그녀는 모든 전시회의 수익을 자선 단체에 기부할 계획이다.
(B) 전시회는 Kozlowski 씨가 원주민들을 찍은 사진들을 바탕으로 이뤄질 것이다.
(C) 그 사진작가는 노숙자들을 대상으로 사진을 찍을 출사 계획에 대해 언급했다.
(D) 몇몇 잡지사들은 그녀의 사진을 사용하기 위해서 조만간 연락을 취할 것이다.

(A) She plans to donate all of the exhibition's profits to charity organizations.
(B) The exhibition will be based on Ms. Kozlowski 's photos of indigenous people.
(C) The photographer mentioned future plans of taking photos of homeless people.
(D) Several magazines and publications will contact her to use her pictures soon.

문제 해설

빈칸에 적합한 내용의 문장을 묻는 문제이다. 빈칸에 앞서 The photographer hopes to contribute to society through his work라며 그 사진작가는 자신의 작품을 통해 사회에 기여할 수 있길 희망하고 있다는 내용이 등장하고 있으며 빈칸 이후에는 The exhibit will last for four months라며 전시회가 넉 달간 계속될 것임을 밝히고 있다. 그러므로 빈칸에 앞서 그 사진작가가 자신의 작품을 통해 사회에 기여할 수 있길 희망하고 있다는 내용이 제시되고 있음을 고려할 때 빈칸에는 자신의 전시회를 통해 사회에 기여할 수 있는 구체적인 방법이 언급되어야 함을 알 수 있다. 따라서 빈칸에는 She plans to donate all of the exhibition's profits to charity organizations, 즉 그녀가 모든 전시회의 수익을 자선 단체에 기부할 계획이라는 내용이 적합하다.

Questions 147-148 refer to the following receipt.

<table>
<tr><td colspan="2">CASH ALLOWANCE RECEIPT</td></tr>
<tr><td colspan="2">DATE 23 November
NAME (IN BLOCK LETTERS) HANK SHREDDER</td></tr>
<tr><td>DETAILED INFORMATION</td><td>AMOUNT</td></tr>
<tr><td>Business travel and meal expenses associated with [147] the accounting conference I will attend in Manhattan, New York from 25 to 26 November</td><td>$1,974</td></tr>
<tr><td>[148] I confirm receipt of the above sum.
Signature Hank Shredder</td><td></td></tr>
</table>

147-148 다음 영수증을 참조하시오.

현금 지급 수당 영수증

날짜 11월 23일
성명 (활자체로 기재) HANK SHREDDER

상세 정보	금액
[147] 11월 25일부터 26일까지 뉴욕, 맨해튼에서 참석할 예정인 회계 컨퍼런스와 관련된 모든 출장 및 식사 지출 비용을 지불하기 위함.	$1,974
[148] 상기 금액의 수령을 확인합니다. 서명 *Hank Shredder*	

어휘 allowance 수당, 지급액 receipt 영수증, 수령, 수납 block letter 활자체 detailed 상세한, 세부적인 expense 지출 비용 associated with ~와 관련된 accounting 회계 attend ~에 참석하다 confirm ~을 확인해 주다 above 상기의, 위의 sum 액수, 총계

147

What will Mr. Shredder do in New York in November?

(A) Sign a new contract
(B) Go on vacation
(C) Hire some accountants
(D) Participate in an event

★★ 세부사항

Shredder 씨는 11월에 뉴욕에서 무엇을 할 것인가?
(A) 새로운 계약을 맺는다.
(B) 휴가를 떠난다.
(C) 몇몇 회계사를 고용한다.
(D) 행사에 참가한다.

토익 분석

시간/시점/요일은 단서와 함께 제시되는 키워드이므로 지문에서 해당 시간/시점/요일이 언급되는 부분만 빠르게 찾아 집중해라.

문제 해설

Shredder 씨는 11월 뉴욕에서 하게 될 일에 대해 묻는 문제이므로 지문에서 11월과 뉴욕, 즉 November과 New York이 등장하는 부분을 중심으로 단서를 파악해야 한다. 영수증에서 the accounting conference I will attend in Manhattan, New York from 25 to 26 November이라며 11월이라는 시점과 New York이란 장소가 등장하며 해당 시점에 열리는 회계 컨퍼런스에 참가한다고 되어 있으므로 (D)가 정답이다.

148

What does Mr. Shredder confirm?

(A) Purchasing new accounting software
(B) Submitting original receipts
(C) Paying hotel costs
(D) Receiving some funds

★ 세부사항

Shredder 씨는 무엇을 확인해 주고 있는가?
(A) 신규 회계 소프트웨어를 구입한 것
(B) 원본 영수증을 제출한 것
(C) 호텔 비용을 지불한 것
(D) 일부 비용을 수령한 것

토익 분석

인명은 키워드이므로 지문에서 인명이 제시되는 부분에서 단서를 살펴봐야 하지만 영수증 자체가 전체적으로 Shredder 씨와 관련된 내용이므로 선택지의 내용을 키워드로 삼아 지문에서 해당 내용이 언급되는지 여부를 빠르게 파악해라.

문제 해설

Shredder 씨의 서명과 함께 confirm이라는 동사가 그대로 활용된 I confirm receipt of the above sum 부분을 통해 바로 위에 적힌 금액의 수령을 확인하고 있으므로 (D)가 정답이다.

149-150 다음 송장을 참조하시오.

New Line Office Supply Warehouse
25200 Carlos Bee Blvd, Hayward, CA 94542 510-212-6313

배송 송장

날짜: 1월 10일
송장 번호: 941796
구매자: Anna Gunn
배송 주소: 540 Pine Street, Daly City, CA 94015

Prima Silver 사무용 책상/워크스테이션 $209.95
Support System 10 책상용 의자 $109.95
Samson 19인치 모니터 $149.95
Samson 컴퓨터 (모델 번호: 안드로메다 X110) $909.90
소계 $1,559.75
[149] 단골 구매 고객 할인$100.00
세금 $86.99
[150] 총계 $1,546.74

New Line Office Supply Warehouse에서 구매해 주셔서 감사합니다.

어휘 office supplies 사무용품 subtotal 중간 합계
frequent shopper 단골 고객 tax 세금

Questions 149-150 refer to the following invoice.

New Line Office Supply Warehouse

25200 Carlos Bee Blvd, Hayward, CA 94542 510-212-6313

Delivery Invoice
Date: Jan 10
Invoice No: 941796
Purchased by: Anna Gunn
Delivery Address: 540 Pine Street, Daly City, CA 94015

Prima Silver Work Desk / Workstation $209.95
Support System 10 Desk Chair $109.95
Samson 19-inch Monitor $149.95
Samson Computer (Model #: Andromeda X110) $909.90
Subtotal $1,559.75
[149] Frequent Shopper Discount$100.00
Tax $86.99
[150] Total $1,546.74

Thank you for shopping at New Line Office Supply Warehouse.

149

★★ 유추

Gunn 씨에 대해 암시되는 것은 무엇인가?
(A) 가게에서 배송품을 직접 찾아갈 것이다.
(B) 사무용품 회사에서 일한다.
(C) New Line Office Supply Warehouse에서 물건을 자주 구매한다.
(D) 다음 주에 책상을 구매할 것이다.

토익 분석

유추 문제의 키워드가 지문 전반에 걸쳐 언급되고 있는 상태에서 적절한 유추 내용을 파악해야 한다면 선택지에 나온 내용을 먼저 파악한 후 선택지의 내용을 유추할 수 있는 근거가 지문에 제시되는지 여부를 역으로 확인하는 방식으로 문제를 풀이하라.

What is suggested about Ms. Gunn?

(A) She will pick up her items from the store.
(B) She works for an office supplies company.
(C) She often shops at New Line Office Supply Warehouse.
(D) She will purchase a desk next week.

문제 해설

송장의 하단 Frequent Shopper Discount, 즉 자주 상품을 구매하는 고객을 위한 할인 혜택이 제공되는 점을 토대로 Gunn 씨는 이 곳에서 물건을 자주 구매하는 단골 고객임을 유추할 수 있다. 따라서 정답은 (C)가 되겠다.

150

★ 세부사항

송장 상에서 지불되어야 하는 총 금액은 얼마인가?
(A) $1,559.75
(B) $1,546.74
(C) $909.90
(D) $86.99

토익 분석

영수증이나 송장에서의 최종 액수를 묻는 문제에는 늘 함정이 포함되어 있다. 즉, 할인을 비롯하여 비용의 일부를 차감 받은 항목이 분명 포함되어 있으므로 이를 꼭 확인하고 최종 액수를 선택하라.

What is the total amount paid on this invoice?

(A) $1,559.75
(B) $1,546.74
(C) $909.90
(D) $86.99

문제 해설

송장 상에서 지불되어야 하는 총 금액은 송장의 맨 마지막 부분에 나와 있는 총액을 통해 알 수 있다. 그러므로 정답은 $1,546.74, 즉 (B)라고 할 수 있다.

Questions 151-153 refer to the following article.

Bangkok, Thailand

[151] Bangkok is a thrilling, vibrant city that has many attractions to excite the modern traveler. Whether you are here to sample Thai culture, taste the delicious food, or simply to shop, Bangkok has something for you.

[151] Things to see:
The Grand Palace is one of the main attractions, and most visitors to the city head there first. This palace was built in the eighteenth century and features many precious Buddha statues.

The market in Chinatown draws huge crowds of tourists on weekends. You can find some fantastic bargains that will make great gifts for people at home. Don't be afraid to bargain, but be polite. [153] Watch out for pickpockets, who operate in this area.

[152] Accommodations:
There are many great budget hotels around the city. [153] Try the Royal Thai Hotel for reasonably priced rooms in a central location (single rooms $10, double $18). The Bangkok Inn is also popular with tourists. It offers rooms with TVs and hot showers in the heart of the tourist district (single rooms $12, double $20).

151-153 다음 기사를 참조하시오.
태국, 방콕
[151] 방콕은 현대 여행객들을 흥분시키는 많은 매력적인 관광지들을 가진 신나고 활기찬 도시이다. 이곳에 태국 문화를 경험하기 위해 왔든, 맛있는 음식들을 맛보기 위해 왔든, 혹은 쇼핑을 위해 왔든 간에, 방콕은 모두를 위한 그 무언가를 가지고 있는 도시이다.

[151] 관광 명소들:
The Grand Palace는 도시 관광객들이 처음으로 방문하는 주요 관광명소이다. 18세기에 세워진 이 궁궐에는 귀중한 불상들이 많이 있다.

차이나 타운에 있는 시장은 주말에 엄청난 관광 인파를 끌어 들인다. 이곳에서 집에 있는 가족들을 위한 훌륭한 선물이 될만한 환상적이고 저렴한 물건들을 찾을 수 있다. 흥정을 두려워하지 말되 정중히 하기 바란다. [153] 이 지역에서 활동하는 소매치기들을 경계해야 한다.

[152] 숙박시설:
도시 주변에는 굉장히 싼 호텔들이 많이 있다. [153] 도심지에 위치한 적절한 가격의 Royal Thai 호텔을 이용해 보는 것도 괜찮다. (1인실-10달러, 2인실-18달러). 관광 지구 중심에 있는 방콕 여관도 여행객들에게 인기가 높으며, TV와 뜨거운 샤워가 가능한 시설을 구비한 방을 제공한다. (1인실-12달러, 2인실-20달러).

어휘 thrilling 스릴 있는 vibrant 자극적인, 활기찬 tourist attraction 관광명소 head 가다, 향하다 main attraction 주요명소 palace 성 draw 끌어들이다 bargain 싸게 사는 물건, 흥정하다 pickpocket 소매치기 accommodation 적응, 순응, 편의, 숙박, 수용 시설 pirated goods 해적판, 복제품

151

In what type of publication would the article mostly likely be found?

(A) An economic report
(B) A business journal
(C) A hotel magazine
(D) A travel guidebook

문제 해설

기사문 초반 Bangkok is a thrilling, vibrant city that has many attractions to excite the modern traveler에서 방콕이 관광객을 많이 유치하는 도시임을 밝히고 있으며 이어서 각각 관광거리와 숙박시설에 대해 구체적으로 나누어 설명하는 부분을 통해 이 기사는 여행 가이드북에서 접할 수 있을만한 기사임을 알 수 있다. 따라서 정답은 (D)가 되겠다.

★ **지문의 종류**

이 기사문은 어떠한 종류의 출간물에서 접할 수 있을 것 같은가?
(A) 경제 보고서
(B) 비즈니스 잡지
(C) 호텔잡지
(D) 여행 가이드북

토익 분석

지문이 포함되어 있을만한 출간물을 묻는 질문에서는 지문의 분야를 유추할 수 있는 어휘나 표현을 찾아본 후 이를 접할 수 있는 출간물의 정체를 파악하라.

★★ 세부사항

관광객들이 차이나 타운에 있는 시장을 방문할 때 주의해야 하는 이유는 무엇인가?
(A) 심각한 교통체증이 발생한다.
(B) 시장에 도둑들이 존재한다.
(C) 시장에 갈 때 택시에서 과한 요금을 청구한다.
(D) 시장에서 많은 복제품들이 판매된다.

토익 분석

세부사항을 묻는 문제는 질문에서 빠른 키워드(핵심어) 파악이 관건이다. 해당 문제에서는 **China town**이 키워드이므로 지문에서 **China town**에 대한 정보가 제공되는 부분을 빠르게 찾아 단서를 파악해야 한다.

Why must tourists be cautious when visiting the market in Chinatown?

(A) There is a lot of traffic on the roads.
(B) There are some thieves in the market.
(C) Taxis charge high prices to go to the market.
(D) Lots of pirated goods are sold at the market.

문제 해설

차이나 타운에 있는 시장을 방문할 때 주의해야 하는 이유이므로 차이나 타운의 시장을 언급하는 부분을 빠르게 찾아야 한다. 기사문 세 번째 단락이 차이나 타운에 대해 다루는 부분이며 여기서 Watch out for pickpockets, who operate in this area라고 말하는 부분을 통해 시장에는 소매치기들이 활동하고 있기 때문에 주의해야 할 필요가 있음을 알 수 있으며, 아울러 지문에서의 pickpockets은 선택지에서 thieves라는 유사표현으로 바뀌어 제시되고 있음에 유의해야 한다. 그러므로 정답은 (B)라고 할 수 있다.

★ 세부사항

Royal Thai 호텔에 대해 알 수 있는 것은 무엇인가?
(A) 중심지에 위치해 있다
(B) 방들이 넓고 깨끗하다.
(C) 호텔에 있는 식당에서 환상적인 태국 음식을 제공한다.
(D) 호텔은 투숙객을 위한 수영장을 보유하고 있다

토익 분석

고유명사는 중요한 키워드이므로 지문에서 **Royal Thai Hotel**이란 호텔명이 제시되는 부분만 빠르게 찾아 그 전후 내용에서 단서를 파악해야 한다.

What is indicated about the Royal Thai Hotel?

(A) It is located in a central area.
(B) Its rooms are spacious and clean.
(C) The restaurant serves fantastic Thai cuisine.
(D) The hotel has a swimming pool for guests to use.

문제 해설

Royal Thai 호텔에 대해 묻고 있으므로 Royal Thai 호텔이 소개되는 부분에서 단서를 찾는 것이 바람직하다. 숙박을 소개하는 마지막 단락 초반 Try the Royal Thai Hotel for reasonably priced rooms in a central location에서 Royal Thai 호텔은 중심지에 위치하고 있다며 위치적인 특징을 정확하게 언급하고 있다. 그러므로 정답은 (A)가 되겠다.

Questions 154-156 refer to the following advertisement.

Roseville Community Center

Located just a short 10-minute drive from downtown Roseville in a scenic mountain setting, the Roseville Community Center (RCC) is the community's new center for leisure, exercise, and relaxation. [154] The RCC is a great place for families and singles to get a massage, play sports, go swimming, and even take a nap in our sunroom.

With a variety of things to keep you busy and a variety of ways to relax, the RCC is an ideal place for family get-togethers and short business meetings, and a comfortable spot to meet other singles. Our on-site coordinator will help you create the perfect plan for your day. [155] For an additional charge, we provide a personal bath accessory package.

For memberships, please call the front desk at 404-555-3242, or send us an e-mail at members@rcc.com. To contact our on-site coordinator, please call 404-575-4331. [156] For more information, photos, directions, and feedback from other members, please visit us at www.rcc.org.

154-156 다음 광고를 참조하시오.

Roseville 지역 문화 센터

Roseville 시내에서 차로 10분 거리의 풍경 좋은 산과 어우러진 지역에 위치해 있는 **Roseville** 지역 센터(RCC)는 지역 사회에서 레저, 운동, 휴식을 위한 새로운 공간입니다. [154] Roseville 지역 센터는 가족 및 개인 단위로 마사지를 받고, 운동 및 수영을 즐기고, 심지어 일광욕실에서 낮잠을 즐길 수 있는 훌륭한 장소입니다.

다채로운 활동과 휴식을 제공하는 RCC는 가족 모임과 단기 사업 회의, 미혼 남녀들의 편안한 만남의 장소로써 최적의 장소입니다. 센터 내 관리자가 여러분의 하루를 위해 완벽한 계획을 세우도록 도와드릴 것입니다. [155] 추가 비용을 지불하시면, 개인 목욕용품을 드립니다.

회원권 문의를 위해서는, 프론트 데스크 404-575-4331로 전화 하시거나, members@rcc.com으로 이메일을 보내시기 바랍니다. 저희 센터 내 관리자와 연락하시려면 404-575-4331로 전화 주십시오. [156] 더 많은 정보, 사진, 오시는 길 또는 다른 회원 분들의 이용 후기를 보시려면 www.rcc.org를 방문하십시오.

어휘 charge 요금 get-together 모임 coordinator 코디네이터, 관리자 on-site 현장의

154

What is indicated about the Roseville Community Center?

(A) It is located in the heart of town.
(B) It offers massages.
(C) It provides catering service.
(D) It has a café in the building.

★★ 진위 / 세부사항

Roseville 지역 문화 센터에 대한 언급된 것은 무엇인가?
(A) 시내 중심부에 위치해 있다.
(B) 마사지 서비스를 제공한다.
(C) 출장 연회 서비스를 제공한다.
(D) 건물 내에 커피숍이 있다.

토익 분석

키워드가 지문 전반에 걸쳐 언급되고 있는 상태에서 적절한 세부사항을 파악해야 한다면 선택지에 나온 내용을 먼저 파악한 후 이들이 지문에서 제시되고 있는지 역으로 확인하는 방식으로 문제를 풀이하라.

문제 해설

Roseville 지역 문화 센터에 대한 언급된 것을 묻는 첫 번째 문제이므로 지문 초반부에서 Roseville 지역 문화 센터가 소개되면서 제시되는 관련 정보에 집중해야 한다. 지문 초반 The RCC is a great place for families and singles to get a massage를 통해 Roseville 지역 문화 센터에는 마사지 서비스를 제공하고 있음을 알 수 있다. 그러므로 정답은 (B)가 되겠다.

★★ 세부사항

추가 요금을 내면 이용 가능한 것은 무엇인가?
(A) 시내에서 오는 교통편
(B) 대형 회의실
(C) 운동 시설의 사용
(D) 목욕용품

토익 분석

세부사항을 묻는 문제는 질문에서 빠른 키워드(핵심어) 파악이 중요하다. 해당 문제에서는 추가비용을 뜻하는 **extra charge**가 키워드이므로 지문에서 **extra charge**가 언급되는 부분을 중심으로 단서를 파악하도록 한다.

What is available for an extra charge?

(A) Transportation from downtown
(B) A large meeting room
(C) Use of the exercise facilities
(D) Bath accessories

문제 해설

추가 비용을 지불할 때 이용이 가능한 것을 묻고 있으므로 추가 비용, 즉 extra charge가 핵심어이다. 따라서 지문에서 extra charge나 이와 유사한 표현이 등장하는 부분을 중심으로 단서를 파악해야 한다. 두 번째 단락 후반에서 For an additional charge, we provide a personal bath accessory package라며 추가 비용을 지급하면 개인 목욕용품도 제공한다는 점을 밝히고 있다. 그러므로 정답은 (D)가 되겠다. 아울러 문제의 extra charge는 지문에서 유사 표현인 additional charge로 바뀌어 제시되고 있음에 유의하도록 한다.

★ 세부사항

광고에 의하면, Roseville 지역 센터로 가는 길 안내는 어떻게 알 수 있는가?
(A) 홈페이지를 방문해서
(B) 관리자에게 전화를 걸어서
(C) 프론트 데스크에 연락해서
(D) 매니저에게 이메일을 보내서

토익 분석

마지막 문제는 항상 지문이 끝나는 부분을 기준으로 역으로 2-3줄씩 내용을 파악하며 단서를 파악하는 것이 가장 효율적이다.

According to the advertisement, how can people get directions to the Roseville Community Center?

(A) By visiting the center's Web site
(B) By calling the coordinator
(C) By contacting the front desk
(D) By e-mailing the manager

문제 해설

Roseville 지역 센터로 가는 길 안내를 알 수 있는 방법을 묻는 마지막 문제이자 길 안내, 즉 directions가 핵심어이다. 그러므로 지문 후반부에서 directions가 언급되는 부분을 중시므로 단서를 파악해야 한다. 지문 후반 For more information, photos, directions, and feedback from other members, please visit us at www.rcc.org라며 길 안내 관련 정보는 홈페이지를 방문하면 알 수 있다는 점을 전달하고 있으므로 정답은 (A)가 되겠다.

Questions 157-159 refer to the following letter.

Superfit Sportswear
490 Over Street
London
England

November 23

Jeremiah Osterland
490 Rinke Strata
Vienna, Austria

Dear Mr. Osterland,

[157] Thank you for your e-mail inquiring about our sportswear products. We are a dynamic, growing company, and we are excited about the prospect of supplying our sportswear to your stores all over Austria.

Superfit Sportswear is a family business established in 1992. Currently, our company has over thirty stores serving the needs of over one million customers throughout England every year. We manufacture and sell a range of products from footwear to sports therapy products.

[158] Please find enclosed our trade catalogue for you to look at. This catalogue contains a list and descriptions of all of our current products.

[159] I have arranged for our sales director, Mr. Rhodes, to fly to Vienna to meet with you on December 12. He will be able to negotiate the terms and conditions of the sales contract with you to create a deal profitable for both parties.

We look forward to doing business with you.

Sincerely,

Paul Goodman

Paul Goodman
Superfit Sportswear

157-159 다음 편지를 참조하시오.

Superfit Sportswear
490 Over Street
London
England

11월 23일

Jeremiah Osterland
490 Rinke Strata
Vienna, Austria

Osterland 씨에게

[157] 저희 스포츠웨어 상품을 문의하셨던 이메일 잘 받았습니다. 저희는 역동적이고, 성장 중에 있는 회사로 오스트리아 전국에 있는 귀하의 매장에 스포츠웨어를 납품할 수 있는 가능성에 기뻐하고 있습니다.

Superfit Sportswear는 1992년 설립된 가족기업입니다. 현재에는 영국 전역 30개 이상의 매장을 갖추고 있어 매년 백만 명 이상 되는 고객님들의 필요한 상품을 공급하고 있습니다. 우리는 신발부터 스포츠 테라피 상품에 이르기까지 다양한 상품을 제조하고 판매합니다.

[158] 귀하가 살펴보실 수 있는 카탈로그를 첨부합니다. 이 카탈로그에는 현재 저희가 생산하는 모든 상품의 목록과 설명서가 포함되어 있습니다.

[159] 판매부장인 Rhodes 씨가 12월 12일 비엔나에 가서 귀하를 만나 뵐 수 있도록 하겠습니다. Rhodes 씨는 귀하와 매매계약 조건을 협상하고 쌍방 간에 이익이 되는 거래를 만들어 낼 것입니다.

귀하와 사업을 함께 할 수 있길 기대합니다.

Paul Goodman
Superfit Sportswear

어휘 inquire 문의하다 prospect 전망, 예상 supply 공급하다, 물건을 대주다 family business 가업 serve the need 필요에 부응하다(채우다) footwear 신발 manufacture 제조하다 Please find enclosed ~를 첨부합니다 look though 살펴보다, 훑어보다 description (상품)설명서 arrange 준비하다, 계획을 짜다 negotiate 협상하다 terms of sale 매매조건 deal 거래, 계약 profitable 이익이 되는 both parties 쌍방, 양당 along with ~와 함께, ~에 더하여 booklet 소책자 discount voucher 할인권

★ 세부사항

Goodman 씨는 어떠한 종류의 의사 표현에 응답하였는가?
(A) 잡지 기사
(B) 주주의 편지
(C) 이메일 문의
(D) 전화 메시지

토익 분석

주어진 지문이 어떠한 종류의 지문에 대한 답변인지는 지문 초반부에서 어떠한 글에 대한 답변인지를 언급하는 부분만 파악하면 된다.

To what kind of communication is Mr. Goodman replying?

(A) A magazine article
(B) A shareholder's letter
(C) An e-mail inquiry
(D) A telephone message

문제 해설

편지 초반 Thank you for your email inquiring about our sportswear products를 통해 굿맨 씨가 상대의 이메일 문의에 대한 답변을 목적으로 편지를 작성했다는 점을 밝히고 있다. 그러므로 정답은 (C)이다.

★★ 세부사항

Goodman 씨는 그의 편지에 무엇을 함께 보냈는가?
(A) 비행기 티켓
(B) 영업용 카탈로그
(C) 할인 쿠폰 책자
(D) 사업 계약서 목록

토익 분석

파트 7에서는 첨부된 것의 정체나 자료의 종류를 묻는 문제가 자주 출제된다. 첨부자료는 대개 지문 후반부에서 특히 enclosed / included / attached와 같은 어휘가 제시되는 부분을 전후하여 단서가 등장한다.

What does Mr. Goodman send along with his letter?

(A) A flight ticket
(B) A trade catalogue
(C) A booklet of discount vouchers
(D) A list of business contacts

문제 해설

편지의 세 번째 단락에서 Please find enclosed our trade catalogue for you to look at. This catalogue contains a list and descriptions of all of our current products라고 언급한 내용을 통해 상품 목록과 상품을 설명한 내용이 담긴 카탈로그를 동봉했음을 알 수 있으므로 정답은 (B)가 적절하다. 아울러 할인 쿠폰 및 사업 계약서와는 무관한 책자이므로 (C)와 (D)를 정답으로 오해하지 않도록 주의해야 한다.

★★ 세부사항

Rhodes 씨가 비엔나로 가는 이유는 무엇인가?
(A) Osterland 씨의 매장 한 곳을 살펴보기 위해서
(B) Osterland 씨와 휴가를 보내기 위해서
(C) 계약조건을 상의하기 위해서
(D) 회사의 현지 지점을 설립하기 위해서

토익 분석

인명이나 지명은 중요한 키워드이므로 해당 문제처럼 인명/지명이 키워드로 언급되는 문제에서는 이들이 제시되는 부분을 전후하여 단서를 파악하는 것이 효율적이다.

Why is Mr. Rhodes going to fly to Vienna?

(A) To examine one of Mr. Osterland's stores
(B) To take a vacation with Mr. Osterland
(C) To discuss the details of a contract
(D) To establish a branch of the company

문제 해설

Rhodes 씨가 비엔나로 가는 이유는 Rhodes라는 인명이 제시되는 부분을 중심으로 파악하는 것이 현명하다. 광고문 말미에서 I have arranged for our sales director, Mr. Rhodes, to fly to Vienna to meet with you on December 12. He will be able to negotiate the terms of the sales contract with you to create a deal profitable for both parties라고 언급하며 당사의 영업 담당 이사인 Rhodes 씨가 12월 12일 Osterland 씨를 만나기 위해 비엔나를 방문할 것이며 이 때 서로에게 이익이 될 수 있는 계약을 할 수 있도록 계약조건을 협상할 예정임을 밝히고 있다. 그러므로 정답은 (C)라고 할 수 있다.

Questions 160-161 refer to the following text message chain.

Sally Murphy [4:44 P.M.] Did you look at the info on the BK Building?

Bobby Carter [4:45 P.M.] Yes, I did. Given that [160] many of our architects and engineers are working off-site, do we need all that space?

Sally Murphy [4:47 P.M.] I really think we do, considering the company is growing so fast.

Bobby Carter [4:48 P.M.] That may not be for a while, though.

Sally Murphy [4:50 P.M.] We have to consider both our short-term and long-term requirements. [161] This building offers plenty of room to allow for staff expansion.

Bobby Carter [4:52 P.M.] Got it. [161] We need room to grow as a company. We wouldn't want to move later on, especially when we start signing contracts with more engineers.

160-161 다음 문자 메시지 대화를 참조하시오.

Sally Murphy [오후 4:44] BK Building에 관한 정보를 확인해 보셨나요?

Bobby Carter [오후 4:45] 네, 봤습니다. [160] 우리 건축가와 엔지니어들이 외부에서 많이 근무하고 있는 것을 고려하면, 우리에게 그 모든 공간이 필요할까요?

Sally Murphy [오후 4:47] 저는 정말로 그렇다고 생각해요, 회사가 이렇게 빠르게 성장하고 있는 것을 감안하면요.

Bobby Carter [오후 4:48] 하지만 그 일은 어느 정도 시간이 지난 후에야 가능할 거예요.

Sally Murphy [오후 4:50] 우리는 단기적인 요건과 장기적인 요건들을 모두 고려해 봐야 합니다. [161] 이 건물은 직원 규모 확대를 수용할 만한 충분한 공간을 제공하고 있습니다.

Bobby Carter [오후 4:52] 알겠습니다. [161] 우리는 하나의 회사로서 성장하기 위한 공간이 필요합니다. 나중에 이전하는 것을 원하는 것은 아닐 테지요, 특히 우리가 더 많은 엔지니어들과 계약을 체결하는 일을 시작하게 되면요.

어휘 info 정보 given that ~을 고려하면 architect 건축가 off-site 외부에서 considering (that) ~을 감안하면 for a while 한동안 though (문장 끝에 쓰여) 하지만

160

Where do Ms. Murphy and Mr. Carter work?

(A) An architectural firm
(B) A moving company
(C) A real estate agency
(D) A local interior design firm

문제 해설

Murphy 씨와 Carter 씨의 직장에 관해 묻고 있으므로 문자 메시지 대화에서 직장을 추측할 수 있을만한 관련 어휘나 표현에 집중해야 한다. 오후 4시 45분에 Carter 씨가 쓴 메시지에서 자사의 직원들을 건축가와 엔지니어들(our architects and engineers)이라고 가리키고 있으므로 이들은 건축 회사에서 근무하고 있음을 유추할 수 있다. 따라서 정답은 (A)가 되겠다.

★ 유추 / 화자들의 직장

Murphy 씨와 Carter 씨는 어디에서 일하는가?
(A) 건축 회사
(B) 이사 전문 회사
(C) 부동산 중개업체
(D) 지역 인테리어 디자인 회사

토익 분석

업종/직장을 묻는 질문은 지문에서 업종/직장과 관련된 어휘나 표현을 파악하는 것이 관건이다

161

At 4:52 P.M., what does Mr. Carter most likely mean when he writes, "Got it"?

(A) They need to improve their existing office space.
(B) A new space will be too expensive.
(C) The building may accommodate plans for future growth.
(D) The property needs structural improvements.

문제 해설

주어진 "Got it"이라는 말은 앞서 Murphy 씨가 This building offers plenty of room to allow for staff expansion이라며 건물의 공간이 직원 규모를 늘리는 데 충분하다는 점을 언급한 것에 대한 답변으로 쓰였으며 바로 뒤이어 Carter 씨도 회사가 성장하기 위한 공간이 필요하다며 We need room to grow as a company라고 이야기하고 있다. 그러므로 "Got it"이라는 말에는 해당 건물이 미래를 위한 성장에 필요하다는 화자의 의도가 포함되어 있음을 알 수 있으므로 (C)가 정답이다.

★★★ 화자 의도

오후 4시 52분에, Carter 씨가 "Got it"이라고 썼을 때 무엇을 의미하는 것이겠는가?
(A) 회사가 현재의 사무 공간을 개선해야 한다.
(B) 새로운 공간이 너무 비쌀 것이다.
(C) 건물이 향후 성장에 대한 계획을 수용할 수 있을 것이다.
(D) 건물에 구조적인 개선 작업이 필요하다.

토익 분석

특정 표현에 담긴 화자의 의도에 대해 이해하기 위해서는 주어진 특정 표현 전후의 내용 파악이 선행되어야 한다. 난이도가 높아지는 경우에는 전체 지문의 내용을 다 파악해야만 풀 수 있는 경우도 발생한다.

162-164 다음 이메일을 참조하시오.

수신: Bandar@bestmail.com
발신: ClaireSaturna@ipi.org

Bandar 씨께,

[162] 저희 International Petroleum Institute (IPI)에 대한 귀하의 많은 후원에 대해 감사드리기 위해 이메일 보냅니다. 한 가지 상기시켜 드리자면, 상파울루에서 열리는 연례 IPI 컨퍼런스에 대한 등록일이 10월 15일이라는 점을 명심하시기 바랍니다.— [1] —. 이번 컨퍼런스를 위해 [163 (C)] 200곳이 넘는 판매업체와 제품 전시, 그리고 강연을 포함한 흥미로운 행사들이 마련되어 있으며, 모든 행사가 도심 한복판에 위치한 최신 컨벤션 시설에서 개최됩니다.— [2] —.

International Petroleum Institute의 프로그램들에 대한 우대 기부자로서, [163 (A)] 저희는 호텔 비용에 대한 20퍼센트 할인 쿠폰과 [163 (D)] 컨벤션홀행의 무료 셔틀 버스 서비스를 제공해 드립니다.— [3] —. 저희 웹 사이트를 방문하셔서 온라인으로 등록하시기 바랍니다. [164] — [4] — 또한 판매업체 부스에 대한 안내도를 포함해 그곳에서 상세한 컨퍼런스 프로그램을 찾아 보실 수 있습니다. 아니면 512-555-8760으로 저희에게 전화를 통해 연락하실 수 있습니다. [163] 귀하의 회원 번호를 준비해 주시기 바랍니다.

안녕히 계십시오.

Anna Bondell
회원 관리 코디네이터

어휘 considerable 많은, 상당한 support 후원, 지원 reminder (메시지 등) 상기시키는 것 keep in mind that ~임을 명심하다 registration 등록 annual 연례적인, 해마다의 in store 마련된 including ~을 포함해 vendor 판매업체 display 전시(품), 진열 state-of-the-art 최신의 facility 시설 right in the heart of ~의 한복판에 preferred 우대되는, 선호되는 contributor 기부자, 기여자 voucher 쿠폰, 상품권 complimentary 무료의 register 등록하다 online 온라인으로 reach ~에게 연락하다 have A ready A를 준비하다

Questions 162-164 refer to the following e-mail.

To: Bandar@bestmail.com
From: ClaireSaturna@ipi.org

Dear Mr. Bandar

[162] I'm writing to thank you for your considerable support for the International Petroleum Institute. As a reminder, registration for the annual IPI Conference in Sao Paulo is October 15. — [1] —. There are exciting things in store for this conference, [163] including over 200 vendors, displays, and lectures, all in a state-of-the-art convention facility right in the heart of town.— [2] —.

As a preferred contributor to the programs at the International Petroleum Institute, [163] we are offering you a voucher for 20% off your hotel and complimentary shuttle service to the convention hall.— [3] —. Visit our Web site to register online. [164]— [4] —. You will also find a detailed conference program there, as well as a map of the vendor booths. You may reach us by phone at 512-555-8760. [163] Please have your membership number ready.

Sincerely,
Anna Bondell
Membership Coordinator

162

★ 유추 / Bandar 씨의 정체

Bandar 씨는 누구일 것 같은가?
(A) 정유회사 임원
(B) 컨퍼런스 조직 책임자
(C) 기자
(D) 교사

토익 분석

인물 유추는 인물의 정체를 유추할 수 있는 관련 어휘나 표현을 파악하는 것이 관건이다.

Who most likely is Mr. Bandar?

(A) An oil company executive
(B) A conference organizer
(C) A journalist
(D) A teacher

문제 해설

Bandar 씨의 정체를 유추해야 하는 문제이므로 지문에서 Bandar 씨의 정체를 추측할 수 있을만한 관련 어휘나 표현이 등장하는 부분을 집중해야 한다. 첫 단락의 시작에서 International Petroleum Institute(국제 석유 협회)에 대한 많은 후원에 감사한다며 I'm writing to thank you for your considerable support for the International Petroleum Institute라고 언급하는 내용 및 두 번째 단락에서 행사 등록에 필요한 회원 번호를 준비해 달라며 Please have your membership number ready라고 이야기하는 부분을 통해 Bandar 씨는 이 협회의 회원임을 추측할 수 있다. 따라서 석유와 관련된 업체에 속한 사람임을 알 수 있으므로 정유회사 임원을 뜻하는 (A)가 정답이다.

163

What is NOT a benefit being offered?

(A) A reduced hotel rate
(B) A hotel room upgrade
(C) Access to hundreds of vendors' booths
(D) Complimentary transportation to the event

문제 해설

제공되는 혜택이 아닌 것을 묻는 문제이므로 이메일에서 제공되는 혜택에 관련된 정보가 제시되는 부분을 빠르게 찾아가야 한다. 두 번째 단락의 a voucher for 20% off your hotel과 complimentary shuttle service to the convention hall에서 (A)와 (D)의 내용을 확인할 수 있으며, 첫 단락의 over 200 vendors를 통해 (C)의 내용도 확인 가능하다. 하지만 호텔 객실 업그레이드는 언급된 바가 없으므로 (B)가 정답이다.

제공되는 혜택이 아닌 것은 무엇인가?
(A) 할인된 호텔 요금
(B) 호텔 객실 업그레이드
(C) 많은 판매업체 부스
(D) 행사장으로 가는 무료 교통편

토익 분석

사실이 아닌 내용[NOT TRUE]을 묻는 문제는 선택지 내용을 파악한 후 지문의 내용과 대조하면서 사실이 아닌 내용을 오답으로 소거하며 정답을 찾아내는 방식으로 풀이하라.

164

In which of the positions marked [1], [2], [3], and [4] does the following sentence best belong?

" You will also find a detailed conference program there, as well as a map of the vendor booths."

(A) [1]
(B) [2]
(C) [3]
(D) [4]

문제 해설

주어진 문장이 위치해야 하는 곳을 묻는 문제이므로 주어진 문장의 의미를 이해한 후 이와 내용적 연계성을 지닌 적절한 위치를 파악해야 한다. 제시된 문장에는 추가 정보를 언급할 때 사용하는 also 및 특정한 곳을 지칭하는 there와 함께 그곳에서 부스 안내도와 상세 컨퍼런스 프로그램을 찾아 볼 수 있다는 의미를 나타낸다. 홈페이지가 언급된 문장 뒤에 위치한 [4]에 들어가 웹 사이트에서 찾아 볼 수 있는 정보를 추가로 언급하는 흐름이 되어야 알맞으므로 (D)가 정답이다.

★★★ 문장 위치 파악

[1], [2], [3], [4]로 표기된 위치들 중에서 다음 문장이 들어가기에 가장 적절한 곳은 어디인가?
"또한 판매업체 부스에 대한 안내도를 포함해 그곳에서 상세한 컨퍼런스 프로그램을 찾아 보실 수 있습니다."
(A) [1]
(B) [2]
(C) [3]
(D) [4]

토익 분석

강사로서 문제풀이 시간을 단축시킬 수 있는 방법으로 제시할만한 방법은 [3] – [4] – [1] – [2] 순서로 정답 비중이 높기 때문에 주어진 문장 내용을 순차적으로 해당 위치에 삽입해보며 내용 연결성을 비교하며 문제를 풀이하는 것이다.

165-167 다음 기사를 참조하시오.

Santa Fe에서 재개장하는 프레지던트 호텔

Darren Pinkman – Santa Fe Weekly

Santa Fe – [165, 166] 시급했던 보수공사로 6개월간 문을 닫았던 President 호텔이 이번 월요일 오전 9시에 다시 문을 연다.

호텔 지배인인 Janice Ha씨는 호텔이 그 어느 때보다 아주 훌륭하다고 말했다. 그녀는 "모든 사람들이 이 오래된 호텔을 좋아했어요."라고 운을 뗀 뒤 "하지만 이 건물 보수 작업은 저희가 현대적인 트렌드를 반영하기 위해선 꼭 해야 했습니다. 이전에 저희는 처리할 수 없었던 관광객들의 요구사항들이 많았습니다. [166] 그에 따라 저희는 최신식 수영장과 체육관을 설치하고 레스토랑의 수준을 향상시키고, 손님들이 즐길 수 있는 극장을 추가했습니다. 이 곳 모든 이들이 호텔의 재개장에 들떠 있고 다시 일터로 복귀할 수 있기를 몹시 기대하고 있어요."라고 말했다.

[166] 디자이너이자 호텔의 소유주인 Chan Hong 씨는 새로운 디자인에 대한 그의 영감을 말했다. 그는 "저는 고객들에게 기억에 남는 경험을 만들어 주고 싶어요."라고 언급한 후 "저는 모든 연령대의 사람들이 이 호텔을 즐길 수 있으면 좋겠어요. 방문 목적이 사업이든 휴가든 간에 말이지요."라고 이야기했다. Hong 씨가 새 호텔이 이제껏 까다로웠던 여행 단체의 요구도 충족시킬 수 있는 시설이 구비되어 있는지 여부에 대한 질문을 받았을 때 "매우 입맛이 까다로운 손님이 와도 매우 자신 있게 응대할 수 있다"고 대답했다.

[167] 새로운 호텔이 주는 즐거움을 최초로 직접 체험한 사람은 바로 Jim Gomez 씨로, 그는 이 곳에서 1주일에 4차례 운동을 한다. Gomez 씨는 "새 체육관은 대단해요." 라고 말했다. 이어서 그는 "그곳은 휴가 때에도 몸매를 유지할 수 있는 모든 것들을 갖추고 있어요. 전 수영장과 레스토랑도 마음에 들어요. 다음에도 당연히 이 호텔에 머무를 겁니다."라고 이야기했다.

President 호텔은 내부와 외부를 막론하고 단연 훌륭해 보인다. 각 객실은 와이드 스크린 TV, 킹 사이즈 침대와 무선 인터넷 접속을 제공하고 있다. 만약 돈을 쓰고 싶다면, 호화로운 Emperor Suite 룸이 지불하는 객실료 만큼 특별한 가치를 제시한다는 점에서 적격이라 할 수 있다. 220달러의 이 고급 방들은 단연 고상함에 딱 들어맞는다.

어휘 carry out 실행하다, 이행하다 claim 주장하다, 단언하다 essential 필수적인 allow 목적어 to do 목적어가 ~하도록 허용하다 keep up with 따라잡다, 쫓다 cope with 대처하다, 처리하다 demand 요구; 수요; 요구하다 state-of-the-art 최신의 can't wait to Vr ~를 기다릴 수 없다. 몹시 하고 싶다. inspiration 영감 be able to do ~할 수 있다 discriminating 차별하는; 날카로운 심미안이 있는 taste 기호, 맛 cater for 음식을 준비하다, 출장 요리를 제공하다, ~에게 음식을 제공하다 delight 기쁨, 기쁘게 하다. regal 훌륭한, 위엄 있는 feel like V-ing 원하다 splurge 과시, 과시하다 exclusive 독점적인; 고급의 fit 적당한, 적절한, 들어맞다 royalty 왕족; 고귀함 publicize 공표하다, 광고하다 facility 설비, 시설 a job vacancy 공석 passionate 열정적인, 정렬적인 improvement 개선, 향상

Questions 165-167 refer to the following article.

President Hotel to Reopen in Santa Fe

By Darren Pinkman – Santa Fe Weekly

Santa Fe – [165, 166] After being closed for six months while much-needed renovations were carried out, President Hotel reopened for business Monday at 9 A.M.

The manager of the hotel, Janice Ha, claims that the hotel is better than ever before. "Everybody loved the old hotel," she claimed, "but this building work was essential in allowing us to keep up with modern trends. We were experiencing a lot of demand from tourists that we couldn't cope with before. As such, [166] we have installed a state-of-the-art swimming pool and gym, upgraded our restaurant, and added a movie theater for our guests to enjoy. Everybody here is excited about the reopening and can't wait to get back to work."

[166] Designer and owner Chan Hong spoke of his inspiration for the new design. "I wanted to create a memorable experience for our guests," he said. "I wanted people of all ages to be able to enjoy the hotel, whether it be for business or pleasure." When asked if he believed the new hotel is equipped to meet the needs of the ever-demanding travel community, Mr. Hong said that he was "extremely confident that it would be able to cater to even the most discriminating of tastes."

[167] One of the first to sample the delights of the new hotel was Jim Gomez, who works out four times a week. "The new gym is great," said Mr. Gomez. "It has everything you need to keep yourself in shape on your vacation. I loved the swimming pool and restaurant, too. I would definitely stay here again."

President Hotel certainly looks regal, both inside and out. Each room is now equipped with a wide-screen TV, a king-sized bed, and wireless Internet access. And if you're feeling like you want to splurge, the luxurious Emperor Suite offers exceptional value for money. Priced at $220, these exclusive rooms are certainly fit for royalty.

165

What is the purpose of the article?

(A) To publicize the reopening of a hotel
(B) To compare several different hotels
(C) To offer free use of facilities to the local community
(D) To advertise job vacancies for staff at a hotel

문제 해설

기사문의 목적을 묻는 문제로 기사문의 주제/목적은 지문 초반부에서 직접적으로 언급되므로 지문 초반부에서 집중적으로 언급하고 있는 중심 소재를 파악하는 것이 중요하다. 기사문 초반 After being closed for six months while much-needed renovations were carried out, President Hotel reopened for business Monday at 9 A.M.라며 반 년간의 보수공사 끝에 다시 개장하는 호텔을 소개하는 부분을 통해 기사문의 주제는 바로 호텔의 재개장을 전달하기 위함임을 알 수 있다. 따라서 정답은 (A)이다.

★★ **지문의 목적**

이 기사문의 목적은 무엇인가?
(A) 호텔의 재개장을 홍보하기 위해서
(B) 몇몇의 다른 호텔들을 비교하기 위해서
(C) 지역사회에 무료시설 사용을 제공하기 위해서
(D) 호텔에서 일하는 직원의 공석을 광고하기 위해서

토익 분석

기사문의 주제/목적은 단락 구분이 있는 경우 첫 번째 단락 초반 2-3문장에서 제시된다. 다만 주제/목적 문제의 난이도가 높아지는 경우 주제/목적은 두 번째 단락의 초반 2-3문장에서 다뤄진다

166

What is NOT mentioned about President Hotel?

(A) It will be open on Christmas Day.
(B) It has a swimming pool.
(C) It was closed for six months.
(D) It is owned by Mr. Hong.

문제 해설

기사문 첫 번째 단락 초반 After being closed for six months를 통해 이 호텔이 반 년간 문을 닫았던 사실을 알 수 있으며, 이어서 두 번째 단락 중반에서 we have installed a state-of-the-art swimming pool라고 언급하는 부분을 통해 최신 수영장을 구비했음을 파악할 수 있다. 마지막으로 세 번째 단락 초반 Designer and owner Chan Hong이라고 소개하는 부분을 통해 이 호텔의 소유주가 Hong 씨라는 점도 밝히고 있다. 따라서 정답은 (A)이다.

★★ **진위**

President 호텔에 대해 언급되지 않은 것은 무엇인가?
(A) 크리스마스 날에 개장할 것이다.
(B) 수영장을 가지고 있다.
(C) 6개월간 문을 닫았다.
(D) Hong 씨가 소유하고 있다.

토익 분석

사실이 아닌 한 가지 내용을 묻는 문제[NOT TRUE]는 선택지를 키워드로 삼아 각 선택지의 내용이 지문에서 언급되는지 여부를 파악하는 방식으로 풀이하는 것이 효율적이다.

167

What is suggested about Jim Gomez?

(A) He stayed at the hotel with his wife and children.
(B) He works in the hotel industry.
(C) He is passionate about exercising.
(D) He helped plan the improvements to the fitness center.

문제 해설

Jim Gomez 씨에 관해 유추하고 있는 내용을 묻고 있으므로 지문에서 Jim Gomez이라는 인명이 제시되는 부분을 중심으로 언급되는 관련 정보를 파악한 후 이를 토대로 그에 관해 유추할 수 있는 내용을 선택지에서 택일해야 한다. 기사문의 네 번째 단락 초반 One of the first to sample the delights of the new hotel was Jim Gomez, who works out four times a week라며 Jim Gomez 씨가 1주일에 4회나 운동하는 사람이라 소개하고 있다. 따라서 이를 통해 Jim Gomez 씨는 운동을 굉장히 좋아하는 사람임을 유추할 수 있으므로 정답은 (C)가 되겠다.

★★ **유추**

Jim Gomez 씨에 관해 암시하고 있는 내용은 무엇인가?
(A) 그는 그의 아내와 아이들과 호텔에서 머물렀다.
(B) 그는 호텔 업계에서 일한다.
(C) 그는 운동에 열정적이다.
(D) 그는 헬스 클럽 보수 계획을 도왔다.

토익 분석

특정 인물에 대해 유추할 수 있는 내용을 묻는 문제의 경우 지문에서 특정 인물에 대한 정보가 집중적으로 소개되는 부분에서 제시되는 내용을 토대로 특정 인물에 대해 유추할 수 있는 내용을 파악해야 한다. 다만 키워드가 지문 전반에 걸쳐 언급되는 경우에는 선택지의 내용을 키워드로 삼아 지문에서 해당 내용이 언급되는지 여부를 빠르게 파악하며 문제를 풀이한다.

168-171 다음 온라인 채팅을 참조하시오.

Molly Vernon [오후 12:08] Mike, 회사 웹 사이트 좀 한 번 봐 주시겠어요? [168] 제 컴퓨터로 우리 제품들의 사진을 볼 수가 없어요. 당신 컴퓨터에는 보이나요?

Mike Snow [오후 12:13] 아뇨, 보이지 않는 게 분명해요. 이렇게 된지 오래됐나요?

Molly Vernon [오후 12:14] 아마 몇 시간 정도 밖에 되지 않았을 거예요. [169] 구매한 제품에 대한 후기를 작성하고 싶어 하시는 고객 한 분으로부터 막 연락을 받았는데, 지금 보이지 않으신대요. 오늘 이른 시간이나 어제도 불만 사항이 없었고요. 우리 IT 담당 팀에게 알려 주시겠어요?

Mike Snow [오후 12:15] Larry, 우리 웹 사이트의 온라인 매장 코너에 있는 이미지 파일에 뭔가 문제가 발생했어요.

Larry McKee [오후 12:18] 이상하네요… [170] 그 파일들이 삭제된 것 같아요.

Mike Snow [오후 12:19] 백업 파일을 보관하고 있어야 할 텐데요.

Larry McKee [오후 12:20] 만일을 위해 항상 그렇게 하죠. 지금 다시 업로드 할게요.

Mike Snow [오후 12:21] 잘됐네요. 그리고 [171] 온라인으로 간단한 해명 글을 발송해서 모든 사람들에게 수정됐다고 알려야 할 겁니다.

Molly Vernon [오후 12:22] 171 그건 제가 처리할게요.

어휘 take a look at ~을 한 번 보다 go on long 오래 지속되다 no more than 불과, ~ 뿐인 contact ~에게 연락하다 review ~에 대한 후기를 쓰다, ~을 평가하다 complaint 불만 let A know A에게 알리다 happen to ~에게 발생되다 looks like ~인 것 같다 remove ~을 없애다, 제거하다 just in case 만일을 위해 explanation 해명, 설명 tell A that A에게 ~라고 말하다 fix ~을 고치다 take care of ~을 처리하다

Questions 168-171 refer to the following online chat discussion.

Molly Vernon [12:08 P.M.] Mike, would you mind taking a look at the company Web site? [168] I can't see the pictures of our products on my computer. Do you see them on yours?

Mike Snow [12:13 P.M.] No, I sure don't. Has this been going on long?

Molly Vernon [12:14 P.M.] Probably no more than a few hours. [169] I was just contacted by a potential customer who wanted to review the item she'd purchased but couldn't see it anymore. There were no complaints earlier today or yesterday. Would you let the IT team know?

Mike Snow [12:15 A.M.] Larry, something happened to the image files on the online store section of our Web site.

Larry McKee [12: 18 P.M.] That's strange… [170] Looks like they've been removed.

Mike Snow [12:19 P.M.] I hope we've kept backup files.

Larry McKee [12:20 P.M.] We always do, just in case. I'll upload them again now.

Mike Snow [12:21 P.M.] Good. [171] And we'll need to send a short explanation online and tell everyone that it is fixed.

Molly Vernon [12:22 P.M.] I'll take care of that.

168

★ 문제점

Vernon 씨가 보고하고 있는 문제점은 무엇인가?
(A) 온라인 구매가 처리되지 않고 있다.
(B) 부정확한 연락처가 회사의 웹 사이트에 기재되어 있다.
(C) 회사의 웹 사이트가 해킹된 것처럼 보인다.
(D) 제품 사진들이 온라인 매장 코너에서 보이지 않는다.

토익 분석

첫 번째 문제로 등장하는 구체적인 문제점은 주로 첫 번째 단락 초반 2-3문장을 통해 제시된다. 채팅 지문의 경우 문제점은 주로 첫 번째 / 두 번째 대화 라인에서 언급된다.

What problem does Ms. Vernon report?

(A) Online purchases are not processing.
(B) Incorrect information is listed on the company's Web site.
(C) The company's Web site appears to have been hacked.
(D) Product photos cannot be viewed in the online store section.

문제 해설

Vernon 씨가 언급하는 문제점을 묻고 있으므로 온라인 채팅 초반 Vernon 씨가 작성한 내용에서 언급하고 있는 구체적인 문제점을 파악해야 한다. Vernon 씨는 첫 대화에서 컴퓨터로 제품 사진들을 볼 수 없다며 I can't see the pictures of our products on my computer라고 이야기하고 있으므로 정답은 (D)가 되겠다.

169

From whom did Ms. Vernon learn about the problem?

(A) An accountant
(B) An IT coworker
(C) A customer
(D) The company president

★★ 세부사항

Vernon 씨는 누구로부터 문제에 대해 알게 되었는가?
(A) 회계사
(B) IT 담당 동료 직원
(C) 고객
(D) 회사의 사장

토익 분석

채팅 지문에서 특정 인명이 제시되는 문제의 단서는 주로 해당 인물의 대화 내용에서 제시된다.

문제 해설

Vernon 씨가 문제점을 알게 된 출처를 묻고 있으므로 문제점을 언급하는 부분을 중심으로 단서를 파악해야 한다. Vernon 씨는 12시 14분에 후기를 작성하고 싶어 하는 고객에게서 연락을 받고 제품이 보이지 않는다는 사실을 알게 되었다며 I was just contacted by a customer who wanted to review the item she'd purchased, but couldn't see it anymore라고 이야기하고 있다. 따라서 문제점을 인식하게 된 출처는 고객임을 알 수 있으므로 (C)가 정답이다.

170

At 12:19 P.M., what does Mr. Snow mean when he writes, "I hope we've kept backup files"?

(A) He is afraid that the company has lost a lot of money.
(B) He wants his coworker to explain the procedures for handling files.
(C) He is looking for clients' financial transaction records.
(D) He hopes all of the pictures are still available.

★★★ 화자의 의도

오후 12시 19분에, Snow 씨가 "I hope we've kept backup files"라고 썼을 때 무엇을 의미하겠는가?
(A) 회사가 많은 돈을 잃었을까 걱정하고 있다.
(B) 자신의 동료직원이 파일을 다루는 절차를 설명해 주기를 원한다.
(C) 고객의 금융 거래 기록을 찾고 있다.
(D) 모든 사진들이 여전히 이용 가능하기를 바라고 있다.

토익 분석

특정 표현에 담긴 화자의 의도에 대한 이해하기 위해서는 주어진 특정 표현 전후의 내용 파악이 선행되어야 한다. 난이도가 높아지는 경우에는 전체 지문의 내용을 다 파악해야만 풀 수 있는 경우도 발생한다

문제 해설

화자의 의도를 묻는 문제이므로 주어진 표현이 제시되는 부분을 전후하여 제시되는 문맥에 집중해야 한다. 해당 문장은 "백업 파일을 보관했기를 바란다"는 의미를 나타내는데, 이는 앞서 McKee 씨가 파일들이 삭제된 것 같다며 Looks like they've been removed라고 말한 것에 대한 반응에 해당된다. 따라서 백업 파일을 이용해 해당 사진들을 다시 이용할 수 있기를 바라는 마음에서 한 말이라는 것을 알 수 있으므로 이와 같은 의미로 쓰인 (D)가 정답이다.

171

What will Ms. Vernon most likely do next?

(A) Update her personal profile
(B) Contact the safety office
(C) Contact the IT team.
(D) Post a note online

★★ 세부사항

Vernon 씨는 곧이어 무엇을 할 것 같은가?
(A) 자신의 개인 프로필을 업데이트하는 일
(B) 보안 담당 팀에 연락하는 일
(C) IT 팀에 연락하는 일
(D) 온라인으로 메시지를 게시하는 일

토익 분석

채팅 후 취하게 될 행동에 대한 단서는 주로 채팅 종료 직전 두 개의 대화 라인에서 제시된다.

문제 해설

Vernon 씨는 곧이어 무엇을 할 것인지 묻는 마지막 문제이므로 인터넷 채팅 후반부에서 단서를 파악하는 것이 바람직하다. 맨 마지막 메시지에 Vernon 씨가 '그 일을 내가 처리하겠다'고 알리고 있는데, 이는 바로 앞서 Snow 씨가 온라인으로 해명 글을 올리는 것을(we'll need to send a short explanation online) 언급한 것에 대한 대답이므로 온라인 메시지 게시를 뜻하는 (D)가 정답이다.

**Sweetwater Lake State Park
이용 가능한 활동**

[172] Sweetwater Lake State Park에서, 여러분께서는 낚시와 카누 타기, 하이킹, 소풍, 오두막에서의 캠핑 또는 숙박, 그리고 보트 타기를 즐기실 수 있습니다. 여러분의 다음 번 모임을 위해 저희 단체 고객용 홀을 대여하시기 바랍니다! [174 (C)] 공원 내에 악어들이 살고 있으므로 방문 전에 악어 대비 안전 팁을 읽어 보시기 바랍니다. — [1] —
낚시: Sweetwater Lake State Park는 26,810에이커의 규모이며, [174 (C)] 호수 자체에 70종이 넘는 물고기 종이 서식하고 있습니다. 저희는 낚시용 교각과 보트 선착장을 보유하고 있습니다. 저희 국립 공원의 물가에서 낚시하는 데 낚시 허가증은 필요치 않습니다. 공원 내에서 사용하실 수 있는 낚시 장비 대여에 관해 문의하시기 바랍니다. — [2] —
카누 타기: Sweetwater Lake의 구불구불한 물길을 탐험해 보십시오. 공원 내에서 카누를 대여하시거나, 보유하고 계신 카누 또는 카약을 가져 오셔도 됩니다. — [3] —
숙박:
[173] 물만 제공되는 장소에서부터 모든 장비 연결이 가능한 장소에 이르기까지, 46곳의 캠프장에서 선택하십시오.
방충망 처리가 된 쉼터에서 머무르실 수 있습니다.
역사적인 저희 오두막 중의 하나를 대여하십시오. 이 오두막은 2인실부터 6인실까지 마련되어 있으며, [174 (B)] 몇몇 곳은 장애인 이용 가능 시설입니다.
하이킹: 도보로 숲을 탐험해 보세요. [175] Sweetwater Forest 산책로의 4분의 1마일에 해당되는 곳은 장애인 이용 가능 구역입니다. 저희 대화형 지도를 통해 더 많은 정보를 확인해 보십시오. [175] — [4] — 장애인용 산책로를 보실 수 있는 링크를 클릭하시기 바랍니다
[174 (D)] 자원 봉사자: 저희 자원 봉사자 페이지를 방문하셔서 도움을 제공하실 수 있는 방법을 확인해 보십시오.

어휘 paddle 카누를 타다, 노를 젓다 harbor ~가 서식하다 species (동식물의) 종 fishing pier 낚시용 교각 boat ramp 선착장 twists and turns 구불구불한 길 hookup 장비 연결 screened 방충망 설치가 된 shelter 쉼터

**Sweetwater Lake State Park
Things to Do**

[172] At Sweetwater Lake State Park, you can fish, paddle, hike, picnic, camp or stay in a cabin, and go boating. Rent our group hall for your next reunion!
[174] Alligators live in the park; read our alligator safety tips before your visit.
— [1] —.
Fish: Sweetwater Lake State Park is 26,810-acres, and [174] the lake itself harbors more than 70 species of fish. We have a fishing pier and a boat ramp. You do not need a fishing license to fish from shore in a state park. — [2] —. Ask about borrowing fishing equipment to use in the park.
Paddle: Explore Sweetwater Lake's twists and turns. Rent a canoe in the park or bring your own canoe or kayak. — [3] —.
Stay:
• [173] Choose from 46 campsites, ranging from water only to full hookup sites.
• Stay at a screened shelter.
• Rent one of our historic cabins. These range from two- to six-person cabins, and [174] several are accessible to the handicapped.
Hike: Explore the forest afoot. [175] One-quarter mile of the Sweetwater Forest Trail is handicapped accessible. Learn more on our Interactive Map page.
[175] — [4] —. Click on the link for the Handicapped Trail.
[174] **Volunteers:** Visit our Volunteer page to see how you can help.

172

★★ 세부사항

Sweetwater Lake State Park에 관해 알 수 있는 것은 무엇인가?
(A) 고속도로에서 접근하기 어렵다.
(B) 인공 호수이며, 비교적 새로 생긴 곳이다.
(C) 다양한 활동들이 제공된다.
(D) 입장료가 매우 저렴하다.

토익 분석

키워드가 지문 전반에 걸쳐 언급되는 경우에는 선택지의 내용을 키워드로 삼아 지문에서 해당 내용이 언급되는지 여부를 빠르게 파악하며 문제를 풀이한다.

What is indicated about the Sweetwater Lake State Park?

(A) It is difficult to get to from the highway.
(B) It is a man-made lake and relatively new.
(C) A variety of activities are provided.
(D) The fee for entry is very affordable.

문제 해설

이 경우는 선택지의 내용을 먼저 숙지한 후 선택지의 내용을 키워드, 즉 핵심어로 삼아 지문에서 해당 선택지의 내용이 나오는지 여부만 신속하게 파악하는 것이 시간을 최소화시키며 문제를 풀이하는 관건이다. 해당 장소의 특징이 설명되는 첫 단락 시작 부분에, 낚시와 카누 타기, 하이킹, 소풍, 오두막에서의 캠핑 또는 숙박, 그리고 보트 타기를 즐길 수 있다며 you can fish, paddle, hike, picnic, camp or stay in a cabin, and go boating이라고 언급하고 있으므로 이와 같은 특징을 언급한 (C)가 정답이다.

173

What is indicated about camping at the park?

(A) There are many options available.
(B) There is no electricity at any of the campsites.
(C) There is no camping allowed this year.
(D) Many additional campsites are being constructed.

문제 해설

공원 캠핑에 관한 세부사항을 묻는 문제이므로 지문에서 공원 캠핑에 관한 정보가 제시되는 부분을 빠르게 찾아가야 한다. 숙박 정보가 제시된 중반부의 Stay 항목의 정보를 보면, 46곳의 캠프장에서 선택하라며 Choose from 46 campsites ~라고 되어 있으므로 선택권의 다양성에 대해 언급한 (A)가 정답이다. 바로 뒤이어 제시된 선택 범위에 full hookup sites, 즉 모든 장비 연결이 가능한 장소도 있다고 되어 있으므로 (B)는 오답이다.

★★ 세부사항

공원에서 캠핑하는 것에 관해 알 수 있는 것은 무엇인가?
(A) 이용 가능한 많은 선택권이 있다.
(B) 어느 캠프장에서도 전기를 이용할 수 없다.
(C) 올해는 캠핑이 허용되지 않는다.
(D) 많은 추가 캠프장들이 현재 지어지고 있다.

토익 분석

세부사항을 묻는 문제는 질문에서 빠른 키워드(핵심어) 파악이 관건이다. 해당 문제에서는 지문에 공원 캠핑이 언급되는 부분을 중심으로 단서를 파악해야 한다.

174

What is NOT suggested about Sweetwater Lake State Park?

(A) It is only for in-state residents.
(B) It has options for the handicapped.
(C) It has many forms of wildlife.
(D) It is supported by volunteers.

문제 해설

Sweatwater Lake State Park에 관해 유추 가능한 내용을 묻는 문제로 사실상 지문 전체의 내용이 Sweetwater Lake State Park에 관한 내용임을 고려할 때 선택지의 내용을 먼저 숙지한 후 지문에서 이를 유추할 수 있는 근거가 되는 정보가 제시되는지 여부를 역으로 살펴나가야 할 필요가 있다. Stay 항목과 Hike 항목에 언급된 장애인 이용 가능 시설(several are accessible to the handicapped)을 통해 (B)의 내용을 유추할 수 있고, 초반부의 악어(Alligators live in the park)와 70종이 넘는 물고기(more than 70 species of fish)를 통해 (C)의 내용도 유추가 가능하다. 또한 마지막 부분의 자원 봉사자 관련 정보(Volunteers)를 통해 (D) 또한 유추할 수 있는 내용임을 알 수 있다. 하지만 오직 주 내에 거주하는 주민들만을 위한 장소라는 정보는 전혀 등장하지 않고 있으므로 (A)가 정답이다.

★★★ 유추

Sweetwater Lake State Park에 관해 암시되는 내용이 아닌 것은 무엇인가?
(A) 오직 주 내에 거주하는 주민들만을 위한 곳이다.
(B) 장애인들을 위한 선택권이 있다.
(C) 많은 종류의 야생 동물들이 있다.
(D) 현재 몇몇 자원 봉사자들을 모집하고 있다.

토익 분석

유추 문제의 키워드가 지문 전반에 걸쳐 언급되고 있는 상태에서 적절한 유추 내용을 파악해야 한다면 선택지에 나온 내용을 먼저 파악한 후 선택지의 내용을 유추할 수 있는 근거가 지문에 제시되는지 여부를 역으로 확인하는 방식으로 문제를 풀이해라.

175

In which of the positions marked [1], [2], [3], and [4] does the following sentence best belong?

"Click on the link for the Handicapped Trail."

(A) [1]　　　　　　　　　　(B) [2]
(C) [3]　　　　　　　　　　**(D) [4]**

문제 해설

주어진 문장이 위치해야 하는 곳을 묻는 문제이므로 주어진 문장의 의미를 이해한 후 이와 내용적 연계성을 지닌 적절한 위치를 파악해야 한다. 제시된 문장은 링크를 클릭해 장애인용 산책로를 확인해 보라고 알리는 내용이다. 따라서 Hike 항목에서 장애인이 이용 가능한 산책로가 언급되어 있는 문장 뒤에 위치한 [4]에 들어가 그 산책로를 볼 수 있는 방법을 알려 주는 흐름을 구성하는 것이 논리적으로 타당하므로 (D)가 정답이다.

★★★ 문장의 위치

[1], [2], [3], [4]로 표기된 위치들 중에서 다음 문장이 들어가기에 가장 적절한 곳은 어디인가?
"장애인용 산책로를 보실 수 있는 링크를 클릭하시기 바랍니다."
(A) [1]　　　　　　(B) [2]
(C) [3]　　　　　　(D) [4]

토익 분석

• 문장 위치는 주어진 문장 내용과 앞선 문장 내용과의 연결고리로 활용할 수 있는 접속사, 접속부사, 고유명사, 대명사를 파악하라.
• 강사로서 문제풀이 시간을 단축시킬 수 있는 방법으로 제시할만한 방법은 [3] - [4] - [1] - [2] 순서로 정답 비중이 높기 때문에 주어진 문장 내용을 순차적으로 해당 위치에 삽입해보며 내용 연결성을 비교하며 문제를 풀이하는 것이다.

176-180 다음 이메일을 참조하시오.

수신: Eric Woodhouse, AZA 의학용품
발신: Ryan Taylor, 지배인, Ivy 호텔
날짜: 11월 29일
제목: Ivy 호텔에서의 숙박
첨부: AZAinvoice.txt

친애하는 Woodhouse 씨

귀하와 동료들이 의료학회에 참여하기 위해 몬트리올에 방문하시는 동안 저희 Ivy 호텔에 숙박하시게 된 점 매우 기쁘게 생각합니다. 11월 26일에 하셨던 방문이 즐거우셨기를 바랍니다. [178] 귀하의 신용카드로 지불된 숙박비는 막 처리되었습니다. [176] 이메일에 영수증을 첨부했습니다. [177] 신속한 계산에 감사드립니다.

Ivy 호텔은 아직 신생인지라, 서비스 향상을 개선하기 위한 방법으로 고객의 소리에 항상 귀를 기울이고자 합니다. [176] 만약 귀하와 귀하의 동료들이 저희 호텔에 머무시는 동안 호텔 숙박과 관련된 의견이 있으셨다면 향후에는 저희가 귀하께 더 나은 서비스를 드릴 수 있도록 저희에게 알려주시길 바랍니다.

저희를 방문해 주셔서 매우 기쁩니다. [180] 만약 내년 회의 때 다시 한 번 저희 호텔을 선택해 주신다면 20% 할인 혜택을 제공해드리겠습니다.

Ryan Taylor
지배인
Ivy 호텔

어휘 be pleased that ~여서 기쁘다 medical 의학적인, 의료의 receipt 영수증, 수령, 수취 prompt 즉각의 be keen to Vr ~하길 원하다 feedback 의견, 견해 improve ~을 향상시키다, ~을 개선하다 aspect 양상, 측면, 국면, 관점 pleasure 즐거움, 유쾌함, 쾌적함 discount 할인

수신: Ryan Taylor, 매니저, Ivy 호텔
발신: Eric Woodhouse, AZA 의학용품
날짜: 12월 1일
제목: 답장: Ivy 호텔에서의 숙박

친애하는 Taylor씨

이메일 주신 점 감사드립니다. 저와 동료들은 귀 호텔에서 머무르게 되어 정말 즐거웠습니다. 직원들로부터 많은 도움을 받을 수 있었고, 객실이 넓어서 편히 머무를 수 있었습니다. 저희를 크게 환대해주셨지요.

저와 동료들은 영업 워크숍에 참석하기 위해 다음 달에 Montreal을 다시 방문할 예정 입니다. 가능하다면 저희는 귀 호텔에 머무르는 동안 4개의 객실을 예약하고 싶습니다. 지난번과 같은 객실에 머무르는 것이 가능하겠습니까? [179] 비록 Oak 객실의 욕실이 약간 지저분했지만, 그 외 다른 객실들은 모두 훌륭했습니다.

[180] 물론 저희는 3월 1일로 예정된 다음 컨퍼런스도 귀 호텔에서 개최하고자 합니다.

Questions 176-180 refer to the following e-mails.

To: Eric Woodhouse, AZA Medical Supplies
From: Ryan Taylor, Manager, Ivy Hotel
Date: November 29
Subject: Your stay at the Ivy Hotel
Attachment: AZAinvoice.txt

Dear Mr. Woodhouse,

We were pleased that you and your colleagues chose to stay at the Ivy Hotel during your visit to Montreal for the medical conference. We hope that you enjoyed your stay on November 26. [178] Your credit card payment has just cleared. [176] I have attached your receipt to this email. [177] Thank you for your prompt payment

As the Ivy Hotel is quite new, we are always keen to receive feedback from our customers on ways that we can improve our services. [176] If you or your staff have any comments about any aspect of your stay, please let us know so that we can better serve you in the future.

It was a pleasure to have you stay with us. [180] If you choose the Ivy Hotel again for the next conference, we will offer you a 20% discount.

Sincerely,

Ryan Taylor
General Manager
The Ivy Hotel

To: Ryan Taylor, Manager, Ivy Hotel
From: Eric Woodhouse, AZA Medical Supplies
Date: December 1
Subject: Re: Your stay at the Ivy Hotel

Dear Mr. Taylor,

Thank you for your e-mail. My staff and I thoroughly enjoyed our stay at your hotel. The staff was very helpful, and the rooms were spacious and a pleasure to stay in. You made us feel very welcome.

My staff and I are actually returning to Montreal to attend a sales workshop next month. We would like to book four rooms to stay at your hotel if possible. Would it be possible to stay in the same rooms as the last time? [179] They were all fantastic although the bathroom in the Oak Room was a little dirty.

[180] We would really like to hold our next conference on March 1 in your hotel.

Sincerely,

Eric Woodhouse
Sales Consultant
AZA Medical Supplies

Eric Woodhouse
영업 고문
AZA 의학용품

어휘 thoroughly 대단히 hopeful 희망적인, 장래가 기대되는, 유망한 spacious 널찍한, 광대한, 포괄적인 book ~을 예약하다 fantastic 환상적인 hold ~을 개최하다

176

What is one purpose of the first email?

(A) To advertise a job opening at a hotel
(B) To promote the opening of a new hotel
(C) To request customer comments on a hotel stay
(D) To place an order for medical supplies

문제 해설

첫 번째 이메일의 목적은 첫 번째 단락 하단 I have attached your receipt to this email.을 통해 일차적으로 지난 숙박요금의 정구임을 알 수 있으며 이어서 두 번째 단락 하단 If you or your staff have any comments about any aspect of your stay, please let us know so that we can better serve you in the future을 통해 숙박과 관련한 의견 요청이 또 다른 목적임을 알 수 있다. 따라서 이 중 숙박 관련 의견의 요청을 언급하고 있는 (C)가 정답이 되겠다.

★★ 지문의 목적

첫 번째 이메일의 목적은 무엇인가?
(A) 호텔 구인 광고를 위해서
(B) 새로운 호텔의 개업을 홍보하기 위해서
(C) 호텔 숙박과 관련된 고객의 의견을 구하기 위해서
(D) 의약품을 주문하기 위해서

토익 분석

이메일의 주제/목적은 이메일 초반 2-3문장의 내용을 통해 파악할 수 있으며 주제/목적 문제의 선택지들은 굳이 먼저 읽어볼 필요가 없다.

177

In the first email, the word "prompt" in paragraph 1, line 4, is closest in meaning to

(A) delayed
(B) late
(C) financial
(D) punctual

문제 해설

주어진 문장 내에서 prompt는 신속한 결제를 요구하는 부분에서 '빠르고 신속한'이란 뜻으로 사용된 어휘이므로 이에 대한 유사어로는 punctual이 적절하다. 따라서 정답은 (D)이다.

★★ 유사어

첫 번째 이메일, 첫 번째 단락 다섯 번째 줄 'prompt'와 가장 의미가 유사한 단어는 무엇인가?
(A) 지연된
(B) 늦은
(C) 재무상의
(D) 즉각적인

토익 분석

유사어 문제는 해당 어휘가 포함된 문장을 비롯하여 그 전후 문장 내용을 파악한 후 해당 어휘와 유사한 의미를 지닌 어휘를 선택하라.

★ 세부사항

Taylor 씨는 Woodhouse 씨가 어떠한 수단으로 지불하길
원하는가?
(A) 현금
(B) 신용카드
(C) 수표
(D) 계좌이체

토익 분석

구체적인 결제 수단은 선택지에 나온 결제 수단이 지문에
서 언급되는 부분에 집중해야 한다.

How did Mr. Woodhouse pay Mr. Taylor?

(A) With cash
(B) By credit card
(C) By check
(D) By bank transfer

문제 해설

구체적인 결제 수단에 대해 묻는 질문이므로 무엇보다 지문에서 구체적인 결제수단이 언급되는 부
분에 집중해야 한다. 이메일 첫 번째 단락 하단에서 Your credit card payment has just cleared.라
고 언급하고 있으므로 정답은 (B)가 되겠다.

★★ 세부사항

Woodhouse 씨는 Oak 객실과 관련하여 어떠한 의견을 남
겼는가?
(A) 침대가 깨끗하지 않았다.
(B) 창문이 깨졌다.
(C) 욕실이 더러웠다.
(D) 객실이 환상적이었다.

토익 분석

고유명사는 중요한 키워드이다. 따라서 지문에서 Oak
Room이라는 객실 고유명사가 언급되는 부분을 중심으로
단서를 파악하도록 한다.

What comment does Mr. Woodhouse make about the Oak Room?

(A) The toilet was not functioning.
(B) The window was broken.
(C) The bathroom was messy.
(D) The room was fantastic.

문제 해설

Oak 객실과 관련하여 남긴 의견에 대해 묻고 있으므로 Oak 객실이 소개되는 부분을 중심으
로 단서를 파악해야 한다. 이메일 두 번째 단락 하단에서 They were all fantastic although the
bathroom in the Oak Room was a little dirty라고 언급된 내용을 통해 오크 객실의 화장실이 약
간 지저분했지만 모든 객실은 다 훌륭했음을 밝히고 있다. 그러므로 정답은 (C)라고 할 수 있다. 욕
실이 조금 지저분한 상태를 지칭했으므로 변기만 지저분하다고 지적하고 있는 (A)는 너무 지엽적
이며 fantastic이란 어휘를 중복하여 사용했지만 오크 객실이 환상적인 것이 아니었으므로 이 또한
정답과 거리가 멀다는 점에 주의해야 한다.

★★★ 두 지문 연계 문제

Woodhouse 씨는 언제 특별 할인을 받을 수 있을 것 같은
가?
(A) 11월 26일
(B) 11월 29일
(C) 12월 1일
(D) 3월 1일

토익 분석

해당 문제의 단서가 나와야 할 지문에 단서가 불충분하게
언급된다면 이는 두 지문 연계 문제이다.

When will Mr. Woodhouse most likely receive a special discount?

(A) November 26
(B) November 29
(C) December 1
(D) March 1

문제 해설

Woodhouse 씨는 언제 특별 할인을 받을 수 있을지 묻는 문제이므로 할인에 관련된 정보가 제시
되는 부분부터 파악해야 한다. Taylor 씨는 첫 번째 이메일 종료 직전 If you choose the Ivy Hotel
again for the next conference, we will offer you a 20% discount라며 내년 회의 때 다시 한 번 방
문해 준다면 Woodhouse 씨에게 20% 할인 혜택을 제공할 것임을 안내하고 있다. 그러나 할인 혜택
의 시기가 언급되지 않고 있으므로 해당 문제는 두 지문 연계 문제임을 파악할 수 있다. 그러므로 두
번째 이메일에서 Woodhouse 씨가 내년 회의도 Ivy 호텔에서 개최하고자 한다는 의사 타진과 구체
적인 회의 시점이 등장하는 부분에 집중해야 한다.

두 번째 이메일 하단에서 Woodhouse 씨는 We would really like to hold our next conference on
March 1 in your hotel라며 3월 1일로 예정된 다음 회의도 귀 호텔에서 개최하길 원한다는 의사를
밝히고 있다. 따라서 Woodhouse 씨가 호텔로부터 할인 혜택을 제공받을 수 있는 시점은 바로 내년
3월 1일임을 가늠할 수 있으므로 정답은 (D)가 되겠다.

Questions 181-185 refer to the following article and e-mail.

The Daily News

December 1

For a "Pick-me-up"

Aaron Milton's days [182] revolve around coffee beans, sugary syrups, and cream, with a variety of unique flavors added. His recently opened shop, [183] the Daily Perk, serves a nice selection of deli sandwiches and sugary sweets, but it is the custom coffee drinks that really stand out. [181] By combining his home-grown and roasted coffee beans with a creative flair for flavor combinations, Aaron Milton has become famous as "Mr. Coffee" among store patrons. [185] Mr. Milton, a former school teacher, now produces the best caffeinated beverages in town. Because his drink concoctions are often inspired by the seasons (for example, pumpkin spiced pie during the fall and candy cane delight during the winter holidays), [183] the selection of flavors changes frequently. Even the staff is encouraged to put their own personal touches to the menu and have created several staple items available year-round.

[183] Mr. Milton started the Daily Perk with a loan from his parents, which he was able to repay just after his first year of business.

If you haven't been there yet, The Daily Perk is conveniently located at the corner of Weems Lane and Elm Street. [183 (A)] It opens every morning at 6:30 A.M. For more information, visit their Web site at www.perkup.com.

To: Aaron Milton <amilton@mail.com>
From: Peter Vickers <Pvickers@mail.com>
Subject: Article
Date: December 3

Dear Aaron,

[184] I saw the newspaper story about you in *The Daily News*, and it reminded me that I haven't been to your coffee shop yet. It sounds great, and I hope to stop by soon. [185] We miss you at Crown Pointe Academy. Several students still ask

---

181-185 다음 기사와 이메일을 참조하시오.

The Daily News

12월 1일

"활기를 주는 음료…"

Aaron Milton 씨의 하루는 여러 가지 독특한 맛이 더해진 커피 콩과 달콤한 시럽, 그리고 크림을 중심으로 [182] 돌아간다. 그가 최근에 개장한 매장 The Daily Perk는 [183 (D)] 여러 가지 뛰어난 매장 제조 샌드위치와 달콤한 음식들을 제공하지만, 정말로 눈에 띄는 것은 이곳의 자체 커피 음료들이다. [181] 집에서 재배하고 볶은 커피 콩과 맛의 조화를 위한 창의적인 솜씨가 조합되어, Aaron Milton 씨는 매장 손님들 사이에서 "미스터 커피"라는 별명으로 유명해졌다. [185] 전직 학교 교사인 Milton 씨는, 현재 도시에서 가장 뛰어난 카페인 함유 음료들을 제조한다. 그의 혼합 음료들은 종종 계절에서 영감을 얻기 때문에(예를 들어, 가을철의 호박맛 파이나 겨울 연휴 동안의 캔디 케인 사탕이 있다), [183 (B)] 맛의 종류가 자주 바뀐다. 심지어 직원들조차 메뉴에 각자 원하는 개인적인 취향을 반영하도록 장려되며, 연중 구매 가능한 여러 가지 대표 제품들을 만들어 왔다.

[183 (C)] Milton 씨는 부모님으로부터 자금을 빌려 The Daily Perk를 시작했는데, 불과 사업 시작 1년 만에 모두 되갚을 수 있었다.

아직 그곳에 가보지 않았다면, The Daily Perk는 Weems Ln.과 Elm St.가 만나는 모퉁이에 편리하게 위치해 있다. [183 (A)] 매일 아침 6시 30분에 영업을 시작한다. 더 많은 정보는 웹 사이트 www.perkup.com를 방문해 확인할 수 있다.

어휘 pick-me-up (술, 커피 등) 기운을 돋우는 것 revolve around ~을 중심으로 돌아가다 sugary 달콤한 a variety of 다양한 deli sandwich 매장에서 만든 샌드위치 sweets 단 것, 사탕 custom 맞춤형의 stand out 눈에 띄다, 두드러지다 combine A with B A를 B와 조합하다, 결합하다 home-grown 집에서 만든 creative 창의적인 flair 솜씨, 재능 combination 조화, 혼합 caffeinated 카페인이 함유된 concoction 혼합물 be inspired by ~에서 영감을 얻다 spiced ~ 맛이 들어간 candy cane delight 캔디 케인 사탕 selection 종류 flavor 맛, 풍미 frequently 자주 be encouraged to do ~하도록 장려되다, 권장되다 touch 취향, 솜씨, 느낌 create ~을 만들어 내다 staple 대표적인, 주요한 available 이용 가능한 year-round 연중으로 loan 융자, 대출 re-pay ~을 갚다 conveniently located 편리하게 위치한 at the corner of A and B A와 B가 만나는 모퉁이에

수신: Aaron Milton <amilton@mail.com>
발신: Peter Vickers <Pvickers@mail.com>
제목: 기사
날짜: 12월 3일

Aaron 씨께,

[184] The Daily News에서 당신에 관한 신문 기사를 읽어 보았는데, 기사를 접하고 나니 제가 아직 당신의 커피 매장에 가보지 않았다는 것이 생각나더군요. 멋진 곳이라고 생각되었기 때문에, 곧 들를 수 있기를 바랍니다. [185] 우리는 Crown Pointe Academy에 있던 당신이 그립습니다. 여러 학생들이 여전히 당신에 관해 묻습니다. 이곳은 모든

일이 잘 되고 있습니다. [184] 이번 여름에 과학 연구실을 개조할 예정인데, 이것은 당신이 오랫동안 바랬던 일이라는 것을 알고 있습니다! 모든 작업이 완료되면 와 보셔야 할 것입니다.

곧 뵙겠습니다!
Peter

어휘 remind A that A에게 ~라고 상기시키다 stop by 들르다 miss ~을 그리워하다 Things are going well 모든 것이 잘 되다 renovate ~을 개조하다, 보수하다 lab 연구실, 실험실 beg for ~을 애원하다

---

about you. Things are going well here. [184] We're renovating the science lab this summer, which I know you had been begging for years! You'll have to come see it when all the work is done.

I'll be seeing you soon!
Peter

181

★ 유추 / Milton 씨에 대한 암시 내용

Milton 씨에 관해 암시되는 것은 무엇인가?
(A) 가족 사업에 합류했다.
(B) 부모님께 빚을 지고 있다.
(C) 몇몇 재료를 직접 재배한다.
(D) 진로를 바꿀 계획이다.

토익 분석

특정 인물에 대한 유추 내용은 인명이 제시되는 부분을 중심으로 언급되는 인물 관련 정보를 파악한 후 이를 토대로 선택지에서 특정 인물에 대해 유추 가능한 내용을 정답으로 선택해야 한다.

What is suggested about Mr. Milton?

(A) He joined the family business.
(B) He owes his parents money.
(C) He farms some of his ingredients himself.
(D) He plans to change careers.

문제 해설

Milton 씨의 정체를 유추하는 문제이므로 Milton 씨의 정체를 파악할 수 있는 관련 어휘나 표현이 등장하는 부분에 초점을 맞춰야 한다. 첫 지문의 첫 단락 중반부에서 home-grown and roasted coffee beans라며 집에서 재배한 커피 콩에 대해 언급되는 부분을 통해 Milton 씨가 직접 커피 콩을 재배한다는 것을 유추할 수 있다. 따라서 (C)가 정답이다.

182

★★ 유사어

기사에서, 1번째 단락, 1번째 줄에 있는 단어 "revolve"와 의미가 가장 가까운 어휘는 무엇인가?
(A) 사임하다
(B) 고안하다
(C) 관련되다
(D) 연기하다

토익 분석

유사어 문제는 해당 어휘가 포함된 문장을 비롯하여 그 전후 문장 내용을 파악한 후 해당 어휘와 유사한 의미를 지닌 어휘를 선택하라

In the article, the word "revolve" in paragraph 1, line 1, is closet in meaning to

(A) resign
(B) design
(C) involve
(D) postpone

문제 해설

동사 revolve 뒤로 전치사 around와 함께 커피 콩과 달콤한 시럽, 그리고 크림이 쓰여 있는데, 뒤에 이어지는 내용을 보면 Milton 씨가 개장한 매장의 메뉴와 관련된 것들임을 알 수 있다. 따라서 그의 하루가 매일 이 재료들을 중심으로 지나간다는 의미로 생각할 수 있으므로 '관련되다, 연루되다'라는 의미를 지닌 involve가 유사어로 적합하다. 그러므로 (C)가 정답이다.

183

What is NOT indicated about the Daily Perk?

(A) It only has evening hours.
(B) Its menu changes often.
(C) It has experienced quick success.
(D) It offers a variety of products.

문제 해설

메뉴가 자주 바뀐다는 의미로 쓰인 (B)는 첫 지문 첫 단락 후반부의 the selection of flavors changes frequently 부분에서 확인 가능하며, 빠른 성공의 경험을 뜻하는 (C)는 같은 지문의 두 번째 단락에서 창업을 위해 부모님에게서 빌린 돈을 일년 만에 갚았다고(~ he was able to repay just after his first year of business) 언급한 부분에서 확인할 수 있다. 그리고 다양한 제품의 제공을 말한 (D)도 같은 지문의 첫 단락 시작 부분의 a nice selection of deli sandwiches and sugary sweets에서 찾아 볼 수 있다. 하지만 첫 지문 마지막 단락에 매일 아침 6시 30분에 문을 연다고(It opens every morning at 6:30 A.M.) 했으므로 (A)가 정답이다.

★★★ 진위

The Daily Perk에 관해 알 수 있는 내용이 아닌 것은 무엇인가?
(A) 오직 저녁 시간에만 문을 연다.
(B) 자주 메뉴를 바꾼다.
(C) 빠른 성공을 경험했다.
(D) 다양한 제품을 제공한다.

토익 분석

사실이 아닌 내용(NOT TRUE)을 묻는 문제는 선택지 내용을 파악한 후 지문의 내용과 대조하며 사실 가능성이 적은 선택지를 오답으로 소거하며 정답을 찾아내는 방식으로 풀이하라

184

Why did Mr. Vickers send the e-mail?

(A) To ask Mr. Milton to come to his party
(B) To ask Mr. Milton for a job
(C) To ascertain his interest in an investment opportunity
(D) To invite Mr. Milton to visit the new facilities

문제 해설

Vickers 씨가 이메일을 보낸 목적에 대해 묻고 있다. 주제/목적 문제는 난이도가 높아질수록 그 주제/목적이 지문의 초반부가 아니라 중반부나 후반부에서 제시된다. Vickers 씨가 이메일 초반 The Daily News에서 I saw the newspaper story about you in *The Daily News*, and it reminded me that I haven't been to your coffee shop yet라며 Aaron Milton 씨에 관한 신문 기사를 읽었고 그의 커피 매장에 아직 가보지 않은 사실이 생각났다는 이메일 초반부 내용을 이메일의 목적으로 여길 수 있다. 하지만 이는 이메일의 본격적인 내용을 작성하기에 앞서 등장하는 운을 떼기 위한 도입부일 뿐, 궁극적으로 이메일을 작성하게 된 목적은 단순히 기사를 읽었다는 내용을 전달하고자 함이 아니라 이메일 후반부에서 We're renovating the science lab this summer, which I know you had been begging for years! You'll have to come see it when all the work is done라며 Milton 씨가 수년 간 굉장히 바랬던 연구실의 보수작업이 마무리되었으니 한 번 방문해줄 것을 요청하는 것이 실질적인 이메일의 발송 목적이라 할 수 있다. 그러므로 정답은 (D)가 되겠다.

★★★ 이메일의 목적

Vickers 씨가 이메일을 보낸 이유는 무엇인가?
(A) Milton 씨에게 자신의 파티에 오도록 요청하기 위해
(B) Milton 씨에게 일자리를 부탁하기 위해
(C) 투자 기회에 대한 자신의 관심을 확인하기 위해
(D) Milton 씨에게 새로운 시설을 방문해달라고 초청하기 위해서

토익 분석

지문의 주제/목적은 단락 구분이 있는 경우 첫 번째 단락 초반 2-3문장에서 제시되는 경우가 대부분이다. 다만 주제/목적 문제의 난이도가 높아지는 경우 주제/목적은 두 번째 단락의 초반 2-3문장에서 등장한다. 만약 단락 구분이 없는 지문인 경우 지문 초반 2-3문장에서 주제/목적이 제시되는 경우가 일반적이지만 이 역시 주제/목적 문제의 난이도가 높아지는 경우 지문의 중반부 또는 후반부에서 주제/목적이 언급된다.

185

Where most likely did Mr. Vickers and Mr. Milton work together?

(A) At a coffee shop
(B) At a school
(C) At an advertising agency
(D) At a charity event

문제 해설

Vickers 씨와 Milton 씨는 함께 근무했던 직장을 유추하는 문제로 두 번째 지문의 중반부에 Vickers 씨는 Crown Pointe Academy에 있던 Milton 씨가 그립다며 We miss you at Crown Pointe Academy라고 말하고 있다. 아울러 첫 지문의 첫 단락 중반부에 Milton 씨가 전직 학교 교사라며 Mr. Milton, a former school teacher라고 언급하고 있다. 따라서 이 두 가지 단서를 취합하면 Vickers 씨와 Milton 씨는 학교에서 근무했었음을 유추할 수 있으므로 정답은 (B)가 되겠다.

★★★ 두 지문 연계 문제

Vickers 씨와 Milton 씨는 어디에서 함께 일했을 가능성이 가장 큰가?
(A) 커피 매장
(B) 학교
(C) 광고 대행사
(D) 자선 행사장

토익 분석

두 사람이 서로에게 보내는 각자 다른 두 개의 이메일을 작성하고 있으므로 두 사람과 연계된 내용을 묻는 문제는 두 지문 연계 문제이다.

186-190 다음 기사와 두 이메일을 참조하시오.

다가오는 Barrington Children's Hospital Marathon에 대한 후원업체 결정 • 5월 5일

[188] Pueblo Corporation이 다가오는 Barrington Children's Hospital Marathon 행사를 위한 가장 큰 후원업체가 될 것이라는 사실이 확인되었다. 이 업체의 후원과 관련된 상세 정보는 조만간 발표될 것이다. [188] 이 기업은 전국에서 세 번째로 큰 제약 회사로 순위에 올라 있다.

[186 (A)] Barrington Children's Hospital Marathon 행사는 지난 15년 동안 해마다 개최되어 왔다. 해당 기간 동안, [186 (B)] 1,500만 달러가 넘는 금액이 희귀 질병으로 고통받고 있는 아이들을 돕기 위해 모금되었다. 이 행사는 일반 마라톤(26마일)과 하프 마라톤(13마일)으로 구성되어 있다. 모든 수익금과 기부금은 Barrington Children's Hospital에 기부될 것이다. 참가자들은 각자 기금 마련과 관련된 노력을 기울이도록 장려된다.

[186 (C)] 이번 행사는 다음 달인 6월 16일 토요일에 시작될 것이다. Barrington Children's Hospital Marathon은 하프 마라톤에 10,000명이 넘는 참가자들이, 그리고 일반 마라톤에는 5,000여명의 참가자들이 찾는 전국에서 20번째로 큰 마라톤 행사이다.

어휘 upcoming 다가오는, 곧 있을 be confirmed that ~라는 것이 확인되다 details 세부 사항, 상세 정보 regarding ~와 관련해 in the near future 조만간, 가까운 미래에 be ranked as ~로서 순위에 오르다, ~로 선정되다 pharmaceutical 제약의 hold ~을 개최하다 annually 해마다, 연례적으로 raise (기금 등) ~을 모금하다 suffer from ~로 고통 받다 rare 희귀한 disease 질병 consist of ~로 구성되다 profit 수익 contribution 기부(금) donate ~을 기부하다 participant 참가자 be encouraged to do ~하도록 장려되다 make an effort 노력하다 fundraising 기금 마련, 모금 commence 시작되다

Questions 186-190 refer to the following article and e-mails.

Sponsor decided for the upcoming Barrington Children's Hospital Marathon • May 5

It has been confirmed that the [188] Pueblo Corporation will be the biggest sponsor for the upcoming Barrington Children's Hospital Marathon. Details regarding the sponsorship are to be announced in the near future. [188] The corporation is ranked as the third largest pharmaceutical company in the country.

[186] The Barrington Children's Hospital Marathon has been held annually for the past fifteen years. Over the years, more than $15 million have been raised [186] to help children suffering from rare diseases. The event consists of a marathon (26 miles) and a half marathon (13 miles). All profits and contributions will be donated to the Barrington Children's Hospital. Participants are encouraged to make their own fundraising efforts.

[186] The event will commence next month on Saturday, June 16. The Barrington Children's Hospital Marathon is the twentieth largest marathon in the nation, with over 10,000 participants for the half marathon and about 5,000 participants for the full marathon.

발신: Teresa Martinez ⟨teresamartinez@pueblo.net⟩
수신: Jim Douglas ⟨jimdouglas@pueblo.net⟩
날짜: 5월 10일
제목: Social Interests News와의 인터뷰

[187] Douglas 씨께,

Barrington Children's Hospital Marathon과 관련해 최근에 언론 보도가 나온 뒤로, 다수의 언론 매체들이 인터뷰를 요청해 오고 있습니다. 언론 매체들은 후원업체 결정과 관련된 [187] 우리 홍보부의 의견을 들어 보고 싶어 합니다. 이 매체들 중에서, 가장 명성이 높은 매체인 Social Interests News을 골랐습니다. Social Interests News의 기자 한 분이 인터뷰 일정을 잡기 위해 곧 연락 드릴 것입니다. [190] 일정을 고려해 보면, 5월 12일, 14일, 15일, 그리고 20일에 시간이 있으실 것 같습니다. 이 중에서 하루 시간이 괜찮으셨으면 합니다.

어휘 following ~ 후에 recent 최근의 press release 언론 보도, 보도 자료 multiple 다수의 news media agency 언론 매체 request ~을 요청하다 opinion 의견 decision 결정 out of ~ 중에서 pick out ~을 고르다, 선발하다 reputable 명성 있는 contact ~에게 연락하다 considering ~을 고려하면, 감안하면 it seems like ~인 것 같다 free 시간이 있는 work (일정 등이) 괜찮다, 적합하다

From: Teresa Martinez <teresamartinez@pueblo.net>
To: Jim Douglas <jimdouglas@pueblo.net>
Date: May 10
Subject: Interview with Social Interests News

[187] Dear Mr. Douglas,

Following the recent press release on the Barrington Children's Hospital Marathon, multiple news media agencies have requested an interview. They want to hear [187] our public relations department's opinion on the sponsorship decision. Out of them, I picked out the most reputable agency, Social Interests News. A writer from Social Interests News will contact you soon to schedule an interview. [190] Considering your schedule, it seems like you will be free on May 12th, 14th, 15th, and 20th. I hope one of these days will work.

From: Matthew Stokes <mstokes12@socialinterestnews.com>
To: Jim Douglas <jimdouglas@pueblo.net>
Date: May 10
Subject: Interview Request to Pueblo Corporation

Dear Mr. Jim Douglas,

My name is Matthew and I am a writer at Social Interests News. [187] I already contacted your secretary Teresa Martinez regarding an interview. I have heard about your company's decision to become a sponsor of the upcoming Barrington Children's Hospital Marathon. Our newspaper thought it would be a great opportunity for us to introduce a major sponsor to the public. We have no doubts that the interview will also be [189] beneficial for your company's publicity. [190] Will you be available on any of the following dates: 13, 14, or 16? If not, I can try to accommodate a better time for you.

발신: Matthew Stokes ⟨mstokes12@socialinterestnews.com⟩
수신: Jim Douglas ⟨jimdouglas@pueblo.net⟩
날짜: 5월 10일
Subject: Pueblo Corporation 인터뷰 요청

Jim Douglas 씨께,

제 이름은 Matthew이며, Social Interests News의 기자입니다. [187] 앞서 귀하의 비서이신 Teresa Martinez 씨께 인터뷰와 관련해 연락 드렸습니다. 다가오는 Barrington Children's Hospital Marathon 행사의 후원업체가 되고자 한다는 귀사의 결정에 관해 들었습니다. 이는 일반 대중들에게 주요 후원업체를 소개할 수 있는 아주 좋은 기회가 될 것이라는 생각이 들었습니다. 저희는 이번 인터뷰가 귀사의 대외 홍보에도 [189] 이득이 될 수 있다는 점에 의심의 여지가 없습니다. [190] 귀하께서는 13일과 14일, 또는 16일 중의 하루에 시간이 되시는지요? 그렇지 않으실 경우, 더 편한 시간으로 맞추어 보도록 하겠습니다.

어휘 regarding ~와 관련해 opportunity for A to do A가 ~할 수 있는 기회 introduce ~을 소개하다 major 주요한 have no doubts that ~라는 점에 의심의 여지가 없다 beneficial 이득이 되는 publicity (대외) 홍보 available (사람이) 시간이 나는 following 다음의 If not 그렇지 않다면 accommodate ~을 수용하다

186

What is NOT indicated about the Barrington Children's Hospital Marathon?

(A) It has been held every year for fifteen years.
(B) It is a fundraising event for children with illnesses.
(C) It consists of only a 26-mile marathon.
(D) It will be held mid-June this year.

문제 해설

Barrington Children's Hospital Marathon과 관련된 전반적인 정보가 제시된 첫 지문에, 두 번째 단락의 has been held annually for the past fifteen years와 to help children suffering from rare diseases 부분을 통해 (A)와 (B)에 대한 내용을 확인할 수 있고, 세 번째 단락의 commence next month on Saturday, June 16에서 (D)도 확인 가능하다. 하지만 두 번째 단락에 일반 마라톤(a marathon)과 하프 마라톤(a half marathon)으로 구성된다고 되어 있으므로 (C)가 정답이다.

★★★ 진위

Barrington Children's Hospital Marathon에 관해 알 수 있는 내용이 아닌 것은 무엇인가?
(A) 15년 동안 매년 개최되어 왔다.
(B) 병을 앓고 있는 아이들을 위한 모금 행사이다.
(C) 26마일 길이의 마라톤으로만 구성된다.
(D) 올해는 6월 중순에 개최될 것이다.

토익 분석

사실이 아닌 한 가지 내용을 묻는 문제[NOT TRUE]는 선택지를 키워드로 삼아 각 선택지의 내용이 지문에서 언급되는지 여부를 파악하는 방식으로 풀이하는 것이 효율적이다.

187

Who most likely is Mr. Douglas?

(A) A director of Pueblo Corporation's public relations
(B) A secretary at Pueblo Corporation
(C) A chief editor at Social Interests News
(D) A representative of Barrington Children's Hospital

문제 해설

Martinez 씨가 Douglas 씨에게 보내는 이메일인 두 번째 지문을 보면, Douglas 씨가 언론과 인터뷰하는 일정과 관련된 정보를 전달하면서 our Public Relations Department, 즉 우리 회사 홍보부라며 소속 부서를 알리고 있다. 아울러 세 번째 이메일의 초반부에서 I already contacted your secretary Teresa Martinez regarding an interview라며 이미 귀하와의 인터뷰와 관련하여 비서와 연락을 취한 바 있음을 밝히고 있다. 그러므로 이를 모두 취합하면 수신인인 Douglas 씨는 홍보부 책임자임을 유추할 수 있다. 따라서 (A)가 정답이다.

★★★ 유추 / Douglas 씨의 정체

Douglas 씨는 누구일 가능성이 가장 큰가?
(A) Pueblo의 홍보부장
(B) Pueblo Corporation의 비서
(C) Social Interests News의 편집장
(D) Barrington Children's Hospital의 직원

토익 분석

인물 유추는 인물의 정체를 유추할 수 있는 관련 어휘나 표현을 파악하는 것이 관건이다.

★★ 진위

Pueblo Corporation에 관해 알 수 있는 것은 무엇인가?
(A) 직원들이 마라톤에 참가한다.
(B) 항상 해당 마라톤 행사의 후원업체였다.
(C) 전국에서 가장 큰 제약 회사이다.
(D) 의약품 제조를 전문으로 한다.

토익 분석

사실 내용을 묻는 문제[TRUE]의 키워드가 지문 전반에 걸쳐 언급되는 경우 선택지의 내용을 키워드로 삼아 지문에서 해당 내용이 언급되는지 여부를 빠르게 파악한다. 이 때 선택지를 두 개씩 나눠 두 번에 걸쳐 지문에서의 해당 내용이 제시되고 있는지 확인하는 방식을 권고한다.

What is suggested about Pueblo Corporation?

(A) Its employees are participating in the marathon.
(B) It has always been a sponsor for the marathon.
(C) It is the biggest pharmaceutical company in the country.
(D) It specializes in producing medicinal drugs.

문제 해설

Pueblo Corporation과 관련된 정보가 언급된, 첫 지문의 첫 단락에서 the third largest pharmaceutical company라며 전국에서 세 번째로 큰 제약 회사임을 밝히고 있으므로 의약품 제조를 전문으로 한다는 의미를 나타내는 (D)가 정답이다.

★ 유사어

세 번째 이메일에서, 1번째 단락의 5번째 줄에 있는 단어 **"beneficial"**과 의미가 가장 가까운 것은 무엇인가?
(A) 도움이 되는
(B) 쓸모 없는
(C) 중대한
(D) 대체 가능한

토익 분석

유사어 문제는 해당 어휘가 포함된 문장을 비롯하여 그 전후 문장 내용을 파악한 후 해당 어휘와 유사한 의미를 지닌 어휘를 선택하라

In the third email, the word "beneficial" in the paragraph 1, line 5, is closest in meaning to

(A) helpful
(B) useless
(C) critical
(D) alternative

문제 해설

beneficial 뒤에 전치사 for와 함께 상대방 회사의 홍보가 언급되어 있다. 따라서 이 문장에서 that 절의 주어로 쓰인 the interview와 회사 홍보 사이의 관계를 나타내기 위해 beneficial이 쓰인 것이므로 홍보에 좋다는 의미임을 알 수 있다. 그러므로 '도움이 되는'을 뜻하는 helpful, 즉 (A)가 정답이다.

★★★ 유추 / 두 지문 연계 문제

인터뷰는 언제 진행될 가능성이 가장 큰가?
(A) 5월 13일
(B) 5월 14일
(C) 5월 16일
(D) 6월 16일

토익 분석

• 해당 문제의 단서가 나와야 할 지문에서 단서가 불충분하게 언급된다면 이는 두 지문 연계 문제이다
• 두 번째 혹은 세 번째 문제가 두 지문 연계 문제인 경우 주로 첫 번째 지문에서 문제풀이에 필요한 단서가 제시되며 네 번째 혹은 다섯 번째 문제가 두 지문 연계 문제인 경우 대개 마지막 세 번째 지문에 문제풀이에 필요한 결정적인 단서가 포함되어 있다.

When will the interview be most likely held?

(A) May 13
(B) May 14
(C) May 16
(D) June 16

문제 해설

두 번째 지문의 마지막 부분에서 you will be free on May 12th, 14th, 15th, and 20th라며 Douglas 씨가 시간이 나는 날짜로 언급된 것이 5월 12일, 14일, 15일, 20일임을 밝히고 있다. 하지만 날짜가 제시되고 있음에도 불구하고 인터뷰 진행 일자는 언급되지 않고 있으므로 이는 두 지문 연계 문제라 할 수 있다. 이어서 세 번째 지문에서 Will you be available on any of the following dates: 13, 14, or 16?을 통해 시간이 나는 날짜로 묻는 때가 13일, 14일, 16일임을 밝히고 있다. 따라서 중복되는 날에 해당되는 5월 14일에 인터뷰를 할 것이라 가늠할 수 있으므로 정답은 (B)가 되겠다.

Questions 191-195 refer to the following advertisements and e-mails.

http://www.allhousinglondon.uk

Visiting Professor Seeking Downtown Apartment

Topic: Six-Month Sublease
Date: September 12
Posted by: Reed McMahon

[191, 195] I will be in London from January to June on a teaching assignment at Coleridge College. I am looking for a six-month lease (or sublease) for the upcoming year.

I am not looking for anything luxurious. I'm in the market for a nice, clean [192] one- or two-bedroom apartment with the basic amenities, including a stove and refrigerator. Anything else would be an added bonus. A patio or open balcony would be ideal, as I like to entertain friends and colleagues. I am looking to live near the college, however, as I will not be bringing my car from the United States. [195] My budget is 1,600 American dollars per month, including water, gas, and electricity. [192] I am a non-smoker.

http://www.allhousinglondon.uk

Apartment for Rent in London

Topic: Real Estate and Housing
Date: September 13

Enjoy this great [192] one-bedroom apartment after a thorough renovation of the property. [193] This clean and simple, yet modern apartment will be move-in ready on December 15. It will feature a lovely balcony, new floors throughout, and all new appliances. [192] The apartment is just outside of downtown London, but close to major public transportation hubs. It is an ideal option for students and staff at Coleridge College, as well as the post office and other government buildings. It is less than a kilometer from a major municipal park. [195] £1,000 per month pays for water, sewer, garbage pickups, and general upkeep of the property. The electricity and natural gas will be the responsibility of the tenant. [192] Non-smokers only. A one-time security deposit equal to one month's rent should be paid upon signing the rental agreement.

191-195 다음 두 광고들과 이메일을 참조하시오.

http://www.allhousinglondon.uk

시내에 아파트를 구하는 초빙 교수

게시 제목: 6개월 기간의 전대
날짜: 9월 12일
게시자: Reed McMahon

[191, 195] 저는 Coleridge College에서의 강의를 위해 1월부터 6월까지 London에 있을 예정입니다. 저는 내년을 위해 6개월 기간의 임대(또는 전대) 계약을 찾고 있습니다.

고급스러운 것을 찾고 있는 것이 아닙니다. 가스 레인지와 냉장고 같은 기본적인 편의 시설이 있는 깨끗하고 괜찮은 [192 (B)] 침실 하나 또는 두 개짜리 아파트를 구입하는 데 관심이 있습니다. 그 외의 것들은 추가적인 보너스와 같을 것입니다. 테라스나 개방된 발코니가 있으면 이상적일 텐데, 친구들이나 동료들과 즐거운 시간을 보내고 싶기 때문입니다. 하지만 저는 대학교 근처에서 거주할 계획인데, 미국에서 제 차를 가져가지 않을 것이기 때문입니다. [195] 제 예산은 수도와 가스, 전기를 포함한 비용으로 월 미화 1,600달러입니다. [192 (D)] 저는 비흡연자입니다.

어휘 seek ~을 찾다, 구하다 sublease 전대(임대된 공간을 다시 임대하는 것) assignment (할당) 업무, 일 look for ~을 찾다 lease 임대 계약 upcoming year 내년 luxurious 고급스러운 be in the market for ~을 구입하는 데 관심이 있다 amenities 편의 시설 stove 가스 레인지 refrigerator 냉장고 added 추가된 patio 테라스 ideal 이상적인 colleague 동료직원 look to do ~할 계획이다 however 하지만 budget 예산 including ~을 포함해 electricity 전기

http://www.allhousinglondon.uk

London의 아파트 임대

게시 제목: 부동산 및 주택
날짜: 9월 13일

건물이 완전히 개조된 후의 이 훌륭한 [192 (B)] 침실 하나짜리 아파트를 즐겨 보세요. [193] 이 깨끗하고 단순하면서도 현대적인 아파트는 12월 15일에 입주 준비가 될 것입니다. 이곳은 멋진 발코니와 구석구석 새롭게 깔린 바닥재, 그리고 모두 새로운 가전 기기들을 특징으로 합니다. [192] 이 아파트는 London 시내 바로 외곽에 위치해 있지만 주요 대중 교통 거점들과 가까운 곳에 있습니다. 이곳은 Coleridge College의 학생과 직원들뿐만 아니라 우체국과 기타 정부 관청 근무 직원들에게도 이상적인 선택권입니다. 주요 지역 공원에서 불과 1킬로미터도 떨어지지 않은 곳에 있습니다. [195] 월 1,000파운드로의 비용이면 상수도와 하수 처리, 쓰레기 수거, 그리고 일반적인 건물 관리비를 지불하실 수 있습니다. 전기와 천연 가스는 세입자에게 지불 책임이 있습니다. [192 (D)] 오직 비흡연자만 가능합니다. 한 달의 방세와 동일한 금액으로 한 번만 지불하면 되는 보증금은 임대 계약을 맺는 즉시 지불되어야 합니다.

언제든 부담 없이 제게 926-7399로 연락하시거나 turnerproperties@hmail.net로 이메일을 주세요.

어휘 thorough 철저한, 꼼꼼한 renovation 개조, 보수 property 건물, 부동산 A yet B A하면서도 B한 be move-in ready 입주 준비가 되다 feature ~을 특징으로 하다 throughout 구석구석 appliance 가전 기기 close to ~와 가까운 major 주요한 public transportation 대중 교통 hub 거점, 중심 as well as ~뿐만 아니라 less than ~ 미만의, ~가 채 되지 않는 municipal 지역의, 지방 자치의 garbage pick-up 쓰레기 수거 general 일반적인 upkeep 관리, 유지 responsibility 책임 tenant 세입자 security deposit 보증금 equal to ~와 동일한 rent 방세, 임대료 upon ~하자마자 sign an agreement 계약을 맺다 rental 임대, 대여

수신 Martha Turner 〈turnerproperties@hmail.net〉
발신 Reed McMahon 박사 〈reed.mc@talkmail.com〉
날짜 아파트
제목 9월 14일

Turner 씨께,

시내 바로 외곽에 위치한 새롭게 개조된 침실 하나짜리 아파트에 대한 귀하의 게시물과 관련해 연락 드립니다. [195] 이 아파트는 매우 매력적인 곳으로 보이며, [192 (A)] 제 예산에도 꼭 맞습니다. 안타깝게도, [194] 제가 직접 12월 18일이 되어서야 런던에 도착하게 되어, 아파트를 직접 볼 수 없을 것 같은데요. 건물 사진 몇 장을 보내주실 수 있으신가요? 분명히 아직 개조 공사 중이겠지만, 틀림 없이 공사 이후의 모습을 상상할 수 있습니다. 이 이메일 주소를 이용해 제게 답변하시거나 원하실 경우에 언제든지 제게 전화 주시기 바랍니다.

감사합니다.

Reed McMahon 박사
512.578.6090

어휘 respond to ~에 답변하다, 응답하다 listing 목록, 명단 It sounds 형용사 ~한 것 같다 appealing to ~에게 매력적인, ~의 관심을 끄는 definitely 분명히 fit ~에 적합하다, 알맞다 unfortunately 안타깝게도 be able to do ~할 수 있다 firsthand 직접 obviously 분명히 fill in the blanks 나머지를 상상하다 feel free to do 언제든지 ~하세요, 마음껏 ~하세요

Please feel free to call me at 926-7399 or e-mail me at turnerproperties@hmail.net.

TO	Martha Turner<turnerproperties@hmail.net>
FROM	Dr. Reed McMahon <reed.mc@talkmail.com>
DATE	Apartment
SUBJECT	September 14

Dear Ms. Turner,

I am responding to your listing for the newly renovated one-bedroom apartment just outside of downtown. [195] It sounds very appealing to me and [192] definitely fits in my budget. Unfortunately, I won't be able to see the apartment firsthand, [194] as I won't be in London until December 18. Could you send some pictures of the property? Obviously, it is still being renovated, but I'm sure I can fill in the blanks. Please use this e-mail address to respond or if you wish, feel free to call me anytime.

Thank you.

Dr. Reed McMahon
512.578.6090

191

Why is Dr. McMahon moving?

(A) To teach students
(B) To relocate a laboratory
(C) To get close to a company
(D) To coach professional athletes

문제 해설

Reed 박사가 쓴 글인 첫 지문의 시작 부분을 보면, I will be in London from January to June on a teaching assignment at Coleridge College라며 강의를 위해 1월부터 6월까지 London에 가 있을 예정임을 알리고 있다. 따라서 학생들을 가르치기 위해 이사한다는 것을 알 수 있으므로 (A)가 정답이다.

★★★ 세부사항

McMahon 박사가 이사하는 이유는 무엇인가?
(A) 학생들을 가르치기 위해서
(B) 실험실을 이전하기 위해서
(C) 회사와 가까운 곳에 위치하기 위해서
(D) 전문 스포츠 선수를 지도하는 코치로 일하기 위해

토익 분석

이사/이전하는 이유를 묻는 문제의 경우 지문 초반부에서 이사/이전에 대해 공지하면서 해당 이유를 직접적으로 제시한다. 그리고 대부분 이사/이전은 그 지문을 구성하는 주제/목적이 된다.

192

What aspect of the property does NOT match Dr. Reed's preferences?

(A) The monthly cost
(B) The size
(C) The location
(D) The smoking rules

문제 해설

해당 건물과 관련해 Reed 박사가 보내는 이메일인 세 번째 지문의 초반부에 쓰여 있는 definitely fits in my budget을 통해 (A)의 내용을 확인할 수 있고, 첫 지문 두 번째 단락의 one or two-bedroom apartment와 두 번째 지문 첫 문장의 this great one-bedroom apartment를 통해 (B)도 확인할 수 있다. 또한 첫 지문 맨 마지막의 I am a non-smoker와 두 번째 지문 끝부분의 Non-smokers only를 통해 (D)도 일치하는 사항임을 알 수 있다. 그런데 위치와 관련해, 첫 지문 두 번째 단락에서는 I am looking to live near the college라며 학교와 가까운 곳을 언급하고 있고 두 번째 지문의 중반부에서는 The apartment is just outside of downtown London라며 시내 바로 외곽에 위치해 있고 주요 대중 교통 거점들과 가깝다는 특징을 다루고 있으므로 (C)가 일치하지 않는 조건임을 알 수 있다.

★★★ 두 지문 연계 문제

건물의 어떤 면이 **Reed** 박사의 선호 사항과 일치하지 않는가?
(A) 월간 비용
(B) 크기
(C) 위치
(D) 흡연 규정

토익 분석

해당 문제의 단서가 나와야 할 지문에서 단서가 불충분하게 언급된다면 이는 두 지문 연계 문제이다.

193

★ 세부사항

12월 15일에 발생할 일은 무엇인가?
(A) Turner 씨의 아파트가 판매될 것이다.
(B) McMahon 박사는 런던으로 갈 것이다.
(C) Turner 씨의 아파트가 입주 가능하게 될 것이다.
(D) McMahon 박사는 보증금을 지불할 것이다.

토익 분석

시간/시점/날짜/요일은 단서와 함께 제시되는 키워드이므로 지문에서 해당 시간/시점/날짜/요일이 언급되는 부분만 빠르게 찾아 집중하라.

What will happen on December 15?

(A) Ms. Turner's apartment will be sold.
(B) Dr. McMahon will travel to London.
(C) Ms. Turner's apartment will become available.
(D) Dr. McMahon will pay a deposit.

문제 해설

12월 15일에 발생할 일에 대해 묻는 문제로 12월 15일이란 시점이 키워드이므로 지문에서 해당 날짜가 등장하는 부분을 빠르게 파악하는 것이 관건이다. 두 번째 아파트 임대 광고 초반부에서 This clean and simple, yet modern apartment will be move-in ready on December 15이라며 12월 15일에 아파트가 입주 가능한 상태임을 밝히고 있다. 그러므로 정답은 (C)가 되겠다.

194

★★ 세부사항

McMahon 박사가 요청하는 추가 정보는 무엇인가?
(A) 아파트에 입주 가능 시점
(B) 월세 할인 혜택
(C) 수리 관련직원 연락처
(D) 아파트 사진들

토익 분석

해당 문제의 키워드는 McMahon이지만 McMahon 박사가 이메일 전체 내용을 작성했을 뿐, 해당 문제의 단서가 지문의 McMahon이라는 키워드를 중심으로 제시되는 것은 아니다. 즉, 키워드가 지문 전반에 걸쳐 언급되고 있거나 키워드가 너무 범위가 넓어 키워드로서의 가치가 반감될 때는 선택지에 나온 내용을 먼저 파악한 후 선택지의 내용이 지문에서 등장하는지 여부를 역으로 신속하게 파악하는 방식으로 문제를 풀이하라.

What does Dr. McMahon request?

(A) Dates of apartment availability
(B) A discount on the monthly rent
(C) Renovation staff contact information
(D) Photos of the apartment

문제 해설

McMahon 박사가 요청하는 세부적인 정보이므로 McMahon 박사가 작성한 이메일을 통해 단서를 파악하는 것이 바람직하다. 이메일 중반부에서 McMahon 박사는 as I won't be in London until December 18. Could you send some pictures of the property?라며 자신이 런던에 12월 18일에 도착하는 관계로 직접 아파트를 볼 수 없으므로 대신 사진을 보내줄 수 있는지 묻고 있다. 따라서 McMahon 박사가 요청한 추가 정보는 바로 아파트 관련 사진들임을 알 수 있으므로 정답은 (D)가 되겠다.

195

★★★ 유추 / 두 지문 연계 문제

Turner 씨의 부동산 임대료와 관련하여 유추할 수 있는 것은 무엇인가?
(A) 매달 초에 임대료가 지급되어야 한다.
(B) 임대료가 1600달러 미만이다.
(C) 가스비와 전기비가 포함된 비용이다.
(D) 다른 나라 화폐를 통해 지급하는 것도 가능하다.

토익 분석

유추 문제는 선택지에 나온 내용을 먼저 파악한 후 선택지의 내용을 유추할 수 있는 근거가 지문에 제시되는지 여부를 역으로 확인하는 방식으로 문제를 풀이하는 것이 상대적으로 유추 문제를 빨리 풀이할 수 있도록 도움을 주며 아울러 지문에서 직접적으로 명시되어 내용 확인이 가능한 선택지는 결코 유추 문제의 정답이 될 수 없음을 유의한다.

What can be inferred the rent at Ms. Turner's property?

(A) It must be paid at the beginning of each month.
(B) It is less than 1,600 American dollars.
(C) It includes gas and electricity.
(D) It can be paid using a different currency.

문제 해설

Turner 씨의 부동산 임대료에 관해 묻고 있으므로 우선 Turner 씨가 작성한 아파트 임대 광고문부터 살펴본다. 아파트 임대 광고 후반에 £1,000 per month pays for water, sewer, garbage pickups, and general upkeep of the property라며 1,000파운드로의 비용이면 상수도와 하수 처리, 쓰레기 수거, 그리고 일반적인 건물 관리비를 지불하실 수 있음을 언급하고 있다. 이어서 McMahon 박사가 작성한 이메일 초반 It sounds very appealing to me and definitely fits in my budget라며 자신이 계획하고 있는 예산에도 적합하다고 이야기하고 있다. 앞서 McMahon 박사가 작성한 첫 번째 이메일 후반부에서 My budget is 1,600 American dollars per month, including water, gas, and electricity라며 자신의 예산은 모든 공과금과 임대료를 합쳐 월 1,600달러임을 구체적으로 명시하고 있다. 따라서 이를 통해 McMahon 박사가 런던에서 거주하는 아파트의 월 임대료는 1,600달러 미만임을 유추할 수 있으므로 정답은 (B)가 되겠다.

BELLA AIR
Late Arrival Baggage Form

Dear Bella Air Customers,

We are sorry to inform you about the late arrival of your luggage. Please write down the details below to help us track your belongings and return them to you as soon as possible. [196] A Bella Air clerk will inform you by phone as soon as we find your luggage. Any luggage that can't be found for more than a day should be reported on our company's Web site so instructions can be given.

Date: November 16
[196] Name: Raymond Walker
Local Address: Hotel Quet, Downtown, 984-2 Auckland, New Zealand
Tel: +62 185 0253
Flight No.: K53GC6

Delayed Luggage Information

	Quantity	Descriptions
*Suitcase	1	Small red suitcase with 2 wheels; "Raymond Walker" on the name tag
Backpack		
Handbag		
[197] *Box	1	Small plastic box with "Raymond Walker, Samion Foods" written on it
Other		

From	Harry Homez <hhomez@samionfoods.com>
To	Raymond Walker <rwalker@samionfoods.com>
Subject	Re: Food Samples
Date	November 16, 5:23 P.M.

Dear Mr. Walker

[197] Since we cannot be sure when your luggage will be found and returned, I've sent sauce samples by night shipping. That way, you'll have goods to show the clients at tomorrow's meeting. It's really important that we get feedback about them. [198, 199, 200] There are five flavors packed discretely as well as two small sauce bottles with labels. I sent the items with TWS Shipping to your lodging.

196-200 다음 양식과 이메일, 그리고 웹 페이지를 참조하시오.

BELLA AIR
연착 수하물 양식

Bella Air 고객 여러분,

수하물에 대한 연착 소식을 알려 드리게 되어 사과 드립니다. 물품들을 파악해 가능한 한 빨리 돌려 드리는 데 도움이 될 수 있도록 아래에 상세 정보를 기재해 주시기 바랍니다. [196] 저희 **Bella Air** 직원이 수하물을 찾는 대로 전화로 연락 드릴 것입니다. 하루 이내 찾을 수 없는 모든 수하물은 안내 사항이 제공될 수 있도록 저희 회사의 홈페이지를 통해 게시될 것입니다.

날짜: 11월 16일
[196] 성명: **Raymond Walker**
지역 주소: Hotel Quet, Downtown, 984-2 Auckland, New Zealand
전화번호: +62 185 0253
항공편 번호: K53GC6

연착 수하물 정보

	수량	설명
*여행 가방	1	바퀴가 2개 달린 붉은색 소형 여행 가방, 이름표에 "Raymond Walker"라고 기재됨
배낭		
핸드백		
[197] *상자	1	"Raymond Walker, Samion Foods"라고 쓰여 있는 소형 플라스틱 상자
기타		

어휘 late arrival 연착 baggage 수하물(= luggage) inform ~에게 알리다 write down ~을 적다, 쓰다 details 상세 정보 below 아래에 help A do A가 ~하는 것을 돕다 track ~을 파악하다, 추적하다 as soon as possible 가능한 한 빨리 find out ~을 찾아 내다 list ~을 기재하다 via ~을 통해 so (that) ~할 수 있도록 instructions 안내, 설명, 지시 quantity 수량 description 설명, 묘사 suitcase 여행 가방

발신 Harry Homez 〈hhomez@samionfood.com〉
수신 Raymond Walker 〈rwalker@samionfood.com〉
제목 회신: 식품 샘플
날짜 11월 16일, 오후 5:23

[197] 수하물이 언제 발견되어 되돌려 받으실지 확실치 않으므로 야간 배송으로 소스 샘플들을 보내 드렸습니다. 이를 통해, 이 물품을 가지고 내일 회의에 참석해서 고객님들에게 제품을 보여주시면 됩니다. 견본품에 대한 고객님들의 의견을 수렴하는 것이 정말 중요합니다. [198, 199, 200] 라벨이 붙은 두 개의 소형 소스 병들뿐만 아니라 따로 포장된 다섯 가지 맛이 있습니다. **TWS Shipping**을 통해 당신의 숙소로 이 물품들을 보냈습니다. 배송 물품이 오전 9시 30분까지 도착할 것이므로 소스와 제품 패키지들을 회의에 가져 가셔서 11시에 발표하실 때 보여 드릴 수 있으실 겁니다.

안녕히 계십시오.

Harry Homez
Samion Food

어휘 night shipping 야간 배송 get feedback about ~에 관한 의견을 수렴하다 flavor 맛, 풍미 packed 포장된 discretely 따로, 분리되어 as well as ~뿐만 아니라 label 라벨, 표 lodging 숙소, 숙박 시설

The package will arrive by 9:30 A.M., so you can bring sauces and packages to the meeting and show them when you speak at the meeting at eleven.

Sincerely,

Harry Homez
Samion Foods

---

https://www.twsshipping.co.au/overnight

TWS SHIPPING
신속하고 신뢰할 수 있는 배송 회사

– 배송 정보
배송 출발지:
Samion Foods, 27 Earot Street, Archeis 1, 1UE, AU

배송 도착지:
HOTEL QUET, Downtown, 984-2 Auckland, New Zealand

중량: 0.68kg

( ) 동봉물 (X) 상자 ( ) 지정 패키지

– 야간 배송 선택권
TWS 이른 오전; [200] 내일 오전 9시 30분까지 배송 [$62 지금 배송]
TWS 오전; 내일 오전 11시 30분까지 배송 [$49 지금 배송]
TWS 오후; 내일 오후 3시까지 배송 [$31 지금 배송]
TWS 저녁; 내일 오후 8시 30분까지 배송 [$35 지금 배송]

어휘 expedited 신속히 처리되는 trustful 신뢰할 수 있는 shipment 배송(품), 선적(품) enclosed 동봉된 custom packaging 고객 지정 패키지 overnight 야간의

https://www.twsshipping.co.au/overnight

TWS SHIPPING
The Expedited and Reliable Shipping Company

- Your Shipment Information
Ship from:
Samion Foods, 27 Earot Street, Archeis 1, 1UE, AU

Ship to:
HOTEL QUET, Downtown, 984-2 Auckland, New Zealand

Weight: 0.68 kg

( ) Enclosed   (X) Box   ( ) Custom packaging

- Your Overnight Shipment Options
TWS Early morning; [200] Deliver by 9:30 A.M. tomorrow [$62 Ship Now]
TWS morning; Deliver by 11:30 A.M. tomorrow [$49 Ship Now]
TWS afternoon; Deliver by 3:00 P.M. tomorrow [$31 Ship Now]
TWS evening; Deliver by 8:30 P.M. tomorrow [$35 Ship Now]

196

What is indicated about Bella Air?

(A) It requires customers to include name tags on all pieces of luggage.
(B) It guarantees that missing luggage will be returned in three days.
(C) It will notify Ms. Walker when her luggage is found.
(D) It will reimburse Mr. Walker for her lost luggage.

문제 해설

연착 수화물 양식인 첫 지문의 첫 단락에서 A Bella Air clerk will inform you by phone as soon as we find out your luggage라며 Bella Air 직원이 수하물을 찾는 대로 전화로 연락해 줄 것임을 밝히고 있으며 바로 아래에 해당 양식 작성자 이름이 Raymond Walker 씨로 되어 있으므로 (C)가 정답임을 알 수 있다.

★★ 세부사항

Bella Air에 관해 알 수 있는 것은 무엇인가?
(A) 모든 수하물에 대해 이름표를 포함하도록 고객들에게 요청한다.
(B) 분실된 수하물이 3일 안에 되돌려 보내진다는 점을 보장한다.
(C) Walker 씨의 수하물을 찾을 경우 통보해 줄 것이다.
(D) Walker 씨에게 분실 수하물에 대한 비용을 환급해 줄 것이다.

토익 분석

첫 번째 수화물 양식지는 벨라 항공사의 서류 양식이다. 문제의 키워드가 지문 전반에 걸쳐 언급되고 있거나 키워드가 너무 범위가 넓어 키워드로서의 가치가 반감될 때는 선택지에 나온 내용을 먼저 파악한 후 선택지의 내용이 지문에서 등장하는지 여부를 역으로 신속하게 파악하는 방식으로 문제를 풀이하라.

197

Where did Mr. Walker most likely pack his samples?

(A) In a box
(B) In a refrigerator
(C) In a briefcase
(D) In a backpack

문제 해설

Walker 씨에게 보내는 이메일인 두 번째 지문의 첫 문장에서 I've sent sauce samples by night shipping이라며 언제 수하물을 돌려 받을지 알 수 없어 견본품들을 보냈다는 점을 전달하고 있다. 또한 Walker 씨가 작성한 수화물 양식서에서 "Raymond Walker, Samion Foods"라는 회사명이 쓰여 있는 소형 상자에 해당 견본품들이 들어 있던 것으로 판단할 수 있으므로 (A)가 정답이다.

★★★ 유추 / 두 지문 연계문제

Walker 씨는 견본품을 어디에 넣었을 가능성이 가장 큰가?
(A) 상자
(B) 냉장고
(C) 서류 가방
(D) 배낭

토익 분석

삼중 지문 중 하나가 양식서라면 해당 양식서와 관련된 두 지문 연계 문제는 필히 출제되며 이 경우 문제를 풀이할 수 있는 가장 결정적인 단서는 양식서를 통해 제시된다.

198

What is implied about Mr. Homez?

(A) He is meeting with clients in New Zealand.
(B) He travels frequently for Samion Foods.
(C) He is a Bella Air customer service agent.
(D) He wants clients to review some products.

문제 해설

Homez 씨가 쓴 이메일인 두 번째 지문에서 There are five flavors packed discretely as well as two small sauce bottles with labels. ~ bring sauces and packages to the meeting and show them when you speak at the meeting at eleven이라며 라벨이 붙은 두 개의 소형 소스 병과 따로 포장된 다섯 가지 맛을 보냈고 이 소스와 제품 패키지들을 회의에 가져 가서 발표할 때 보여 주라고 요청하고 있다. 따라서 이를 통해 발표를 들을 사람들이 제품 샘플을 확인해 보길 원한다는 의미임을 유추할 수 있으므로 정답은 (D)가 되겠다.

★★★ 유추 / 세부사항

Homez 씨에 관해 유추할 수 있는 것은 무엇인가?
(A) New Zealand에서 고객들과 만난다.
(B) Samion Foods를 위해 자주 출장을 간다.
(C) Bella Air의 고객 서비스 직원이다.
(D) 고객이 일부 제품을 검토해 보기를 원하고 있다.

토익 분석

두 번째 이메일 전체가 Homez 씨가 작성한 이메일이며 Homez와 관련된 업무 내용이 주를 이루고 있을 뿐만 아니라 지문에서 Homez라는 인명이 등장하는 부분에서 단서가 제시되는 형태도 아니다. 즉, 유추 문제의 키워드가 지문 전반에 걸쳐 언급되고 있는 상태에서 적절한 유추 내용을 파악해야 한다면 선택지에 나온 내용을 먼저 파악한 후 선택지의 내용을 유추할 수 있는 근거가 지문에 제시되는지 여부를 역으로 확인하는 방식으로 문제를 풀이하라. 아울러 이 때 지문에서 사실 여부가 확실하게 드러나는 내용은 유추와 무관한 내용이므로 오답으로 소거해야 한다.

★ 세부사항

이메일에 따르면, **Walker** 씨는 내일 오전 11시에 무엇을
할 것인가?
(A) 배송 물품을 받는다.
(B) 발표를 한다.
(C) 호텔에서 체크아웃한다.
(D) 돌아가는 항공편을 확인한다.

토익 분석

시간/시점/날짜/요일은 단서와 함께 제시되는 키워드이
므로 지문에서 해당 시간/시점/날짜/요일이 언급되는 부
분만 빠르게 찾아 집중하라.

According to the e-mail, what will Mr. Walker do tomorrow at 11 A.M.?

(A) Accept a delivery
(B) Give a presentation
(C) Check out of the hotel
(D) Confirm his return flight

문제 해설

내일 오전 11시라는 구체적인 시점이 키워드이므로 이메일에서 내일 오전 11시라는 시점이 제시되
는 부분을 중심으로 단서를 파악한다. Homez 씨 이메일 말미에서 when you speak at the meeting
at eleven이라며 11시에 메일 수신인인 Walker 씨가 회의에서 발표를 하게 될 예정임을 밝히고 있
다. 따라서 정답은 (B)가 되겠다.

★★★ 유추 / 두 지문 연계 문제

Homez 씨가 배송에 대해 청구받게 될 액수는 얼마일 것
같은가?
(A) 35달러
(B) 31달러
(C) 49달러
(D) 62달러

토익 분석

삼중 지문 중 하나가 양식서라면 해당 양식서와 관련된
두 지문 연계 문제는 필히 출제되며 이 경우 문제를 풀이
할 수 있는 가장 결정적인 단서는 양식서를 통해 제시된
다.

How much was Mr. Homez most likely charged for shipping?

(A) $35.00
(B) $31.00
(C) $49.00
(D) $62.00

문제 해설

두 번째 지문에 Homez 씨는 The package will arrive by 9:30 A.M.라며 자신이 보낸 배송 물품이
오전 9시 30분까지 도착할 것임을 알리고 있다. 아울러 세 번째 지문의 마지막 부분에는 오전 9시
까지 도착하는 서비스의 비용이 $62로 표기되어 있으므로 정답은 (D)가 되겠다.

해설서

101

★ 어형 / 형용사

최근 경제보고서에서는 많은 중소기업들이 사업 초기에 재정적으로 무리하지 않도록 신중하다는 점을 언급했다.

문제 분석

be financially cautious 재정적으로 신중을 기하다

어휘 financially 재정적으로 cautious 주의하는 early stage 초기단계

The recent economic report shows that many small companies are financially ------- in the early stages of their business.

(A) cause
(B) cautious
(C) caution
(D) cautiously

문제 해설

빈칸에 적절한 어형을 묻는 문제이다. 빈칸이 주격보어를 취하는 2형식동사인 be 동사와 부사인 financially 뒤에 위치하고 있으므로 빈칸에는 부사 financially의 수식을 받으며 주격보어의 역할을 행할 수 있는 형용사 어형이 와야 한다. 따라서 빈칸에는 '신중한, 조심스러운'이란 뜻을 지닌 형용사 cautious가 적합하다.

토익 분석

토익에서는 주격보어의 어형을 묻는 문제가 출제되는 경우 대부분 형용사 어형을 중심으로 정답이 제시되고 있다. 아울러 주격 보어 어형을 묻는 동사의 90%는 be 동사가 출제되며 나머지 10% 정도의 비중으로 become/remain 정도가 등장하고 있음을 알아두도록 한다.

102

★★ 어형 / 최상급 형용사

West Sea 대교는 최근 젊은 건축 전문가들에 의해 Asia 지역에서 가장 훌륭한 건축물로 선정되었다.

어휘 recently 최근에 construction structure 건축물 professional 전문가, 전문적인 architecture 건축

West Sea Bridge was recently chosen as the ------- construction structure in Asia by young professionals in architecture.

(A) fine
(B) finer
(C) finest
(D) fineness

문제 해설

빈칸이 정관사인 the와 '건축 구조물'을 뜻하는 복합명사인 construction structure 사이에 위치하고 있으므로 빈칸에는 복합 명사 construction structure를 수식할 수 있는 형용사가 자리해야 한다. 다만 빈칸 뒤에 등장하는 in Asia를 통해 아시아 전역이 대상이며 이는 곧 건축물 선정을 위한 비교 대상이 최소한 셋 이상이 된다는 점을 간과하지 않도록 주의해야 한다. 따라서 West Sea 대교는 아시아 전체 지역에서 가장 훌륭한 건축물로 선정되었다는 문맥이 형성될 수 있도록 빈칸에는 최상급 형용사인 finest가 와야 한다.

토익 분석

셋 이상의 대상을 중심으로 상태의 절대 비교를 표현하기 위해 쓰이는 것이 최상급 형용사이다. 따라서 최상급 형용사를 묻는 경우 비교 대상이 셋 이상임을 나타내는 명사와 함께 쓰이는 전치사구가 등장한다. 대표적으로 in / among / of + 비교 대상이 셋 이상임을 뜻하는 명사라 할 수 있다.

103

Most frozen foods are neither healthy ------- nutritious, so people should avoid eating them regularly.

(A) but
(B) nor
(C) yet
(D) and

문제 해설

빈칸에 적합한 등위 접속사를 묻는 문제이며, 빈칸 앞에 부사 neither이 위치하고 있다. 따라서 빈칸에는 부사 neither과 결합하여 양자부정의 뜻을 지닌 등위 상관 접속사를 구성하는 등위접속사 nor이 와야 한다.

토익 분석

토익에서 출제되는 대표적인 등위 상관 접속사로는 both A and B (A와 B 모두), either A or B (A와 B 둘 중 하나), neither A nor B (A와 B 모두 아닌), not only A but also B (A 뿐만 아니라 B도)가 있다.

★ 접속사 / 등위 상관접속사

대부분의 냉동 음식들은 명백하게 건강에 좋지 않을 뿐만 아니라 영양분도 부족하므로 사람들이 이를 주기적으로 섭취하는 것을 피하는 편이 좋다.

어휘 frozen food 냉동 음식 definitely 명백하게, 분명하게 neither A nor B A와 B 모두 아닌 healthy 건강한, 건강에 좋은 nutritious 영양분이 풍부한, 건강에 좋은 avoid ~을 피하다 regularly 주기적으로, 규칙적으로

104

------- high profits, most pharmaceutical companies are unable to conduct research to improve public health care.

(A) From
(B) Without
(C) Inside
(D) Along with

문제 해설

빈칸에 적합한 전치사를 묻는 문제이다. 빈칸 뒤에는 많은 이익을 뜻하는 high profits가 등장하고 있으며, 빈칸 뒤에는 대부분의 제약회사들은 대중 의료 관리 증진을 위한 다양한 연구를 못한다는 부정적 내용이 제시되고 있다. 그런데 많은 이익이 있음에도 제약회사들이 다양한 연구를 행하지 않는다는 것은 논리적으로 어폐가 있다. 따라서 제약회사들이 다양한 연구를 행하지 않는다는 경우는 연구에 비해 많은 이익이 수반되지 않은 상황이라 할 수 있으므로 빈칸에는 '~가 없는'이란 뜻의 전치사 without이 적합하다.

토익 분석

전치사 along with은 '~와 함께, ~와 더불어'란 뜻을 지니고 있으며 사실 출제되면 제일 자주 틀리는 전치사 중 하나이기도 하다. 따라서 비록 오답으로 제시되었더라고 해도 꼭 알아둬야 할 필요가 있는 전치사이기도 하다.

★ 어휘 / 전치사

많은 이익이 없다면, 대부분의 제약회사들은 대중 의료 관리 증진을 위한 다양한 연구를 행하지 못한다.

문제 분석
conduct research 연구를 행하다

어휘 pharmaceutical company 제약 회사 conduct ~을 행하다 various 다양한 type 종류 improve ~을 개선하다, ~을 향상시키다 public health care 대중 의료 관리

105

★★ 어형 / 과거분사

Cupertino 시 최고의 레스토랑인 Bella Bistro는 시의 금융 지구 근처에 교통이 편리한 곳에 위치하고 있다.

문제 분석

be conveniently located 교통 접근성이 좋은 곳에 위치한

어휘 conveniently 편리하게 financial area 금융 지구 location 위치 located 위치한, 자리잡은

Bella's Bistro, the best restaurant in Cupertino, is conveniently ------- near the financial area of the city.

(A) locate
(B) locating
(C) located
(D) location

문제 해설

빈칸에 적합한 어형을 묻는 문제로 빈칸 앞에 be 동사 is와 '편리하게'란 뜻을 지닌 부사 conveniently가, 빈칸 뒤에는 전치사구인 near the financial area of the city가 등장하고 있으므로 빈칸에는 부사인 conveniently의 수식을 받는 주격 보어의 역할을 하는 형용사 어형이 위치해야 함을 알 수 있다. 따라서 현재분사인 locating과 과거분사인 located 중 정답을 택일해야 하며 빈칸 뒤에 명사 목적어가 존재하지 않고 있다는 점을 고려할 때 빈칸에는 수동태 구조를 구성할 수 있는 과거분사인 located가 와야 한다. 아울러 be conveniently located은 '교통 접근성이 편리한 곳에 위치한'이란 뜻으로 토익 빈출 표현이니만큼 통으로 숙지하는 편이 바람직하다.

토익 분석

토익에선 본래 located를 수식하는 부사로선 conveniently가 부동의 전통적인 어휘로 출제되었지만 신토익 이후에는 전략적인 곳에 위치하고 있다는 뜻을 지닌 be strategically located 뿐만 아니라 부러워할 만큼 목이 좋은 곳에 위치하고 있다는 의미의 be enviously located도 출제되고 있음을 알아두도록 한다.

106

★★ 어형 / 사람명사 및 일반명사 구분

지역 취업 박람회 참가자들의 대부분은 정보 기술 분야에서의 취업을 고려하고 있다.

문제 분석

Almost all of the + 가산 복수명사/불가산명사 거의 ~의 대부분

어휘 almost all 대부분 job fair 취업 박람회 information technology 정보 기술 분야 participant 참석자 participation 참석 participate 참석하다

Almost all of the ------- in the local job fair are considering finding jobs in information technology.

(A) participants
(B) participating
(C) participation
(D) participate

문제 해설

빈칸에 적절한 어형을 묻는 문제이다. 빈칸이 정관사 the 뒤에 위치하고 있으므로 빈칸에는 명사 어형이 필요하다. 선택지에는 '참가자'를 뜻하는 사람명사인 participants와 '참석'을 뜻하는 일반명사인 participation이 동시에 제시되고 있다. 그러나 취업을 고려하는 것은 사람이어야 하므로 빈칸에는 사람명사인 participants가 와야 한다.

토익 분석

토익에서의 명사 어형 문제인 경우 사람을 뜻하는 명사와 사람이 아닌 일반적인 명사가 동시에 제시되며 둘 중 한 가지를 택일하는 방식의 문제가 출제된다. 따라서 이 두 가지 명사를 모두 숙지하는 방식으로 공부하는 편이 바람직하다.

107

If your application meets the criteria of our company, you will receive written
------- that you have been hired.

(A) notify
(B) notifying
(C) notification
(D) notifies

문제 해설

빈칸에 적합한 어형을 묻는 문제이다. 빈칸이 과거분사인 written 뒤에 위치하고 있으므로 빈칸에는 written의 수식을 받는 명사 어형이 와야 한다. 따라서 빈칸에는 '통보, 공지'를 뜻하는 명사 어형인 notification이 적절하다.

토익 분석

토익에서 같은 의미라도 notice는 가산명사로, notification은 불가산명사로 등장하기 때문에 이는 꼭 알아두도록 한다.

★ 어형 / 명사

신청서가 우리 회사의 채용 기준을 충족시킨다면, 채용이 결정되었다는 서면 통보를 받게 될 것이다.

어휘 application 신청, 신청서 criteria 기준, 조건, 평가 notification 통보, 공지

108

Municipal boards of education in each city in California need time ------- for the
new school system.

(A) to prepare
(B) preparing
(C) prepared
(D) prepare

문제 해설

빈칸에 적합한 어형을 묻는 문제이다. 빈칸이 명사 time 뒤에 위치하고 있으며 명사 time은 형용사 역할을 하는 To 부정사구의 수식을 받는다. 따라서 빈칸에는 to prepare이 와야 한다. 아울러 ability(능력), authority(권위, 당국), right(권리), plan(계획), time(시간), effort(노력), chance(기회), opportunity(기회) 등의 명사는 형용사 역할을 하는 To 부정사구의 수식을 받는 대표적인 명사 어휘들임을 숙지하도록 한다.

토익 분석

토익에서는 해당 문제처럼 명사를 수식하는 To 부정사구 형태를 묻기도 하지만 역으로 To 부정사구의 수식을 받는 명사 어휘가 무엇인지 묻는 문제가 출제되기도 하므로 이들을 알아둘 경우 어떠한 유형으로 문제가 출제되더라도 모두 신속하고 정확하게 문제를 풀이할 수 있다.

★★★ 어형 / To 부정사

California 주에 있는 각 도시의 교육 위원회들은 새로운 학제를 준비할 시간적 여유가 필요하다.

문제 분석
time to Vr ~하기 위한 시간

어휘 municipal 시의, 지방자치의 prepare for ~을 준비하다 school system 학제

109

★ 어휘 / 형용사

연구원들이 실험실에서 가연성 화학물질들을 다룰 때는 이를 신중히 취급해야 하며 또한 안전규정을 필히 따라야 한다.

문제 분석

follow the safety instructions 안전 규정을 따르다

어휘 researcher 연구원 handle ~을 다루다, ~을 취급하다 flammable 가연성의, 인화성의 chemicals 화학 물질, 화학 성분 research laboratory 연구 실험실 follow ~을 뒤따르다, ~을 이해하다 safety instructions 안전 수칙, 안정 규정 careful 신중한, 꼼꼼한 operational 가동하는, 작동하는 reliable 믿을만한, 신뢰할만한

When researchers handle the flammable chemicals in the research laboratory, they must be ------- and follow the safety instructions.

(A) tentative

(B) careful

(C) operational

(D) reliable

문제 해설

빈칸에 적절한 형용사 어휘를 묻는 문제이다. 빈칸 앞에는 실험실 연구원들이 가연성 화학물질을 취급한다는 내용이, 빈칸 뒤에는 안전 규정을 필히 따라야 한다는 내용이 등장하고 있으므로, 빈칸에는 실험실의 연구원들의 상태가 어떠한지 설명할 수 있는 형용사 어휘가 위치해야 한다. 따라서 실험실 연구원들이 가연성 화학물질을 취급한다는 내용과 안전 규정을 필히 따라야 한다는 내용을 고려할 때 빈칸에는 연구원들이 가연성 화학물질을 다룰 때 신중을 기해야 한다는 문맥을 구성할 수 있도록 '조심스러운, 신중한'이란 뜻을 지닌 형용사 careful이 적합하다.

토익 분석

토익에서 careful/carefully는 자주 등장하는 어휘이며 무엇보다 'be careful with ~에 주의하는 / pay careful attention ~에 꼼꼼하게 신경을 쓰다 / give careful consideration to ~을 충분히 고려하다 / on careful consideration of ~에 대한 신중한 숙고'란 뜻을 지닌 표현들을 숙지해두는 것이 좋다. 또한 토익에서는 carefully와 유사한 어휘로 meticulously란 상대적으로 낯선 어휘가 출제된 바 있음을 알아두도록 한다.

110

★★ 어형 / 과거분사

국내 건설 활동은 작년에 약 15% 감소하였는데, 이는 주택 건설 부문에서 장기화된 불황에 의해 초래된 것이다.

문제 분석

fall about ~ ~ 정도 하락하다

어휘 domestic 국내의 fall ~이 하락하다, ~이 떨어지다, ~이 감소하다 prolonged 길어진 slump 불황 housing construction sector 주택 건설 부문

Domestic construction activities fell about 15% last year, ------- by a prolonged slump in the housing construction sector.

(A) led

(B) lead

(C) leading

(D) be led

문제 해설

빈칸에 적절한 어형을 묻는 문제이다. 빈칸 뒤는 절이 아닌 구의 형태를 지니고 있으므로 절을 구성할 수 있는 동사 어형인 lead와 be led는 오답으로 소거해야 한다. 그러므로 과거분사인 led와 현재분사인 leading 중 정답을 택일해야 한다. 무엇보다 빈칸 뒤에 명사인 목적어가 존재하지 않는다는 점과 국내 건설 활동의 15% 감소가 '장기화된 불황에 의해' 초래된 것이란 수동적 의미를 구성하는 전치사구 by a prolonged slump가 제시되고 있음을 고려할 때 빈칸에는 과거분사인 led가 위치해야 한다.

토익 분석

토익에선 동사 lead는 과거분사인 led 뿐만 아니라 현재분사인 leading도 자주 묻는다. 토익에서는 현재분사 leading이 '업계를 선도하는'이란 뜻을 지닌 어휘로 출제되며 대표적으로 leading company (일류 회사), leading role(주도하는 역할), leading researcher(수석 연구원) 등이 있으므로 알아두도록 한다.

111

There are retail shops, beauty shops, restaurants, and art galleries ------- walking distance for most residents in the city.

(A) inside
(B) within
(C) until
(D) from

문제 해설

빈칸에 적합한 전치사를 묻는 문제이다. 빈칸 앞에는 소매점, 미용실, 식당, 그리고 미술관들이 있다는 내용이, 빈칸 이후에는 걸어갈 수 있는 거리가 언급되고 있으므로 빈칸에는 걸어갈 수 있는 거리 이내이거나 혹은 걸어갈 수 있는 거리를 넘어선다는 내용을 구성할 수 있는 전치사가 필요하다. 따라서 빈칸에는 '~이내에'란 뜻을 지닌 전치사 within이 와서 걸어갈 수 있는 거리 이내라는 의미를 구성할 수 있어야 한다.

토익 분석

토익에서 출제되는 전치사 문제 중에서 다른 전치사에 비해 상대적으로 출제 비중이 높은 대표적인 전치사가 바로 within으로 within은 기간/거리/공간과 모두 함께 쓰이는 것이 가능하다. 따라서 토익에서는 within seven days of purchase(구매한 지 7일 이내)처럼 기간과 함께 쓰이는 용례와 within 10 miles(10마일 이내)와 같이 거리와 쓰이는 용례도, 마지막으로 within the company(시내에서)처럼 공간과 함께 쓰이는 용례가 모두 함께 출제되고 있음을 알아두도록 한다.

★★ 어휘 / 전치사

소매점, 미용실, 식당, 그리고 미술관들은 모두 이 도시에서 주민들이 걸어갈 수 있는 거리 이내에 있다.

문제 분석

within walking distance 걸어갈 수 있는 거리 이내에

어휘 retail shop 소매점 beauty shop 미용실 art gallery 미술관 walking distance 걸어갈 수 있는 거리 resident 거주민

112

------- our company is growing in terms of revenue, we are not yet strong enough to compete with other foreign companies.

(A) When
(B) Even though
(C) In case
(D) Nonetheless

문제 해설

빈칸이 부사절 앞에 위치하고 있으므로 부사절과 주절의 내용을 논리적으로 적절하게 연결시켜줄 수 있는 부사절 접속사가 와야 한다. 부사절은 회사가 수익 면에서 성장하고 있다는 내용이나 주절은 다른 외국 회사들과 경쟁을 할 수 있을 정도로 경쟁력이 있지 않은 상태임을 지적하며 부사절과 주절의 내용이 서로 상충되는 문맥임을 제시하고 있다. 따라서 빈칸에는 역접 관계를 나타내는 부사절 접속사 Even though가 적합하다.

토익 분석

역접 관계를 나타내는 대표적인 부사절 접속사로 even though, although, though가 있으며 전치사로서는 in spite of, despite, notwithstanding이, 접속부사로서는 nevertheless, nonetheless, however, but 등이 있다. 따라서 이들을 혼동하지 않고 정확하게 구분하여 인식할 수 있도록 한다.

★★ 접속사 / 부사절 접속사

비록 우리 회사가 수익 면에서는 성장하고 있지만, 다른 외국 회사들과 경쟁을 해낼 수 있을 만큼 경쟁력이 있지는 않다.

문제 분석

형용사 + enough to Vr ~하기에 충분히 ~한

어휘 in terms of ~라는 점에서 revenue 수익 compete with ~과 함께 경쟁하다 foreign 외국의

113

★★ 재귀대명사

Lisa Jones 씨는 그녀 자신이 북미 지역에서 우수한 싱어
송라이터이자 성공한 가수임을 입증했다.

문제 분석

prove oneself + N 자신이 N임을 입증하다

어휘 prove ~을 입증하다 B as well as A A뿐만 아니라
B도 outstanding 뛰어난, 출중한

Lisa Jones has proved ------- a successful singer as well as an outstanding songwriter in North America.

(A) she
(B) her
(C) hers
(D) herself

문제 해설

빈칸에 적합한 대명사를 묻는 문제이다. 빈칸이 동사인 has proved 뒤에 위치하고 있으므로 빈칸에는 목적어 역할을 해줄 수 있는 대명사가 필요하며 구조적으로는 빈칸에 주격 인칭대명사 she를 제외한 목적격 인칭대명사 her, 소유대명사 hers, 그리고 재귀대명사 herself가 위치할 수 있다. 하지만 빈칸 앞에는 Lisa Jones 씨가 입증했다는 내용이, 빈칸 뒤에는 북미 지역에서 우수한 싱어송라이터이자 성공한 가수란 내용이 등장하고 있으므로 빈칸에는 Lisa Jones 씨가 북미 지역에서 우수한 싱어송라이터이자 성공한 가수라고 입증한 대상을 지칭할 수 있는 대명사가 와야 한다. 하지만 목적격 인칭대명사 her는 구체적으로 어떤 여성을 지칭하고 있는지 불분명하며 소유대명사인 hers는 '그녀의 것'이란 의미가 전반적인 문맥에 적합하지 않다. 따라서 빈칸에는 Lisa Jones 씨 자신을 지칭하는 재귀대명사 herself가 자리하여 Lisa Jones 씨는 그녀 자신이 북미 지역에서 우수한 싱어송라이터이자 성공한 가수임을 입증했다는 문맥을 구성하는 것이 논리적으로 타당하다.

토익 분석

토익에서 재귀대명사는 동사의 목적어로 쓰이는 대명사 목적어로의 용례를 묻는 문제와 S+V+O 구조의 완전한 절 뒤에서 쓰이는 수식어인 부사로서의 용례를 묻는 문제가 출제되고 있다. 물론 이 경우는 To + Vr + O / V-ing + O 뒤에서 부사로서 쓰이는 재귀대명사의 용례를 묻는 문제로 바뀌어 출제될 수도 있음에 주의해야 한다. 아울러 재귀대명사 관용표현으로 by oneself를 주로 묻지만 이는 by one's own으로 바뀌어 출제될 수도 있음을 알아두도록 한다.

114

★★ 어형 / 형용사

우리 회사의 새로운 공장에서 근무하길 원하는 외국인은
누가 되든 관련된 취업 허가증을 신청해야만 한다.

어휘 foreigner 외국인 apply for ~에 신청하다, ~에 지원
하다 work permit 취업 허가증, 근로 허가증 relevant 연
관된, 관련 있는

Any foreigner who wants to work at our new factory for over a month must apply for a ------- work permit.

(A) relevance
(B) relevancies
(C) relevant
(D) relevantly

문제 해설

빈칸에 적합한 어형을 묻는 문제로 빈칸이 '취업 허가증'을 뜻하는 복합명사 work permit 앞에 위치하고 있으므로 명사를 수식하는 형용사 어형이 필요하다. 따라서 빈칸에는 '연관된, 관련 있는'이란 뜻을 지닌 형용사 relevant가 와야 한다.

토익 분석

명사 permit은 허가증이란 뜻을 지니고 있으며 토익에서는 취업 허가증이란 의미의 work permit, 주차 허가증이란 의미의 parking permit, 그리고 건축 허가를 뜻하는 building permit이 출제된 바가 있음을 알아두도록 한다.

115

------- discourage wasteful use, the newly revised law will raise the cost of water and electricity next year.

(A) In order to
(B) Thanks to
(C) Due to
(D) With regard to

문제 해설

빈칸에 적합한 표현을 묻는 문제이다. 빈칸 뒤에 discourage wasteful use란 구가 등장하고 있지만 discourage란 동사가 동명사인 V-ing 형태가 아닌 동사원형인 형태를 유지하고 있으므로 빈칸에는 전치사가 위치할 수 없다. 따라서 빈칸에는 구를 형성하고 이끌지만 전치사가 아닌 표현이 와야 하므로 목적/의도의 뜻을 지니며 To 부정사구를 구성하는 in order to가 와야 한다. 아울러 '~덕분에'란 뜻의 Thanks to와 '~로 인해'란 뜻의 Due to 그리고 '~에 관해'란 뜻을 지닌 With regard to 는 모두 전치사이므로 모두 오답으로 소거해야 한다.

토익 분석

목적/의도의 뜻을 지닌 To 부정사구는 in order to Vr 외에도 so as to Vr도 알아둬야 하며 이들 이 확장하여 목적/의도의 뜻을 지닌 부사절 접속사를 이룰 경우 so that S + can/may + Vr이나 in order that S + can/may + Vr의 형태를 지니게 되며 이들 또한 토익에서 자주 묻는 표현늘이니 꼭 숙지하도록 한다.

★★ 어휘 / To 부정사구

과도한 소비를 막고자, 새로 개정된 법은 내년에 수도와 전기세를 인상시킬 것이다.

문제 분석

in order to Vr ~하기 위해서

어휘 discourage ~을 낙담시키다, ~을 단념시키다 wasteful use 과도한 사용 raise ~을 인상하다, ~을 들어올리다 electricity 전기 in order to Vr ~하기 위해서 thanks to ~덕분에 due to ~로 인해 with regard to ~에 관해, ~에 관련하여

116

According to the report, construction for the new stadium complex in Oakland is ------- 80 percent complete.

(A) currently
(B) frequently
(C) so far
(D) once

문제 해설

빈칸에 적합한 부사 어휘를 묻는 문제이다. 빈칸에 앞서 Oakland에 위치한 새로운 종합 경기장 건설이 언급되고 있으며, 빈칸 이후에는 준공의 80퍼센트에 도달한 상태임을 밝히고 있다. 아울러 be 동사가 현재 시제인 is이므로 전체 문맥은 새로운 종합 경기장 건설 공사가 현재 전체 공정의 80퍼센트에 도달한 상황임을 설명하고 있는 내용임을 알 수 있다. 따라서 빈칸에는 '현재의'란 뜻을 지닌 부사 currently가 적절하다.

토익 분석

빈칸이 현재시제인 be 동사 is/are과 형용사류인 형용사, 분사 또는 전치사구 사이에 위치하는 경우 현재의 상태임을 강조하기 위한 목적으로 빈칸에 currently, presently, now와 같은 부사 어휘를 선택하도록 요구하는 유형의 문제가 자주 출제되는 경향이 있음을 알아두도록 한다. 이러한 어휘 문제의 출제 경향도 정리해서 알아두면 어휘 문제도 5초면 풀 수 있는 내공을 지니게 된다. 완전한 시험 대비와 이에 따른 좋은 성적이라는 결과는 모든 시험을 앞두고 알아둬야 하는 모든 데이터를 얼마나 일목요연하게 잘 정리해서 숙지하는가에 있다. 세상에 날로 먹을 수 있는 건 회와 과일 뿐이다.

★★ 부사 어휘

보고서에 따르면, Oakland에 위치한 새로운 종합 경기장 건설은 현재 준공의 80퍼센트에 도달한 상태이다.

어휘 stadium complex 종합 경기장 complete ~을 종료하다, ~을 끝내다, 완전한, 철저한 currently 현재의 frequently 종종, 자주 once 한 번, 예전에, 일단 ~하면

★ 소유격 대명사

Mandoo Heavy Machines 사는 한국에서의 큰 성공을 거두며 국제 시장에 자사의 존재를 알릴 수 있었다.

문제 분석

be able to Vr ~하는 것이 가능하다
introduce oneself on/to 자신을 ~에게 소개하다

어휘 introduce ~을 소개하다, ~을 도입하다
international market 국제 시장 huge 거대한, 엄청난

Mandoo Heavy Machines was able to introduce itself on international markets with ------- huge success in South Korea.

(A) whose
(B) whom
(C) those
(D) its

문제 해설

빈칸에 적합한 접속사 혹은 대명사를 묻는 문제이다. 빈칸이 형용사인 huge와 명사인 success 앞에 위치하고 있고 더불어 두 개의 절이 제시되고 있는 구조가 아니므로 접속사가 아닌 명사 success를 수식할 수 있는 소유격 대명사가 와야 한다. 따라서 빈칸에는 소유격 대명사 its가 적절하다.

토익 분석

명사의 범위를 제한하는 존재를 한정사라고 하며 대표적으로 관사, 소유격 대명사, 수량사가 있으며 이 중 토익에서는 한정사 문제로 소유격 대명사와 수량사를 출제하고 있다. 수량사를 묻는 문제는 매달 등장하지 않지만 소유격 대명사를 묻는 문제는 매달 출제되고 있다. 수량사를 묻는 경우 many + 가산 복수명사 / much + 불가산명사 / other + 가산 복수명사 / each(every) + 가산 단수명사 / a few(few) + 가산 복수명사 / a little(little) + 불가산명사 / a plenty of + 가산 복수명사 및 불가산명사 / a number of + 가산 복수명사 / numerous + 가산 복수명사 / a variety of(various) + 가산 복수명사 / (almost) all(most/some) + 가산 복수명사 및 불가산명사 등을 중심으로 출제하고 있음을 알아두도록 한다.

118

★★ 어형 / 부사

고객이 Bella 화장품 TV 상업 광고의 일부 변경을 요청했을 때는 그 광고 제작 과정이 거의 끝날 무렵이었다.

어휘 process 과정 commercial 상업적인, 상업 광고
advertisement 광고 complete 완료된

The process of creating the TV commercial for Bella Cosmetics was ------- complete when the client asked for some changes.

(A) nearer
(B) nearest
(C) nearby
(D) nearly

문제 해설

빈칸에 적합한 어형을 묻는 문제이다. 빈칸이 be 동사 was와 동사가 아닌 형용사로서 쓰인 complete 사이에 위치하고 있으므로 형용사 complete를 수식하는 부사 어형이 와야 한다. 따라서 빈칸에는 '거의, 대부분'이란 뜻을 지닌 nearly가 적절하다.

토익 분석

토익에서는 부사 nearly는 almost를 대체하여 쓰이는 것이 가능하며 숫자를 수식하는 부사로서의 용례도 자주 묻고 있다. 아울러 near 역시 거리/공간적으로 '가까이에, 가까운 장소로'란 뜻을 지닌 부사로 쓰이는 것이 가능하나 해당 문장은 광고 제작 과정이 거의 다 끝났을 무렵이라는 시점 또는 단계를 뜻하므로 문맥상 부사로서의 near은 빈칸에 부적절하다. 무엇보다 토익에선 부사 near이 아닌 전치사 near의 용례를 묻는 문제가 출제되고 있음을 알아두도록 한다. 아무리 내가 김씨 집안의 아들이지만 아무 김씨 집안에 들어가서 그 집 아들이라고 주장할 순 없는 노릇이다. 어디서 쓰이고 어떻게 출제되는지 정확하게 알아두도록 한다.

119

Based on their resumes and recommendation letters, the final two candidates seem ------- qualified for our sales director position.

(A) high
(B) successfully
(C) equally
(D) punctually

문제 해설

빈칸에 적합한 부사 어휘를 묻는 문제이다.빈칸 앞에는 최후에 남은 두 명의 후보자들이 언급되고 있으며 빈칸 뒤에는 영업이사직에 적격인 상태임을 밝히는 내용이 등장하고 있다. 빈칸에 위치해야 할 부사 어휘는 무엇보다 두 명의 후보자가 모두 영업이사직에 적격인 상태임을 구체적으로 설명할 수 있어야 한다는 점을 고려해야 한다. 따라서 빈칸에는 '동등하게'란 뜻을 지닌 equally가 적절하다.

토익 분석

앞서 정리했듯이 부사 high와 부사 highly는 그 의미가 서로 다르다. 토익에서는 high를 묻는 문제는 출제되지 않고 highly를 묻는 혼동 부사 어휘 혹은 어형 문제가 출제되고 있으며 주로 highly qualified for / highly responsible for / highly recommended 등이 그 출제 대상이라 할 수 있다.

★★ 어휘 / 부사

그들의 이력서와 추천서를 토대로, 최종 두 명의 후보자가 모두 영업 이사직에 적격인 것으로 보인다.

문제 분석

seem + 형용사 ~인 상태인 것처럼 보이다

어휘 based on ~을 토대로, ~을 바탕으로 resume 이력서 recommendation letter 추천서 candidate 후보자 seem ~인 것처럼 보이다. ~인 상태인 것으로 보이다 be qualified for ~에 적격이다 equally 동등하게 punctually 시간대로, 늦지 않게

120

The cost of gasoline has become ------- high that many people commuting to work are unable to pay for their commute without a pay raise.

(A) so
(B) very
(C) too
(D) such

문제 해설

빈칸에 적합한 어휘를 묻는 문제로 빈칸이 has become의 형용사 주격 보어인 high 앞에 위치하고 있고 뒤이어 that 절의 형태가 이어지고 있다. 그러므로 빈칸에는 형용사 high를 수식하며 that 절과 함께 쓰여 휘발유 가격이 너무 비싸서 직장까지 통근하는 사람들이 급여 인상이 없이는 교통비를 감내할 수 없다는 결과 부사절을 구성할 수 있는 부사 어휘가 와야 한다. 따라서 that 절과 함께 쓰여 이러한 결과 부사절 접속사를 만들어내는 부사 어휘는 so가 유일하므로 빈칸에는 so가 적절하다. 아울러 'so + 형용사/부사 + that + 주어 + 동사~'는 '매우 ~하여 ~라는 결과를 낳는다'는 의미의 부사절 접속사임을 전체적으로 숙지하도록 한다.

토익 분석

결과 부사절 접속사인 'so + 형용사/부사 + that + 주어 + 동사~'는 so 뒤에 형용사 어형과 부사 어형 중 어떠한 어형이 적합한지 택일할 것을 묻는 문제도 출제되고 있다. 이 경우 so 앞쪽에서 맨 처음으로 보이는 동사(준동사)가 be/become이면 이들의 보어 역할을 할 수 있는 형용사 어형을 선택해야 하며, 그 외 일반적인 동사가 자리하면 이들을 수식할 수 있는 부사 어형을 선택해야 한다. 추가로 선택지에 나와 있는 부사 very와 too는 모두 that 절과 함께 쓰일 수 없으며 such는 형용사로 'such + 부정관사 + 형용사 + 명사 + that + 주어 + 동사~'의 구조를 취하는 것이 보통이나 경우에 따라 such는 가산 복수명사 및 불가산명사를 바로 수식하며 'such + 가산복수명사 / such + 불가산명사'로 쓰일 수 있다는 점을 고려할 때 이 또한 오답으로 소거해야 한다.

★★ 어휘 / 부사

휘발유 가격이 너무 비싸서 직장까지 통근하는 많은 사람들은 급여 인상 없이는 그들의 교통비를 감당할 수가 없다.

문제 분석

So + 형용사 / 부사 + that S + V 매우 ~해서 ~하는 결과를 낳다

어휘 commute to work 통근하다 be unable to Vr ~할 수가 없다 pay raise 급여 인상

121

★★ 어형 / 동사

항공기 조종사들의 부분 파업으로 인해 남부 휴양 도서인 Cayo Costa로 가는 약 200개의 항공편이 취소될 것이다.

어휘 about ~에 관해, 약, 대략 southern 남쪽의, 남부의 resort 휴양지 due to ~로 인해 partial 부분적인 strike 파업

About 200 flights to the southern resort island of Cayo Costa ------- due to the pilots' partial strike.

(A) canceling
(B) cancels
(C) will be canceled
(D) have canceled

문제 해설

빈칸에 알맞은 동사 어형을 묻는 문제이다. 동사 어형 문제는 우선 절을 구성할 수 없는 준동사형태를 오답으로 먼저 소거한 후 주어/동사 수 일치 - 태 - 시제 순으로 고려하며 풀이하는 것이 효율적이다. 그러므로 canceling을 먼저 오답으로 소거해야 한다. 이어서 주어가 About 200 flights로 복수 주어이므로 단수동사 형태인 cancels는 부적절하며 빈칸 이후에는 cancel이란 동사의 목적어가 등장하지 않고 있으므로 수동태가 적절하기에 능동태를 구성하는 have canceled 또한 오답이 되겠다. 따라서 빈칸에는 will be canceled가 와야 한다.

토익 분석

토익에서는 행사를 개최한다는 뜻을 지닌 동사 hold, host 그리고 연기/지연한다는 postpone 그리고 취소한다는 cancel의 경우 능동태를 구성하는 어형보다 수동태를 구성하는 be held/be hosted/be postponed/be canceled란 어형을 주로 묻고 있음을 알아두도록 한다.

122

★★ 어휘 / 형용사

이사회는 회사에서 10년 이상 근속한 일부 성실한 직원들에게 보상을 해줄 것이다.

어휘 the board of directors 이사회 reward 보상, ~에게 보상을 하다 dedicated 헌신적인, 전념하는 temporary 일시적인 promotional 홍보의, 판촉의

The board of directors is going to reward some ------- employees who have been with the company for over ten years.

(A) dedicated
(B) satisfied
(C) temporary
(D) promotional

문제 해설

빈칸에 적합한 형용사 어휘를 묻는 문제이다. 빈칸 앞에는 이사회가 보상할 것이란 내용이 등장하고 있으며, 빈칸 뒤에는 회사에서 10년 이상 근속한 직원이라는 보상을 받는 대상임을 알려주고 있다. 그러므로 빈칸에는 회사에서 10년 이상 근속하여 보상을 받게 되는 직원들이 어떠한 직원들인지를 적절하게 묘사할 수 있는 형용사 어휘가 필요하며, 10년 이상 근속하여 회사로부터 보상을 받게 되는 직원이라면 오랜 기간 동안 성실하고 꾸준하게 근무한 직원이라 할 수 있으므로 빈칸에는 '헌신적인, 전념하는'이란 뜻을 지닌 과거분사 형태의 형용사인 dedicated가 와야 한다.

토익 분석

'헌신적인, 전념하는'이란 뜻을 지닌 과거분사 형태의 형용사로는 dedicated 외에도 이와 동일한 의미로 쓰일 수 있는 devoted도 함께 알아두는 것이 바람직하다.

123

Ms. Whitman established her own post-impressionism style after she was -------
by many impressionist artists in Europe.

(A) presented
(B) reminded
(C) influenced
(D) determined

★★ 어휘 / 과거분사

Whiteman 씨가 유럽의 많은 인상주의 화가들에 의해 영향을 받은 후 자신만의 독자적인 후기 인상주의 방식을 창조하였다.

어휘 establish ~을 설립하다, ~을 확립하다, ~을 제정하다 remind ~을 상기시키다 influence 영향, ~에게 영향을 미치다 determine ~을 결정하다

문제 해설

빈칸에 적절한 동사 어휘를 묻는 문제이며 전체적으로 Whiteman 씨가 유럽의 많은 인상주의 화가들에 의해 무엇인가가 이뤄진 후 자신만의 후기 인상주의 방식을 창조했다는 내용이 등장하고 있다. 따라서 Whiteman 씨가 많은 인상주의 화가들에 의해 영향을 받고 난 후 이를 토대로 자신만의 후기 인상주의 방식을 창조했다는 문맥이 타당하므로 빈칸에는 영향을 받는다는 의미를 구성할 수 있도록 '영향을 받은'이란 뜻을 지닌 과거분사인 influenced가 와야 한다.

토익 분석

비록 오답으로 제시되었지만 동사 present에 대해선 제대로 알고 있어야 한다. 동사 present는 present sby with sth의 형태로 쓰이지만 present sth to sby 형태로 변환이 가능하며 모두 sby에게 sth을 주다/수여하다/제시하다란 의미로 쓰인다. 이 때 선치사의 변화에 주의해야 하며 이들이 각각 수동태로 전환되는 경우 sby be presented with sth/sth be presented to sby란 형태가 된다는 점도 함께 알아두도록 한다.

124

The institute ------- the brand power of major foreign companies based on their
global market shares and export volumes.

(A) built
(B) evaluated
(C) nominated
(D) attracted

★★ 어휘 / 동사

그 기관은 전 세계 시장의 점유율과 수출 물량을 토대로 해외 주요 대기업들이 브랜드 파워를 평가했다.

어휘 institute 전문 기관 be based on ~에 바탕을 두다, ~에 근거를 두다 market share 시장 점유율 export 수출 volume 부피, 규모, 체적, 양

문제 해설

빈칸에 적절한 동사 어휘를 묻는 문제로 빈칸 앞에는 전문 기관이, 빈칸 뒤에 해외 주요 대기업들의 브랜드 파워와 그들의 전 세계 시장의 점유율과 수출 물량을 토대로 한다는 내용이 등장하고 있다. 따라서 해당 기관이 전 세계 시장의 점유율과 수출 물량이란 자료를 근거로 하여 해외 주요 대기업들의 브랜드 파워와 관련하여 무엇을 했는지 나타낼 수 있는 동사 어휘가 필요하므로 빈칸에는 '평가하다'란 뜻을 지닌 동사 evaluated가 와야 한다.

토익 분석

'평가하다'란 뜻을 지닌 동사로 evaluate 외에도 동사 assess(명사 - assessment)와 동사 appraise(명사 - appraisal)을 함께 숙지하도록 한다.

★★★ 어휘 / 부사

우리 회사의 이사진은 본래 수요일에 New York을 향해 출발하기로 계획했었으나 악천후로 인해 출발이 지연되었다.

어휘 board members 이사진 set out for ~를 향해 출발하다 be held up by ~에 의해 지연되다 inclement weather 악천후

Our board members ------- planned to set out for New York on Wednesday but were held up by the inclement weather.

(A) inadvertently   (B) precisely
(C) knowingly   **(D) initially**

문제 해설

빈칸에 적합한 의미의 부사 어휘를 묻는 문제로, 빈칸을 전후하여 이사진이 수요일에 New York을 향해 출발하기로 계획했지만 악천후로 인해 지연되었다는 내용이 언급되고 있다. 따라서 이는 이사진들이 예정된 일정대로 출발을 못하게 되어 다른 날에 출발할 수 밖에 없음을 나타내므로 수요일에 New York을 향해 출발하려고 했던 일정은 악천후가 발생하기 이전 본래 계획했던 일정이 되어버린 상황임을 알 수 있으므로 빈칸에는 '최초의, 처음에, 본래'란 뜻을 지닌 부사 initially가 적절하다.

토익 분석

동사 initiate는 무엇인가를 새롭게 혹은 처음으로 시작/시행/실시한다는 의미를 지니고 있으며 토익에서는 initiate a new program (새로운 프로그램을 시작하다) / initiate a reform (개혁을 실시하다) / initiate a project (프로젝트를 시행하다)와 같은 표현이 어휘 문제로 출제된 바 있다. 아울러 형용사인 initial은 최초 혹은 초기를 뜻하는 형용사로 토익에서 initial investment (초기 투자) / initial cost (초기 비용) / initial negotiations (초기 협상) / initial stage (초기 단계)가 어휘 문제로 등장하기도 했다. 물론 initial은 복수명사 형태인 initials로 쓰여 이름의 첫 글자를 의미할 수도 있다. 마지막으로 또 다른 명사 initiative는 이전 토익에선 주도권(take initiative)이나 진취적인 정신/독창성의(demonstrate initiative)의 뜻으로 쓰이는 경우를 묻기도 했지만 최근 토익에서는 주로 program/plan이란 뜻으로 쓰이는 경우만 묻는 경향이 있음을 알아두도록 한다.

 접속사 once

★★ 어휘 / 부사

유명한 영국의 음악 잡지인 Classic은 어제 McDonald 씨가 어떠한 노래이든 한 번만 듣고서도 이를 기타로 연주할 수 있다고 보도했다.

어휘 fame 유명한 report 보도, 보도문, ~을 보도하다 recite ~을 읊다, ~을 암송하다, ~을 낭독하다 once 한 번, 예전에, 일단 ~하면

According to famed British music magazine Classic, Mr. McDonald can play any song on the guitar after hearing it just -------.

(A) once   (B) again
(C) now   (D) yet

문제 해설

빈칸에 적합한 부사 어휘를 묻는 문제이다. 빈칸 앞에는 McDonald 씨가 어떠한 노래이든 듣고서 이를 기타로 연주하며 노래할 수 있다는 내용이 제시되고 있으며 빈칸은 듣고 난 후라는 뜻의 전치사구인 after hearing it just 뒤에 위치하고 있다. 그러므로 빈칸에는 hearing과 함께 '단지, 그저, 딱, 막'이란 뜻을 지닌 부사 just와 어울릴 수 있는 어휘가 필요함을 알 수 있다. 따라서 빈칸에는 노래를 딱 한 번만 듣고서도 기타로 이를 연주하며 노래를 할 수 있다는 문맥을 구성할 수 있도록 '한 번, 1회'를 뜻하는 부사 어휘인 once가 와야 한다.

토익 분석

하나의 어휘가 여러 가지 품사의 역할을 하며 여러 의미로 쓰이는 경우가 발생하는데 대표적으로 once가 이에 해당한다. 부사 once가 횟수를 나타낼 때는 한 번이 되지만 시점을 언급할 때는 이전에 한 때가 되며 접속사로 쓰일 때는 '일단 ~하면'이란 뜻을 지니며 조건 부사절을 이끄는 부사절 접속사가 된다는 점은 기본적으로 모두 알아두어야 한다. 다만 토익에서는 주로 접속사로서의 once를 묻는 문제가 자주 출제되는 경향이 있다.

127

The customer service manager requested that all questions from customers
------ answered quickly and courteously.

(A) are
(B) were
(C) will be
(D) be

★★★ 어형 / 동사

고객 서비스 담당자는 고객으로부터의 모든 질문들에 신속하고 정중하게 답변할 것을 요구했다.

어휘 request ~을 요청하다, ~을 요구하다 quickly 빠르게, 신속하게 courteously 정중하게

문제 해설

주절의 동사가 요청/요구를 뜻하는 request인 경우, 이는 종속절인 명사절의 동사에 타당성/당위성/강제성의 의미를 부여하며 'should + 동사원형' 형태를 구성한다. 하지만 이미 주절의 동사인 request가 강하게 무엇인가를 할 것을 요청/요구하는 의미를 지니고 있으며 이로 인해 should가 타당성/당위성/강제성 중복으로 생략이 되어 결과적으로 동사원형인 본동사의 형태만 유지하게 된다. 그러므로 빈칸에는 be 동사의 원형인 be가 와야 한다.

토익 분석

종속절의 동사가 동사원형인 형태를 유지하게 하는 대표적인 주절의 동사로는 insist (주장) / ask, demand, request, require (요청/요구) / command, order (명령) / suggest, propose, advise, recommend (제안/권고) 등이 있다. 다만 토익에서는 command, order (명령)은 출제되지 않으므로 이는 참고만 하도록 한다. 아울러 이성 판단의 형용사가 쓰여도 같은 결과가 발생하는데 토익에서 출제될 수 있는 대표적인 이성 판단의 형용사로는 necessary (필요한) / important (중요한) / mandatory (의무적인, 필수적인) / imperative (의무적인, 필수적인) / essential (필수적인)이 있음을 꼭 숙지하도록 한다. 이들을 인식하지 못한 상태에서는 어떻게 문제를 풀이해도 풀었다고 잠시만 행복할 뿐 궁극적으로는 모두 공허한 오답이 된다.

128

Some city officials said that factory ------ will be introduced to improve Beijing's
air quality and the health of citizens.

(A) close
(B) closed
(C) closely
(D) closure

★★★ 어휘 / 복합 명사

몇몇 시 공무원들은 Beijing시 대기의 질과 시민들의 건강을 개선시키고자 공장 폐쇄가 시행될 것이라 언급했다.

어휘 official 공무원, 공식적인 be introduced to Vr ~가 시행되다 air quality 대기의 질 citizen 시민 closure 폐쇄

문제 해설

빈칸이 동사인 will be introduced 앞에 위치하고 있으므로 동사를 수식할 수 있는 부사 closely를 먼저 떠올릴 수 있으나 closely가 '가까이, 면밀하게'란 뜻을 지니고 있음을 고려할 때 Beijing시 대기의 질과 시민들의 건강을 개선시키고자 조만간 시행될 것이란 전체적인 문맥에 적절하지 않으므로 오답으로 처리해야 한다. 이어서 '폐쇄된'이란 뜻을 지닌 과거분사 closed가 명사인 factory를 후치수식하는 경우를 생각해볼 수 있지만 폐쇄된 공장은 조만간 시행되는 대상이라 할 수 없을 뿐만 아니라 공장 factory는 가산명사이자 폐쇄된 공장은 구체적인 대상으로 부정관사 또는 정관사를 대동해야 하기 때문에 이 또한 오답이다. 그렇다면 조만간 시행될 수 있는 대상이자 동사인 will be introduced 앞에서 주어 역할을 할 수 있는 대상이 필요하므로 빈칸에는 공장 폐쇄라는 뜻을 형성할 수 있는 명사 closure이 와야 적합하다.

토익 분석

복합명사의 기본적인 성격과 의미 구성의 특징을 살펴보자면 두 개 이상의 명사가 모여 하나의 명사 단어를 이루는 복합명사 N1 + N2에서 N2에 따라 복합명사가 가산인지 불가산인지가 결정이 된다. 이를테면 고객만족을 뜻하는 customer satisfaction은 satisfaction이 불가산명사이기 때문에 결국 customer satisfaction은 불가산명사로 취급된다. 하지만 rental car의 경우 car이 가산명사이므로 이는 궁극적으로 가산명사로 여겨진다. 따라서 가산 단수명사는 a rental car, 가산 복수명사로는 rental cars라고 쓰게 된다. 또한 복합명사의 의미는 크게 N1을 위한 N2, 또는 N1을 N2 하는 것 혹은 N1에 대한 N2이란 의미로 구성된다. 예컨대 customer satisfaction은 customer를 위한 satisfaction의 의미로 구성이 된 복합명사라 한다면 문제에선 제시된 factory closure은 factory를 closure하는 것 또는 factory에 대한 closure이란 뜻으로 형성된 복합명사라 할 수 있다.

★★ 접속사 / 형용사절 접속사

몇몇 분석가들은 회사 수익원에 피해를 줄 소지가 있는 정보의 공유를 피하곤 한다.

어휘 analyst 분석가 often 종종, 자주 avoid ~을 피하다 client 고객 damage ~에게 피해를 입히다, ~을 파손하다 revenue 수익 stream 흐름

Some analysts often avoid sharing information ------- may damage their company's revenue streams.

(A) who

(B) which

(C) whose

(D) what

문제 해설

빈칸을 전후하여 두 개의 절이 위치하고 있는 구조이므로 빈칸에는 이 두 개의 절을 연결해줄 수 있는 적절한 접속사가 와야 한다. 우선 명사절/형용사절 접속사와 관련된 문제를 풀이할 때는 빈칸 뒤에 등장하는 절의 구조가 완전한 절의 구조인지 혹은 불완전한 절이 구조인지부터 살피는 것이 현명하다. 빈칸 이후에 주어 또는 목적어가 빠진 불완전한 절이 등장할 때는 who, whom, which, what 및 선행사를 취하는 that 중에서 한 가지가 정답이 되며, 만약 이 중 두 개 이상이 접속사가 동시에 선택지에 제시되고 있다면 선행사를 살펴보고 이에 부합하는 접속사를 정답으로 선택하면 된다. 문제에서도 빈칸 이후에 주어가 빠진 불완전한 절이 등장하고 있으므로 빈칸에는 who와 which가 올 수 있다. 다만 선행사로 '정보'를 뜻하는 information. 즉 사람이 아닌 명사가 제시되고 있음을 고려할 때 빈칸에는 who가 아닌 which가 적절하다.

토익 분석

접속사 whose는 완전한 절의 구조와 함께 해야 하며 사람/사물을 모두 선행사로 취할 수 있으며 이 외에도 사람/사물을 모두 선행사로 취하는 것이 가능한 접속사로는 that이 있다. 아울러 what은 선행사 자체를 취하지 않는다는 특징을 알아두어야 한다.

★★ 접속사 / 부사절 접속사

사람들이 조만간 쓰레기 매립지에서 살길 원하지 않으려면 시청은 시장에서의 비닐 봉투 사용을 금지해야만 한다.

어휘 ban ~을 금하다 plastic bag 비닐 봉지 land fill 쓰레기 매립지 sooner or later 조만간, 머지 않아 unless ~하지 않는다면 whether ~인지 아닌지

The city government must ban plastic bags in markets ------- people want to live on a landfill sooner or later.

(A) whether

(B) where

(C) unless

(D) how

문제 해설

빈칸이 두 절 사이에 위치하고 있으므로 빈칸에는 적절한 접속사가 위치해야 한다. 빈칸 앞에는 시청은 시장에서의 비닐 봉투 사용을 금해야 한다는 내용이 언급되고 있으며, 빈칸 이후에는 사람들이 조만간 쓰레기 매립지에서 살길 원한다는 내용이 등장하고 있다. 하지만 사람들이 쓰레기 매립지에서 살길 원하기에 시청이 시장에서의 비닐 봉투 사용을 금지해야 한다는 문맥은 서로 상충되는 내용이자 논리적으로 부적절하다. 도리어 사람들이 쓰레기 매립지에서 살길 원하지 않으려면 시청이 서장에서의 비닐 봉투 사용을 금지해야 한다는 문맥이 타당하다. 따라서 빈칸에는 부정적 조건 부사절을 구성할 수 있는 '만약~가 아니라면'이란 뜻을 지닌 부사절 접속사 unless가 적합하다.

토익 분석

대표적인 조건 부사절 접속사로는 if, once, unless, in case that, in the event that, on the condition that이 있으며 아울러 이 때 if의 격식체/문어체 표현이라 할 수 있는 providing/ provided that, assuming that, supposing that도 함께 필히 숙지하도록 한다. 이를 알아놓지 않으면 조건 부사절 접속사인 if가 정답인 문제가 분명함에도 불구하고 막상 선택지에 if가 보이지 않아 결국 오답을 선택하게 되는 눈이 먼 비운의 주인공이 될 수도 있다. 사전에 미리미리 대비하여 정답을 아는 문제인데 정답을 선택하지 못하는 아이러니한 상황은 피해가는 것이 상책이다.

Questions 131-134 refer to the following information.

The Haru Battery you have purchased was designed to last for approximately three years or about 30,000 miles. When your battery finally dies, you should dispose of it ------- **131.** . Please do not just throw it in a trash can. Most municipalities currently recommend users not ------- **132.** their dead batteries away with trash.

Most experts say discarded batteries can cause fires and explosions if they ------- **133.** loose in boxes or bags with metal items. That's why our company offers a quick and easy disposal method to customers. ------- **134.** . When you turn them over to us, our recycling specialists take care of them in the proper fashion at no additional charge.

고객님이 방금 구매하신 **Haru** 건전지는 대략 3년 이상, 3만 마일을 주행할 수 있도록 제작되었습니다. 건전지의 수명이 다 하면 해당 건전지를 적절하게 폐기하셔야 합니다. 수명이 다된 건전지를 쓰레기통에 그냥 버리시면 안 됩니다. 대부분 도시에서는 현재 수명이 다 된 건전지를 단순히 쓰레기와 함께 버리지 말 것을 권고하고 있습니다.

대부분 전문가들은 폐기된 건전지들이 상자나 가방에 금속 물질과 함께 허술하게 보관되는 경우 화재와 폭발을 유발할 수 있다는 점을 언급하고 있습니다. 따라서 당사는 고객님께 폐기된 건전지를 신속하고 용이하게 폐기하는 법을 제공해드립니다. 고객님께서는 고객님 주변에 있는 저희 재활용 센터에 폐기된 건전지를 반납하시기만 하면 됩니다. 고객님께서 폐기된 건전지를 반납하시면, 당사의 재활용 전문가들이 반납된 건전지를 추가 비용이 없이 적절한 방식으로 처리해드립니다.

어휘 last ~가 지속되다 nevertheless 그럼에도 불구하고 dispose of ~을 폐기하다 properly 적절하게, 알맞게 throw ~을 버리다 trash can 쓰레기통 municipality 지방자치체, 시당국 currently 현재의, 지금의 expert 전문가 discarded 폐기된 explosion 폭발 store ~을 보관하다, ~을 저장하다 loose 헐겁게, 느슨하게 metal 철, 금속 disposal 폐기 method 방법, 수단 turn sth over to ~를 건네주다, ~을 넘겨주다 recycling specialist 재활용전문가 in the proper fashion 적절한 방식으로 additional charge 추가비용

131

(A) immediately
(B) properly
(C)confidentially
(D) respectively

★★ 어휘 / 부사

토익 분석

'알맞게, 타당하게, 적절하게'란 뜻을 지닌 부사 어휘로는 properly 뿐만 아니라 appropriately도 함께 숙지하시는 것이 바람직하다.

문제 해설

빈칸에 적합한 부사 어휘를 묻는 문제이다. 빈칸에 앞서 수명이 다 된 건전지를 폐기한다는 내용이 등장하고 있고 빈칸 이후에는 쓰레기통에 수명이 다 된 건전지를 버리지 말 것을 요청하고 있다. 따라서 이는 결국 수명이 다 된 건전지를 쓰레기통에 함부로 버리지 않도록 해야 한다는 내용으로 귀결되어야 하므로 빈칸에는 '적절하게'란 뜻을 지닌 부사 properly가 와야 한다.

132

(A) throw
(B) to throw
(C) throwing
(D) thrown

★★★ 어형 / to 부정사

토익 분석

동사 recommend는 목적어로는 to 부정사가 아닌 V–ing란 동명사 형태 또는 명사절 접속사 that과 함께 명사절을 취하지만 사람 목적어 뒤에 이은 목적격 보어 자리에는 To 부정사 어형을 취해야 한다는 점을 혼동하지 않도록 주의해야 한다.

문제 해설

빈칸에 적합한 어형을 묻는 문제로 빈칸이 동사 recommend와 목적어 users 뒤에 위치하고 있다. 무엇보다 동사 recommend는 권고/조언의 대상인 사람 또는 사람에 준하는 대상이 목적어로 제시되는 경우 목적격 보어로 to 부정사 형태를 취한다. 따라서 빈칸에는 to 부정사 어형인 to throw가 위치해야 한다.

133

★★★ 동사 어형

토익 분석

무엇보다 시간 부사절/조건 부사절의 경우 현재시제를 통해 미래시제를 표현한다는 시제적 특징을 고려할 때 빈칸에는 **will be stored**가 아닌 **are stored**를 선택해야 한다. 이 부분은 무엇보다 알면서도 실수를 자주 범하기 쉬운 부분이니만큼 각별히 주의해야 한다.

(A) stores
(B) are stored
(C) stored
(D) will be stored

문제 해설

빈칸에 적절한 동사 어형을 묻는 문제이다. 빈칸이 복수주어인 they와 형용사인 loose 그리고 수식 어구인 전치사구 in boxes or bags 및 with metal items 사이에 등장하고 있으므로 이를 통해 동사 뒤에 명사 목적어가 존재하지 않고 있음을 알 수 있다. 그러므로 단수동사인 stores와 능동태를 구성하는 stored는 모두 오답이다. 아울러 주절의 동사가 can cause, 즉 미래시제이므로 if로 시작하는 부사절의 동사 시제 역시 미래시제여야 함을 알 수 있다.

134

★★★ 빈칸 문장 추론

(A) 고객님의 차고에 남아 있는 충전지들은 안전상의 문제를 초래할 수도 있습니다.
(B) 오래된 건전지들과 새로운 건전지들, 또는 서로 다른 종류의 건전지들이나 다른 제조사들의 건전지들을 혼용하지 마세요.
(C) 새로운 소형 건전지들은 휴대전화와 전동기가 포함된 전기 장비에서 사용됩니다.
(D) 고객님께서는 고객님 주변에 있는 저희 재활용 센터에 폐기된 건전지를 반납하시기만 하면 됩니다

(A) Some batteries left in your garage can cause several safety concerns.
(B) Please do not combine old and new batteries or different types or makes of batteries.
(C) New small-size batteries are used in mobile phones and motor-driven electric tools.
(D) All you have to do is return your dead battery to one of our recycling centers in your area.

문제 해설

빈칸에 적합한 내용을 지닌 문장을 묻는 문제이다. 빈칸에 앞서 That's why our company offers a quick and easy disposal method to our customers라며 회사에서 고객님께 용이하고 신속하게 폐기된 건전지를 폐기하는 방법을 제공한다는 내용이 등장하고 있으며 빈칸 이후에는 When you turn them over to us, our recycling specialists take care of them in the proper fashion at no additional charge, 즉 폐기된 건전지를 저희에게 반납하면, 당사의 재활용 전문가들이 반납된 건전지를 추가 비용이 없이 적절한 방식으로 처리할 것이란 내용이 제시되고 있다. 따라서 빈칸에는 빠르고 신속하게 건전기를 폐기하는 방법을 구체적으로 언급하는 내용이 와야 함을 가늠할 수 있으므로 고객님 주변에 있는 재활용 센터에 폐기된 건전지를 반납하기만 하면 된다는 내용이 언급되고 있는 All you have to do is return your dead battery to one of our recycling centers in your area가 정답이다.

Questions 135-138 refer to the following e-mail.

From: customerservice@diamondcinemas.com
To: rwillis12@bizwiz.com
Date: October 11
Subject: Emerald Member Status

Dear Rochelle Willis,

Congratulations! Our records ------- that your recent purchase qualifies you as
an emerald member. The emerald membership can be attained by purchasing
135.
over $250 worth of movie tickets within a year. As thanks, we are sending you
five free movie tickets and eight coupons for free popcorn. This status also gives
you special -------to our exclusive movie premieres. The next level, which is
136.
the ruby membership, can be acquired by spending over $400 on movie tickets
within a year. -------.
137.

We thank you again for your -------and we look forward to seeing you at our
138.
movie theaters nationwide.

Sincerely,
Diamond Cinemas Customer Service

발신: customerservice@diamondcinemas.com
수신: rwillis12@bizwiz.com
일자: 10월 11일
제목: Emerald 회원자격

Rochelle Willis 씨에게,

축하드립니다! 고객님의 최근 구매액으로 Emerald 회원 자격이 되었음을 기록상 확인하게 되었습니다. Emerald 회원자격은 1년에 250달러 이상 영화를 관람하셔야 획득이 가능합니다. 감사의 표시로서, 5장의 무료 영화 관람권과 무료로 팝콘을 드실 수 있는 8장의 쿠폰을 보내드립니다. Emerald 회원 자격을 보유하시면 회원만을 위한 시사회에 참여하실 수도 있습니다. Emerald 회원보다 한 단계 높은 회원자격은 Ruby 회원이며 이는 년간 400달러 이상 영화를 관람하시면 획득하시게 됩니다. Ruby 회원은 8장의 무료 영화 관람권과 12장의 무료 팝콘 쿠폰을 받게 됩니다.

다시 한 번 항상 저희 극장을 아껴주셔서 감사를 드리고 전국에 있는 저희 극장에서 고객님을 볼수 있길 바랍니다.

Diamond Cinema 고객서비스

어휘 record 기록, ~을 기록하다 indicate ~을 나타내다, ~을 가리키다, ~을 지적하다, ~을 표시하다 qualify as ~로서 적격이다 attain ~을 획득하다 status 현황, 상태 access to ~에 대한 접속, ~에 대한 접근, ~에 대한 이용 exclusive 독점적인, 배타적인, 단독적인 premier 시사회, 초연 acquire ~을 획득하다 spend (돈/시간)을 쓰다 within ~이내에 look forward to ~를 기대하다, ~을 바라다 nationwide 전국적인

135

(A) indicate
(B) indication
(C) indicating
(D) has indicated

문제 해설

빈칸에 적합한 어형을 묻는 문제이다. 빈칸이 주어인 Our records와 목적어 역할을 하는 명사절인 your recent purchase qualifies you as a Emerald member 사이에 위치하고 있으므로 빈칸에는 동사가 위치해야 한다. 따라서 명사인 indication과 준동사 indicating은 오답이며 동사 indicate와 has indicate 중 주어가 Our records가 복수주어임을 고려할 때 동사는 복수동사 형태인 indicate가 적합하다.

★★ 어형 / 동사

토익 분석

토익에선 동사 indicate 외에도 '조짐, 징후'라는 뜻을 지닌 명사 indication과 '지표'를 뜻하는 명사 indicator, 그리고 '~를 나타내는'이란 뜻을 지닌 형용사인 be indicative of가 모두 출제된 바 있으므로 이들을 모두 숙지하도록 한다.

136

(A) excess   **(B) access**
(C) advice   (D) assess

문제 해설

빈칸에 적합한 명사 어휘를 묻는 문제이다. 빈칸 앞에 This status also gives you special이라며 Emerald 회원 자격이 회원에게 특별한 무엇인가를 제공한다는 내용이 등장하고 있으며 빈칸 뒤에는 to our exclusive movie premiers, 즉 회원만을 위한 시사회가 전치사 to와 함께 등장하고 있다. 그러므로 빈칸에는 Emerald 회원만이 누릴 수 있는 혜택으로 회원을 위한 시사회가 있다는 문맥을 구성할 수 있도록 '접근, 접속, 이용'이란 뜻을 지닌 명사 access가 와야 한다.

★★★ 어휘 / 명사

토익 분석

동사 access는 전치사가 없이 명사 목적어를 직접 취하는 타동사이며 명사 access는 전치사 to와 함께 (have) access to라는 형태로 쓰인다는 점을 꼭 숙지하며 이를 통해 동사 access와 명사 access를 구분할 수 있도록 해야 한다.

★★★ 빈칸 문장 추론

(A) 처음 방문한 고객이라면, Diamond Cinema 멤버십 프로그램에 등록하세요.
(B) Ruby 멤버십은 8편의 무료 영화 티켓과 12개의 무료 팝콘 쿠폰을 드립니다.
(C) 영화 티켓은 환불 및 교환이 되지 않습니다.
(D) 영화관에 외부 음식과 음료를 반입하실 수 없습니다.

토익 분석

빈칸에 적합한 내용의 문장을 묻는 문제의 경우, 지문의 전반적인 내용 흐름을 파악하고 빈칸 위치에 따라 제시되는 내용적 특징을 이해하며 내용적 연관성이 없는 어휘나 표현이 제시되는 선택지를 빠르게 오답으로 소거해 나가며 정답을 택일하는 것이 가장 효율적인 풀이 방법이다. 아울러 함께 출제된 다른 문제들을 먼저 풀이하고 난 후 가장 마지막으로 풀이하는 것이 바람직하다.

(A) If you are a first-time customer, please join our Diamond Cinemas membership program
(B) Ruby members receive 8 free movie tickets and 12 free popcorn coupons.
(C) Movie tickets are non-refundable and non-exchangeable.
(D) Please do not bring outside food or drinks into the movie theater.

문제 해설

빈칸에 적합한 내용을 지닌 문장을 묻는 문제이다. 빈칸에 앞서 The next level, which is the ruby membership, can be acquired by spending over $400 on movie tickets within a year, 즉 Emerald 회원보다 한 단계 높은 회원 자격은 Ruby 회원이며 이는 년간 400달러 이상 영화를 관람하면 해당 자격을 획득하게 된다는 내용을 설명하고 있다. 따라서 내용적 연계성을 고려할 때 빈칸에는 Ruby 회원 자격을 획득하면 8장의 무료 영화 관람권과 12장의 무료 팝콘 쿠폰을 받게 된다는 구체적인 혜택이 언급된 Ruby members receive 8 free movie tickets and 12 free popcorn coupons가 위치해야 한다.

138

★★ 명사 어휘

토익 분석

명사 loyalty 뿐만 아니라 '충직한, 충성스러운'이란 뜻을 지닌 형용사인 loyal도 꼭 알아두어야 하며 아울러 충성도가 높은 고객/팬/지지자를 의미하는 loyal customers/fans/supporters란 표현들도 함께 숙지하도록 한다.

(A) honesty
(B) assistance
(C) loyalty
(D) improvement

문제 해설

빈칸에 적합한 명사 어휘를 묻는 문제이다. 빈칸에 앞서 최근 1년 간 250달러 이상의 영화를 구매한 것에 대해 언급하고 이에 대한 감사의 인사를 전달하고 있으며 빈칸 이후에는 we look forward to seeing you at our movie theaters nationwide, 즉 전국에 있는 극장들에서 고객님을 볼 수 있길 기대하고 있다는 내용이 제시되고 있다. 따라서 빈칸에는 극장에서 자주 영화를 관람해주는 고객에 대한 감사를 표현할 수 있도록 고객의 '충성도'를 뜻하는 명사 loyalty가 와야 한다.

Questions 139-142 refer to the following e-mail.

To: Melina Ramos Sandoval<mrs@watchmedia.com>
From: Customer Service <welcome@nationwidejobs.com>
Date: 25 October
Subject: About Your Registration

Dear Ms. Sandoval,

Welcome to the Nationwide Jobs Network, one of the leading online profession matchmakers in the country. Your personal information, **139.** your address and work experience, will be securely kept only in our database if you allow us to do so.

The collected information will be used to analyze your job preferences, and we will provide it to employers who are **140.** a job applicant just like **141.** . Regular e-mail notifications about job openings in your area will be sent after you subscribe to our service.

142. . Therefore, we handle your personal information very carefully. If you want to join us, please visit our Web site at www.njn.com or call 1-888-926-7677.

Thank you.

Truly yours,

Nationwide Jobs Network
Customer Service

139

(A) and
(B) such as
(C) as well as
(D) now that

문제 해설

빈칸에 적합한 전치사 내지는 접속사를 묻는 문제로 빈칸 앞에는 '개인 정보'를 뜻하는 your personal information이, 빈칸 뒤에는 '귀하의 주소 및 직장 경력'을 의미하는 your address and work experience가 등장하고 있다. 이를 통해 앞서 언급된 개인 정보가 이를테면 주소나 직장 경력을 의미한다는 것임을 알 수 있으므로 빈칸에는 '~와 같은, 이를테면'의 뜻을 지닌 전치사 such as가 위치해야 한다.

발신: Melina Ramos Sandoval〈mrs@watchmedia.com〉
수신: 고객 서비스〈welcome@njn.com〉
일자: 10월 25일
제목: 귀하의 등록에 관해

Sandoval 씨께,

국내의 대표적인 인터넷 직업 소개 사이트인 Nationwide Jobs Network에 오신 것을 환영합니다. 귀하의 주소와 직업 경력과 같은 개인정보는 귀하께서 허용하신다면 저희 데이터베이스에 안전하게 보관될 것입니다.

수집된 정보는 귀하의 취업 성향을 분석하는데 이용되며 그 결과는 귀하와 같은 취업 지원자들을 물색 중인 고용주들에게 제공됩니다. 저희 서비스에 가입하시면 귀하가 거주 중인 지역의 일자리에 관해 정기적으로 이메일을 통해 알려드립니다.

저희는 누구나 신원 도용의 피해자가 될 수 있다는 점을 알고 있습니다. 그러므로 저희는 귀하의 개인 정보를 매우 신중하게 다루고 있습니다. 만약 귀하가 저희 서비스에 가입하시고자 한다면 www.njn.com를 방문해 주시거나 1-888-926-7399로 연락을 주시면 됩니다.

감사합니다.

Nationwide Jobs Network
고객서비스

어휘 leading 선도하는 profession 직업 matchmaker 소개업체, 소개자 personal information 개인 정보 securely 안전하게 be kept in our database ~이 데이터베이스에 보관되다 allow ~을 허용하다 collected 수거된 be used to Vr ~하기 위해 사용되다 analyze ~을 분석하다 job preferences 취업 성향 employer 고용주 job applicant 취업 지원자 like ~와 같은 notification 통보, 알림 job opening 일자리 subscribe to ~에 가입하다, ~을 구독하다 carefully 신중하게, 꼼꼼하게

★★ 어휘 / 전치사

토익 분석

뒤이은 내용이 앞선 내용에 대한 상세한 예에 해당되는 내용이 제시되고 있는 구조에서 이에 적합한 전치사를 묻는다면 such as가 적절하다. 만약 접속부사가 필요하다면 for example나 for instance를 선택해야 한다. 만약 뒤이은 내용이 앞선 내용에 대한 주제나 소재가 등장하고 있는 구조라면 이 때는 전치사 such as가 아니라 about, on, regarding, concerning, as to, as for을 선택하는 것이 바람직하다.

140

★★ 어휘 / 동사 + 전치사 표현

토익 분석

토익에 대비해서는 '~을 찾다, ~을 물색하다'란 뜻을 지니고 있는 표현으로 search for 외에도 look for과 seek을 함께 숙지하도록 한다.

(A) looking into
(B) laying off
(C) relying upon
(D) searching for

문제 해설

빈칸에 적합한 동사 어휘를 묻는 문제로, 빈칸 앞에는 '고용주'를 뜻하는 employers who가, 빈칸 뒤에는 '취업 지원자'인 job applicant가 등장하고 있다. 따라서 빈칸에는 고용주가 취업 지원자를 어떻게 하고자 하는지 언급할 수 있는 동사 어휘가 필요하다. 이보다 앞서 Welcome to the Nationwide Jobs Network, one of the leading online profession matchmakers in the country라며 국내의 대표적인 인터넷 직업 소개 사이트인 Nationwide Jobs Network에 오신 것을 환영한다는 내용이 제시되고 있음을 고려할 때 빈칸에는 취업 지원자를 물색 중인 고용주라는 의미를 형성할 수 있는 동사가 적합하다. 따라서 빈칸에는 searching for이 위치해야 한다.

141

★ 대명사 / 목적격 인칭 대명사

토익 분석

무엇보다 like는 동사 외에도 '~처럼, ~같이'란 뜻을 지닌 전치사로서도 쓰일 수 있다. 하지만 like가 동사로 쓰이든 전치사로 쓰이든 뒤이은 자리에는 공통적으로 이들의 목적어 역할을 할 수 있는 목적격 인칭대명사가 와야 한다.

(A) me
(B) you
(C) ours
(D) us

문제 해설

빈칸에 적합한 인칭대명사를 묻는 문제로 빈칸에 앞서 '취업 지원자'를 뜻하는 job applicant 및 부사 just와 함께 쓰여 '~와 같은'이란 뜻을 형성하는 전치사 like가 등장하고 있다. 그러므로 빈칸에는 '누구'와 같은 취업 지원자인지 이를 구체적으로 언급할 수 있는 인칭대명사가 와야 한다. 아울러 해당 이메일이 취업을 주선하는 인터넷 직업 소개 사이트인 Nationwide Jobs Network에서 취업을 희망하는 Sandoval 씨에게 발송된 것임을 고려할 때 빈칸에는 Sandoval 씨를 지칭하는 인칭대명사 you가 적합함을 알 수 있다.

142

★★ 빈칸 문장 추론

토익 분석

파트 6 빈칸에 적합한 문장의 내용을 묻는 문제에 대한 풀이 방법을 제시하고 있는 시중의 기본서들이나 파트별 전략서를 보면 관사라던가 아니면 대명사라던가 여러 가지 요소들을 살펴보며 빈칸에 적절한 내용을 지닌 문장을 선택하는 방식을 언급하는 경우가 많다. 사실 그러한 방법은 같은 유형의 문제이지만 토익에 비해 지문의 내용이 어렵고 복잡할 뿐만 아니라 지문의 길이가 긴 편인 공무원/편입/국가 자격증 영어 시험 부류에 적합한 문제 풀이 방식이다. 하지만 파트6는 지문의 길이가 짧고 내용도 그리 어려운 편이 아니므로 이러한 방법을 적용해서 풀게 되면 오히려 시간만 더 소요되는 결과가 발생하게 된다. 때로는 사공이 많으면 배가 산으로 간다. 파트6의 지문은 전체 내용을 정독하며 한 번에 모든 문제를 풀이하는 것이 현명하므로 지문 전반적인 내용의 흐름을 파악한 상태에서 내용적 연계성을 토대로 해당 문제를 풀이하는 단순한 풀이 방식이 가장 효율적이라 할 수 있다.

(A) We know anyone can be a victim of identity theft.
(B) Customer satisfaction has always been our top priority.
(C) Our job database is usually updated monthly.
(D) Your résumé has recently been reviewed by the board members.

문제 해설

빈칸에 적절한 내용을 지닌 문장을 묻는 문제이다. 빈칸 뒤에는 인과 관계, 즉 '따라서, 그러므로'란 뜻을 지닌 접속부사 therefore이 위치하고 있으며 이어서 we handle your personal information very carefully라며 귀하의 개인 정보를 매우 신중하게 다루고 있다는 내용이 등장하고 있다. 따라서 빈칸에는 개인 정보를 신중하게 다루게 될 이유가 제시되어야 하므로 저희는 누구나 신원도용의 피해자가 될 수 있다는 점을 알고 있다는 내용이 담긴 We know anyone can be a victim of identity theft가 적합하다.

Questions 143-146 refer to the following letter.

April 5

Dr. Nina Lee
5th Avenue #310
Phoenix, AZ 50505

Dr. Michael Westen
25200 Carlos Bee Blvd #302
Hayward, CA 94542

Dear Dr. Michael Westen:

Thank you for your invitation to Hayward for the urban economy conference ------- by California State University. It was ------- an honor to receive the invitation.
143. **144.**

Unfortunately, I am already committed during the period of your event. -------.
145.

I am working on getting an equally qualified faculty member from Arizona State University that would be willing to come. If you think this person is qualified, he or she could go in my -------. If you have any further questions, please do not hesitate to get in touch with me.
146.

Best regards,

Dr. Nina Lee
Professor
The Department of Economics
Arizona State University

143

(A) interested
(B) specialized
(C) scheduled
(D) organized

문제 해설

빈칸에 적합한 과거분사 형태의 형용사 어휘를 묻는 문제이다. 빈칸에 앞서 Thank you for your invitation to Hayward for the urban economy conference 라며 도시경제학 컨퍼런스란 행사에 초청을 받았다는 내용이 언급하고 있으며, 빈칸 이후에는 California State University, 즉 캘리포니아 주립대학교라는 기관이 등장하고 있다. 아울러 이후 Unfortunately, I am already committed during the period of your event에서 도시경제학 컨퍼런스를 your event, 즉 귀 행사라고 언급하고 있다. 따라서 이를 통해 캘리포니아 주립대학교가 바로 도시경제학 회의의 주최 기관임을 파악할 수 있으므로 빈칸에는 '주최되는'이란 뜻을 지닌 과거분사인 organized가 와야 한다.

4월 5일

Nina Lee 박사
5번가 310호
Phoenix, AZ 50505

Michael Westen 박사
25200번지 Carlos Bee가 302호
Hayward, CA 94542

Michael Westen 박사님께

캘리포니아 주립 대학교에서 주최하는 Hayward 시 도시 경제학 컨퍼런스에 초청해주셔서 감사드립니다. 초청장을 받게 되어 정말 영광입니다.

안타깝게도, 제가 이미 귀 행사가 예정된 시기에 선약이 있습니다. 그래서 그 행사에 참석을 할 수가 없어서 굉장히 죄송하게 생각합니다.

제가 Arizona 주립대에서 근무하는 교원 중에서 동등한 자격을 갖고 귀 행사에 참여할 수 있는 분을 찾고 있습니다. 만약 그 분이 자격이 된다고 여기신다면, 저를 대신하여 회의에 참석하실 수도 있으리라 생각합니다. 추가적인 질문이 있으시면, 제게 주저하지 마시고 연락을 주십시오.

Nina Lee 박사
교수
경제학부
Arizona 주립대학교

어휘 invitation 초청 urban 도시의 conference 회의 organize ~을 주최하다, ~을 정돈하다, ~을 설립하다 quite 매우 committed 전념하는, 헌신적인, 약속된 period 기간, 주기 equally 동등하게 qualified 자격을 지닌, 적격의 in one's place ~를 대신하여 be willing to Vr 기꺼이 ~을 하다, 흔쾌히 ~을 하다, ~을 할 의사가 있다 further 추가적인 hesitate to Vr ~하는 것을 주저하다 get in touch with ~와 연락을 하다

★★ 어휘 / 형용사(과거분사)

144

★★★ 어휘 / 부사

토익 분석

부사 so의 경우 뒤에는 필히 부사 so의 수식을 받는 형용사 또는 또 다른 부사가 위치해야 하며 부사 much는 비교급 형태의 형용사/부사만 수식할 수 있다는 점을 알아두도록 한다.

(A) very
(B) so
(C) quite
(D) much

문제 해설

빈칸에 적합한 어휘를 묻는 문제로 빈칸이 부정관사 an과 명사 honor 앞에 위치하고 있다. 부사 very는 '부정관사 a/an + very + 형용사 + 명사'의 어순을, 부사 so는 'so + 형용사 + 부정관사 a/an + 명사'의 어순을, 부사 'quite는 quite + 부정관사 a/an + (형용사) + 명사'의 어순으로 구성된다. 그러므로 이 모든 점들을 고려할 때 an honor 앞 빈칸에 자리해야 하는 부사는 바로 quite임을 알 수 있다.

145

★★ 빈칸 문장 추론

(A) 컨퍼런스에 참석하지 못하게 되어 죄송하게 생각합니다.
(B) 귀하께서 시간을 내어 이 행사에 참석하시는 것을 고려해주시기 바랍니다.
(C) 5월 1일 이전에 등록하는 경우 회원은 250달러이며 비회원은 350달러입니다.
(D) 이 중요한 행사에 참석하겠다고 동의를 해주신 점에 미리 감사를 드립니다.

(A) I am very sorry that I will not be able to participate in the conference.
(B) Please consider making time to commit yourself to this great opportunity.
(C) The registration fee before May 1 is $250 for a member, and $350 for a non-member.
(D) Thank you in advance for agreeing to participate in this important event.

문제 해설

빈칸에 적합한 내용의 문장을 묻는 문제이다. 빈칸에 앞서 Unfortunately, I am already committed during the period of your event라며 이미 귀 행사가 예정된 시기에 선약이 있음을 밝히고 있으며 빈칸 이후에는 I am working on getting an equally qualified faculty member from Arizona State University that would be willing to come, 즉 Arizona 주립대에서 근무하는 교직원 중에서 자기만큼이나 적격이며 행사에 참여할 수 있는 분을 구하고 있음을 밝히고 있으며 이는 자신의 회의 불참에 따른 대안임을 가늠할 수 있다. 따라서 빈칸에는 그 행사에 참석을 할 수가 없어서 굉장히 죄송하게 생각한다며 회의 불참에 따른 사과/유감을 밝히는 내용이 담긴 I am very sorry that I will not be able to participate in the conference가 와야 한다.

146

★★ 어휘 / 명사

토익 분석

토익에서 출제되는 place는 해당 문제처럼 '자리, 입지'를 뜻하는 명사로서 묻고 있으며 이와 관련된 대표적인 표현이 '~를 대신하여'란 뜻을 지닌 in place of가 있다. 물론 place는 '장소'를 뜻하며 이 때 venue란 어휘를 대신하여 사용할 수 있다는 점도 알아둬야 한다. 그리고 동사 place는 명사 order/advertisement와 함께 쓰여 '~을 주문하다 / ~에 대한 광고를 내다'란 의미를 구성하는 부분도 토익에서 출제가 가능한 부분이라 할 수 있다.

(A) place
(B) expertise
(C) perspective
(D) presentation

문제 해설

빈칸에 적절한 명사 어휘를 묻는 문제이다. 빈칸에 앞서 I am working on getting an equally qualified faculty member from Arizona State University that would be willing to come이라며 Arizona 주립대에서 근무하는 교원 중에서 자신만큼 적격이며 행사에 참여할 수 있는 분을 구하는 중이라 밝히고 있으며 빈칸 이후에는 If you think this person is qualified, he or she could go라며 이 분이 자격을 갖췄다고 여긴다면 그분이 Hayward 시를 방문하여 회의에 참석할 수도 있을 것이란 내용이 등장하고 있다. 따라서 이는 회의에 불참하게 된 자신을 대신하여 회의에 참석하는 것이니만큼 빈칸에는 '자신을 대신하여'란 의미를 형성할 수 있는 명사 place가 위치해야 한다.

Questions 147-148 refer to the following e-mail.

From: Office King Customer Service <infor@officeking.com>
To: Isabella Choi <ischoi@kamongcorp.com>
Subject: Order #1123
Date: 11 September

Dear Isabella Choi,

147 Your order has been cancelled as you requested. For your reference, here is a summary of your September 9 order.

Order #1123 Apple 110 BK Printer
Status: Cancelled

148 According to our policy, you will get a full refund within three business days.

If you need some further information, please visit us at www.officeking.com, or call us at 1-800-692-9815.

We always appreciate your business.

Office King

147-148 다음 이메일을 참조하시오.

발신: Office King Customer Service <infor@officeking.com>
수신: Isabella Choi <ischoi@kamongcorp.com>
제목: 주문번호 1123
날짜: 9월 11일

Isabella Choi 씨께,

147 요청하신 바와 같이 귀하의 주문은 취소되었습니다. 참고용으로, 귀하의 9월 9일 문에 대한 요약 내용을 보내드립니다.

주문번호 1123 Apple 110 BK Printer
상태: 취소

148 당사 방침에 따라, 3일 이내에 전액 환불을 받으시게 됩니다.

추가 정보가 필요하실 경우, www.officeking.com을 방문하시거나 1-800-692-9815로 저희에게 전화주시기 바랍니다.

귀하의 거래에 항상 감사드립니다.

Office King

어휘 order 주문(품) cancel ~을취소하다 request 요청하다 reference 참고 summary 요약 according to ~에따라 policy 정책 full refund 전액환불 within ~ 이내에 further 추가의 appreciate ~에 대해 감사하다 business 거래

147

Why was the e-mail sent?
(A) To inquire about a refund policy
(B) To inform a customer of a sales promotion
(C) To confirm an order cancellation
(D) To correct a mistake

★ 이메일의 발송 목적

이메일이 발송된 이유는 무엇인가?
(A) 환불정책에 관해 문의하기 위해
(B) 고객에게 판촉행사에 관해 알리기 위해
(C) 주문 취소를 확인하기 위해
(D) 실수를 수정하기 위해

토익 분석

이메일의 주제/목적은 이메일 초반 2~3문장의 내용을 통해 파악할 수 있으며 주제/목적 문제의 선택지는 굳이 먼저 읽어볼 필요가 없다.

문제 해설

이메일의 발송 목적에 대해 묻고 있으므로 이메일 초반부에서 발송 목적에 관한 정보를 파악하는 것이 현명하다. 지문 시작 부분에서 요청에 따라 주문이 취소되었고 참고를 위해 주문과 관련된 요약 내용을 보낸다며 Your order has been cancelled as you requested. For your reference, here is a summary of your September 9 order.라고 말하고 있으므로 이를 통해 주문 취소확인이 이메일 발송 목적임을 알 수 있다. 그러므로 (C)가 정답이다.

148

What is suggested about Ms. Choi?
(A) She has already paid for the item.
(B) She will get a full refund in one week.
(C) She will receive a printer in three days.
(D) She has been offered a special discount.

★ 세부사항

Choi 씨에 관해 알 수 있는 것은 무엇인가?
(A) 이미 제품에 대한 비용을 지불했다.
(B) 일주일 후에 전액 환불을 받을 것이다.
(C) 3일 후에 프린터를 받을 것이다.
(D) 특별 할인을 제공받았다.

토익 분석

다만 키워드가 지문 전반에 걸쳐 언급되는 경우에는 선택지의 내용을 키워드로 삼아 지문에서 해당 내용이 언급되는지 여부를 빠르게 파악하며 문제를 풀이한다.

문제 해설

Choi 씨에 관해 알 수 있는 내용을 묻고 있다. 이메일 중반부를 보면, you will get a full refund이라며 전액 환불을 받을 것이라 언급하고 있으므로 이는 비용을 이미 지불한 경우에만 가능한 것이다. 따라서 정답은 (A)가 되겠다.

창의적 글쓰기 수강 학생들에게 알립니다!
연례 Sandstone Short Story Writing Contest가 시작되었습니다.

[149] 현재 마감시한인 10월 30일까지 계속 참가작이 접수되고 있습니다. 모든 단편 소설 작품은 1,000자와 4,000자 사이의 길이에 해당되어야 하며, 어떤 주제도 가능합니다. 유명 작가들로 구성된 심사 위원단이(공포 소설가 Samuel J. Kingston 씨, 미스터리 소설가 Janice Bonderman 씨, 그리고 에세이 작가 Diana Jacobi 씨) 참가작들을 심사합니다.

두 가지 다른 연령대에 대해 수여되는 여러 상이 있습니다.
-16세 이하
-17세에서 19세 사이

[151] 대상인 Most Promising Writer 수상자는 1,000달러 상당의 대학 장학금과 두 곳의 대형 출판사 방문을 위한 3일간의 경비가 전액 부담되는 뉴욕으로의 여행, 그리고 Sandstone Beacon Gazette을 통한 단편 소설 출간과 같은 혜택을 받게 됩니다.

[150] 참가 신청서는 지역 내 모든 학교의 영어 교사들을 통해 받으실 수 있습니다. 해당 양식은 우편으로 아래 주소로 제출해 주십시오.
Sandstone Short Story Writing Contest
사서함 번호 50
Sandstone, VA 65455

모든 신예 작가들께 행운을 빌어 드립니다!

어휘 creative writing 창의적 글쓰기 annual 연례적인 entry 참가작 accept ~을 받아 들이다 up until ~까지 계속 deadline 마감시한 short story 단편 소설 in length 길이가 ~인 panel 위원단 noted 유명한 author 작가 judge ~을 심사하다 numerous 수많은, 여러 prize 상 award ~을 수여하다 category 부문, 항목 winner 수상자 receive ~을 받다 scholarship 장학금 publishing house 출판사 publication 출간, 게재 registration form 신청서, 등록 양식 available 이용 가능한, 구할 수 있는 send A in A를 제출하다 P.O.Box 사서함 budding 신예의

Attention Creative Writing Students!
The annual Sandstone Short Story Writing Contest has begun.

[149] Entries are being accepted from now the deadline of October 30. All short stories should be between 1,000 and 4,000 words in length and can be on any topic. A panel of noted authors—horror novelist Samuel J. Kingston, mystery writer Janice Bonderman and essayist Diana Jacobi—will judge the entries.

There will be numerous prizes awarded in two different age categories:
—Ages 16 and under
—Ages 17-19

[151] The winner of the major prize of Most Promising Writer will receive a $1,000 university scholarship, a three-day all-expenses-paid trip to New York to visit two major publishing houses and publication of his or her short story in the Sandstone Beacon Gazette.

[150] Registration forms are available from English teachers at all local area schools. Send the forms by mail to:
Sandstone Short Story Writing Contest
P.O.Box 50
Sandstone, VA 65455

Best of luck to all budding writers out there!

149

★ **세부사항**

모든 참가작은 반드시 언제까지 접수되어야 하는가?
(A) 10월 3일
(B) 10월 16일
(C) 10월 19일
(D) 10월 30일

토익 분석

시간/시점/요일을 묻는 문제에선 지문에서 시간/시점/요일이 언급되는 부분에만 빠르게 찾아 집중하라.

What date must all entries be received by?
(A) October 3
(B) October 16
(C) October 19
(D) October 30

문제 해설

모든 참가작의 접수 마감시한에 대해 묻고 있으므로 지문에서 구체적인 날짜가 제시되는 부분을 중심으로 단서를 파악해야 한다. 지문 초반부에 마감시한인 10월 30일까지 접수가 가능하다며 Entries are being accepted from now the deadline of October 30이라 언급하고 있으므로 (D)가 정답이다.

150

Where should registration forms be sent?

(A) To Samuel J. Kingston
(B) To the local newspaper
(C) To a special Post Office Box number
(D) To the local community center

문제 해설

참가 신청서를 보내야 하는 곳에 대해 묻고 있다. 마지막 단락에서 Send the forms in by mail to라며 참가 신청서를 보내야 하는 주소를 알려 주고 있으며 이 주소 중에 포함되어 있는 사서함 번호, 즉 P.O. Box 50를 언급하고 있는 (C)가 정답이다.

★ 세부사항

참가 신청서는 어디로 발송되어야 하는가?
(A) Samuel J. Kingston 씨
(B) 지역 신문사
(C) 특별 사서함 번호
(D) 지역 문화 센터

토익 분석

참가 신청서를 접수하는 장소라는 세부사항을 묻는 문제이므로 지문에서 접수처에 해당되는 내용이 어디에서 제시되고 있는지 스캐닝을 통해 빠르게 파악하도록 한다.

151

What will the top prize winner get?

(A) A full four-year university scholarship
(B) A week's stay in New York with all expenses paid
(C) A chance to meet top publishers
(D) An internship at a popular magazine company

문제 해설

대상 수상자에게 주어지는 혜택을 묻고 있으므로 대상 수장자가 얻게 되는 혜택이 등장하는 부분을 빠르게 찾아가야 한다. 세 번째 단락에서 The winner of the major prize of Most Promising Writer will receive a $1,000 university scholarship, a three-day all-expenses-paid trip to New York to visit two major publishing houses라며 대상 수상자는 천 달러의 장학금 및 뉴욕으로 가서 두 곳의 대형 출판사를 방문하는 3일간의 여행 상품을 받게 된다는 점을 언급하고 있다. 그러므로 (C)가 정답이다.

★★ 세부사항

1위 수상자는 무엇을 받을 것인가?
(A) 4년 전액 대학 장학금
(B) 모든 경비가 부담된 뉴욕으로의 일주일 숙박
(C) 최고의 출판업자들을 만날 수 있는 기회
(D) 유명 잡지사의 특채

토익 분석

세부사항을 묻는 문제는 질문에서 빠른 키워드(핵심어) 파악이 중요하다. 다만 질문에서의 키워드는 지문에서 유사 어휘나 표현으로 바뀔 수 있다. 해당 문제의 경우 대상 수상자에게 주어지는 혜택을 묻고 있으므로 지문에서 대상 수상자, 즉 **top prize winner** 또는 이와 유사한 표현이 등장하는 부분을 스캐닝을 통해 빠르게 찾아야 한다. 지문에서는 **top prize winner**이 The winner of the major prize로 바뀌어 제시되고 있다.

Aurora Lane [14:18]
어디 계세요? 대회의실 B에 계신가요?

Holly White [14:19]
네, 마지막 발표가 막 시작되었습니다.

Aurora Lane [14:21]
그 후에 여전히 Sally Murphy 박사님의 인공 지능 발표회에 가고 싶으신가요? [153] 이 발표는 대회의실 C에서 열립니다.

Holly White [14:23]
물론이죠, 그 발표는 놓치지 않을 겁니다. [152] 그분의 발표는 언제나 매우 흥미롭거든요.

Aurora Lane [14:25]
전적으로 동의합니다. [152, 153] 제가 당신 자리를 하나 맡아 놓을까요?

Holly White [14:26]
그렇게 해 주시면 좋죠. 정말 감사합니다. 그곳에서 뵙겠습니다.

어휘 presentation 발표(회) artificial intelligence 인공 지능 hold ~을 개최하다, 열다 miss ~을 놓치다, 지나치다 interesting 흥미로운 I can't agree with you more 전적으로 동의합니다 Would you like me to do? 제가 ~해 드릴까요? save a seat 자리를 하나 맡다

Questions 152-153 refer to the following text message chain.

Aurora Lane [14:18]
Where are you? You are in conference room B?

Holly White [14:19]
Yeah, the last presentation has just begun.

Aurora Lane [14:21]
You still wanna go to Dr. Sally Murphy's artificialintelligence presentation afterward? [153] It will be held in conference room C.

Holly White[14:23]
Of course. I wouldn't miss it. [152] Her presentations are always very interesting.

Aurora Lane [14:25]
I can't agree with you more. [152, 153] Would you like me to save you a seat?

Holly White[14:26]
That would be good. Thanks a lot. I'll see you there.

152

★★★ 화자 의도

14시 25분에, Lane 씨가 "I can't agree with you more"라고 썼을 때 무엇을 의미할 가능성이 가장 큰가?
(A) Murphy 박사의 이론을 뒷받침할 증거가 없다고 생각한다.
(B) White 씨가 그의 연설에서 실수한 부분이 있다고 확신하고 있다.
(C) White 씨의 발표에 대단히 깊은 인상을 받았다.
(D) Murphy 박사의 연설에 대한 White 씨의 의견에 동의하고 있다.

토익 분석

특정 표현에 담긴 화자의 의도에 대한 이해하기 위해서는 주어진 특정 표현 전후의 내용 파악이 선행되어야 한다. 난이도가 높아지는 경우에는 전체 지문의 내용을 다 파악해야만 풀 수 있는 경우도 발생한다

At 14:25, what does Ms. Lane most likely mean when she writes, "I can't agree with you more"?

(A) She thinks there is no evidence to support Dr. Murphy's theory.
(B) She is certain Ms. White is mistaken in his speech.
(C) She was very impressed with Ms. White's presentation.
(D) She agrees with Ms. White's opinion of Dr. Murphy's speech.

문제 해설

주어진 "I can't agree with you more"이란 말은 "더 이상 동의할 수 없다"와 같이 해석 가능하며, 이에 앞서 White 씨가 Murphy 박사의 발표가 항상 흥미롭다며 Her presentation is always very interesting라고 언급한 부분에 대한 답변으로 제시되었다. 아울러 바로 뒤이어 Lane 씨가 Would you like me to save you a seat?라며 자리를 맡아 줄지 묻고 있다. 그러므로 I can't agree with you more라는 말에는 자신도 그 발표를 보러 간다는 의도가 포함된, 남자의 의견에 동의하는 것을 강조하는 말임을 알 수 있다. 따라서 (D)가 정답이다.

153

★★★ 사실 유추

Lane 씨에 관해 무엇이 사실일 것 같은가?
(A) White 씨에 앞서 대회의실 C로 갈 것이다.
(B) Murphy 박사 다음으로 발표를 할 것이다.
(C) 이미 행사를 위해 대회의실을 예약해 두었다.
(D) White 씨와 함께 인공 지능에 관한 논문을 쓰고 싶어 한다.

토익 분석

문자 메시지 상에 등장하는 특정 인물에 대한 적절한 유추 내용을 파악해야 하는 경우, 선택지에 나온 내용을 먼저 파악한 후 해당 인물의 대화 내용에서 선택지의 내용을 유추할 수 있는 근거가 지문에 제시되는지 여부를 역으로 확인하는 방식으로 문제를 풀이하라.

What is probably true about Ms. Lane?

(A) She will go to conference room C before Ms. White.
(B) She will give a presentation after Dr. Murphy.
(C) She has already reserved a conference room for an event.
(D) She wants to write a thesis on artificial intelligence with Ms. White.

문제 해설

14시 21분에 Lane 씨가 Murphy 박사의 발표가 대회의실 C에서 열린다고 말한 뒤로 그 박사 발표와 관련된 의견을 얘기하면서 자신이 자리를 맡아 줄 것인지 Would you like me to save you a seat for you?라고 묻고 있다. 따라서 이를 통해 Lane 씨는 해당 발표가 개최되는 대회의실 C로 White 씨에 앞서 가 있을 것임을 유추할 수 있으므로 (A)가 정답이다.

Questions 154-155 refer to the following article.

The World Economy Leader
Business News

September 13, Los Angeles—Lance Merrier, Vice President of Apple Republic Corporation, released a statement on Tuesday stating that the company is going through with plans to open stores in Chicago, Atlanta, New York, and New Orleans within the next year.

Mr. Merrier admitted mistake on his part last year, when the company first tried to expand. He confessed that the main problem with the unsuccessful expansion was that the company was not yet strong enough financially to make that kind of move. He acknowledged that the company had misjudged its value. With a strong marketing campaign and a revitalized mission, the company maintains that the expansion will be far easier this time.

[155] Los Angeles-based Apple Republic Corporation was founded by Christopher Lee and [154] maintained a clean and classic style marketed at middle-aged adults. The company will begin adding a younger line of clothing in the spring in its new stores. The company will keep a close watch on how well its first foray into children's clothing starts out. Early projections have the four new stores bringing in record numbers, but no one at the company is going to believe it until they see it.

154

What is suggested about Apple Republic Corporation?

(A) It moved its main office to Los Angeles.
(B) It recently closed half its stores.
(C) It carries children's clothing.
(D) Its merchandise is currently limited to adults.

문제 해설

기사문 세 번째 단락 초반 a clean and classic style marketed at middle-aged adults를 통해 회사의 제품이 현재 성인을 대상으로 하는 제품으로 한정되어 있음을 유추할 수 있다.

155

Where is Apple Republic Corporation currently located?

(A) In Chicago   (B) In New York
(C) In Los Angeles   (D) In New Orleans

문제 해설

Apple Republic 사의 본거지에 대해 묻고 있으며 선택지를 통해 단서가 도시 이름으로 제시될 것임을 미리 추측할 수 있다. 따라서 지문에서 도시의 이름이 언급되는 부분을 빠르게 찾아보며 단서를 파악하는 것이 현명하다. 기사 세 번째 단락 초반 Los Angeles-based Apple Republic Corporation을 통해 Apple Republic 사는 로스앤젤레스에 위치하고 있는 회사임을 알 수 있으므로 정답은 (C)라고 할 수 있다.

154-155 다음 기사를 참조하시오.

The World Economy Leader
비즈니스뉴스

9월 13일, 로스앤젤레스 – Apple Republic Corporation 의 부사장 Lance Merrier 씨는 내년에 시카고, 아틀란타, 뉴욕, 뉴올리언즈에 새로운 매장을 열겠다는 구상을 화요일에 발표했다.

Merrier 씨는 그가 맡은 부분에서의 실수를 인정했다. 성공적이지 못했던 사업 확장의 가장 큰 문제점은 그러한 확장을 진척시키기에 작년에 회사가 재정적으로 충분히 건실하지 못했던 점이라고 언급했다. Merrier 씨는 회사가 회사의 가치에 대해 잘못 판단했다고 시인했다. 강력한 마케팅 캠페인과 활력을 불어넣은 목표로 금번에는 사업 확장이 훨씬 수월해질 것이라 주장한다.

[155] 로스앤젤레스에 본사를 두고 있는 Apple Republic Corporation 는 Christopher Lee 씨가 창립하였고 [154] 중년층을 대상으로 깔끔하고 고전적인 스타일을 유지해왔다. Apple Republic 사는 봄철에 새로운 매장에서 젊은 층을 위한 새로운 의류제품을 선보일 예정이다. Apple Republic Corporation 는 아동복 시장에 어떻게 진입할 것인지 주의를 기울여 살펴볼 것이다. 초기 예상으로는 4개 매장에서 기록적인 매출을 이끌어낼 것이라고 예측되지만, 실제로는 회사 내 누구도 보기 전까진 믿지 않을 것이다.

어휘 order 주문(품) cancel ~을취소하다 foray 시도 request 요청하다 reference 참고 summary 요약 according to ~에따라 policy 정책 full refund 전액환불 within ~ 이내에 further 추가의 appreciate ~에 대해 감사하다 business 거래

★★ 유추

Apple Republic 사에 대해 암시되는 내용은 무엇인가?
(A) 본사를 샌프란시스코로 이전했다.
(B) 최근에 매장의 반을 폐쇄했다.
(C) 아동복을 판매한다.
(D) 회사의 제품은 현재 성인용으로 국한되어 있다.

토익 분석

유추 문제의 키워드가 혹은 키워드에 관한 내용이 지문 전반에 걸쳐 언급되고 있는 상태에서 적절한 유추 내용을 파악해야 한다면 선택지에 나온 내용을 먼저 파악한 후 선택지의 내용을 유추할 수 있는 근거가 지문에 제시되는지 여부를 역으로 확인하는 방식으로 문제를 풀이하라.

★ 세부사항

Apple Republic 사는 어디에 위치하고 있는가?
(A) 시카고   (B) 뉴욕
(C) 로스앤젤레스   (D) 뉴올리언즈

토익 분석

Apple Republic 사의 본거지에 해당하는 도시 이름을 묻는 문제이므로 선택지에 제시된 도시 이름을 살펴본 후 지문에서 도시 이름이 등장하는 부분 전후 내용을 살펴 Apple Republic 사의 본거지를 파악하도록 한다.

156-157 다음 회람을 참조하시오.

수신: **Harvey Davis** 박사, 수석 레지던트
발신: **Dana Kamon** 박사, 소아과장
제목: [156] 간호 인력 부족

병동 주변에서 들리는 소문을 통해 알고 계시겠지만, 인력 부족 문제가 아주 큰 방해가 되고 있습니다. [156] 우리 모두는 간호사들이 추가로 필요하다는 점과 예산이 빠듯하다는 점을 알고 있습니다. [157] 저는 더 많은 직무 분담을 제안하고자 하는데, 아마 이는 적어도 위기에 대한 임시 해결책이 될 수 있을 것이기 때문입니다.

물론, 장기적으로는, 정규직 간호사들을 고용해야 하지만, [157] 소아과와 1년 넘게 직무 분담을 해온 것은 꽤 효과적이었습니다. 그것이 완벽한 상황임을 말씀 드리고자 하는 것은 아니지만, 직원 부족 문제를 다루는 데 있어 효과적이었습니다.

어휘 chief resident 수석 레지던트 Pediatrics 소아과 nursing 간호직 shortage 부족 buzz (사람들의) 웅성댐, 소문 ward 병동 distraction 방해 budget 예산 tight 빠듯한 propose ~을 제안하다 job sharing 직무 분담 possibly 아마 at least 최소한, 적어도 temporary 임시의 solution 해결책 crisis 위기 in the long term 장기적으로 hire ~을 고용하다 work well 효과가 좋다, 잘 되어 가다 situation 상황 cover 다루다

Questions 156-157 refer to the following memorandum.

To: Dr. Harvey Davis, Chief Resident
From: Dr. Dana Kamon, Head of Pediatrics
[156] Subject: Nursing shortages

As you know from the buzz around the wards, the staff shortages are becoming too much of a distraction. [156] We all know we need more nurses, but the budget is tight. [157] I wanted to propose more job sharing, which might be at least a temporary solution to the crisis.

Of course, in the long term, we need to hire full-time nurses but [157] here in Pediatrics where we have had job sharing for over a year, we feel it works well. I'm not saying it's a perfect solution, but to cover shortages of staff, it has worked.

156

★ 문제점

어떠한 문제가 논의되고 있는가?
(A) 병원 내 침대의 부족
(B) 너무 많이 긴 시간의 교대 근무를 하는 의사들
(C) 소아과 병동 내의 환자 관리
(D) 간호 인력 문제

토익 분석

첫 번째 문제로 등장하는 구체적인 문제점은 주로 첫 번째 단락 초반 2–3문장을 통해 제시된다

What is the issue being discussed?

(A) A shortage of hospital beds
(B) Doctors working too many long shifts
(C) Patient care in the pediatric ward
(D) A nurse staffing problem

문제 해설

논의되고 있는 문제점에 대해 묻고 있으며 문제점은 지문 초반부에서 직접적으로 제시되는 경향이 있다. 회람 제목에 적힌 Nursing shortages을 비롯해, 첫 단락에 추가 간호사들이 필요하다며 We all know we need more nurses라고 언급하고 있으므로 간호 인력 문제를 뜻하는 (D)가 정답임을 알 수 있다.

157

★★ 세부사항

Kamon 박사에 의해 제안되고 있는 해결책은 무엇인가?
(A) 간호사들에 의한 직무 분담
(B) 더 많은 정규직 의사들의 고용
(C) 간호 인력의 감축
(D) 각 병동에 대한 의사들의 교대 근무

토익 분석

마지막 문제는 항상 마지막 단락의 내용이 끝나는 부분부터 역순으로 한 문장씩 내용을 확인하며 단서를 파악하는 것이 효율적이다. 특히 해결책을 묻는 문제인 경우 구체적인 해결책은 마지막 단락에서 제시된다.

What is the solution being suggested by Dr. Kamon?

(A) Job sharing by the nurses
(B) Hiring more full-time doctors
(C) Cutting the nursing staff
(D) Rotating doctors from ward to ward

문제 해설

Kamon 박사에 의해 제안되고 있는 해결책에 대해 묻고 있다. 따라서 Kamon 씨가 보낸 회람에서 인력 부족에 따른 해결책이 제시되는 부분을 빠르게 찾아가야 한다. 회람 첫 단락의 마지막 부분에서 Kamon 씨는 직무 분담을 제안하고 싶다며 I wanted to propose more job sharing라고 이야기하고 있으며 이어서 두 번째 단락에서도 직무 분담이 효과가 좋다며 here in Pediatrics where we have had job sharing for over a year, we feel it works well라고 말하고 있다. 따라서 간호사들의 직무 분담을 뜻하는 (A)가 정답임을 알 수 있다.

Questions 158-160 refer to the following advertisement.

The Sea World
The Pacific Ocean Hotel

Good day to you, and welcome to the Pacific Ocean Hotel. We hope you will thoroughly enjoy your stay. If you are looking for a restaurant with delicious food and the best view in town, look no further than the Sea World, our hotel restaurant located on the first floor. Chef Albert Condoza will be serving up some of the freshest catch of the day all evening long, and there is a table waiting just for you.

[158] The Sea World is open Tuesday through Sunday from 11:00 A.M. to 11:30 P.M. [159] If you are in your room and would like to order room service, we have a room service menu posted in every room. You can order anything from the Sea World menu during regular restaurant hours.

Come and visit this Sunday between 1:00 P.M. and 3:00 P.M. You can enjoy the shrimp and crab feast. [160] All you need to do is bring this advertisement with you to the restaurant, and you can enjoy unlimited amount of succulent crab meat and giant shrimp.

158

At what time does the restaurant open on Wednesdays?

(A) 11:00 A.M.
(B) 11:30 A.M.
(C) 1:00 P.M.
(D) 3:00 P.M.

문제 해설

식당이 문을 여는 시간에 대해 묻고 있으므로 식당의 영업시간과 관련된 내용이 언급되는 부분을 빠르게 찾아야 한다. 광고문 두 번째 단락 초반 The Fresh Catch is open Tuesday through Sunday from 11:00 A.M. to 11:30 P.M.에서 언급된 내용을 통해 월요일을 제외하고는 모두 오전 11시에 개장함을 알 수 있다. 따라서 정답은 (A)이다.

158-160 다음 광고문을 참조하시오.

The Sea World
The Pacific Ocean Hotel

안녕하세요, **Pacific Ocean** 호텔에 오신 것을 환영합니다. 계시는 동안 즐거운 시간을 보내시길 기원합니다. 시내에서 맛있는 요리와 최고의 전망을 모두 갖춘 식당을 찾고 계시다면, 그 어느 곳보다도 저희 호텔 1층에 위치한 **Sea World**를 찾으세요. **Albert Condoza** 주방장이 그 날 바로 잡은 가장 신선한 생선요리를 저녁 내내 제공할 것이며, 여러분을 위해 준비될 것입니다.

[158] **Sea World**는 화요일에서 일요일까지 오전 11시부터 오후 11시 30분까지 영업합니다. [159] 만약 객실에서 룸서비스를 신청하고 싶으시면, 모든 객실에 룸서비스 메뉴가 준비되어 있습니다. 식당의 정규 영업 시간 동안 씨 월드 메뉴에 있는 모든 음식을 주문하실 수 있습니다.

이번 주 일요일 오후 1시에서 오후 3시 사이에 방문해주세요. 새우와 게를 마음껏 즐기실 수 있습니다. [160] 이 광고지를 식당에 가져오시기만 하면, 육즙이 가득한 게살과 커다란 새우를 무한정 드실 수 있습니다.

어휘 thoroughly 매우 많이 delicious 맛있는 view 전망 chef 주방장 catch 어획량 all evening long 저녁 내내 post ~을 게시하다 shrimp 새우 crab 게 feast 축제 all you need to do is ~하기만 하면 된다 unlimited 무제한의 succulent 즙이 많은 crab meat 게살

★ **세부사항**

식당은 수요일에 몇 시에 개장하는가?
(A) 오전 11시
(B) 오전 11시 30분
(C) 오후 1시
(D) 오후 3시

토익 분석

시간/시점/요일을 묻는 문제에선 지문에서 시간/시점/요일이 언급되는 부분에만 빠르게 찾아 단서를 파악하라.

159

★★ 진위

룸 서비스에 대해 언급되지 않은 것은 무엇인가?
(A) 전체 메뉴를 포함한다.
(B) 저렴한 가격의 상품을 제공한다.
(C) 영업하는 시간 동안 이용할 수 있다.
(D) 씨 월드에서 가져오는 음식이다.

토익 분석

진위를 묻는 문제는 질문에서 빠른 키워드(핵심어) 파악이 중요하다. 해당 문제는 룸 서비스에 관해 사실인 내용을 묻는 문제이므로 지문에서 룸 서비스라는 키워드가 언급되는 부분을 스캐닝을 통해 빠르게 파악한 후 전후 내용을 통해 단서를 파악하는 것이 효율적이다.

What is NOT indicated about the room service?

(A) It includes the full menu.
(B) If offers many items at low prices.
(C) It is available during business hours.
(D) Its food is from the Sea World.

문제 해설

룸 서비스와 관련된 사실 확인 문제이므로 우선 룸 서비스가 소개되는 부분을 빠르게 파악해야 할 필요가 있다. 광고문 두 번째 단락에서 룸 서비스에 대해 If you are in your room and would like to order room service, we have a room service menu posted in every room. You can order anything from the Fresh Catch menu during regular restaurant hours라고 언급하는 내용을 통해 식당이 영업하는 시간에 어떠한 메뉴든 객실로 가져다 준다는 점을 알 수 있다. 하지만 가격은 언급된 바 없으므로 정답은 (B)가 되겠다.

★★ 세부사항

Pacific Ocean 호텔이 일부 고객들에게 제공하는 것은 무엇인가?
(A) 식당의 할인 쿠폰
(B) 무료 룸 서비스
(C) 무료 해산물 음식
(D) 특별 수중 발레 공연

토익 분석

마지막 문제는 항상 마지막 단락의 내용이 끝나는 부분부터 역순으로 한 문장씩 내용을 확인하며 단서를 파악하는 것이 효율적이다. 해당 문제는 지문 마지막 단락에서 선택지에서 언급된 것 중 고객에게 제공되는 것으로 언급된 대상을 정답으로 택일하도록 한다.

What will the Pacific Ocean Hotel offer some of its clients?

(A) A discount coupon for the restaurant
(B) Complimentary room service
(C) Free seafood meals
(D) Special water ballet shows

문제 해설

Pacific Ocean 호텔에서 고객에게 제공하는 것을 묻고 있으며, 이는 광고문 말미에서 All you need to do is bring this advertisement with you to the restaurant, and you can enjoy unlimited amount of succulent crab meat and giant shrimp라고 언급된 내용을 통해 광고지를 들고 오는 특정 고객들에게는 무제한으로 게살과 새우 같은 해산물을 제공할 것임을 알 수 있다. 따라서 정답은 (C)이다.

Questions 161-163 refer to the following memorandum

From: Wesley Kim, Personnel Manager
To: All employees
Date: 13 September 15
Subject: Maintenance Work

Dear colleagues:

[163] Please be advised that our underground parking lot will be unavailable from October 2 through October 5 due to maintenance work. — [1] —. We have decided to expand the underground parking lot to provide room for more vehicles. It is scheduled to reopen on Monday, October 6. [162] Employees who drive to work are encouraged to use nearby parking lots such as the downtown public parking lot, and the company will reimburse any parking costs. — [2] —. [161] Also, employees can discuss with their department heads the possibility of working from home if they have a long commute. — [3] —.

We will have ten additional parking spaces once the maintenance work has been completed. — [4] —. If you are a full-time employee and have worked over three years, you can get one of them via lottery. Please call me at ext. 1123 to enter the lottery.

Thank you for your understanding and cooperation in advance.

Wesley Kim
Personnel Manager
Hayward Accounting Firm

161-163 다음 회람을 참조하시오.

발신: **Wesley Kim**, 인사부장
수신: 전 직원
날짜: 9월 13일
제목: 시설 관리 작업

동료 직원 여러분,

[163] 시설 관리 작업으로 인해 우리 지하 주차장을 10월 2일부터 5일까지 이용할 수 없다는 점에 유의하시기 바랍니다. 우리는 차량들이 들어갈 충분한 공간을 제공하기 위해 지하 주차장을 확장하기로 결정했습니다. 주차장은 10월 6일 월요일에 다시 문을 열 예정입니다. [162] 차를 운전해 출근하는 직원들은 시내 공영주차장과 같은 인근의 주차장들을 이용하시기를 권해 드리며, 발생되는 모든 주차 비용은 환급해 드릴 것입니다. 또한, [161] 통근 거리가 길 경우에 소속 부서장과 재택 근무 여부를 논의하실 수 있습니다.

이번 시설 관리 작업이 완료되고 나면 10개의 추가 주차 공간이 생깁니다. 정규직 직원이면서 3년 넘게 재직해 오신 직원이라면, 제비 뽑기 방식을 통해 이 공간들 중의 하나를 배정 받으실 수 있습니다. 이 제비 뽑기를 하려면 제게 내선번호 1123으로 전화 주십시오.

여러분의 양해와 협조에 대해 미리 감사 드립니다.

Wesley Kim
인사부장
Hayward Accounting Firm

어휘 maintenance 시설 관리 Please be advised that ~ 임에 유의하세요 underground parking lot 지하 주차장 unavailable 이용할 수 없는 due to ~로 인해 be scheduled to do ~할 예정이다 reopen 다시 문을 열다, 재개장하다 be encouraged to do ~하도록 권고되다 nearby 근처의 such as ~와 같은 reimburse ~을 환급해 주다 incur (비용) ~을 발생시키다 department head 부서장 possibility 가능성 work from home 자택 근무하다 commute 통근 additional 추가의 once 일단 ~하면, ~하자마자 via ~을 통해 lottery 추첨, 제비뽑기 ext.(extention) 내선전화(번호) enter ~에 참가하다 cooperation 협조 in advance 미리

161

What can employees discuss with their supervisors?

(A) Transition to permanent employment
(B) A lottery drawing for a parking space
(C) The possibility of telecommuting
(D) Reimbursement for their travel expenses

문제 해설

직원들의 각자의 직장 상사와 논의할 수 있는 것이 무엇인지 묻고 있으므로 지문 초반부에서 키워드인 직장 상사, 즉 supervisors 또는 이와 유사한 표현이 제시되는 부분을 중심으로 논의 소재를 파악하는 것이 현명하다. 회람 첫 단락에서 Also, employees can discuss with their department heads the possibility of working from home if they have a long commute라며 통근 거리가 긴 직원들의 경우에 소속부서장과 자택 근무 가능성에 관해 논의할 수 있음을 밝히고 있다. 이 때 키워드인 supervisors는 지문에서 department heads로 바뀌어 등장하고 있다. 따라서 정답은 (C)가 되겠다.

★★ 세부사항

인사부장의 말에 따르면, 직원들은 각자의 상사와 무엇에 관해 이야기할 수 있는가?
(A) 정규직 채용으로의 전환
(B) 주차 공간에 대한 제비 뽑기
(C) 자택 근무의 가능성
(D) 출장 경비에 대한 환급

토익 분석

세부사항을 묻는 문제는 질문에서 빠른 키워드(핵심어) 파악이 중요하며 해당 키워드가 등장하는 부분을 중심으로 단서를 파악하는 것이 관건이다. 다만 질문에서의 키워드는 지문에서 유사 어휘나 표현으로 바뀔 수 있다

★★★ 사실 유추

시내 공영 주차장에 관해 사실일 것 같은 내용은 무엇인가?
(A) 10월 6일에 다시 문을 열 것이다.
(B) 유료 주차장이다.
(C) Hayward Accounting Firm에서 멀리 떨어져 있다.
(D) 최근에 확장되었다.

토익 분석

유추 문제의 키워드(핵심어) 파악이 중요하며 지문에서 해당 키워드가 등장하는 부분을 중심으로 제공되는 정보를 토대로 유추 가능한 선택지의 내용을 정답으로 택일해야 한다.

What is probably true of the downtown public parking lot?

(A) It will reopen on October 6.
(B) It charges for parking.
(C) It is far from Hayward Accounting Firm.
(D) It was recently expanded.

문제 해설

시내 공영 주차장에 관해 사실일 것 같은 내용을 유추해야 하는 문제이므로 지문에서 downtown public parking lot란 키워드가 등장하는 부분에서 제시되는 정보를 빠르게 찾아 관련 정보를 토대로 사실 가능성이 높은 내용을 파악해야 한다. 첫 단락에서 Employees who drive to work are encouraged to use nearby parking lots such as downtown public parking lot, and the company will reimburse any parking costs라며 시내 공영 주차장과 같은 인근 주차장에 주차하여 발생하는 모든 비용은 회사에서 환급해줄 것이란 방침을 알리고 있다. 따라서 이를 통해 주차장이 유료 주차장임을 유추할 수 있으므로 이에 대해 언급한 (B)가 정답이다. 아울러 해당 주차장이 인근 주차장(nearby parking lots) 중의 한 예시로 언급되어 있으므로 (C)는 오답임에 주의하도록 한다.

★★★ 문장의 위치

[1], [2], [3], [4]로 표기된 위치들 중에서 다음 문장이 들어가기에 가장 적절한 곳은 어디인가?
"우리는 차량들이 들어갈 충분한 공간을 제공하기 위해 지하 주차장을 확장하기로 결정했습니다."
(A) [1]
(B) [2]
(C) [3]
(D) [4]

토익 분석

강사로서 문제풀이 시간을 단축시킬 수 있는 방법으로 제시할만한 방법은 [3] – [4] – [1] – [2] 순서로 정답 비중이 높기 때문에 주어진 문장 내용을 순차적으로 해당 위치에 삽입해보며 내용 연결성을 비교하며 문제를 풀이하는 방법을 권고한다.

In which of the positions marked [1], [2], [3], and [4] does the following sentence best belong?

"We have decided to expand the underground parking lot to provide room for more vehicles."

(A) [1]
(B) [2]
(C) [3]
(D) [4]

문제 해설

주어진 문장이 위치해야 하는 곳을 묻는 문제이므로 주어진 문장의 의미를 이해한 후 이와 내용적 연계성을 지닌 적절한 위치를 파악해야 한다. 제시된 문장은 주차 공간 확장과 관련된 회사의 결정을 알리는 내용이다. 따라서 확장 공사를 위한 일정을 언급하는 첫 단락의 첫 문장 뒤에 위치해 지하 주차장 공사에 대한 이유를 알리는 흐름이 되어야 자연스러우므로 (A)가 정답이다.

Questions 164-167 refer to the following e-mail.

To: Chris Bundy <cbundy@dahmercorp.com>
From: Yuliana Lim <ylim@trentonhotel.com>
Subject: Trenton Hotel Reservation Inquiry
Date: August 19

Dear Mr. Bundy,

I just received your e-mail regarding your upcoming reservations at our hotel. [164] You are correct that your September stay will be eligible for our reward points plan for frequent guests. — [1] —.

In your e-mail, you mentioned that you would like to check in early on September 1. As you are probably aware, our normal check-in time is not until 2 P.M.but we will do our best to have your room ready by noon. — [2] —. You may call the front desk in advance to ask about this. If you choose to turn up early and your assigned room is still being prepared, [165] you may leave your luggage with the front desk staff, and they will store it securely while you relax or walk around town.

[166] You are also correct about the issue regarding your July reservation at our hotel. Due to a computer error, we failed to refund the $100 security deposit after you checked out. I have now personally made sure that the amount was deposited back into your account this morning. — [3] —. [167] I apologize for this oversight and any inconvenience it may have caused you. To make amends for this mistake, I have arranged for you to receive a gift certificate that can be exchanged for two tickets to see any film at the nearby Odeon Cinema.

If you have any further questions, please contact me directly at 555-5674. — [4] —.

Regards,

Yuliana Lim
Trenton Hotel Reservations Manager

164-167 다음 이메일을 참조하시오.

발신: Chris Bundy <cbundy@dahmercorp.com>
수신: Yuliana Lim <ylim@trentonhotel.com>
제목: Trenton 호텔 예약 문의
날짜: 8월 9일

Bundy 씨께,

저희 호텔 예약에 관한 이메일을 방금 받았습니다. [164] 귀하의 9월 투숙이 단골 고객들을 위한 보상 포인트 방침에 해당한다는 점은 맞습니다.

이메일에 귀하는 9월 1일 예정된 시간보다 일찍 입실하길 바란다고 언급하셨습니다. 알고 계시듯이 일반적인 입실 시간은 2시부터지만, 12시까지 객실을 준비할 수 있도록 노력하겠습니다. 이와 관련해서는 안내 데스크에 미리 연락해 여쭤보시길 바랍니다. 만약 일찍 오셨는데 객실이 준비 중이면, 안내 데스크 직원들에게 짐을 맡기셔도 됩니다. [165] 잠시 쉬거나 마을 주변을 산책하시는 동안에 직원들이 짐을 안전하게 보관해드릴 것입니다.

[166] 귀하의 7월 예약에 관한 사안 또한 정확합니다. 컴퓨터 오류로 인해 저희는 귀하가 퇴실한 이후 보증금 100달러를 돌려드리지 못했습니다. 오늘 아침 보증금이 귀하의 계좌로 다시 입금되는 것을 직접 확인했습니다. [167] 업무 누락과 이로 인해 겪으셨을지도 모를 고객님의 불편함에 사과를 드립니다. 이를 보상해드리고자, 근처 Odeon 극장에서 원하시는 영화를 보실 수 있는 두 장의 영화 상품권을 준비했습니다.

추가로 질문이 있으신 경우, 555-5674로 제게 직접 문의하시기 바랍니다.

Yuliana Lim
Trenton 호텔 예약 관리자

164

What is the purpose of the e-mail?

(A) To inform a guest that a check-out time has been changed
(B) To request that a guest send an advance payment
(C) To notify a guest that a room is unavailable on a certain date
(D) To confirm that a guest is eligible for a special program

문제 해설

이메일의 목적은 대개 이메일 초반에서 직접적으로 언급되는 것이 일반적이다. 이메일 초반 You are correct that your September stay will be eligible for our reward points plan for frequent guests를 통해 손님이 특별 프로그램에 대한 자격 요건을 갖추고 있다는 사실을 확인해주고자 하는 목적의 이메일임을 알 수 있다. 따라서 정답은 (D)가 되겠다.

★★ 지문의 목적

이메일의 목적은 무엇인가?
(A) 체크 아웃 시간이 변경되었음을 손님에게 알리기 위해서
(B) 고객에게 선불금을 요청하기 위해서
(C) 특정 날짜에 방이 없음을 손님에게 알리기 위해서
(D) 손님이 특별 프로그램에 대한 자격 요건을 갖추고 있음을 확인해주기 위해서

토익 분석

이메일의 주제/목적은 이메일 초반 2-3문장의 내용을 통해 파악할 수 있으며 주제/목적 문제의 선택지들은 굳이 먼저 읽어볼 필요가 없다.

★★ 진위

Trenton 호텔에 대해 언급된 것은 무엇인가?
(A) 피트니스 센터 옆에 위치하고 있다.
(B) 최근 일부 객실을 보수했다.
(C) 손님의 가방을 보관해준다.
(D) Bundy 씨에게 할인된 객실 요금에 대해 통보했다.

토익 분석

진위 문제의 키워드가 지문 전반에 걸쳐 언급되는 경우에는 선택지의 내용을 키워드로 삼아 지문에서 해당 내용이 언급되는지 여부를 빠르게 파악하며 문제를 풀이한다.

What is mentioned about the Trenton Hotel?

(A) It is situated next to a fitness center
(B) It has recently renovated some of its rooms.
(C) It allows guests to store their bags.
(D) It has notified Mr. Bundy about reduced room rates.

문제 해설

Trenton 호텔과 직접적으로 관련이 있는 정보가 제시되는 부분에 집중해야 할 필요가 있다. 첫 번째 단락은 이메일의 목적이 드러나는 부분이며 마지막 단락은 초반부 내용을 통해 호텔에서 발생한 컴퓨터 오류로 인한 문제점이 언급되는 부분임을 알 수 있다. 따라서 두 번째 단락을 중심으로 단서를 파악하는 것이 바람직하며, 구체적으로 두 번째 단락 후반 you may leave your luggage with the front desk staff, and they will store it securely while you relax or walk around town을 통해 호텔에서는 손님의 짐을 보관해준다는 점을 파악할 수 있다. 그러므로 정답은 (C)이다.

166

★★ 세부사항

지난 번 Trenton 호텔에 투숙했을 당시, Bundy 씨는 어떠한 문제점을 경험했는가?
(A) 룸서비스가 초과 청구되었다.
(B) 자신의 보증금을 받지 못했다.
(C) 개인 소지품의 일부를 분실하였다.
(D) 표준 입실 시간에 입실하는 것이 불가했다.

토익 분석

실질적으로 마지막 문제이며 마지막 문제의 단서는 마지막 단락에서 제시되므로 마지막 단락 후반부에서 역순으로 내용을 확인해가며 단서를 파악하는 것이 효율적이다.

What problem did Mr. Bundy experience when he last stayed at the Trenton Hotel?

(A) He was overcharged for room service.
(B) He did not receive his security deposit.
(C) He lost some of his personal belongings.
(D) He was unable to check in at the standard time.

문제 해설

이메일의 마지막 단락 초반 You are also correct about the issue regarding your July reservation at our hotel. Due to a computer error, we failed to refund the $100 security deposit after you checked out라고 언급된 내용을 통해 지난 7월에 투숙했을 때 컴퓨터 오류로 인해 퇴실 이후에도 보증금 100달러를 돌려주지 못했음을 알 수 있다. 따라서 정답은 (B)가 되겠다.

167

★★★ 문장의 위치

[1], [2], [3], [4]로 표기된 위치들 중에서 다음 문장이 들어가기에 가장 적절한 곳은 어디인가?
"이러한 누락과 이로 인해 겪으셨을지도 모를 고객님의 불편함에 사과를 드립니다."
(A) [1]
(B) [2]
(C) [3]
(D) [4]

토익 분석

강사로서 문제풀이 시간을 단축시킬 수 있는 방법으로 제시할만한 방법은 [3] - [4] - [1] - [2] 순서로 정답 비중이 높기 때문에 주어진 문장 내용을 순차적으로 해당 위치에 삽입해보며 내용 연결성을 비교하며 문제를 풀이하는 것이다.

In which of the positions marked [1], [2], [3], and [4] does the following sentence best belong?

"I apologize for this oversight and any inconvenience it may have caused you."

(A) [1]
(B) [2]
(C) [3]
(D) [4]

문제 해설

주어진 문장이 위치해야 하는 곳을 묻는 문제이므로 주어진 문장의 의미를 이해한 후 이와 내용적 연계성을 지닌 적절한 위치를 파악해야 한다. 우선 주어진 문장 I apologize for this oversight and any inconvenience it may have caused you는 이러한 누락과 이로 인해 겪으셨을지도 모를 불편함에 사과한다는 내용이므로 이에 앞서 불편함을 초래할 만큼 무엇을 누락/간과했는지 이를 밝히는 내용이 위치해야 함을 알 수 있다. 따라서 고객의 불편함을 초래할 수도 있었을 업무상의 누락 사항, 즉 보증금 미반납과 보상 포인트 방침 미적용에 관해 모두 밝힌 직후인 [3]이 적절한 위치임을 알 수 있다. 그러므로 정답은 (C)가 되겠다.

Questions 168-171 refer to the following article.

Calvert City News
A Chance to Escape the City

By Kelly McGowan

MAY 23—Rather than focusing on activities and restaurants based here in Calvert City, [169] I decided to make this week's column a little different by discussing the beautiful town of Grey Bridge, just 20 kilometers north of the city limits. Grey Bridge is a quaint, peaceful little town that offers everyone a chance to escape the noise and chaos of the city. It also [168] boasts a surprising number of things to do and places to eat. Below, you can read my suggestions for planning an enjoyable day-trip to Grey Bridge.

(8:30 A.M.) When you arrive, you should head straight for Dale Bakery. Although it is primarily a bakery, selling various breads and pastries to customers, it also has a dining area and boasts a limited, yet delicious menu. It has been a long-time fixture in Grey Bridge, and it has become particularly well-known for its delicious breakfast offerings. Try the full English breakfast with some freshly brewed coffee.

(9:45 A.M.) After gaining energy from your delicious breakfast, I recommend taking a walk along nearby Glenford River. Not only is the entire river area picturesque, but it contains several sites of interest. During your walk, stop to check out the many sculptures and murals at the Balgay Art Park, and don't miss the Alton Farm Petting Zoo, which will be of particular interest to young children.

(1:30 P.M.) Once you've worked up an appetite walking along the river, head back into town and visit Alma's Country Kitchen for lunch. Although it has not been open long, it has already established itself as one of the town's premier eateries. [170] Alma's serves dishes that are made using only produce from nearby farms and suppliers, and I would specifically single out its expertly-cooked grilled salmon and chopped salad for special praise. Its menu can be viewed online at www.almascountrykitchen.co.uk. Be warned, however, that you may face a long wait if you go there on the weekend. [171] Also, it's possible to take out certain foods, such as baguettes and baked potatoes, which means you can enjoy them in nearby Meadow Park if you choose. This is a great choice when the weather is nice

(3:00 P.M.) For the remainder of your day in Grey Bridge, try taking a guided tour of Grey Bridge Cathedral. This stunning building was built in the late-fifteenth century and is preserved and maintained by the Grey Bridge Cultural Heritage Society. [171] One wing of the cathedral has been converted into an art gallery, which features various artworks from local painters and sculptors. Admission to both the cathedral and its gallery is free from Monday to Thursday. At all other times, a ticket must be purchased at the main entrance. Check www.greybridgecathedral.org for current rates.

[171] Do you have any of your own suggestions regarding what to do during daytrips to Grey Bridge? If so, please send your thoughts to ggilford@calvertnews.org.

168-171 다음 기사를 참조하시오.

Calvert City 뉴스

도시에서 벗어날 수 있는 기회
Kelly McGowan

5월 23일–이곳 Calvert City에서 벌어지는 활동과 레스토랑들에 초점을 맞추는 대신, 우리 도시 경계에서 북쪽으로 불과 20킬로미터 밖에 떨어지지 않은 아름다운 마을인 Grey Bridge 에 관한 이야기를 하는 것으로 [169] 이번 주의 칼럼을 조금 다르게 작성하기로 결정했습니다. Grey Bridge는 오래되고 평화로운 작은 마을로서, 모든 사람들에게 도시의 소음과 혼란스러움으로부터 벗어날 수 있는 기회를 제공해 줍니다. 이곳은 또한 놀랄 정도로 많은 활동과 음식을 즐길 수 있는 장소를 [168] 자랑합니다. 다음을 보시면, Grey Bridge로의 즐거운 당일 여행 계획에 관한 제 제안들을 읽어 보실 수 있습니다.

(오전 8시 30분) 도착하시면, 곧장 Dale Bakery으로 향하셔야 합니다. 기본적으로는 다양한 빵과 패스트리들을 고객들에게 판매하는 제과점이지만, 또한 식사 공간으로서 제한적이면서도 맛이 뛰어난 메뉴를 자랑합니다. 이곳은 Grey Bridge의 터줏대감 같은 곳이며, 맛있는 아침 식사 제공 서비스로 특히 잘 알려져 온 곳입니다. 갓 내린 커피와 함께 완전한 영국식 아침 식사를 즐겨 보시기 바랍니다.

(오전 9시 45분) 맛있는 아침 식사로 에너지를 얻으신 후에는, 근처의 Glenford River를 따라 산책해 보시기를 권해 드립니다. 강 전체 지역이 그림 같은 풍경을 지니고 있을 뿐만 아니라, 사람들이 관심을 끄는 여러 지점들이 포함되어 있습니다. 산책하시는 동안, 잠시 멈춰 Dalgay Art Park에 있는 여러 조각품과 벽화들을 확인해 보시기 바라며, 특히 어린이들의 관심을 끌 수 있는 Alton Farm Petting Zoo도 놓치지 마십시오.

(오후 1시 30분) 강을 따라 걸으면서 식욕을 북돋우셨다면, 다시 마을로 돌아가 점심 식사를 위해 Alma's Country Kitchen을 방문해 보십시오. 개장한지 오래된 곳은 아니지만, 이미 이 마을 최고의 식당들 중 한 곳으로서의 명성을 얻은 곳입니다. [170] Alma's는 오직 인근의 농장과 공급업체들을 통해 구입한 농산물만을 사용한 요리를 제공하며, 저는 특히 전문적으로 조리된 그릴에 구운 연어와 잘게 자른 샐러드를 꼽아 칭찬하고 싶습니다. 이곳의 메뉴는 www.almascountrykitchen.co.uk에서 온라인으로 보실 수 있습니다. 하지만 주말에 가실 경우에 긴 대기 시간과 맞닥뜨리실 수 있다는 점에 주의하시기 바랍니다. 또한, [171] 바게트나 구운 감자 등과 같은 특정 음식을 포장해 가실 수 있는데, 이는 원하실 경우 근처에 있는 Meadow Park에서 이 음식들을 즐기실 수 있다는 것을 의미합니다. 이는 날씨가 좋을 경우 아주 좋은 선택입니다.

(오후 3시) Grey Bridge 에서의 남은 시간 동안에는, 가이드를 동반한 Grey Bridge Cathedral 견학을 한 번 해 보십시오. 이 놀라운 건물은 15세기 후반에 지어졌으며, Grey Bridge Cultural Heritage Society에 의해 보존 및 유지 관리되고 있습니다. [171] 이 대성당의 한 부속 건물은 미술관으로 개조되었으며, 지역 미술가와 조각가들이 만든 다양한 미술품들을 특징으로 하고 있습니다. 성당과 미술관 모두 월요일부터 목요일까지 입장료가 무료입니다. 그 외의 다른 날에는, 중앙 출입구에서 티켓을 구입하실 수 있습니다. www.greybridgecathedral.org을 통해 현재의 요금을 확인해 보십시오.

[171] Grey Bridge에서의 당일 여행 동안 할 수 있는 활동과 관련된 여러분만의 의견이 있으신가요? 그러시다면, 여러분의 생각을 ggilford@calvertnews.org로 보내 주시기 바랍니다.

어휘 single out A for special praise ~만 꼽아 칭찬하다, ~을 지목해 칭찬하다 remainder 나머지, 남은 것 wing 부속 건물

168

★★ 유사어

1번째 단락, 5번째 줄에 있는 단어 "boasts"와 의미가 가장 가까운 어휘는 무엇인가?
(A) 수여하다
(B) 발표하다
(C) 갖추게 하다
(D) 제공하다

토익 분석

유사어 문제는 해당 어휘가 포함된 문장을 비롯하여 그 전후 문장 내용을 파악한 후 해당 어휘와 유사한 의미를 지닌 어휘를 선택하라

The word "boasts" in paragraph 1, line 8, is closest in meaning to

(A) awards
(B) announces
(C) equips
(D) offers

문제 해설

boasts 뒤에 목적어로 제시된 a surprising number of things to do and places to eat는 할 수 있는 일과 먹을 곳이 아주 많다는 의미의 명사구인데, 이는 해당 마을에서 제공하는 것과 같으므로 boasts 의 유사어로는 '제공하다'를 뜻을 지닌 offers가 적합하다고 할 수 있다. 그러므로 (D)가 정답이다.

169

★★★ 유추

McGowan 씨의 칼럼에 관해 암시되는 것은 무엇인가?
(A) 자주 Grey Bridge에 초점을 맞춘다.
(B) 보통 인터뷰를 포함한다.
(C) 해당 출판물의 주간 특집 기사이다.
(D) 해당 출판물의 최신 칼럼이다.

토익 분석

유추 문제의 키워드가 혹은 키워드에 관한 내용이 지문 전반에 걸쳐 언급되고 있는 상태에서 적절한 유추 내용을 파악해야 한다면 선택지에 나온 내용을 먼저 파악한 후 선택지의 내용을 유추할 수 있는 근거가 지문에 제시되는지 여부를 역으로 확인하는 방식으로 문제를 풀이하라.

What is suggested about Ms. McGowan's column?

(A) It often focuses on Grey Bridge.
(B) It ordinarily includes interviews.
(C) It is a weekly feature in a publication.
(D) It is the publication's newest column.

문제 해설

McGowan 씨의 칼럼에 관해 유추할 수 있는 내용을 묻는 문제이나 사실상 기사문 전체의 내용이 McGowan 씨의 칼럼이므로 선택지의 내용을 먼저 숙지한 후 기사에서 이를 유추할 수 있는 정보가 제시되는지 여부를 파악하며 역으로 정답을 찾는 것이 현명하다. 첫 단락의 시작 부분에 필자는 이번 주의 칼럼은 조금 다르게 쓰기로 했다며 I decided to make this week's column a little different라고 언급하고 있다. 따라서 이를 토대로 해당 칼럼은 매주 실리는 칼럼임을 유추할 수 있으므로 이를 언급하고 있는 (C)가 정답이다. 아울러 이 내용을 통해 이미 지속적으로 실리고 있는 칼럼임을 알 수 있으므로 (D)는 오답이 되겠다.

170

According to the article, what is true about Alma's Country Kitchen?

(A) It offers a wide variety of baked goods.
(B) It opens for business at 1:30 P.M. every day.
(C) It uses only locally-sourced ingredients.
(D) It is generally less busy on weekends.

문제 해설

Alma's Country Kitchen에 관해 사실인 내용을 묻고 있으므로 기사문에서 Alma's Country Kitchen이 등장하는 부분을 중심으로 단서를 파악해야 한다. Alma's Country Kitchen과 관련된 정보가 제시된 네 번째 단락에서 Alma's는 오직 인근의 농장과 공급업체들을 통해 구입한 농산물만을 사용한 요리를 제공한다며 Alma's serves dishes that are made using only produce from nearby farms and suppliers라고 언급하고 있으므로 이를 토대로 (C)가 정답임을 알 수 있다. 아울러 주말에는 대기 시간이 길다는 말이 있으므로 (D)는 오답이다.

★★ 진위

기사 내용에 따르면, **Alma's Country Kitchen**에 관해 사실인 것은 무엇인가?
(A) 아주 다양한 제과 제품을 제공한다.
(B) 매일 오후 1시 30분에 영업을 위해 문을 연다.
(C) 오직 현지에서 구한 재료만을 사용한다.
(D) 일반적으로 주말에 덜 바쁘다.

토익 분석

세부사항을 묻는 문제는 질문에서 빠른 키워드(핵심어) 파악이 중요하며 해당 키워드가 등장하는 부분을 중심으로 단서를 파악하는 것이 관건이다. 다만 질문에서의 키워드는 지문에서 유사 어휘나 표현으로 바뀔 수 있다

171

What is NOT a recommendation made by Mr. McGowan?

(A) Purchasing a ticket for the cathedral in advance
(B) Taking restaurant food to a local park
(C) Visiting an exhibition of paintings
(D) Submitting ideas for things to do in Grey Bridge

문제 해설

McGowan 씨가 권하는 사항이 아닌 내용을 묻고 있는 문제이나, McGowan 씨가 권고하는 내용은 지문 전반에 걸쳐 등장하고 있다. 그러므로 선택지의 내용을 간략하게 정리해 이를 키워드로 활용하여 지문에서 해당 내용이 제시되고 있는지 여부를 파악하며 문제를 풀이해야 한다. 네 번째 단락에서 Meadow Park에서 음식을 즐기는 일, it's possible to take out certain foods, ~ you can enjoy them in nearby Meadow Park을 통해 (B)의 내용을, 다섯 번째 단락에서 언급하는 미술관으로 개조된 곳, One wing of the cathedral has been converted into an art gallery에서 (C)의 내용을 확인할 수 있다. 또한 마지막 단락에서 Grey Bridge에서의 여행과 관련된 의견을 전해 달라고 요청하는 부분, Do you have any of your own suggestions ~ daytrips to Grey Bridge?에서 (D)의 내용도 확인 가능하다. 하지만 성당 입장과 관련해 미리 티켓을 구입하라는 내용은 찾아 볼 수 없으므로 (A)가 정답이다.

★★★ 진위

McGowan 씨가 권하는 사항이 아닌 것은 무엇인가?
(A) 미리 성당 입장권을 구입하는 것
(B) 레스토랑 음식을 갖고 지역 공원으로 가는 것
(C) 그림들이 전시된 곳을 방문하는 것
(D) **Grey Bridge**에서의 활동에 대한 아이디어를 제출하는 것

토익 분석

진위 문제의 키워드가 지문 전반에 걸쳐 언급되는 경우 선택지의 내용을 키워드로 삼아 지문에서 해당 내용이 언급되는지 여부를 빠르게 파악하며 문제를 풀이해야 한다.

Questions 172-175 refer to the online chat discussion.

Neil Webster [오전 09:34]: 안녕하세요, Lora, 주문 번호 3920의 환불 문제에 무슨 일이 생긴 건지 아시나요? 고객께서 진행 상황을 알고 싶어 하세요.

Lora McDaniel [오전 09:35]: [172] 요가 매트와 아령이 포함된 주문 아니었나요? 이미 처리된 것으로 생각했는데요.

Neil Webster [오전 09:36]: 그 고객께서는 아직 비용을 받지 못했다고 말씀하셨어요. [173] 그분께서 제품을 반품하고 환불을 요청하신지 벌써 2주나 됐어요.

Lora McDaniel [오전 09:37]: 그럼 무슨 일이지 모르겠네요. 고객 서비스부에 확인해 봅시다.

Lora McDaniel [오전 09:39]: [174] Max, 주문 번호 3920에 대한 환불 처리 상황 좀 확인해 주시겠어요? 그 고객께서 여전히 비용을 받지 못하셨어요.

Max Francis [오전 09:42]: 처리 과정에서 실수가 있었던 것 같습니다. 제가 바로 해 드릴 수는 있지만, [175] 그 고객께서 비용을 돌려 받으시기까지 여전히 일주일이 걸릴 겁니다. 그래도 괜찮은가요?

Neil Webster [오전 09:43]: [175] 어쩔 수 없을 것 같아요. 하지만 처리해 주시는 것에 대해 감사 드립니다.

어휘 refund 환불(금) progress 진행 상황, 진척 contain ~을 포함하다 process ~을 처리하다 receive ~을 받다 payment 지불(금) since ~한 이후로 return ~을 반품하다, 반환하다 request ~을 요청하다 what's going on 어떻게 된 일인지 then 그럼, 그렇다면 check with ~에게 확인해 보다 look up (컴퓨터나 자료 등을 통해) ~을 확인해 보다, 찾아 보다 It looks like ~인 것 같다 immediately 즉시, 바로 it can't be helped 어쩔 수 없는 일이다 take care of ~을 처리하다 though (문장 끝에서) 하지만

Neil Webster [09:34 A.M.]: Hey Lora, do you know what's happening to the refund on order #3920? The customer wants to know the progress.

Lora McDaniel [09:35 A.M.]: [172] Wasn't that the order containing the yoga mat and dumbbells? I thought they were already processed.

Neil Webster [09:36 A.M.]: The customer said that he hasn't received the payment yet. [173] It has already been two weeks since he returned the products and requested a refund.

Lora McDaniel [09:37 A.M.]: I'm not sure what's going on then. Let me check with customer services.

Lora McDaniel [09:39 A.M.]: [174] Max, can you look up the refund process on order #3920? The customer still hasn't received the payment.

Max Francis [09:42 A.M.]: It looks like there was a mistake in the processing. I can work on it immediately, [175] but it will still take a week for the customer to receive the payment. Is that alright?

Neil Webster [09:43 A.M.]: [175] I guess we don't have a choice. Thanks for taking care of it though.

172

★ 화자의 직장

메시지 작성자들은 어느 업계에서 근무하고 있는가?
(A) 부동산 중개업체
(B) 운동 장비 매장
(C) 회계 법인
(D) 피트니스 센터

토익 분석

업종/직장을 묻는 질문은 지문에서 업종/직장과 관련된 어휘나 표현을 파악하는 것이 관건이다.

What type of business do the writers work for?
(A) A real estate agency
(B) An exercise equipment store
(C) An accounting firm
(D) A fitness center

문제 해설

화자들의 직장에 대해 묻는 문제이다. 9시 35분 메시지에 고객의 주문품으로 요가 매트와 아령, 즉 yoga mat와 dumbbells이 언급되고 있으므로 화자들의 직장으로는 운동 장비를 판매하는 업체가 적절함을 알 수 있다. 따라서 (B)가 정답이다.

173

What did the customer ask for?

(A) A refund on a previous order
(B) A change in shipping address
(C) An addition to an order
(D) An update on the order delivery

문제 해설

고객의 요청 사항을 묻고 있다. 9시 36분 메시지에서 2주 전에 제품을 반품하고 환불을 요청했다며 he returned the products and requested a refund라고 이야기하고 있다. 따라서 이를 통해 주문품에 대한 환불 요청이 이뤄지고 있음을 알 수 있으므로 (A)가 정답이다.

★★ 세부사항

고객은 무엇을 요청하고 있는가?
(A) 이전의 주문품에 대한 환불
(B) 배송 주소의 변경
(C) 주문 사항의 추가
(D) 주문품 배송에 대한 정보

토익 분석

고객의 요청사항을 묻고 있으므로 채팅하는 사람들의 대화 내용에서 고객의 요청사항이 언급되는 대화 내용을 파악하는 것이 관건이다. 각 대화자의 초반 대화 내용의 일부 주요 단어들만 확인하는 스캐닝을 통해 고객의 요청 사항이 등장하는지 여부를 빠르게 파악할 수 있다.

174

Why does Ms. McDaniel contact Mr. Francis?

(A) To ask for advice on product delivery
(B) To look up where the returned package is
(C) To find out if she can get a refund for her order
(D) To know why a refund has not been processed yet

문제 해설

McDaniel 씨가 Francis 씨에게 연락하는 이유를 묻고 있으므로 McDaniel씨의 대화 내용에서 Francis 씨에게 연락하는 이유를 파악해야 한다. McDaniel 씨가 Francis 씨에게 말을 거는 9시 39분 메시지에서, 주문 번호 3920에 대한 환불 처리 상황을 확인해 달라며 Max, can you look up the refund process on order #3920?라고 말하고 있다. 따라서 해당 환불 문제의 미처리 이유 확인이 Francis 씨에게 연락하는 목적임을 알 수 있으므로 정답은 (D)가 되겠다.

★★ 세부사항

McDaniel 씨가 Francis 씨에게 연락하는 이유는 무엇인가?
(A) 제품 배송에 대한 조언을 요청하기 위해
(B) 반품된 배송 물품이 어디 있는지 알아 보기 위해
(C) 자신의 주문품에 대한 환불을 받을 수 있는지 확인해 보기 위해
(D) 환불 문제가 아직 처리되지 않은 이유를 알아 보기 위해

토익 분석

인터넷 채팅 지문에서 특정 인물과 관련된 문제는 우선 해당 인물의 대화 내용에서 단서를 파악하는 것이 우선이며 해당 인물의 대화 내용에서 단서가 언급되지 않는 경우 그 이후 제시되는 대화 내용을 살펴보도록 한다.

175

At 9:43 A.M., what does Mr. Webster most likely mean when he writes, "I guess we don't have a choice."?

(A) He wants Mr. Francis to process the problem immediately.
(B) He is accepting the fact that it will inevitably take time to fix the problem.
(C) He does not understand why the processing takes so long.
(D) He is asking for additional help from customer services.

문제 해설

주어진 문장인 "I guess we don't have a choice."는 어쩔 수가 없을 것 같다는 의미를 지니고 있으며 이는 앞서 Francis 씨가 환불 처리가 되는 데 일주일이 걸릴 것이라고 언급하면서 그래도 괜찮은지 묻는 질문, 즉 it will still take a week for the customer to receive the payment. Is that alright? 에 대한 답변으로 제시되고 있다. 그리고 바로 뒤이어 처리해 주는 것에 대해 감사하다는 말을 덧붙이는 것으로 볼 때 주어진 문장인 "I guess we don't have a choice." 에는 시간이 걸리더라도 그렇게 처리해야 하는 상황임을 인지하고 있다는 화자의 의도가 포함되어 있음을 가늠할 수 있다. 따라서 어쩔 수 없이 시간이 걸리는 것을 받아 들인다는 의미의 (B)가 정답이다.

★★★ 화자의 의도

오전 9시 43분에, Webster 씨가 "I guess we don't have a choice."라고 썼을 때 무엇을 의미할 가능성이 가장 높은가?
(A) Francis 씨가 즉시 문제를 처리해 주기를 원한다.
(B) 문제를 해결하는 데 불가피하게 시간이 걸린다는 사실을 받아 들이고 있다.
(C) 처리 과정이 오래 걸린 이유를 이해하지 못하고 있다.
(D) 고객 서비스 부서에 의한 추가 도움을 요청하고 있다.

토익 분석

특정 표현에 담긴 화자의 의도에 대한 이해하기 위해서는 주어진 특정 표현 전후의 내용 파악이 선행되어야 한다. 난이도가 높아지는 경우에는 전체 지문의 내용을 다 파악해야만 풀 수 있는 경우도 발생한다.

176-180 다음 편지와 이메일을 참조하시오.

Simmons Heat & Air

9월 2일
Jessie Spano 씨
Dunder Miflin 기업
Swanson 가 9923
테네시 주 92929 내시빌

Spano 씨께,

지난 며칠간 저희 기록을 살펴본 결과, [178] 귀하의 회사에 설치했던 난방 시설이 거의 1년 전에 구매되었다는 것을 알게 되었습니다. [176] 이 메시지는 시스템 점검을 받아보시라고 권해드리기 위한 것입니다. 귀하의 계약서에 언급된 바와 같이, 귀하가 구입하신 제품은 5년 동안 보증수리가 가능하오니, 결함이 있는 부속품들을 무료로 교체하실 수 있습니다. 시스템 방문 점검을 받으시기 편한 일정을 이메일로 보내주시기만 하면 됩니다.

현재 기계가 잘 작동된다고 생각하실 지 몰라도, 전체적인 점검을 하여 마모되거나 고장날 만한 것이 없는지 확인하는 일은 절대 나쁘지 않습니다. 그것이 장기적으로 볼 때 큰 돈을 절약하는 것입니다. [177] 겨울철에는 많은 점검 요청, 가정 방문, 그리고 수리 서비스들로 인해 매우 바쁘기 때문에 지금이 서비스를 받기에 최적의 시기라 할 수 있습니다.

겨울철 동안 안락하고 따뜻하실 수 있도록 가능한 빨리 저희에게 연락주세요. 606-555-0994로 전화 주시거나 customerservice@simmonshna.com으로 이메일을 주세요.

J. K. Simmons J. K. Simmons
사장
Simmons Heat & Air

어휘 go through 살펴보다, 조사하다 examine 검토하다, 점검하다 as noted 언급된 대로 come with ~이 딸려오다 warranty 보증(서) defective 결함있는, 하자있는 parts 부품 for free 무료로 come by 방문하다 overall 전반적인 close to ~에 가깝다 wear out 마모되다 in the long run 장기적으로 besides 게다가, 뿐만 아니라 get busy 바빠지다 get in touch with ~와 연락하다 cozy 안락한

Questions 176-180 refer to the following letter and e-mail

Simmons Heat & Air

September 2
Ms. Jessie Spano
Dunder Miflin Corp.
9923 Swanson Street
Nashville, TN 92929

Dear Ms. Spano,

We were going through our records in the past few days and [178]found that the heating unit you installed at your company was purchased almost a year ago. [176] This message is a recommendation to have your system examined. As noted in your contract, your purchase comes with a five-year warranty, so you can have any defective parts replaced for free. Just send us an e-mail to schedule a convenient time for us to come by and check the unit.

Even if you think the unit is working fine right now, it is never a bad thing to have an overall check up and make sure nothing is close to wearing out or breaking. It will save you lots of money in the long run. [177] Now is the best time to schedule a service check because the winter months can get very busy with requests, house calls, and service repairs.

Get in touch with us as soon as you can to ensure that you are cozy and warm throughout the winter months. You can call us at 606-555-0994 or e-mail at customerservice@simmonshna.com.

Sincerely,

J. K. Simmons *J. K. Simmons*
President
Simmons Heat & Air

수신: customerservice@simmonshna.com
발신: jspano@dundermif.com
날짜: 4월 5일
제목: 난방 시설 점검

Simmons 씨께,

현재 저희의 난방 시설 점검에 관한 편지를 받았습니다. [178] 귀하의 말씀이 맞습니다. 저희가 구매 이후 한번도 시설을 점검하지 않았습니다. 시설이 효율적으로 작동되고 있는지 확인하기 위해 적절한 점검을 받아야 할 시간인 것 같습니다. 다음 주 중에 방문해 주실 수 있나요?

저는 또한 서비스 기사님이 저희 냉방 시스템을 점검해주시길 바랍니다. [179] 현재 저희 에어컨이 낡아서 말썽이 많기 때문에 새로운 제품을 구매하려 [180] 물색 중에 있습니다. 근무시간이 오전 9시부터 오후 6시까지이니, 서비스

To: customerservice@simmonshna.com
From: jspano@dundermif.com
Date: September 5
Subject: Heating Unit Inspection

Dear Mr. Simmons,

I received your letter about inspecting my current heating system. [178] You are correct: our unit has not been examined since we purchased it. I do think it is time we should get a proper inspection to ensure that it is running efficiently. Would it be possible to send someone out next week?

I also would like the service technician to check our current air conditioning system. We are [180] looking into getting a new one because [179] our current one is getting old and unreliable. We are in the office from 9 A.M. until 6 P.M., so you can send a service technician any time we are here. Just e-mail and inform me when your technician will be coming by.

Thank you.

Jessie Spano
Director of Operations
Dunder Miflin Corp.

기사님을 근무시간 중에만 보내주시면 됩니다. 기사님이 언제 오실지만 이메일로 알려 주세요.

감사합니다.

Jessie Spano
관리이사
Dunder Miflin Corp.

어휘 assessment 평가 technician 기술자 air-conditioning system 냉방 시스템 unreliable 믿을 수 없는 inform 통보하다

176

What is the purpose of the letter?

(A) To recommend a service
(B) To report test retake days
(C) To cancel an appointment
(D) To inquire about a replacement part

문제 해설

편지의 목적은 주로 편지의 초반부에서 직접적으로 제시된다 편지의 첫 번째 단락 중반 This message is a recommendation to have your system examined를 통해 편지의 목적은 상대에게 시스템 점검을 권하기 위함임을 알 수 있다. 따라서 정답은 (A)이다.

★ 편지의 목적

이 편지의 목적은 무엇인가?
(A) 서비스를 추천하기 위해서
(B) 재시험 날짜를 보고하기 위해서
(C) 약속을 취소하기 위해서
(D) 교환 부품에 대해 문의하기 위해서

토익 분석

편지의 주제/목적은 단락 구분이 있는 경우 첫 번째 단락 초반 2-3문장에서 제시된다. 다만 주제/목적 문제의 난이도가 높아지는 경우 주제/목적은 두 번째 단락의 초반 2-3문장에서 다루게 된다는 점에 주의한다.

177

According to Mr. Simmons, why should an inspection be scheduled promptly?

(A) Winter weather has damaged some components.
(B) A manufacturing error has been detected.
(C) The warranty will expire at the end of the fall.
(D) It will be difficult to schedule an inspection in winter.

문제 해설

편지의 두 번째 단락 후반 Now is the best time to schedule a service check because the winter months can get very busy with requests, house calls, and service repairs를 통해 겨울철에는 요청이나 방문 등으로 바빠지기 때문에 지금 즉시 서비스를 받도록 권고하고 있음을 알 수 있다. 그러므로 정답은 (D)이다.

★★ 세부사항

Simmons 씨에 따르면, 즉시 점검 일정을 잡아야 하는 이유는 무엇인가?
(A) 겨울 날씨가 몇몇 부품을 손상시켰다.
(B) 제조 결함이 감지되었다.
(C) 가을이 끝나면 보증기간이 만료된다.
(D) 겨울철에는 점검 일정을 잡기 어렵다.

토익 분석

세부사항을 묻는 문제는 질문에서 빠른 키워드(핵심어) 파악이 중요하며 해당 키워드가 등장하는 부분을 중심으로 단서를 파악하는 것이 관건이다. 다만 질문에서의 키워드는 지문에서 유사 어휘나 표현으로 바뀔 수 있다. 해당 문제에서는 inspection / scheduled이 키워드에 해당된다고 할 수 있다. 따라서 지문에서 점검 또는 구체적인 일정을 잡거나 언급하는 내용이 제시되는 부분을 빠르게 찾아야 할 필요가 있다.

178

★★★ 두 지문 연계 문제

Dunder Miflin 기업에 있는 난방 시설은 언제 점검되었는
가?
(A) 1주 전
(B) 1달 전
(C) 1년 전
(D) 2년 전

토익 분석

해당 문제의 단서가 나와야 할 지문에 단서가 불충분하게
언급된다면 이는 두 지문 연계 문제이다

When was the heating system at Dunder Miflin Corp. inspected?

(A) One week ago
(B) One month ago
(C) One year ago
(D) Two years ago

문제 해설

편지의 첫 번째 단락 초반 found that the heating unit you installed at your company was
purchased almost a year ago에서 1년 전에 구입했다고 밝히고 있으며, 두 번째 지문 첫 번째 단락
중반 Your are correct: our unit has not been examined since we purchased it에서 구입한 이래로
점검을 받아 보지 않았음을 밝히고 있으므로, 구입한 시점인 1년 전에 점검이 되었다는 사실을 파악
할 수 있다. 그러므로 정답은 (C)이다.

179

★★★ 유추

Dunder Miflin 기업의 에어컨 시스템에 대해 암시되는 내
용은 무엇인가?
(A) 고장이 났다.
(B) 제대로 작동하지 않는다.
(C) 점검을 받은 적이 없다.
(D) 최근에 설치되었다.

토익 분석

유추 문제의 키워드(핵심어) 파악이 중요하며 지문에서
해당 키워드가 등장하는 부분을 중심으로 제공되는 정보
를 토대로 유추 가능한 선택지의 내용을 정답으로 택일해
야 한다.

What is suggested about Dunder Miflin Corp.'s air-conditioning system?

(A) It is broken.
(B) It is not in good working order.
(C) It has never been inspected.
(D) It was installed just recently.

문제 해설

Dunder Miflin 기업의 에어컨 시스템에 대해 암시하는 내용을 묻고 있으므로 에어컨 시스템에 관
한 정보가 제시되는 부분에 집중한 후 이를 토대로 에어컨 시스템에 대해 유추할 수 있는 내용을 파
악해야 한다. 두 번째 지문 두 번째 단락 중반 our current one is getting old and unreliable라고 언
급되는 내용을 통해 현재의 에어컨 시스템은 오래 되어 믿을만하지 못하다는 점을 알 수 있고, 이를
토대로 현재의 에어컨은 안정적으로 작동하지 않고 있음을 유추할 수 있으므로 정답은 (B)라 할 수
있다.

180

★★ 유사어

이메일에서, 두 번째 단락 두 번째 줄의 "looking into"와
가장 유사한 의미를 지니는 어휘는 무엇인가?
(A) 예상하다
(B) 조사하다
(C) 관찰하다
(D) 연구하는

토익 분석

유사어 문제는 해당 어휘가 포함된 문장을 비롯하여 그
전후 문장 내용을 파악한 후 해당 어휘와 유사한 의미를
지닌 어휘를 선택하라

In the e-mail, the phrase "looking into" in paragraph 2, line 2, is closest in
meaning to

(A) expecting
(B) investigating
(C) observing
(D) researching

문제 해설

두 번째 단락 두 번째 줄의 We are looking into getting a new one은 이는 현재의 에어컨 시스템이
낙후되어 새로운 에이컨 시스템을 찾고 있다는 내용이므로 질문의 looking into의 유사어로는 '조
사하다'란 뜻을 지닌 investigate가 가장 적절하다고 할 수 있다. 따라서 정답은 (B)이다.

Questions 181-185 refer to following memo and e-mail.

MEMO

From: Nancy Palosi, Executive Assistant, Office of the Vice President
To: Carmina Falcone, Chief Financial Officer
Date: September 13
Subject: Bixby Inc. Tour

[181,182] The itinerary has unfortunately been changed for the Bixby Inc. facilities tour next month starting in El Paso and ending in San Antonio. I have listed the new dates and times of your new flights from Seattle to El Paso as well as from El Paso to San Antonio below. Your flight from San Antonio returning to Seattle has not been determined yet. I will give that information to you as soon as I have it.

Flight E443 departing Seattle 10:00 A.M. September 19
Arrive El Paso 12:50 P.M. September 19
Flight F559 departing El Paso 2:40 P.M. September 21
Arrive San Antonio 4:30 P.M. September 21

Mr. Stern's flight arrives in El Paso a few hours before you, so he has asked if you could contact him once you have landed. The two of you will then proceed to Bixby Inc.'s El Paso plant and commence the tour. Because of the arrival time of your flight, [183] the meeting was moved back to 2 P.M.

To: Nancy Palosi <npalosi@millerco.com>
From: David Thornbush <guestservice@grandritz.com>
Date: September 11
Subject: Your requests for Ms. Falcone and Mr. Stern

[183] This is a confirmation of the reservation you made over the phone last week for Ms. Carmina Falcone and Mr. Daniel Stern at the Grand Ritz Hotel. [185(A),(C)] Two single rooms have been booked on the executive floor. All their business needs will be met inside their rooms. [185(B)] Each room is equipped with a computer with Internet access, a printer, and a fax machine. I received the package that was sent by courier from your company in Seattle. It will be placed in Ms. Falcone's room when she arrives.

[184] As Mr. Stern is arriving around 10 A.M., I have arranged an early check-in time of 10:30 A.M. free of charge. [183] Mr. Stern and Ms. Falcone will have full use of conference room C at 2 P.M. on the day of their arrival. Conference room C is located on basement level one. [185] We have also reserved a special dinner for our two guests at our hotel restaurant, The Olive. The meals will be charged to the guests' account. If you have any other questions at all about their stay, please contact us before their arrival, and I am sure we can assist you with any request you might have. Thank you.

Mina Sohn
Service Manager
Grand Ritz Hotel, El Paso

181-185 다음 회람과 이메일을 참조하시오.

회 람
발신: Nancy Palosi, 부사장실 비서실장
수신: Carmina Falcone, 수석회계사
날짜: 9월 13일
제목: Bixby 사 순방

[181,182] 다음 달 El Paso에서 시작하여 San Antonio에서 끝나는 Bixby 사 시설물 순방 일정이 유감스럽게도 변경되었습니다. 그리고 El Paso에서 San Antonio까지의 새로운 비행 일자와 더불어 Seattle에서 El Paso 까지의 시간을 아래에 적어 놓았습니다. San Antonio에서 시애틀로 돌아오는 비행편은 아직 정해지진 않았지만, 제가 알게 되는 즉시 알려드리겠습니다.

비행편 E443 9월 19일 오전 10시 Seattle 출발
9월 19일 오후 12시 50분 El Paso 도착
비행편 F559 9월 21일 오후 2시 40분 El Paso 출발
9월 21일 오후 4시 30분 San Antonio도착

Stern 씨께서 El Paso에 당신보다 몇 시간 일찍 도착하므로, 도착하시면 그에게 연락해 주시기를 원하십니다. 그후 두 분께서는 Bixby 사의 El Paso공장으로 출발하여 순방을 시작할 예정입니다. 귀하가 탑승하는 비행기의 도착 시간 때문에 [183] 회의가 오후 2시로 연기되었습니다

수신: Nancy Palosi <npalosi@millerco.com>
발신: David Thornbush<guestservice@grandritz.com>
날짜: 9월 11일
제목: Falcone 씨와 Stern 씨에 대한 요청사항

[183] 지난 주 Grand Ritz 호텔에 유선상으로 하신 Carmina Falcone 씨와 Daniel Stern 씨의 예약 건에 대한 확인 메일입니다. [185(A),(C)] 두 개의 1인실이 귀빈층에 예약되어 있을 것입니다. 모든 사무용 집기들이 객실 안에 있을 것입니다. [185(B)] 각 객실들은 인터넷 사용이 가능한 컴퓨터, 프린터, 그리고 팩스기기를 갖추고 있습니다. 저는 시애틀에 있는 귀사에서 보내신 택배를 받았습니다. 그것을 팔콘 씨가 도착하면 받으실 수 있도록 객실에 가져다 두겠습니다.

[184] Stern 씨가 거의 오전 10시에 도착하시기 때문에, 입실시간을 10시 30분으로 추가비용이 없이 정해놓았습니다. [183] Stern 씨와 Falcone 씨는 도착 당일 오후 2시부터 C 회의실을 단독으로 사용하실 수 있습니다. C 회의실은 지하 1층에 위치해 있습니다. [185] 저희는 또한 두 분을 위해 호텔식당인 The Olive에 특별 저녁식사를 준비해놨습니다. 식사비는 두 분의 객실 요금에 청구될 것입니다. 두 분의 숙박에 대해 문의가 있으시면, 두 분이 도착하시기 전에 미리 연락을 주시면 어떠한 요청사항에 대해서도 도와드릴 것을 약속드립니다. 감사합니다.

Mina Sohn
서비스 담당자
Grand Ritz Hotel, El Paso

★ 회람의 목적

Palosi 씨의 회람의 주된 목적은 무엇인가?
(A) 출장의 새로운 일정을 요청하기위해서
(B) 누가 출장을 갈 것인지 결정하기 위해서
(C) 출장 일정의 변경을 확인하기 위해서
(D) 계획된 회의를 취소하기 위해서

토익 분석

회람의 주제/목적은 이메일 초반 2-3문장의 내용을 통해 파악할 수 있으며 주제/목적 문제의 선택지들은 굳이 먼저 읽어볼 필요가 없다.

What is the main purpose of Ms. Palosi's memo?

(A) To request a new date for the trip
(B) To determine who will go on the trip
(C) To confirm a change in travel plan
(D) To cancel a planned meeting

문제 해설

회람의 목적에 대해 묻고 있으며 회람의 목적은 초반부에 직접적으로 언급되는 비즈니스 서신이므로 지문 초반부에서 집중적으로 다루고 있는 중심 소재를 파악하는 것이 관건이다. Palosi 씨가 쓴 회람의 첫 번째 단락 초반 The itinerary has unfortunately been changed for the Bixby Inc. facilities tour next month starting in El Paso and ending in San Antonio를 통해 출장 일정이 변경되었음을 전달하기 위한 목적의 회람임을 알 수 있으므로 정답은 (C)가 적절하다.

★★ 세부사항

시설물 견학은 어디에서 이루어질 것인가?
(A) El Paso
(B) San Antonio
(C) Seattle와 El Paso
(D) El Paso와 San Antonio

토익 분석

도시 이름을 묻는 문제에선 지문에서 도시 이름이 언급되는 부분을 중심으로 단서를 파악한다.

Where will the facilities tour take place?

(A) In El Paso
(B) In San Antonio
(C) In Seattle and El Paso
(D) In El Paso and San Antonio

문제 해설

시설물 견학이 이뤄지는 곳에 대해 묻고 있으며 선택지를 통해 단서가 도시 이름을 중심으로 제시될 것임을 사전에 알 수 있다. 따라서 지문에 등장하는 도시의 이름을 중심으로 시설물 견학, 즉 facilities tour이 언급되는 부분을 신속하게 찾아야 한다. 회람의 첫 번째 단락 초반 The itinerary has unfortunately been changed for the Bixby Inc. facilities tour next month starting in El Paso and ending in San Antonio을 통해 facilities tour, 즉 시설물 견학은 El Paso에서 시작하여 San Antonio에서 종료될 것임을 밝히고 있으므로 정답은 (D)가 되겠다.

★★ 두 지문 연계문제

두 손님의 회의는 어디에서 열릴 것인가?
(A) 호텔 회의실
(B) San Antonio 사무실
(C) El Paso 시설물
(D) Falcone 씨의 사무실

토익 분석

두 번째 문제에서 네 번째 문제까지가 주로 두 지문 연계 문제가 출제되는 부분이다. 따라서 이 부분에서 해당 문제의 단서가 나와야 할 지문에 단서가 불충분하게 언급된다면 이는 두 지문 연계 문제이다.

Where will the two guests hold their meeting?

(A) In a hotel conference room
(B) In the San Antonio office
(C) At the El Paso facilities
(D) In Ms. Falcone's office

문제 해설

이메일의 초반 This is a confirmation of the reservation you made over the phone last week for Ms. Carmina Falcone and Mr. Daniel Stern at the Grand Ritz Hotel을 통해 Falcone 씨와 Stern 씨를 위한 호텔의 객실이 예약되었음을 알 수 있다. 또한 회람의 마지막 단락 하단 the meeting was moved back to 2 P.M.을 통해 회의 시간이 2시로 예정되어 있음을 확인할 수 있다. 마지막으로, 이메일 두 번째 단락 초반 Mr. Stern and Ms. Falcone will make full use of conference room C at 2 P.M. on the day of their arrival에서 Stern 씨와 Falcone 씨가 도착 당일 오후 2시에 회의실 C를 사용할 것임을 밝히고 있으므로 회의가 열리는 곳은 호텔 회의실임을 파악할 수 있다. 따라서 정답은 (A)가 되겠다.

184

What is mentioned about Mr. Stern's arrival?

(A) It will be delayed because his flight was canceled.
(B) It will take place before the documents from the office arrive.
(C) It will be earlier than standard hotel check-in time.
(D) It will be after Ms. Falcone has arrived.

문제 해설

이메일의 두 번째 단락 초반 As Mr. Stern is arriving around 10 A.M., I have arranged an early check-in time of 10:30 A.M. free of charge라고 언급된 내용을 통해 Stern 씨는 거의 10시쯤 도착하며 그를 위해 10시 30분에 무료 조기 입실의 편의를 제공할 것임을 밝히고 있으므로 정답은 (C)가 되겠다.

★★ 세부사항

Stern 씨의 도착에 관해 언급된 것은 무엇인가?
(A) 그의 비행편이 취소되었기 때문에 연기될 것이다.
(B) 사무실에서 서류가 오기 전에 도착할 것이다.
(C) 일반적인 호텔의 입실시간보다 빨리 도착할 것이다.
(D) Falcone 씨가 도착한 후에 도착할 것이다.

토익 분석

인명이나 지명은 중요한 키워드이므로 해당 문제처럼 인명/지명이 키워드로 언급되는 문제에서는 이들이 제시되는 부분을 전후하여 단서를 파악하는 것이 효율적이다.

185

What is NOT mentioned about the guest rooms that have been reserved?

(A) They are single rooms.
(B) They have office equipment.
(C) They are on the same floor.
(D) They are adjacent to the dining room.

문제 해설

이메일의 첫 번째 단락 초반 Two single rooms have been booked on the executive floor을 통해 두 개의 1인실이 같은 층에 예약되었음을 알 수 있으며, 이어서 Each room is equipped with a computer with Internet access, a printer, and a fax machine에서 객실에 사무기기가 구비되어 있고 인터넷 접속도 가능함을 파악할 수 있다. 따라서 (A), (B), (C)가 모두 지문에서 언급된 사실이다. 다만 식당에 대해서는 이메일의 두 번째 단락 중반에서 We have also reserved a special dinner for our two guests at our hotel restaurant, The Olive라고 언급된 내용이 전부인데, 여기서는 단지 호텔 식당인 올리브에 두 사람을 위한 특별 식사를 준비했음을 밝히고 있을 뿐, 객실과 식당과의 상대적 위치에 대해 가늠할 수 있는 내용은 전혀 등장하지 않고 있다. 그러므로 정답은 (D)라고 할 수 있다.

★★★ 사실 확인

예약된 객실에 대해 언급되지 않은 것은 무엇인가?
(A) 1인실이다.
(B) 사무집기들이 갖춰져 있다.
(C) 같은 층에 있다.
(D) 식당에 근접해있다.

토익 분석

사실이 아닌 내용[NOT TRUE]을 묻는 문제는 선택지 내용을 파악한 후 이를 간단히 정리하여 키워드로 삼은 후 지문의 내용과 대조하며 사실이 아닌 선택지를 오답으로 소거하며 정답을 찾아내는 방식으로 풀이한다.

186-190 다음 제품 설명과 고객 후기, 그리고 온라인 응답을 참조하시오.

Flywheel Knife Sharpener

[186 (B), 186 (D)] 가정에서 요리를 하시기로 단단히 마음먹은 분이시거나 조리용 칼을 사용하시는데 능숙하신 요리사이신가요? 그러시다면, Flywheel Knife Sharpener야말로 날이 있는 모든 주방기구들을 단번에 갈아주는 이상적인 주방 조리대 도구일 것입니다. 무엇보다도, 이 제품은 표면이 거칠고, 가벼우며, 최적의 성능을 위해 제조된 제품입니다!

특징: 끝이 다이아몬드로 된 연마휠이 포함되어 있어 최고의 성능과 안전뿐만 아니라 [186 (A)] 신뢰성과 내구성까지 제공해 드립니다. 이 제품의 방수 기능은 모든 환경에서 칼 연마를 가능하게 해주므로, 가장 어려운 주방조건에서도 칼을 갈 수 있습니다.

품질 보증: 저희는 모든 부품들과 수리 작업에 대한 10년 기간의 품질 보증 서비스를 포함하고 있으며, 이는 시중의 다른 어떤 브랜드와 견줄 수 없는 표준 서비스입니다. 이는 이 제품이 잦은 사용에도 오랜 기간 사용할 수있음을 보증해 드리는 것입니다.

구매 정가: 250달러 / Flywheel Products 단골 이용 회원: 199달러

어휘 determined 단단히 마음먹은, 단호한 seasoned 능숙한, 경험 많은 knife-wielding 칼을 사용하는, 칼질하는 ideal 이상적인 counter 조리대 appliance 기구, 도구 sharpen ~을 갈다, 날카롭게 하다 bladed 칼이 달린 tool 도구 in a snap 단번에 best of all 무엇보다도 rugged 거친 lightweight 가벼운, 경량의 built for ~를 위해 만들어진 performance 성능, 기능 feature 특징 enclosed 포함된, 들어있는 tipped 끝이 ~로 된 endurance 내구성 gear 장비, 장치 allow for ~을 가능하게 하다 hard use 잦은 사용 regular purchase price 구매 정가

---

www.flywheelcountertopappliances.uk/2345/mn

홈　　　제품 소개　　　**이용 후기**　　　자주하는 질문

평가: ★★★★★

저는 이보다 더 인상적인 칼연마기를 본 적이 없습니다! [187] 저는 요리사도 아니며, [188] 제 아내가 모든 요리를 담당하고 있지만, 저는 전문 칼 제작자입니다. 저는 직업으로 맞춤 제작용 칼을 만드는 일을 합니다. 저는 주방용 칼과 군용칼, 그리고 사냥용 칼과 같은 모든 종류의 칼을 만듭니다. 제가 주기적으로 무역 박람회로 출장을 다니기 때문에, Flywheel Sharpener의 무게는 제게 이상적입니다. 저는 이 제품을 가지고 계속해서 여기저기 갖고 다녀야 합니다. 이 제품은 제 출장용 승합차에서 가장 핵심적인 제품입니다. 저는 특히 여러 가지 속도에서 조절이 가능한 경사각까지 포함된 제품 특징들로 깊은 인상을 받고 있습니다. 아주 좋은 제품입니다. 적극 추천 합니다!

[190] 게시자, David Baker
8월 29일

어휘 be impressed by ~에 깊은 인상을 받다 maker 제작자 custom 맞춤 제작의 for living 직업으로 tactical knife 군용 칼 regularly 주기적으로 trade show 무역박람회 weight 무게 from place to place 여기저기 mainstay 중심(이 되는 것) adjustable 조절 가능한 bevel angle 경사각 post ~을 게시하다
www.flywheelcountertopappliances.uk/2345/mn/response

Questions 186-190 refer to the following product description, customer's review, and online response.

Flywheel Knife Sharpener

[186 (B), 186 (D)] Are you a determined home kitchen cook or a seasoned knife-wielding chef? Well, the Flywheel Knife Sharpener is the ideal kitchen-counter appliance that sharpens all bladed kitchen tools in a snap. Best of all, it is rugged, lightweight, and built for performance!

Features: The enclosed diamond-tipped sharpening wheels provide superior performance and safety, [186 (A)] as well as reliability and endurance. Its waterproof gears allow for knife sharpening in all environments you can sharpen your knives in the toughest kitchen conditions.

Warranty: We include a ten-year warranty on all parts and labor—a standard not met by any other brand on the market. This is our guarantee that the product will provide years of hard use.

Regular purchase price: $250.00 / Flywheel Products Loyalty members price: $199.00

---

www.flywheelcountertopappliances.uk/2345/mn

HOME　　　　　PRODUCTS　　　　　**REVIEW**　　　　　FAQ

Rating : ★★★★★

I've never been more impressed by a knife sharpener! [187] I am not a chef [188] and my wife does all the cooking, but I am a professional knife maker. I make custom knives for a living. I make all kinds of knives kitchen knives, tactical knives, and hunting knives. I regularly travel to trade shows, so the weight of the Flywheel Sharpener is ideal for me. I need to move it from place to place constantly. It is a mainstay on my travelling van. I am particularly impressed by its various features from the different speeds to the adjustable bevel angles. Well done. Highly recommended!

[190] Posted by David Baker
August 29

www.flywheelcountertopappliances.uk/2345/mn/response

HOME   PRODUCTS   **REVIEW**   FAQ

Thank you for your kind comments, Mr. Baker. At Flywheel, we are committed to serving customers—particularly customers who need a reliable, powerful tool in order to get the job done. You said you travel for work, [188] but what about the wife? Couldn't she use a Flywheel Sharpener on her kitchen countertop? [189] We'd like to recommend a lighter version of your sharpener: the Flywheel Knife Sharpener Express. It has all of the features of your sharpener, but in a slightly lighter package. It also comes in a variety of colors, so your wife can match her appliances for a clean, coherent look in the kitchen. See it on our Web site at : www.flywheelcountertopappliances/sharpeners/express Again, thanks for your vote of confidence, and keep on sharpening!

[190] Posted by Flywheel Customer Service on August 29.

홈   제품 소개   **이용 후기**   자주하는 질문

귀하의 친절한 의견에 감사드립니다, Baker 씨. 저희 Flywheel 사에서는 고객 여러분께, 특히 작업을 완수하시는데 있어 신뢰할 수 있고 강력한 도구를 필요로 하시는 고객들께 서비스를 제공해 드리는데 전념하고 있습니다. 귀하께서는 업무 때문에 출장을 다니신다고 하셨는데, [188] 아내 분은 어떤가요? 아내 분은 주방 조리대에서 Flywheel Sharpener를 사용하실 수 있지 않을까요? [189] 저희는 갖고 계신 칼 연마기보다 더 가벼운 버전인 Flywheel Knife Sharpener Express를 추천해 드리고자 합니다. 갖고 계신 연마기가 지닌 모든 특징들을 포함하고 있지만, 조금 더 가벼운 패키지에 해당됩니다. 또한 다양한 색상으로 출시되고 있으므로 아내 분께서 깔끔하고 주방과 어울리는 모습을 갖춘 기기를 사용하실 수 있습니다. 저희 홈페이지인 www.flywheelcountertopappliances/sharpeners/express를 확인해 보시기 바랍니다. 다시 한 번, 귀하의 확신에 찬 말씀에 감사드리며, 지속적으로 즐거운 연마 작업하실 수 있기를 바랍니다!

[190] 게시자, Flywheel 고객 서비스 부서, 8월29일

어휘 be committed to -ing ~하는데 전념하다, 헌신하다 reliable 신뢰할 수 있는 get A p.p. A가 ~되게 하다 countertop 조리대 come in (색상 등) ~로 출시되다

186

What is NOT mentioned in the product description as a feature of the knife sharpener?

(A) It is very reliable.
(B) It is suitable for professional chefs.
(C) It is larger than competitors' knife sharpeners.
(D) It is great for the home kitchen.

문제 해설

첫 지문의 첫 단락에서 Are you a determined home kitchen cook or a seasoned knife-wielding chef? Well, the Flywheel Knife Sharpener is the ideal이라며 Flywheel Knife Sharpener를 이상적으로 사용할 수 있는 사람들과 관련해 집에서 요리하는 사람과 칼을 사용하는데 능숙한 요리사가 언급되어 있으므로 (B)와 (D)는 옳은 내용이다. 또한 바로 다음 단락에서는 provide superior performance and safety, as well as reliability라며 신뢰성을 제공한다는 내용도 있으므로 (A)도 확인할 수 있다.

★★★ 진위

제품 설명에서 칼 연마기의 특징으로 언급되지 않은 것은 무엇인가?
(A) 매우 신뢰할 수 있다.
(B) 전문 요리사들에게 적합하다.
(C) 경쟁사의 연마기보다 더 크다.
(D) 자택 주방용으로 좋은 제품이다.

토익 분석

이중 지문의 첫 번째 문제는 첫 번째 지문에서 단서가 제시된다. 아울러 사실 내용을 묻는 문제[TRUE]의 키워드가 지문 전반에 걸쳐 언급되는 경우 선택지의 내용을 키워드로 삼아 지문에서 해당 내용이 언급되는지 여부를 빠르게 파악한다.

187

What is indicated in the customer review?

(A) The sharpener comes with detailed instructions.
(B) Mr. Baker is not a chef.
(C) Flywheel products come in a variety of colors.
(D) The sharpener is very heavy.

문제 해설

고객 후기인 두 번째 지문의 하단에 작성자가 David Baker 씨로 되어 있고, 이 지문의 시작 부분에 자신을 I am not a chef라고 언급하고 있으므로 (B)가 정답임을 알 수 있다.

★★ 사실 확인

고객 후기에서 알 수 있는 것은 무엇인가?
(A) 해당 연마기 제품에 상세한 안내가 포함되어 있다.
(B) Baker 씨는 요리사가 아니다.
(C) Flywheel 사의 제품들은 다양한 색상으로 출시된다.
(D) 해당 연마기는 매우 무겁다.

토익 분석

사실 내용을 묻는 문제[TRUE]의 키워드가 지문 전반에 걸쳐 언급되는 경우 선택지의 내용을 키워드로 삼아 지문에서 해당 내용이 언급되는지 여부를 빠르게 파악한다. 이 때 선택지를 두 개씩 나눠 두 번에 걸쳐 지문에서의 해당 내용이 제시되고 있는지 확인하는 방식을 권고한다.

188

★★ 유추 / 두 지문 연계 문제

제조사의 답변에 관해 유추할 수 있는 내용은 무엇인가?

(A) 제조사는 Baker 씨가 요리를 위한 또 다른 제품을 구매하길 원한다.

(B) 제조사는 Baker 씨가 품질 보증 서비스의 기간을 연장하길 원한다.

(C) 제조사는 Baker 씨에게 다음 구매에 대한 할인을 제공하고자 한다.

(D) 제조사는 Baker 씨가 자사의 수석 연구원이 되어 주길 원한다.

토익 분석

- 삼중 지문에 따른 문제에서 특정인에 대한 세부정보를 묻거나, **probably**, **most likely**, **imply**, **suggest**를 대동하는 유추 문제가 출제된다면 이들은 두 지문 연계 문제일 가능성이 매우 높다.
- 삼중 지문의 두 지문 연계 문제는 대개 두 번째 문제와 네 번째 문제(2-4) 또는 세 번째 문제와 다섯 번째 문제(3-5)로 짝지어 출제되는 경향이 있다.
- 유추 문제의 키워드가 혹은 키워드에 관한 내용이 지문 전반에 걸쳐 언급되고 있는 상태에서 적절한 유추 내용을 파악해야 한다면 선택지에 나온 내용을 먼저 파악한 후 선택지의 내용을 유추할 수 있는 근거가 지문에 제시되는지 여부를 역으로 확인하는 방식으로 문제를 풀이하라

What is suggested in the manufacturer's response?

(A) They want Mr. Baker to purchase another model for cooking.

(B) They want Mr. Baker to extend a warranty.

(C) They want to offer Mr. Baker a discount on his next purchase.

(D) They want Mr. Baker to be their new head researcher.

문제 해설

Baker 씨는 후기 초반부에서 my wife does all the cooking이라며 아내가 가정에서의 모든 요리를 전담하고 있다는 점을 밝히고 있다. 이어서 후기에 대한 제조사 답변에 해당되는 세 번째 지문의 중반부를 보면 what about the wife? Couldn't she use a Flywheel Sharpener on her kitchen countertop?라며 Baker 씨의 아내를 지칭해 아내도 Flywheel Sharpener 제품을 주방에서 사용할 수 있지 않을까 묻고 있다. 이는 아내를 위해 다른 모델을 구입하도록 권하는 내용에 해당되므로 이를 토대로 제조사는 Baker 씨가 요리 용도로 또 다른 제품을 구매하길 원하고 있음을 유추할 수 있다. 그러므로 (A)가 정답이다.

189

★★★ 세부사항

Flywheel Knife Sharpener Express가 Baker 씨에게 추천되는 이유는 무엇일 것 같은가?

(A) 저렴하다.　　　　　　　(D) 무게가 가볍다.

(B) 식기 세척기에 사용할 수 있다.　(C) 조립하기 쉽다.

토익 분석

세부사항을 묻는 문제는 질문에서 빠른 키워드(핵심어) 파악이 중요하며 해당 키워드가 등장하는 부분을 중심으로 단서를 파악하는 것이 관건이다.

Why would the Flywheel Knife Sharpener Express be recommended for Ms. Baker?

(A) It is inexpensive.　　　　(B) It is dishwasher proof.

(C) It is easy to assemble.　　**(D) It is lightweight.**

문제 해설

Flywheel Knife Sharpener Express라는 제품 이름이 제시된 세 번째 단락 중반부에서 We'd like to recommend a lighter version of your sharpener: the Flywheel Knife Sharpener Express이라며 Baker 씨의 아내에게 추천하는 제품으로 언급하면서 더 가벼운 제품 유형이라고 소개하고 있으므로 무게의 가벼움을 의미하는 (D)가 정답이다.

★★★ 유추 / 두 지문 연계 문제

제조사의 응답 날짜를 통해 알 수 있는 것은 무엇인가?

(A) 대응이 매우 빠르다.

(B) 서두르지 않는다.

(C) 마케팅에 관심이 있다.

(D) 경쟁사들보다 더 많이 판매하고있다.

토익 분석

- 삼중 지문의 두 지문 연계 문제는 대개 두 번째 문제와 네 번째 문제(2-4) 또는 세 번째 문제와 다섯 번째 문제(3-5)로 짝지어 출제되는 경향이 있다.
- 해당 문제의 단서가 제시되어야 할 지문에서 단서가 불충분하게 등장한다면 이는 두 지문 연계 문제임을 파악해야 한다. 해당 문제의 경우 제조사의 답변 작성 날짜만 봐서는 사실상 단서를 온전하게 파악할 수 없기 때문에 바로 두 지문 연계문제임을 눈치채야 한다.

What is suggested by the date of the manufacturer's response?

(A) They respond very quickly.

(B) They take their time.

(C) They are interested in marketing.

(D) They are outselling their competitors.

문제 해설

Baker 씨에게 쓴 제조사의 응답 메시지 날짜를 확인할 수 있는 세 번째 지문의 맨 마지막에서 Posted by Flywheel Customer Service on August 29라며 작성 날짜가 8월 29일로 되어 있다. 아울러 이는 두 번째 지문의 맨 마지막 Posted by David Baker과 August 29을 통해 Baker 씨가 쓴 메시지의 작성 날짜로 되어 있는 8월 29일과 같은 날짜이므로 고객 의견에 대한 대응 속도가 매우 빠르다는 것을 유추할 수 있다. 따라서 정답은 (A)가 되겠다.

Questions 191-195 refer to the following letters and invoice.

Jack Stanford
1123 Pine St.
Queen City, CA 92152

Snape's Second-Hand Books
45 Capon St.
Los Angeles, CA 94721

Dear Mr. Snape,

I visited Snape's Second-hand Books at the Antiquarian Book Fair in California last year. I noticed that you have a variety of products in reliable condition, so I ordered some books through your Web site. As I take great care of my books and am not interested in collecting any damaged books, I always check the descriptions to learn about the condition of a book before I place an order. I expected the products I ordered not to have any defects but when I inspected the products upon arrival, [191,192] I found that the cover of *Timmy's Voyage as a a Captain* had not been attached properly and looks like it has been rebound several times. [193] However, given your store policy, I cannot send the book back. [191] Please reply to me as soon as possible to solve this frustrating situation.

Sincerely,

Jack Stanford

INVOICE

Snape's Second-Hand Books
45 Capon St.
Los Angeles, CA 94721

Jack Stanford
1123 Pine St.
Queen City, CA 92152

Item Number -------------------------Book Title -------------------------Price

[192] BK 1123	Timmy's Voyage as a Captain	$94.25
[194] BC 6030	New Line of the World	$58.00
CJ 7399	How Should I Live	$86.00
KS 9013	Behind the History	$131.00
	Total	$369.25

191-195 다음 두 통의 편지와 거래 내역서를 참조하시오.

Jack Stanford
1123 Pine St.
Queen City, CA 92152

Snape's Second-Hand Books
45 Capon St.
Los Angeles, CA 94721

Snape 씨께,

저는 작년에 California에서 열린 Antiquarian Book Fair에서 Snape's Second-hand Books를 방문했습니다. 다른 제품들과 비교해 귀하께서는 믿음이 가는 다양한 제품들을 보유하고 계시다는 점을 알게 되어서 귀사의 홈페이지에서 몇몇 도서들을 구입했습니다. 저는 제 책을 매우 소중히 다룰 뿐 아니라, 손상된 도서들을 수집하는 것엔 관심이 없기 때문에, 주문을 하기 전에 책들의 상태를 파악할 수 있도록 항상 설명된 내용들을 확인합니다. 저는 제품에 어떠한 결함도 없었다고 생각했지만, [191, 192] 제품이 도착하자마자 점검해 봤을 때, Timmy's Voyage as a Captain의 표지는 제대로 부착되지 않았을 뿐만 아니라 여러 번 제본된 것처럼 보였습니다. [193] 하지만 귀사의 방침으로 인해 이 도서를 다시 반송할 수가 없네요. [191] 실망스러운 이 상황을 해결할 수 있도록 가능한 빠른 답변을 주시기 바랍니다.

안녕히 계십시오.

Jack Stanford

어휘 notice that ~임을 알아차리다 reliable 믿을만한 compared to ~와 비교해 harmful 해가 되는 interested in ~에 관심이 있는 collect ~을 수집하다 damaged 손상된 careful 신중한 description 설명, 묘사 find out ~을 알아내다 whether A or not A인지 아닌지 make an order 주문하다 defect 결함 inspect ~을 점검하다 upon ~하자마자, ~할 시에 arrival 도착 find that ~임을 파악하다 attach ~을 부착하다 completely 제대로, 완전히 rebind ~을 제본하다 reply 답변하다 solve ~을 해결하다 frustrating 실망감을 주는 situation 상황

거래 내역서

From: Snape's Second-Hand Books
45 Capon St.
Los Angeles, CA 94721

To: Jack Stanford
1123 Pine St.
Queen City, CA 92152

제품 번호 ---------도서 제목 ---------가격

[192] BK 1123	Timmy's Voyage as a Captain	$94.25
[194] BC 6030	New Line of the World	$58.00
CJ 7399	How Should I Live	$86.00
KS 9013	Behind the History	$131.00
	총액	$369.25

Snape's Second-Hand Books
'저희는 여러분이 원하는 모든 도서를 제공합니다'
45 Capon St.
Los Angeles, CA 94721

Jack Stanford
1123 Pine St.
Queen City, CA 92152

Stanford 씨께,
[195] 저는 직접 모든 도서들을 신중하게 점검하며 저희 홈페이지에 그 도서의 상태에 관한 설명을 작성합니다. 귀하로부터 편지를 받았을 때, 60년도 더 이전에 최초 소유주가 그 책을 제본했었다는 사실이 기억났습니다. 따라서, 그 책은 제가 받은 이후로는 원 상태 그대로를 유지해 온 것입니다.

[194] 귀하께서 도서에 대해 실망하고 계신다는 점을 알고 있기에, 이를 보상해 드릴 수 있도록 구매하신 도서 중 가장 저렴한 도서에 대해 지불하신 비용을 환불해드리겠습니다.

회사를 대신하여, 불편을 끼쳐 드려 사과드립니다.

귀하의 이해와 협조에 관해 미리 감사의 말씀을 전합니다.

Sean Snape
최고 경영자

어휘 carefully 신중히 by oneself 직접, 스스로 original 최초의, 원래의 owner 소유주 decade 10년 since ~ 이래로 understand (that) ~임을 알다 disappointed 실망한 make up to ~에게 보상해주다, ~을 만회하다 payment 지불, 지급 비용 least expensive 가장 덜 비싼 pay back ~을 환불해주다 on behalf of ~를 대표하여 apologize for ~를 사과하다 in advance 미리, 앞서서

Snape's Second-Hand Books
'We Offer You Every Book You Want'
45 Capon St.
Los Angeles, CA 94721

Jack Stanford
1123 Pine St.
Queen City, CA 92152

Dear Mr. Stanford,

[195] I can tell you that I carefully check all our books myself and write the descriptions of their conditions on our Web site. When I received your letter, I remembered that the book was rebound by the original owner over six decades years ago. Therefore, the book has been in its original condition since I received the book.

I understand you are disappointed, so to try to make it up to you, [194] your payment for the least expensive book your purchased will be paid back.

On behalf of our company, I apologize for any inconvenience we may have caused you.

Thank you for your understanding and cooperation in advance.

Sean Snape
Sean Snape
Chief Executive Officer

191

★★★ 편지의 발송 이유

Stanford씨가 Snape 씨에게 편지를 쓴 이유는 무엇인가?
(A) 부정확한 비용 청구서에 대해 이의를 제기하기 위해
(B) 최근에 주문한 것들을 취소하기 위해
(C) 한 제품의 상태에 대해 항의하기 위해
(D) 분실된 물품에 대해 문의하기 위해

토익 분석

편지의 주제/목적은 단락 구분이 있는 경우 첫 번째 단락 초반 2~3문장에서 제시되지만 주제/목적 문제의 난이도가 높아지는 경우 주제/목적이 두 번째 단락의 초반 2~3문장에서 다뤄지는 것이 보통이다. 하지만 주제/목적의 난이도가 가장 높아지는 경우 출제 비중이 높진 않지만 상대적으로 내용이 긴 지문의 주제/목적이 지문 후반부, 즉 지문 종료 직전에 제시되기도 한다. 따라서 분량이 긴 지문의 경우 첫 번째/두 번째 단락에서 주제/목적이 드러나지 않는 경우 다른 문제들을 먼저 풀이하고 가장 마지막으로 주제/목적 문제를 풀이하는 것도 현명한 방법이라 할 수 있다.

Why did Mr. Stanford write to Mr. Snape?

(A) To dispute an inaccurate bill
(B) To cancel recently placed orders
(C) To object to an item's condition
(D) To inquire about a missing item

문제 해설

Stanford 씨가 쓴 편지인 첫 번째 지문의 마지막 부분에서 I found that the cover of Timmy's Voyage as a Captain had not been attached properly and looks like it has been rebound several times와 Please reply me as soon as possible to solve this frustrating situation라며 제품을 점검했을 때 표지가 제대로 부착되어 있지 않았고 여러 번 제본된 것처럼 보인다는 문제점을 언급하면서 이 실망스러운 상황을 해결할 수 있도록 답변해 달라고 요청하고 있음을 알 수 있다. 따라서 편지의 발송 이유는 제품 상태에 대한 항의에 있음을 알 수 있으므로 (C)가 정답이다.

192

How much did Mr. Stanford most likely pay for a book with a cover problem?

(A) $94.25
(B) $58.00
(C) $86.00
(D) $131.00

문제 해설

겉장에 문제가 있는 도서에 관련된 내용은 첫 번째 편지에 등장하고 있지만 해당 도서에 얼마를 지불했는지 단서가 제공되고 있지 않으므로 이 문제는 두 지문 연계 문제임을 알 수 있다. 첫 지문의 마지막 부분에서 I found that the cover of Timmy's Voyage as a Captain had not been attached properly and looks like it has been rebound several times 라며 Timmy's Voyage as a Captain란 도서의 표지가 제대로 부착되어 있지 않았다는 문제점을 언급하고 있다. 이어서 두 번째 지문인 거래 내역서에서 해당 도서의 가격이 $94.25로 제시되고 있으므로 이를 통해 Stanford 씨는 Timmy's Voyage as a Captain를 구매할 때 $94.25를 지불했을 것이라 생각할 수 있다. 따라서 (A)가 정답이다.

★★ 두 지문 연계 문제

Stanford 씨는 겉장에 문제가 있는 도서에 대해 얼마를 지불했겠는가??
(A) $94.25
(B) $58.00
(C) $86.00
(D) $131.00

토익 분석

- 해당 문제의 단서가 나와야 할 지문에서 단서가 불충분하게 언급된다면 이는 두 지문 연계 문제이다.
- 삼중 지문 중 하나가 양식서라면 해당 양식서와 관련된 두 지문 연계 문제는 필히 출제되며 이 경우 문제를 풀이할 수 있는 가장 결정적인 단서는 양식서를 통해 제시된다
- 삼중 지문의 두 지문 연계 문제는 대개 두 번째 문제와 네 번째 문제(2-4) 또는 세 번째 문제와 다섯 번째 문제(3-5)로 짝지어 출제되는 경향이 있다.

193

What is suggested about Snape's Second-Hand Books?

(A) It does not have an online store.
(B) It does not have much inventory.
(C) It does not sell illustrated books.
(D) It does not allow product returns.

문제 해설

Stanford 씨가 작성한 첫 번째 편지가 종료되는 부분에서 However, given your store policy, I cannot send the book back라며 Snape's Second-Hand Books의 방침으로 인해 책을 반품할 수가 없다는 없음을 언급하고 있다. 따라서 이를 통해 Snape's Second-Hand Books 사는 도서의 반품을 허용하지 않는다는 방침을 유지하고 있음을 유추할 수 있다. 따라서 정답은 (D)가 되겠다.

★★★ 유추

Snape's Second-Hand Books에 관해 알 수 있는 것은 무엇인가?
(A) 온라인 매장을 보유하고 있지 않다.
(B) 재고를 많이 갖고 있지 않다.
(C) 삽화가 있는 책들을 판매하지 않는다.
(D) 제품 반품을 허용하지 않는다.

토익 분석

해당 유추 문제의 키워드는 Snape's Second-Hand Books 이지만 Snape's Second-Hand Books에 대한 내용이 편지 전반에 걸쳐 제시되고 있다. 즉, 유추 문제의 키워드가 지문 전반에 걸쳐 언급되고 있거나 키워드의 범위가 너무 넓어 키워드로서의 가치가 반감될 때는 선택지에 나온 내용을 먼저 파악한 후 이를 간단하게 정리하여 키워드로 삼아 선택지의 유추 내용이 가능한 근거가 지문에서 등장하는지 여부를 역으로 신속하게 파악하는 방식으로 문제를 풀이해야 한다.

★★★ 두 지문 연계 문제

Stanford 씨가 Snape's Second-Hand Books 사에 반송할 도서는 무엇인가?
(A) Timmy's Voyage as a Captain
(B) New Line of the World
(C) How Should I Live
(D) Golden Island

토익 분석

- 해당 문제의 단서가 나와야 할 지문에서 단서가 불충분하게 언급된다면 이는 두 지문 연계 문제이다.
- 삼중 지문 중 하나가 양식서라면 해당 양식서와 관련된 두 지문 연계 문제는 필히 출제되며 이 경우 문제를 풀이할 수 있는 가장 결정적인 단서는 양식서를 통해 제시된다

Which of the books will Mr. Stanford receive a refund for?

(A) Timmy's Voyage as a Captain
(B) New Line of the World
(C) How Should I Live
(D) Golden Island

문제 해설

Stanford 씨가 Snape's Second-Hand Books 사에 반송할 도서에 관한 내용은 두 번째 편지에서 언급되고 있지만 막상 구체적으로 반송하게 될 도서명이 제시되지 않고 있으므로 이는 두 지문 연계 문제임을 알 수 있다. 비용 환불과 관련해, 마지막 지문의 마지막 부분에서 your payment for the least expensive one will be paid back라며 가장 저렴한 도서의 비용에 대해 환불해 주겠다고 쓰여 있다. 아울러 두 번째 지문인 거래 내역서에서 가장 저렴한 가격의 도서는 New Line of the World 을임을 알 수 있다. 따라서 정답은 (B)이다.

195

★★ 사실 확인

두 번째 편지에 언급된 내용은 무엇인가?
(A) Snape 씨가 직접 제품들을 점검한다.
(B) Snape 씨의 제품이 아직 배송되지 않았다.
(C) Snape 씨가 곧 대체 물품을 받을 것이다.
(D) Snape 씨가 평가를 위해 책을 전문가에게 보낼 것이다.

토익 분석

특별한 키워드가 없이 지문 전체의 내용에 관한 진위를 묻는 문제의 경우, 선택지에 나온 내용을 먼저 파악한 후 선택지의 내용을 간단하게 정리하여 이를 키워드로 삼아 지문에서 해당 내용이 등장하는지 여부를 역으로 신속하게 파악하는 방식으로 문제를 풀이해야 한다. 하지만 시간이 부족한 경우에는 건너뛰어야 할 문제 유형이기도 하다.

What is stated in the second letter?

(A) Mr. Snape inspected the products himself.
(B) Mr. Snape's item has not been mailed yet.
(C) Mr. Snape will mail a replacement soon.
(D) Mr. Snape will send a book to an expert for evaluation.

문제 해설

두 번째 편지의 마지막 지문 시작 부분에서 I carefully check all our books by myself라며 Snape 씨는 자신이 직접 모든 도서들을 신중하게 점검하고 있음을 밝히고 있으므로 이에 대해 언급한 (A)가 정답이다.

Questions 196-200 refer to the following the e-mail, Web page, and article.

To: Shurred Nuhans <shurrednuhans@nexusgarage.com>
From: Nathan Phillips<nphillips@nexusgarage.com>
Subject : Request
Date : 13 January

Dear Mr. Nuhans

I carefully ask that our company consider entering the PATC Virtual Business Tournament. The contest, established by the Portugal& American Trade Cooperation (PATC), [196] asks participants to improve and conduct business plans that make an imaginary company stable and continuous.

Participation in this contest would bring high benefits to our company. We know that some of the participants are in non-decision-making positions in their groups, but the contest will demand a wide range of leadership practices from them. In the process, some of them can [197] find out about the realities and complexities of an entrepreneur's work. Furthermore, they are likely to use the skills obtained or improved from the competition such as [197] team work, research, and problem solving when they do their actual work. Moreover, participating in the competition [197] can serve as a promotion to the public. Approximately seven months after the last tournament, [200] about more than a half of the eighty-five companies that participated in the event reported an improvement in business results.

Information about the participation is on the PATC Website, www.patc.org.

Sincerely,

Nathan Phillips
Nexus Garage Corporation

http//www.PATC.org/events/tournament_information

PATC Virtual Business Tournament

Entry Information

Registration for this year's tournament is from 12 May to 12 June whereas the tournament starts on 8 October. More than two teams from a same company cannot be enrolled. [198] A rank for each team will be posted on 14 October and will receive an honor during a ceremony on 19 November at Hotel Hilltop, Sydney, Australia.

196-200 다음 이메일과 홈페이지, 그리고 기사문을 참조하시오.

수신 : Shurred Nuhans <shurrednuhans@nexusgarage.com>
발신 : Nathan Phillips<nphillips@nexusgarage.com>
제목: 요청
날짜: 1월 13일

Nuhans 씨께,

저는 우리 회사가 PATC Virtual Business Tournament에 참가하는 것을 신중하게 요청을 드립니다. 이 대회는 Portugal& American Trade Cooperation (PATC)에 의해 설립되었으며, [196] 참가자들에게 가상의 회사가 안정적으로 지속될 수 있도록 회사 경영 계획을 향상시키고 이를 실행할 것을 요구합니다.

이 대회의 참가는 우리 회사에 많은 이득을 가져다 줄 것입니다. 일부 참가자들은 소속 회사에서 결정권이 없는 직책에 있는 사람들이라는 것을 알지만, 이 대회는 이들에게 아주 다양한 범위의 리더십의 실행을 요구할 것입니다. 그 과정에서, 일부 사람들은 [197(A)] 기업인의 업무가 지닌 현실성과 복잡함에 관해 알게 됩니다. 더욱이, 이 사람들은 [197(D)] 팀 워크나 연구, 그리고 해결책 모색과 같이 대회를 통해 얻거나 개선되는 능력들을 실제 회사에서 근무할 때 사용하게 될 가능성이 있습니다. 이 경연대회에 참가하는 일은 우리 제품들을 위한 신규매장들을 개장하는 것과 같은 [197(C)] 일반 대중들을 대상으로 하는 홍보의 역할을 할 수 있습니다. 지난 번 대회가 종료된 후 7개월 동안, [200] 행사에 참가했던 85개의 기업들 중에서 약 절반이 넘는 회사에서 영업 실적의 향상을 알렸습니다.

대회 참가와 관련된 정보는 PATC 홈페이지에 게재되어 있습니다.

Nathon Phillips
Nexus Garage Cop

어휘 ask that ~하도록 요청하다 consider -ing ~하는 것을 고려하다 enter ~에 참가하다 establish ~을 확립하다, 설립하다 ask A to do A에게 ~하도록 요청하다 participant 참가자 improve ~을 개선하다, ~을 향상시키다 conduct ~을 실시하다, 수행하다 be likely to do ~할 가능성이 있다 obtain ~을 얻다 competition 경연대회 serve as ~의 역할을 하다 promotion 홍보, 판촉 approximately 약, 대략(=about) more than a half 절반이 넘는 improvement 개선, 향상 business result 영업 실적

http//www.PATC.org/events/tournament_information

PATC Visual Business Tournament

참가정보

올해의 토너먼트에 대한 참가 등록은 5월 12일부터 6월 12일까지이지만 토너먼트 행사는 10월 8일에 시작됩니다. 동일한 회사에 소속된 복수 이상의 팀들은 등록할 수 없습니다. [198] 각 팀에 대한 순위는 10월 14일에 게시될 것이며, Australia의 Sydney에 있는 Hotel Hilltop에서 11월 19일에 열리는 기념행사에서 상을 수상하게 됩니다.

어휘 registration for ~에 대한 등록, 참가 신청 whereas ~인 반면에 enroll ~을 등록시키다 rank 순위 post ~을 게시하다 receive an honor 상을 받다, 영예를 받다

Nexus 사의 가상적 돌파구

(10월 15일)–PATC Virtual Business Tournament 행사는 많은 회사에서 출전한 팀들에게 가상의 회사를 성공적으로 운영하는 방법을 찾도록 요구했다. [199] 영국에서 출전한 많은 팀들이 이 행사가 시작된 이후로 참가해왔지만 한 번도 우승한 적이 없었다. 하지만 [198, 199, 200] Nexus Garage 사를 대표하는 팀이 90개가 넘는 회사에서 출전한 109개의 팀들로 구성된 경쟁 부문에서 3위를 차지했다. 이와 같은 승리를 거둔 팀은 Nathon Phillips 씨에 의해 인솔되었다. 이 팀은 PATC Virtual Business 시상식에서 상을 수상하게 될 것이다.

어휘 virtual 가상의, 실질적인 breakthrough 돌파구 require A to do A에게 ~하도록 요구하다 how to do ~하는 법 operate ~을 운영하다 successfully 성공적으로 join 참가하다 since ~ 이래로 however 하지만 delegate ~을 대표하다 third rank 3위 field 부문, 분야 consist of ~로 구성되다 represent ~을 대표하다 victorious 승리한, 승리를 거둔 lead ~을 인솔하다, 지휘하다 honor ~에게 상을 주다, ~에게 영예를 주다

A Virtual Breakthrough For Nexus

(October 15)—The PATC Virtual Business Tournament required teams from many companies to find out how to operate a virtual business successfully. [199] Many teams from England joined the event before but had never won until now. Indeed, [198, 199, 200] the team representing Nexus Garage Corp. took third rank in a field consisting of 109 teams from over ninety companies. The victorious team was led by Mr. Nathan Phillips. The team will be honored at the PATC Virtual Business Awards.

196

★★★ 세부사항

PATC 대회 참가자들의 목적은 무엇인가?
(A) 국제 거래 계약을 수주한다.
(B) 잠재 책임자들을 교육하기 위한 자료를 제작한다.
(C) 존재하지 않는 회사를 경영한다.
(D) 비즈니스 홈페이지를 디자인한다.

토익 분석

행사의 목적은 행사가 소개된 직후에서 언급되므로 이 부분에 집중해야 할 필요가 있다.

What is the goal of participants in the PATC tournament?
(A) To secure an international agreement
(B) To create materials for training prospective managers
(C) To run a nonexistent company
(D) To design a business Web site

문제 해설

해당 행사의 목적이 설명된 첫 지문의 첫 단락에서 asks participants to improve and conduct business plans that make an imaginary company stable and continuous라며 참가자들에게 가상의 회사를 안정적이고 지속적으로 만드는 비즈니스 계획을 향상시키고 수행할 것을 요구하고 있다. 간단히 말해, 존재하지 않는 회사를 운영해 보는 것을 의미하므로 (C)가 정답임을 알 수 있다.

197

★★★ 진위

Phillips 씨가 PATC 대회 참가에 따른 장점으로 언급하지 않은 내용은 무엇인가?
(A) 책임자들이 수행하는 업무들에 대한 더 나은 이해
(B) 지역 기업들에게 투자할 수 있는 더 많은 기회
(C) 회사의 제공 서비스에 대한 대중들의 더 나은 인식
(D) 직원들 간의 개선된 협력

토익 분석

세부사항을 묻는 문제는 질문에서 빠른 키워드(핵심어) 파악이 중요하며 해당 키워드가 등장하는 부분을 중심으로 단서를 파악하는 것이 관건이다. 다만 질문에서의 키워드는 지문에서 유사 어휘나 표현으로 바뀔 수 있다. 아울러 세부사항/진위 문제의 경우 정독보다는 일부 단어들만 파악하며 관련 내용이 등장하고 있는지 여부를 빠르게 확인할 수 있는 스캐닝을 통해 풀이하는 것이 바람직하다.

What does Mr. Phillips NOT say is a benefit of participating in the PATC tournament?
(A) Better understanding of the tasks that managers perform
(B) Increased opportunities to invest in regional companies
(C) Greater public awareness of a company's offerings
(D) Improved cooperation among employees

문제 해설

행사 참여에 따른 장점을 묻는 문제이므로 장점, 즉 benefit이 키워드라 할 수 있다. 따라서 지문에서 benefit 또는 이와 유사한 어휘가 제시되는 부분 또는 정독보다는 일부 단어들만 확인하는 스캐닝을 통해 행사 참여에 대한 장점이 언급되는 내용이 등장할만한 부분인지 여부를 파악해야 한다. 첫 지문의 두 번째 단락에 제시된 정보들 중에서 find out about realities and complexities of an entrepreneur's work라며 기업인의 업무가 지닌 현실성과 복잡함에 관해 알게 될 것이라는 내용이 (A)에 해당되는 내용이고, 팀워크(team work)와 같은 능력을 사용하는 일은 (D)에, 그리고 serve as a promotion to the public, 즉 일반 대중들을 대상으로 한 홍보의 역할을 한다는 내용은 (C)에 해당되는 내용이다. 하지만 지역 기업들에 대한 투자는 언급된 바 없으므로 (B)가 정답이다.

198

What most likely is true about Mr. Phillips?

(A) He will be invited to a celebratory event.
(B) He is being considered for a managerial position.
(C) He has taken part in interactive online competitions before.
(D) He recommends implementing new management practices.

문제 해설

세 번째 지문의 중간 부분에서 the team representing Nexus Garage Corp. took third rank ~ The victorious team was led by Nathon Phillips라며 Phillips 씨가 이끄는 팀이 3위를 차지했다는 내용이 언급되며 있다. 아울러 두 번째 지문의 끝부분에서 will receive an honor during a ceremony on 19 November at Hotel Hilltop, Sydney, Australia라며 시상식에서 상을 받게 될 것이라 밝히고 있다. 따라서 이를 취합하면 Phillips 씨는 시상식에 초청받아 수상하게 될 것이라 유추할 수 있으므로 (A)가 정답임을 알 수 있다.

Phillips 씨에 관해 사실일 가능성이 높은 내용은 무엇인가?
(A) 기념 행사에 초청될 것이다.
(B) 책임자 자리에 대해 고려되고 있다.
(C) 예전에 온라인 상호 교류 경연대회에 참가한 적이 있었다.
(D) 새로운 경영 관행들을 시행하도록 권했다.

토익 분석

삼중 지문에 따른 문제에서 특정인에 대한 세부정보를 묻거나, probably, most likely, imply, suggest를 대동하는 유추 문제는 두 지문 연계 문제일 가능성이 매우 높다.

199

What is suggested about Nexus Garage Corporation?

(A) Its services are in great demand.
(B) It does business in England.
(C) It will formulate new business strategies in October.
(D) It registered two teams for the PATC tournament.

문제 해설

세 번째 지문에서 Many teams from England joined the event before but had never won until now. Indeed, the team representing Nexus Garage Corp. took third rank in a field consisting of 109 teams라며 영국에서 출전한 팀들은 이 행사가 시작된 이후로 한 번도 우승한 적이 없었지만 Nexus Garage 사를 대표하는 Phillips 씨의 팀이 3위를 했다는 말을 통해 영국을 대표하여 대회에 참여한 회사임을 유추할 수 있다. 따라서 Nexus Garage 사는 영국에서 비즈니스를 하는 회사라는 사실을 가늠할 수 있으므로 (B)가 정답이다.

★★★ 유추

Nexus Garage 사에 관해 유추할 수 있는 내용은 무엇인가?
(A) 서비스에 대한 수요가 많다.
(B) 영국에서 비즈니스를 한다.
(C) 10월에 새로운 사업 전략을 만들어 낼 것이다.
(D) PATC 토너먼트에 두 개의 팀을 등록했다.

토익 분석

해당 유추 문제의 키워드는 Nexus Garage이지만 Nexus Garage에 대한 내용이 기사 전반에 걸쳐 제시되고 있다. 즉, 유추 문제의 키워드가 지문 전반에 걸쳐 언급되고 있거나 키워드의 범위가 너무 넓어 키워드로서의 가치가 반감될 때는 선택지에 나온 내용을 먼저 파악한 후 이를 간단하게 정리하여 키워드로 삼아 선택지의 유추 내용이 가능한 근거가 지문에서 제시되는지 여부를 역으로 신속하게 파악하는 방식으로 문제를 풀이해야 한다.

200

What is indicated about the most recent PATC tournament?

(A) It was sponsored by a Brazilian hotel chain.
(B) It saw the introduction of a set of new criteria.
(C) It drew participation from more companies than last year's event.
(D) It received more press coverage than last year's tournament.

문제 해설

기사에 해당되는 세 번째 지문의 중간에 109 teams from over ninety companies라며 90개가 넘는 회사를 대표하여 출전한 109개의 팀들이 참가했음을 보도하고 있다. 아울러 첫 지문의 두 번째 단락 끝부분에서는 eighty-five companies participated in the event라며 작년 행사에 85개의 회사가 참여했음을 언급하고 있다. 따라서 이 두 가지 사실을 토대로 작년에 비해 더 많은 회사들이 참여했다는 점을 유추할 수 있으므로 (C)가 정답임을 알 수 있다.

★★★ 세부사항 / 두 지문 연계 문제

가장 최근에 열린 PATC 대회에 관해 알 수 있는 것은 무엇인가?
(A) 브라질 호텔 체인 회사의 후원을 받았다.
(B) 일련의 새로운 기준이 도입된 것을 경험했다.
(C) 작년의 행사보다 더 많은 회사로부터의 참여를 이끌어 냈다.
(D) 작년의 토너먼트보다 더 많은 언론의 취재를 받았다.

토익 분석

삼중 지문에서 특정 대상에 관련된 정보를 묻는 문제가 출제되는 경우, 이 때 두 개 지문에서 특정 대상에 대한 정보를 공통적으로 다루고 있다면 이는 두 지문 연계 문제라 할 수 있다. 해당 문제 역시 첫 번째 지문과 세 번째 지문이 집중적으로 PATC 대회에 대해 다루고 있으므로 이는 두 지문 연계 문제이다. 아울러 관련 내용이 굉장히 광범위하게 등장하고 있으므로 선택지의 내용을 먼저 접한 후 이를 토대로 문제를 풀이하는 것이 현명하다. 이를테면 (A)의 경우 브라질 호텔이 두 개 지문에서 모두 언급된 바 없으므로 이는 스캐닝 기법만 통해서도 오답임을 파악할 수 있는데 이러한 방식으로 두 개의 지문 중 하나의 지문에서 선택지의 특정 정보가 제시되고 있는지 여부를 파악하도록 한다.

PART 5

101 토익에 나오는 practice

★ 어휘 / 전치사

Star 상표는 1950년도에 등록되었으며 거의 70년간 사용되어왔다.

어휘 register ~을 등록하다 be in operation ~이 운영되다, ~이 가동되다 almost 거의

The 74 Star brand was registered in 1950 and has been in operation ------- almost 70 years.

(A) for
(B) since
(C) within
(D) after

문제 해설

빈칸에 적절한 전치사를 묻는 문제로 빈칸 뒤에는 almost 70 years, 즉 거의 70년이라는 기간이 등장하고 있으므로 빈칸에는 기간을 표현할 수 있는 전치사가 필요하다. 따라서 빈칸에는 '~동안'이란 뜻을 지닌 기간 전치사인 for이 와야 한다.

토익 분석

대표적인 기간 전치사로는 for / over / in / during이 있으며 일반적으로 숫자를 대동하는 기간에는 for를, 기간을 나타내는 명사를 대동하는 경우에는 during을 취한다. 아울러 since가 전치사인 경우에는 과거시점과 함께 쓰이며 전치사 within은 기간과 함께 쓰일 수 있지만 이 경우 '~이내에'란 뜻을 지니므로 주어진 문장의 의미와는 부적절하다.

102

★★★ 어형 / 형용사 & 혼동 형용사 어휘

Washington 씨는 뛰어난 지식과 능력에도 불구하고, 다른 직원들과 고객들을 배려하지 않는다.

문제 분석

be considerate of ~를 배려하다

어휘 knowledge 지식 ability 능력 considerate 배려가 깊은, 이해심이 많은 colleague 직장 동료 considerable 상당한, 꽤 consideration 고려, 배려

For all his knowledge and abilities, Mr. Washington is very not ------- of other colleagues and clients.

(A) consider
(B) considerable
(C) consideration
(D) considerate

문제 해설

빈칸에 적합한 어형을 묻는 문제이다. 빈칸이 주격 보어를 취하는 2형식 동사인 be 동사 is 뒤에 위치하고 있으므로 빈칸에는 주격 보어 역할을 할 수 있는 형용사 또는 명사가 올 수 있지만 주어인 Washington 씨와 '고려'를 뜻하는 명사 consideration이 동격 관계를 형성할 수 없으므로 형용사인 보어가 필요하다. 그러나 선택지에는 considerate과 considerable 두 개의 형용사가 제시되고 있으므로, 결과적으로 형용사 어형뿐만 아니라 제시된 두 개의 형용사 중 문맥에 적합한 의미를 지닌 형용사를 선택해야 하는 어형과 어휘 구분이 복합된 상대적으로 난이도가 높은 문제가 되겠다. 따라서 두 개의 형용사 considerate과 considerable 중에서 다른 직원들과 고객들을 배려하지 않는다는 문맥을 형성할 수 있는 '배려하는'이란 뜻을 지닌 형용사 considerate을 선택해야 한다.

토익 분석

해당 형용사가 빈칸 뒤 전치사 of 및 다른 직장 동료들/고객들이란 사람과 함께 쓰일 수 있어야 함을 고려할 때, 빈칸에는 '양/정도가 상당한 상태'를 언급하는 considerable이 아니라 '배려하고 이해심이 많은 상태'를 뜻하는 considerate가 적절하다. 아울러 '~을 배려하는'이란 뜻을 지닌 be considerate of란 표현은 필히 기억해두도록 한다.

103

Presently, the government is trying hard to find ------- ways to carry out more effective residential welfare policies.

(A) practice
(B) practical
(C) practicing
(D) practically

문제 해설

빈칸에 적합한 어형을 묻는 문제로 빈칸이 '방법'을 뜻하는 명사 ways 앞에 위치하고 있으므로 빈칸에는 명사 ways를 수식하는 형용사 어형이 위치해야 한다. 따라서 빈칸에는 '실용적인'이란 뜻을 지닌 형용사 practical이 적합하다.

토익 분석

토익에선 형용사 practical 뿐만 아니라 명사 practice에 대해서도 자주 묻고 있다. 우선 명사 practice는 '관습, 관례, 관행'이란 뜻을 지니고 있으며 이를 테면 fair trade practices는 공평한 무역 관행이라 할 수 있다. 덧붙여 명사 practice는 '기량, 숙련'을 뜻하기도 하므로 have great practice라고 하면 기술이나 솜씨가 뛰어나다는 것을 표현한다. 아울러 변호사/의사와 같은 전문가들이 개인적으로 영리 활동을 하는 것 또한 practice라고 한다. 예를 들자면 malpractice는 의료사고를 뜻하며 a lawyer in practice라고 하면 변호사로서 개업하고 변호사로서 영리 활동을 행하는 것을 의미한다. 토익에 대비하여 이러한 의미의 명사 practice를 필히 숙지해야 한다.

★어형 / 형용사

현재, 정부는 좀 더 효과적인 주거복지 정책을 시행할 수 있는 실용적인 방법을 강구하고자 굉장히 노력하고 있다.

문제 분석

ways to Vr ~하는 방법

어휘 presently 현재 practical 실용적인 carry out ~을 시행하다 effective 효과적인 residential 거주의 welfare policy 복지정책

104

The new battery charger is ------- with almost all types of mobile phones on the domestic market.

(A) popular
(B) compatible
(C) innovative
(D) concerned

문제 해설

빈칸에 적절한 형용사 어휘를 묻는 문제이다. 빈칸에 앞서 새로운 충전기란 제품이 등장하고 있으며 빈칸 뒤에는 국내 시장에 출시된 거의 대부분의 휴대 전화들이 제시되고 있다. 휴대폰 충전기란 상품으로 인해 이와 쉽게 연계가 가능한 인기가 많다는 popular 또는 혁신적이란 innovative를 정답으로 우선시할 수 있겠으나 popular는 뒤이은 with 이하에 사람들이 등장하여 그 사람들에게 인기를 얻고 있다는 의미를 형성하며 innovative는 with 이하에 혁신을 이루게 하는 구체적인 수단이 제시되어야 한다. 하지만 문제에서 with 이하는 국내 시장에 출시된 거의 대부분의 휴대 전화들이란 almost all types of mobile phones이 등장하고 있으므로 이들은 모두 오답으로 소거해야 한다. 또한 concerned는 걱정을 하거나 관심을 갖고 있는 상태를 뜻하고 있으므로 휴대폰 충전기란 주어와 같이 쓰일 수 없다. 따라서 빈칸에는 새로운 충전기가 국내 시장에 출시된 대부분의 휴대 전화들과 사용이 가능하다는 문맥을 구성할 수 있도록 호환이 가능하다는 뜻을 지닌 compatible이 적합하다.

★★★ 어휘 / 형용사

새로운 충전기는 국내 시장에 출시된 거의 대부분의 휴대 전화와 호환이 가능하다.

어휘 battery charger 충전기 type 종류 mobile phone 휴대전화 domestic 국내의 be compatible with ~와 호환이 가능한, ~와 병행이 가능한 innovative 혁신적인 unavailable 이용이 불가한, 구매가 불가한

105

★★ 어휘 / 명사

회사는 소비자 프로필이 기록되어 한시적으로 보관이 될 것임을 보장하였다.

어휘 give assurance that ~라는 것을 보장하다 profile 개요, 분석표, 경력, 측면 모습 record 기록, ~을 기록하다 limited 제한된, 한정된 value 가치 ahead 앞서

The company gave assurance that consumer profiles will be recorded and kept for a limited ------- of time.

(A) part
(B) amount
(C) value
(D) ahead

문제 해설

빈칸이 과거분사 형태의 형용사인 limited 뒤에 위치하고 있으며 선택지가 명사 어휘를 중심으로 구성되어 있기 때문에 빈칸에 적합한 명사 어휘를 묻는 문제임을 알 수 있다. 아울러 빈칸 앞에 '제한된, 한정된'이란 뜻의 limited와 빈칸 뒤에 '시간'을 뜻하는 time이 위치하고 있음을 고려할 때 빈칸에는 한정된 시간의 양을 언급할 수 있는 amount가 적절하다.

토익 분석

토익에 대비하여 명사 amount는 금전과 관련해선 '액수, 금액, 총액'이라는 뜻으로 쓰이지만 그 외에는 '양'을 뜻하는 어휘로 쓰인다는 점을 알아두도록 한다.

106

★★ 어휘 / 명사

연구 실험실에서 인화성 물질을 취급하기 전에 사전 안전 규정을 필히 준수해야한다.

어휘 safety 안전 handle ~을 다루다, ~을 취급하다 flammable 인화의, 불이 붙기 쉬운 chemical 화학물질 laboratory 실험실 speculation 심사숙고, 사색, 투기 manual 수동의, 설명서 precaution 주의, 예방조치 inspector 조사관, 검사관

Safety ------- must be taken before handling the flammable chemicals in the research laboratory.

(A) speculation
(B) manuals
(C) precautions
(D) inspectors

문제 해설

빈칸이 동사인 must be 앞에 위치하고 있으므로 빈칸에는 '안전'을 뜻하는 safety란 명사와 결합하여 문맥에 적합한 주어를 구성할 수 있는 명사 어휘가 와야 한다. 연구 실험실에서 인화성 물질을 취급하기에 앞서 필히 취해야 하는 대상을 지칭하는 명사 어휘여야 하므로 빈칸에는 safety와 함께 안전 예방조치란 의미를 구성할 수 있는 precautions가 적합하다.

토익 분석

토익에서는 안전과 관련된 복합명사가 많이 다뤄진 편이라 할 수 있다. 대표적으로 '안전 규정'을 뜻하는 safety regulations, '안전 기준'을 뜻하는 safety standards, '사전 안전 규정'을 뜻하는 safety precautions, 그리고 '안전 검사'를 뜻하는 safety inspection 등은 기본적으로 숙지하고 있도록 한다.

107

Mr. Kiesling will work at the company's Moscow branch office, ------- three of his colleagues will work in Seoul.

(A) while
(B) in case
(C) during
(D) that

★★ 접속사 / 부사절 접속사

Kiesling 씨는 회사의 Moscow 지점에서 근무하지만, 그의 직장 동료 세 명은 서울 지점에서 근무하게 된다.

어휘 work at ~에서 일하다, ~에서 근무하다 branch office 지사, 지점 colleague 직장동료 while ~하는 동안에, ~인 반면에 in case ~인 경우에 대비하여, ~인 경우에는 during ~하는 동안

문제 해설

빈칸을 전후하여 등장한 두 개의 절과 하나의 마침표를 통해 빈칸에 적합한 접속사를 묻는 문제임을 알 수 있으므로 우선 전치사 during은 오답으로 소거해야 한다. 아울러 that은 명사절/형용사절 접속사로 쓰일 땐 콤마와 함께 쓰이지 못하므로 이 또한 오답이 되겠다. 그러므로 while과 in case (that)이란 부사절 접속사 중 정답을 택일해야 하며 두 절의 내용이 Kiesling 씨가 회사의 Moscow 지점에서 근무하는 반면 그의 직장 동료 세 명은 서울 지점에서 근무하게 된다는 서로 상반되는 내용이 제시되고 있음을 고려할 때 빈칸에는 역접 관계를 뜻하는 부사절 접속사가 와야 한다. 따라서 빈칸에는 '~인 반면에'란 뜻을 지닌 while이 적절하다.

토익 분석

부사절 접속사 while은 '~인 반면에'란 뜻으로 역접 관계를 나타내며 이는 whereas로 대체할 수 있다는 점과 아울러 '~하는 동안'이란 의미의 시간 부사절 접속사로 쓰이기도 한다는 점을 알고 있어야 한다.

108

According to marketing experts, customers usually make purchasing decision ------- two minutes.

(A) towards
(B) within
(C) about
(D) up to

★★ 어휘 / 전치사

시장 전문가에 따르면, 고객들은 대개 2분 안에 구매를 할 것인지 여부에 대한 결정을 내린다고 한다.

어휘 marketing expert 마케팅 전문가 usually 대개, 일반적으로 purchasing decision 구매 결정 towards ~를 향해 about ~에 관해, 약, 대략 up to 최대 ~에 달하는

문제 해설

빈칸에 적합한 전치사를 묻는 문제로 빈칸 뒤에는 2분이란 시간이 등장하고 있다. 그러므로 빈칸에는 시간과 함께 쓰이는 것이 가능한 전치사가 필요하며 또한 빈칸에 앞서 구매 결정을 내린다는 make purchasing decision이 위치하고 있음을 고려할 때 2분이란 시간은 구매 결정을 내리기 위한 제한 시간임을 가늠할 수 있다. 따라서 빈칸에는 '~이내에'란 뜻을 지닌 within이 와야 한다. 아울러 about이나 over 또한 시간과 함께 쓰이는 것이 가능하나 숫자를 대동하는 about은 '대략, 약'이란 뜻의 부사로 대략 어느 정도 수치인지를 나타낼 뿐이고 전치사 up to 역시 대동하는 숫자가 최대치라는 의미를 지닐 뿐이므로 이들 모두 오답으로 처리해야 한다.

토익 분석

숫자 앞에서 '대략, 약'이란 뜻으로 숫자를 수식하는 대표적인 부사 어휘로는 about, approximately, almost, nearly, around, roughly 등이 있다. 덧붙여 최대치를 뜻하는 up to, 최소한을 뜻하는 at least 그리고 정확히 해당 수치만 언급하는 just와 only도 함께 알아둬야 할 필요가 있다.

★ 어형 / 부사

첨단 기술이 지속적으로 발전해오고 있기 때문에, 자동차들은 그 어느 때보다 주행 안정성을 강화시키는 더 많은 전자 기능들을 구비하고 있다.

문제 분석

be equipped with ~가 구비되다
in order to Vr ~하기 위해서

어휘 high technology 첨단 기술 be equipped with ~을 구비하다, ~이 장착되다 electronic feature 전자 기능 in order to Vr ~하기 위해서 enhance ~을 강화하다 driving stability 주행 안정성 continual 지속적인

As high technologies have been ------- developing, cars are equipped with more electronic features than ever in order to enhance their driving stability.

(A) continue
(B) continues
(C) continual
(D) continually

문제 해설

빈칸에 적합한 어형을 묻는 문제로 빈칸이 has been과 developing 사이에 위치하고 있으므로 빈칸에는 developing이라는 준동사를 수식할 수 있는 부사가 위치해야 한다. V-ing 형태나 To 부정사 형태와 같은 준동사들은 어떠한 품사의 역할을 하더라도 기본적으로 준동사이므로 이들은 부사의 수식을 받게 된다는 점을 잊지 않도록 해야 한다. 따라서 빈칸에는 부사 어형인 continually가 적절하다.

 동사에 따라 달라지는 전치사

★★ 어휘 / 동사

부사장님은 한 직원에게 기자회견을 11월 23일로 재조정하라고 언급했다.

문제 분석

reschedule A for B A의 일정을 B로 재조정하다

어휘 vice president 부사장, 부회장 press conference 기자회견 host ~을 개최하다 postpone ~을 연기하다 prolong ~을 늘리다, ~을 연장하다

The vice president asked one of his employees to ------- the press conference for November 23.

(A) host
(B) reschedule
(C) postpone
(D) prolong

문제 해설

빈칸에 적합한 동사를 묻는 문제로 빈칸에는 for November 23, 즉 11월 23일이란 시점과 어울리는 동사가 필요하므로 host/reschedule/postpone 중에서 정답을 택일해야 한다. 그러나 이 중 전치사 for을 취할 수 있는 동사는 reschedule 뿐이다.

토익 분석

동사에 따라 전치사가 달라지는 경우가 발생한다. 이를테면 정해진 시간이나 날짜 앞에는 일반적으로 전치사 on을 취하는데, 동사 host가 이에 해당한다. 아울러 (re)schedule/plan은 날짜, 시간, 요일 앞에 전치사 for을 취하지만 postpone은 날짜, 시간 요일 앞에 전치사 to/until이 온다. 이들은 모두 토익에서 출제가 되고 있는 부분이므로 각각의 동사에 따른 전치사를 명확하게 파악하여 숙지하도록 한다.

111

Ace Electronics has recently launched a ------- of innovative and high-performance computers.

(A) length
(B) portion
(C) series
(D) shortage

★★ 어휘 / 명사

Ace Electronics 사는 최근에 혁신적이고 우수한 성능을 지닌 일련의 컴퓨터 제품들을 출시했다.

어휘 recently 최근에 launch ~을 출시하다 innovative 혁신적인 high-performance 우수한 성능의 length 길이 portion 부분, 일부, 양, 분량, 인분 series 시리즈, 일련, 연작 shortage 부족

문제 해설

빈칸에 적합한 명사 어휘를 묻는 문제로 빈칸 뒤에는 컴퓨터 제품들을 뜻하는 computers가 등장하고 있다. 따라서 여러 컴퓨터 제품들을 포함할 수 있는 명사 어휘가 필요하므로 빈칸에는 '시리즈, 일련, 연작'을 뜻하는 명사 series가 위치해야 한다.

토익 분석

명사 series는 단/복수 형태가 동일한 명사로 이 series란 명사만 단독적으로 출제되는 경우는 없다. 항상 a series of란 표현 자체가 출제되는 만큼 이 표현을 알아두는 것이 바람직하다. 또한 비록 오답으로 제시되었지만 '~의 일부'를 뜻하는 a portion of 그리고 '~의 부족'을 의미하는 a shortage of는 토익에서 출제된 전력이 있는 표현이므로 꼭 숙지하도록 한다.

112

As a token of our apology, ------- is a $50 gift certificate we hope you will accept as a gesture of good will.

(A) attach
(B) attachment
(C) attached
(D) attaching

★★★ 어형 및 도치 / 과거분사 & 주격 보어 도치

사과의 의미로, 50달러에 달하는 상품권을 동봉해 보내 드리며 호의의 표시로 받아 들여 주시기를 희망합니다.

문제 분석

As a token of ~의 표시로서

어휘 token 표시 apology 사과 attach ~을 첨부하다 gift certificate 상품권 gesture 몸동작, 표시 good will 선의, 호의

문제 해설

빈칸에 적합한 어형을 묻는 문제이다. 우선 빈칸이 be 동사 is 앞에 위치하고 있으므로 주어 역할을 할 수 있는 명사가 필요하다고 여기어 attachment라는 명사 어형을 정답으로 택하곤 한다. 그러나 실제 주어는 50달러라는 상품권이므로 빈칸에는 상품권이 첨부되었음을 뜻하는 과거분사 형태의 형용사 attached가 와야 한다.

토익 분석

토익에서 주격 보어를 강조하고자 하는 도치 구문 관련 문제는 항상 동사 attach, enclose, include와 연계되어 출제되고 있다는 경향을 숙지하도록 한다.

★★ 어형 / To 부정사

BK 사는 직원들이 외국어를 구사할 수 있는 적절한 방법을 가르치는 특별 언어 과정을 제공한다.

어휘 offer ~을 제공하다 proper 알맞은, 적절한

BK Corporation offers special language courses to teach employees the proper way ------- foreign languages.

(A) speak
(B) to speak
(C) speaking
(D) spoken

문제 해설

빈칸에 적합한 어형을 묻는 문제이다. 빈칸이 명사인 way 뒤에 위치하고 있으므로 명사 way를 수식함과 동시에 foreign languages를 목적어로 취할 수 있는 어형이 필요하며, 명사 way는 To 부정사의 후치 수식을 받는 어휘이므로 빈칸에는 to speak가 적절하다.

토익 분석

토익에서 To 부정사의 후치 수식을 받는 명사 어휘로 출제 비중이 높은 편에 속하는 명사어휘로는 authority, ability, plan, time, way, effort, chance, opportunity가 있음을 필히 숙지하도록 한다.

★ 어휘 / 전치사

정부는 중동 지역의 일부 국가들에서 원유와 천연가스의 수입량을 늘릴 예정이다.

어휘 volume 부피, 규모, 권 crude oil 원유 natural gas 천연가스 import ~을 수입하다

The government will increase the volume of crude oil and natural gas imported ------- some countries of the Middle East.

(A) within
(B) from
(C) after
(D) throughout

문제 해설

빈칸에 적합한 전치사를 묻는 문제로 빈칸 앞에는 수입되는 원유와 천연가스 양을 뜻하는 the volume of crude oil and natural gas imported가, 빈칸 뒤에는 중동 지역의 일부 국가들을 뜻하는 some countries of the Middle East가 등장하고 있다. 따라서 원유와 천연가스를 수입하는 출처로서의 중동 지역의 일부 국가들을 지칭할 수 있는 전치사가 필요하므로 빈칸에는 '~로부터'란 뜻을 지닌 전치사 from이 와야 한다.

115

------- takes the chief executive officer job, the business situation facing our company is too difficult to expect a quick and sharp improvement.

(A) Whichever
(B) Whoever
(C) Since
(D) Even though

★★★ 접속사 / 복합 관계부사 & 부사절 접속사

누가 최고 경영자 직을 맡더라도, 우리 회사가 직면한 사업 환경이 빠르고 급속하게 나아질 것이라 기대하기엔 무리가 있다.

어휘 chief executive officer 최고 경영자 sharp 날카로운, 급격한, 뚜렷한 improvement 향상, 개선 face ~에 직면하다

문제 해설

빈칸에 적절한 접속사를 묻는 문제로 빈칸이 부사절을 이끄는 부사절 접속사 자리에 위치하고 있다. 아울러 해당 부사절은 주어가 없는 불완전한 구조의 절임을 고려할 때 완전한 구조의 절과 함께 쓰이는 since와 even though는 바로 오답으로 처리해야 한다. 따라서 불완전한 구조의 절과 함께 쓰이는 복합 관계부사인 whichever과 복합 관계대명사 whoever 중 정답을 택일해야 하며 빈칸 이후 takes the chief executive officer job, 즉 최고 경영직을 맡는다는 내용이 제시되고 있음을 고려할 때 빈칸에는 Whichever이 아닌 Whoever이 적합하다.

토익 분석

Whoever, Whomever, Whatever, Whichever은 복합 관계대명사라 칭하며 Whenever, Wherever, However은 복합 관계부사라 일컫는다. 기본적으로 복합 관계사는 선행사를 취하지 않는다는 특징을 지니고 있으며 Whoever, Whomever, Whatever, Whichever은 모두 불완전한 구조의 절과 함께 쓰이는 반면 Whenever, Wherever, However은 완전한 절의 구조와 함께 쓰인다는 구조적 특징을 명확하게 파악해야 한다. 또한 However은 뒤에 형용사 혹은 부사를 필히 대동한다는 특징을 알고 있어야 한다.

116

Entrepreneurs usually read newspapers and business magazines in order to obtain ------- information about the recent consumer trends.

(A) assigned
(B) obscure
(C) sensitive
(D) accurate

★★ 어휘 / 형용사

사람들은 대개 다양한 사회 현상에 대한 정확한 정보를 획득하고자 신문과 잡지를 읽는다.

어휘 obtain 획득하다 obscure 모호한

문제 해설

빈칸에 적절한 형용사 어휘를 묻는 문제이다. 빈칸 앞에는 사람들이 신문과 잡지를 읽는다는 내용이 등장하고 있으며 빈칸 이후에는 사회 현상과 관련된 정보가 등장하고 있다. 따라서 사람들이 얻고자 하는 정보의 성격을 언급할 수 있는 형용사가 필요하므로 빈칸에는 '정확한'이란 뜻을 지닌 accurate가 위치하여 사람들이 사회 현상에 대한 정확한 정보를 얻고자 신문이나 잡지를 읽는다는 문맥을 구성하는 것이 바람직하다.

토익 분석

아울러 '민감한'이란 뜻의 sensitive가 information과 함께 쓰이는 경우 이는 민감한 정보, 즉 기밀 정보란 뜻으로 지금까지 토익에선 이에 관해 confidential information이 출제되었으나 최근엔 sensitive information이 새롭게 출제된 바 있으므로 이를 무조건 익혀두도록 한다.

117

★★ 어휘 / 형용사

Godong Landscaping Service사가 적절한 가격으로 회사가 새로운 정원을 조성하는 공사를 감리해줄 수 있으므로 최종적으로 공사를 감독하는 회사로 선정되었다.

문제 분석

given that ~라는 점을 고려할 때

어휘 landscaping 조경 choose ~을 선택하다 given that ~라는 점을 고려할 때 project 프로젝트, 공사 supervise ~을 감독하다 compact 소형의, 아주 조밀한 considerable 상당한, 꽤 sharp 날카로운

Godong Landscaping Service was chosen to supervise the construction of a new company garden given that it can do the project at a ------- price.

(A) compact

(B) considerable

(C) sharp

(D) reasonable

문제 해설

빈칸에 적합한 명사를 묻는 문제이다. 빈칸 뒤에 가격을 뜻하는 price가 등장하고 있으므로 빈칸에는 price와 함께 쓰일 수 있는 형용사이자 전체 문맥에 적합한 뜻을 지닌 형용사 어휘를 선택해야 한다. 우선 '소형의, 아주 조밀한'이란 뜻의 compact는 price와 함께 쓰일 수 없는 어휘이며 이어서 considerable은 price와 함께 상당한 가격이란 의미를 형성할 수 있으나 문맥에 적합하지 않으므로 이들은 모두 오답이다. 아울러 sharp는 price가 아닌 상승/증가를 뜻하는 rise/increase 또는 하락을 뜻하는 drop/decline/decrease 등과 함께 쓰이는 것이 적합하다. 따라서 빈칸에는 적절한 가격으로 인해 공사 감리사로 선정이 되었다는 논리적으로 타당한 문맥을 구성할 수 있는 형용사 reasonable이 와야 한다.

토익 분석

가격/비용과 관련된 형용사 어휘 문제를 묻는 문제는 토익에서 아주 오랫동안 출제되어 온 전통적인 문제지만 그럼에도 불구하고 여전히 신토익에서도 등장하고 있으며 주로 affordable/competitive/reasonable이란 형용사들이 정답으로 제시되고 있음을 알아두도록 한다.

118

★★ 접속사 / 결과 부사절 접속사

새로운 아파트들은 수익성이 매우 좋아서 향후 몇 년 간 아파트 재건축 계획들이 종종 발표될 것이다.

문제 분석

so + 형용사/부사 + that + 주어 + 동사~ 매우 ~해서 ~라는 결과를 낳다

어휘 usually 대개, 일반적으로 profitable 수익성이 좋은 reconstruction project 재건축 계획 pop up ~이 발생하다, ~이 나타나다 such as ~와 같은 therefore 따라서, 고로, 그러므로

New apartments are usually so profitable ------- reconstruction projects often pop up for the next several years.

(A) such as

(B) that

(C) which

(D) therefore

문제 해설

빈칸을 중심으로 두 개의 절들이 등장하고 있으므로 빈칸에는 적절한 접속사가 필요하다. 그러므로 전치사 such as와 인과 관계를 나타내는 접속부사 therefore는 오답으로 소거해야 한다. 아울러 빈칸 뒤 reconstruction projects often pop up for the next several years는 완전한 구조의 절이므로 불완전한 구조의 절과 함께 쓰이는 which 역시 오답으로 처리해야 한다. 빈칸에 앞선 so profitable은 수익이 좋다는 원인/이유가 되며 빈칸 이후의 향후 몇 년간 아파트 재건축 계획들이 발표될 것이란 의미는 그에 따른 결과라 할 수 있다. 따라서 결과적 의미의 부사절을 구성하기 위해선 'so 형용사/부사 that 주어 + 동사~' 구조가 필요하므로 빈칸에는 that이 와야 한다.

토익 분석

결과 부사절 접속사에서는 so와 that 사이에 형용사 어형과 부사 어형 중 어떠한 어형이 위치해야 하는지 묻는 문제 또한 숙지하고 있어야 할 문제 유형이다. 이 때는 so 앞 쪽에서 맨 처음으로 접하는 동사 혹은 준동사가 be/become이라면 so that 사이에는 형용사, 그 외 동사가 오면 so that 사이에는 부사가 와야 한다는 점을 알아두도록 한다.

119

Our hotel suites feel like your own private paradise since the hotel is located on the island of Borneo and it is ------- only by boat.

(A) transported
(B) accessible
(C) operated
(D) adjacent

★★ 어휘 / 형용사

우리 호텔은 Borneo 섬에 위치하고 있으며 배를 통해서만 접근이 가능하므로 호텔 객실들은 고객님만의 개인적인 안식처처럼 느껴질 것입니다.

어휘 suite 객실 private 사적인 transport ~을 운송하다 accessible 이용이 가능한, 접근이 가능한 adjacent 인접한

문제 해설

빈칸에 적절한 형용사 어휘를 묻는 문제로 빈칸 앞에는 호텔이 Borneo 섬에 있다는 위치적 특징에 대해 언급하고 있으며 빈칸 이후에는 배라는 교통수단을 통해서라는 내용이 제시되고 있다. 그러므로 배라는 교통수단과 Borneo 섬에 있는 호텔을 연계한다면 배라는 교통수단을 이용해서 그 호텔에 갈 수 있다는 내용이 구성되는 것이 논리적으로 타당하다. 따라서 빈칸에는 '접근이 가능한'이란 뜻을 지닌 형용사 accessible이 와야 한다.

토익 분석

형용사 accessible 외에도 명사 access는 전치사 to와 함께 쓰인다는 점과 동사 access는 전치사가 없이 명사 목적어를 바로 취하는 타동사라는 점을 꼭 숙지하도록 한다.

120

Rhode Island was one of the ------- gateways to the city of New York for the Scot-Irish, who moved to the United States in the early nineteenth century.

(A) principal
(B) outgoing
(C) eligible
(D) constant

★★★ 어휘 / 형용사

Rhode Island는 19세기 초 미국으로 이주해오는 스코틀랜드와 아일랜드 사람들이 New York 시로 입국하는 주요한 관문 중 한 곳이었다.

어휘 gateway 관문 move to ~로 들어가다, ~로 이주하다 principal 주요한 eligible 자격을 갖춘 constant 지속적인

문제 해설

빈칸에 알맞은 형용사 어휘를 묻는 문제로 빈칸이 관문을 뜻하는 명사 gateways 앞에 위치하고 있으므로 관문에 적절한 의미를 지닌 형용사가 필요하다. 아울러 이 관문은 19세기 초 미국으로 이주해오는 스코틀랜드와 아일랜드 사람들이 New York 시로 입국하려면 필히 거쳐 가야 하는 곳임을 고려할 때 이 곳은 이민자들이 통과해야 하는 주된 관문이라 할 수 있다. 그러므로 빈칸에는 '주요한, 주된'이란 뜻의 principal이 적합하다.

토익 분석

우선 형용사 outgoing은 외향적인 성격을 뜻하며 eligible은 자격을 갖춘 상태를 뜻하며 모두 사람에게만 쓰일 수 있으므로 이들은 오답이다. 형용사 constant는 지속적이고 일정한 상태를 뜻하는데 이는 역으로 생각하면 심정/성질/성격적 상태의 변화가 존재하는 대상에게만 쓸 수 있다는 것이다. 따라서 관문과 같이 심정/성질/성격적 상태의 변화가 없는 무생물 대상과는 어울리지 않기 때문에 오답이 된다. 그런데 지속적인 관문이라는 의미가 적합하다고 여겨서 constant를 정답으로 선택했다가 오답이라 당황했다면 세상에 한발 차이로 아깝게 놓치거나 실패하는 일들은 부지기수이니 너무 자괴감에 빠지지 않도록 하며 아울러 이를 통해 어휘 문제를 풀이할 때는 단순한 자신의 해석에 대해 집중하는 것이 중요한 것이 아니라 출제자의 의도 및 어휘의 쓰임새를 파악하는 것이 필수적이라는 교훈을 얻게 된 것이니 도리어 기쁘다고 해야 할 일이다. 가장 가치가 있는 것은 이 곳에서 틀리고 토익 고사장에선 틀리지 않는 것이다.

121

★★ 어형 / 부사

그 자료에 따르면, 우리 직원들의 생산성은 다른 경쟁사
들의 생산성에 비해 현저하게 더 높다고 했다.

어휘 productivity 생산성 rival company 경쟁사
significantly 상당하게, 꽤

According to the data, the productivity of our employees was ------- higher than that of rival companies.

(A) significance
(B) significant
(C) more significant
(D) significantly

문제 해설

빈칸에 적절한 어형을 묻고 있으며 빈칸은 be동사인 was와 주격 보어인 비교급 형용사 higher 사이
에 위치하고 있다. 따라서 빈칸에는 형용사를 수식하는 부사가 필요하므로 significantly라는 부사
어형이 와야 한다.

토익 분석

토익에서는 비교급 형용사를 수식하는 대표적인 부사 어휘로 significantly와 considerably를 묻는
문제도 출제되고 있으므로 이에 대비하여 이 둘을 필히 숙지하도록 한다.

122

★★★ 대명사 / 부정 형용사 + 대명사

우리 시립 미술관이 보유하고 있는 세계적으로 유명한 그
림들은 하나 하나가 500년 이상된 작품들이어서 이를 관
람하고자 해마다 수백만 명의 관객들이 방문하고 있다.

어휘 famous 유명한 painting 그림 municipal 시의, 시
립의, 지방자치의 visitor 방문객

------- of the world famous paintings in our municipal gallery is over 500 years old, and we receive millions of visitors each year.

(A) They
(B) All
(C) Each one
(D) Other

문제 해설

빈칸에 적합한 어휘나 표현을 묻는 문제이다. 빈칸이 문두의 주어 자리에 위치하고 있으므로 주어
역할을 할 수 있는 명사나 대명사가 와야 함을 알 수 있다. 주격 대명사인 They는 단수동사인 is에
적합하지 않을 뿐만 아니라 of the world's most famous paintings in our municipal gallery란 전
치사구의 수식을 받기에 부적절한 인칭 대명사이므로 오답이다. All이 가산 복수명사와 함께 쓰이
는 부정 형용사나 가산 복수명사에 대한 부정 대명사로 쓰이는 경우 복수로 취급 받기 때문에 단수
동사인 is와 함께 쓰일 수 없으므로 이 또한 오답이다. Other은 부정 대명사로 쓰이는 것이 불가하
므로 이 역시 오답으로 소거해야 한다. 반면에 Each는 부정 형용사로 가산 단수명사와 쓰일 수 있을
뿐만 아니라 단독적으로 부정 대명사로 쓰일 수 있으며, 어떠한 경우라도 단수로 처리되어 단수동
사와 함께 쓰인다. 따라서 빈칸에는 부정 형용사인 Each와 부정 대명사인 one이 함께 결합된 each
one이 와야 한다.

토익 분석

부정 형용사나 부정 대명사로 출제되는 비중이 가장 높은 어휘들을 손꼽자면 바로 each/every라 할
수 있다. 무엇보다 each/every는 가산 단수명사와 쓰이므로 동사 또한 단수동사 형태를 취하게 된다.
반면에 each는 부정 형용사뿐만 아니라 부정 대명사로서 쓰이는 것이 가능하지만 every는 부정 형
용사로는 쓰이지만 부정 대명사로는 사용이 불가하다는 점을 필히 숙지해야 한다.

123

Domestic steel production rose ------- this year maintaining our company in second position after Haru Steel.

(A) mostly
(B) conspicuously
(C) technically
(D) marginally

★★★ 어휘 / 부사

국내 철강 생산량은 올해 소폭으로 증가했으며 이로 인해 철강 생산량에 있어 Haru Steel에 이어 2위를 차지할 수 있었었다.

어휘 domestic 국내의 steel 철강 production 생산 maintain ~을 유지하다 mostly 대부분, 주로, 거의 conspicuously 두드러지게, 현저하게 technically 기술적으로 marginally 가까스로, 조금만, 소폭으로, 가장자리에

문제 해설

빈칸에 알맞은 부사 어휘를 묻는 문제로 빈칸이 '상승하다'란 뜻을 지닌 동사 rise의 과거 시제 형태인 rose 뒤에 위치하고 있으므로 '상승하다'란 뜻을 지닌 동사를 수식할 수 있는 부사 어휘가 필요하다. 상승/증가와 연관된 부사 어휘라면 상승/증가의 폭이 크거나 혹은 적다는 의미를 형성할 수 있는 뜻을 지닌 부사 어휘뿐이다. 따라서 빈칸에는 '소폭으로, 경미하게'란 뜻을 지닌 부사 어휘인 marginally가 적합하다.

토익 분석

상승/증가/변화와 연관된 부사 어휘라면 상승/증가/변화의 폭이 크거나 혹은 적다는 의미를 형성할 수 있는 뜻을 지닌 부사 어휘라 할 수 있다. 상승/증가/변화의 폭이 크다는 의미를 지닌 대표적인 부사 어휘로는 considerably, significantly, substantially, sharply, dramatically, markedly가 되겠다. 반면에 싱숭/증가/변화의 폭이 적다는 뜻을 지닌 부사 이휘로는 slightly, marginally를 알아두어야 한다. 덧붙여 점진적으로 증가하거나 감소하는 경우도 발생할 수 있으므로 이를 표현할 수 있는 incrementally, gradually 또한 숙지하는 편이 바람직하다.

124

We can't improve our competitiveness in the global market ------- we develop innovative technologies to commercialize.

(A) because
(B) neither
(C) when
(D) unless

★★ 접속사 / 부사절 접속사

상업화시킬 수 있는 혁신적인 기술들을 개발하지 못한다면, 우리는 세계 시장에서 경쟁력을 향상시키지 못할 것이다.

어휘 hardly 거의 ~할 것 같지 않다 improve ~을 향상시키다, ~을 개선하다 competitiveness 경쟁력 innovative 혁신적인 commercialize ~을 상업화하다

문제 해설

빈칸이 두 절 사이에 위치하고 있으므로 빈칸에 적합한 접속사를 묻는 문제이다. 무엇보다 neither은 접속사가 아니므로 우선적으로 이를 오답으로 소거해야 한다. 빈칸 앞에는 세계 시장에서 경쟁력을 향상시키지 못할 것이란 내용이 등장하고 있으며 빈칸 뒤에는 우리가 상업화시킬 수 있는 혁신적인 기술들을 개발한다는 내용이 언급되고 있다. 하지만 상업화시킬 수 있는 혁신적인 기술들을 개발하는데 세계 시장에서 경쟁력을 향상시키지 못한다는 것은 어폐가 있다. 따라서 빈칸에는 혁신적인 기술들을 개발하지 못한다는 의미를 형성할 수 있도록 부사절 접속사인 unless가 와야 한다.

125

★★ 어휘 / 동사

많은 영업 직원들은 젊은 소비자의 관심을 끌기 위해 sns 및 다양한 인터넷 블로그를 지속적으로 사용하고 있다.

어휘 consistently 지속적으로 various 다양한 consumer 소비자 call out 크게 부르다, 소집하다, 요구하다 appeal to ~에 호소하다, ~을 매료하다

Many salespeople are consistently using social network services and various online blogs to ------- young consumers.

(A) call out
(B) manage
(C) advertise
(D) appeal to

문제 해설

빈칸에 적합한 동사구를 묻는 문제이다. 빈칸 앞에는 많은 영업 직원들이 sns 및 다양한 인터넷 블로그를 지속적으로 사용하고 있다는 내용이 등장하고 있으며 빈칸 뒤에는 젊은 소비자들이 언급되고 있다. 그러므로 빈칸에는 많은 영업 직원들이 sns 및 다양한 인터넷 블로그를 이용하는 것과 젊은 소비자들과의 상관 관계를 설명할 수 있는 동사구가 필요하다. 따라서 sns 및 다양한 인터넷 블로그를 이용하는 것은 젊은 소비자들의 관심을 끌기 위한 목적으로 행하는 것임을 가늠할 수 있으므로 빈칸에는 '~에 호소하다/~를 매료하다'란 뜻을 지닌 appeal to가 와야 한다.

126

★ 어형 / 형용사

만약 고객들이 더욱 구체적인 정보를 원한다면, 그들은 질문을 좀 더 상세하게 해야 한다.

어휘 detailed 세부적인 specify ~을 구체화하다 specific 구체적인, 상세한 specifics 세부사항

If customers want more ------- information, they should make their questions more detailed.

(A) specify
(B) specific
(C) specifics
(D) specifically

문제 해설

빈칸에 적합한 어형을 묻는 문제로, 빈칸이 information이란 명사 앞에 위치하고 있으므로 명사를 수식할 수 있는 형용사 어형이 필요하다. 그러므로 빈칸에는 '구체적인'이란 뜻을 지닌 형용사인 specific이 와야 한다.

토익 분석

무엇보다 specific은 형용사일 뿐만 아니라 specifics란 복수명사 형태로 쓰여 세부적인 내용을 뜻할 수도 있다는 점을 꼭 숙지하도록 한다.

127

According to the market analysis report, Gaby Technologies' price ------- will not bring any changes to the domestic market.

(A) reductions
(B) anticipations
(C) exchanges
(D) sensations

문제 해설

빈칸에는 '가격'을 뜻하는 명사 price와 결합하여 문맥에 부합하는 의미를 지닌 복합명사를 구성하는 명사 어휘가 필요하다. 무엇보다 가격과 연관되어 쓰일 수 있는 대표적인 복합 명사의 의미라면 가격 인상/인하 또는 가격 할인 정도라 할 수 있으며 이 중 시장 내 변화를 이루기 위해 행해지는 조치라고 한다면 가격 인하나 가격 할인이 그에 해당된다고 볼 수 있다. 따라서 빈칸에는 '감소, 감축, 절감' 등을 뜻하는 명사 reductions가 적합하다.

★★ 명사 어휘

시장 분석 보고서에 따르면, Gaby Technologies 사의 가격 인하는 국내 시장에 어떠한 변화도 가져오지 못할 것이라 한다.

어휘 market analysis 시장 분석 domestic 국내의 anticipation 기대 exchange 교환, ~을 교환하다 sensation 감각, 느낌, 대소동

128

Some economists predict that the pace of economic recovery will slow down without a ------- improvement in the fourth quarter.

(A) marked
(B) broad
(C) intensive
(D) respective

문제 해설

빈칸에 적절한 형용사 어휘를 묻는 문제로 빈칸 뒤에 회복/상승/향상을 뜻하는 improvement가 위치하고 있으므로 빈칸에는 회복/상승/향상과 연관되어 쓰일 수 있는 형용사 어휘가 필요하다. 따라서 4분기에서의 현저한 경기 향상이 없이 경제 회복의 속도가 더디어 질 것으로 예측했다는 내용이 논리적으로 타당하므로 빈칸에는 marked가 위치해야 한다.

★★ 어휘 / 형용사

일부 경제학자들은 4분기에서의 두드러지는 경기 향상이 없이 경제 회복의 속도가 더디어 질 것으로 예측했다.

어휘 economist 경제학자 predict ~을 예측하다 pace 속도 economic recovery 경제 회복 slow down 느려지다, 더디어 지다 improvement 향상, 개선 marked 두드러지는, 현저한 broad 넓은 intensive 격렬한, 집중적인 respective 상대적인

129

★★ 어형 / To 부정사

그 시장은 우리 도시를 우리 주변 몇몇 도시들에 살고 있는 사람들을 위한 문화, 관광 그리고 경제의 중심지로 변모시킬 계획이다.

어휘 mayor 시장 plan to Vr ~할 계획이다 cultural 문화의 economic 경제의 hub 중심, 중핵 several 몇몇 transform ~의 모양을 바꾸다

The mayor plans ------- our city into a cultural, tourist, and economic hub for people living in the cities around us.

(A) to transform
(B) transforming
(C) transformed
(D) transformation

문제 해설

빈칸에 적합한 어형을 묻는 문제로 빈칸이 plans라는 동사 뒤에 위치하고 있다. 그러므로 빈칸에는 plans라는 동사의 목적어 역할을 할 수 있는 어형이 필요하다. 다만 이 목적어 역할을 행하는 명사는 빈칸 뒤 city라는 또 다른 명사를 목적어로 취할 수 있는 명사이어야 한다. 그러므로 transformation이란 일반명사와 transformed란 과거분사는 오답이다. 따라서 transforming과 to transform이란 어형 중에 정답을 택일해야 하나, plan이란 동사는 준동사 형태의 목적어로 to 부정사 형태만을 취하므로 빈칸에는 to transform이 와야 한다.

★★★ 어형 / 동사의 어형 및 시제

예상치 못한 시청각 시스템의 오작동으로 인해, 우리의 마케팅 워크숍은 추후 공지가 있을 때까지 연기되었다.

어휘 unexpected 예기치 못한, 예상하지 못한 audiovisual system 시청각 시스템 malfunction 오작동, 오류 notice 공지, 통보 postpone ~을 연기하다

Due to an unexpected audiovisual system malfunction, our marketing workshop ------- until further notice.

(A) will postpone
(B) has been postponed
(C) to postpone
(D) have postponed

문제 해설

빈칸에 적절한 시제가 반영된 동사 어형을 묻는 문제이므로 우선 준동사인 To 부정사 to postpone부터 오답으로 소거해야 한다. 그리고 시제가 반영된 동사의 어형을 묻는 문제는 주어/동사의 수 일치 – 태 – 시제 순으로 어형을 파악하는 것이 시간을 절약하며 효율적으로 문제를 풀이하는데 도움이 된다. 주어가 our marketing workshop이란 단수주어이므로 단수동사 형태가 필요하다는 점을 고려하면 have postponed는 오답이다. 이어서 postpone은 타동사로 명사인 목적어를 취하지만 빈칸 뒤에는 목적어가 제시되지 않고 있으므로 능동태가 아닌 수동태가 적합하다. 하지만 will postpone/have postponed은 능동태를 구성하는 동사의 어형이므로 이들 역시 모두 오답으로 소거해야 한다. 따라서 빈칸에는 has been postponed가 적합하다.

Questions 131-134 refer to the following article.

Delicious Treat in Kenshington

Luke's Ice Cream was ----131.---- in 2004 when Ms. Luke, a German immigrant to the United States of America, bought an old clothing plant on Pine Street. This plant had gone out of business and was put up for sale at a knockdown price. Ms. Luke spent all of her savings to buy it and hired several ----132.---- employees to start her ice cream company.

----133.---- new ice cream flavors, she used some of her family's favorite traditional recipes. Then, she enhanced the flavors with a wide variety of produce, including strawberries, plums, apples, and even nuts. ----134.----. They quickly became highly popular, and there are now seven Luke's Ice Cream store locations in Boston.

Kenshington 지역의 별미

Luke Ice Cream은 미국으로 이주한 독일인 Luke 씨가 Pine 가에 위치한 오래된 의류 공장을 구입하여 2004년도에 설립되었다. 이 공장은 파산된 상태에서 헐값에 매물로 나온 상태였다. Luke 씨는 저축한 모든 돈을 들여 그 공장을 구입했고 아이스크림 회사를 창업하기 위해 몇 명의 경력 직원들을 채용하였다.

새로운 맛의 아이스크림을 개발하기 위해, 그녀는 집안에서 좋아하는 전통 아이스크림 제조법의 일부를 사용했다. 그리고 그녀는 딸기, 자두, 사과 그리고 심지어는 견과류를 포함한 다양한 농산물을 활용하여 아이스크림의 맛을 더욱 풍부하게 만들었다. 새로운 아이스크림의 맛은 진하고, 부드럽고 그리고 담백하다. 새로 개발된 아이스크림들은 사람들 사이에서 엄청난 인기를 구가하고 있으며 Boston 시에는 현재 7개의 판매점이 있다.

어휘 immigrant 이주민 plant 공장 be gone out of business 파산하다 put up for sale 매물로 나오다 knockdown price 엄청나게 저렴한 가격 savings 저축, 저축금 hire ~를 채용하다 flavor 맛 favorite 좋아하는, 선호하는 traditional 전통적인 recipe 조리법 enhance ~을 강화하다 a wide variety of 다양한 produce 농산물, ~을 생산하다 plum 자두 nut 견과류 gain ~을 얻다, ~을 획득하다 huge 엄청난, 거대한 popularity 인기, 대중성 describe A as B A를 B로 묘사하다 rich 맛이 진한, 맛이 풍부한 buttery 버터가 든, 부드러운, 지방이 많은 delicate 섬세한, 민감한, 예민한, 맛이 담백한

131 ────────────

(A) find
(B) found
(C) founding
(D) founded

★★★ 어형 / 동사

토익 분석

동사 found 외에도 설립을 뜻하는 명사 founding, 근간이나 바탕을 뜻하는 명사 foundation, 그리고 설립자를 뜻하는 명사 founder도 함께 숙지하도록 한다.

문제 해설

빈칸에 적합한 동사 어형을 묻는 문제로, 빈칸이 주격 보어를 취하는 2형식 동사인 be 동사 was 뒤에 등장하고 있으므로 빈칸에는 명사 혹은 형용사가 위치해야 한다. 무엇보다 be 동사 뒤에는 동사의 원형이 올 수 없으므로 find는 오답이다. 아울러 found는 동사 find의 과거시제/과거분사 형태이기도 하지만 '설립하다, 창립하다'란 뜻을 지닌 동사의 원형인 found이기도 하다. 그러나 동사 find의 과거시제로 쓰인 found는 결국 동사이므로 오답이며, 과거분사 형태로 쓰인 found는 Luke Ice Cream이란 회사가 2004년에 발견되었다는 부적절한 내용을 형성하므로 이 역시 오답일 수 밖에 없다. 마지막으로 '설립하다, 창립하다'란 뜻을 지닌 동사 found 역시 be 동사 뒤에 자리할 수 없으므로 오답이 되겠다. 그리고 '설립, 창립'이란 뜻의 명사 founding은 주어인 Luke Ice Cream과 동격 관계를 구성할 수 없으므로 오답임을 알 수 있다. 그러므로 빈칸에는 Luke Ice Cream이란 회사가 2004년도에 창립되었다는 문맥을 형성할 수 있는 founded란 과거분사가 적절하다.

★★ 어형 / 과거분사

토익 분석

토익에서는 특히 노련하거나, 기술적으로 완숙하거나, 전문적인 프로라거나, 혹은 일이나 업무에 열성적이거나 성실하다는 뜻을 지닌 어휘들, 즉 정리하자면 experienced, skilled, professional, dedicated, devoted와 같은 어휘들은 자주 출제되는 편이므로 이들을 꼭 숙지해야 한다.

(A) experiences
(B) experience
(C) experiencing
(D) experienced

문제 해설

빈칸에 적절한 어형을 묻는 문제로 빈칸 뒤에 employees, 즉 직원들을 뜻하는 가산 복수명사가 위치하고 있으므로 빈칸에는 이들이 경력이 많고 노련한 직원이라는 뜻을 형성할 수 있는 형용사 어휘가 와야 한다. 따라서 빈칸에는 '노련한, 경험 많은'이란 의미의 과거분사 형태의 형용사인 experienced가 적절하다.

133

★★ 어형 / To 부정사

토익 분석

동일한 의미를 지닌 부사구인 in order to Vr / so as to Vr 도 함께 알아두어야 한다.

(A) To invent
(B) Invents
(C) Had invented
(D) Invention

문제 해설

빈칸에 적합한 동사 어형을 묻는 문제이다. 빈칸이 주절인 she used some of her family's favorite traditional recipes를 수식하는 부사구 앞자리에 위치하고 있으므로 빈칸에는 절을 구성하는 동사 형태인 invents/had invented는 올 수가 없다. 또한 명사 invention이 또 다른 명사인 flavors를 목적어로 취할 수 없으므로 Invention 또한 오답으로 소거해야 한다. 따라서 그녀가 집안에서 좋아하는 전통 아이스크림 제조법의 일부를 사용한 것은 바로 새로운 아이스크림 맛을 개발하기 위한 목적임을 파악할 수 있으므로 빈칸에는 '목적/의도'의 부사구를 형성할 수 있는 To 부정사 어형인 To invent가 와야 한다.

★★★ 빈칸 문장 추론

(A) 사실 아이스크림에 많은 설탕과 지방이 포함되어 있다는 사실은 널리 알려져 있다.
(B) 일부 견과류는 다른 재료들에 비해 약간 비싸다.
(C) 새로운 아이스크림의 맛은 진하고, 부드럽고 그리고 담백하다.
(D) 일부 아이스크림 제품들은 우유 가격의 인상으로 인해 인기가 감소할 것이다.

(A) In fact, it is widely known that ice cream has a lot of sugar and fat in it.
(B) Some fruits are slightly more expensive than other ingredients.
(C) The new ice cream flavors have been described as rich, buttery, and delicate.
(D) Some ice cream products will be declining in popularity because of the rising cost of milk.

문제 해설

빈칸에 적합한 내용의 문장을 묻는 문제이다. 빈칸에 앞서 she enhanced the flavors with a wide variety of produce, including strawberries, plums, apples, and even nuts라며 그녀가 딸기, 자두, 사과 그리고 심지어는 견과류를 포함한 다양한 농산물을 활용하여 아이스크림의 맛을 더욱 풍미있게 만들었음을 밝히고 있으며 빈칸 이후에는 They quickly became highly popular, and there are now seven Luke's Ice Cream store locations in Boston이라며 새로 개발된 아이스크림들이 사람들 사이에서 빠른 시간 내에 엄청난 인기를 얻었다는 내용과 함께 Boston 시에는 현재 7개의 판매점이 있다는 내용이 등장하고 있다.

그렇다면 빈칸에는 새로운 아이스크림들의 풍미있는 맛이 어떠한지 구체적으로 밝히고 호평하고 있는 내용이 위치하고 이로 인해 현재 사람들 사이에서 엄청난 인기를 구가하여 Boston 시에 벌써 7개의 판매점이 생겼다는 내용으로 마무리가 되는 것이 논리적으로 적절하다. 따라서 빈칸에는 새로운 아이스크림의 맛은 진하고, 부드럽고 그리고 담백하다는 내용이 담긴 The new ice cream flavors have been described as rich, buttery and delicate가 와야 한다.

Questions 135-138 refer to the following e-mail.

From: Jennifer Lawrence <jlawrence@powerelectric.com>
To: John Morrison <johnm@bellastore.com>
Date: September 9
Subject: Price Changes

Dear Mr. Morrison:

Please accept this e-mail as notification of a slight rate adjustment, ------- **135.** October 1. The adjustment is a result of increased transportation costs ------- **136.** the last twelve months.

A summary of rate changes is located at the bottom of this e-mail. We anticipate no additional rate adjustments for the next full year.

Should you have any further questions regarding our services, please contact our company at 692-9815. ------- **137.** .

Thank you for understanding that this price increase means that we can ------- **138.** superior quality standards for our products and services in the coming year.

Very truly yours,

Jennifer Lawrence
Chief Executive Officer
Power Electro, Inc.

발신: Jennifer Lawrence <jlawrence@powerelectro.com>
수신: John Morrison <johnm@bellastore.com>
일자: 9월 9일
제목: 가격 변동

Morrison 씨에게:

지금 보내드리는 이메일은 10월 1일 부로 시행되는 약간의 가격 변동에 대한 공지로 받아 주시기 바랍니다. 해당 가격 변동은 최근 1년 간 운송비 증가에 따른 결과입니다.

가격 변화의 전반적인 개요는 이메일 하단에 위치하고 있습니다. 내년 한 해 동안에는 추가적인 가격 인상이 없을 것으로 예상하고 있습니다.

저희 서비스에 관한 별도의 질문이 있으시면, 692-9815를 통해 저희 사무실로 연락을 주십시오. 그러면 저희 고객 상담원들이 기꺼이 도움을 드릴 것입니다.

이번 가격 인상이 향후 저희 제품과 서비스의 월등한 품질 기준을 유지할 수 있을 것임을 약속드리며 이해해주셔서 감사드립니다.

Jennifer Lawrence
최고경영자
Power Electro 사

어휘 accept A as B A를 B로 받아들이다 notification 통보, 전달, 공지, 알림 slight 약간의 rate adjustment 가격변동, 비용변동 effective 효과적인, 유효한, 시행하는 transportation costs 운송비용 rate changes 가격변경, 비용변경 be located ~가 위치하다 at the bottom of ~의 하단에 anticipate ~을 기대하다, ~을 예상하다 additional 추가적인 further 추가적인 regarding ~에 관해 price increase 가격인상 superior 우월한, 월등한 quality standards 품질기준 in the coming year 다가오는 해에 priority 우선, 상위, 중요

135

(A) acute
(B) good
(C) effective
(D) entitled

문제 해설

빈칸에 적합한 형용사 어휘를 묻는 문제이다. 빈칸에 앞서 Please accept this e-mail as notification of a slight rate adjustment라며 지금 보내드리는 이메일을 약간의 가격 변동에 대한 공지로 받아 주시기 바란다는 내용이 등장하고 있으며 빈칸 이후에는 10월 1일이라는 구체적인 시점이 제시되고 있다. 따라서 10월 1일은 가격 변동이 시행되는 시점임을 가늠할 수 있으므로 빈칸에는 '유효한, 시행되는'이란 뜻을 지닌 effective란 형용사가 위치해야 한다.

★★어휘 / 형용사

토익 분석

형용사인 effective는 대부분 '효과적인'이란 뜻으로 알고 있지만 토익에서는 '유효한, 시행되는'이란 의미로 쓰이는 effective도 자주 접할 수 있을 뿐만 아니라 어휘/어형 문제로서 출제되기도 한다는 점을 꼭 알아두도록 한다.

★★ 어휘 / 전치사

토익 분석

토익에선 전치사 over 외에도 **the last / the past** + 시간 명사 앞에 올 수 있는 또 다른 기간 전치사로서 **for / in**이 출제될 수 있다는 점을 꼭 알아두도록 한다.

(A) with
(B) until
(C) over
(D) following

문제 해설

빈칸에 적절한 전치사를 묻는 문제이다. 빈칸에 앞서 이 가격 변동은 증가된 운송비로 인해 초래된 결과임을 밝히고 있으며 빈칸 이후에는 최근 12개월이란 기간이 등장하고 있다. 따라서 증가된 운송비는 최근 1년 간 발생한 현상임을 알 수 있으므로 빈칸에는 최근 12개월 동안이란 기간을 언급할 수 있는 기간 전치사인 over이 와야 한다.

137

★★★ 빈칸 문장 추론

(A) 저희는 해외 고객들과 소통하는 것에 어려움이 있습니다.
(B) 마케팅은 고객의 요구와 고객의 만족에 관한 것입니다.
(C) 저희 고객 상담원들이 기꺼이 도움을 드릴 것입니다.
(D) 고객을 위한 더 나은 서비스야말로 모든 상점과 식당이 중시하는 것입니다.

(A) We have great difficulty communicating with overseas clients.
(B) Marketing is concerned with customer needs and customer satisfaction.
(C) Our customer service representatives will be happy to assist you.
(D) Better service for all customers should be a priority for every store and restaurant.

문제 해설

빈칸에 적합한 내용을 지닌 문장을 묻는 문제로 빈칸에 앞서 Should you have any further questions regarding our services, please contact our company at 692-9815라며 자사의 서비스에 관한 별도의 질문이 있으면, 692-9815를 통해 회사로 연락을 줄 것을 요청하고 있다. 그러므로 빈칸에는 회사로 연락을 했을 경우 제공받는 서비스, 즉 자사의 고객 상담원이 기꺼이 도움을 줄 것이란 내용이 담긴 Our customer service representatives will be happy to assist you가 위치하는 것이 논리적으로 타당하다.

138

★★어휘 / 동사

(A) examine
(B) maintain
(C) organize
(D) accomplish

문제 해설

빈칸에 적합한 동사 어휘를 묻는 문제로 빈칸 앞에는 we can이, 빈칸 뒤에는 the superior quality standards for our products and services in the coming year이 제시되며 궁극적으로 향후 자사의 제품 및 서비스에 대한 품질 기준을 어떻게 할 것인지 언급하고 있다. 따라서 이후에도 지속적으로 품질 기준을 유지하거나 강화한다는 내용을 구성할 수 있는 동사 어휘가 논리적으로 적절함을 알 수 있으므로 빈칸에는 '유지하다'란 뜻을 지닌 동사 maintain이 위치해야 한다.

Questions 139-142 refer to the following letter.

Homestead Corporation
51 Benson Street
Bronx, New York 10465

May 10

Aura Lane Manufacturing, Inc.
7401 Fifth Avenue
New York, New York 10055

To whom it may concern:

We intend ------- a new office copier before the end of the fiscal year. We
139.
would like to consider one of your copiers and wonder if you have a model that
would suit our needs.

Our company is a little small, and the copier would be shared by twenty
employees. We make ------- 7,800 copies a month and prefer a machine that
140.
uses regular paper. -------.
141.

Since our fiscal year ------- on June 30, we hope to hear from you before then.
142.

Sincerely yours,

Jim Preston
Personnel Manager
Homestead Corporation

Homestead 사
Benson 가 51번지
Bronx, New York 10465

5월 10일

Aura Lane 제조사
Fifth 가 7401번지
New York, New York 10055

담당자 분께

저희는 올 회계연도가 가기 전에 귀사의 새로운 사무용
복사기를 구매하고자 합니다. 구매대상으로 귀사의 복사
기를 고려하고 있으며 저희가 원하는 요구사항을 총족시
킬 수 있는 제품을 보유하고 있는지 궁금합니다.

저희 회사는 소규모인지라 복사기는 대개 20명의 직원들
이 사용하고 있습니다. 저희는 한 달에 대략 7천 8백 부
정도를 복사하며 일반 복사용지를 사용하는 복사기를 선
호합니다. 저희는 또한 귀사의 품질보증과 수리 서비스에
관해 알고 싶습니다.

저희 회계연도가 6월 30일부로 종료되기 때문에, 귀사로
부터 그 이전에 답변을 접할 수 있길 바랍니다.

Jim Preston
인사부장
Homestead 사

어휘 intend to Vr ~를 하려고 의도하다, ~을 하고자 계획
하다 consider ~을 고려하다, ~라 여기다 suit ~에 적합
하다, ~에 어울리다 generally 일반적으로, 대개 run 뛰
다, ~을 인쇄하다, ~을 복사하다, ~을 경영하다, ~에 입
후보하다 fiscal year 회계연도 hear from ~에게 소식을
듣다, ~에게 답변을 듣다 as soon as possible 최대한 빨
리

139

(A) purchase
(B) purchasing
(C) having purchased
(D) to purchase

문제 해설

빈칸에 적합한 어형을 묻는 문제로 빈칸이 동사 intend 뒤에 위치하고 있으므로 빈칸에는 동사
intend의 목적어 역할을 할 수 있는 동사 purchase의 명사 어형이 필요하다. 따라서 이론적으로는
to purchase/purchasing이란 형태가 모두 가능하지만 intend가 미래 지향적 의미를 지닌 동사이므
로 목적어로는 과거/현재 지향적인 V-ing 형태보다 역시 미래적 의미가 강한 준동사 형태인 to Vr
형태가 적합하다. 따라서 빈칸에는 to purchase가 위치해야 한다.

★★ 어형 / To 부정사

토익 분석

미래적 의미가 강한 동사들은 역시 미래적 의미를 지닌
준동사인 To Vr 형태를 목적어로 취한다. 반면에 과거/현
재적 의미가 강한 동사들은 또한 과거/현재적 의미가 반
영된 V-ing 형태를 목적어로 취한다. 이는 마치 옷을 입
을 때 같은 색상으로 맞춰 입거나 혹은 옷의 색상과 화장
의 색조를 맞추는, 이를 테면 '깔맞춤'과 같은 원리라고 할
수 있다. 예를 들자면 agree, want, wish, hope, decide,
promise 등은 to Vr 형태와 함께 쓰이고 enjoy, finish,
postpone, give up, mind, avoid 등은 V-ing 형태와 함께
쓰이는 것이 적절하게 잘빠진 모양새라 할 수 있다.

★★ 어형 / 부사

토익 분석

무엇보다 **approximately**는 '대략, 약'이란 뜻을 지닌 부사 어휘로 숫자 수식 어휘로 자주 출제되는경향이 있음을 알아두도록 한다.

(A) approximate
(B) approximating
(C) approximately
(D) approximation

문제 해설

빈칸에 적합한 어형을 묻는 문제로 빈칸이 7,800이란 숫자 앞에 등장하고 있다. 따라서 숫자 수식은 부사가 한다는 점을 고려할 때 빈칸에는 approximately라는 부사 어형이 적합하다.

141

★★ 명사 어휘

(A) 저희는 또한 귀사의 제품 품질 보증과 수리 서비스에 관해 알고 싶습니다.
(B) 스캐너와 합쳐진 인쇄기는 일종의 복사기 기능도 갖추고 있습니다.
(C) 저희는 기꺼이 귀하가 요청한 견적을 제공해드리고자 합니다.
(D) 그 회사는 마감시한이 지켜지지 못한 점에 실망스러움을 표현했습니다.

(A) We would also like to know about your warranty and repair service.
(B) A printer which is combined with a scanner can function as a kind of photocopier.
(C) We are happy to supply you with the estimate you requested.
(D) The company expressed disappointment at the deadline being missed.

문제 해설

빈칸에 적합한 내용을 지닌 문장을 묻는 문제이다. 빈칸에 앞서 복사기 구매를 밝히고 있으며 이어서 월 7,800장 정도를 복사한다며 자사의 복사기 운용에 관한 특징을 언급하는 내용이 등장하고 있음을 고려할 때 빈칸에는 구매자 측이 원하는 복사기의 기능/성능, 또는 복사기 구매와 관련된 조건, 혹은 문의하고자 하는 내용 등이 제시되어야 할 필요가 있다. 따라서 빈칸에는 귀사의 제품 품질 보증과 수리 서비스에 관해 알고 싶다는 내용이 포함된 We would also like to know about your warranty and repair service가 적합하다.

142

★★ 어형 / 동사

토익 분석

파트 6의 동사 어형 문제를 풀이하다 보면, 분명 미래 시제여야 하는데 막상 선택지에는 조동사 + 본동사(동사원형) 형태의 동사 어형이 제시되지 않는 경우가 있다. 이 때는 선택지에서 현재시제-현재시제 진행상 순서대로 정답을 택하면 된다.

(A) end
(B) ends
(C) has ended
(D) ended

문제 해설

빈칸에 적합한 동사 어형을 묻는 문제이다. 우선 주어인 our fiscal year이 단수 주어이므로 단수동사 형태를 취해야 하며, end는 6월 30일이란 전치사구 on June 30와 함께 쓰이는 자동사이므로 능동태를 유지해야 한다. 마지막으로 편지가 작성된 날은 5월 10일이고, 회계 연도가 끝나는 시점은 6월 30일이므로 미래 시제가 필요하다. 다만 회계 연도가 끝나는 시점은 6월 30일로 정해져 있고 정해진 미래라 시간이 지나면 필연적으로 다가오는 미래는 현재 시제로 표현한다는 점을 고려할 때 빈칸에는 ends가 와야 함이 옳다.

Questions 143-146 refer to the following e-mail.

From: David Kiesling <dkiesling@samsonelectronics.com>
To: Linda Kim <lindakim@businessworld.com>
Date: November 23
Subject: Investment Opportunity

Dear Ms. Kim:

I obtained your name from Ms. Betty Hwang, one of your board members.

We ------- in manufacturing liquid displays utilized for car navigation systems,
143.
computers, and various control panels for home appliances.

Because of the superior quality of our semiconductors, and because of the
increasing popularity of our products in the industry, we want to seize the
opportunity ------- immediately; however, in order to do so, we are asking for
144.
the help of outside investors.

I believe this is a great opportunity for a profitable investment. ------- are our
145.
pamphlets explaining our services and the expansion plans.

-------. Please let me know when I should call to make an appointment.
146.

Thank you.

Very truly yours,

David Kiesling
Finance Director
Samson Electronics

발신: David Kiesling <dkiesling@samsonelectronics.com>
수신: Linda Kim <lindakim@businessworld.com>
일자: 11월 23일
제목:투자 기회

Kim 님께

귀사의 이사진 중 한 분인 Betty Hwang 씨에게 귀하를 소개받았습니다.

당사는 자동차 항법장치, 컴퓨터, 그리고 가전제품에 쓰이는 다양한 제어화면에 활용되는 액정화면을 전문적으로 제조하는 회사입니다.

당사 반도체의 우수한 품질과 제품에 대한 업계의 인기 상승 덕분에 당장이라도 사세를 확장할 수 있는 기회를 얻을 수 있길 원하지만 그러기 위해서는 외부 투자가들의 도움을 요청해야 합니다.

저는 이것이 수익성이 좋은 투자 기회라고 믿습니다. 첨부된 것은 저희의 서비스와 사업확장 계획을 설명하는 소책자입니다.

저는 다음 주 초에 귀하와 만남을 갖고 이 놀라운 투자 기회에 대해 논의하고 싶습니다. 약속을 잡기 위해 언제 연락드리면 좋을지 알려주시기 바랍니다.

감사합니다.

David Kiesling
재정 이사
Samson Electronics

어휘 obtain ~을 얻다, ~을 획득하다 board members 이사진 specialize in ~가 전문이다 manufacture ~을제조하다 liquid 액체의 liquid display 액정화면 be utilized for ~로 활용되다 navigation system 항법장치 various 다양한 control panel 제어 화면 home appliances 가전제품 superior 우월한, 월등한 quality 품질, 자질 seize ~을 잡다, ~을 쥐다 opportunity 기회 immediately 즉시, 바로 however 그러나 in order to Vr ~하기 위해서 ask for ~을 요청하다 outside 바깥의, 외부의 investor 투자가 profitable 수익성이 좋은 investment 투자 attach ~을 첨부하다, ~을 부착하다 pamphlet 소책자 expansion plan 사업확장계획 make an appointment 약속을 하다, 예약을 하다

143

(A) make
(B) enroll
(C) specialize
(D)participate

★★어휘 / 동사

토익 분석

토익에 대비하여 동사 specialize는 specialize in이란 표현까지 함께 익혀야 하며 아울러 특기라는 뜻을 지닌 명사 specialty와 전문가를 의미하는 specialist까지 같이 알아둬야 한다.

문제 해설

빈칸에 적합한 동사 어휘를 묻는 문제로 빈칸 이후에 in manufacturing liquid displays utilized for navigation systems, computers, and various control panels for home appliances라며 자동차 항법장치, 컴퓨터, 그리고 가전제품에 쓰이는 다양한 제어화면에 활용되는 액정화면을 제조한다는 내용이 등장하고 있다. 그러므로 빈칸에는 이러한 제품을 전문적으로 제조하는 회사라며 자사를 소개하는 내용을 구성할 수 있도록 '전문화하다'란 뜻을 지닌 동사 specialize가 와야 한다.

★★★ 어형 / To 부정사

(A) expand
(B) expanding
(C) expanded
(D) to expand

문제 해설

빈칸에 적합한 어형을 묻는 문제로 빈칸이 명사인 the opportunity 뒤에 위치하고 있다. 무엇보다 명사 opportunity는 토익에서 ability, authority, right, time, plan, effort, chance와 함께 To 부정사구의 수식을 받는 대표적인 명사 어휘로 출제되고 있다. 따라서 빈칸에는 명사 the opportunity를 후치수식하며 형용사 역할을 하는 To 부정사 어형이 위치해야 한다.

145

★★★ 어형 / 과거분사

토익 분석

이 문제 유형은 항상 attach/enclose/include란 동사의 명사 어형, 즉 attachment/enclosure/inclusion을 대상으로 출제되고 있다는 점을 꼭 숙지하도록 한다.

(A) Attach
(B) Attached
(C) Attaching
(D) Attachment

문제 해설

빈칸에 적합한 어형을 묻는 문제이다. 대부분 이 유형의 문제를 처음 접하는 경우 빈칸이 be 동사 are 앞에 위치하고 있으므로 첨부된 것이 소책자들이란 해석과 함께 빈칸에는 첨부된 것이란 주어 역할을 행할 수 있는 명사 어형인 attachment가 위치해야 할 것이라 생각하며 이를 정답으로 선택하는 전형적인 오답 유도 과정을 착실하게 따라간다. 그러나 문맥을 정확히 파악해보자면 자사의 서비스와 사업 확장을 설명하는 소책자들이 이메일에 첨부된 것이라 할 수 있으며 이때 한 가지 간과하지 말아야 할 것은 주어인 our pamphlets가 be 동사 are 뒤에 위치하고 있는, 주어와 동사가 도치된 상태라는 점이다. 따라서 빈칸에는 첨부된 상태를 뜻하는 attached라는 과거분사 형태의 형용사가 자리해야 하며, 결과적으로 해당 문장은 주격보어인 attached를 강조하는 도치구문이라 할 수 있다. 사실상 이 문제는 오답인 명사 attachment를 혼동할 수 있는 대표적인 문제 유형임을 필히 숙지하도록 한다.

146

★★ 빈칸 문장 추론

(A) 일단 갱신이 이뤄지고 나면, 귀하의 계약서를 꼼꼼하게 검토하십시오.
(B) 저희는 핵심기술 개발에 필요한 충분한 자금을 제공하는 것에 실패하였습니다.
(C) 저는 다음 주 초에 귀하와 만나서 이 놀라운 투자 기회에 대해 논의하고 싶습니다.
(D) 저희 투자는 일자리를 늘리고 생활의 수준을 향상시킬 수 있습니다.

(A) Once the updates are made, please review your contract carefully.
(B) We have failed to provide sufficient funds for developing key technologies.
(C) I would like to discuss this exciting offer with you early next week.
(D) Our investment will increase job opportunities and improve living standards.

문제 해설

빈칸에 적합한 내용의 문장을 묻는 문제로 빈칸 이후에는 Please let me know when I should call to make an appointment, 즉 Linda Kim 씨와 만남을 갖기 위해서는 언제 연락을 취해야 하는지 알려줄 것을 요청하는 내용이 제시되고 있다. 따라서 만남의 목적은 앞서 소개된 투자 기회에 대해 논의하기 위해 추진되는 미팅임을 파악할 수 있으므로 빈칸에는 다음 주 초에 귀하와 만나서 이 놀라운 투자 기회에 대해 논의하고 싶다는 의중을 전달하는 I would like to discuss this exciting offer with you early next week가 와야 한다.

Questions 147-148 refer to the following text message.

From: Walter White, Friday, 26 October, 9:30 A.M.

Ms. Glennane, I'm at the convention center in Boston. [147] I'm here to fix the Internet network system, but I don't think I can do it by myself. The convention center is a huge space with many offices and conference rooms. And the employees working here want to get the Internet network system to work properly before they leave for the day. [148] Would you mind calling Mr. Parker and asking him to come to work with me? Unfortunately, I don't have his mobile phone number. I'm sorry to bother you. Please call me back after you contact Mr. Parker.

147-148 다음 문자 메시지를 참조하시오.

발신: Walter White, 10월 26일, 금요일, 오전 9:30

Glennane 씨, 저는 보스턴에 있는 컨벤션 센터에 와 있습니다. [147] 저는 이 호텔의 인터넷 네트워크 시스템을 수리하기 위해 왔습니다. 하지만 저 혼자 이 일을 할 수 있을 것 같지 않습니다. 이 컨벤션 센터는 대규모 공간에 많은 사무실과 대회의실을 갖추고 있고, 이곳에 근무하는 직원들은 퇴근 전에 인터넷을 다시 사용할 수 있기를 원합니다. [148] Parker 씨에게 전화하셔서 이곳으로 와서 저와 함께 작업하도록 요청해 주시겠습니까? 안타깝게도, 제가 그분의 휴대 전화번호를 모릅니다. 번거롭게 해드려 죄송합니다. Parker 씨에게 연락해 보신 후에 제게 다시 전화 주십시오.

어휘 fix ~을 고치다, 바로 잡다 by oneself 혼자, 스스로 huge 엄청난, 막대한 besides 게다가 get A back A를 돌려받다 leave for the rest of the day 남은 하루 일과를 마치고 퇴근하다 Would you mind -ing? ~해 주시겠습니까? ask A to do A에게 ~하도록 요청하다 unfortunately 안타깝게도 bother ~을 방해하다 contact ~에게 연락하다

147

What problem does Mr. White mention?

(A) Mr. Parker called in sick this morning.
(B) He has some repair work he can't do alone.
(C) A colleague is not answering the phone.
(D) He doesn't know the exact location of a convention center.

문제 해설

문제점에 대해 묻고 있으며 문제점은 대부분 지문 초반부에서 직접적으로 제시되고 있다. 메시지 발신인인 White 씨는 메시지 초반 I'm here to fix the Internet network system, but I don't think I can do it by myself라며 인터넷 네트워크 수리를 위해 한 컨벤션 센터에 와 있다고 알리면서 이 일을 혼자 할 수 없을 것 같다는 문제점을 함께 언급하고 있다. 따라서 (B)가 정답이다.

★ 문제점

White 씨는 어떠한 문제점을 언급하고 있는가?
(A) Parker 씨가 오늘 아침에 전화로 병가를 냈다.
(B) 혼자 할 수 없는 수리 작업이 있다.
(C) 한 동료 직원이 연락되지 않고 있다.
(D) 컨벤션 센터의 정확한 위치를 알지 못한다.

토익 분석

첫 번째 문제로 등장하는 구체적인 문제점은 주로 첫 번째 단락 초반 2-3 문장을 통해 제시되며 단락 구분이 없는 경우 지문 초반 2-3 문장에서 문제점에 대한 단서를 파악할 수 있다.

148

What does Mr. White want Ms. Glennane to do?

(A) Install audiovisual equipment
(B) Contact a coworker
(C) Cancel a corporate event
(D) Reschedule a conference at a hotel

문제 해설

White 씨가 Glennane 씨에게 원하는 것이 무엇인지 묻고 있으므로 문자 메시지 후반부에서 White 씨의 구체적인 요구사항을 파악해야 한다. 문자 메시지 시작 부분에서 Glennane 씨가 수신인임을 알 수 있으며, 문자 메시지 후반부에서는 Would you mind calling Mr. Parker and asking him to come to work with me?라며 Parker 씨에게 전화해서 자신이 있는 곳으로 와줄 것을 요청해 달라는 부탁을 하고 있다. 따라서 (B)가 정답이다.

★ White 씨의 요청사항

White 씨는 Glennane 씨가 무엇을 해주길 원하는가?
(A) 시청각 장비를 설치한다.
(B) 동료에게 연락한다.
(C) 기업 행사를 취소한다.
(D) 호텔에서의 회의 일정을 재조정한다.

토익 분석

• 마지막 문제는 항상 마지막 단락의 내용이 끝나는 부분부터 역순으로 한 문장씩 내용을 확인하며 단서를 파악하는 것이 효율적이다.
• 특히 요청/요구/제안/추천/권장/조언과 관련된 내용을 묻는 문제는 주로 마지막 문제로 출제되며 단서는 대부분 지문이 끝나는 마지막 2-3문장을 중심으로 제시된다.

149-151다음 송장을 참조하시오.

송장
Starz Service LTD
"항상 여러분께서 필요로 하시는 것을 배송해 드립니다."

발급인: Starz Service LTD.
1188 Mission Blvd, San Francisco, CA 94712

수령인: Ash Williams 박사
Ash Williams Hospital
310 Harder Road, Hayward, CA 94542

주문 날짜: 6월 25일
[150] 배송 날짜: 6월 29일

제품 코드	제품	단가	수량
44BK	[149] 탈지면 상자	$25.00	15 / $375.00
73KG	[149] 소독약 상자	$78.00	10 / $780.00
[151] *49GS	[149] 의료용 마스크	$3.25	10 / $32.50
42SK	[149] 위생 장갑	$2.50	20 / $50.00

총액: $1,237.50

저희 **Starz Service LTD**는 미국 서부 지역에서 가장 큰 의료용품 공급업체 중의 하나입니다. 귀하의 거래에 대해 항상 감사 드립니다.

[151] * 49GS는 현재 품절 상태이므로 다음 주 화요일에 배송해 드리겠습니다.

어휘 invoice 송장 unit price 단가 quantity 수량 absorbent cotton 탈지면 disinfectant 소독약 sanitary 위생의 medical supplies 의료용품 provider 공급업체 currently 현재 out of stock 품절된, 재고가 없는

149

★ 회사의 정체/ 유추

Starz Service LTD는 어떠한 회사일 것 같은가?
(A) 제약회사
(B) 종합병원
(C) 의료용품 회사
(D) 배송회사

토익 분석
업종/직장을 묻는 질문은 지문에서 업종/직장과 관련된 어휘나 표현을 파악하는 것이 관건이다

Questions 149-151 refer to the following invoice.

INVOICE

Starz Service LTD
"We Always Get You What You Need"

From: Starz Service LTD.
1188 Mission Blvd, San Francisco, CA 94712

To: Dr. Ash Williams
Ash Williams Hospital
310 Harder Road, Hayward, CA 94542

Order Date: June25
[150] Delivery Date: June 29

Item Code	Item	Unit Price	Quantity
44BK	[149] Absorbent Cotton Box	$25.00	15 / $375.00
73KG	[149] Disinfectant Box	$78.00	10 / $780.00
[151] *49GS	[149] Medical Mask	$3.25	10 / $32.50
42SK	[149] Sanitary Gloves	$2.50	20 / $50.00

TOTAL AMOUNT : $1,237.50

Starz Service LTD is one of the largest suppliers in the western part of the United States. We thank you for your business.

[151] * We will deliver 49GS next Tuesday because they are currently out of stock.

What type of business is Starz Service LTD?

(A) A pharmaceutical company
(B) A general hospital
(C) A medical supplies company
(D) A shipping company

문제 해설

Starz Service LTD라는 회사가 어느 업종에 종사하는 회사인지 묻는 문제이므로 회사의 정체를 추측할 수 있을 만한 관련 어휘나 표현이 제시되는 부분에 집중해야 한다. 송장에서 이 업체에서 판매하는 제품이 표기된 도표에 탈지면(Absorbent Cotton Box), 소독약(Disinfectant Box), 의료용 마스크(Medical Mask), 위생 장갑(Sanitary Gloves)가 표기된 것을 토대로 Starz Service LTD라는 회사는 의료용품 업체임을 유추할 수 있다. 따라서 (C)가 정답이다.

150

According to the invoice, what will probably happen on June 29?

(A) Mr. William's order will be shipped.
(B) A payment will be made to the hospital.
(C) A regular inventory check will be taken.
(D) New medical products will be released.

문제 해설

6월 29일에 발생할 일에 대해 유추할 수 있는 내용을 묻는 문제이므로 6월 29일이라는 시점이 제시되는 부분에서 언급되는 정보를 토대로 사실 가능성이 높은 내용을 유추해야 한다. 송장 중반부에 표기된 배송 날짜 항목(Delivery Date: June 29)에서 6월 29일이란 날짜가 배송일자임을 파악할 수 있으며 아울러 이 송장의 수령인이 Ash Williams 박사라는 점 또한 알 수 있다. 따라서 이를 토대로 6월 29일에는 Ash Williams 박사에게 물품들이 배송될 것임을 유추할 수 있으므로 (A)가 정답이다.

★ 유추

송장 내용에 따르면, 6월 29일에 무슨 일이 있을 것 같은가?
(A) Williams 씨의 주문이 배송될 것이다.
(B) 병원으로 비용이 지불될 것이다.
(C) 정기 재고 조사가 있을 것이다.
(D) 새로운 의료용 제품이 출시될 것이다.

토익 분석

유추 문제의 키워드(핵심어) 파악이 중요하며 지문에서 해당 키워드가 등장하는 부분에서 제공되는 정보를 토대로 유추 가능한 선택지의 내용을 정답으로 택일해야 한다.

151

What is suggested about the masks?

(A) They will be delivered on June 29.
(B) They will come in a variety of colors.
(C) They won't be manufactured any more.
(D) They are currently unavailable.

문제 해설

마스크에 관해 알 수 있는 세부 정보를 묻는 문제이므로 송장 제품 목록에서 마스크가 등장하는 부분을 찾아 마스크와 관련된 정보를 파악해야 한다. 송장 마지막 별 표시 부분에서 We will deliver 49GS next Tuesday because they are currently out of stock이라며 제품 코드가 49GS인 의료용 마스크는 현재 품절상태라 다음 주 화요일에 배송된다는 점을 전달하고 있다. 따라서 (D)가 정답이다. 아울러 별(*) 표시가 등장하는 부분은 언제나 출제되는 문제를 풀 수 있는 단서를 포함하고 있다는 점도 간과하지 않도록 한다.

★★ 세부사항

마스크에 관해 알 수 있는 것은 무엇인가?
(A) 6월 29일에 배송될 것이다.
(B) 다양한 색상으로 출시될 것이나.
(C) 더 이상 생산되지 않을 것이다.
(D) 현재 완전히 품절된 상태이다.

토익 분석

별(*) 표시가 등장하는 경우 이 부분의 내용을 토대로 풀이해야 하는 문제가 필히 출제된다.

152-153 다음 영수증을 참조하시오.

영수증 번호: 7374-1123

이 번호를 분실하지 마십시오. 저희 고객 서비스 직원들로부터 도움을 받기를 원하실 경우 필요합니다.

Chuck Finley 씨로부터 납입됨: Khandar Theater에 대한 44달러의 지불 비용.
11월 23일, 오후 6시 15분에 XXXX-0909로 끝나는 신용카드로 청구됨
* 귀하의 티켓은 환불 불가입니다.

152 이 영수증은 12월 12일 오후 7시에 열리는 음악 축제에 참석하는 Chuck Finley 씨를 위한 것입니다.

153 이 영수증을 출력하셔서 극장으로 지참하고 오십시오. 콘서트가 시작되기 한 시간 전에 오셔야 저희가 매표소에서 귀하의 성함과 좌석 번호를 확인해 드릴 수 있으니 유의 바랍니다.

어휘 receipt 영수증 representative 직원 receive ~을 받다 charge ~을 청구하다 ending in ~로 끝나는 non-refundable 환불되지 않는 so that ~할 수 있도록 하고자

Questions 152-153 refer to the following receipt.

Receipt Number: 7374-1123

 DO NOT lose this number. You will need it if you want to get help from our customer service representatives.

Received from Chuck Finley: $44 payment to Khandar Theater
Charged to the credit card ending in XXXX-0909 on November 23, 6:15 P.M.
* Your ticket is non-refundable.

152 • This receipt is for Mr. Chuck Finley for the music festival on December 12, 7:00 P.M.

153 • Please print this receipt and bring it with you to the theater. Please arrive one hour before the concert begins so that we can check your name and seat number at the ticket counter.

152

★ 세부사항

Finley 씨는 12월 12일에 무엇을 할 것인가?
(A) 티켓을 구매한다.
(B) 음악 행사에 참석한다.
(C) 신규 신용카드를 받는다.
(D) 지역 축제를 준비한다.

토익 분석

시간/시점/요일을 묻는 문제에선 지문에서 시간/시점/요일이 언급되는 부분만 빠르게 찾아 단서를 파악한다.

What will Mr. Finley do on December 12?

(A) Purchase a ticket
(B) Attend a musical event
(C) Receive a new credit card
(D) Organize a local festival

문제 해설

Finley 씨가 12월 12일에 무엇을 할 것인지 묻고 있으므로 영수증에서 12월 12일이라는 날짜가 제시되는 부분을 중심으로 단서를 파악해야 한다. 영수증 중반부에서 This receipt is for Mr. Chuck Finley in the music festival on December 12, 7:00 P.M.이라며 음악 축제에 참석하는 Chuck Finley 씨를 위한 영수증이라 되어 있으므로 Finley 씨는 12월 12일에 음악 축제에 참석할 것임을 알 수 있다. 따라서 정답은 (B)가 되겠다.

153

★★ 세부사항 / 요청

Finley 씨가 요청 받는 것은 무엇인가?
(A) 제 시간에 도착한다.
(B) 신청서를 작성한다.
(C) 신분증을 제시한다.
(D) 영수증을 지참하고 온다.

토익 분석

요청/요구/제안/추천/권장/조언과 관련된 내용을 묻는 문제는 주로 마지막 문제로 출제되며 단서는 대부분 지문이 끝나는 마지막 2-3문장을 중심으로 제시된다.

What is Mr. Finley asked to do?

(A) Make a reservation
(B) Fill out an application form
(C) Present his identification card
(D) Bring a receipt with him

문제 해설

영수증이 Finley 씨에게 요청한 내용을 묻는 마지막 문제이므로 영수증 후반에서 Finley 씨에게 요청하고 있는 사항이 무엇인지 파악해야 한다. 영수증 하단을 보면 Please print this receipt and bring it with you to the theater이라며 영수증을 출력해 극장으로 지참하고 올 것을 요청하고 있다. 그러므로 정답은 (D)가 되겠다.

Questions 154-155 refer to the following advertisement.

Elk Wood Cabins

Elk Wood Park Service is pleased to announce a project to build 25 beautiful log cabins by Raccoon Lake in Elk Wood National Park. Work is expected to begin in approximately two weeks. If all goes according to plan, we hope to have the site prepared and the main structural foundations in place within a month. That may seem like quite a huge task, but we are desperate to have everything finished before the summer season begins. The new cabins at Raccoon Lake should be completed by June this year.

[155] There will be two types of cabins available: standard cabins that have two floors and sleep up to 5 people and group cabins that have three floors and sleep up to 10 people. Both kinds of cabins will be fully air conditioned and will have modern bathrooms, including hot tubs. [154] The kitchens in both cabin types will be equipped with a full range of appliances, including a refrigerator, microwave, washing machine, and gas range.

[155] The Elk Wood cabins will be conveniently located beside beautiful Raccoon Lake. This will make them perfect for anyone who wishes to escape the city heat and enjoy some fishing, swimming, and water sports in the national park. Contact an agent from the Elk Wood Park Service today to make an advance booking for one of the cabins.

[155] Most cabins will be available to rent starting June 4.
Contact us at 555-6892 for further details.

154-155 다음 광고를 참조하시오.

Elk Wood Cabins

저희 Elk Wood 공원 서비스는 Elk Wood 국립공원 내의 Raccoon 호수 옆에 25개의 아름다운 통나무집을 건축하는 계획을 발표하게 되어 기쁩니다. 작업은 약 2주 후에 시작될 예정입니다. 계획대로 진행된다면, 한 달 이내에 부지 정리와 주요 구조적인 기초 작업을 위한 준비가 될 것으로 기대합니다. 막대한 업무로 보이나, 저희는 여름철이 시작되기 전에 모든 것들을 완료시키기 위해 필사적으로 애쓰고 있습니다. Raccoon 호수의 새 통나무집은 올해 6월까지 완공될 것입니다.

[155] 이용 가능한 객실은 두 종류입니다: 기본 객실은 두 개의 층으로 되어 있고 5명까지 수용 가능 합니다. 그룹 객실은 세 개의 층으로 되어 있고 10명까지 수용 가능합니다. 두 종류의 객실 모두 냉난방 장치가 되어있고, 욕조를 포함한 현대식 화장실이 구비되어 있습니다. [154] 또한 주방에는 냉장고와 전자레인지, 식기 세척기와 가스레인지 등 모든 종류의 주방 기기들이 갖추어져 있습니다.

[155] 엘크 우드 통나무집은 아름다운 Raccoon 호수 옆에 편리하게 위치해 있습니다. 도시의 열기를 피해 국립공원에서 낚시와 수영, 수상 스포츠를 즐기고자 하는 사람이라면 누구에게나 최적의 장소입니다. 통나무집의 사전 예약을 원하신다면, Elk Wood 공원 서비스의 직원에게 오늘 연락하세요!

[155] 6월 4일부터 대부분의 객실이 이용 가능합니다.
자세한 내용은 555-6892로 문의하세요.

어휘 cabin 오두막집, 통나무집, 객실, 선실 log cabin 통나무집 approximately 약, 대략 be equipped with ~이 갖추어진, 구비된 a full range of 다양한, 많은 appliance 기기

154

What is stated about the cabins?

(A) Construction began two weeks ago. **(B) Kitchen appliances are included.**
(C) The bedrooms are very spacious.   (D) They cannot accommodate large groups.

문제 해설

두 번째 단락 하단 부분에서 The kitchens in both cabin types will be equipped with a full range of appliances, including a refrigerator, microwave, washing machine, and gas range라고 언급된 내용을 통해 통나무집은 주방기기들이 모두 갖춰진 상태임을 알 수 있으므로 정답은 (B)이다.

★★ 진위

통나무집에 관해 언급된 내용은 무엇인가?
(A) 공사는 2주 전에 시작되었다
(B) 주방 기기들이 포함되어 있다
(C) 침실이 매우 넓다
(D) 많은 인원을 수용할 수는 없다

토익 분석

사실 내용을 묻는 문제[TRUE]의 키워드가 지문 전반에 걸쳐 언급되는 경우 선택지의 내용을 키워드로 삼아 지문에서 해당 내용이 언급되는지 여부를 빠르게 파악한다. 이 때 선택지를 두 개씩 나눠 두 번에 걸쳐 지문에서의 해당 내용이 제시되고 있는지 확인하는 방식을 권고한다.

155

What information is NOT included in the advertisement?

(A) The date the first cabins open   (B) The cabin styles available
(C) The cost of a cabin rental   (D) The location of the cabins

문제 해설

광고 지문 맨 하단에 Most cabins will be available to rent starting June 4라며 임대 시작이 6월 4일임을 밝히고 있으며 두 번째 단락 초반부에서 There will be two types of cabins available이라며 두 가지 종류의 통나무집을 이용할 수 있다는 점을 언급하고 있다. 마지막으로 세 번째 단락 초반부에서 The Elk Wood cabins will be conveniently located beside beautiful Raccoon Lake에서 통나무집의 구체적인 위치를 전달하고 있다. 하지만 통나무집의 사용료와 관련된 내용은 등장하지 않고 있으므로 정답은 (C)라 할 수 있다.

★★ 진위

광고에 언급된 정보가 아닌 것은 무엇인가?
(A) 통나무집의 첫 개장 일자
(B) 이용 가능한 통나무집의 종류
(C) 통나무집 사용료
(D) 통나무집의 위치

토익 분석

사실이 아닌 내용[NOT TRUE]을 묻는 문제는 선택지 내용을 파악한 후 이를 간단히 정리하여 키워드로 삼은 후 지문의 내용과 대조하며 지문에서 언급된 내용의 선택지를 오답으로 소거하며 정답을 찾아내는 방식으로 풀이하도록 한다.

Anna Gunn 오후 2:11
있잖아요, [157] 제 이메일에 있는 모임 초대장을 여는 방법을 모르겠어요. 실은, 직원들을 위한 온라인 비즈니스 강좌에 처음 참석하는 거라서요. 저 좀 도와주실래요?

Harrison Morgan 오후 2:13
아주 쉽습니다. 이메일을 통해 우리에게 부여된 접속 코드를 입력하시기만 하시면 됩니다. 코드는 GS6929815입니다.

Anna Gunn 오후 2:15
화면에 "접속 코드가 틀렸습니다. 다시 시도해 주십시오."라고 나와요. 접속 코드에 무슨 문제라도 있는 건가요?

Harrison Morgan 오후 2:16
잠시만요. 제가 대신 확인해 볼게요.

Anna Gunn 오후 2:17
제가 받은 이메일 초대장에 문제가 있을 수도 있어요.

Harrison Morgan 오후 2:19
아, 죄송해요. [156] 제가 엉뚱한 접속 코드를 알려 드렸네요. 제 실수입니다. 접속 코드 JA870613을 입력해 보세요.

Anna Gunn 오후 2:20
네, 이제 되네요!

Harrison Morgan 오후 2:23
좋습니다. 제가 한 가지만 더 말씀 드릴게요. 모니터 화면의 하단에 무음 버튼이 보이시나요? [157] 마이크는 사용하실 필요가 없기 때문에 그것을 클릭하시면 됩니다.

어휘 how to do ~하는 법 actually 실은, 사실은 attend ~에 참석하다 It's a piece of cake 식은 죽 먹기이다 access code 접속 코드 assign ~을 배정하다, 할당하다 through ~을 통해 try 시도하다 Hold on 잠시만요 receive ~을 받다 work 작동되다, 효과가 있다 Right on 잘 됐다, 잘 했어 mute 무음의 at the bottom of ~의 하단에

Questions 156-157 refer to the following online chat discussion.

Anna Gunn 2:11 P.M.
Hey, [157] I don't know how to open the meeting invitation in my e-mail. Actually, it's my first time attending an online business course for employees. Can you help me?

Harrison Morgan 2:13 P.M.
It's a piece of cake. All you have to do is enter the access code from the e-mail. It's GS6929815.

Anna Gunn 2:15 P.M.
It says, "Your access code is not right. Please try again." Something's wrong with the access code.

Harrison Morgan 2:16 P.M.
Hold on. Let me check that for you.

Anna Gun n2:17 P.M.
There might be a problem with the e-mail invitation I received.

Harrison Morgan 2:19 P.M.
[156] Oh, I'm sorry. I gave you the wrong access code. It's my mistake. Please enter the access code JA870603

Anna Gunn 2:20 P.M.
Yeah, it's working!

Harrison Morgan 2:23 P.M.
Okay. Let me tell you one more thing. You see the mute button at the bottom of the monitor screen? [157] You don't need to use your microphone, so you should click it.

156

★★ 화자의 의도

오후 2시 19분에, Morgan 씨가 "Oh, I'm sorry"라고 쓴 것이 의미하는 바는 무엇일 것 같은가?
(A) Gunn 씨 없이 비즈니스 워크숍을 시작해야 한다.
(B) Gunn 씨에게 엉뚱한 정보를 알려 주었다.
(C) 아직 문제의 원인을 찾지 못했다.
(D) 해당 비즈니스 강좌에 등록하지 않을 것이다.

토익 분석

특정 표현에 담긴 화자의 의도에 대한 이해하기 위해서는 주어진 특정 표현 전후의 내용 파악이 선행되어야 한다.

At 2:19 P.M., what does Ms. Morgan most likely mean when she writes, "Oh, I'm sorry"?

(A) She needs to start a business workshop without Ms. Gunn.
(B) She has given Ms. Gunn wrong information.
(C) She hasn't found the cause of a problem yet.
(D) She will not register for the business course.

문제 해설

주어진 문장인 "Oh, I'm sorry"는 기본적으로 미안/유감이라는 의미를 지니고 있다. 이어서 Morgan 씨는 I gave you the wrong access code라며 잘못된 접속 코드를 전달했음을 밝히고 있다. 따라서 이를 토대로 오후 2시 19분에 Morgan 씨가 "Oh, I'm sorry"라고 말한 내용에는 자신이 Gunn 씨에게 부적절한 정보를 제공한 것에 대한 미안함이 반영되었음을 가늠할 수 있으므로 정답은 (B)가 되겠다.

157

What is probably true about Ms.Gunn?

(A) She has recently bought a new headset.
(B) She will lead a business seminar tomorrow.
(C) She doesn't need to speak during the online course.
(D) She hasn't received an e-mail invitation.

문제 해설

Gunn 씨에 대해 사실일 가능성이 높은 내용을 유추해야 하는 문제이므로 Gunn 씨와 관련된 정보를 파악하는 것이 우선이며 이를 토대로 사실 가능성이 높은 내용을 추측해야 한다. 무엇보다 Gunn 씨가 Morgan 씨와 지문 전반에 걸쳐 대화 내용이 제시되고 있으므로 선택지의 내용을 정리한 후 이를 키워드로 삼아 선택지의 내용을 유추할 수 있을만한 근거가 제시되고 있는지 여부를 파악하는 방식으로 문제를 풀이하는 편이 현명하다. 마지막 메시지에서 Morgan 씨는 Gunn 씨에게 마이크를 사용할 필요가 없다며 You don't need to use your microphone이라고 말하고 있다. 이는 지문 초반 Gunn 씨가 수강하는 직원용 온라인 비즈니스 강좌(online business course for employees)와 관련된 내용이다. 따라서 이를 토대로 해당 강좌를 듣는 동안 마이크를 사용해 말을 할 필요가 없음을 유추할 수 있으므로 정답은 (C)가 되겠다.

★★★ 세부사항 / 유추

Gunn 씨에 관해 사실일 것 같은 내용은 무엇인가?
(A) 최근에 새로운 헤드폰을 구입했다.
(B) 내일 비즈니스 세미나를 이끌 것이다.
(C) 온라인 강좌 중에 말을 할 필요가 없다.
(D) 이메일 초대장을 받지 못했다.

토익 분석

유추 문제의 키워드가 혹은 키워드에 관한 내용이 지문 전반에 걸쳐 언급되고 있는 상태에서 적절한 유추 내용을 파악해야 한다면 선택지에 나온 내용을 먼저 파악한 후 선택지의 내용을 유추할 수 있는 근거가 지문에 제시되는지 여부를 역으로 확인하는 방식으로 문제를 풀이한다. 이 때 선택지를 두 개씩 나눠 두 번에 걸쳐 지문에서의 해당 내용이 제시되고 있는지 확인하는 방식을 추천한다.

158-160 다음 기사문을 참조하시오.

현실 세계의 비즈니스에 대한 집중 조명

9월 15일-업계를 선도하는 임원인 Brian McCallister 씨는 몇 년 전에 St. Olaf Industrial Institute에서 강의를 시작했으며, [158] 자신의 강의에서 실제 비즈니스 활동에 관련되어 있는 초청 연사들에게 연설을 하도록 주기적으로 요청하고 있다. — [1] —.

이 비즈니스 리더들은 St. Olaf Industrial Institute의 마케팅 및 경제학 입문 강좌에 등록되어 있는 학생들에게 각자의 경험을 공유하고 있다. — [2] —. [159] 이 교수의 목표는 학생들이 강의실에서 공부하는 이론과 그들이 이를 현실적으로 적용시키는 방법 사이의 연결 고리를 만들도록 돕는 데 있다.

이 객원 강사들은 일상 생활에서 얻는 교훈이 컴퓨터와 인쇄물을 통해 읽는 그 어떤 것만큼 중요할 수 있다는 것을 가르쳐 준다. — [3] —. 그는 학생들에게 제안하여 친척이나 친구, 그리고 지인들을 포함한 강의실 참관자를 초대하여 그들의 현실적인 경험을 공유하게 하며, 특히 문제 해결, 협업, 그리고 수행 능력과 관련해 공유한다.

McCallister 씨의 학생들은 각자 궁금해 하는 비즈니스 관계자에게 와서 질문하도록 권장도 받는다. McCallister 씨의 학생들은 모두 그 연사들이 흥미롭다는 데 동의한다. [160] 비록 이 강좌에 학생들이 다양한 지역 회사에서 인턴으로 근무하는 몇 주 동안의 기간이 포함되어 있기는 하지만, 초청 연사들은 비즈니스 업계에 대한 매우 다른 시각을 제공한다. — [4] —. 이 강좌의 초점은 비즈니스 업계에 존재하는 장애물을 극복하는 체계성과 전략에 맞춰져 있다.

어휘 be engaged in ~에 관여되어 있다, ~에 종사하다 acquaintance 지인 particularly 특히 when it comes to ~에 관해서라면 be encouraged to do ~하도록 권고되다, 권장되다 ask A to do A에게 ~하도록 요청하다 associated with ~와 관련된 agree that ~임에 동의하다 include ~을 포함하다 perspective 관점, 시각

Questions 158-160 refer to the following article.

Spotlight on real-world business

September 15—Industry leading executive Brian McCallister began teaching at St. Olaf Industrial Institute a few years ago and [158] regularly invites guest speakers who are engaged in real-world business activities to speak in his classes. — [1] —.

These business leaders share their experiences with the students enrolled in introductory marketing and economics courses at St. Olaf. — [2] —. [159] The professor's objective is to help students to make connections between the theories they study in the classroom and their practical applications in their future careers.

The visitors show them that the lessons in everyday life can be just as important as anything they read in their computer and printed literature. — [3] —. He lets students propose and invite their own classroom guests, including relatives, friends, and acquaintances, to share their experiences in the real world particularly when it comes to problem solving, collaboration, and execution.

Mr. McCallister's students are encouraged to ask people associated with business they are curious about to come to speak, as well. McCallister's students all agree that the speakers are interesting. [160] Although the class includes a few weeks in which students work as interns in various local companies, the guest speakers provide a very different perspective of the world of business. — [4] —. The focus is on organization and strategies to overcome obstacles in the industrial business world.

158

★★★ 기사의 주제

기사는 무엇을 다루고 있는가?
(A) 향후 업계 선도자들이 각자의 은퇴를 계획하는 방법
(B) 해외 유학을 가는 한 학생의 흔치 않은 기회
(C) 학생들이 각자의 과제 시간을 계획하는 방법
(D) 한 강사의 강의 실무 수업

토익 분석

기사문의 주제/목적은 단락 구분이 있는 경우 첫 번째 단락 초반 2-3문장에서 제시된다. 다만 주제/목적 문제의 난이도가 높아지는 경우 주제/목적은 두 번째 단락의 초반 2-3문장에서 다뤄진다

What does the article discuss?
(A) How future industry leaders can plan their retirement
(B) A student's unusual opportunity to study abroad
(C) A way for students to plan their homework time
(D) An instructor's classroom practice

문제 해설

기사문의 주제/목적은 기사문 전반부, 즉 첫 번째 단락과 두 번째 단락 부분에서 직접적으로 언급되고 있다. 기사문의 첫 단락에서 Industry leading executive Brian McCallister began teaching at St. Olaf Industrial Institute a few years ago and regularly invites guest speakers who are engaged in real-world business activities to speak in his classes라며 업계 전문가인 Brian McCallister 씨가 자신의 강의에 주기적으로 연사를 초청해 연설을 하도록 요청하고 있음을 언급하고 있으며 이러한 방식의 강의가 진행되는 목적과 방식 등을 설명하는 내용 중심으로 기사문이 구성되어 있다. 따라서 강의 운영과 관련해 주기적으로 진행하는 일은 일종의 관행으로 볼 수 있으므로 이와 같은 의미에 해당되는 (D)가 정답이다

159

According to the article, what is Mr. McCallister's goal?

(A) To expand students' exposure to real-world industry practices
(B) To find ways businesses can work more efficiently
(C) To create literature that is better suited to students' needs
(D) To teach students to make better public presentations

문제 해설

McCallister 씨의 목적을 묻는 질문이므로 기사문에서 McCallister 씨의 목적이 언급되는 부분, 즉 goal이란 키워드 혹은 이와 유사한 어휘가 제시되는 부분을 스캐닝을 통해 빠르게 파악하는 것이 관건이다. 두 번째 단락에서 McCallister 씨는 The professor's objective is to help students to make connections between the theories they study in the classroom and their practical applications in their future careers라며 학생들이 강의실에서 공부하는 이론과 그들이 이를 현실적으로 적용시키는 방법 사이의 연결고리를 만들도록 돕는 것이 목표라고 보도하고 있다. 따라서 이는 현실의 업계에 관해 학생들이 더 잘 알 수 있게 한다는 의미이므로 이와 같은 내용에 해당되는 (A)가 정답이다.

기사에 따르면, 학생들에 대한 **McCallister** 씨의 목적은 무엇인가?
(A) 현실 세계의 업계 실무에 대한 학생들의 노출을 늘리는 것
(B) 기업들이 더욱 효율적으로 일을 할 수 있는 방법을 찾는 것
(C) 학생들이 필요로 하는 것에 더 적합한 인쇄물을 만드는 것
(D) 학생들에게 대중 발표를 더 잘 하도록 가르치는 것

토익 분석

세부사항을 묻는 문제는 질문에서 빠른 키워드(핵심어) 파악이 중요하며 해당 키워드가 등장하는 부분을 중심으로 단서를 파악하는 것이 관건이다. 다만 질문에서의 키워드는 지문에서 유사 어휘나 표현으로 바뀔 수 있다. 해당 문제의 경우, **goal**이란 키워드가 지문에서는 **objective**로 바뀌어 제시되고 있다.

160

In which of the positions marked [1],[2],[3], and [4] does the following sentence best belong?

"The focus is on organization and strategies to overcome obstacles in the industrial business world."

(A) [1]
(B) [2]
(C) [3]
(D) [4]

문제 해설

주어진 문장이 위치해야 하는 곳을 묻는 문제이므로 주어진 문장의 의미를 이해한 후 이와 내용적 연계성을 지닌 적절한 위치를 파악해야 한다. 우선 제시된 문장 "The focus is on organization and strategies to overcome obstacles in the industrial business world."는 비즈니스 업계의 장애물을 극복하는 체계성과 전략에 초점이 맞춰져 있다는 의미를 지니고 있다. 목적에 대해 구체적으로 언급하고 있는 내용인 만큼 이에 앞선 내용은 무엇의 목적인지 해당 대상이 위치해야 한다. 따라서 해당 강좌는 학생들이 실제로 회사에서 인턴으로 근무하는 과정이 포함되어 있지만 초청 연사들은 비즈니스에 따른 다른 시각을 제공한다는 의미를 지닌 문장 뒤 [4]에 위치하며 전반적으로 해당 강좌의 목적은 인턴 기회뿐만 아니라 근무 중에 겪는 비즈니스 업계에 존재하는 장애물을 극복하는 체계성과 전략에 맞춰져 있음을 설명하는 흐름이 되어야 논리적으로 타당하므로 정답은 (D)가 되겠다.

[1],[2],[3], [4]로 표기된 위치들 중에서 다음 문장이 들어가기에 가장 적절한 곳은 어디인가?
"초점은 비즈니스 업계에 존재하는 장애물을 극복하는 체계성과 전략에 맞춰져 있다."
(A) [1]
(B) [2]
(C) [3]
(D) [4]

토익 분석

강사로서 문제풀이 시간을 단축시킬 수 있는 방법으로 제시할만한 방법은 [3] – [4] – [1] – [2] 순서로 정답 비중이 높기 때문에 주어진 문장 내용을 순차적으로 해당 위치에 삽입해보며 내용 연결성을 비교하며 문제를 풀이하는 방법을 권고한다.

발신: 리베카 제닝톤 〈rjenington@goodtravel.com〉
수신: 마이클 윌슨 〈michaelw@heymail.net〉
제목: 휴가
날짜: 5월 9일 15:46

안녕하세요, 귀하의 여행사 담당자인 리베카 제닝톤입니다. [161] 고객님의 휴가 세부사항을 확인하고 싶습니다. 고객님은 전화상으로 제게 7월 2일에 이태리로 가시겠다고 말씀하셨습니다. 가능하긴 하지만, 항공료는 개인당 620 달러입니다. [162] 고객님께서 휴가 날짜를 조정하실 수 있으십니까? 만약 휴가를 일주일 늦춰 7월 9일 날 출발하시는 것이 가능하다면 항공료는 개인당 450 달러로 많이 인하됩니다. 이에 대해 고객님께서 원하시는 바를 제게 알려주세요.

그리고 고객님께서 예약하실 호텔에 대해 몇 가지 질문이 있습니다. 성인 2명과 아동2명을 포함하여 총 4명이 이번 휴가를 떠날 거라고 말씀하셨습니다. 큰 가족용 객실 하나와 그 보다 작은 두 개의 객실 중 어떤 것을 원하시나요? [162] 만약 가족용 객실을 선호하신다면, 가격대에 비해 훌륭한 시설을 구비한 프린스 호텔을 추천합니다. 이 호텔의 객실은 욕조와 TV, 그리고 컴퓨터를 갖추고 있으며 무료로 인터넷에 접속할 수 있는 무선 와이파이를 제공합니다.

가능한 한 빨리 1-800-7767-3232로 전화하셔서 고객님의 의사를 알려주셨으면 합니다.

Rebecca Jenington

어휘 travel agent 여행사 직원 details 세부사항 fly 날다, 비행하다 flexible 융통성이 있는, 탄력이 있는 delay ~을 지연시키다, ~을 연기하다 mention ~을 언급하다 adult 성인 represent 대표하다 excellent value for money 가격대에 효율이 좋은 wireless 무선의 access 접근, 접속, 이용 connection 연결 preference 선호, 취향 for free 무료로

Questions 161-164 refer to the following e-mail.

From: Rebecca Jenington<rjenington@goodtravel.com>
To: Michael Wilson <michaelw@heymail.net>
Subject: Vacation
Date: May 9, 15:46

Hi. This is Rebecca Jenington, your travel agent. [161] I want to check on the details of your vacation with you.— [1] —. [162] You told me on the phone that you wanted to fly to Italy on July 2. This is possible, but the flight will cost $620 per person. [162] — [2] —. Could you be more flexible with your vacation dates? If you were to delay your vacation and fly one week later on July 9, the cost would be much cheaper at $450 per person. Let me know what you want to do about this.

I also have some questions about the hotel that you would like to book. — [3] —. You mentioned that there are four people going on vacation: two adults and two children. Would you like one large family room or two smaller rooms? [162] If you would like a family room, I would recommend the Prince Hotel as it represents excellent value for the price. The rooms in this hotel come with a hot tub, a TV, and a computer and have wireless Wi-Fi access for connection to the Internet for free. — [4] —.

Please call me as soon as possible at 1-800-7767-3232 to let me know your preferences.

Regards,
Rebecca Jenington

161

★★ 이메일의 목적

이메일의 목적은 무엇인가?
(A) Wilson 씨에게 독일에서의 할인된 휴가를 제안하기 위해서
(B) Wilson 씨에게 이번 휴가가 취소된 것을 알려주기 위해서
(C) Wilson 씨에게 여행자 보험 상품을 광고하기 위해서
(D) Wilson 씨에게 휴가 계획에 대한 몇 가지 질문을 하기 위해서

토익 분석

이메일의 주제/목적은 이메일 초반 2-3문장의 내용을 통해 파악할 수 있으며 주제/목적 문제의 선택지들은 굳이 먼저 읽어볼 필요가 없다.

What is the purpose of the e-mail?

(A) To offer Mr. Wilson a discounted vacation package to Italy
(B) To inform Mr. Wilson that his vacation has been cancelled
(C) To promote a travel insurance package to Mr. Wilson
(D) To ask Mr. Wilson some questions about his vacation arrangements

문제 해설

이메일의 목적은 우선 첫 번째 단락 초반부에서 제시되는 내용에 집중해야 한다. 이메일 첫 번째 단락 초반 I want to check on the details of your vacation with you에서 고객의 여행상품의 몇 가지 세부사항에 대해 확인하고자 이메일을 한다는 내용이 언급된 바 있고 이어서 두 번째 단락 초반 I also have some questions about the hotel that you would like to book에서도 예약한 호텔에 관련해서도 몇 가지 질문할 내용이 있음을 밝히고 있으므로 궁극적으로 이메일의 목적은 휴가 상품에 대한 질문을 하기 위함임을 알 수 있다. 따라서 정답은 (D)가 되겠다.

162

What is suggested about Mr. Wilson?

(A) He manages a big hotel chain.
(B) He is a celebrated travel writer.
(C) He has spoken with Ms. Jenington.
(D) He will lead a workshop in July.

문제 해설

Wilson 씨에 대해 암시되는 내용을 묻고 있다. 지문 초반 Jenington 씨는 You told me on the phone that you wanted to fly to Italy on July 2라며 Wilson 씨가 전화상으로 자신에게 7월 2일에 이태리로 출발할 것이라 밝혔음을 언급하고 있다. 따라서 이를 통해 Wilson 씨는 Jenington 씨에게 전화 연락을 통해 사전에 먼저 여행에 관해 논의한 적이 있음을 유추할 수 있다. 그러므로 정답은 (C)가 되겠다.

★★ 유추

Wilson 씨에 대해 암시되는 내용은 무엇인가?
(A) 그는 대형 호텔 체인을 경영하고 있다.
(B) 그는 유명한 여행 작가이다.
(C) 그는 Jenington 씨와 이야기를 나눈 적이 있다.
(D) 그는 7월에 워크숍을 주재한다.

토익 분석

유추 문제의 키워드가 혹은 키워드에 관한 내용이 지문 전반에 걸쳐 언급되고 있는 상태에서 적절한 유추 내용을 파악해야 한다면 선택지에 나온 내용을 먼저 파악한 후 선택지의 내용을 유추할 수 있는 근거가 지문에 제시되는지 여부를 역으로 확인하는 방식으로 문제를 풀이한다. 이 때 선택지를 두 개씩 나눠 두 번에 걸쳐 지문에서의 유추 근거가 제시되고 있는지 확인하는 방식을 추천한다.

163

In which of the positions marked [1],[2],[3], and [4] does the following sentence best belong?

"Could you be more flexible with your vacation dates?"

(A) [1]
(C) [3]
(B) [2]
(D) [4]

문제 해설

주어진 문장은 "귀하의 휴가 날짜를 조정하실 수 있으십니까?"란 내용을 지니고 있다. 따라서 이를 전후하여 휴가 날짜를 변경할 수도 있을만한 이유나 휴가 날짜를 변경함에 따라 뒤따르는 장점이나 혜택에 관한 내용이 제시되어야 함을 가늠할 수 있다. 첫 번째 단락 초반 You told me on the phone that you wanted to fly to Italy on July 2. This is possible, but the flight will cost $620 per person이라며 7월 2일 이태리로의 여행이 가능하지만 비행기 요금이 개인당 620달러임을 언급하고 있다. 그 이후에는 If you were to delay your vacation and fly one week later on July 9, the cost would be much cheaper at $450 per person이라며 휴가를 일주일 늦춰 7월 9일에 가면 요금은 개인당 450달러로 낮아진다는 내용을 밝히고 있다. 따라서 귀하의 휴가 날짜를 변경하실 수 있는지 질문하는 내용은 바로 그 사이에 위치해야 함을 알 수 있다. 그러므로 정답은 (B)가 되겠다.

★★ 문장의 위치

지문 내 표시된 [1], [2], [3], [4] 중에서 주어진 문장이 지문 내에 위치하기에 적합한 곳은 어디인가?
"귀하의 휴가 날짜를 조정하실 수 있으십니까?"
(A) [1]
(B) [2]
(C) [3]
(D) [4]

토익 분석

강사로서 문제풀이 시간을 단축시킬 수 있는 방법으로 제시할만한 방법은 [3] - [4] - [1] - [2] 순서로 정답 비중이 높기 때문에 주어진 문장 내용을 순차적으로 해당 위치에 삽입해보며 내용 연결성을 비교하며 문제를 풀이하는 것이다.

164

What does Ms. Jenington NOT mention about the Prince Hotel?

(A) It represents excellent value for the price.
(B) Each of its rooms is fitted with a hot tub.
(C) Family suites are available at the hotel.
(D) Every room provides free Internet access.

문제 해설

Prince 호텔과 관련하여 언급되지 않은 내용을 묻고 있으므로 prince 호텔이 소개되는 부분을 빠르게 파악한 후 그 부분을 중심으로 단서를 파악해야 할 필요가 있다. 이메일 두 번째 단락 하단 If you would like a family room, I would recommend the Prince Hotel as it represents excellent value for the price을 통해 가격 대비 우수한 프린스 호텔에 대해 소개하고 있음을 알 수 있으며, 이어서 The rooms in this hotel come with a hot tub, a TV, and a computer에서 Prince 호텔 각 객실에는 욕조, 텔레비전, 그리고 컴퓨터가 구비되어 있을 뿐만 아니라 인터넷 접속을 위한 무선 와이파이도 제공하고 있음을 파악할 수 있다. 따라서 정답은 (D)가 되겠다.

★★ 진위

Jenington 씨가 Prince 호텔과 관련하여 언급되지 않은 내용은 무엇인가?
(A) 그 호텔은 가격에 비해 훌륭한 시설을 구비하고 있다.
(B) 각 객실에는 욕조를 구비되어 있다.
(C) 이 호텔에서는 가족용 객실을 이용할 수 있다.
(D) 모든 객실은 무료 인터넷 서비스를 제공한다.

토익 분석

진위 문제의 키워드가 제시되는 부분을 중심으로 키워드에 대한 진위 여부를 파악할 수 있는 모든 정보가 집중적으로 몰려 있는 경우에는 선택지 내용을 키워드로 삼을 필요가 없다.

세이프벳 보험
193 레이크 스트릿
어스틴, 텍사스 49302
(800) 2020-5830

7월 4일

샬롯 헨더슨 씨께,

[165] 저희 보험 상품에 관한 추가 정보를 요청하셨던 7월 1일의 전화통화와 관련하여 편지를 씁니다. 동봉된 회사 상품 소개 책자를 참조하십시오.

상품 소개 책자에서 저희는 현재 제공하고 있는 다양한 종류의 보험 상품의 대략적인 내용을 살펴보실 수 있습니다. [167] 저는 이 기회를 빌려 사고나 응급상황의 경우 고객님과 고객님의 부군이 모두 보상을 받을 수 있는 Total Cover 보험을 추천해드리고 싶습니다. 이 보험은 1년에 1200달러(또는 한 달에 100달러) 정도의 비용 밖에 들지 않으며 고객님이 거주하시는 지역에서 가장 인기 있는 보험 상품입니다.

저희는 적절한 보험을 선택하는 것이 간혹 스트레스를 받고, 번거로운 일이라는 것을 잘 알고 있습니다. 그것이 바로 저희가 최근에 보험 관련 세미나를 준비한 이유라고 할 수 있습니다. 세미나는 Austin 시청에서 한 달에 한 번, 토요일에 개최되고 대략 한 시간 정도 걸립니다. [166] 이 세미나는 어떤 보험 상품이 고객님에게 적합한지 결정을 돕고자 마련되었습니다. 이 세미나에서 고객님은 보험에 대한 성실한 조언가에 고객님의 개인적인 상황을 상담할 기회를 가지실 수 있습니다.

보험 세미나에 대한 추가 정보나 약관내용의 상세한 정보를 원하신다면, 인터넷 홈페이지 www.safebetinsurance.com을 방문해 주십시오.

Safebet을 선택하여 주셔서 감사합니다. 좋은 하루 보내십시오.

Judy Pennington
보험 개발 부장
Safebet Insurance

어휘 insurance 보험 with regard to ~에 대해, ~와 관련하여 further information 추가 정보 enclose 동봉하다 brochure 소책자 outline 개요; 요점을 말하다 policy 보험증권 opportunity 기회 region 지역 appropriate 적절한 overwhelming business 피곤한 일 hold 개최시키다 be held 개최되다 approximately 대략 dedicated 헌신적인 further information 추가정보 terms and conditions 약관 내용 valid 효력 있는, 유효한 spouse 배우자

165

★ **편지의 목적**

이 편지의 목적은 무엇인가?
(A) 보험 상품의 약관 내용을 요약하기 위해서
(B) 고객이 요청했던 대로 추가 상품 정보를 제공하기 위해서.
(C) 수신자에게 회사 직책을 제안하기 위해서
(D) 새로운 매장의 개장을 알리기 위해서

토익 분석

편지의 주제/목적은 단락 구분이 있는 경우 주로 첫 번째 단락 초반 2-3문장에서 제시되며 주제/목적 문제의 선택지들은 굳이 먼저 읽어볼 필요가 없다.

Questions 165-167 refer to the following letter.

Safebet Insurance
193 Lake Street
Austin, TX 49302
(800) 2020-5830

July 4

Dear Ms. Charlotte Henderson,

[165] I am writing with regard to our telephone conversation held on July 1, during which you requested further information on our insurance packages. Please find enclosed a company brochure.

In the brochure, the various types of insurance that are currently being offered are outlined. [167] I would like to take this opportunity to recommend our Total Cover policy, which would cover both you and your husband in the event of an accident or emergency. This policy is priced at just $1,200 per year (or $100 per month) and is our most popular program with our clients in your region.

I understand that choosing an appropriate insurance policy can often be a stressful and overwhelming business. That is why we at Safebet Insurance have recently set up some insurance seminars. These are held one Saturday a month at the Austin town hall and last for approximately one hour. [166] These seminars are designed to help you decide just which insurance package is right for you. At these sessions, you can also take the chance to speak to one of our dedicated advisers about your own personal situation.

For further information on our insurance seminars and for detailed information on our terms and conditions, please visit our website at www.safebetinsurance.com.

Thank you for choosing Safebet. I wish you a pleasant day.

Sincerely,
Judy Pennington
Insurance Development Head
Safebet Insurance

What is the purpose of the letter?

(A) To outline the terms and conditions of an insurance policy
(B) To provide further product information as requested by a client
(C) To offer the reader a position within the company
(D) To announce the opening of a new store

문제 해설

편지의 목적에 대해 묻고 있으므로 편지 초반부에서 언급되는 소재를 파악해야 할 필요가 있다. 편지 첫 번째 단락 초반 I am writing with regard to our telephone conversation held on July 1, during which you requested further information on our insurance packages을 통해 편지는 고객이 요청한 추가 정보를 제공하기 위해 작성되었음을 알 수 있다. 그러므로 정답은 (B)이다.

166

What is the purpose of the seminar sessions?

(A) To train new employees in sales techniques
(B)To provide education in the area of Website design
(C) To discuss the company's sales figures with board members
(D) To help customers choose the appropriate insurance policy

문제 해설

세미나의 목적에 대해 묻고 있으므로 지문에서 세미나가 소개되는 부분을 중심으로 단서를 파악해야 한다. 편지의 세 번째 단락 하단에서 These seminars are designed to help you decide just which insurance package is right for you라고 언급하는 내용을 통해 세미나의 목적은 고객이 적절한 보험을 선택할 수 있도록 도와주기 위해 개최됨을 파악할 수 있으므로 정답은 (D)가 되겠다.

★★ 세부사항

세미나의 목적은 무엇인가?
(A) 신입직원들에게 영업기술에 대한 훈련을 시키기 위해서
(B) 웹사이트 디자인 분야에 관한 교육을 제공하기 위해서
(C) 이사회 임원들과 회사 영업 실적을 토론하기 위해서
(D) 소비자가 적절한 보험증권을 선택하도록 도와주기 위해서

토익 분석

세부사항을 묻는 문제는 질문에서 빠른 키워드(핵심어) 파악이 중요하며 해당 키워드가 등장하는 부분을 중심으로 단서를 파악하는 것이 관건이다. 다만 질문에서의 키워드는 지문에서 유사 어휘나 표현으로 바뀔 수 있다

167

What is NOT mentioned about the Total Cover policy?

(A) It costs twelve hundred dollars a year.
(B) The policy would be valid for both Mrs. Henderson and her spouse.
(C) Ms. Henderson's children would be covered by the policy.
(D) It is the company's best-liked insurance program in the local area.

문제 해설

토탈 커버 보험에 대한 사실 확인 질문이므로 토탈 커버 보험이 소개되는 부분을 중심으로 관련 내용을 살펴봐야 할 필요가 있다. 편지의 두 번째 단락 중반 I would like to take this opportunity to recommend our Total Cover policy, which would cover both you and your husband in the event of an accident or emergency라고 제시된 내용을 통해 이 보험은 가입자와 가입자의 배우자에게 모두 적용이 되는 보험상품임을 알 수 있으며, 이어서 This policy is priced at just $1,200 per year and is our most popular program with our clients in your region라고 밝히는 내용을 통해 1년에 소요되는 비용이 1200달러이며, Henderson 씨가 거주하는 지역에서 가장 인기가 많은 보험상품이란 점도 알 수 있다. 따라서 정답은 (C)가 되겠다.

★★ 진위

Total Cover 보험에 대해 언급되지 않은 내용은 무엇인가?
(A) 일 년에 1200 달러 비용이 소요된다.
(B) 보험은 Henderson 씨와 그의 배우자 모두에게 유효하다.
(C) Henderson 씨의 아이들도 이 보험으로 보장받을 수 있다.
(D) 그 지역에서 가장 인기 있는 보험 상품이다.

토익 분석

진위 문제의 키워드가 제시되는 부분을 중심으로 키워드에 대한 진위 여부를 파악할 수 있는 모든 정보가 집중적으로 몰려 있는 경우에는 선택지 내용을 키워드로 삼을 필요가 없다.

5월 10일—기자 회견에서 **Scolan** 건설의 회장 **Lyle Vines**는 **Canton** 공원 복원 계획에 회사가 150만 달러를 기부할 것이라고 밝혔다

지난 2년간 공원 복원 계획에 대한 재정적 지원이 지속적으로 감소해, 자금이 크게 필요한 상태였다. "**Scolan** 사의 후한 기부에 굉장히 기쁩니다." 라며 **Canton** 공원 위원회의 **Betty Judge** 위원은 "**Canton** 지역의 공원들을 유지하고 개선하겠다는 목표에 확실한 도움이 될 것입니다." 라고 말했다.

[168] 캔톤 공원 복원 계획(**Canton Parks Restoration Initiative**)은 **Canton** 주변의 공원과 운동장 시설들을 개선하기 위한 작업으로, 5년 전 **Canton** 공원 위원회(**Canton Parks Commission CPC**)에 의해 설립되었다. 처음 시작했을 당시에는 지역 정부에서 자금을 제공했으나, [169] 2년 전 **Canton** 시 위원회가 **Canton** 공원 복원 계획을 위한 자금을 신규 상업 지구 지원에 사용하기로 결정했다. **Canton** 공원 복원 계획은 그 이후로 자금 확보에 어려움을 겪고 있었다.

마침내 6개월 전부터 **CPC**는 지역 내 기업들에게 기부금을 요청하기 시작했다. "우리는 우리 공원들의 아름다움을 보여주는 책자와 편지를 여러 기업들에게 보냈습니다." 라고 **Judge** 씨는 말했다. 책자 속 사진들은 몇 년에 걸친 공원의 경관들과 아이들이 놀고 있는 사진들을 다수 포함하고 있었다. "**Vines** 씨가 캔톤 공원 복원 계획에 기부관련 문의를 하기 전까지, [170] 우리는 그가 이전에 이 지역 거주자였다는 것을 전혀 몰랐습니다." 라고 **Judge** 씨는 말했다.

Canton의 시민들과 지역장들은 **Canton** 공원 복원 계획이 받을 추가 자금에 대해 반가워하고 있다. 시의원인 **Carl Nesmith**는 **Vines** 씨 기업이 한 기부에 대해 치하했다. 시의회는 공원들에 명예 명판을 배치하는 것을 논의했다. "**Canton**은 지역 사회 일원 모두에게 이로운 아름다운 공원들이 여러 개 있습니다." **Vines** 씨가 기부를 발표하며 말했다. [171] "사실 처음 이 공원들에서 놀면서 건설에 매력을 느끼기 시작했습니다. 놀이터 속 모래사장에 작은 도시들을 만들며 보낸 시간이 아니었다면 나는 다른 직업을 선택했을 수도 있었습니다. 이번 기부로 지역 사회가 계속 공원을 즐기게 도움이 되었으면 좋겠습니다."

Michael Pyke,
현지 기자

어휘 plaque 명판

Questions 168-171 refer to the following article.

May 10—Scolan Construction's president, Lyle Vines, stated at a press conference that the company would donate 1.5 million dollars to the Canton Parks Restoration Initiative over the next year.

With the initiative's financial support having decreased over the last two years, the funding is greatly needed.

"Our organization couldn't be happier with Scolan's generous donation," said Canton Parks commissioner Betty Judge. "It will certainly help us in our objective of maintaining and improving the parks in Canton.

[168] The Canton Parks Restoration Initiative was established five years ago by the Canton Parks Commission (CPC) to help improve park and playground facilities around Canton. When it was first started, the local government provided funding for the initiative, [169] but two years ago, the Canton City Council voted to use the revenue for CPC to fund a new commercial district. The initiative has had difficulties finding funding since then.

Finally, CPC began asking for donations from companies in the area six months ago. "We sent out letters to many companies with a pamphlet showing the beauty of our parks," Ms. Judge stated. The photographs in the pamphlets showed the parks throughout the years, and many had children playing in them. [170] "We had no idea that Mr. Vines is a former resident, until he called and asked about making a contribution to the initiative," Ms. Judge said.

Citizens and community leaders of Canton are pleased about the increased funding the initiative will receive. Councilman Carl Nesmith lauded Mr. Vines for his company's donation. The city council has talked about placing honorary plaques in the parks. "Canton has a number of beautiful parks that are very beneficial to everyone in the community," said Mr. Vines when announcing the donation, [171] "My fascination with building actually began when I would play at these parks. If it weren't for the time I spent making little cities in the sandboxes at playgrounds, I may have chosen a different career. I just hope this donation helps the community continue to enjoy the parks."

Michael Pyke,
Local Reporter

168

★ **세부사항**

Canton 공원 복원 계획은 언제 시작되었는가?
(A) 6개월 전
(B) 1년 전
(C) 2년 전
(D) 5년 전

토익 분석

세부사항을 묻는 문제는 질문에서 빠른 키워드(핵심어) 파악이 중요하며 해당 키워드가 등장하는 부분을 중심으로 단서를 살펴보는 것이 관건이다. 해당 문제는 the Canton Parks Restoration Initiative가 등장하는 부분 주변의 정보를 빠르게 스캐닝을 하면서 단서를 파악해야 한다.

When was the Canton Parks Restoration Initiative started?
(A) Six months ago
(B) One year ago
(C) Two years ago
(D) Five years ago

문제 해설

칸톤 공원 복원 계획이 시작된 시점에 대해 묻는 질문이므로 칸톤 공원 복원 계획, 즉 the Canton Parks Restoration Initiative이라는 키워드가 제시되는 부분을 중심으로 단서를 파악해야 한다. 기사문 세 번째 단락 초반 The Canton Parks Restoration Initiative was established five years ago by the Canton Parks Commission (CPC) to help improve park and playground facilities around Canton를 통해 칸톤 공원 복원 계획은 5년 전에 시작된 사업임을 알 수 있다. 따라서 정답은 (D)이다.

169

According to the article, why was the initiative losing financial support?

(A) The funding from the local government was redistributed.
(B) The cost of maintenance increased too much.
(C) Residents of Canton were moving away from the city.
(D) Further maintenance work was no longer needed.

★★ 세부사항

기사에 따르면, Canton 공원 복원 계획이 재정 지원을 잃었던 이유는 무엇인가?
(A) 지방 정부가 지원한 자금이 재분배되었기 때문에
(B) 유지 보수 비용이 너무 증가해서
(C) Canton 지역의 주민들이 지역에서 이사를 가서
(D) 상기 유지 보수 작업이 더 이상 필요하지 않았기 때문에

토익 분석

세부사항을 묻는 문제는 질문에서 빠른 키워드(핵심어) 파악이 중요하며 해당 키워드가 등장하는 부분을 중심으로 단서를 파악하는 것이 관건이다.

문제 해설

칸톤 공원 복원 계획의 재정 문제와 관련된 내용이 직접적으로 언급되는 부분을 파악해야 할 필요가 있다. 기사문 세 번째 단락 하단 but two years ago, the Canton City Council voted to use the revenue for CPC to fund a new commercial district에서 2년 전에 시의원들이 Canton 공원 복원 계획에 지원될 자금으로 새로운 상업지구 개발을 지원하기로 했다는 내용을 통해 정답은 (A)임을 알 수 있다.

170

Who is NOT a current resident of Canton?

(A) Lyle Vines
(B) Betty Judge
(C) Carl Nesmith
(D) Michael Pyke

★★ 세부사항

현재 Canton 지역 주민이 아닌 사람은 누구인가?
(A) Lyle Vines
(B) Betty Judge
(C) Carl Nesmith
(D) Michael Pyke

토익 분석

인명이나 지명은 중요한 키워드이므로 해당 문제처럼 선택지가 모두 인명/지명으로 구성된 경우, 지문에서 선택지에 제시된 인명/지명이 제시되는 부분을 전후하여 문제가 요구하는 단서를 파악하는 것이 효율적이다.

문제 해설

Canton 지역 주민이 아닌 사람의 이름을 파악해야 하므로 인명이 등장하는 부분을 중심으로 현재 거주민인지 과거 거주민인지 여부를 가늠할 수 있는 부가정보가 함께 제시되는지 여부에 집중해야 할 필요가 있다. 기사문 네 번째 하단 "We had no idea that Mr. Vines is a former resident, until he called and asked about making a contribution to the initiative," Ms. Judge said를 통해 Vines 씨가 이전 거주민임을 알 수가 있다. 그러므로 정답은 (A)이다.

171

What does Mr. Vines mention about the parks in Canton?

(A) They are not used by members of the community.
(B) They led him to his career in construction.
(C) Companies in the area should provide support for them.
(D) All parks should have a plaque giving information about donors.

★★★ 유추

Vines 씨가 Canton 지역의 공원들에 대해 암시한 내용은 무엇인가?
(A) 지역 사회의 일원들이 공원들을 사용하지 않는다.
(B) 공원들이 그를 건설 분야로 이끌었다.
(C) Canton 지역의 회사는 공원에 지원을 제공해야 한다.
(D) 모든 공원은 기증자에 대한 정보를 제공하는 명패가 있어야 한다.

토익 분석

유추 문제의 키워드(핵심어) 파악이 중요하며 지문에서 해당 키워드가 등장하는 부분에서 제공되는 정보를 토대로 유추 가능한 선택지의 내용을 정답으로 택일해야 한다.

문제 해설

Vines 씨에 대해 유추할 수 있는 내용의 근거를 이해하는 것이 순서이므로 무엇보다 지문에서 vines 씨가 언급되는 내용, 또는 그가 언급하는 내용에 집중해야 한다. 기사문 다섯 번째 단락 하단 "My fascination with building actually began when I would play at these parks. If it weren't for the time I spent making little cities in the sandboxes at playgrounds, I may have chosen a different career."에서 Vines 씨는 공원 놀이터에서 작은 도시들을 짓고 놀면서 건축에 대한 매력을 느끼기 시작했고 이런 시기가 없었다면 다른 직업을 선택했을지도 모른다는 내용이 언급되고 있다. 이를 통해 공원에서 보냈던 시간과 놀이가 오늘날 건축가로서의 그를 만들어냈음을 유추할 수 있으므로 정답은 (B)가 되겠다.

172-175 온라인 채팅을 참조하시오.

Jim Preston (오후 4:10)
[172] Valentina와 저는 6시에 저녁 식사를 일찍 할 생각인데요. 같이 가실 분 계신가요?

April Armstrong (오후 4:11)
어쩌면요. [172] 어디로 가실 생각이신가요?

Jim Preston (오후 4:12)
[172, 173] Fifth Avenue에 있는 중식당에 가 볼까 합니다. The Great Wall이라고 불리는 곳입니다. 음식이 정말로 훌륭하다고 들었거든요.

Mary Barnes (오후 4:13)
아, 이런! 운이 없으시네요. John과 제가 지난 주에 그곳에 들렀어요. [173, 174] 아쉽게도, 그곳은 이미 문을 닫았어요.

Jim Preston (오후 4:14)
그런 줄은 몰랐어요. [174] 안타깝네요. 인터넷에 올라와 있는 후기는 아주 좋았는데요.

Mary Barnes (오후 4:16)
Pine Street에 있는 한식당인 Chosun Dynasty에 가 보는 것은 어때요? 한국식 바비큐는 드셔 보셨나요?

Jim Preston (오후 4:18)
그거 좋겠네요. 몇 달 전에 로스앤젤레스로 출장 갔을 때 한국식 바비큐를 먹었어요. 정말로 맛있었어요. 다른 분들도 그곳에 가실래요?

April Armstrong (오후 4:19)
네, 저도 한국 음식을 좋아합니다. 저도 끼워 주세요.

Jim Preston (오후 4:20)
좋습니다. 오후 6시에 로비에서 만납시다. 괜찮으신가요?

Mary Barnes (오후 4:20)
괜찮습니다. 6시 30분에 그곳에서 뵙겠습니다.

April Armstrong (오후 4:22)
음… [175] 하지만 저는 6시 30분이 지나서야 사무실 밖으로 갈 수 있을 거예요. Jim, 전 다음 달에 출시될 신제품 디자인을 마쳐야 해요. 하지만 오후 7시 30분까지는 그곳으로 갈게요.

어휘 care to do ~하고 시다 try ~에 한 번 가 보다 exception 훌륭함, 뛰어남 out of luck 운이 없는 stop by ~에 들르다 unfortunately 아쉽게도, 안타깝게도 review 후기, 의견, 평가 pretty good 아주 좋은 Why don't we ~? ~하는 게 어때요? go on a business trip 출장을 가다 cuisine 음식, 요리 All righty 좋습니다, 알겠습니다. not A until B B나 되어야 A하다 get out of ~ 밖으로 나가다 release ~을 출시하다 by (기한) ~까지

Questions 172-175 refer to the following online chat discussion.

Jim Preston (4:10 P.M.)
[172] Valentina and I are going to stop for an early dinner at 6 P.M. Anyone care to join us?

April Armstrong (4:11 P.M.)
[173] Maybe. Where are you thinking of going?

Jim Preston (4:12 P.M.)
[172, 173] We can try the Chinese restaurant on Fifth Avenue. It's called The Great Wall. I heard their food is exceptional.

Mary Barnes (4:13 P.M.)
Oh, man! You are out of luck. John and I stopped by there last week. [173, 174] Unfortunately, it has already closed for business.

Jim Preston (4:14 P.M.)
I didn't know that. [174] That's too bad. The reviews were pretty good on the Internet.

Mary Barnes (4:16 P.M.)
Why don't we go to the Korean restaurant, Chosun Dynasty, on Pine Street? Have you ever tried Korean barbeque?

Jim Preston (4:18 P.M.)
That would be great. I had Korean barbeque several months ago when I went on a business trip to Los Angeles. It was really good. You guys want to go there?

April Armstrong (4:19 P.M.)
Yeah, I like Korean cuisine, too. count me in.

Jim Preston (4:20 P.M.)
All righty. Meet me in the lobby at 6:30 P.M. Is that okay?

Mary Barnes (4:20 P.M.)
Yes, that works. I'll see you at 6:30 P.M.

April Armstrong (4:22 P.M.)
Um… [175] I won't get out of the office until 6:30 P.M., though. Jim, I have to finish the designs for our new products, which will be released next month. But I'll get there by 7:30 P.M.

172

★ 인터넷 채팅 주제

메시지 작성자들은 무엇에 관해 이야기하고 있는가?
(A) 기업 행사를 주최할 장소
(B) 식사에 초대할 사람
(C) 저녁 식사를 할 장소
(D) 고객들과 Los Angeles에서 만날 시간

토익 분석

인터넷 채팅 지문의 주제/목적은 채팅 초반 3개의 채팅 라인에서 집중적으로 다루는 중심 소재를 파악하는 것이 관건이다.

What are the writers talking about?

(A) Where to host a corporate event
(B) Who to invite a meal
(C) Where to go for dinner
(D) When to meet with clients in Los Angeles

문제 해설

인터넷 채팅 주제에 대해 묻고 있으므로 채팅 초반부에서 집중적으로 다루고 있는 중심 소재를 파악하는 것이 관건이다. Jim Preston 씨가 오후 4시 10분에 Valentina and I are going to stop for an early dinner at 6 P.M. Anyone care to join us?라며 오후 6시에 저녁식사를 하러 갈 것인데 함께 갈 사람이 있는지 묻고 있으며 이어서 April Armstrong 씨가 어느 식당으로 갈 것인지 반문하고 있다. 따라서 인터넷 채팅 주제는 저녁식사 장소임을 파악할 수 있으므로 정답은 (C)가 되겠다.

173

What is indicated about the Chinese restaurant?

(A) It has moved to a new location.
(B) It received very poor reviews.
(C) It is no longer in business.
(D) It offers a special menu after 6:30 P.M.

문제 해설

중식당에 대해 알 수 있는 내용을 묻고 있으므로 인터넷 채팅에서 중식당이 언급되는 부분에 초점을 맞춰야 한다. 4시 12분 메시지에서 Preston 씨가 중식당을 언급하고 있으며 이 식당과 관련해 바로 다음 메시지에서 Barnes 씨가 그곳은 이미 문을 닫은 곳이라며 it has already closed for business 이라고 말하고 있다. 따라서 더 이상 영업하지 않는다는 곳임을 알 수 있으므로 (C)가 정답이다.

★★ 진위

중식당에 관해 알 수 있는 것은 무엇인가?
(A) 새로운 곳으로 이전했다.
(B) 아주 형편 없는 평가를 받았다.
(C) 더 이상 영업하지 않는다.
(D) 오후 6시 이후에 특별 메뉴를 제공한다.

토익 분석

진위 문제의 키워드가 제시되는 부분을 중심으로 키워드에 대한 진위 여부를 파악할 수 있는 모든 정보가 집중적으로 몰려 있는 경우에는 선택지 내용을 키워드로 삼을 필요가 없다.

174

At 4:14 P.M., what does Mr. Preston mean when he writes "That's too bad"?

(A) He has a prior engagement.
(B) He cannot meet a deadline for his project.
(C) He wanted to try Chinese food.
(D) He thinks a new restaurant is too far away.

문제 해설

"That's too bad"라는 그거 참 안 되었네요 정도에 해당하는 의미이자 좋지 않은 상황에 대한 유감을 언급하는 표현으로 바로 앞서 Barnes 씨가 it has already closed for business라며 한 중식당이 이미 문을 닫았다고 이야기하는 부분에 대한 답변으로 제시되었다. 뒤이어 온라인 상의 후기가 아주 좋았다는 The reviews were pretty good on the Internet이란 말이 덧붙는 것으로 보아 Preston 씨는 그곳의 음식을 먹어 보고 싶었지만 먹을 수 없게 되어 아쉬움을 드러내고 있음을 알 수 있다. 따라서 이와 같은 의미에 해당되는 (C)가 정답이다.

★★ 화자의 의도

오후 4시 14분에, Preston 씨가 "That's too bad"라고 썼을 때 무엇을 의미하는가?
(A) 선약이 있다.
(B) 자신의 프로젝트에 대한 마감시한을 충족할 수 없다.
(C) 중국 음식을 한번 먹어 보고 싶어 했다.
(D) 새로운 레스토랑이 너무 멀리 떨어져 있다고 생각한다.

토익 분석

특정 표현에 담긴 화자의 의도에 대한 이해하기 위해서는 주어진 특정 표현 전후의 내용 파악이 선행되어야 한다. 난이도가 높아지는 경우에는 전체 지문의 내용을 다 파악해야만 풀 수 있는 경우도 발생한다

175

What will Ms. Armstrong do next?

(A) Work on a project design
(B) Meet her colleagues in the lobby.
(C) Go to a new restaurant
(D) Leave for a business trip

문제 해설

Armstrong 씨는 무엇을 할 것인지 이후 행동이나 계획에 대해 묻는 마지막 문제이므로 인터넷 채팅 지문 후반부에 등장하는 Armstrong 씨의 이야기에 집중해야 한다. 채팅 종료 직전 Armstrong 씨는 6시 30분이 지나서야 나갈 수 있고 오후 7시 30분까지는 그 식당으로 가겠다며 I won't get out of the office until 6:30 P.M., though. Jim, I have to finish the designs for our new products, which will be released next month. But I'll get there by 7:30 P.M.이라고 말하고 있다. 따라서 이를 통해 Armstrong 씨는 프로젝트를 마무리하기 위한 작업을 할 것이라는 (A)가 정답이다.

★★ 세부사항

Armstrong 씨는 무엇을 할 계획인가?
(A) 조금 늦게 동료들에게 합류할 것이다.
(B) 오늘밤에 초과 근무를 할 것이다.
(C) 새로운 레스토랑으로 갈 것이다.
(D) 출장을 떠날 것이다.

토익 분석

특정 인물의 미래 행동은 해당 인물의 마지막 채팅 내용에서 동사를 중심으로 관련 단서를 파악한다.

Santa Maria 호텔

[176] 투스카니의 보석으로 알려진 Santa Maria 호텔은 이탈리아의 경사가 완만한 지형과 풍성한 포도농장들 속에 위치해 있습니다. 50개의 [177] 객실을 갖추고 있는 이 호텔은 WCHL로부터 4개의 다이아몬드 인증을 받았으며, 많은 유명 고객들의 성원을 받고 있습니다. 손님들은 이탈리아의 "고풍스런 모습"을 즐길 수 있지만, 저희 시설은 그와는 완전 반대입니다. 저희 객실은 초고속 무선 인터넷, 평면 TV, 프리미엄 케이블 채널 등이 갖추어져 있고, 시설로는 최고의 수영장, 노천탕, 운동시설, 비즈니스 센터 그리고 무료 유럽식 아침식사가 포함되어 있습니다.

호텔 산타 마리아는 세 가지 타입의 객실을 제공해 드립니다:

■ **플래티넘** 두 명의 고객을 위해 준비된 이 객실은 프리미엄 린넨을 갖춘 하나의 킹사이즈 침대가 있으며, 개인 발코니에서 포도농장을 볼 수 있고, 무료 아침 룸서비스, 그리고 스파 시설과 스팀 샤워 시설을 갖추고 있습니다. [180] 하루 저녁에 372유로이며, 세금과 수수료가 포함된 가격입니다.

■ **골드** 네 명의 고객을 위해 준비된 이 객실은 개인 발코니에서 정원 경치를 볼 수 있고, 무료 아침식사, 킹사이즈 침대 하나, 그리고 소파 겸 접이식 침대 하나 혹은 퀸사이즈 침대 두 개, 그리고 스팀 샤워시설을 갖추고 있습니다. 2명이 하루 저녁에 285유로로 이용하실 수 있고, 손님 추가 시 30유로가 추가되며, 세금과 수수료가 포함된 가격입니다.

■ **실버** 이 객실들은 8명의 인원까지 수용할 수 있는 조인트 특실이 되도록 연결할 수 있으며, 4명씩 분리할 수도 있습니다. 우리 정원과 같은 높이인 지상 1층에 위치해 있어 여러분들은 모든 호텔 시설을 손쉽게 이용할 수 있습니다. 객실은 킹사이즈 침대 하나와 소파 겸 접이식 침대 하나 혹은 퀸사이즈 침대 두 개를 포함하고 있습니다. 각 4명까지 하룻밤 객실 하나당 250유로이며, 세금과 수수료가 포함된 가격입니다.

예약 현황을 알아보시려면, 저희 홈페이지 www.smhotel.it을 방문하시거나 510-445-4331번으로 전화 주시기 바랍니다.

어휘 touted ~로 알려진, ~로 칭찬받는 be nestled in ~에 자리잡다 rolling landscape 완만한 경사의 풍경 fruitful vineyards 풍성한 포도농장 50-room establishment 50개의 객실을 갖춘 건물 receive recognition 인정을 받다 patronage 성원, 후원 amenities 편의시설 be equipped with ~을 갖추고 있다 flat-screen television 평면 TV facility 시설 elite pool 최고의 풀장 hot tub 스파 complimentary 무료의, 칭찬하는 European breakfast (간단한) 유럽식 아침식사 intended for ~을 위해 설계된 up to two guests 두 명의 게스트까지 feature ~을 포함하다, ~을 특징으로 하다 premium linen 최고의 린넨 private balcony 개인 발코니 plus taxes and fees 세금과 수수료 별도 courtyard views 정원 광경 couch pullout bed 소파 겸 접이식 침대 on our garden level 지상 1층에 위치한 have easy access to ~을 쉽게 이용하다

수신 : reservations@smhotelfrontdesk.it
발신 : smcgowan@bkmail.uk
날짜 : 10월 9일
제목 : 예약 변경

예약을 변경하기 위해 온라인 예약 현황에 로그인을 하려 했으나, 설정해 두었던 사용자명과 암호가 작동되지 않습니다. 제가 잘못 받아 적었는지, 시스템이 작동하고 있지

Hotel Santa Maria

[176] Touted as the Jewel of Tuscany, Hotel Santa Maria is nestled in the rolling landscape and fruitful vineyards of Italy. Our 50-room [177] establishment has received 4-diamond recognition by the Worldwide Chamber of Hotels and Lodging (WCHL) and enjoys the patronage of many elite guests. While guests can enjoy Italy's "Old World," our amenities are anything but that. Our rooms are equipped with high-speed wireless Internet, flat-screen televisions, and premium cable channels, and our facility includes an elite pool and hot tub, fitness facility, business center, and complimentary European breakfast.

Hotel Santa Maria offers three types of rooms:

• **Platinum** Intended for up to two guests, this room features a king-sized bed with premium linens, vineyard views from a private balcony, complimentary morning room service, and a jetted tub and steam shower. [180] €372 per night, including taxes and fees.

• **Gold** Intended for up to 4 guests, this room has courtyard views from your own balcony, free breakfast, a kingsized bed and a couch pullout bed or 2 queen-sized beds, and a steam shower. €285 per night for 2 guests + €30 for each additional guest, including taxes and fees.

• **Silver** These rooms can be connected to make a joint suite rooming up to 8 guests or kept separate for up to 4 guests. Situated on our garden level, you will have easy access to all the hotel's amenities. Rooms include a king-sized bed and a couch pullout bed or 2 queen-sized beds. €250 per night per room (up to four guests each), including taxes and fees.

To check our availability, please visit our website at www.smhotel.it or call us at 510-445-4331.

To: reservations@smhotelfrontdesk.it
From: smcgowan@bkmail.uk
Date: 9 Oct.
Subject: Change to Reservation

I just tried logging into my online reservation to make a change, but the username and password I had set up are not working. I do not know if I did not write it down correctly or if your system is not working. Either way, I need to make a change to my reservation, reference #110074.

[180] Originally, my daughter and her husband were going to join my husband and me on our trip to Tuscany, and we decided to go spend five nights and six days there. So I booked a 2-room Silver Suite. [179] However, my husband just learned that he would go on a business trip to at that point. (He would be in London by that time.) [180] Thus, I need to change our reservation from two rooms to one. But while we're making that change, I would also like to upgrade from a Silver to a Platinum room.

This will be our first trip to Tuscany, so we are very excited. If you could direct me to a reputable tourist firm, I would appreciate your assistance. Please also reply to confirm the above changes in my reservation.

Thank you.
Silvia McGowan

않은지 모르겠네요. 어느 쪽이든, 예약번호는 110074인데, 저의 예약을 변경해야 할 것 같습니다.
[180] 원래, 제 딸 부부가 우리 부부와 투스카니 여행을 함께 하기로 했었고, 저희는 투스카니에서 5박 6일의 지내기로 결정했습니다. 그래서 두 개의 방이 있는 silver suite로 예약도 했습니다. [179] 그러나, 제 남편이 막 그 시점에 출장을 가야 한다는 일정을 알게 되었습니다. (그때가 되면 제 남편은 런던에 있을 것입니다.) [180] 따라서, 두 개의 객실에서 하나의 객실로 바꿀 필요가 있을 것 같아요. 그런데 예약을 변경하면서 객실도 실버에서 플래티넘으로 향상시키길 원합니다.
이번이 투스카니로 가는 첫 여행입니다. 그래서 우리는 매우 기대하고 있어요. 신뢰할 수 있을만한 여행사와 연결시켜주신다면 감사하겠습니다. 그리고 제 예약 현황 변경도 확인해 주시기 바랍니다.
감사합니다.
Silvia McGowan

어휘 online reservation 온라인 예약 write down correctly ~을 정확하게 받아 적다 either way 둘 중 어느 쪽이든 originally 원래, 애초 upgrade from A to B A에서 B로 업그레이드하다 direct A to B ~A를 B에게 보내다 reputable 유명한, 명성이 높은 tourist firm 여행사 confirm ~을 확인하다

176

What is mentioned about the hotel?

(A) It sits on a historic site.
(B) It is centrally located.
(C) It was recently remodeled.
(D) It has scenic views.

★★ 진위

호텔에 관해 언급된 내용은 무엇인가?
(A) 역사적인 장소에 위치하고 있다.
(B) 시내 중심에 위치해 있다.
(C) 최근에 리모델링이 되었다.
(D) 좋은 경치를 갖고 있다.

문제 해설

호텔에 관해 언급된 내용을 묻고 있는 진위 문제이며 키워드가 hotel이긴 하나 광고문 전체의 내용이 호텔에 관한 내용이므로 실질적으로 키워드라 할 수 없다. 따라서 선택지의 내용을 키워드로 삼아 지문에서 해당 내용이 언급되는지 여부를 빠르게 파악해야 한다. 광고 초반 Touted as the Jewel of Tuscany, Hotel Santa Maria is nestled in the rolling landscape and fruitful vineyards of Italy라며 Santa Maria 호텔은 경사가 완만한 지형과 풍성한 포도농장 속에 위치하고 있음을 언급하고 있으므로 정답은 (D)가 되겠다.

토익 분석

사실 내용을 묻는 문제[TRUE]의 키워드가 지문 전반에 걸쳐 언급되는 경우 선택지의 내용을 키워드로 삼아 지문에서 해당 내용이 언급되는지 여부를 빠르게 파악한다. 이 때 선택지를 두 개씩 나눠 두 번에 걸쳐 지문에서의 해당 내용이 제시되고 있는지 확인해 보도록 한다.

177

In the advertisement, the word "establishment" in paragraph 1, line 2, is closest in meaning to

(A) expansion
(B) foundation
(C) accommodation
(D) corporation

★★ 유사어

광고문의 1번째 단락, 3번째 줄에 있는 단어 "establishment"와 의미가 가장 유사한 단어는 무엇인가?
(A) 확장
(B) 설립
(C) 숙박시설
(D) 기업

문제 해설

해당 어휘인 establishment에 앞서 Santa Maria 호텔에 대해 설명하고 있으며 이후에는 50개의 객실을 갖추고 있다는 점과 WCHL로부터 4개의 다이아몬드 인증을 받았다는 사실을 언급하고 있다. 따라서 이 때 establishment는 결국 앞서 설명하고 있는 Santa Maria 호텔을 지칭하는 명사라 할 수 있으므로 이에 대한 유사어로는 '숙박/숙박시설'을 뜻하는 accommodation이 적절하다. 그러므로 정답은 (C)가 되겠다.

토익 분석

유사어 문제는 해당 어휘가 포함된 문장을 비롯하여 그 전후 문장 내용을 파악한 후 해당 어휘와 가장 유사한 의미를 지닌 어휘를 선택한다.

178

★★ 세부사항

McGowan 씨가 이메일을 통해 문의하는 것은 무엇인가?
(A) 입실 시간
(B) 유명 여행사
(C) 투스카니의 치안 상태
(D) 업그레이드 비용

토익 분석

특별한 키워드가 없이 지문 전체의 내용을 토대로 진위/특정 세부정보를 묻는 문제의 경우, 선택지에 나온 내용을 먼저 파악한 후 선택지의 내용을 간단하게 정리하여 이를 키워드로 삼아 지문에서 해당 내용이 등장하는지 여부를 역으로 신속하게 파악하는 방식으로 문제를 풀이한다. 이 때 선택지를 두 개씩 나눠 두 번에 걸쳐 지문에서의 해당 내용이 제시되고 있는지 확인하는 방식을 권고한다.

What does Ms. McGowan inquire about in the e-mail?

(A) Check-in time
(B) **Famous travel agency**
(C) Public safety in Tuscany
(D) The price of upgrade

문제 해설

이메일 마지막 단락 초반 맥고완 씨가 This will be our first trip to Tuscany, so we are very excited. If you could direct me to a reputable tourist firm, I would appreciate your assistance 라며 이번이 첫 투스카니 여행이므로 신뢰할 만한 여행사와 연결시켜주면 고맙겠다는 생각을 밝히고 있다. 따라서 정답은 (C)가 되겠다.

179

★★ 세부사항

McGowan 씨는 예약을 변경하기 위해 어떤 이유를 제시하고 있는가?
(A) 여행 예산이 변경되었다.
(B) 여행 날짜가 바뀌었다.
(C) 여행 목적지가 바뀌었다.
(D) 인원 수가 바뀌었다

토익 분석

예약 변경에 관한 이유를 묻고 있으므로 지문에서 예약 변경에 대한 내용이 시작되는 부분을 스캐닝을 통해 빠르게 파악한 후 전후 내용을 정독하며 예약 변경의 이유를 살펴보는 것이 바람직하다.

What reason does Ms. McGowan give for changing his reservation?

(A) The budget for his trip has changed.
(B) His travel dates have changed.
(C) His travel destination has changed.
(D) **The number of guests has changed.**

문제 해설

예약을 변경하려는 이유를 묻는 문제로, 이메일 두 번째 단락에서 However, my husband just learned that he would go on a business trip to at that point. (He would be in London by that time.)라며 남편이 출장 일정으로 인해 여행에 참석하지 못할 것이며 여행할 때가 되면 남편은 런던에 머물며 업무를 처리할 것이란 이유를 제시하며 궁극적으로 여행 인원이 줄어 들었다는 사실을 언급하고 있다. 그러므로 (D)가 정답이다.

180

★★★ 두 지문 연계문제

McGowan 씨는 호텔 숙박료로 얼마를 지불할 것 같은가?
(A) € 1,250
(B) € 1,425
(C) € 1,860
(D) € 2,232

토익 분석

• 해당 문제의 단서가 나와야 할 지문에서 단서가 불충분하게 제시된다면, 또는 문제에서 정답을 취합하기 위한 두 개의 정보가 서로 다른 지문에 위치하고 있음이 드러나는 경우 이는 두 지문 연계 문제라 할 수 있다. 해당 문제 역시 호텔 광고 지문에선 객실 숙박료 관련 정보만 제공할 것이고 막상 어느 객실에 머무를 것인지는 객실에 관한 정보는 맥고완 씨의 이메일에서 등장하게 될 것임은 사전에 충분히 파악할 수 있는 부분이기도 하다.

• 두 지문 연계 문제는 가장 마지막에 풀이하는 것이 현명하다. 두 지문 연계 문제의 풀이에 소요되는 시간을 절약하기 위한 좋은 방법은 바로 각 지문에서만 단서가 제시되는 문제들을 먼저 풀이하며 각 지문이 지닌 정보를 최대한 많이 파악하고 이해한 상태에서 두 지문 연계 문제를 마지막으로 접하여 풀이하는 것이다.

How much will Ms. McGowan most likely pay for the hotel charges?

(A) € 1,250
(B) € 1,425
(C) **€ 1,860**
(D) € 2,232

문제 해설

구체적인 객실별 호텔 숙박료는 첫 번째 호텔 광고 지문에 언급되어 있는 반면 McGowan 씨가 구체적으로 자신과 자신의 사위 부부가 머물 객실이 무엇인지는 이메일에서 다뤄지는 내용일 수 밖에 없으므로 이를 토대로 해당 문제가 두 지문 연계 문제임을 파악할 수 있다. 이메일 두 번째 단락 초반에서 맥고완 씨는 Originally, my daughter and her husband were going to join my husband and me on our trip to Tuscany, and we decided to go spend five nights and six days there라며 McGowan 씨는 남편과 사위 부부와 함께 5박 6일 간의 일정으로 투스카니를 여행하려고 했었던 본래 계획을 언급하고 있다. 이어서 이메일 두 번째 단락 후반에서 McGowan 씨는 Thus, I need to change our reservation from two rooms to one. But while we're making that change, I would also like to upgrade from a Silver to a Platinum room이라며 객실을 두 개에서 하나로, 그리고 객실도 실버에서 플래티넘으로 업그레이드를 시키길 원한다는 의사를 밝히고 있다. 이어서 광고 지문을 살펴보면 플래티넘 객실은 1박 숙박료가 €372이다. 5박 6일 간의 일정이므로 마지막 날은 당연히 호텔에 투숙할 이유가 없다. 따라서 호텔엔 5일간 머무를 것이므로 맥고완 씨는 숙박료로 € 1,860를 지불할 것임을 가늠할 수 있다. 그러므로 정답은 (C)가 되겠다.

Questions 181-185 refer to the following memo and e-mail.

To: Carson Center Building Tenants
From: Ms. Natalie Mills, Colbert Management Company
Date: May 22

[181] Colbert Management Company will [182] assume the management of the Carson Center building starting June 1. We will be committed to complete satisfaction of all the tenants.

Below is a list of contacts you should know.

[185] On-Site Maintenance
[183, 185] Maintenance Manager, Mr. Jung Ah Choi<jachoi@colbert.com>
All maintenance issues are to be directed to Ms. Choi.

Legal Department
[183] Administrative Assistant, Mr. Matthew Perry
<mperry@colbert.com>

General Management
[183] Office Manager, Ms. Rebecca Hales <rhales@colbert.com>

Colbert Management Company
1-303-555-1276

From: Natasha Dawson <ndawson@brownfinance.com>
[183] To: Jung Ah Choi <jachoi@colbert.com>
Date: June 5
Subject: Security Code

My name is Natasha Dawson. I work at Brownstone Finance. Our offices are located on the third floor at the Carson Center building. [184] We need to reset the code for our security system. The system lost power over the weekend and has since been turned back on. Unfortunately, the security code was reset, and we need a new one. Could you please send someone over to assist us with this problem immediately? We do not want our offices unprotected over the weekend.

Sincerely,
Natasha Dawson

181-185 다음 회람과 이메일을 참조하시오.

수신: Carson Center 건물 세입자
발신: Natalie Mills, Colbert Management Company
날짜: 5월 22일

[181] Colbert Management Company는 6월 1일부터 Carson Center 건물의 관리 업무를 [182] 담당하게 되었습니다. 관리 업무에 관해 모든 세입자들께 완전한 만족을 드리고자 최선을 다하겠습니다.

아래는 세입자 분들께서 필요한 연락처 명단입니다.

[185] 현장유지 관리
[183, 185] 유지관리부장, Jung Ah Choi 씨 <jachoi@colbert.com>
모든 건물 관리 사항들은 Jung Ah Choi 씨에게 전달됩니다.

법무부서
[183] 업무비서, Matthew Perry 씨 <mperry@colbert.com>

총무관리
[183] 총무부장, Rebecca Hales 씨 <rhales@colbert.com>

Colbert Management Company
1-303-555-1276

발신: Natasha Dawson<ndawson@brownfinance.com>
[183] 수신: Jung Ah Choi <jachoi@colbert.com>
날짜: 6월 5일
제목: 보안 코드

제 이름은 Natasha Dawson입니다. 저는 Brownstone Finance에서 근무하고 있습니다. Carson Center 3층에 위치한 [184] 저희 회사는 보안 시스템 코드를 재설정해야 합니다. 보안 시스템의 전원이 주말동안 꺼져 있었고, 그 이후 다시 전원이 들어왔습니다. 안타깝게도, 보안 코드가 재설정되어서 새로운 코드가 필요합니다. 이 문제를 즉시 해결해 주실 분을 보내주실 수 있을까요? 주말 내로 처리했으면 합니다.

Natasha Dawson

어휘 be committed to ~에 전념하다 tenant 세입자 contact 연락, ~에 연락하다 maintenance 보수유지관리 administrative 관리의, 행정의 reset ~을 재설정하다 security system 보안 시스템 since 그 이래로, ~이기 때문에 turn back on 다시 전원이 들어오다, 다시 전원을 켜다 unfortunately 안타깝게도, 불행하게도 send over ~을 파견하다, ~를 보내다 immediately 즉시 unprotected 보호받지 못한, 무방비의

181

★ 세부사항

Colbert Management Company는 어떠한 업종의 회사인가?
(A) 부동산 관리 회사
(B) 건설회사
(C) 토지 주택개발 회사
(D) 보안회사

토익 분석

사명은 중요한 키워드이므로 해당 문제처럼 사명이 키워드로 언급되는 문제에서는 지문에서 사명이 등장하는 부분을 전후하여 단서를 파악하는 것이 효율적이다.

What kind of business is Colbert Management Company?

(A) A property management company
(B) A construction company
(C) A housing development company
(D) A security company

문제 해설

Colbert Management Company의 업종에 대해 묻고 있으므로 무엇보다 Colbert Management Company란 사명이 제시되는 부분에 집중해야 한다. 회람 첫 번째 단락 초반 Colbert Management Company will assume the management of the Carson Center building starting June 1에서 Colbert Management Company가 Carson Center 건물의 관리업무를 담당한다는 점을 알리는 부분을 통해 이 회사는 부동산 관리 회사임을 알 수 있다. 따라서 정답은 (A)이다.

182

★★★ 유사어

회람의 1번째 단락 3번째 줄에 있는 단어 "assume"과 의미가 가장 유사한 단어는 무엇인가?
(A) 채용하다
(B) 가정하다
(C) 담당하다
(D) 심사숙고하다

토익 분석

유사어 문제는 해당 어휘가 포함된 문장을 비롯하여 그 전후 문장 내용을 파악한 후 해당 어휘와 유사한 의미를 지닌 어휘를 선택하라

In the memo, the word "assume" in paragraph 1, line 1, is closes in meaning to

(A) hire
(B) suppose
(C) undertake
(D) deliberate

문제 해설

주어진 문장 내에서 assume은 다른 업체가 하던 업무를 담당하게 되었다는 의미로 사용이 되고 있으므로 이와 동일한 의미를 지닌 표현으로는 undertake가 적절하다고 할 수 있다. 다만 assume에는 추정하거나 가정하다라는 뜻도 포함이 되어 있지만 이 문장 내에서는 그러한 의미로 사용된 것이 아니므로 (B)를 정답으로 택하는 우를 범하지 않도록 주의해야 한다.

★★ 진위

회람에서 언급하는 내용은 무엇인가?
(A) Carson Center 건물은 새로운 세입자를 물색하고 있다.
(B) 인터넷 연결 수리 작업이 이뤄질 것이다.
(C) Colbert Management Company는 일부 직원에 대한 해고를 단행할 것이다.
(D) 도움을 제공하는 다양한 사람들에게 연락할 수 있다.

토익 분석

특별한 키워드가 없이 지문 전체의 내용을 토대로 진위/특정 세부정보를 묻는 문제의 경우, 선택지에 나온 내용을 먼저 파악한 후 선택지의 내용을 간단하게 정리하여 이를 키워드로 삼아 지문에서 해당 내용이 등장하는지 여부를 역으로 신속하게 파악하는 방식으로 문제를 풀이하는 것이 현명하다.

What is indicated in the memo?

(A) The Carson Center building is seeking new tenants.
(B) Internet connections are being repaired.
(C) Colbert Management Company will fire some staff.
(D) Various individuals may be contacted for assistance.

문제 해설

첫 번째 회람에 있는 목록에서 볼 수 있듯이 세입자들에게 도움을 제공하는 각 분야에 따라 담당자가 다르며 연락처 또한 다르다. 그러므로 세입자들이 원하는 도움을 받고자 하는 분야에 따라 그에 적합한 담당자에게 연락을 해야 함을 알 수 있으므로 정답은 (D)가 되겠다.

184

What is the purpose of Ms. Dawson's e-mail?

(A) To report lost building keys
(B) To check the cost of installing a lock
(C) To receive assistance with a security system
(D) To request information about the management office

★★ 이메일의 목적

Dawson 씨가 이메일을 작성한 목적은 무엇인가?
(A) 잃어버린 건물 열쇠를 보고하기 위해서
(B) 자물쇠 설치 비용을 확인하기 위해서
(C) 보안 시스템에 대한 도움을 받기 위해서
(D) 관리 사무소에 대한 정보를 요청하기 위해서

토익 분석

대부분 이메일의 주제/목적은 이메일 초반 2~3문장의 내용을 통해 파악할 수 있다.

문제 해설

Dawson 씨가 작성한 이메일 초반 We need to reset the code for our security system에서 Dawson 씨는 보안 시스템의 코드를 재설정해야 함을 밝히고 있으며 이어서 Could you please send someone over to assist us with this problem immediately?라고 질문하며 이 문제를 바로 처리해줄 수 있는 사람을 보내줄 수 있는지 여부를 묻고 있다. 이를 통해 Dawson 씨는 보안 시스템 코드 재설정에 대한 도움을 줄 수 있는 인력을 보내도록 요청하고자 이메일을 작성했음을 알 수 있다. 그러므로 정답은 (C)가 되겠다.

185

To what office did Ms. Dawson send the e-mail?

(A) On-Site Maintenance
(B) Technical Support
(C) Legal Department
(D) General Management

★★ 두 지문 연계 문제

Dawson 씨가 이메일을 발송한 곳은 어느 부서인가?
(A) 현장 유지 관리
(B) 기술 지원
(C) 법무부서
(D) 총무 관리

토익 분석

• 두 지문 연계 문제는 가장 마지막에 풀이하는 것이 현명하다. 두 지문 연계 문제의 풀이에 소요되는 시간을 절약하기 위한 좋은 방법은 바로 각 지문에서만 단서가 제시되는 문제들을 먼저 풀이하며 각 지문이 지닌 정보를 최대한 많이 파악하고 이해한 상태에서 두 지문 연계 문제를 마지막으로 접하여 풀이하는 것이다.

• 수/발신자와 날짜 그리고 제목이 있는 서신을 접할 때는 이들을 꼭 모두 읽어보고 본문으로 들어간다.

문제 해설

두 번째 지문인 이메일의 수신자 부분 Jung Ah Choi <jachoi@colbert.com>를 통해 Dawson 씨는 Jung Ah Choi 씨에게 이메일을 발송한 것임을 확인할 수 있다. 이어서 이를 토대로 첫 번째 지문인 회람의 각 지원 분야별 담당자 목록을 살펴보면 Jung Ah Choi 씨의 담당 부서가 On-Site Maintenance, 즉 현장 유지 관리 부서임을 파악할 수 있다. 따라서 정답은 (A)가 되겠다. 많은 이들이 파트7의 문제를 풀 때, 특히 수/발신자와 날짜 그리고 제목이 있는 서신을 접할 때 시간이 촉박하다는 이유로 이 부분을 등한시하고 바로 본문으로 들어가 본문의 내용만 중시하는 경우를 자주 접할 수 있는데 강사로서 결코 그러지 말라고 진심을 담아 조언하고 싶다. 해당 문제와 같이 수/발신자 또는 날짜가 문제를 풀이함에 있어 결정적인 단서 역할을 하는 경우가 발생하기 때문이다. 또한 해당 이메일이 보안 시스템의 문제점으로 인해 작성한 이메일이므로 무의식 중에 기술 지원 분야 쪽을 떠올리며 막연하게 (B)를 정답으로 생각할 수도 있으나, 회람의 목록을 살펴보면 기술 지원 분야는 애당초 기재된 바가 없으며 무엇보다 Jung Ah Choi 씨는 기술 지원 분야/부서의 담당자가 아니란 점을 간과하지 않도록 한다.

http://phreshpaint.com
인테리어 디자인----- 페인트 작업----- 견적 받아보기---------- 연락처

Phresh Paint와 함께 비용을 절약해 보세요!

당사는 가정 인테리어 디자인 도색 서비스를 전문으로 합니다. 당사의 도색 작업 담당자들은 친절하고 경험이 많습니다. 저희는 도료 선택과 도색 작업에서부터 도료가 건조된 후의 실내 물품의 재정리에 이르기까지 여러분께서 해당 과정의 모든 단계에 [186] 만족하시기를 원합니다.

견적가는 새로 도색을 해야 하는 방의 수와 그 크기에 따라 다양합니다. 방의 수에 따른 기본 비용이 있으며 선택되는 색상과 방의 크기에 따라 추가 비용이 지불됩니다.

기본적인 작업 비용은 다음과 같습니다.

방 1개 = 200달러, [188] 방 2개 = 400달러, 방 3개 = 800달러

맞춤 견적을 받아보시려면, 희망하시는 작업에 관한 세부 정보를 주문서에 기입해주시기 바랍니다.
[187] * 가을 Phresh Paint Pass 서비스: 9월부터 11월까지, 매주 월요일과 화요일로 예정된 작업 주문에 대한 추가 비용을 최대 30퍼센트까지 할인해드리고 있습니다.

어휘 specialize in ~을 전문으로 하다 friendly 친절한 experienced 경험 많은 be pleased with ~에 만족하다 step 단계 process 과정 select ~을 선택하다 rearrange ~을 재배치하다, 재정리하다 dry 건조되다, 마르다 depend on ~에 따라 다르다, ~에 달려 있다 the number of ~의 수, 숫자 base rates 기본 요금 custom 맞춤 제공의, 맞춤 제작의 estimate 견적(서) complete ~을 작성 완료하다 order form 주문서 details 상세 정보 reduce ~을 할인하다 up to 최대 ~까지

Questions 186–190 refer to following webpage, order form, and e-mail.

http://phreshpaint.com
Interior Design---------- Painting---------- Receive an Estimate ------------- Contact

Save money with Phresh Paint!

Our company specializes in interior design painting services for your home. Our painters are friendly and experienced. We want you to be [186] pleased with every step of the process from selecting the paint and the painting job to rearranging the items in the room after the paint dries.

Our price depends on the number of rooms and their sizes. We have base rates for the number of rooms, and an additional fee is paid depending on the colors chosen and the size of the rooms.

Our base rates are:

1 room = $200, [188] 2 rooms = $400, and 3 rooms = $800.

For a full custom estimate, complete the order form with details about the work you need done.

[187] * Fall Phresh Paint Pass: From September through November, we are reducing the additional fees for orders scheduled on Mondays & Tuesdays by up to 30%!!!

Phresh Paint 작업 주문서	
제출 날짜	5월 29일, 월요일
성명	Brooklyn Oliver
이메일 주소	a_mail to:bkoliver@dogmail.com
전화번호	832-713-5555
주소	7530 Rugsby , Las Vegas, NV 10104
서비스 요청 날짜	6월 17일
필요한 작업	[188, 189] 제 주방과 거실이 도색되어야 합니다. 아직 색상은 결정하지 않았습니다. 두 가지 색상을 고르는데 있어 도움이 필요합니다. 각 방마다 하나의 색상으로 도색을 하고자 합니다.
기타 정보	주방이 매우 작습니다. [189] 거실은 주방 크기의 두 배입니다. 이 서비스에 대한 비용 견적이 필요합니다. 또한 가능하시다면, [187] 다음 주 화요일에 작업이 이뤄지길 원합니다.

어휘 assistance 도움 pick out ~을 고르다 twice the size of ~의 두 배 크기인

Phresh Paint Job Order Form	
Submission Date	Monday, May 29
Name	Brooklyn Oliver
E-mail address	a_mail to:bkoliver@dogmail.com
Telephone	832-713-5555
Address	7530 Rugsby, Las Vegas, NV 10104
Request Service Date	June 17
What Is Needed	[188, 189] My kitchen and living room need to be painted. I have not decided on the colors yet. I will need assistance picking out two colors, one for each room.
Comments	The kitchen is very small. [189] The living room is twice the size of the kitchen. I need an estimate of the cost for the service. [187] Also, I would like the job to be done next Tuesday, if possible.

To	Brooklyn Oliver
From	Brandon McDonald
Date	June 1
Subject	Service Estimate
Attachment	Service #: 12345098AFC

Hello Brooklyn,

Thanks for contacting Phresh Paint.

We would be happy to provide an estimate for completing both rooms and suggest some colors. We have staff on-hand to help! [190] In regard to picking out colors, please feel free to call our office at 832-456-8202. Our interior design specialist is willing to talk over suggestions based on your favorite colors. As for the price quote, we will need to measure your rooms and it will also depend on the colors you end up choosing.

I have noted your name on our calendar for next Tuesday, so we hope to talk to you soon about your colors!

Sincerely,
Phresh Paint

수신	Brooklyn Oliver
190발신	Brandon McDonald
날짜	6월 1일
제목	서비스 견적
첨부	서비스 번호: 12345098AFC

안녕하세요, Brooklyn 씨,

Phresh Paint에 연락을 주셔서 감사드립니다.

두 개의 방을 도색하는 작업에 대한 견적 비용을 제공하고 색상을 제안할 수 있게되어 기쁘게 생각합니다. 고객님께 도움을 드릴 수 있는 직원들이 상시 대기 중입니다. [190] 색상 선택과 관련해서는, 832-456-8202를 통해 사무실로 언제든지 연락주시기 바랍니다. 인테리어 디자인 전문가가 고객님께서 선호하시는 색상들을 바탕으로 기꺼이 도색에 필요한 색상을 제안해드릴 것입니다. 견적가에 관해 말씀을 드리자면, 저희가 고객님의 방 크기를 측정하고 고객님께서 최종적으로 선택하시는 색상에 따라 정해질 것입니다.

제가 다음 주 화요일에 있을 작업 일정에 고객님의 성함을 기입했으므로, 고객님께서 원하시는 색상에 관해 논의할 수 있길 바랍니다.

Phresh Paint

어휘 inquiry 문의 complete ~을 완료하다, 완수하다 have A on-hand A가 대기하다 in regards to ~에 관해서는 feel free to do 언제든지 ~하세요, 마음껏 ~하세요 specialist 전문가 be willing to do 기꺼이 ~하다 over ~에 관해 favorite 선호하는, 가장 좋아하는 based on ~에 근거를 둔, ~에 바탕을 둔 quote 견적, 견적을 내다 measure ~을 측정하다 end up V-ing ~하는 결과를 낫다, 결국에는 ~를 하게 되다 note ~을 적다, ~을 필기하다, ~에 유의하다

186

In the Web page, the word "pleased" in paragraph 1, line 2, is closest in meaning to

(A) confused
(B) satisfied
(C) thoughtful
(D) offered

★★ 유사어

홈 페이지에서, 1번째 단락의 2번째 줄에 있는 단어 "pleased"와 의미가 가장 가까운 것은 무엇인가?
(A) 혼란스러운
(B) 만족한
(C) 사려 깊은
(D) 제공된

토익 분석

유사어 문제는 해당 어휘가 포함된 문장을 비롯하여 그 전후 문장 내용을 파악한 후 해당 어휘와 유사한 의미를 지닌 어휘를 선택한다. 아울러 이중 지문 및 삼중 지문에서는 두 지문 연계 문제가 아니라 각각의 지문에서 단서가 명확하게 제시되는 문제들을 우선적으로 풀이하는 것이 바람직하므로 유사어 문제를 가장 먼저 풀이하는 것도 하나의 좋은 방법이다.

문제 해설

해당 문장의 We want you to be pleased with every step of the process ~을 그대로 해석해 보면, 고객인 상대방이 모든 단계에 대해 기뻐하기를 원한다는 의미를 나타낸다. 이는 고객이 서비스에 만족하는 것과 같으므로 '만족한'을 뜻하는 satisfied, 즉 (B)가 정답이다.

★★★ 유추 / 두 지문 연계 문제

Oliver 씨에 대해 유추할 수 있는 내용은 무엇인가?
(A) 그는 할인 혜택을 받게 될 것이다.
(B) 그는 최근에 새로운 주택으로 이사를 갔다.
(C) 그는 이미 부엌에 도색할 색상을 선택했다.
(D) 그의 일정은 매우 유동적이다.

토익 분석

- 별(*) 표시가 등장하는 경우 이 부분의 내용을 토대로 풀이해야 하는 문제가 필히 출제된다.
- 해당 문제의 단서가 나와야 할 지문에서 단서가 불충분하게 제시된다면, 또는 문제에서 정답을 취합하기 위한 두 개의 정보가 서로 다른 지문에 위치하고 있음이 드러나는 경우 이는 두 지문 연계 문제라 할 수 있다.
- 유추 문제의 키워드가 혹은 키워드에 관한 내용이 지문 전반에 걸쳐 언급되고 있는 상태에서 적절한 유추 내용을 파악해야 한다면 선택지에 나온 내용을 먼저 파악한 후 선택지의 내용을 유추할 수 있는 근거가 지문에 제시되는지 여부를 역으로 확인하는 방식으로 문제를 풀이한다. 이 때 선택지를 두 개씩 나눠 두 번에 걸쳐 지문에서의 유추 근거가 제시되고 있는지 확인하는 방식을 추천한다.

What can be inferred about Mr. Oliver?

(A) He will receive a discount.
(B) He recently moved into a new house.
(C) He has already chosen the colors for his kitchen.
(D) His schedule is very flexible.

문제 해설

Oliver 씨에 대해 유추할 수 있는 내용을 묻는 질문이다. Oliver 씨가 작성한 주문서 하단에서 Also, I would like the job to be done next Tuesday, if possible이라며 다음 주 화요일에 작업을 하길 원한다는 점을 밝히고 있다. 아울러 홈페이지 하단에서 **Fall Phresh Paint Pass: From September through November, we are reducing the additional fees for orders scheduled on Mondays & Tuesdays by up to 30%!!!라며 가을 Phresh Paint Pass 서비스를 안내하며 9월부터 11월까지 매주 월요일과 화요일로 예정된 작업 주문에 대한 추가 비용을 최대 30퍼센트까지 할인 혜택을 제공한다는 점을 밝히고 있다. 따라서 이 두 가지 사실을 토대로 Oliver 씨는 작업에 따른 추가 비용에 있어 30퍼센트 할인 혜택을 받게 될 것임을 유추할 수 있다. 그러므로 정답은 (A)가 되겠다.

★★ 두 지문 연계 문제

Oliver 씨는 자신의 서비스에 대해 얼마를 지불할 것 같은가?
(A) 100달러
(B) 200달러
(C) 400달러
(D) 800달러

토익 분석

- 삼중 지문에 따른 문제에서 특정인에 대한 세부정보를 묻거나, **probably, most likely, imply, suggest**를 대동하는 유추 문제는 두 지문 연계 문제일 가능성이 매우 높다.
- 해당 문제의 단서가 나와야 할 지문에서 단서가 불충분하게 제시된다면, 또는 문제에서 정답을 취합하기 위한 두 개의 정보가 서로 다른 지문에 위치하고 있음이 드러나는 경우 이는 두 지문 연계 문제라 할 수 있다.
- 돈의 액수가 제시되는 관련 정보가 언급되는 지문이 등장하는 경우 이와 관련된 두 지문 연계 문제가 출제되는 경향이 있으므로 이를 두 지문 연계 문제를 풀이하는 연결고리로 활용하도록 한다.

How much will Mr. Oliver most likely pay as a base rate?

(A) $100
(B) $200
(C) $400
(D) $800

문제 해설

두 번째 지문의 What Is Needed 항목을 보면 My kitchen and living room need to be painted라며 Oliver 씨는 주방과 거실에 도색 작업이 필요하다는 점을 알리고 있다. 아울러 홈페이지 중반부에서 2 rooms = $400, 즉 방 2개에 대한 작업이 400달러라고 밝힌 바 있다. 따라서 이를 취합하면 주방과 거실의 도색 작업에 소요되는 비용은 400달러임을 파악할 수 있으므로 (C)가 정답이다.

189

What is NOT true about Mr. Olive?

(A) His kitchen is smaller than his living room.
(B) He is a regular customer of Phresh Paint.
(C) He has not yet chosen paint colors for the rooms.
(D) He plans on having two rooms repainted.

문제 해설

Oliver 씨에 관해 사실이 아닌 내용을 묻는 진위 문제이므로 Oliver 씨가 작성한 작업 주문서를 중심으로 단서를 파악해야 할 필요가 있다. Oliver 씨는 작업 주문서의 Comments 부분에서 My kitchen and living room need to be painted이라며 부엌과 거실을 도색할 계획임을 언급하고 있으며 이어서 The living room is twice the size of the kitchen라며 거실의 크기는 부엌 크기의 두 배임을 밝히고 있다. 또한 I have not decided on the colors yet이라며 아직 색상을 선택하지 못한 상태임을 알리고 있다. 하지만 Oliver 씨가 Phresh Paint 사의 단골 손님임을 알 수 있는 내용은 등장한 바 없으므로 (C)가 정답임을 파악할 수 있다.

★★ 진위

Oliver 씨에 관해 사실이 아닌 내용은 무엇인가?
(A) 그의 부엌은 거실보다 크기가 작다.
(B) 그는 Phresh Paint 사의 정규 고객이다.
(C) 그는 아직 색상을 선택하지 못했다.
(D) 그는 두 개의 방을 도색할 계획을 지니고 있다.

토익 분석

특정 인물이 작성한 지문이 등장할 때, 그 해당 인물에 관련된 내용의 진위 여부를 묻는 경우 그 사람이 작성한 지문을 중심으로 단서를 파악하는 것이 바람직하다. 이 문제는 Oliver 씨에 관련된 내용의 진위 여부를 묻는 문제이므로 Oliver 씨가 작성한 작업 주문서를 토대로 선택지의 진위 여부를 확인해야 한다.

190

According to Mr. McDonald, what can Phresh Paint do?

(A) Paint the entire home
(B) Clean the kitchen and the living room after the job
(C) Expand the size of the kitchen
(D) Offer color choices over the phone

문제 해설

McDonald 씨가 Phresh Paint 사가 할 수 있는 것으로 언급한 내용이 무엇인지 묻는 문제이다. Phresh Paint의 직원 McDonald 씨가 작성한 세 번째 지문인 이메일 중반부를 보면, In regards to picking out colors, please feel free to call our office at 832-456-8202라며 Oliver 씨가 색상 선택과 관련해 도움이 필요하다고 알린 것과 관련해 언제든지 사무실로 연락하여 이에 대해 논의할 수 있음을 전달하고 있다. 따라서 (D)가 정답이다.

★★ 세부사항

McDonald 씨에 따르면, Phresh Paint 사가 할 수 있는 것은 무엇인가?
(A) 주택 전체를 도색한다.
(B) 작업 후에 주방과 거실을 청소한다.
(C) 주방의 크기를 확장한다.
(D) 전화상으로 색상 선택권을 제공한다.

토익 분석

• 특정 인물이 작성한 지문이 등장할 때, 그 해당 인물에 언급한 세부사항을 묻는 경우, 그 사람이 작성한 지문을 중심으로 단서를 파악하는 것이 바람직하다.
• 해당 키워드에 관한 내용이 지문 전반에 걸쳐 언급되는 상황에서 지문 전체의 내용을 토대로 진위/특정 세부 정보를 묻는 문제의 경우, 선택지에 나온 내용을 먼저 파악한 후 선택지의 내용을 간단하게 정리하여 이를 키워드로 삼아 지문에서 해당 내용이 등장하는지 여부를 역으로 신속하게 파악하는 방식으로 문제를 풀이하는 것이 효율적이다. 이 때 선택지를 두 개씩 나눠 두 번에 걸쳐 지문에서의 해당 내용이 언급되고 있는지 여부를 확인하는 방식을 권고한다.

191-195 다음 홈페이지와 목록, 그리고 기사문을 참조하시오.

Http://www.whatshot.ca

이번 달

행사명: Summer Sand Sculpture Contest
장소: Teriland Beach, Helson Tribon
날짜: 9월20일~22일
수준: 전문가 및 아마추어
연락처: Skyla Bonnie : sbonnie@eosandssculpture.ca

이 행사는 최근 3년간 연례적으로 개최되었습니다. 올해, [191] 전 세계에서 78명의 전문가들과 아마추어들이 대회 초청을 받았습니다. 참가자들은 개인 또는 팀으로 참여할 수도 있습니다. 이 대회는 매우 인기가 높으며, 작년 한 해에만 대략 [193] 10,000명의 관중이 참여하였는데, 이는 Helson Tribon에서 개최된 해변 행사들 중에서 가장 참여인원이 많다고 할 수 있습니다. Teriland Beach는 백사로 덮인 장거리의 해변입니다. Helson Tribon은 Rabitory와 인접해 있습니다. 아울러 행사 중에는, 3일간 지속되는 라이브음악, 다양한 음식과 음료, 공예품 판매점, 그리고 관람객들을 위한 모래 예술 강좌가 있을 예정입니다. 입장료는 무료입니다만, 주차장을 이용하시는 분께는 7달러의 요금이 부과될 것입니다.

어휘 hold ~을 개최하다 annually 연례적으로 whether to Vr ~을 해야 할지 말아야 할지 participant 참가자 attendance 참가자 수 among ~ 사이에서 covered by ~로 뒤덮인 in the vicinity of ~의 인근에 있는 moreover 게다가, 더욱이 a wide selection of 다양한 beverage 음료 craft 공예품 vendor 판매점, 판매업체, 판매상 entry fee 입장료 parking lot 주차장 charge A B A에게 B를 부과하다

Questions 191-195 refer to the following Web page, list and article.

Http://www.whatshot.ca

THIS MONTH

Event Name: Summer Sand Sculpture Contest
Location:Teriland Beach, Helson Tribon
Dates: 20-22 September
Level:Professional and amateur
Contact:Skyla Bonnie: sbonnie@eosandssculpture.ca

This event has been held annually for the past three years. [191] This year, over 78 professional and amateur participants were invited from around the world. Participants can decide whether to work solo or as a team. The contest is very popular and [193] recorded about 10,000 spectators last year, which was the highest attendance among the beach events held in Helson Tribon. Teriland Beach is a long beach covered in white sand. Helson Tribon is in the vicinity of Rabitory. Moreover, during the event, there will be live music for three days, a wide selection of food and beverages, craft vendors, and sand art lessons for visitors. No entry fee for anyone, but those who use the parking lot will be charged $7.

Third Annual Summer Sand Sculpture Contest 입상자

* 개인 참가자*

	성명	국적	작품 제목
1위	Henry Tyson	호주	Blue Mermaid
2위	William McGowan	캐나다	Pod of Dolphin
3위	Angus Truman	미국	Hearst Castle
4위	[195] Pitution Queset	브라질	Safari Jungle
5위	James McQueen	캐나다	Sea Creatures

어휘 winner 입상자, 수상자 contestant 대회 참가자 nationality 국적

Winners of the Third Annual Summer Sand Sculpture Contest

* For Solo Contestants *

	Name	Nationality	Work Title
First Prize	Henry Tyson	Australia	Blue Mermaid
Second Prize	William McGowan	Canada	Pod of Dolphin
Third Prize	Angus Truman	U.S.	Hearst Castle
Fourth Prize	[195] Pitution Queset	Brazil	Safari Jungle
Fifth Prize	James McQueen	U.K.	Sea Creatures

Rabitory에서 어떠한 일이 있는가?
[195] Ophelia Parker

올해의 Summer Sand Sculpture Contest가 지난 주로 종료되었으며, 이는 여름을 즐길 수 있었던 아주 좋은 기회였다. 좋은 날씨로 덕분에 [193] 관람객들의 수는 이전 대회에 비해 두 배로 늘었다.

What's new in Rabitory?
[195] By Ophelia Parker

This year's Summer Sand Sculpture Contest ended last weekend, and it was a great way to end the summer. Thanks to nice weather, [193] the number of visitors doubled compared to that of the previous event.

The contest [192] drew numerous solo and team contestants. They made masterpieces by using local sand and water. Shells, seaweed, driftwood, and other materials from nature were used in the sculptures as well.

[194] Henry Tyson from Australia took first place again by beating William McGowan from Canada with his *Blue Mermaid* sculpture, which was decorated with sea weed and seashells. All the sculptures were beautiful, but [195] I personally liked *Safari Jungle* best. The lower part of the sculpture was filled with driftwood, something I had never seen before.

I'm sure all the spectators also enjoy themselves. Some professional sculptors volunteered to help participants create better artworks during the event. With music and artisans, the event gave us all unforgettable memories.

이번 대회는 많은 개인 및 팀 참가자들을 [192] 유치하였다. 이들은 현지 모래와 물을 이용하여 멋진 작품들을 제작하였다. 조개 껍질과 해초, 유목, 그리고 기타 자연 재료들 또한 조각품의 일부가 되었다.

[194] 호주 출신의 Henry Tyson씨가 해조와 조개 껍질로 장식된 Blue Mermaid로 캐나다 출신의 William McGowan 씨를 누르고 다시 한 번 1위를 차지했다. 모든 모래 조각 작품들은 아름다웠지만, [195] 개인적으로는 Safari Jungle 이 가장 마음에 들었다. 이 작품의 하단에는 예전에 보지 못한 유목으로 가득 채워져 있었다.

모든 관람객들도 즐거운 시간이 되었을 행사였다고 확신한다. 참가자들이 대회 기간 중 더 나은 작품을 만들 수 있도록 몇몇 모래 조각 전문가들이 자원하여 이들에게 도움을 주었다. 음악 및 모래 조각 장인들을 통해 이 행사는 우리에게 잊지 못할 기억을 선사해주었다.

어휘 thanks to ~로 인해, ~ 덕분에 double 두 배가 되다 compared to ~와 비교해 previous 이전의 draw ~을 끌어 들이다 numerous 수많은 masterpiece 뛰어난 작품, 걸작 shell 조개 껍질 seaweed 해초 driftwood 유목 material 재료 sculpture 조각품 beat ~을 물리치다, 이기다 decorate ~을 장식하다 personally 개인적으로 filled with ~으로 가득 찬 spectator 관람객 volunteer 자원하다 artworks 작품, 예술품 artisan 장인, 기능공 unforgettable 잊지 못할

191

What is indicated about the contestants?

(A) They are all amateurs.
(B) They are from a variety of countries.
(C) They are acquainted with Ms. Bonnie.
(D) They are requested to register in advance.

★ 세부사항

참가자들에 관해 알 수 있는 것은 무엇인가?
(A) 모두 아마추어들이다.
(B) 다양한 국가 출신이다.
(C) Bonnie 씨와 아는 사이이다.
(D) 미리 등록하도록 요청 받고 있다.

토익 분석

세부사항을 묻는 문제는 질문에서 빠른 키워드(핵심어) 파악이 중요하며 해당 키워드가 등장하는 부분을 중심으로 단서를 파악하는 것이 관건이다. 다만 질문에서의 키워드는 지문에서 유사 어휘나 표현으로 바뀔 수 있다. 해당 문제는 참석자의 특징에 대해 묻는 초반부 문제로 contestant가 키워드이며 지문 초반에서 참석자가 언급되는 부분을 중심으로 단서를 파악해야 한다. 물론 문제의 contestant는 지문에서 유사어인 participants로 바뀌어 등장하고 있다.

문제 해설

참석자의 특징을 묻는 첫 번째 문제이므로 첫 번째 지문 초반부에서 키워드인 contestant, 즉 참석자가 언급되는 부분을 중심으로 단서를 파악해야 한다. 첫 번째 지문 시작 부분에서 inviting over 78 professional and amateur participants from around the world라며 키워드인 contestant와 유사한 participants와 함께 전 세계에서 78명이 넘는 전문가 및 아마추어 참가자들이 대회 참석 초청을 받았다는 점을 알리고 있다. 따라서 다양한 국가 출신임을 의미하는 (B)가 정답이다.

★★ 유사어

기사에서, 2번째 단락 1번째 줄의 단어 "**drew**"와 의미가 가장 가까운 어휘는 무엇인가?
(A) 수상했다
(B) 상상했다
(C) 옮겼다
(D) 끌어 들였다

토익 분석

유사어 문제는 해당 어휘가 포함된 문장을 비롯하여 그 전후 문장 내용을 파악한 후 해당 어휘와 유사한 의미를 지닌 어휘를 선택한다. 아울러 이중 지문 및 삼중 지문에서는 두 지문 연계 문제가 아니라 각각의 지문에서 단서가 명확하게 제시되는 문제들을 우선적으로 풀이하는 것이 바람직하므로 유사어 문제를 가장 먼저 풀이하는 것도 하나의 좋은 방법이다.

In the article, the word "drew" in the paragraph 2, line 1, is closest in meaning to
(A) won
(B) pictured
(C) moved
(D) attracted

문제 해설

해당 문장에서 drew의 주어로 경연 대회를 뜻하는 The contest가 위치하고 있고 drew 뒤에는 참가자를 의미하는 contestants가 목적어로 등장하고 있다. 따라서 동사 drew는 이 둘 사이의 관계를 나타내야 하므로 '~을 끌어 들이다, ~을 유치하다'란 의미로 쓰였음을 가늠할 수 있으며 실제로도 대회가 많은 참여자들을 유치했다는 문맥을 형성하고 있다. 따라서 이와 가장 유사한 의미를 지니는 attract, 즉 (D)가 정답이다.

★★★ 진위 / 유추 / 두 지문 연계 문제

올해의 행사에 관해 사실이라 유추할 수 있는 내용은 무엇인가?
(A) 10,000 명이 넘는 방문객들이 찾아 왔다.
(B) 참석하는데 1인당 5달러의 비용이 들었다.
(C) 처음으로 Teriland Beach에서 개최되었다.
(D) 작년 행사 기간보다 더 길게 개최되었다.

토익 분석

- 진위/유추 복합 문제에서 제시되는 키워드는 이와 관련된 내용이 여러 지문에서 전반적으로 다뤄지고 있으므로 이들은 두 지문 연계 문제로 출제된다. 아울러 삼중 지문에서 특정 대상에 관련된 정보를 묻는 문제가 출제되는 경우, 이 때 두 개 지문에서 특정 대상에 대한 정보를 공통적으로 다루고 있다면 이는 두 지문 연계 문제라 할 수 있다.
- 문제의 키워드가 지문 전반에 걸쳐 언급되고 있거나 키워드의 범위가 너무 넓어 키워드로서의 가치가 반감될 때는 선택지에 나온 내용을 먼저 파악한 후 이를 간단하게 정리하여 키워드로 삼아 선택지의 유추 내용이 가능한 근거가 지문에서 제시되는지 여부를 역으로 신속하게 파악하는 방식으로 문제를 풀이해야 한다. 이 때 선택지를 두 개씩 나눠 두 번에 걸쳐 지문에서의 해당 내용이 언급되고 있는지 여부를 확인하는 방식을 추천한다.
- 진위 문제와 유추 문제가 복합된 문제는 파트7에서 문제 풀이에 가장 많은 시간이 소요되는 유형의 문제이므로 시간이 부족한 상황에선 건너 뛰는 것이 현명하다.

What most likely is true of this year's event?
(A) It had more than 10,000 visitors.
(B) It cost $5 per person to attend.
(C) It was held in Teriland Beach for the first time.
(D) It was longer than last year's event.

문제 해설

해당 문제는 진위 문제이자 유추 문제이므로 사실상 파트7에서 접할 수 있는 가장 까다로운 유형의 문제라고 할 수 있다. 어차피 지문 전반에 걸쳐 올해의 경연대회에 대한 내용이 다뤄지고 있으므로 this year's event는 별반 도움이 되지 못하는 키워드이다. 따라서 선택지의 내용을 먼저 간략하게 정리한 후 이를 키워드로 삼아 지문에서 이를 유추할 수 있는 근거가 제시되는지 여부를 살펴보는 방식으로 문제를 풀이해야 한다. 세 번째 기사문 첫 단락에서 the number of visitors doubled compared to that of the previous event라며 관람객들의 숫자가 이전의 행사에 비해 두 배임을 알리고 있다. 아울러 첫 지문의 초반부에는 recorded about 10,000 people last year이라며 작년 행사에는 약 만 명의 관람객이 참여 했었음을 밝히고 있다. 따라서 이 두 가지 정보를 취합한 후, 이를 토대로 올해 행사에는 작년의 두 배, 즉 2만 명의 관람객이 참여했음을 유추할 수 있으므로 정답은 (A)가 되겠다.

194

What is implied about Mr. Tyson?

(A) He has won the competition previously.
(B) He has given sand sculpting lessons.
(C) He used driftwood in his sculpture.
(D) He recently moved to Canada.

문제 해설

Tyson 씨에 대한 유추 내용을 묻고 있으므로 우선 Tyson 씨에 관한 내용이 언급되고 있는 지문에서 Tyson 씨와 관련된 해당 정보를 파악한 후 이를 선택지의 내용과 대조하며 유추 근거로 활용이 가능한지 여부를 확인해야 한다. 세 번째 기사문의 세 번째 단락에서 Henry Tyson from Australia took first place again by beating William McGowan from Canada with his *Blue Mermaid* sculpture, which was decorated with sea weed and seashells이라며 Tyson 씨가 McGowan씨를 물리치고 다시 한 번 1위를 차지했다는 내용을 보도하고 있다. 따라서 이를 토대로 Tyson 씨는 이전에도 이 대회에 참여하여 우승한 경력이 있었음을 가늠할 수 있으므로 정답은 (A)가 되겠다.

★★ **유추**

Tyson 씨에 관해 유추할 수 있는 내용은 무엇인가?
(A) 이전에 경연대회에서 우승했었다.
(B) 모래 조각 강좌를 제공했다.
(C) 자신의 조각품에 유목을 사용했다.
(D) 최근에 Canada로 이주했다.

토익 분석

특정인에 대한 유추 가능한 내용을 묻는 문제의 경우, 해당 인물의 정보가 언급되고 있는 내용을 파악한 후 이를 토대로 유추 가능한 내용이 담긴 선택지를 정답으로 택일하는 방식으로 문제를 풀이해야 한다.

195

Whose sculpture did Ms. Parker like the most?

(A) Tyson's
(B) McGowan's
(C) Truman's
(D) Queset's

문제 해설

세 번째 지문인 기사문의 세 번째 단락에서 I personally liked *Safari Jungle* best이라며 Parker 씨는 개인적으로 *Safari Jungle*란 작품이 좋았음을 밝히고 있다. 이어서 두 번째 지문에서 해당 작품을 조각한 참석자의 이름은 Pitution Queset으로 되어 있다. 따라서 Parker 씨가 선호하는 조각품은 Pitution Queset 씨 작품임을 알 수 있으므로 정답은 (D)가 되겠다.

★★ **두 지문 연계 문제**

Parker 씨는 누구의 조각품을 가장 마음에 들어 했는가?
(A) Tyson 씨의 작품
(B) McGowan 씨의 작품
(C) Truman 씨의 작품
(D) Queset 씨의 작품

토익 분석

• 삼중 지문의 두 지문 연계 문제는 대개 두 번째 문제와 네 번째 문제(2-4) 또는 세 번째 문제와 다섯 번째 문제(3-5)로 짝지어 출제되는 경향이 있다.

• 두 지문 연계 문제는 가장 마지막에 풀이하는 것이 현명하다. 두 지문 연계 문제의 풀이에 소요되는 시간을 절약하기 위한 좋은 방법은 바로 각 지문에서만 단서가 제시되는 문제들을 먼저 풀이하며 각 지문이 지닌 정보를 최대한 많이 파악하고 이해한 상태에서 두 지문 연계 문제를 마지막으로 접하여 풀이하는 것이다.

• 이중/삼중 지문에서 등장하는 책의 이름/작품의 이름은 항상 두 지문 연계 문제와 연관되어 출제가 되고 있다. 따라서 이들이 제시되는 지문이 등장하는 경우 이들을 연결고리로 하여 풀이해야 하는 두 지문 연계 문제가 등장할 것임을 염두에 두어야 한다.

196-200 다음 기사와 광고, 그리고 후기를 참조하시오.

Griphin Hotels가 새로운 가족을 맞이하다

BEIJING (3월 10일) – Griphin 사가 President Hotel Group
에 합병되었다. Griphin 사는 President Hotel Group과 비
교해 소규모의 기업이지만 지역 내 독자적인 호텔 체인
을 보유하고 있다. Griphin사의 호텔들을 인수하여, 현재
President사는 Beijing 지역에 11개의 호텔과 1,800개가
넘는 객실들을 보유하게 되었다.

이 인수에 앞서, 196, 198 President사는 President Travel
Suites로 널리 알려져 있었는데, 이는 특별히 출장 방문하
는 고객들을 대상으로 한 비즈니스 호텔이었다. Griphin사
가 보유한 네 곳의 지점에는 1924년에 건설된 고급 Foxy
Hotel과 바로 작년에 영업을 시작한 최고급 호텔인 Wales
Inn이 포함되어 있다.

President사의 대변인인 Brian Parkman씨는 "President
Hotel Group은 Griphin사가 한 식구가 된 것을 환영합
니다," 라며 196 "Griphin 사는 Beijing에서 평판이 좋아,
President 사의 기존 호텔들의 부족한 부분을 완벽하게
보완해줄 수 있습니다."라고 했다.

President 사의 정기 고객들은 이제 Griphin 사가 소유했
던 호텔들에 머무를 때도 포인트를 적립할 수 있으며 쿠
폰을 사용하는 것이 가능하다.

어휘 be merged with ~과 합병이 되다 compared to ~
와 비교해 acquire ~을 얻다, 인수하다 property 건물, 부
동산 acquisition 인수 be widely known for ~로 널리 알
려져 있다 business traveler 출장 여행객 include ~을 포
함하다 deluxe 고급의 upscale 최고급의 launch ~을 출
시하다, 공개하다 spokesperson 대변인 reputable 명성
이 높은 complement 보완 existing 기존의 earn ~을 얻
다 voucher 쿠폰, 상품권

Question 196-200 refer to the following article, advertisement, and review.

Griphin Hotels Get New Family

BEIJING (10 March)—Griphin Inc. merged with President Hotel Group. Griphin Inc. is a small company compared to President Hotel Group. It owns a hotel chain in the local area. By acquiring Griphin properties, President Hotel Group currently owns 11 hotels and more than 1,800 guest rooms in Beijing.

Before the acquisition, 196, 198 President was widely known for its President Travel Suites, which were designed specifically for business travelers. Griphin's four branches include the deluxe Foxy Hotel, built in 1924, and the Wales Inn, an upscale hotel that was launched just last year.

"President Hotel Group welcomed Griphin Inc. to be a part of them," said President spokesperson Brian Parkman. 196 "Griphin is reputable in Beijing, and they will be a perfect complement to President's existing hotels."

President's loyal members are now able to earn points and apply vouchers when they stay at Griphin Hotels.

Beijing City Center
197 Beijing을 방문하십니까? 도심에서 머무르시길 원하십
니까? 그러시다면 President 호텔 중 한 곳에서 숙박하십
시오. 시내 지역에서 가장 많이 찾는 저희 호텔들을 아래
에서 확인하실 수 있습니다.

Atlanta Hotel
편의 시설로는, 무선 인터넷 서비스, 2인용 침대, 55인치
TV, 그리고 실내 수영장이 있습니다. 이 호텔은 모든 분들
이 필요로 하는 모든 서비스를 제공할 준비가 되어 있습
니다. 가족들에게 아주 적합한 호텔입니다!

Heart Grand
새로 장식한 저희 객실과 200 최근에 보수된 식당에서 조
용하게 식사를 즐겨보십시오. 또한 인근 영화관과 쇼핑
몰, 그리고 기타 도심 지역의 관광 명소를 방문하실 수도
있습니다.

Hotel Polish
공항으로 가는 교통비는 무료이자, 비즈니스 센터로서 완
벽하게 보수된 호텔이라서 198 이 호텔은 출장을 오시는
분들께 적합한 호텔입니다. 회의실들과 무료 무선 인터넷
서비스를 제공하고 있습니다.

Tradition D. Inn
오래되었지만 편리한 호텔이며 현대식 호텔들과 마찬가
지로 각 객실마다 2인용 침대, 평면 TV와 무선 인터넷 서
비스가 포함되어 있습니다. 매력적인 장식, 구미가 당기

Beijing City Center
197 Visiting Beijing? Want to stay in the city center? Then stay at one of the President's hotels. Below are our most popular hotels in the downtown area.

Atlanta Hotel
Our amenities include wireless Internet service, double beds, 55-inch TVs, and an inside swimming pool. This hotel is ready to provide everything for everyone. Great for Families!

Heart Grand
Try our newly decorated guest rooms and enjoy quiet dining at 200 our recently renovated eatery. You can also visit nearby theaters, shopping malls, and other city attractions.

Hotel Polish
With no fee for transportation to the airport and a perfectly remodeled business center, 198 this is the best hotel for business travelers. It has conference rooms and complimentary wireless Internet service.

Tradition D. Inn
This old-fashioned but convenient inn includes double beds, flat TVs, and

wireless Internet service in each room, like a modern hotel. It features a charming decor, appetizing free breakfast, and nearby public transportation. This is a beautiful place to stay during your holiday in Beijing.

Or have a look at our other hotels in Beijing. Choosing President is choosing the best.

는 무료 아침식사를 제공하며 인근 대중교통을 이용할 수 있습니다. 이 호텔은 여러분이 Beijing에서 휴가를 보내는 동안 머무시기에 좋은 아름다운 풍경을 지니고 있는 호텔입니다.

이외에도 Beijing에 위치한 다른 저희 호텔들도 확인해보시기 바랍니다. President 를 선택하는 것은 최고를 선택하는 것입니다!

어휘 amenities 편의시설 try ~을 한 번 해 보다 dining 식사 recently renovated 최근에 개조된 eatery 식당 nearby 근처의 attraction 명소, 명물 fee 요금 transportation 교통편 complimentary 무료의 business trip 출장 old-fashioned 오래된, 구식의 convenient 편리한 charming 매력적인 decor 장식 appetizing 구미가 당기는 free 무료의 have a look at ~을 한 번 보다 choose ~을 선택하다

Heart Grand
☆☆☆☆

[200] I really enjoyed my stay at the Heart Grand. My room was quite relaxing, and all my meals at the hotel restaurant were delightful. The hotel provided me with excellent service as well, but [199] I would have liked transportation, such as a shuttle service, to the airport. Since it was my first visit, catching a taxi to the airport was difficult, and it wasn't cheap. Other than this problem, I enjoyed my stay at Heart Grand.

Andrew Kim

Heart Grand
☆☆☆☆

[200] Heart Grand에서 정말로 즐겁게 머물렀습니다. 객실은 상당히 편안했으며, 호텔 레스토랑에서의 모든 식사는 굉장히 만족스러웠습니다. 호텔은 훌륭한 서비스를 제공해주기도 했지만, [199] 저는 공항행 서틀버스와 같은 교통편이 필요했습니다. 첫 방문인지라 공항으로 가는 택시를 잡아 타는 것조차 어려웠으며, 요금도 저렴하지 않았습니다. 이 문제 외에는, Heart Grand에서의 숙박은 만족스러웠습니다.

Andrew Kim

어휘 quite 상당히, 꽤 relaxing 느긋한, 여유로운 provide sby with sth ~에게 ~을 제공하다 as well 또한, 마찬가지로 such as ~와 같은 since ~이기 때문에, ~이후로 catch (교통편) ~을 이용하다 other than ~ 외에는, ~을 제외하고

196

What does the article suggest about President Hotel Group?

(A) It is relocating its headquarters.
(B) It has discontinued its loyalty club.
(C) It specializes in luxury hotels.
(D) It wants to appeal to a wider variety of customers.

★★★ 유추

President Hotel Group에 관해 암시하고 있는 내용은 무엇인가?
(A) 본사를 이전하는 중이다.
(B) 전용 고객용 클럽을 종료했다.
(C) 고급 호텔을 전문으로 한다.
(D) 더 다양한 고객들의 마음을 사로잡고 싶어 한다.

문제 해설

첫 번째 지문 전반에 걸쳐 President Hotel Group에 관한 내용이 언급되고 있는 President Hotel Group이라는 키워드는 그다지 쓸모가 있는 키워드라 할 수 없다. 따라서 선택지의 내용을 키워드로 삼아 지문에서 이를 유추할 수 있을 만한 근거가 제시되는지 여부를 파악하는 것이 바람직하다. President Hotel Group을 다룬 첫 번째 기사문 두 번째 단락에서 President was widely known for its President Travel Suites, which were designed specifically for business travelers 라며 President Hotel Group사는 President Travel Suite란 호텔로 인한 유명세를 지니고 있는데 President Travel Suite은 주로 출장을 오는 고객들을 대상으로 하는 호텔임을 밝히고 있다. 이어지는 다음 단락에서는 they will be a perfect complement to President's existing hotels 라며 Griphin 사가 President사가 보유한 기존 호텔들이 부족한 부분을 완벽하게 보완해 줄 것임을 알리고 있다. 따라서 정답은 (D)가 되겠다.

토익 분석

유추 문제의 키워드가 지문 전반에 걸쳐 언급되고 있거나 키워드의 범위가 너무 넓어 키워드로서의 가치가 반감될 때는 선택지에 나온 내용을 먼저 파악한 후 이를 간단하게 정리하여 키워드로 삼아 선택지의 이후 내용이 가능한 근거가 지문에서 제시되는지 여부를 역으로 신속하게 파악하는 방식으로 문제를 풀어야 한다. 이 때 선택지를 두 개씩 나눠 두 번에 걸쳐 지문에서의 해당 내용이 언급되고 있는지 여부를 확인하는 방식을 추천한다.

★ 진위

광고에서 네 개의 호텔의 공통점으로 언급하고 있는 내용
은 무엇인가?
(A) 모두 수영장을 보유하고 있다.
(B) 아주 오래 전에 건설되었다.
(C) Beijing 시내에 위치해 있다.
(D) 출장 여행객들에게 할인 혜택을 제공한다.

토익 분석

광고문은 네 개의 호텔들을 광고하는 내용으로 구성되어
있으므로 특별한 키워드가 등장하지 않는 문제이다. 특정
키워드가 없이 지문 전체의 내용을 토대로 특정 세부정보
를 묻는 문제의 경우, 선택지에 나온 내용을 먼저 파악한
후 선택지의 내용을 간단하게 정리하여 이를 키워드로 삼
아 지문에서 해당 내용이 등장하는지 여부를 역으로 신속
하게 파악하는 방식으로 문제를 풀이한다. 이 때 선택지
를 두 개씩 나눠 두 번에 걸쳐 지문에서의 해당 내용이 언
급되고 있는지 여부를 확인하는 방식을 추천한다.

What do the four hotels mentioned in the advertisement have in common?

(A) They all have swimming pools.
(B) They were all built a long time ago.
(C) They are all located in downtown Beijing.
(D) They all offer discounts to business travelers.

문제 해설

광고 지문에만 집중하면 되는 만큼 진위 문제임에도 크게 부담이 되지 않는 문제이다. 광고의 시작
부분에서 Visiting Beijing? Want to stay in the city center? Then stay at one of the President's
hotels. Below are our most popular hotels in the downtown area라고 언급하는 부분을 통해 해
당 호텔들은 모두 Beijing에 위치한 호텔들임을 알 수 있다. 따라서 정답은 (C)가 되겠다.

198

★★★ 유추 / 두 지문 연계 문제

Griphin 사가 보유하지 않았던 호텔은 무엇일 것 같은가?
(A) Atlanta Hotel
(B) Hotel Polish
(C) Heart Grant
(D) Tradition D. Inn

토익 분석

• 삼중 지문의 두 지문 연계 문제는 대개 두 번째 문제와
 네 번째 문제(2-4) 또는 세 번째 문제와 다섯 번째 문
 제(3-5)로 짝지어 출제되는 경향이 있다.
• 삼중 지문에 따른 문제에서 특정 대상에 대한 세부정보
 를 묻거나, probably, most likely, imply, suggest를 대
 동하는 유추 문제는 두 지문 연계 문제일 가능성이 매
 우 높다.
• 두 번째 혹은 세 번째 문제가 두 지문 연계 문제인 경우
 주로 첫 번째 지문에서 문제풀이에 필요한 단서가 제시
 되며 네 번째 혹은 다섯 번째 문제가 두 지문 연계 문제
 인 경우 대개 마지막 세 번째 지문에 문제풀이에 필요
 한 연결고리로 활용될 수 있는 결정적인 단서가 포함되
 어 있다.

Which hotel is most likely NOT Griphin's property?

(A) Atlanta Hotel
(B) Hotel Polish
(C) Heart Grand
(D) Tradition D. Inn

문제 해설

첫 번째 지문인 기사문의 두 번째 단락에서 President was widely known for its President Travel
Suites, which were designed specifically for business travelers라며 President Hotel Group사
는 President Travel Suite란 호텔로 인한 유명세를 지니고 있는데 President Travel Suite은 주로
출장을 오는 고객들을 대상으로 하는 호텔임을 밝히고 있다. 아울러 두 번째 지문인 광고에서 Hotel
Polish에 관해 this is the best hotel for business travelers이라며 출장 온 사람들에게 최적의 호텔
임을 홍보하는 내용이 제시되고 있다. 따라서 이와 같은 특징이 언급된 Hotel Polish는 본래 출장
여행객들을 대상으로 운영하는 호텔을 보유하던 President사의 호텔임을 유추할 수 있으므로 (B)
가 정답이다.

199

What disappointed Mr. Kim about his stay?

(A) The unfriendly staff
(B) The high price of the room
(C) The low quality of the restaurant
(D) The lack of affordable transportation

★★ 세부사항

Kim 씨가 숙박 기간에 실망했던 점은 무엇인가?
(A) 불친절한 직원들
(B) 높은 객실 요금
(C) 레스토랑의 낮은 수준
(D) 저렴한 비용의 교통 편의 부족

토익 분석

숙박시설이 등장하는 이중/삼중 지문인 경우 숙박시설에 대한 장/단점을 묻는 문제. 그리고 특정인이 머물렀던 숙박시설이 어디인지 혹은 머물렀던 숙박시설에 관한 세부적인 정보를 묻거나 유추하는 두 지문 연계 문제는 필히 출제되고 있다는 점을 숙지하도록 한다.

문제 해설

Kim 씨가 숙박 기간에 실망했던 점은 그가 작성한 이용 후기를 통해 파악할 수 있다. 세 번째 지문인 이용 후기 중반부에서 Kim 씨는 I would have liked transportation, such as a shuttle service, to the airport. Since it was my first visit, catching a taxi to the airport was difficult, and it wasn't cheap 이라며 Kim 씨는 셔틀 버스와 같은 교통편이 필요했고, 택시를 이용하는 것조차 쉽지 않았지만 그 비용 또한 저렴하지 않았다는 문제점을 언급하고 있다. 따라서 이를 통해 Kim 씨는 호텔 측의 교통 편의와 관련된 불만이 있었음을 알 수 있으므로 (D)가 정답이다.

200

What information is provided about the hotel in which Mr.Kim has stayed?

(A) Its restaurant has been redone.
(B) It provides free Internet service.
(C) It is available for conference.
(D) It includes a gift shop.

★★ 두 지문 연계 문제

Kim 씨가 머물렀던 호텔에 관해 제공된 정보는 무엇인가?
(A) 레스토랑이 보수되었다.
(B) 무료 인터넷 서비스를 제공한다.
(C) 회의를 하기 위해 이용할 수 있다.
(D) 선물 매장이 포함되어 있다.

토익 분석

- 삼중 지문의 두 지문 연계 문제는 대개 두 번째 문제와 네 번째 문제(2-4) 또는 세 번째 문제와 다섯 번째 문제(3-5)로 짝지어 출제되는 경향이 있다
- 두 번째 혹은 세 번째 문제가 두 지문 연계 문제인 경우 주로 첫 번째 지문에서 문제풀이에 필요한 단서가 제시되며 네 번째 혹은 다섯 번째 문제가 두 지문 연계 문제인 경우 대개 마지막 세 번째 지문에 문제풀이에 필요한 연결고리로 활용할 수 있는 결정적인 단서가 포함되어 있다.
- 두 지문 연계 문제는 가장 마지막에 풀이하는 것이 현명하다. 두 지문 연계 문제의 풀이에 소요되는 시간을 절약하기 위한 좋은 방법은 바로 각 지문에서만 단서가 제시되는 문제들을 먼저 풀이하며 각 지문이 지닌 정보를 최대한 많이 파악하고 이해한 상태에서 두 지문 연계 문제를 마지막으로 접하여 풀이하는 것이다.

문제 해설

Kim 씨가 머물렀던 호텔에 대한 내용은 Kim 씨가 작성한 이용 후기와 호텔 광고에서 모두 다뤄지고 있음을 고려할 때 해당 문제는 두 지문 연계 문제임을 알 수 있다. Kim 씨가 쓴 이용 후기 초반 I really enjoyed my stay at the Heart Grand라며 Kim 씨는 Heart Grand에서 즐겁게 숙박했음을 언급하고 있다. 아울러 광고 지문에서 Heart Grand와 관련된 정보를 살펴보면 our recently renovated eatery이라며 최근에 보수된 식당이 언급하고 있다. 따라서 두 가지 정보를 취합하면 Kim 씨가 머무른 Heart Grand의 식당이 최근 리뉴얼되었음을 유추할 수 있으므로 (A)가 정답이다.

101

★ 어형 과거분사

새로 나온 청바지 한 벌의 권장 소비자 가격인 $43는 1주일 전 가격에 비해 $7가 할인된 가격이다.

어휘 retail price 소매가 pair 한 쌍, 한 벌 blue jeans 청바지

The ------- retail price of a pair of new blue jeans, $43, is about $7 less than it was a week ago.

(A) suggested
(B) suggest
(C) suggests
(D) suggesting

문제 해설

빈칸에 적합한 어형을 묻는 문제로 빈칸이 소매가를 뜻하는 retail price라는 복합명사 앞에 위치하고 있으므로 빈칸에는 이를 수식하는 형용사 역할이 가능한 어형이 위치해야 한다. 그러므로 빈칸에는 과거분사 suggested 또는 현재분사 suggesting 중 정답을 택일해야 한다. 이 소매가는 새로 출시된 청바지 한 벌을 구매하고자 소비자에 의해 지불되어야 하는 가격으로 대개 제조사에 의해 제시되는 권장 소비자 가격을 뜻한다. 따라서 빈칸에는 '권고되는, 제안되는'이란 뜻을 지닌 과거분사 형태의 형용사인 suggested가 적절하다.

토익 분석

토익에선 명사 앞에 적합한 분사 형태의 형용사로서 대개 과거분사가 출제되고 명사 뒤에서 명사를 후치수식하는 분사 형태의 형용사로는 현재분사가 주로 출제되는 경향이 있다.

102

★ 대명사 / 소유격 대명사

그 지역 비즈니스 잡지는 양 사의 변호사들이 현재 그들의 선택사항들을 검토하고 있다고 보도했다.

어휘 currently 현재의 review ~을 검토하다 option 선택사항

A local business magazine says lawyers from both companies are currently reviewing ------- options.

(A) they
(B) their
(C) them
(D) themselves

문제 해설

빈칸에 적합한 인칭대명사를 묻는 문제이다. 빈칸이 가산 복수명사인 options 앞에 위치하고 있으므로 빈칸에는 유일하게 명사를 수식할 수 있는 인칭대명사이자 한정사인 소유격대명사 their이 와야 한다.

103

The film *"The Twenty Cats"*, which was modestly budgeted, ------- expectations at the box-office last year.

(A) believed
(B) expressed
(C) exceeded
(D) accomplished

문제 해설

빈칸에 적합한 동사 어휘를 묻는 문제로 빈칸이 '기대, 예상'을 뜻하는 expectations 앞에 위치하고 있다. '기대, 예상'이란 명사와 함께 쓰일 수 있는 동사 어휘라면 기대/예상을 초과하거나 혹은 기대/예상에 못 미친다는 의미를 형성할 수 있는 동사가 전부라 할 수 있다. 그러므로 빈칸에는 '초과하다'란 뜻을 지닌 동사 어휘 exceeded가 와야 함이 옳다.

토익 분석

토익에 대비하여 동사 exceed와 동의어 관계인 동사 surpass까지 함께 알아두는 것이 바람직하다.

★★ 어휘 / 동사 어휘

영화 "Twenty Cats"는 그다지 많지 않은 예산으로 제작된 영화지만 작년 영화 매출 부분에서 예상을 초월하는 큰 성공을 거두었다.

어휘 modestly 겸손하게, 얌전하게, 많지 않은 budget 예산, 예산을 짜다 box office 매표소, 흥행 매상 exceed ~을 초과하다 accomplish ~을 이루다, ~을 성취하다

104

Some employees are very self-centered and greedy, so they are ------- of other colleagues in the company.

(A) impossible
(B) unaware
(C) inconsiderate
(D) uncourteous

문제 해설

빈칸에 적합한 형용사 어휘를 묻는 문제이다. 빈칸에 앞서 일부 직원들은 매우 자기 중심적이고 욕심이 많은 성격임을 밝히고 있으며 빈칸 이후에는 회사의 직장 동료들이 언급되고 있다. 그러므로 빈칸에는 자기 중심적이고 욕심이 많은 일부 직원들과 직장 동료들과의 상태를 설명할 수 있는 형용사가 와야 함을 알 수 있다. 따라서 빈칸에는 이들에 대한 배려가 없다는 의미를 형성할 수 있는 inconsiderate이 와야 한다.

토익 분석

무엇보다 형용사 (in)considerate만 익히지 말고 be (in)considerate of란 표현 자체를 알아두도록 한다.

★★ 어휘 / 형용사

일부 직원들은 매우 자기 중심적이고 욕심이 많아서, 같은 회사에서 근무하는 다른 직장 동료들을 배려하지 않는다.

문제 분석

be inconsiderate of ~에 대한 배려가 없는

어휘 self-centered 자기 중심적인 greedy 욕심이 많은, 탐욕스러운 be inconsiderate of ~을 배려하지 않는, ~에 이해심이 많지 않은 unaware ~을 모르는, ~을 인식하지 못하는 uncourteous 무례한, 거친

105

★ 어휘 / 부사

올 2분기 공장 설비 부문의 기업 투자는 작년 동기 대비 3퍼센트 상승했다.

문제 분석

be compared to ~와 비교되다

어휘 corporate investment 기업 투자 plant and machinery 공장 설비 second quarter 2분기 compared to ~와 비교하여 period 기간

Corporate investment in plant and machinery rose 3 percent in the second quarter compared to the same period a year -------.

(A) ago
(B) now
(C) past
(D) away

문제 해설

빈칸에 적합한 어휘를 묻는 문제로 빈칸이 a year 뒤에 위치하고 있으므로 빈칸에는 1년 동안이나 1년 전 혹은 1년 후 정도란 의미를 형성할 수 있는 어휘가 필요하다. 아울러 빈칸에 앞서 올 2분기 공장 설비 부문 기업 투자가 3퍼센트 상승했으며 이는 동일한 기간과 비교해서 나온 수치임을 언급하고 있다. 따라서 이미 상승한 수치이므로 작년 대비 동일한 기간과의 비교여야 함을 알 수 있으므로 빈칸에는 1년 전이란 뜻을 만들어 내는 부사 ago가 와야 한다.

106

★★ 어형 / 동사 어형

내일 있을 이사회가 끝난 후에, 사장님은 우리가 제약 산업 분야로 사업을 확대할 것인지 여부를 결정지을 것이다.

문제 분석

expand one's business into ~로 사업을 확대하다

어휘 board meeting 이사회 whether ~인지 아닌지 expand ~을 확장하다 pharmaceutical industry 제약 산업

After the board meeting tomorrow, our president ------- whether we will expand our business into the pharmaceutical industry.

(A) deciding
(B) is decided
(C) have decided
(D) will decide

문제 해설

빈칸에 적합한 동사의 어형을 묻고 있으며, 동사 어형 문제는 일반적으로 주어/동사의 수 일치 – 태 – 시제 순으로 적절한 동사 어형을 파악하는 것이 효율적이다. 우선 절을 구성할 수 없는 준동사 형태인 deciding은 오답으로 소거해야 한다. 이어서 주어인 our president가 단수주어이므로 복수동사 형태인 have가 포함된 have decided도 오답이며 빈칸 뒤에 목적어 역할을 행하는 명사절인 whether we will expand our business into the pharmaceutical industry이 등장하고 있음을 고려할 때 수동태가 아닌 능동태가 적절하다. 아울러 내일 있을 이사회가 끝난 후에 결정이 이뤄지는 것이니만큼 시제로는 미래 시제가 알맞다. 따라서 이 모든 점을 감안할 때 빈칸에는 will decide가 와야 한다.

107

Newly developed subway cars have ------- seats as large-sized commercial buses with sixty seats.

(A) as many
(B) as much
(C) so many
(D) so much

문제 해설

빈칸이 동사 have와 명사인 목적어 seats 사이에 위치하고 있으므로 빈칸에는 가산 복수명사인 seats를 수식할 수 있음과 동시에 as large-sized commercial buses with 60 seats와 호응할 수 있어야 한다. 따라서 빈칸에는 as-as 동등비교구문을 구성하며 as large-sized commercial buses with 60 seats에서 대형 상업용 버스가 지닌 60석이란 좌석 수와 동수를 의미하는 as many가 적절하다.

★★ as - as 동등 비교구문

새로 개발된 지하철 차량들은 60석을 지닌 대형 상업용 버스와 동일한 좌석 수를 보유하고 있다.

문제 분석

A as many + 가산 복수명사 + as B / A as much + 불가산 명사 + as B B와 동일한 수/양의 A

어휘 newly 새롭게 developed 개발된 large-sized 대형 크기의 commercial 상업 광고, 상업적인

108

The local newspaper reported that Countryside& Mills and Kamon Farming will consolidate through a ------- merger next week.

(A) strategy
(B) strategic
(C) strategize
(D) strategically

문제 해설

빈칸에 적합한 어형을 묻는 문제로 빈칸이 '합병'을 뜻하는 명사 merger 앞에 위치하고 있으므로 명사를 수식할 수 있는 형용사 어형이 필요하다. 따라서 빈칸에는 형용사 어형인 strategic이 적절하다.

★ 어형 / 형용사

그 지역 신문은 다음 주에 Countryside & Mills 사와 Kamon 농장이 전략적 합병을 통해 하나의 회사로 통합될 것이라 보도했다.

어휘 local 지역, 지역주민, 지역의 report 보도, ~을 보도하다 consolidate ~을 통합하다, ~을 강화하다, ~가 공고해지다 through ~을 통해, ~을 관통하는, ~을 지나서 merger 합병

109

★ 어휘 / 전치사

우리 회사의 야유회는 악천후로 인해 내일모레로 재조정되었다.

어휘 outing 야외 행사 reschedule ~을 재조정하다 the day after tomorrow 내일 모레 inclement 혹독한, 엄동의

Our company outing has been rescheduled ------- the day after tomorrow due to the inclement weather.

(A) for
(B) during
(C) until
(D) on

문제 해설

빈칸에 적합한 전치사를 묻는 문제이다. 전반적으로 악천후로 인해 회사의 야외행사 일정이 내일모레로 재조정되었음을 의미하고 있으며 빈칸 뒤에는 내일 모레라는 재조정 시점이 등장하고 있으므로 빈칸에는 기일 지정의 의미를 지닌 전치사 for이 와야 한다.

토익 분석

토익에 대비하여 동사 (re)schedule은 전치사 for과 함께 쓰이고 동사 postpone은 전치사 until과 함께 쓰인다는 점은 필히 숙지해야 한다.

110

★★ 어휘 / 부정 형용사

많은 고객들은 그들이 구매한 제품에 대한 특별한 품질 보증으로 인해 몇 번이고 계속하여 Mimi 백화점을 찾는다.

어휘 time and time again 몇 번이고 계속하여, 지속적으로, 되풀이하여 thanks to ~덕분에 special 특별한 guarantee 보증, 보호, 약속, ~을 보증하다, ~을 장담하다 purchase ~을 구매하다 plenty 풍요, 넉넉함, 많은, 풍부한

Many customers come back time and time again to Mimi's Department Store because of the special guarantee on ------- items purchased.

(A) all
(B) each
(C) every
(D) plenty

문제 해설

빈칸에 적합한 어휘를 부정 형용사를 묻는 문제로 빈칸이 '제품'을 뜻하는 가산 복수명사 items 앞에 위치하고 있다. 무엇보다 each와 every는 가산 단수명사하고만 사용이 가능한 부정 형용사이므로 이들은 오답으로 소거해야 한다. 또한 all과 plenty는 모두 가산 복수명사와 불가산명사를 취하며 다수/다량을 표현할 수 있지만 plenty는 a plenty of라는 형태로 가산 복수명사 및 불가산명사를 취해야 한다는 점을 고려할 때 빈칸에는 all이 와야 함이 옳다.

111

The World Economy is the second ------- distributed magazine in the United States and Canada.

(A) wide
(B) wider
(C) more widely
(D) most widely

문제 해설

빈칸이 과거분사 형태의 형용사인 distributed 앞에 위치하고 있으므로 빈칸에는 형용사를 수식하는 부사가 필요하다. 아울러 미국과 캐나다에서 유통되고 있는 모든 잡지들 중에서 두 번째로 광범위하게 유통되고 있음을 고려할 때 비교 대상이 최소한 셋 이상임을 알 수 있으므로 빈칸에는 최상급 부사 어형인 most widely가 와야 한다.

World Economy 잡지는 미국과 캐나다 지역에서 두 번째로 많이 광범위하게 유통되고 있는 잡지이다.

어휘 distribute ~을 배포하다, ~을 나눠주다, ~을 유통하다 wide 넓은 widely 넓게

112

Dr. Andrew Lee, one of the most prominent economists in California, ------- a new labor economics theory last year.

(A) terminated
(B) supervised
(C) interpreted
(D) invented

문제 해설

빈칸 앞에는 California 지역에서 가장 저명한 경제학자인 Andrew Lee 박사가 등장하고 있으며, 빈칸 이후에는 새로운 노동 경제학 이론이 제시되고 있으므로 빈칸에는 새로운 노동 경제학 이론이란 목적어를 취할 수 있는 적절한 의미의 동사가 필요하다. 따라서 빈칸에는 새로운 노동 경제학 이론을 세웠다는 문맥을 구성할 수 있는 invented가 적합하다. 아울러 동사 invent는 '발명하다'란 뜻으로만 생각하는 경우가 많은데 '상상력/창의력을 동원하여 새로운 것을 만들어내거나 고안하다'는 뜻이므로 발명품에만 국한시켜서 생각하지 않도록 한다.

토익 분석

동사 terminate는 무엇인가를 종료시키거나 종결시킨다는 뜻을 지니고 있으며 토익에서는 주로 계약을 뜻하는 contract나 장기 임대를 뜻하는 lease, 또는 논의를 뜻하는 discussion과 함께 쓰여 계약/임대를 종결시키거나 해지시킨다는 의미, 그리고 논의를 끝내다란 의미로 접하게 된다.

Andrew Lee 박사는 California 지역에서 가장 지명한 경제학자 중 한 사람으로 작년에 새로운 노동 경제학 이론을 세웠다.

어휘 prominent 저명한 economist 경제학자 labor economics 노동 경제학 theory 이론 terminate ~을 종결시키다, ~의 종말을 이루다 supervise ~을 감독하다, ~을 관리하다 interpret ~을 해석하다 invent ~을 개발하다, ~을 고안하다

★★ 어휘 / 형용사

그 분기별 매출 보고서에 따르면, **Last Ship** 해운사의 수익은 2분기 말에 급격한 상승 기조를 보였다.

어휘 quarterly 분기의 merchant 상인, 상업적인, 상선의 wealthy 넉넉한, 부유한 drastic 급격한, 강렬한, 과감한 compare ~을 비교하다, ~을 비유하다 worsening 악화

According to the quarterly sales report, Last Ship Merchant Marine's revenue showed a ------- improvement at the end of the second quarter.

(A) wealthy
(B) drastic
(C) comparing
(D) worsening

문제 해설

빈칸에 적합한 형용사 어휘를 묻는 문제로 빈칸이 '향상, 개선'을 뜻하는 명사 improvement 앞에, 그리고 '보여주다'란 뜻의 동사 showed 뒤에 등장하고 있다. '향상, 개선'을 뜻하는 명사 improvement를 수식하는 형용사라면 향상/개선된 폭이 어느 정도 되는지 이를 설명할 수 있는 형용사이어야 한다. 즉, 향상의 폭이 크거나 미약하단 의미를 형성할 수 있는 형용사가 필요하다는 것이다. 따라서 빈칸에는 '급격한, 강렬한'이란 뜻의 형용사 drastic이 적절하다.

 꼼꼼하게, 신중하게

★★★ 어휘 / 부사

그 최고 경영자는 휴가를 떠나기에 앞서 우리 회사에 아직 처리되지 않은 중요한 사업 현안들을 세심하게 처리했다.

어휘 chief executive officer 최고 경영자 take care of ~을 처리하다, ~을 돌보다 pending 미정의, 결정되지 않은 go on vacation 휴가를 가다 accurately 정확하게

The chief executive officer ------- took care of pending business issues important to our company before going on vacation.

(A) accurately
(B) increasingly
(C) meticulously
(D) correctly

문제 해설

빈칸에 알맞은 부사 어휘를 묻는 문제이다. 빈칸을 중심으로 최고 경영자가 휴가를 떠나기에 앞서 아직 처리되지 않은 중요한 사업적 현안들을 처리했다는 내용이 제시되고 있다. 최고 경영자가 처리한 것이 회사에게 중요한 사업 현안들임을 고려할 때 빈칸에는 중요한 사업 현안들 어떻게 처리했는지 표현할 수 있는 부사가 필요하다. 그러므로 빈칸에는 업무 처리와 연계하여 쓰일 수 있는 '세심하게'란 뜻의 부사 meticulously가 와야 한다.

토익 분석

'꼼꼼하게/신중하게'란 뜻을 지닌 대표적인 부사 어휘로는 carefully, closely, meticulously, fastidiously, scrupulously 등이 있다.

115

Many scholars offered their ------- to Dr. McDonald for his remarkable accomplishments.

(A) congratulate
(B) congratulations
(C) congratulating
(D) congratulatory

문제 해설

빈칸이 소유격 대명사인 their 뒤에 위치하고 있으므로 빈칸에는 소유 대상을 언급하는 명사가 와야 한다. 따라서 빈칸에는 명사 어형인 congratulations가 적합하다. 아울러 대명사 중 명사를 수식할 수 있는 유일한 한정사는 소유격 대명사임을 상기하도록 한다.

토익 분석

동사 offer은 offer + 간접 목적어 + 직접 목적어, 즉 목적어를 두 개 취하는 동사이지만 간접 목적어와 직접 목적어 순서로 그 위치가 바뀐다면 offer + 직접 목적어 + to 간접 목적어 구조로 지니게 된다. 이 때 전치사는 대개 to가 등장하지만 일부 동사의 경우 동사에 따라 전치사가 달라질 수 있다. 예전 토익에서는 동사에 따라 변화하는 전치사에 대해 출제했었지만 오늘날의 토익에서는 이 부분에 대한 출제 비중은 거의 없다시피 할 정도로 극히 미미하다.

많은 학자들은 McDonald 씨의 훌륭한 업적에 축하를 전달했다.

문제 분석

offer sth to sby ~에게 ~을 제공/제안/전달하다

어휘 scholar 학자 offer ~을 제공하다, ~을 제안하다 congratulations 축하 remarkable 놀라운, 주목할만한, 훌륭한 accomplishment 업적, 성취 congratulate ~을 축하하다 congratulatory 축하의

116

When there is a problem with our database system, you should ------- contact the technology support department as quickly as possible.

(A) ever
(B) always
(C) precisely
(D) efficiently

문제 해설

빈칸에 적합한 부사 어휘를 묻는 문제이다. 빈칸에 앞서 데이터 베이스 시스템에 문제가 발생할 때를 언급하고 있으며 빈칸을 중심으로는 항상 기술지원부로 최대한 신속하게 연락을 취해야 한다는 내용을 제시하며 데이터 베이스 시스템에 문제가 발생했을 시에 취해야 할 조치에 대해 밝히고 있다. 문제를 풀이함에 있어 가장 결정적인 단서는 바로 기술지원부로 최대한 신속하게 연락을 취해야 한다는 내용의 조치이며 이는 데이터 베이스 시스템에 문제가 발생하는 경우 언제나 반복적으로 이뤄져야 하는 행동이라는 점이다. 따라서 빈칸에는 '항상, 언제나'란 뜻을 지닌 빈도 부사 always가 와야 한다.

토익 분석

토익에서 출제되었던 대표적인 빈도 부사 어휘로는 always, frequently, often, generally, typically, regularly 등이 있다.

★★ 어휘 / 빈도 부사

우리 데이터 베이스 시스템에 문제가 발생하면, 여러분은 항상 기술지원부로 최대한 신속하게 연락을 취해야 합니다.

어휘 technology support department 기술지원부 as quickly as possible 최대한 빠르게, 최대한 신속하게

117

★★ 어휘 / 동사

지구 온난화와 수질 오염은 어류를 포함한 모든 지구상의 생명체의 멸종을 초래할 수 있을 정도로 위협적이다.

문제 분석

동사 cause는 cause + 목적어 + to Vr 형태의 5형식 구조를 구성하는 것이 가능하다. 따라서 동사 cause는 목적어 뒤에 위치하는 to 부정사 형태의 목적격 보어의 형태를 묻는 문제도 출제되고 있으므로 이 또한 필히 알아두도록 한다.

어휘 global warming 지구 온난 화 pollution 오염 threaten ~을 위협하다 extinction 멸종 species 종자

Global warming and water pollution threaten to ------- the extinction of all life on earth, including fish species.

(A) lead
(B) prevent
(C) survive
(D) cause

문제 해설

빈칸에 적합한 동사 어휘를 묻는 문제이다. 빈칸 앞에는 지구 온난화와 수질 오염의 위협이, 빈칸 뒤에는 어류를 포함한 지구상의 모든 생명체의 멸종이 제시되고 있다. 따라서 지구 온난화와 수질 오염의 위협은 어류를 포함한 지구상의 모든 생명체의 멸종을 초래할 수 있는 원인/이유가 될 수 있으므로 빈칸에는 '~을 초래/야기하다'란 뜻을 지닌 동사 cause가 와야 함이 옳다.

118

★★ 어휘 / 접속부사

다양한 일자리들은 다양한 기술을 지닌 숙련된 직원들이 필요하며, 따라서 그에 맞는 여러 가지 의무 정년 퇴직 연령을 정해야 한다.

어휘 different 다른, 다양한 skilled 숙련된, 능숙한, 유능한, 기술이 좋은 however 그러나 furthermore 더욱이, 덧붙여 therefore 따라서, 고로 often 종종, 자주

Different jobs require different skilled employees, and should ------- have various mandatory retirement ages.

(A) however
(B) furthermore
(C) therefore
(D) often

문제 해설

빈칸에 적합한 부사 어휘를 묻는 문제이며 빈칸이 조동사 should와 본동사 have 사이에 위치하고 있다. 조동사 should 앞에 있는 등위접속사 and는 앞뒤로 절을 대등하게 연결할 수 있으며 주어가 동일한 경우 뒤에 오는 절의 주어는 생략이 가능하다. 그러므로 조동사 should에 앞선 생략된 주어는 바로 '다양한 일자리들'을 뜻하는 Different jobs 임을 알 수 있다. 또한 등위 접속사 and에 앞선 내용이 다양한 일자리들은 다양한 기술을 지닌 숙련된 직원들을 필요로 한다는 내용이, 빈칸 이후에는 그에 따른 결과로 다양한 일자리들은 각각에 적합한 정년 퇴직 연령을 지녀야 한다는 내용이 등장하고 있으므로 빈칸에는 인과 관계를 표현할 수 있는 therefore이란 부사가 와야 한다.

토익 분석

인과 관계를 뜻하는 대표적인 접속부사로 so, therefore, thus, as a result, hence 등이 있고 역접 관계를 나타내는 대표적인 접속부사로 however, but, nonetheless, nevertheless, on the contrary 등이 있다. 그리고 추가 의미를 나타내는 대표적인 접속부사로 moreover, furthermore, in addition, additionally 등을 알아두도록 한다.

119

The economic crisis of a nation usually develops ------- a global phenomenon that must be solved by international efforts.

(A) for
(B) into
(C) from
(D) with

문제 해설

빈칸에 알맞은 전치사를 묻는 문제이다. 빈칸에 앞서 한 국가의 경제 위기가 대개 확대가 된다는 내용이 등장하고 있으며, 빈칸 이후에는 국제 공조를 통해 해결되어야 하는 세계적인 문제란 내용이 언급되고 있다. 그러므로 빈칸에는 한 국가의 경제 위기가 국제 공조를 통해 해결되어야 하는 세계적인 문제로 확대가 된다는 문맥을 형성할 수 있는 전치사가 필요하다. 따라서 빈칸에는 모양, 상태, 성격 등이 변화됨을 뜻하는 전치사 into가 적합하다.

토익 분석

전치사 into는 '~안으로'란 뜻을 지니고 있는 전치사이지만 막상 토익에서는 전치사 into의 기본적인 의미를 묻기 보다는 모양, 상태, 성격 등이 변화됨을 뜻하는 전치사 into에 쓰임새에 대해 집중적으로 묻고 있으며 특히 동사 merge, consolidate, incorporate, break 등과 함께 쓰이는 into에 대해 출제된 바가 있음을 상기하도록 한다.

★★★ 어휘 / 전치사

한 국가의 경제 위기는 대개 국제 공조로 인해 해결되어야 하는 세계적인 문제로 확대되곤 한다.

어휘 economic 경제의 crisis 위기 develop ~을 개발하다, ~을 발전하다, ~을 만들다, ~을 키우다, ~이 성장하다 phenomenon 현상 solve ~을 해결하다 international efforts 국제적인 노력, 국제적인 공조

120

The company spokesperson said board members are ------- to have an influential entrepreneur, Mr. Simpson, as their CEO.

(A) thrill
(B) thrilling
(C) thriller
(D) thrilled

문제 해설

빈칸에 적합한 어형을 묻는 문제로 빈칸이 명사나 형용사를 주격 보어로 취하는 2형식 동사인 be 동사 뒤에 위치하고 있다. 무엇보다 명사로서의 thrill/thriller은 각각 '흥분'과 '오싹하게 하는 것'이란 뜻으로 '이사진'을 뜻하는 board members와는 동격이라 할 수 없으므로 이들은 모두 오답이다. 그렇다면 빈칸에는 주격 보어로 형용사가 위치해야 하며 동사 thrill이 be 동사 뒤에 형용사로 자리하려면 현재분사인 thrilling 또는 과거분사 thrilled 중 한 가지 어형을 선택해야 한다. 이사진이 영향력 있는 기업인인 Simpson 씨를 그들의 최고 경영자로 영입하게 되어 기쁘다는 문맥을 형성할 수 있어야 하므로 빈칸에는 thrilled가 와야 한다.

토익 분석

토익에서는 대표적인 감정/기분 동사인 interest, satisfy, disappoint, embarrass, thrill, fascinate, confuse, please가 사람명사와 함께 주로 과거분사 형태로 쓰여 그 사람이 해당 '감정/기분'을 직접 느끼고 있는 상태임을 묻는 문제가 집중적으로 출제되는 경향이 있음을 숙지하도록 한다.

★★ 어형 / 감정-기분 동사의 과거분사

그 회사의 대변인은 이사진이 영향력 있는 기업인인 Simpson 씨를 그들의 최고 경영자로 영입하게 되어 기쁘다고 언급했다.

어휘 spokesperson 대변인 board members 이사진 influential 영향력 있는 entrepreneur 사업가, 기업 인 thrill 흥분, 오싹함, 오싹하게 하다, 가슴 설레게 하다 thrilling 오싹한, 소름이 끼치는, 감격적인 thriller 오싹하게 하는 것, 흥미진진한 것

121

★ 어형 / 부사

우리 시 관광 버스의 노선들은 강북 지역과 강남 지역으로 나뉘어서 운영되고 있다.

문제 분석

부사 separately는 '별개로, 따로'란 뜻을 지니고 있으며 이와 유사한 어휘로는 individually가 있다. 대개 individual 이란 어휘를 접하면 '개인의'란 뜻을 떠올리는 경우가 많지만 이는 '개인의'란 뜻 뿐만 아니라 '개별적인'이란 뜻도 가능하다라는 점을 꼭 기억해야 한다. 과거 토익에서 be sold individually라 하여 '개별적으로(낱개로) 판매되다'란 표현이 출제된 바 있으며 물론 individually가 아닌 separately가 정답으로 제시된 적도 있다.

어휘 tour bus 관광버스 route 길, 노선 operate ~을 작동하다, ~을 가동하다 separate ~을 나누다, ~을 분리하다

Our city's tour bus routes are operated ------- for the north of the river and south of the river areas.

(A) separate
(B) separating
(C) separation
(D) separately

문제 해설

빈칸 앞에 위치한 Our city's tour bus routes are operated가 주어, 이어지는 be 동사 are, 그리고 주격보어인 과거분사 형태의 형용사인 operated가 완전한 구조(2형식)의 절이므로 빈칸에는 완전한 구조의 절에 부가되는 수식어인 부사가 위치하여 궁극적으로 형용사인 과거분사 operated를 수식해야 한다. 따라서 빈칸에는 부사 어형인 separately가 적절하다.

122

★★ 어휘 / 명사

대기업들은 공공이익을 위한 다양한 활동을 후원함으로써 기업이 지녀야 할 사회적 책무를 필히 행해야 한다.

문제 분석

토익에서 자주 접할 수 있는 형용사 social이 포함된 대표적인 표현으로는 social network service (소셜 네트워크 서비스), social welfare (사회 복지), social security system (사회 보장 제도), 그리고 social infrastructure (사회 인프라 시설) 등이 있다.

어휘 major company 대기업 carry out ~을 행하다 sponsor ~을 후원하다 various 다양한 public interest 공공이익 development 개발, 발전 promotion 홍보, 판촉

Major companies must carry out the social ------- of a business by sponsoring various activities for public interests.

(A) ties
(B) responsibilities
(C) developments
(D) promotions

문제 해설

빈칸에는 '사회적인'이란 뜻을 지닌 형용사 social과 어울리는 적합한 명사 어휘가 와야 한다. 대기업들이 공공이익을 위한 다양한 활동을 후원하는 것은 기업으로서의 사회적 책임 내지는 직무를 다하는 것이라 할 수 있으므로 빈칸에는 '책임, 책무'를 뜻하는 명사 responsibilities가 적절하다.

123

------- the new business plan is not cost effective and environmentally friendly, there will be problems approving it.

(A) Since
(B) While
(C) Although
(D) Unless

문제 해설

빈칸이 부사절 앞에 위치하고 있으므로 빈칸에는 부사절 접속사가 위치해야 한다. 부사절은 새로운 사업 계획안은 비용 효율이 좋지 않고 친환경적이지 않다는 내용이며 이어지는 주절은 이를 승인하는데 있어서 문제가 있다는 내용이다. 따라서 부사절은 주절의 결과를 초래하는 이유/원인에 해당되는 내용이므로 빈칸에는 이유 부사절 접속사인 Since가 적합하다.

토익 분석

부사절 접속사에 대해선 전반적으로 이미 숙지된 상태여야 하며 절대로 틀리는 일이 있어서는 안 되는 부분이기도 하다. 고득점을 목표로 시험에 대비하여 공부하는 자라면 다른 사람들의 기억 속에서 자신의 존재가 잊히는 것보다 내가 학습을 통해 응당 기억해야 할, 혹은 기억해야 하는 내용이 잊히는 것을 더욱 두려워하고 경계해야 할 정도가 되어야 한다. 더군다나 그 내용이 문제로 출제가 되었을 때 놓지지 않아야 할 출제 비중이 높은 내용이라면 더욱 더 그러하다.

★★ 접속사 / 부사절 접속사

새로운 사업 계획안은 비용 효율이 좋지 않고 친환경적이지 않기 때문에, 이를 승인하는데 문제가 발생할 수 밖에 없다.

어휘 cost effective 가성비가 좋은, 비용 효율이 좋은 environmentally friendly 친환경적인 approve ~을 승인하다, ~을 결재하다 since ~이기 때문에, ~이후에 while ~하는 동안에, ~인 반면에 although 비록 ~지만 unless ~이지 않다면

124

The plant manager could not find replacement parts for some of the broken conveyor belts because the component suppliers have ------- in stock.

(A) none
(B) every
(C) them
(D) little

문제 해설

빈칸에 적합한 어휘를 묻는 문제로 빈칸이 have란 동사와 in stock이란 전치사구 사이에 위치하고 있으므로 빈칸에는 have란 동사의 목적어 역할을 할 수 있는 명사 또는 대명사가 필요하다는 점을 알 수 있다. 무엇보다 every는 부정 형용사로 명사나 대명사를 대동하여 쓰이는 것은 가능하나 부정대명사로서 단독적으로 쓰이는 것은 불가하므로 오답이다. 목적격 인칭대명사 them 역시 동사 have의 목적어로 쓰이는 것이 가능하나 이를 쓰는 경우 부품을 제공하는 모든 업체들이 교체용 부품을 재고에 보유하고 있기 때문에, 공장장은 고장 난 컨베이어 벨트에 대한 교체용 부품을 수령하지 못했다는 모순되는 내용을 구성하게 되므로 이 또한 오답이다. 아울러 little은 부정대명사로 사용할 수 있으나 수가 아닌 극소량을 언급하며 재고에 보유하고 있는 것은 바로 the replacement parts, 즉 교체용 부품들이란 가산 복수명사 형태임을 고려할 때 오답이 되겠다. 따라서 모든 부품 제공업체들이 재고에 교체용 부품들을 전혀 보유하고 있지 않은 상태여야 공장장이 고장 난 컨베이어 벨트에 대한 교체용 부품을 물색하지 못하고 있다는 타당한 문맥이 형성될 수 있으므로 빈칸에는 부정대명사로 전혀 존재하지 않음을 뜻하는 none이 와야 한다.

★★★ 대명사 / 부정 대명사

부품을 제공하는 모든 업체들의 재고가 동이 난 상태인지라 공장장은 고장 난 컨베이어 벨트에 대한 교체용 부품을 찾지 못하고 있다.

어휘 plant manager 공장장 replacement parts 교체용 부품 broken 고장이 난, 부서진 components supplier 부품 제공 업체 in stock 재고가 있는

125

★★ 어휘 / 형용사

Sarah Scofield 씨는 작년에 초기 투자금 2만 5천 달러를 가지고 회사를 창업하였다.

어휘 launch ~을 시작하다, ~을 출시하다 investment 투자 attentive 주의 깊은, 세심한, 친절한 initial 최초의 instant 즉각적인 appealing 호소하는, 마음을 이끄는, 매력적인

Ms. Sarah Scofield launched her company with an ------- investment of twenty-five thousand dollars last year.

(A) attentive
(B) initial
(C) instant
(D) appealing

문제 해설

빈칸에 적절한 형용사 어휘를 묻는 문제이다. 빈칸에 앞서 Sarah Scofield 씨가 창업을 했다는 내용이 등장하고 있으며 빈칸 이후에는 투자금 2만 5천 달러를 언급하고 있다. 그러므로 투자금 2만 5천 달러는 회사를 창업하기 위한 초기 투자금이란 점을 파악할 수 있으므로 빈칸에는 '최초의, 초기의'란 뜻을 지닌 형용사 어휘인 initial이 적합하다.

토익 분석

동사 initiate는 무엇인가를 새롭게 혹은 처음으로 시작/시행/실시한다는 의미를 지니고 있으며 토익에서는 initiate a new program (새로운 프로그램을 시작하다) / initiate a reform (개혁을 실시하다) / initiate a project (프로젝트를 시행하다)와 같은 표현이 어휘 문제로 출제된 바 있다. 아울러 형용사인 initial은 최초 혹은 초기를 뜻하는 형용사로 토익에서 initial investment (초기 투자) / initial cost (초기 비용) / initial negotiations (초기 협상) / initial stage (초기 단계)가 어휘 문제로 등장하기도 했다. 물론 initial은 복수명사 형태인 initials로 쓰여 이름의 첫 글자를 의미할 수도 있다. 마지막으로 또 다른 명사 initiative는 이전 토익에선 주도권(take initiative)이나 진취적인 정신/독창성의(demonstrate initiative)의 뜻으로 쓰이는 경우를 묻기도 했지만 최근 토익에서는 주로 program/plan이란 뜻으로 쓰이는 경우만 묻는 경향이 있음을 알아두도록 한다.

126

★★★ 어휘 / 동사

그 외국 회사는 지난 주에 새로운 사업을 하기 위해 한국의 법과 규정을 준수할 의사가 있음을 밝혔다

어휘 intention 의도, 의사 comply with ~을 따르다, ~을 준수하다, ~을 지키다 regulations 규정 accomplish ~을 이루다, ~을 성취하다 authorize ~을 승인하다, ~을 허가하다

The foreign company expressed its intention last week to ------- with the laws and regulations of South Korea to do new business.

(A) accomplish
(B) comply
(C) authorize
(D) designate

문제 해설

빈칸에 적합한 동사 어휘를 묻는 문제로 빈칸이 한국의 법과 규정을 뜻하는 with the laws and regulations of South Korea란 전치사구와 새로운 사업을 행하기 위해서라는 뜻의 부사구 to do new business 앞에 위치하고 있다. 그러므로 빈칸에는 한국에서 새로운 사업을 행하기 위해서 한국의 법과 규정에 어떻게 대처할 것인지를 언급할 수 있는 동사 어휘가 와야 함을 알 수 있다. 따라서 외국에서 새로운 사업을 하려면 그 나라의 법과 규정을 준수하며 합법적인 사업 활동을 해야 하는 것이 논리적으로 타당하므로 빈칸에는 '준수하다, 부합하다, 따르다'란 뜻을 지닌 동사 어휘인 comply가 와야 한다.

토익 분석

앞서 언급한 comply with과 함께 동일한 의미이지만 comply의 품사가 각각 형용사와 명사로 변형이 이뤄진 상태의 표현인 be compliant with / be in compliance with도 꼭 숙지하도록 한다.

127

Most of the meat processing companies will need more farmlands to raise more cows, ------- the beef consumption increases.

(A) unless
(B) provided that
(C) although
(D) now that

★★★ 접속사 / 부사절 접속사

만약 소고기 소비량이 증가한다면, 대부분의 육류 가공 회사들은 소를 키우기 위한 더 많은 경지가 필요할 것이다.

어휘 meat processing 육가공 farmland 경지, 농지 beef consumption 소고기 소비 provided that 만약 ~라면 now that ~이기 때문에

문제 해설

빈칸이 두 절 사이에 위치하고 있으므로 빈칸에는 적절한 접속사가 위치해야 한다. 빈칸에 앞서 육류 가공 회사들은 소를 키우기 위한 더 많은 경지가 필요할 것이란 내용이 등장하고 있고, 빈칸 뒤에는 소고기 소비량이 증가한다는 내용이 제시되고 있다. 그렇다면 빈칸에는 소고기 소비량이 증가하기 때문이라는 의미를 형성할 수 있는 이유 부사절 접속사나 또는 소고기 소비량이 증가한다는 전제 조건의 뜻을 나타낼 수 있는 조건 부사절 접속사가 와야 함을 알 수 있다. 따라서 빈칸에는 조건 부사절 접속사인 provided that이 적합하다.

토익 분석

조건 부사절 접속사 if를 대체할 수 있는 provided that / providing that / assuming that / supposing that / on the condition that, 이유 부사절 접속사 because, since, as 등을 대체할 수 있는 now that, 그리고 양보 부사절 접속사 although 등을 대체할 수 있는 granted that / granting that / admitting that은 필히 숙지하고 있어야 한다.

128

According to the recent market analyst report, our company's G7 ------- BK's X10 for the last three years.

(A) were outsold
(B) will outsell
(C) has been outselling
(D) would have been outsold

★★ 어형 / 동사

최근 시장 분석 보고서에 따르면, 최근 3년 간 우리 회사의 G7 제품은 BK 사의 X10 제품보다 더 많이 판매되었다고 한다.

어휘 recent 최근의 market analysis report 시장 분석 보고서 outsell ~보다 많이 판매하다, ~보다 더 좋은 값으로 판매하다

문제 해설

빈칸에 적합한 동사 어형을 묻는 문제이다. 주어인 our company's G7이 단수 주어이므로 단수 동사 어형이어야 하며 빈칸 뒤에 BK's X10이란 목적어가 등장하고 있으므로 수동태가 아닌 능동태 구조이어야 한다. 아울러 지난 3년 간이란 for the last three years란 부사구를 고려할 때 시제는 현재 완료 시제가 적절하다. 따라서 이 모든 부분을 고려할 때 빈칸에는 have been outselling이와야 한다.

129

★★★ 어휘 / 형용사

화려한 예술성은 최근 아시아 문화가 전 세계에서 독특한 문화로 여겨지는 주요한 이유 중 하나이다.

어휘 brilliant 훌륭한, 화려한, 찬란한 be identified as ~로 확인이 되다, ~로 여겨지다 unique 독특한 chief 우두머리, 상관, 주요한 straight 직선의, 연속한, 똑바른, 곧장, 솔직한 reliable 믿을만한, 신뢰할만한 adept 숙련된, 능숙한, 숙달자

Brilliant artistry is one of the ------- reasons why various Asian cultures have recently been identified as unique.

(A) chief
(B) straight
(C) reliable
(D) adept

문제 해설

빈칸에 알맞은 형용사 어휘를 묻는 문제이다. 빈칸에 앞서 화려한 예술성을 뜻하는 Brilliant artistry가, 빈칸 이후에는 최근 아시아 문화가 전 세계에서 독특한 문화로 여겨지는 주요한 이유란 내용인 reasons why various Asian cultures have recently been identified as unique 앞에 위치하고 있다. 그러므로 이를 통해 현재 아시아 문화가 전 세계에서 독특한 문화로 여겨지게 된 근간에는 바로 화려한 예술성이라는 대표적인 이유가 있음을 알 수 있다. 따라서 빈칸에는 '주요한'이란 뜻을 지닌 형용사 chief가 와야 한다.

130

★★★ 접속사 / 명사절 접속사

최근에 주 정부는 최대 기간시설 건설 공사 중 하나인 Spokane과 Seattle간 놓이는 새로운 고속도로 건설 공사를 어느 회사가 맡을 것인지 결정하였다.

어휘 state government 주 정부 infrastructure 시설, 기반, 사회 간접자본

The state government recently decided ------- companies will build a new highway between Spokane and Seattle, one of the largest infrastructure projects in the area.

(A) which
(B) each
(C) where
(D) those

문제 해설

빈칸을 사이에 두고 제시된 두 개의 절을 이어줄 수 있는 적절한 접속사를 묻는 문제이다. 빈칸 앞에는 the government이란 주어와 동사인 decided가 등장하고 있으므로 빈칸 이후의 절은 동사 decided의 목적어 역할을 하는 명사절이 제시되고 있음을 알 수 있다. 아울러 해당 명사절은 companies란 주어와 will build란 동사 그리고 a new highway란 목적어를 모두 지니고 있는 완전한 구조의 절이므로 우선적으로 완전한 구조의 절과 함께 쓰이는 where이란 접속사를 서둘러 정답으로 여길 소지가 있다. 그러나 where이 자리하면 문맥이 부자연스럽기 때문에 이는 오답으로 소거해야 한다. 대부분 정기토익에선 which란 접속사가 주어나 목적어가 빠진 불완전한 구조의 절과 함께 쓰이는 관계 대명사의 용례에 대해서만 집중적으로 묻는 경향이 있어서 다들 이 부분에만 집중하여 학습하곤 한다. 하지만 which/what/whose는 바로 뒤에 명사를 취하는 관계 형용사로 완전한 구조의 절과 함께 쓰이는 용례가 있다는 점도 간과하지 않도록 주의해야 한다. 따라서 빈칸에는 which가 와서 정부가 최대 기간시설 건설 공사 중 하나인 Spokane과 Seattle을 잇는 새로운 고속도로 건설 공사를 어느 회사가 맡을 것인지 결정하였다라는 적절한 문맥을 구성할 수 있도록 해야 한다.

토익 분석

이미 신토익에서 which가 관계 형용사로 쓰이는 쓰임새에 관한 문제가 출제되기도 한 만큼 이에 대해 숙지하여 향후에 다시 출제될 경우에 대비해야 할 필요가 있다.

Questions 131-134 refer to the following e-mail.

To: Emily Brunt <ebrunt@brightwing.co.nz>
From: Alicia Morgan <amorgan@bluedot.org.nz>
Date: June 12
Subject: About Your Interview

Dear Ms. Blunt,

We have received your application for the job ------- **131.** as a caterer at Blue Dot Catering Services. We have been searching for job candidates who have an immense amount of experience in the catering industry. After reviewing your resume and references, we have found you have a long and ------- **132.** career in the business. ------- **133.**.

We would like to invite you in for a job interview. We are scheduling a ------- **134.** interview time for June 25 at 10 A.M. This schedule may be altered according to circumstances. If you want to change the time or date the time or date, please feel free to call me at 924-7332.

Thank you. Have a good day.

Alicia Morgan
Head of Personnel
Blue Dot Catering Services

수신: Emily Brunt 〈ebrunt@brightwing.co.nz〉
발신: Alicia Morgan 〈amorgan@bluedot.org.nz〉
일자: 6월 12일
제목: 귀하의 면접에 관해

Blunt 씨께,

Blue Dot 출장 요리 서비스에서 출장 요리사로 근무하고자 하는 귀하의 지원서를 접수했습니다. 저희는 출장요리 업계에서 아주 많은 경험을 지닌 지원자를 찾고 있습니다. 귀하의 이력서와 추천서를 검토한 결과 귀하가 장기간의 경력 및 탁월함에 있어 출중하다고 파악했습니다. 귀하는 우리 회사의 가장 적합한 후보자 중 하나입니다.

귀하와 면접을 보고 싶습니다. 6월 25일 오전 10시로 귀하와의 잠정 인터뷰를 계획하고 있습니다. 이 일정은 경우에 따라 변경 될 수 있습니다. 면접 시간 혹은 날짜를 변경하시려면 924-7332로 연락을 주십시오.

감사합니다. 좋은 하루 되십시오.

Alicia Morgan
인사부장
Blue Dot 출장요리서비스

어휘 application 신청, 지원, 신청(지원)서 caterer 출장 요리사 search for ~을 찾다, ~을 물색하다 job candidate 취업 지원자 an immense amount of ~의 많은 양 catering industry 출상 요리업계 resume 이력서, ~을 재개하다 reference 참고, 참조, 추천서 respected 존중 받는, 훌륭한, 높이 평가되는 schedule 일정, 일정을 정하다 alter ~을 바꾸다, ~을 변경하다 according to ~에 따르면 circumstance 환경 feel free to Vr 주저하지 말고 ~을 하다

131

(A) training   (B) responsibility
(C) opening   (D) description

문제 해설

빈칸에 적합한 명사 어휘를 묻는 문제이다. 빈칸 앞에는 We have received your application for the job, 즉 취업 지원서를 접수했다는 내용이, 빈칸 이후에는 as a caterer at Blue Dot Catering Services라며 Blue Dot 출장 요리 서비스에서 출장 요리사로 근무하고자 한다는 내용이 언급되고 있다. 따라서 해당 지원서는 바로 Blue Dot 출장 요리 서비스에서 출장 요리사로 취업하기 위한 용도의 지원서임을 알 수 있으므로 빈칸에는 일자리를 뜻하는 복합명사를 구성할 수 있도록 opening이 위치해야 한다.

★ **어휘 / 복합 명사**

토익 분석

명사 job이 포함된 복합명사는 토익에서 꾸준하게 출제되어 온 복합명사라 할 수 있다. 명사 job과 관련된 대표적인 복합명사로는 job training (실무교육), job interview (취업 면접), job offer (구인, 일자리 제공), job openings (구인, 채용), job application (취업 지원, 취업 지원서), job search (구직 활동), job description (직무 설명), job experience (직장 경력), job fair (취업 박람회), job posting (구인 공고), job responsibility (책무)가 있다.

132

(A) respect   **(B) respected**
(C) respecting   (D) respects

문제 해설

빈칸에는 respected란 과거분사와 respecting이란 현재분사 중 한 가지를 정답으로 선택해야 한다. 아울러 뒤이어 We would like to invite you in for a job interview, 즉 귀하와 면접을 하고 싶다는 내용이 등장하고 있음을 고려할 때 빈칸에는 상대의 직장 경력이 오래 되었을 뿐만 아니라 대단하게 느껴져서 존중을 받을 만한 직장 경력이라는 내용을 구성하는 것이 논리적으로 적합하다. 따라서 빈칸에는 '존중 받는, 존경 받는'이란 뜻을 지닌 과거분사 respected가 와야 한다.

★★ **어형 / 과거분사**

토익 분석

토익에선 명사 앞에 위치하는 일반적인 동사의 분사 어형으로는 주로 과거분사 어형을 묻고 명사 뒤에 위치하는 분사 어형으로는 대개 현재분사 어형을 묻는 경향이 있다.

133

★★ 빈칸 문장 추론

(A) 이제 귀하는 면접을 잘 보는 방법에 대해 궁금해할 것입니다.
(B) 귀하는 당사에 가장 적격인 지원자 중 한 분입니다.
(C) 이 요리 경연대회는 유명한 국제 요리 대회입니다.
(D) 우리 회사는 귀하의 새로운 요리법과 요리 기술을 숙지하는 것에 관심이 있습니다.

(A) Now you're wondering how to make the interview go really well.
(B) You are one of the most qualified candidates for our company.
(C) This cooking contest is a popular international culinary competition.
(D) Our company is interested in learning about your new recipes and cooking techniques.

문제 해설

빈칸에 적합한 내용을 지닌 문장을 묻는 문제이다. 빈칸에 이어 We would like to invite you in for a job interview, 즉 귀하와 면접을 하고 있다는 내용이 등장하고 있음을 고려하면 빈칸에는 상대가 회사에서 찾고 있는 인재라는 내용을 지닌 You are one of the most qualified candidates for our company가 와야 함이 옳다.

★★★ 어휘 / 형용사

(A) joint
(B) exclusive
(C) tentative
(D) preliminary

문제 해설

빈칸에 적합한 형용사 어휘를 묻는 문제로 빈칸을 중심으로 6월 25일 오전 10시로 면접 일정을 잡겠다는 내용이 언급되고 있다. 또한 빈칸 이후에는 This schedule may be altered according to circumstances라며 해당 일정은 상황에 따라 변경이 가능할 수도 있음을 밝히고 있다. 따라서 이를 통해 6월 25일 오전 10시로 정해진 면접 일정은 확실하게 정해진 것이 아닌 임시 일정임을 알 수 있으므로 빈칸에는 '임시적인'이란 뜻을 지닌 tentative가 와야 한다.

Questions 135-138 refer to the following letter.

May 21

Ms. Sarah Fox
8248 Central Avenue
Houston, TX 77025

Dear Ms. Fox,

We are very pleased to inform you that the Waco Recycling Program will commence in your area on April 5. Residents who would like to participate in the ------- **135.** will be issued a green wheeled -container. To ------- **136.** a container, please call 1-800-575-4331.

Curbside recycling will take place twice a month, rather than once a week, as initially proposed. -------, **137.** trips to neighborhoods will be less frequent, which will lower fuel costs and emissions.

A list of recyclable materials can be found in the enclosed brochure. For more information on schedules of citywide recycling programs, visit www. wacorecycling.org. -------. **138.**

Sincerely yours,

Thomas Lee
Manager of Waco Recycling Program

5월 21일

Ms. Sarah Fox
8248 Central Avenue
Houston, TX 77025

Fox 님께,

저희는 Waco 재활용프로그램이 4 월 5일에 귀하가 거주하는 지역에서 시작될 것임을 알려드리게 되어 매우 기쁘게 생각합니다. 이 프로그램에 참여하시고자 하는 주민 분들은 바퀴가 달린 녹색 용기를 지급받을 것입니다. 이 용기를 요청하려면 1-800-575-4331로 연락을 주십시오.

도로가에 내놓은 물품의 재활용은 본래 제안대로 일주일에 한 번이 아니라 한 달에 두 번 이뤄질 것입니다. 결과적으로 인근 지역으로의 이동 횟수가 줄어들어 연료비와 배기가스 배출량이 감소하게 될 것입니다.

동봉된 소책자에서 재활용 물품의 목록을 찾을 수 있습니다. 도시 전역의 재활용 프로그램들의 일정에 관련된 더 많은 정보를 원하시면, 저희 홈페이지인 www.wacorecycling.org를 방문해 주십시오. 여러분께서 이 중요한 프로그램에 참여하시길 바랍니다.

감사합니다
Thomas Lee
Waco 재활용 프로그램 매니저

어휘 be pleased to Vr ~하게 되어 기쁘다 inform ~에게 알리다, ~에게 전달하다 commence ~이 시작하다 resident 거주민 participate in ~에 참석하다 issue 문제, 안건, 쟁점, ~을 발급하다, ~을 발행하다 wheeled 바퀴가 달린 container 용기 curbside 도로가 take place ~이 벌어지다, ~이 발생하다 rather than ~라기보다는 ~인 initially 초기에, 최초에 propose ~을 제안하다 trip 여행 neighborhood 이웃 frequent 종종, 자주 lower ~을 낮추다 fuel cost 연료비 emission 배출, 배기, 배기가스 recyclable 재활용이 가능한 materials 자료, 재료 enclosed 동봉된 brochure 소책자 citywide 도시전역에 걸쳐

135

(A) initiative
(B) hearing
(C) competition
(D) exhibition

★★★ 어휘 / 명사

토익 분석

토익에선 명사 initiative 뿐만 아니라 형용사로 최초를 뜻하는 initial과 동사로 '시행/개시하다'란 뜻을 지닌 initiate 또한 출제되고 있으므로 이들을 모두 숙지하도록 한다.

문제 해설

빈칸에 적합한 명사 어휘를 묻는 문제이다. 빈칸에 앞서 We are very pleased to inform you that the Waco Recycling Program will commence in your area on April 5라며 Waco 재활용프로그램이 4 월 5 일에 귀하가 거주하는 지역에서 시작될 것임을 알려드리게 되어 매우 기쁘게 생각한다는 내용이 언급되고 있으며 빈칸이 포함된 부분은 참석하길 원하는 주민들을 뜻하는 Residents who would like to participate in the~가 등장하고 있으므로 빈칸에는 거주민들이 참여하는 대상, 즉 4월 5일에 시행되는 Waco 재활용 프로그램을 뜻하는 the Waco Recycling Program을 지칭하는 명사가 와야 함을 알 수 있다. 따라서 빈칸에는 '프로그램/계획'을 뜻하는 명사인 initiative가 적절하다.

★★ 어휘 / 동사

(A) prepare
(B) return
(C) repair
(D) request

문제 해설

빈칸에 적합한 동사 어휘를 묻는 문제이다. 빈칸에 앞서 Residents who would like to participate in the initiative will be issued a green-wheeled container라며 4월 5일에 시행되는 Waco 재활용 프로그램에 참여하길 원하는 주민들은 바퀴가 달린 초록색의 용기를 지급받게 될 것임을 언급하고 있으며, 빈칸 이후에는 해당 용기를 뜻하는 a container과 함께 please call 1-800-575-4331라며 연락을 해달라는 내용이 제시되고 있다. 그러므로 빈칸에는 전화를 걸어야 하는 목적, 즉 해당 용기를 요청하고자 한다는 내용을 구성할 수 있는 동사가 필요하므로 빈칸에는 '요청하다'란 뜻을 지닌 동사 request가 위치해야 함이 옳다.

137

★★ 어휘 / 접속부사

토익 분석

인과 관계를 표현하는 대표적인 접속부사로는 so, thus, therefore, hence, as a result 등이 있으며 이들은 모두 접속부사 문제로 자주 등장하므로 이들 모두 꼭 숙지하도록 한다.

(A) After all
(B) Furthermore
(C) As a result
(D) In fact

문제 해설

빈칸에 적합한 표현을 묻는 문제이다. 빈칸에 앞서 Curbside recycling will take place twice a month, rather than once a week, as initially proposed라며 도로가에 내놓은 물품의 재활용은 본래 제안대로 일주일에 한 번이 아니라 한 달에 두 번 이뤄질 것임을 안내하고 있으며 빈칸 이후에는 trips into neighborhoods will be less frequent, which will lower fuel costs and emissions라며 이로 인해 인근 지역으로의 이동 횟수가 줄게되어 연료비와 배기가스 배출량이 감소되는 결과를 얻게 될 것이란 점을 밝히고 있다. 따라서 빈칸에는 인과 관계를 뜻하는 As a result가 와야 함이 옳다.

138

★★ 빈칸 문장 추론

(A) We hope that you will take part in this important program.
(B) Your container will arrive at your door within seven days.
(C) Please make sure not to put broken glass into the container.
(D) The city has invested an enormous sum in this project.

문제 해설

빈칸에 적합한 내용을 지닌 문장을 묻는 문제이다. 빈칸에 앞서 Waco 재활용 프로그램의 시행에 대해 구체적으로 언급해왔으며 빈칸 직전에는 For more information on schedules of citywide recycling programs, visit www.wacorecycling.org라며 도시 전역의 재활용 프로그램들의 일정에 관련된 더 많은 정보를 원하면, www.wacorecycling.org를 방문해줄 것을 요청하고 있다. 그러므로 재활용 프로그램 시행에 관한 자세한 정보를 제공하는 지문을 마무리하는 내용으로 빈칸에 적합한 것은 주민들이 이 중요한 프로그램에 참여하시길 바란다는 의미를 지닌 We hope that you will take part in this important program가 되겠다.

Questions 139-142 refer to the following memo.

MEMORANDUM

From: Anna Hopewell, Personnel Director
To: All employees
Date: June 8
Subject: The Resignation of Ms. Lisa Evans

Ms. Lisa Evans announced yesterday that she will ------- **139.** as President of Blue Jet Airlines next Monday to start her own aviation business. She was very instrumental in shaping our growth and direction as the nation's leading low-cost airliner. She made a considerable contribution to the expansion of our company. ------- **140.** .

We have undertaken formal organizational changes within the company. Ms. Isabella Choi, our vice president, will take over the duties of Ms. Evans. We expect Ms. Choi to bring her ------- **141.** experience in airline planning, finance, marketing, and leadership to this new position. We are confident that our new president ------- **142.** our company to new levels of excellence with your support.

Thank you for all your efforts to keep us strong.

회람

발신: **Anna Hopewell**, 인사 담당 이사
수신: 전 직원
일자: 6월 8일
제목: **Lisa Evans** 씨의 사임

Lisa Evans 씨는 어제 **Blue Jet** 항공사의 사장직을 사임하고 다음 주 월요일에 자신의 항공사업을 시작한다고 발표했습니다. 대표님은 우리 회사를 성장시키고 국내 저가 항공 분야의 선두 기업인 우리 회사가 나아갈 방향을 결정함에 있어 큰 도움을 주셨습니다. 또한 우리 회사의 사업확장에 지대한 공헌을 하였습니다. 저희는 수 년 간에 걸친 대표님의 노고와 지도력에 감사를 전하고 싶습니다.

저희는 내부적으로 공식적인 인사 개편을 시도했습니다. **Isabella Choi** 부사장님께서 대표님의 업무를 대신할 것입니다. 저희는 신임 대표님께서 항공기획, 재무, 마케팅 및 리더쉽 분야에서 쌓아온 풍부한 경험으로 새로운 직무 수행에 임해주시기를 기대합니다.

새로운 대표님께서 여러분의 성원을 바탕으로 당사를 좀 더 새롭고 우수한 회사가 될 수 있도록 이끌어 주실 것이라 확신합니다.

우리가 항상 업계 최고 회사가 될 수 있도록 노력해주신 여러분께 감사드립니다.

어휘 step down as ~라는 직책에서 사임하다 aviation 항공 be instrumental in ~에 도움이 되다 shape 형상, 모양, ~을 구체화하다, ~을 실현하다, ~을 형성하다 leading 선도하는 low-cost airline 저가항공사 major 주요한, 큰 considerable 꽤, 상당한 contribution 기여, 기고, 기부 expansion 확장, 확대 undertake ~을 착수하다, ~을 시작하다, ~을 떠맡다 formal 공식적인, 형식적인, 정식의 organizational 조직적인, 구조적인, 조직화에 관한 within the company 사내에서 take over ~을 맡다 duty 세금, 업무, 근무 confidential 확신이 있는, 자신이 있는 excellence 우수함 support 지원, 성원, 후원, ~을지지하다, ~을 후원하다

139

(A) serve
(B) assume
(C) lay off
(D) step down

★★★ 어휘 / 동사

문제 해설

빈칸에 적합한 동사 어휘를 묻는 문제이다. 빈칸 뒤 to start her own aviation business라며 자신만의 항공사업, 즉 창업을 한다는 내용이 등장하고 있으므로 이를 통해 빈칸에는 Blue Jet 항공사의 사장직에서 물러난다는 내용을 구성할 수 있는 동사 어휘가 와야 한다. 따라서 빈칸에는 '사임하다'란 뜻을 지닌 step down이 적절하다.

140

(A) 그녀는 미래에 당사에 열정과 프로페셔널리즘을 가져올 것입니다.
(B) 이전 대표님은 매출 증진을 위해 혁신적인 아이디어와 방법을 활용하셨습니다.
(C) 당사는 여러분의 헌신 덕분으로 선두업체 중 하나가 되었습니다.
(D) 저희는 수년 간에 걸친 대표님의 노고와 지도력에 감사를 전하고 싶습니다.

(A) She will bring passion and professionalism to our airline company in the future.
(B) The former president has used innovative ideas and methods to increase our sales.
(C) Our company is recognized as one of the leading companies thanks to your dedications.
(D) We would like to express our appreciation for her hard work and leadership over the years.

문제 해설

빈칸에 적합한 내용의 문장을 묻는 문제이다. 빈칸에 앞서 Ms. Lisa Evans announced yesterday that she will step down as President of Blue Jet Airlines next Monday to start her own aviation business라며 Lisa Evans 씨가 어제부로 Blue Jet 항공사의 사장직을 사임하고 다음 주 월요일부터 자신의 항공사업을 시작할 것임을 발표했다는 내용과 함께 She made a considerable contribution to the expansion of our company라며 Evans씨가 회사 발전에 지대한 공헌을 했다는 그녀의 업적이 소개되고 있다. 그러므로 이를 통해 정리하자면, Evans 씨는 회사의 발전에 큰 기여를 한 사장이었고 이젠 창업을 위해 사임하게 된 상황임을 파악할 수 있다. 따라서 빈칸에는 곧 헤어지게 될 Evans 씨가 그간 회사를 경영하고, 회사를 발전시킨 공로에 대한 감사의 말인 We would like to express our appreciation for her hard work and leadership over the years가 위치하는 것이 논리적으로 적절하다.

141

토익 분석

동사 extend는 '시간/길이를 연장하다/범위를 넓히다'란 뜻을 지니고 있으며 동사 extend에선 두 가지 형용사가 파생된다. 문제에서 접한 '광범위한/종합적인'이란 뜻을 지닌 extensive란 형용사와 더불어 '(시간/길이가) 연장된/쭉 뻗은'이란 의미를 가지고 있는 extended란 과거분사 형태의 형용사가 있다. 간단히 정리하자면 범위가 넓고 종합적인 상태를 의미하는 형용사로는 extensive가 적절하며 시간/길이가 연장된 상태를 표현해야 할 때는 extended가 적합하다. 이를테면 research는 extensive가, contract/deadline 같은 경우에는 extended가 알맞다고 할 수 있다. 무엇보다 토익에선 이 두 가지 형용사가 모두 출제되므로 이들을 모두 알아두어야 한다. 그렇지 않은 경우 정기토익을 접하는 과정에서 분명 후회할 일이 발생할 수 있다.

(A) to extend
(B) extend
(C) extended
(D) extensive

문제 해설

빈칸에 적합한 어형을 묻는 문제로, 빈칸이 '경험'을 뜻하는 명사 experience 앞에 위치하고 있으므로 빈칸에는 형용사 어형이 와야 함을 알 수 있다. 그러나 extended와 extensive가 모두 형용사이므로 문맥에 적합한지 여부를 통해 정답을 택일해야 한다. 그러므로 experience에 이어 airline planning, finance, marketing, 즉 항공기획, 재무, 마케팅과 같이 다양한 분야가 제시되고 있으므로 빈칸에는 '광범위한, 종합적인'이란 뜻을 지닌 extensive가 적절하다.

142

(A) lead
(B) will lead
(C) is led
(D) has led

문제 해설

빈칸에 적합한 동사 어형을 묻는 문제이다. 빈칸 앞 주어가 our new president란 단수주어이며 빈칸에 이어 our company란 목적어가 등장하고 있으므로 동사는 단수동사이자 수동태가 아닌 능동태를 구성할 수 있는 어형이 와야 한다. 아울러 빈칸에 앞서 We have undertaken formal organizational changes within the company. Ms. Isabella Choi, our vice president, will take over the duties of Ms. Evans라며 회사 내에서 공식적인 인사 개편이 있었고 그 결과 현재 회사의 부사장인 Isabella Choi 씨가 Evans씨에 이어 새로운 사장으로 부임하게 되었음을 전달하고 있다. 따라서 새로운 사장인 Isabella Choi 씨가 향후에 회사를 경영하게 될 것이니만큼 동사는 미래시제여야 함을 알 수 있으므로 빈칸에는 능동태/미래시제가 반영된 동사어형인 will lead가 위치해야 한다.

Questions 143-146 refer to the following article.

BK Petrochemical announced Thursday that it ------ **143.** Won International in a deal valued at 120 million dollars.

Mr. Andrew Kim, the spokesperson of BK Petrochemical, said this morning the company purchased Won International to bolster its overseas operations and increase its global ------ **144.** He also said BK Petrochemical aims to double its global sales by the end of next year.

------ **145.** Therefore, many industry experts strongly believe this acquisition will make BK Petrochemical the top leading producer and vendor of petrochemical goods since Won International is expected to offset its weakest point.

BK Petrochemical plans ------ **146.** Won International's current workforce and to hire additional staff over the next two years.

BK Petrochemical 사는 지난 목요일에 Won International 사를 1억 2천만 달러 상당의 거래로 인수했다고 발표했다.

BK Petrochemical 사의 대변인인 Andrew Kim 씨는 오늘 오전 회사가 해외 영업을 강화하고 해외 경쟁력을 높이고자 Won International 사를 인수했다고 발표했다. 또한 BK Petrochemical 사가 내년 말까지 해외 매출을 두 배로 증가시킬 계획임을 언급했다.

Won International 사는 강력한 영업망과 영업력으로 유명하다. 따라서 업계 전문가들은 이번 인수로 인해 BK Petrochemical 사의 가장 큰 약점이 상쇄될 것이기 때문에 BK Petrochemical 사가 석유 화학 제품의 주요 생산업체이자 공급업체가 될 것으로 굳게 믿고 있다.

BK Petrochemical 사는 Won International 사의 현재 인력을 유지하고 향후 2년 동안 추가 인력을 고용할 계획이다.

어휘 petrochemical 화학적인 announce ~을 발표하다 deal 거래 valued 소중한, 가치가 있는 spokesperson 대변인 bolster ~을 강화하다, ~을 강화하다, ~을 받치다 overseas operations 해외 영업 aim to Vr ~을 목적으로 하다 double 두 배의, ~을 두 배로 늘리다, ~을 배가하다 therefore 따라서, 고로, 그러므로 industry expert 산업전문가 strongly 강력하게 acquisition 인수, 획득 leading 선도하는, 주도하는 producer 생산업체, 생산자 vendor 판매자, 공급입체 goods 상품, 제품 offset ~을 상쇄하다 plan to Vr ~할 계획이다 maintain ~을 유지하다, ~을 주장하다 current 현재의 workforce 노동력, 인력 sales network 영업망 A be regarded as B A를 B로 여기다 large corporation 대기업 recruit ~을 채용하다 talent 재능, 재능이 있는 사람 accomplish ~을 이루다, ~을 달성하다 make use of ~을 이용하다 recently 최근에 updated 갱신된, 개량된 production facilities 생산 시설

143

(A) sold
(B) acquired
(C) organized
(D) merged

★★★ 어휘 / 동사

문제 해설

빈칸에 적합한 동사 어휘를 묻는 문제로, 빈칸이 Won International이란 회사 이름 앞에 위치하고 있지만 선택지에 있는 동사 어휘들은 모두 회사와 함께 쓰이는 것이 가능하므로 사실상 단순히 이들의 의미를 파악하는 정도만 가지고선 문제가 풀리지 않는다. 그러므로 빈칸 이후 Mr. Andrew Kim, the spokesperson of the BK Petrochemical, said this morning the company purchased Won International이라며 BK Petrochemical 사가 Won International 사를 매입했음을 직접적으로 밝히는 부분을 통해 빈칸에는 회사를 인수했다는 내용을 구성할 수 있는 동사 어휘가 적절함을 알 수 있다. 따라서 빈칸에는 '인수하다'란 뜻을 지닌 acquired가 와야 한다.

144

★★★ 어형 & 어휘 / 명사

(A) compete
(B) competition
(C) competitor
(D) competitiveness

문제 해설

빈칸에 적합한 어형/어휘를 묻는 문제이다. 빈칸이 increase 뒤에 위치하고 있으며 빈칸 앞에는 global이란 형용사가 등장하고 있으므로 빈칸에는 increase의 목적어이자 형용사 global의 수식을 받는 명사가 필요하다. 그러나 동사 compete를 제외한 competition/competitor/competitiveness 가 모두 명사 어휘이기 때문에 단순히 빈칸에 명사 어형이 와야한다는 점만 파악한들 문제가 풀리지 않는다. 그러므로 앞선 to bolster its overseas operations, 즉 해외 영업을 강화시킨다는 문맥과 궤를 함께 하려면 전세계적인 경쟁력을 증가시킨다는 내용이 구성되어야 하므로 빈칸에는 그 어느 명사 어휘보다도 '경쟁력'을 뜻하는 명사 competitiveness가 적합하다.

145

★★★ 빈칸 문장 추론

(A) Won International 사는 강력한 영업망과 영업력으로 유명하다.
(B) 이는 북미지역에서 안정적인 운영이 이뤄지고 있는 최고 회사들 중 하나로 여겨지고 있다.
(C) BK Petrochemical 사의 이사회는 내년에 뛰어난 외국 인들을 채용하기로 결정을 내렸다.
(D) 우리는 BK Petrochemical 사의 최근 개량된 생산시설 들을 사용하여 이 목적을 달성할 것이다.

(A) Won International is known for its strong sales network and sales power.
(B) It is regarded as one of the best managed large corporations in North America.
(C) The board of BK Petrochemical made the big decision to recruit foreign talent next year.
(D) We will accomplish this goal by making use of BK Petrochemical's recently updated production facilities.

문제 해설

빈칸에 적합한 내용의 문장을 묻는 문제로, 빈칸에 앞서 Mr. Andrew Kim, the spokesperson of BK Petrochemical, said this morning the company purchased Won International to bolster its overseas operations and increase its global competitiveness라며 해외 경쟁력을 높이기 위한 해외 영업을 강화하고자 Won International 사를 인수하겠다는 목적이 언급되고 있다. 아울러 빈칸 이후에는 Therefore, many industry experts strongly believe this acquisition will make BK Petrochemical the top leading producer and vendor of petrochemical goods라며 대부분의 업계 전문가들은 BK Petrochemical 사가 석유화학제품의 주요 생산업체이자 공급업체가 될 것으로 굳게 믿고 있다는 내용이 등장하고 있다. 무엇보다 이에 앞서 Therefore이란 인과 관계를 뜻하는 접속사가 위치하고 있음을 고려할 때, 빈칸에는 인수한 Won International 사가 강력한 영업망과 영업력이란 장점을 지닌 회사라는 내용이 담긴 Won International is known for its strong sales network and sales power가 자리하여 BK Petrochemical 사가 석유화학제품의 주요 생산업체이자 공급업체가 될 수 밖에 없는 이유를 제시해야만 한다.

146

★★ 어휘 / 동사

(A) maintain
(B) seek
(C) offer
(D) encourage

문제 해설

빈칸에 적합한 동사 어휘를 묻는 문제로 빈칸이 '계획하다'란 뜻을 지닌 동사 plans to와 Won International 사의 현재 인력을 의미하는 Won International's current workforce 사이에 위치하고 있다. 그러므로 빈칸에는 Won International 사의 현재 인력을 어떻게 처리할 것인지 알려주는 동사 어휘를 선택해야 하며 이를 위해선 빈칸 이후에 to hire additional staff over the next two years라며 향후 2년 간 추가적으로 직원을 채용할 것이라 언급되는 부분에 유의해야 한다. 추가로 직원을 채용하겠다는 것은 현재 인력은 그대로 고용을 유지한다는 내용과 맥을 함께하므로 빈칸에는 '유지하다'란 뜻을 지닌 동사 maintain이 와야 한다.

Questions 147-148 refer to the following flyer.

[147] **Broughton MegaBowl**
is offering a selection of special discounts to our customers:

[148] **Wednesday** – Receive a coupon for a free cold drink for every game played!
Thursday – Buy two games of bowling and get one free!
Friday – Half-priced bowling for groups of over six people!
Saturday – A 50% discount for bowlers on all food and beverages purchased!

Thank you for your custom.

147–148 다음 전단지를 참고하시오.

[147] Broughton MegaBowl는
저희 고객님들에게 특별 할인을 제공하고 있습니다

[148] 수요일 – 한 경기 하실 때마다 무료 음료를 드실 수 있는 쿠폰을 받으세요!
목요일 – 볼링 2게임을 치면 한 경기는 공짜입니다!
금요일 – 일행이 6명 이상인 경우 볼링 경기 요금이 반값입니다!
토요일 – 볼링을 치는 고객님이 구매하는 모든 음식과 음료를 50% 할인해드립니다!

애용해 주셔서 감사합니다

어휘 custom 단골손님, 거래처 a series of 연속의, 일련의 publicize 광고하다 a job vacancy (일자리)공석 bowling alley 볼링장

147

What is the purpose of the flyer?

(A) To promote a series of discounts
(B) To publicize new opening times
(C) To advertise job vacancies at a bowling alley
(D) To inform customers of changes to the drinks menu

문제 해설

전단지 상단에 Broughton MegaBowl is offering a selection of special discounts to our customers라고 언급한 부분을 통해 이는 여러 할인 행사들을 홍보하기 위한 목적의 전단지임을 알 수 있다. 따라서 정답은 (A)이다.

★**전단지의 목적**

이 전단지의 목적은 무엇인가?
(A) 일련의 할인 혜택들을 홍보하기 위해서
(B) 새 개장시간을 알리기 위해서
(C) 볼링장에서 일자리를 광고하기 위해
(D) 고객들에게 바뀐 음료 메뉴를 알리기 위해

토익 분석

전단지(광고지)의 제목만으로도 광고의 주제/목적, 또는 광고하고자 하는 상품이나 서비스가 무엇인지 파악하는 것이 가능하다.

148

What will bowling customers receive on Wednesday?

(A) Discounts on food and drink products
(B) Discounts on the price of bowling games
(C) Free bowling games
(D) Complimentary beverages

문제 해설

수요일에 받을 수 있는 혜택은 전단지에서 수요일이란 시점이 적힌 부분을 통해 파악할 수 있다. Wednesday – Receive a coupon for a free cold drink for every game played!라며 전단지에서는 수요일에 경기마다 무료 음료를 마실 수 있는 쿠폰이 발급되고 있음을 알 수 있으므로 정답은 무료음료를 뜻하는 (D)가 되겠다. 아울러 지문의 free cold drink가 선택지에서는 유사 표현인 complimentary beverages로 바뀌어 제시되고 있음을 간과하지 않도록 유의해야 한다.

★ **세부사항**

수요일에 볼링 고객들은 무엇을 받을 수 있는가?
(A) 음식과 음료의 할인
(B) 볼링 게임 가격 할인
(C) 무료 볼링 게임
(D) 무료 음료

토익 분석

시간/시점/요일을 묻는 문제에선 지문에서 시간/시점/요일이 언급되는 부분만 빠르게 찾아 그 주변에서 단서를 파악한다.

149-150 다음 메시지를 참조하시오.

수신: April Wilson
날짜: 11월 2일(월)
시간: 오후 2시 25분
통화자: Jim Mathers
내용: 맞춤 부엌 수리
전화번호: 434-555-0214

메시지: Mathers 씨가 수요일 오전 9시로 잡혀 있던 미팅을 미뤄달라고 요청했는데, 요청하셨던 타일 샘플이 연기됐기 때문이랍니다. 목요일에 도착한다고 합니다. [149] Mathers 씨는 금요일 오전 10시부터 오후 2시까지 시간이 가능하시다고 하니 유선상으로 일정을 다시 잡으시기 바랍니다. [150] 또한, 당신이 그에게 보내주기로 했던 부엌 치수 도면 초안을 아직 기다리고 있다고 합니다.

메시지 접수자: Debra Morgan

어휘 custom kitchen 맞춤 부엌 renovation 수리공사 request a postponement of ~의 연기를 요청하다 be delayed 늦어지다 be available on Friday 금요일에 시간이 나다 reschedule 일정을 다시 잡다 in addition 게다가 wait on ~을 기다리다 sketch 초안 kitchen dimensions 부엌 치수

Questions 149-150 refer to the following message.

For: April Wilson
Date: Monday, November 2
Time: 2:25 P.M.
Caller: Jim Mathers
Of: Custom Kitchen Renovations
Phone: 434-555-0214

Message: Mr. Mathers has requested a postponement of your meeting with him, which was to be held on Wednesday at 9 A.M., as the tile samples you requested have been delayed. They should arrive by Thursday. [149] He is available on Friday between 10 A.M. and 2 P.M. Please call him to reschedule. [150] In addition, he is still waiting on the sketch of your kitchen dimensions you were to send him.

Taken by: Debra Morgan

149

★ 메시지의 목적

Mathers 씨가 Wilson 씨에게 연락한 이유는 무엇인가?
(A) 그녀가 주문한 타일을 변경하기 위해
(B) 그녀에게 회사 소책자를 요청하기 위해
(C) 회의 시간을 새로 정하기 위해
(D) 구직 인터뷰를 요청하기 위해

토익 분석

메모지의 목적은 메시지를 남기게 된 목적이 언급되는 부분을 통해 파악할 수 있다.

Why did Mr. Mathers call Ms. Wilson?

(A) To make some changes to her tile order
(B) To request a company brochure from her
(C) To arrange a new time for a meeting
(D) To request a job interview

문제 해설

Mathers 씨가 전화를 한 이유를 묻고 있으므로 메시지 초반부에서 메시지를 남기는 목적이 언급되는 부분에 집중하도록 한다. 메시지 초반 Mathers 씨는 He is available on Friday between 10 A.M. and 2 P.M. Please call him to reschedule 이라며 만날 일정의 연기와 그 이유를 설명한 후 만날 수 있는 시간을 제시하고 있으므로 회의 시간을 재조정하기 위해 남긴 메시지라 할 수 있다. 그러므로 정답은 (C)가 되겠다.

150

★ 요청/제안 사항

Mathers 씨가 Wilson 씨에게 요청한 것은 무엇인가?
(A) 사무실 치수에 관한 정보를 전해준다.
(B) 새 책상의 배송을 준비한다.
(C) 자신이 요청한 치수를 제출한다.
(D) 거실 가구들을 구입한다.

토익 분석

요청/요구/제안/추천/권장/조언과 관련된 내용을 묻는 문제는 주로 마지막 문제로 출제되며 단서는 대부분 지문이 끝나는 마지막 2~3문장을 중심으로 제시된다.

What does Mr. Mathers want Ms. Wilson to do?

(A) Give him some information about the size of her office
(B) Arrange for the delivery of a new desk
(C) Submit the measurements he requested
(D) Purchase some living room furniture

문제 해설

Mathers 씨가 Wilson 씨에게 요청한 것에 대해 묻는 요청/제안 유형의 문제이며 요청/제안 문제는 지문 후반부에서 단서가 제시된다. 메시지의 마지막 부분 In addition, he is still waiting on the sketch of your kitchen dimensions you were to send him 이라며 게다가 그에게 보내주기로 했던 부엌 치수 도면 초안을 아직 기다리고 있음을 밝히고 있다. 그러므로 정답은 (C)가 되겠다.

Questions 151-152 refer to the following online chat discussion.

Lynn Jacobs [3:11 P.M.]
151 Hey Cedric, can I ask you how the product design is getting along? Our client wants to check our progress this week.

Cedric Clark [3:13 P.M.]
I'm working on the colors right now. I don't know whether to use bright colors or dark colors.

Lynn Jacobs [3:15 P.M.]
Can you send me a sample of both? I'll let you know how I feel.

Cedric Clark [3:16 P.M.]
Thanks! 152 I just sent them to your e-mail.

Lynn Jacobs [3:18 P.M.]
Are you sure? 152 My inbox is still empty.

Cedric Clark [3:20 P.M.]
Sorry. I accidentally sent it to your old e-mail account. Do you mind checking again?

Lynn Jacobs [3:21 P.M.]
I got it. I like the brightly colored version better.

151–152 다음 온라인 채팅을 참조하시오.

Lynn Jacobs [오후 3:11]
안녕하세요, Cedric 씨, 151 제품 디자인이 어떻게 되어 가고 있으신지 여쭤 봐도 될까요? 고객께서 이번 주말까지 진행 상황을 확인하고 싶어 하십니다.

Cedric Clark [오후 3:13]
지금 색상 작업을 하는 중입니다. 밝은 색을 사용할지 아니면 어두운 색으로 할지 모르겠어요.

Lynn Jacobs [오후 3:15]
두 가지 모두에 대한 샘플을 제게 보내 주시겠어요? 제 생각을 알려 드릴게요.

Cedric Clark [오후 3:16]
감사합니다! 152 방금 이메일로 보내드렸습니다.

Lynn Jacobs [오후 3:18]
확실하신가요? 152 제 수신함이 여전히 비어 있는데요.

Cedric Clark [오후 3:20]
죄송해요. 실수로 예전 이메일 계정으로 보내 드렸어요. 다시 한 번 확인해 보시겠어요?

Lynn Jacobs [오후 3:21]
받았습니다. 저는 밝게 색상 처리된 버전이 더 마음에 들어요.

어휘 how A is getting along A가 어떻게 되어 가고 있는지 progress 진행 상황, 진척 by (기한) …까지 work on ~에 대한 작업을 하다 whether to do A or B A를 할지 B를 할지 bright 밝은 both 둘 모두 inbox 수신함 empty 비어 있는 accidentally 실수로, 잘못하여 account 계정 Do you mind -ing? ~해 보시겠어요? brightly colored 밝게 색이 들어간

151

What type of business does Mr. Clark most likely work for?

(A) An art college
(B) An auto manufacturer
(C) An accounting firm
(D) A design agency

문제 해설

화자의 직장을 유추하는 문제이므로 화자의 직장을 유추할 수 있을만한 관련 어휘나 표현이 등장하는 부분에 초점을 맞춰야 한다. 지문 시작 부분에 Jacobs 씨는 Clark 씨에게 can I ask you how the product design is getting along?이라며 제품 디자인이 어떻게 되어 가고 있는지 묻고 있으며 이를 통해 Clark 씨는 디자인 업체에 근무하고 있다는 것을 추측할 수 있다. 그러므로 (D)가 정답이다.

★★ 유추

Clark 씨는 무슨 종류의 업체에서 근무하고 있을 것 같은가?
(A) 미술 대학
(B) 자동차 제조사
(C) 회계 법인
(D) 디자인 업체

토익 분석

업종/직장을 유추하는 질문에서는 지문에서 업종/직장과 관련된 어휘나 표현을 파악하는 것이 관건이다

152

At. 3:18 P.M. what does Ms. Jacobs most likely mean when she writes, "Are you sure"?

(A) She is questioning Mr. Clark's color choice.
(B) She is asking if Mr. Clark sent the e-mail.
(C) She is wondering if Mr. Clark could start the product design project.
(D) She is surprised by the progress Mr. Clark has made.

문제 해설

주어진 문장인 "Are you sure?"은 확실한지 묻는 내용으로 이는 바로 앞서 Clark 씨가 이메일로 전송했다며 I just sent them to your e-mail라고 말한 것에 대한 답변으로 제시되고 있다. 바로 뒤이어 Jacobs 씨는 자신의 수신함이 여전히 비어 있다며 My inbox is still empty라고 언급하고 있다. 따라서 Jacobs 씨가 "Are you sure?"이라고 말한 내용에는 Clark 씨가 자신에게 이메일을 제대로 보냈는지 재차 확인하고자 하는 의도가 포함된 표현임을 알 수 있다. 그러므로 정답은 (B)가 되겠다.

★★ 화자의 의도

오후 3시 18분에, Jacobs 씨가 "Are you sure?"이라고 쓴 것이 의미하는 바는 무엇일 것 같은가?
(A) Clark 씨가 선택한 색상을 묻고 있다.
(B) Clark 씨가 이메일을 보냈는지 묻고 있다.
(C) Clark 씨가 제품 디자인 프로젝트를 시작할 수 있을지 궁금해 하고 있다.
(C) Clark 씨가 이뤄낸 작업 진도에 놀라고 있다.

토익 분석

특정 표현에 담긴 화자의 의도에 대한 이해하기 위해서는 주어진 특정 표현 전후의 내용 파악이 선행되어야 한다. 난이도가 높아지는 경우에는 전체 지문의 내용을 다 파악해야만 풀 수 있는 경우도 발생한다

내 계정

[153] Prototype Shopping에 오신 것을 환영합니다, Chastain 님! 현재 귀하께서는 그 어느 때보다 더 편리하게 저희 온라인 식료품 쇼핑 계정을 이용하시고 귀하만을 위한 맞춤 쇼핑 서비스를 찾아가실 수 있습니다! 시간을 내셔서 새롭게 개선된 저희 쇼핑 홈페이지를 둘러보시기 바랍니다. 확인해 보실 수 있는 특징들은 다음과 같습니다.

– 더욱 편리해진 홈페이지 내 탐색 기능
– [154 (A)] 더욱 자세한 설명을 곁들인 개선된 제품사진
– [154 (B)] 저희 고객들의 민감한 금융 데이터를 보장해 드리는 강화된 암호화 체계가 그 어느 때보다 안전해졌습니다!
– [154 (D)] 개인 맞춤 쇼핑 서비스를 위해 실시간으로 채팅하실 수 있는 기능을 포함한 향상된 온라인 고객 서비스 도구들

어휘 account 계정 access ~을 이용하다, ~에 접근하다 grocery 식료품 reach ~에 도달하다, 접근하다 customized 개인 맞춤형의(= personalized) than ever 그 어느 때보다 take time to do 시간내어 ~하다 view ~을 보다 improved 개선된, 향상된(= increased) among ~ 중에서, ~ 사이에서 feature 특징, 기능 discover ~을 발견하다, 찾다 navigation (경로 등의) 탐색 detailed 상세한 description 설명, 묘사 heightened 강화된 encryption 암호화 ensure ~을 보장하다 sensitive 민감한 financial 금융의, 재정의 secure 안전한 tool 도구, 공구 including ~을 포함해

153

★ 유추

Chastain씨는 누구일 것 같은가?
(A) 온라인 쇼핑객
(B) 은행 임원
(C) 은행 컨설턴트
(D) 해당 홈페이지의 디자이너

토익 분석

인물 유추는 인물의 정체를 유추할 수 있는 관련 어휘나 표현을 파악하는 것이 관건이다.

154

★★ 진위

새로운 홈페이지에 관해 언급되지 않은 것은 무엇인가?
(A) 이전보다 더 높은 해상도의 사진
(B) 더 뛰어난 정보 보안
(C) 모든 서비스 요금에 대한 목록
(D) 개인맞춤 쇼핑을 위한 채팅서비스

토익 분석

새로운 홈페이지에 관해 언급되지 않은 내용을 묻는 문제이므로 지문에서 새로운 홈페이지의 변경 사항에 대해 정리 열거하고 있는 부분에 집중해야 한다.

Questions 153-154 refer to the following Web site.

My Account

[153] Welcome to Prototype Shopping, Ms. Chastain! Now you can access your online grocery shopping account and reach our customized shopping for you more easily than ever! Please take time to view our newly improved shopping Web site. Among the features you will discover are:

- Easier navigation of the Website
- [154] Better pictures of products with more detailed descriptions
- [154] Heightened encryption that ensures our customers' sensitive financial data is more secure than ever before
- Increased online customer service tools, [154] including the ability to chat live for your personalized shopping.

153

Who most likely is Ms. Chastain?

(A) An online shopper　　(B) A grocery store manager
(C) A bank consultant　　(D) A Web site designer

문제 해설

Chastain씨의 정체를 유추해야 하는 문제이므로 안내문 초반 Chastain 씨의 정체를 추측할 수 있을만한 관련 어휘나 표현을 파악하는 것에 집중해야 한다. 첫 단락에서 Chastain 씨에게 Welcome to Prototype Shopping, Ms. Chastain!이라며 환영 인사를 하는 부분, 이어서 편리하게 온라인 쇼핑계정을 이용하고 자신만의 맞춤형 쇼핑 서비스로 찾아갈 수 있다며 Now you can access your online grocery shopping account and reach our customized shopping라고 언급하는 부분을 통해 Chastain 씨는 인터넷 쇼핑객임을 알 수 있다. 따라서 (A)가 정답이다.

154

What is NOT mentioned as a new feature of the Web site?

(A) Pictures with higher resolution　　(B) Greater information security
(C) A listing of all service fees　　(D) Chatting service for customized shopping

문제 해설

새로운 홈페이지에 관해 언급되지 않은 것을 묻는 문제이므로 홈페이지에 대해 소개하는 부분에서 제시되는 정보를 파악해야 한다. 두 번째 단락에서 새로운 홈페이지에 대한 정보를 다루고 있으며 (A)에서 말하는 이전보다 높은 해상도의 사진은 Better pictures에서, (B)에 언급된 보안 기능은 Heightened encryption that ensures our customers' sensitive financial data ~ 부분에서, 그리고 (D)의 맞춤쇼핑을 위한 채팅은 the ability to chat live for your personalized shopping 부분에서 각각 찾아볼 수 있다. 하지만 서비스 요금 목록을 제시된 바가 없으므로 (C)가 정답이다.

Questions 155-157 refer to the following e-mail.

To: Employees at Daily Best Corporation
From: Michael Moore<mm@dbc.com>
Date: June 15
RE: Save the Date!

You are invited to a dinner honoring Richard Hutchson's 45 years of hard work and dedication. [156] Richard started working for Daily Best Corporation at the age of 16, when he worked as a temporary office boy. As the years passed, Richard slowly worked his way up the chain. By the age of 26, he had both earned his master's in Accounting from California State University and been established as the head accountant in the bookkeeping department. Finally, at age 45, Richard joined our corporate staff as vice president of Financial Affairs, where he spent the remainder of his career. Richard will be retiring at the end of the month and is looking forward to spending his days relaxing with his wife of 38 years, his 4 children, and his 9 grandchildren, all of whom live in the area.

[157] If you would like to speak at Richard's retirement dinner, please e-mail Ms. Bakinsale with your intention by June 20. Each employee is permitted to bring one guest to the event. Please RSVP to Ms. Bakinsale to let her know if you will be attending by June 20.

We hope to see you there.

Sincerely,

Michael Moore
President and CEO
Daily Best Corporation

155-157 다음 이메일을 참조하시오

수신 : Daily Best 사의 전 직원
발신 : Michael Moore ⟨mm@dbc.com⟩
날짜 : 6월 15일
제목 : 그날은 비워두세요!

Richard Hutchson 씨의 45년 간의 노고와 헌신을 기념하는 저녁 만찬에 여러분을 초대합니다. [156] Richard 씨는 16세에 우리 회사의 임시 사환으로 업무를 시작했습니다. 시간이 지나면서 Richard 씨는 회사에서 단계적으로 승진을 하게 됩니다. 26세가 되었을 때, 그는 California 주립 대학에서 회계학 석사 학위를 받았고, 그와 동시에 우리 경리부에서 수석 회계사로 자리매김하게 됩니다. 마침내 45세의 나이에 Richard 씨는 재무담당 부사장으로 회사 임원진에 합류하게 되었고, 그 부서에서 남은 임기를 보냈습니다. Richard 씨는 이달 말에 퇴임할 예정이며, 38년 동안 함께 한 아내, 같은 지역에 거주하는 4명의 자녀들 및 9 명의 손주들과 함께 편안한 노후를 보낼 기대에 차 있습니다.

[157] Richard 씨의 퇴임 저녁 만찬에서 발표를 하고 싶으신 분들은 Bakinsale 씨에게 발표의 요지와 함께 6월 20일까지 이메일을 보내주시기 바랍니다. 각 직원들은 한 명씩 게스트를 만찬 장소에 동행할 수 있습니다. 참석 여부를 6월 20일까지 Bakinsale 씨에게 알려주기 바랍니다.

그럼 만찬 장소에서 만나기를 바랍니다.

Michael Moore
사장 겸 CEO,
Daily Best 사

어휘 be invited to ~에 초대되다 hard work and dedication 노고와 헌신 office boy 사환 as the years passed 시간이 흘러 work one's way up the chain 승진의 길을 걷다 master's in Accounting 회계학 석사(학위) head accountant 수석 회계사 bookkeeping department 경리부 corporate staff 회사 임원진 Vice President of Financial Affairs 재무부(담당) 부사장 the remainder of his career 자신의 남은 임기 look forward to -ing ~을 기대하다 spend 시간 -ing ~에 시간을 보내다 relax with ~와 편안한 시간을 보내다 retirement dinner 퇴임(은퇴) 기념 파티 intention 의도, 목적 be permitted to do ~해도 된다는 허가를 얻다 RSVP (répondez sil vous plaît) (참가 또는 불참에 대해) 응답바람

155

What was Mr. Hutchson's position when he started working at Daily Best Corporation?

(A) Accountant
(B) Office Assistant
(C) Finance Officer
(D) Vice President

문제 해설

Baker 씨가 Daily Best 사에서 근무를 시작했을 때 그의 직책이 무엇이었는지 묻는 문제이므로 Baker 씨에 대해 소개하는 부분에서 그의 근무 초기 직책에 관한 정보를 파악하는 것이 현명하다. 이메일 초반 Richard started working for Daily Best Corporation at the age of 16, when he worked as a temporary office boy라며 Richard 씨가 16세에 회사에서 처음 근무할 때 직책이 임시 사환이었음을 밝히고 있다. 따라서 이를 통해 사무 보조를 뜻하는 (B)가 정답임을 알 수 있다.

★★ 세부사항

Hutchson 씨가 Daily Best 사에서 근무를 시작했을 때 직책은 무엇이었는가?

(A) 회계사
(B) 사무 보조
(C) 재무 부장
(D) 부사장

토익 분석

인명은 중요한 키워드이므로 해당 문제처럼 인명/지명이 키워드로 언급되는 문제에서는 이들이 제시되는 부분을 전후하여 단서를 파악하는 것이 효율적이다.

156

★★ 세부사항

Hutchson 씨는 언제 퇴직하는가?
(A) 6월 15일
(B) 6월 20일
(C) 6월 30일
(D) 7월 1일

토익 분석

시간/시점/요일을 묻는 문제에선 지문에서 시간/시점/요일 관련 표현이 언급되는 부분을 중심으로 단서를 파악해야 한다.

When will Mr. Hutchson retire?

(A) June 15
(B) June 20
(C) June 30
(D) July 1

문제 해설

Hutchson 씨의 퇴직 일자가 언제인지 세부사항을 묻는 문제이다. 따라서 지문에서 구체적인 시점이 언급되는 부분만 집중하는 스캐닝을 통해 등장하는 시점이 퇴직과 관련이 있는지 여부를 빠르게 파악해야 한다. 이메일의 첫 번째 단락 후반 Richard will be retiring at the end of the month라며 Hutchson 씨는 이달 말일에 퇴직할 것임을 알리고 있다. 아울러 이메일의 발송 일자가 6월 15일임을 고려할 때 Hutchson 씨의 퇴직 일자는 6월 30일임을 가늠할 수 있으므로 정답은 (C)가 되겠다.

157

★★ 세부사항

만약 직원들이 연설을 하고 싶다면 무엇을 해야 하는가?
(A) 연설문을 작성한다.
(B) 연설 자료를 제출해야 한다.
(C) 신청서를 작성한다.
(D) Bakinsale 씨에게 연락한다.

토익 분석

• 세부사항을 묻는 문제는 질문에서 빠른 키워드(핵심어) 파악이 관건이다. 문제에 등장하는 If로 시작하는 절이 키워드이므로 지문에서 스캐닝을 통해 If절의 내용이 제시되는 부분을 빠르게 파악해야 한다.
• 마지막 문제는 항상 마지막 단락의 내용이 끝나는 부분부터 역순으로 한 문장씩 내용을 확인하며 단서를 파악하는 것이 효율적이다.

What are employees asked to do if they want to give a speech?

(A) E-mail Mr. Hutchson
(B) Submit the contents of the speech
(C) Complete an application
(D) Contact Ms. Bakinsale

문제 해설

직원들이 연설을 하려면 무엇을 해야 하는지 묻는 문제이므로 이메일에서 make a speech가 언급되는 부분을 중심으로 단서를 파악해야 한다. 이메일 후반 최고 경영자인 Moore 씨는 If you would like to speak at Richard's retirement dinner, please email Ms. Bakinsale with your intention by June 20라며 Richard 씨의 퇴임 저녁 만찬에서 발표를 하고 싶으신 직원들은 Bakinsale 씨에게 발표의 요지와 함께 6월 20일까지 이메일을 보내줄 것을 요청하고 있다. 따라서 정답은 (D)가 되겠다.

Questions 158-160 refer to the following article.

[158] **New Restaurant Set to Open Soon**

By John Wilson – New Jersey Daily Telegraph

Jersey City—[158] Soul Food Café will be opening its doors this Friday for breakfast at 8:00 A.M. [159] Soul Food Café is the welcome addition to the area's main street restaurants.

The owner of Soul Food Café, Linda Hamilton, says, "Soul Food Café will specialize in down-home country style meals. [159] We are different from other restaurants in that we offer a lower calorie, healthier version of good country cooking by using healthier oils and cookingpractices. We want our customers to enjoy high-quality entrées that are not high in fat and cholesterol. Our goal is to make the customers want to come back and maybe even become a little healthier in the meantime."

Ms. Hamilton, the former head chef at Creole's Home Cooking, started her plans for her own restaurant over two years ago. After looking at several spaces around the city for her restaurant, she bought the former carpet store on the main street location and had it fully restored and renovated. [167] She explains, "I worked with the designers personally to get this place looking exactly like some of the southern restaurants I went to as a kid in Alabama."

Soul Food Café is beautiful both inside and outside. We will soon see if many residents will patronize the restaurant like Linda and her eager staff hope. [166] Soul Food Café will be open daily from 8:00 A.M. to 9:00 P.M. except for Sundays, when it will open for brunch starting at 10:00 A.M.

158-160 다음 기사를 참조하시오.

[158] 새로운 레스토랑 개점 임박

John Wilson – New Jersey Daily Telegraph

Jersey 시티 – [158] Soul Food Café는 이번 주 금요일 오전 8시에 아침식사를 위해 개점할 것이다. [159] Soul Food Café는 이 지역 중심가에 있는 레스토랑들에 더하여 환영할 만한 새로운 레스토랑이다.

Soul Food Café의 사장 Linda Hamilton 씨는 "Soul Food Café는 남부 시골 스타일의 음식을 만드는 것을 전문으로 합니다. [159] 고객 여러분들을 위해 건강에 좋은 기름과 조리법을 이용한 저칼로리의 시골풍 건강식을 제공한다는 점에서 다른 레스토랑들과 차별화됩니다. 저희는 고객님들이 저지방, 저콜레스테롤로 만들어진 품격있는 남부 지역 스타일의 음식을 드시길 원합니다. 저희의 목표는 고객님들이 다시 방문하여, 저희의 음식을 지속적으로 드시도록 하여 좀 더 건강하실 수 있도록 하는 것입니다."라고 말했다.

Hamilton 씨는 Creole's 홈 쿠킹의 주방장으로 일했으며, 2년 전에 본인 소유의 레스토랑을 갖는 계획을 세웠다. 시 전역에 걸쳐 여러 지역을 둘러본 후에, 그녀는 메인 가에 위치한 카펫 상점을 사들여 레스토랑으로 수리하였다. [167] Hamilton 씨는 "제가 어린 시절 알라바마에서 갔었던 남부 레스토랑을 기억하며 그와 똑같이 보이도록 하기 위해 설계자들과 함께 작업을 했습니다."라고 말했다.

Soul Food Café는 내부와 외부 모두가 아름답다. 우리는 Linda 씨와 그의 열렬한 직원들의 바람처럼 많은 주민들이 단골이 될지 곧 알게 될 것이다. [166] Soul Food Café는 일요일을 제외하고는 오전 8시에 개점하여 오후 9시까지 영업하며, 일요일은 브런치와 함께 오전 10시에 개점한다.

어휘 addition to ~에 추가 specialize in ~을 전문으로 하다 down-home 남부 특유의, 남부적인 be different from ~와 다르다 in that ~라는 점에서 practice 관행 entrée 앙트레, 주 요리 former 과거의 renovate ~을 보수하다 patronize ~을 단골로 하다 brunch 브런치 food preparation 조리 entrepreneur 기업인, 사업가

158 ———

What is the purpose of the article?

(A) To explain food preparation techniques
(B) To review local restaurants
(C) To describe an entrepreneur's business strategy
(D) To publicize the opening of a new restaurant

문제 해설

기사문의 제목 New Restaurant Set to Open Soon과 기사 초반 Soul Food Café will be opening its doors this Friday for breakfast at 8:00 A.M.에서 새로운 레스토랑에 대해 알리고자 하는 목적의 기사문임을 파악할 수 있으므로 정답은 (D)가 되겠다.

★ **지문의 목적**

이 기사문의 목적은 무엇인가?
(A) 음식 조리법을 설명하기 위해서
(B) 지역 레스토랑을 평가하기 위해서
(C) 한 경영인의 사업 전략을 설명하기 위해서
(D) 새로운 레스토랑의 개업을 알리기 위해서

토익 분석

기사문의 주제/목적은 단락 구분이 있는 경우 대개 첫 번째 단락 초반 2–3문장에서 제시된다.

159

★★★ 진위

Soul Food Café에 대해 언급되지 않은 것은 무엇인가?
(A) Creole's Home Cooking의 소유이다.
(B) 저칼로리의 음식을 판매한다.
(C) 도심과 가깝다.
(D) 매일 아침 8시에 개점할 것이다

토익 분석

사실이 아닌 내용을 묻는 문제의 키워드가 지문 전반에 걸쳐 언급되는 경우 선택지의 내용을 키워드로 삼아 지문에서 해당 내용이 언급되는지 여부를 빠르게 파악한다. 이 때 선택지를 두 개씩 나눠 두 번에 걸쳐 지문에서의 해당 내용이 제시되고 있는지 확인하는 방식을 권고한다.

What is NOT mentioned about Soul Food Café?

(A) It is owned by Creole's Home Cooking.
(B) It serves low-calorie meals.
(C) It is close to downtown.
(D) It will open at 8:00 A.M. almost every day.

문제 해설

기사문 초반 Soul Food Café is the welcome addition to the area's main street restaurants를 통해 Soul Food Café가 시 중심가에 있음을 알 수 있으며, 두 번째 단락 초반 We are different from other restaurants in that we offer a lower calorie에서 저칼로리의 음식을 제공하는 곳임을 파악할 수 있으며, 마지막으로 기사문 말미 Soul Food Café will be open daily from 8:00 A.M. to 9:00 P.M. except for Sundays, when it will open for brunch starting at 10:00 A.M.에서 일요일만 오전 10시에 개점한다고 언급하고 있으므로, 거의 매일 오전 8시에 개점한다는 점 또한 알 수 있다. 그러므로 정답은 (A)이다.

160

★★★ 유추

Hamilton 씨에 대해 암시되는 것은 무엇인가?
(A) 모든 요리를 즐긴다.
(B) 업계에 처음 뛰어들었다.
(C) 인테리어 디자인을 도왔다.
(D) 그녀는 건축 전문이다.

토익 분석

유추 문제의 키워드가 제시되는 부분을 중심으로 해당 키워드에 대한 유추 정보를 파악하는 것이 관건이다.

What is suggested about Ms. Hamilton?

(A) She enjoys all cuisine.
(B) She is new to the industry.
(C) She helped design the interior.
(D) She specializes in architecture.

문제 해설

Hamilton 씨에 대해 시사하는 내용에 대해 묻는 유추문제이므로 Hamilton 씨와 직접적으로 관련 있는 내용을 살펴보며 유추근거로 활용할 수 있을만한 내용이 있는지 여부를 살펴봐야 한다. 기사문 세 번째 단락 하단에서 Hamilton 씨가 She explains, "I worked with the designers personally to get this place looking exactly like some of the southern restaurants I went to as a kid in Alabama."라며 자신이 어릴 때 갔던 알라바마 식당의 모습과 동일한 모습으로 만들기 위해 직접 설계자들과 협업했다고 언급하는 부분을 통해 Hamilton 씨가 인테리어 디자인을 도왔다는 점을 유추할 수 있다. 따라서 정답은 (C)이다.

Questions 161-163 refer to the following form.

We thank you for choosing to purchase a Pegasus Electronics mobile phone. [163] If you made your purchase between July 1 and July 31, you are entitled to a gift pack containing Pegasus Electronics accessories, including a case, a set of earphones, and a protective screen cover.

[161] Once you have completed this form by entering the requested details below, send it, along with an original proof of purchase, to Pegasus Electronics Head Office, Johnson Technology Park, Edmonton, Alberta T5A 0FH. Should you have any questions, please do not hesitate to contact Pegasus Electronics' customer service department at customerservice@pegasus.ca.

[162] I confirm that I would like to be sent a free set of Pegasus Electronics mobile phone accessories. _X_

Name: ___Brendan Baker___
Address: ___55 Joseph Street___
City/Province/Postal code: ___Bracebridge, ON P1L 5JY___
Phone number: ___555-9231___
E-mail address:
Purchased mobile phone model: S350   S400   _X_ S450

Delivery of your items may take up to two weeks. This offer is a limited-time offer that ends on August 30. The offer does not extend to purchases made outside of Canada, or purchases made on our Web site. Also, persons currently employed by Pegasus Electronics are not permitted to take advantage of this offer.

By supplying your e-mail address, you indicate that you wish to receive Pegasus Electronics' monthly newsletter, which contains information about forthcoming phone models and special discounts.

161

What is suggested about Pegasus Electronics?

(A) It is headquartered in Edmonton.
(B) It will discontinue production of mobile phones on August 30.
(C) It has created a store membership plan for customers.
(D) It has recently launched a new model of mobile phone.

문제 해설

Pegasus 전자에 대해 유추할 수 있는 내용을 묻는 문제이므로 Pegasus 전자에 관한 정보를 숙지하고 난 후 회사에 관해 유추할 수 있는 내용을 파악해야 한다. 양식지 두 번째 단락 초반 Once you have completed this form by entering the requested details below, send it, along with an original proof of purchase, to Pegasus Electronics Head Office, Johnson Technology Park, Edmonton, Alberta T5A 0FH에서 작성한 서류양식을 구매 기록과 함께 Pegasus 전자 본사가 있는 Johnson 기술공원으로 보낼 것을 요청하고 있으며 주소지 중 Edmonton 시임을 확인할 수 있으므로 정답은 (A)이다.

161-163 다음 양식을 참조하시오.

Pegasus 전자의 휴대 전화를 구입하기로 결정해 주셔서 감사드립니다. [163] 7월 1일부터 7월 31일 사이에 구매를 하셨다면 Pegasus 전자의 케이스, 이어폰 세트 및 보호 화면 커버가 포함된 악세사리 증정품을 받으실 수 있습니다.

[161] 하단에 요청된 세부 사항들을 입력하여 양식을 완료한 후, 구매 기록과 함께 Pegasus 전자 본사가 있는 Pegasus Electronics Head Office, Johnson Technology Park, Edmonton, Alberta T5A 0FH로 발송해 주십시오. 질문이 있으시다면 Pegasus 전자의 고객 서비스 부서인 customerservice@pegasus.ca로 연락해 주시길 바랍니다.

[162] 저는 Pegasus 전자의 핸드폰 악세사리가 담긴 무료 선물을 받고 싶음을 확인합니다. X

이름: Brendan Baker
주소: 55 Joseph Street
도시/지역/우편번호 Bracebridge, On PqL 5JY
전화번호: 555-9231
이메일 주소:
구매한 휴대폰 모델명: S350 S400 X S450

귀하의 품목이 배송되는데 최대 2주까지 걸릴 수 있습니다. 이 할인행사는 8월 30일에 끝나는 한정된 기회입니다. 이 행사는 캐나다 및 우리 웹사이트 이외에서 구매한 상품에는 해당되지 않습니다. 또한 Pegasus 전자에 현재 고용되어 있는 직원들은 이 행사에 참여할 수 없습니다.

이메일 주소를 제공하면, 귀하는 Pegasus 전자의 출시 예정인 폰 모델들과 특별 할인 등에 관한 정보가 들어있는 월간 소식지를 받고 싶다는 의사 표시로 간주됩니다.

어휘 be entitled to Vr ~을 할 자격요건을 갖추다 claim ~을 주장하다, ~을 요구하다, ~을 제기하다 along with ~과 함께 proof 증거, 증빙자료, 증명 hesitate 주저하다, 망설이다 extend 연장하다, 확장하다, 늘리다 forthcoming 다가오는, 준비된, 뒤따르는

★★ 유추

Pegasus 전자에 대해 암시되는 내용은 무엇인가?
(A) Edmonton에 본사를 두고 있다.
(B) 8월 30일자부로 휴대 전화 생산을 중단할 것이다
(C)고객들을 위한 매장 회원제 상품을 제작했다
(D) 최근 신규 휴대 전화 모델을 출시했다.

토익 분석

유추 문제의 키워드가 혹은 키워드에 관한 내용이 지문 전반에 걸쳐 언급되고 있는 상태에서 적절한 유추 내용을 파악해야 한다면 선택지에 나온 내용을 먼저 파악한 후 선택지의 내용을 유추할 수 있는 근거가 지문에 제시되는 지 여부를 역으로 확인하는 방식으로 문제를 풀이한다.

162

★★ 세부사항

Baker 씨가 서류를 작성한 이유는 무엇인가?
(A) 제품 교환을 요구하기 위해서
(B) 서비스에 대한 견해를 전달하기 위해서
(C) 제품에 대한 환불을 요청하기 위해서
(D) 무료 제품을 수령하기 위해서

토익 분석

문제의 키워드가 혹은 키워드에 관한 내용이 지문 전반에 걸쳐 언급되고 있는 상태에서 세부적인 내용을 파악해야 한다면 선택지에 나온 내용을 먼저 파악한 후 이를 키워드로 삼아 지문에 해당 내용이 제시되는지 여부를 역으로 확인하는 방식으로 문제를 풀이한다.

Why did Mr. Baker fill out the form?

(A) To ask that a product be exchanged
(B) To give feedback about a service
(C) To request a refund on a product
(D) To receive complimentary items

문제 해설

Baker 씨가 서류를 작성한 이유는 서류 작성을 시작하는 부분, 즉 서류 양식지 중반 I confirm that I would like to be sent a free gift of Pegasus Electronics mobile phone accessories을 통해 무료 제품을 수령하기 위해 작성하는 것임을 알 수 있으므로 정답은 (D)가 되겠다.

163

★★★ 유추

Baker 씨에 대해 유추할 수 있는 것은 무엇인가?
(A) 그는 이전에 Pegasus 전자의 직원이었다.
(B) 그는 Pegasus 전자 홈페이지에서 휴대 전화를 주문했다.
(C) 그는 Pegasus 전자의 월간 소식지를 수령하고 싶어한다.
(D) 그는 7월에 Pegasus 전자의 휴대 전화를 구매했다.

토익 분석

• 유추 문제의 키워드가 혹은 키워드에 관한 내용이 지문 전반에 걸쳐 언급되고 있는 상태에서 적절한 유추 내용을 파악해야 한다면 선택지에 나온 내용을 먼저 파악한 후 선택지의 내용을 유추할 수 있는 근거가 지문에 제시되는지 여부를 역으로 확인하는 방식으로 문제를 풀이한다. 이 때 선택지를 두 개씩 나눠 두 번에 걸쳐 지문에서의 유추 근거가 제시되고 있는지 확인하는 방식을 추천한다.

• 문제의 키워드가 혹은 키워드에 관한 내용이 지문 전반에 걸쳐 언급되고 있는 상태에서 세부적인 내용을 파악해야 한다면 선택지에 나온 내용을 먼저 파악한 후 이를 키워드로 삼아 지문에 해당 내용이 제시되는지 여부를 역으로 확인하는 방식으로 문제를 풀이한다. 이 때 선택지를 두 개씩 나눠 두 번에 걸쳐 지문에서 해당 내용이 제시되고 있는지 확인하는 방식을 추천한다.

What is implied about Mr. Baker?

(A) He is a former employee of Pegasus Electronics.
(B) He ordered a mobile phone from Pegasus Electronics' Web site.
(C) He would like to receive Pegasus Electronics' monthly newsletter.
(D) He bought a Pegasus Electronics mobile phone in July.

문제 해설

Baker 씨에 대해 유추할 수 있는 내용에 관해 묻는 문제이므로 지문에서 Baker 씨에 관한 정보를 숙지한 후 이를 토대로 유추 가능한 사실을 파악해야 한다. 서류 양식지 중반 I confirm that I would like to be sent a free gift of Pegasus Electronics mobile phone accessories에서 Baker 씨가 무료 제품을 수령하기 위해 이 서류 양식지를 작성하고 있음을 알 수 있으며, 아울러 서류 양식지 초반 If you made your purchase between July 1 and July 31, you are entitled to a gift pack containing Pegasus Electronics accessories을 통해 무료 상품은 7월 1일에서 31일 사이에 Pegasus 에서 제품을 구매한 사람에게만 해당되는 혜택임을 파악할 수 있으므로 궁극적으로 Baker 씨는 7월에 Pegasus 제품을 구매한 고객임을 유추할 수 있다. 따라서 정답은 (D)라고 할 수 있다.

Questions 164-167 refer to the following letter.

August 10
Professor Jim Moore
Gentech Enterprises, 290 Swallow Court, Hackney, London, UK, E15 6PP

Dear Professor Moore,

— [1] —. [166] We truly appreciate your decision to join our pool of contributing experts here at Stem Cell Monthly. We have strived to assemble a team of the most experienced professionals from the fields of stem cell engineering and gene therapy.

[165] We meet with all of our contributing experts annually at the International Genetics Conference in January. — [2] —. Next year's event will be held at the Wilshire Hotel in Los Angeles. [164] All experts are expected to attend this event, [166] in addition to monthly meetings with our editorial team via teleconference. [164] Our editorial team handles the bulk of the writing for the journal, but our contributing experts provide their invaluable knowledge, expertise, and advice on all issues and developments related to the field. — [3] —. [164] As a contributing expert, you will be expected to fulfill the following duties:

- Report recent developments in stem cell research
- Recommend leading figures for interviews
- Write occasional columns about your field of research
- Answer letters from readers that our staff cannot adequately answer

[167] Within the next two weeks, we will contact you with more details, including contact information for our other contributing experts, in case you would like to confer with them on any topics. [167] During this time, we suggest that you familiarize yourself with our journal by reading through the three issues we previously mailed to you. — [4] —. This will help you get a good idea of our style and content.

All of us here look forward to working with you!

Warm regards,

Beatrice Hopper
Chief Editor
Stem Cell Monthly

164-167 다음 편지를 참조하시오.

8월 10일
Jim Moore 교수
Gentech Enterprises, 290 Swallow Court, Hackney, London, UK, E15 6PP

Moore교수님께,

[166] Stem Cell Monthly 잡지에 기고해주실 전문가로 합류하기로 해주신 점 정말 감사합니다. 줄기 세포 공학과 유전자 치료 분야에서 가장 경험이 많은 전문가들로 집필진을 구성하기 위해 굉장히 노력했습니다.

[165] 저희는 매년 1월 모든 전문 집필진과 국제 유전학 회의에서 만납니다. 내년 행사는 로스앤젤레스의 Wilshire 호텔에서 개최됩니다. [164] 모든 기고 전문가들은 [166] 매달 편집팀과 원격 화상 회의를 하는 것과 더불어 이 연례행사에도 참석해야 합니다. [164] 저희 편집팀이 잡지에 기고되는 원고의 대부분을 처리하지만, 전문 집필진은 이 분야와 관련된 모든 사안과 소식에 대한 귀중한 정보, 전문 지식 및 조언을 제공합니다. [164] 전문 집필진으로서, 교수님께서는 다음의 의무를 이행하여 주시기 바랍니다.

– 줄기 세포 연구에 관한 최근의 발전 보고
– 인터뷰를 위한 주요 인물 추천하기
– 귀하의 연구 분야에 대해 비정기적 칼럼 기고
– 저희 직원이 대답하지 못하는 독자의 편지에 대한 응답

[167] 2주 안에 더 자세한 내용과 함께 연락을 드릴 것이며, 다른 전문 집필진과 기사 주제들에 관해 상의하고 싶을 때를 대비하여 다른 전문가들의 연락처도 제공해드릴 것입니다. [167] 그동안, 저희가 이전에 우편으로 보내드린 세 권의 잡지를 숙지하여 저희 잡지에 익숙해지시기를 제안합니다. 저희 잡지의 스타일과 내용을 파악하는데 도움을 줄 것입니다.

모두 교수님과 함께 일하기를 고대하고 있습니다.

Beatrice Hopper
편집장
Stem Cell Monthly

어휘 contributing 기여하는, 기고하는, 기부하는 strive to ~을 하고자 노력하다 assemble ~을 조립하다, ~을 만들다 experienced 경험이 많은, 노련한 gene 유전자 therapy 치료 annually 연례적으로 monthly meeting 월간 회의 editorial team 편집팀 via ~을 통해 teleconference 원격 회의 handle ~을 다루다, ~을 취급하다 invaluable 매우 소중한, 가치가 있는, 귀중한 expertise 전문성 related to ~과 관련이 있는 fulfill ~을 행하다 duties 의무 stem cell 줄기세포 in case ~인 경우에 confer with ~와 의논하다, ~와 협의하다 familiarize with ~에 익숙하다

164

★★★ 편지의 목적

편지의 목적은 무엇인가?
(A) Moore 교수를 회의에 초빙하여 연설을 하도록 요청하기 위해서
(B) 새로운 과학 잡지 발간을 발표하기 위해서
(C) 기사를 제출할 때의 가이드라인을 설명하기 위해서
(D) 직무를 간단히 설명하기 위해서

토익 분석

편지의 주제/목적은 단락 구분이 있는 경우 첫 번째 단락 초반 2-3문장에서 제시되는 경우가 대부분이다. 다만 주제/목적 문제의 난이도가 높아지는 경우 주제/목적은 두 번째 단락의 초반 2-3문장에서 다뤄지는 경우가 많다. 무엇보다 주제/목적 문제는 난이도가 높아질수록 주제/목적이 지문 초/전반이 아니라 중/후반부에서 나오게 된다는 점을 알아두도록 한다.

What is the purpose of the letter?

(A) To invite Professor Moore to speak at a conference
(B) To announce the release of a new science journal
(C) To describe guidelines for submitting articles
(D) To outline the responsibilities of a position

문제 해설

편지의 첫 번째 단락은 전문 집필진으로 합류한 결정에 대한 감사인사가 주를 이루고 있으나 두 번째 단락의 전체적인 내용을 고려할 때 단순히 감사의 인사를 전하기 위한 목적의 편지라 볼 수 없다. 따라서 구체적으로 전문 집필진이 해야 할 일과 따라야 할 의무에 대해서 집중적으로 소개하고 있는 두 번째 단락의 내용을 고려할 때 편지의 목적은 직무에 대한 설명을 언급하기 위함임을 알 수 있다. 따라서 정답은 (D)가 되겠다.

165

★★ 세부사항

Moore 교수와 정기적으로 연락하는 사람은 누구인가?
(A) 런던에 거주하는 과학자들
(B) 정부 공무원들
(C) 월간 줄기세포 잡지 구독자들
(D) 편집팀 직원들

토익 분석

문제의 키워드가 혹은 키워드에 관한 내용이 지문 전반에 걸쳐 언급되고 있는 상태에서 세부적인 내용을 파악해야 한다면 선택지에 나온 내용을 먼저 파악한 후 이를 키워드로 삼아 지문에 해당 내용이 제시되는지 여부를 역으로 확인하는 방식으로 문제를 풀이한다. 이 때 선택지를 두 개씩 나눠 두 번에 걸쳐 지문에서 해당 내용이 제시되고 있는지 확인하는 방식을 추천한다.

With whom is Professor Moore expected to stay in regular contact?

(A) London-based scientists
(B) Government officials
(C) Stem Cell Monthly subscribers
(D) Editorial team members

문제 해설

Moore 교수와 정기적으로 연락하는 사람에 대해 묻고 있으므로 지문에서 구체적인 연락 수단이 언급되는 부분을 찾아 Moore 교수와 정기적으로 연락을 취하는 대상에 관한 정보를 파악해야 한다. 두 번째 단락 중반 in addition to monthly meetings with our editorial team via teleconference 에서 Moore 교수는 잡지사 편집팀과 원격 월별 회의를 통해 주기적으로 만남을 갖게 될 것이란 사실을 밝히고 있으므로 정답은 (D)가 되겠다.

166

In which of the positions marked [1],[2],[3], and [4] does the following sentence best belong?

"We truly appreciate your decision to join our pool of contributing experts here at Stem Cell Monthly."

(A) [1]
(B) [2]
(C) [3]
(D) [4]

★★ 문장의 위치—

[1], [2], [3], [4]로 표기된 위치들 중에서 다음 문장이 들어가기에 가장 적절한 곳은 어디인가?
"Stem Cell Monthly 잡지에 기고해주실 전문가로 합류하기로 해주신 점 정말 감사합니다."
(A) [1]
(B) [2]
(C) [3]
(D) [4]

토익 분석

강사로서 문제풀이 시간을 단축시킬 수 있는 방법으로 제시할만한 방법은 [3] – [4] – [1] – [2] 순서로 정답 비중이 높기 때문에 주어진 문장 내용을 순차적으로 해당 위치에 삽입해보며 내용 연결성을 비교하며 문제를 풀이하도록 한다.

문제 해설

주어진 문장이 위치해야 하는 곳을 묻는 문제이므로 주어진 문장의 의미를 이해한 후 이와 내용적 연계성을 지닌 적절한 위치를 파악해야 한다. 주어진 문장 "We truly appreciate your decision to join our pool of contributing experts here at Stem Cell Monthly"은 Stem Cell Monthly 잡지에 기고해주실 전문가로 합류하기로 해주신 점 정말 감사하다는 내용으로 이는 합류하게 될 팀과 팀이 해야 하는 일에 대해 소개하는 내용에 앞서 제시되어야 한다. 따라서 주어진 문장은 편지 초반 We have strived to assemble a team of the most experienced professionals from the fields of stem cell engineering and gene therapy에 앞서 위치하는 것이 적절하므로 정답은 (A)가 되겠다.

167

What is Professor Moore encouraged to do within the next two weeks?

(A) Forward his contact details
(B) Organize a meeting with other contributors
(C) Register for an upcoming conference
(D) Review some publications

★★ 세부사항

Moore 교수는 오는 2주 동안 무엇을 해야 하는가?
(A) 그의 연락처를 발송한다.
(B) 다른 기고자들과의 회의를 준비한다.
(C) 추후에 있을 회의에 등록한다.
(D) 일부 출판물을 검토한다.

토익 분석

기간이 키워드인 경우 우선 지문에서 해당 기간이 언급되는 부분을 빠르게 찾아 그 전후 내용에서 단서를 파악한다.

문제 해설

Moore 교수가 향후 2주 동안 무엇을 해야 하는지 묻는 마지막 문제이므로 편지 후반부에서 2주라는 기간이 제시되는 부분을 중심으로 단서를 파악해야 한다. 편지 마지막 단락 초반 Within the next two weeks를 통해 향후 2주간이란 기간에 해당되는 내용이 그 이후에 제시되고 있을 것임을 알 수 있으며, 이어서 During this time, we suggest that you familiarize yourself with our journal by reading through the three issues we previously mailed to you라고 언급하는 내용을 통해 향후 2주 동안 이전에 발송된 잡지를 숙지하며 이에 익숙해지도록 요청하고 있음을 알 수 있다. 그러므로 정답은 (D)가 되겠다.

168-171 다음 기사문을 참조하시오.

교통 위원회가 산책로 건설을 승인하다

CASTRO VALLEY (7월 14일)— [168] **Castro Valley** 교통위원회는 도시에서 가장 붐비는 열 개의 거리에 보행자 통로를 구축하는데 300,000달러를 사용하는 사안을 표결에 부쳐 승인을 얻었다. 이 허가는 **Castro Valley**에 살고 있는 보행자들이 보행자 통로들의 위험한 교통 상황과 긴 대기 시간에 대해 불만을 토로해 시가 안전 감사를 실시한 후 바로 허가된 것이다. 감사원들은 보행자들이 제기한 문제들을 내년 내에 처리되어야 한다는 데 동의했다. 이 보행자 통로들은 보행자들이 교통흐름을 방해하지 않고 길을 건널 수 있도록 할 것이며, [169] 특히 관광객들이 많이 몰리는 시기에는 강변지구의 심한 교통체증으로 인해 고생하는 운전자들에겐 희소식이라 할 수 있다.

Castro Valley의 시장인 Simon Livingston 씨가 3월 12일 교통 위원회에 보행자 통로 건설을 제안했다. Livingston 씨는 11월 **Castro Valley** 지역 주민들을 대상으로 실시한 연구 결과를 언급했다. [168] 그 연구는 **Castro Valley** 인구의 10퍼센트만이 도시에서 조깅 또는 산책을 즐기고 있음을 보여주었다. 인근 도시에 비슷한 산책로가 건설된 경우를 근거해서, Livingston 씨는 보행자 통로 건설이 산책이나 조깅을 하는 인구를 3배 정도 증가시킬 것이라고 믿는다.

건설을 위한 초기 단계에서 필요 시 도로의 차선을 일시적으로 차단할 수도 있다. 이런 경우 우회로가 표시될 것이다. [170] 초기 건설 단계를 거치면, 보행자 통로들은 야간에도 접근하기 쉽도록 도색이 될 것이며 조명 또한 추가될 것이다. 첫 번째 통로 건설은 8월 3일에 시작될 것이며 이후 4개월 이내에 10개 모두 완성될 것이다.

어휘 transit council 교통 위원회 approval 승인, 결재 pedestrian 보행자 walkway 인도, 통로, 보도 traffic conditions 교통 상태 crosswalk 횡단보도 conductor 차장, 지휘자, 시행자 audit 회계 감사 address 주소, 연설, 연설하다, 수취인을 기입하다, 다루다, 취급하다 hinder 방해하다 riverside 강가 congest 충만하다, 혼잡하게 하다 relate 관련시키다, 연관되다, 연결되다 outcome 결과 population 인구 surrounding 둘러쌓는 recreational 휴양의, 오락의, 기분전환의 initial 초기의, 최초의 phase 단계 accessible 접근할 수 있는, 이용 가능한 detour 우회, 우회로, 우회하다

Questions 168-171 refer to the following article.

Transit Council Approves Walkways Construction

CASTRO VALLEY(July 14)— [168] The Transit Council of Castro Valley has voted in approval of a using $300,000 to build pedestrian walkways over ten of the busiest streets in the city. — [1] —. The approval comes after the city conducted a safety audit following complaints from pedestrians living in Castro Valley about dangerous traffic conditions and long waiting times at pedestrian crosswalks. The conductors of the audit agreed that the issues brought up by pedestrians should be addressed within the next year. — [2] —. The walkways will allow pedestrians to cross roads without hindering the flow of traffic, which will also make drivers happy, [169] especially during the tourist season, when traffic around the riverside district can be very congested.

Mr. Simon Livingston, Mayor of Castro Valley, suggested the construction of the walkways to the transit council on March 12. Mr. Livingston related the outcome of a study of residents of Castro Valley that was conducted in November. — [3] —. [168] The study shows that only 10 percent of the population in Castro Valley enjoyed jogging or walking in the city. Based on happenings when similar walkways were constructed in surrounding cities, Mr. Livingston believes that the amount of people who walk or jog recreationally or for exercise could triple.

The initial phase for the construction will include temporarily closing down lanes on the road when necessary. Detours will be marked at these times. [170] After the initial construction, the walkways will be painted and have lights added to make them accessible to residents at night. — [4] —. Construction on the first walkway will begin on August 3, and all ten will be completed within 4 months.

168

★★★ 지문의 목적

기사문의 목적이 무엇인가?
(A) 교통위원회 후보자들에 대한 간단한 신상 정보를 제공하기 위해서
(B) 새로운 통근용 고속도로에 대한 세부 정보를 제공하기 위해서
(C) 보행자를 만족시킬 프로젝트를 설명하기 위해서
(D) 의회 사무소를 보수할 근로자들을 모집하기 위해서

토익 분석

기사문의 주제/목적은 단락 구분이 있는 경우 첫 번째 단락 초반 2-3문장에서 제시된다. 다만 주제/목적 문제의 난이도가 높아지는 경우 주제/목적은 두 번째 단락의 초반 2-3문장에서 등장하는 경향이 있다.

What is a purpose of the article?

(A) To report some plans to attract tourists
(B) To give details about a new commuter expressway
(C) To explain a project that caters to pedestrian
(D) To recruit workers to renovate council offices

문제 해설

기사문의 첫 번째 단락은 전체적으로 보도 건설과 관련된 공사를 시 교통위원회에서 승인했다는 내용과 이 공사안이 나오게 된 배경과 과정에 대한 설명이 제시되고 있다. 따라서 실질적으로 기사문에서 이 보도 건설 공사의 어떠한 부분을 다루는 것이 목적인지 그 세부적인 내용은 두 번째 단락 하단 The study shows that only 10 percent of the population in Castro Valley enjoyed jogging or walking in the city. Based on happenings when similar walkways were constructed in surrounding cities, Mr. Livingston believes that the amount of people who walk or jog recreationally or for exercise could triple에서 거주민 중 10퍼센트만이 산책이나 조깅을 즐긴다는 설문 결과와 함께 보도 건설 공사가 행해지면 산책이나 조깅을 하는 인구가 3배 정도 증가할 것이란 예측을 전달하는 부분을 통해 지문의 목적은 공사의 세부사항을 설명하기 위함임을 알 수 있다. 그러므로 정답은 (C)이다.

169

What is indicated about Castro Valley?

(A) There are many problems year-round with traffic near the riverside district.
(B) More than 10,000 people enjoy walking recreationally in the city.
(C) The number of residents has tripled over the last few years.
(D) The riverside district is popular among tourists.

문제 해설

기사문의 첫 번째 단락 말미 especially during the tourist season, when traffic around the riverside district can be very congested에서 특히 관광객이 많이 몰리는 시기에 강변 지구에서의 교통량은 많아진다는 내용을 통해 강변 지역이 관광객들이 많이 찾는 지역임을 유추할 수 있다.

170

What is scheduled to be done as part of the construction?

(A) The streetlights on roads will be replaced.
(B) New roads for car only will be added.
(C) The walkways will be painted to be more noticeable to pedestrians.
(D) Lanes for walking and jogging will be separated.

문세 해설

기사문의 마지막 단락 하단 After the initial construction, the walkways will be painted and have lights added to make them accessible to residents at night을 통해 초기 공사 이후에는 보도가 도색이 될 것이며 야간에도 거주민들이 쉽게 접근할 수 있도록 등이 추가될 것임을 알 수 있으므로 정답은 (C)라고 할 수 있다. 아울러 (B)의 경우, 자칫 정답으로 착각할 수도 있는데, 기사는 공사장 인근 도로가 아니라 공사가 행해지고 도로의 차선들이 일시적으로 폐쇄되어(closing down lanes on the road) 사용할 수 없는 상태임에 주의하도록 한다.

171

In which of the positions marked [1],[2],[3], and [4] does the following sentence best belong?

"Construction on the first walkway will begin on August 3, and all ten will be completed within 4 months."

(A) [1]
(B) [2]
(C) [3]
(D) [4]

문제 해설

주어진 문장이 위치해야 하는 곳을 묻는 문제이므로 주어진 문장의 의미를 이해한 후 이와 내용적 연계성을 지닌 적절한 위치를 파악해야 한다. 주어진 문장 Construction on the first walkway will begin on August 3, and all ten will be completed within 4 months은 첫 번째 보도에 대한 공사는 8월 3일에 시작될 것이며, 4개월 이내에 열 곳의 모든 보도가 완료될 것이란 내용으로 첫 번째 보도 공사의 시작일과 최종 완공 시점에 관한 정보가 모두 언급되어 있다. 따라서 공사의 초기 단계에 실시될 작업이 언급된 마지막에 단락에 속해 있는 [4]에 어울리는 문장임을 알 수 있으므로 (D)가 정답이다.

★★★ 유추

Castro Valley에 관해 유추할 수 있는 것은 무엇인가?
(A) 강변 지구 주변은 일년 내내 많은 만성적 교통 문제들이 있다.
(B) 만 명 이상 사람들이 취미로 도심 속 산책을 한다.
(C) 주민 인구가 지난 몇 년 동안 3배로 뛰었다.
(D) 강변 지역은 관광객들에게 인기가 좋다.

토익 분석

유추 문제의 키워드가 혹은 키워드에 관한 내용이 지문 전반에 걸쳐 언급되고 있는 상태에서 적절한 유추 내용을 파악해야 한다면 선택지에 나온 내용을 먼저 파악한 후 선택지의 내용을 유추할 수 있는 근거가 지문에 제시되는지 여부를 역으로 확인하는 방식으로 문제를 풀이한다. 이 때 선택지를 두 개씩 나눠 두 번에 걸쳐 지문에서의 유추 근거가 제시되고 있는지 확인하는 방식을 추천한다.

★★★ 세부사항

건설 과정에서 예정되어 있는 일은 무엇인가?
(A) 도로에 가로등이 교체될 것이다.
(B) 새로운 자동차 전용도로가 추가될 것이다.
(C) 보행자들의 눈에 잘 띌 수 있도록 보행자용 보도가 도색될 것이다.
(D) 산책이나 조깅을 할 수 있는 보도가 분리될 것이다.

토익 분석

세부사항을 묻는 문제는 질문에서 빠른 키워드(핵심어) 파악이 중요하다. 해당 문제에서는 스캐닝을 통해 공사에 대한 정보가 제시되는 부분을 빠르게 파악하는 것이 관건이다.

★★★ 문장의 위치

[1],[2],[3], [4]로 표기된 위치들 중에서 다음 문장이 들어가기에 가장 적절한 곳은 어디인가?
"첫 번째 보도에 대한 공사는 8월 3일에 시작될 것이며, 4월 이내에 열 곳의 모든 보도가 완료될 것이다."
(A) [1]
(B) [2]
(C) [3]
(D) [4]

토익 분석

강사로서 문제풀이 시간을 단축시킬 수 있는 방법으로 제시할만한 방법은 [3] – [4] – [1] – [2] 순서로 정답 비중이 높기 때문에 주어진 문장 내용을 순차적으로 해당 위치에 삽입해보며 내용 연결성을 비교하며 문제를 풀이하는 것이다.

172-175 다음 온라인 채팅을 참조하시오.

Kelly Han 1:25 P.M.
여러분, 문제가 생겼어요. [173] 도움이 필요해요.

Isabella Choi 1:26 P.M.
무슨 일이에요? 뭐가 잘못되었어요?

Kelly Han 1:28 P.M.
어디신가요? 사무실에 있어요, 아니면 사무실로 돌아가는 길이신가요?

William Smith 1:29 P.M.
[173] 저는 아직 점심식사 중이에요. 15분 정도 후에 사무실로 복귀할 겁니다.

Isabella Choi 1:30 P.M.
저는 막 들어왔어요. 뭘 도와드리면 될까요?

Kelly Han 1:31 P.M.
[172] 제가 제 책상 위에 중요한 서류를 두고 왔어요. 30분 뒤에 발표를 하는데 그 서류가 필요해요.

Isabella Choi 1:32 P.M.
잠시만요. 제가 가서 확인해볼게요.

William Smith 1:33 P.M.
발표가 목요일이지 않았나요?

Kelly Han 1:35 P.M.
맞아요, 그랬어요. 그런데 사장님이 목요일에 한국으로 출장을 가셔야 해서 일정이 앞당겨졌어요.

Isabella Choi 1:36 P.M.
VIP Sports 사 발표 파일을 말씀하신 게 맞나요?

Kelly Han 1:37 P.M.
맞아요. 그 파일을 빨리 가져다 주실 수 있을까요? 지금 8층에 있는 회의실에 있어요.

Isabella Choi 1:39 P.M.
좋아요. 그리로 갈게요.

Kelly Han 1:40 P.M.
정말 다행이에요! 고마워요. 제가 신세 한번 지네요.

어휘 in trouble 곤란을 겪다 walk in ~로 들어오다 leave 떠나다, ~을 남겨두다 hold on 기다리다 be scheduled on ~로 일정이 잡히다 move forward 앞으로 전진하다, 일정이 앞당겨지다 take a business trip to ~로 출장을 가다 ASAP = As soon as possible 최대한 빨리 relief 안도, 다행 owe ~에게 빚을 지다

Questions 172-175 refer to the following online chat discussion.

Kelly Han 1:25 P.M.
Hey guys, I'm in trouble. [173] I need some help.

Isabella Choi 1:26 P.M.
What's up? Something's wrong?

Kelly Han 1:28 P.M.
Where are you? Are you in the office, or are you on your way back?

William Smith 1:29 P.M.
[173] I'm still at lunch. I'll be back at the office in fifteen minutes.

Isabella Choi 1:30 P.M.
I've just walked in. Do you need my help?

Kelly Han 1:31 P.M.
[172] I've left some important documents on my desk. I need them for my presentation in about half an hour.

Isabella Choi 1:32 P.M.
Hold on. I'll check it out.

William Smith 1:33 P.M.
Wasn't your presentation scheduled on Thursday?

Kelly Han 1:35 P.M.
Yes, it was. But it has been moved forward because the CEO is going on a business trip to South Korea on Thursday.

Isabella Choi 1:36 P.M.
You mean the VIP Sports presentation file?

Kelly Han 1:37 P.M.
Right. Could you get it to me ASAP? I'm in the conference room on the eighth floor.

Isabella Choi 1:39 P.M.
Okay. On my way.

Kelly Han 1:40 P.M.
What a relief! Thanks a lot. I owe you one.

172

★ Han 씨의 문제점

Han 씨의 문제점은 무엇인가?
(A) 그녀는 직장까지 갈 수 있는 교통수단이 없다.
(B) 그녀의 노트북 컴퓨터가 고장이 났다.
(C) 그녀가 서류를 가지고 오지 않았다.
(D) 그녀는 마감시한을 맞추기 어려울 수도 있다.

토익 분석

문자 메시지/인터넷 채팅 지문 상에 등장하는 특정 인물에 관한 정보는 해당 인물의 대화 내용에서 단서를 확인하는 방식으로 문제를 풀이한다.

What is Ms. Han's problem?

(A) She cannot find a ride to work.
(B) She has broken her laptop computer..
(C) She hasn't brought some documents.
(D) She may not be able to meet a deadline.

문제 해설

Han 씨의 문제점은 Hans 씨의 메시지 내용을 통해 파악해야 한다. Han 씨는 오후 1시 31분에 I've left some important documents on my desk. I need them for my presentation in about half an hour라며 발표에 필요한 중요한 서류를 책상 위에 두고 왔음을 밝히고 있다. 따라서 정답은 (C)가 되겠다.

173

At 1:29 P.M., what does Mr. Smith mean when he writes, "I'm still at lunch"?

(A) He can't help Ms. Han.
(B) He will not give a presentation today.
(C) He can't start working right now.
(D) He is currently enjoying his food.

★★★ 화자의 의도

오후 1시 29분에, Smith 씨가 "I'm still at lunch"라고 썼을 때 무엇을 의미할 가능성이 가장 높은가?
(A) 그는 Han 씨를 도울 수 없다.
(B) 그는 오늘 발표를 하지 않는다.
(C) 그는 지금 바로 업무를 시작할 수 없다.
(D) 그는 현재 점심식사를 하고 있다.

토익 분석

특정 표현에 담긴 화자의 의도에 대한 이해하기 위해서는 주어진 특정 표현 전후의 내용 파악이 선행되어야 한다. 난이도가 높아지는 경우에는 전체 지문의 내용을 다 파악해야만 풀 수 있는 경우도 발생한다.

문제 해설

주어진 "I'm still at lunch."라는 말은 여전히 점심식사를 하고 있다는 의미이며 이는 오후 1시 25분에 Han 씨가 I need help라며 도움이 필요하다고 이야기하는 내용에 대한 답변으로 언급되고 있다. 또한 이후 오후 1시 31분에 Han 씨가 I've left some important documents on my desk. I need them for my presentation in about half an hour라며 발표에 필요한 중요한 서류를 책상 위에 두고 왔음을 밝히고 있다. 따라서 Smith 씨가 "I'm still at lunch"라고 말한 부분에는 점심식사 중이라 Han 씨에게 도움을 줄 수 없다는 화자의 의도가 포함되어 있음을 가늠할 수 있으므로 정답은 (A)가 되겠다.

174

What is suggested about Mr. Smith?

(A) He will be giving a presentation on Thursday.
(B) He currently works at VIP Sports Corporation.
(C) He will meet with an important client this afternoon.
(D) He hasn't been informed of the presentation schedule change.

★★★ Smith 씨에 대한 유추

Smith 씨에 대해 유추할 수 있는 것은 무엇인가?
(A) 그는 목요일에 발표를 할 것이다.
(B) 그는 현재 VIP Sports 사에서 근무하고 있다.
(C) 그는 오늘 오후에 중요한 고객과 만날 것이다.
(D) 그는 발표 일정이 변경되었다는 사실을 전달받지 못했다.

토익 분석

문자 메시지/인터넷 채팅 지문 상에 등장하는 특정 인물에 대한 적절한 유추 내용을 파악해야 하는 경우, 선택지에 나온 내용을 먼저 파악한 후 해당 인물의 대화 내용에서 선택지의 내용을 유추할 수 있는 근거가 지문에 제시되는지 여부를 역으로 확인하는 방식으로 문제를 풀이한다. 여기서 유추 근거가 충분하지 않은 경우 해당 인물의 대화 내용의 전후 대화 내용까지 고려하여 풀이하도록 한다.

문제 해설

Smith 씨에 대해 유추할 수 있는 내용을 묻고 있으므로 우선 Smith 씨에 관한 정보를 파악하는 것이 우선이다. 오후 1시 33분에 Smith 씨는 Wasn't your presentation scheduled on Thursday?이라고 이야기하며 Han 씨의 발표가 목요일로 예정되어 있지 않은지 반문하고 있다. 이어서 Han 씨는 오후 1시 35분에 Yes, it was. But it has been moved forward because the CEO is going on a business trip to South Korea on Thursday라며 사장님이 목요일에 한국으로 출장을 가야 해서 발표 일정이 앞당겨졌음을 언급하고 있다. 따라서 이를 통해 Smith 씨는 발표 일정이 변경되었다는 점을 사전에 전달받지 못했음을 알 수 있다. 그러므로 정답은 (D)가 되겠다.

175

What will Ms. Choi most likely do next?

(A) Leave for a business travel
(B) Bring important papers to Ms. Han
(C) Prepare for some research
(D) Send an e-mail to Mr. Smith

★ Choi 씨의 미래 행동

Choi 씨는 이후에 무엇을 할 것인가?
(A) 출장을 간다.
(B) 중요한 서류를 Han 씨에게 가져다 준다.
(C) 연구를 준비한다.
(D) Smith 씨에게 이메일을 보낸다.

토익 분석

채팅 후 취하게 될 행동에 대한 단서는 주로 채팅 종료 직전 두 개의 대화 라인에서 제시된다.

문제 해설

Choi 씨가 채팅 이후에 취하게 될 행동에 대해 묻고 있으므로 Choi 씨의 마지막 메시지와 메시지 전후 내용을 토대로 단서를 파악해야 한다. Choi 씨는 오후 1시 39분에 Okay. On my way라며 곧 Han 씨가 있는 8층 회의실로 갈 것임을 밝히고 있으며 이는 앞서 Han 씨가 오후 1시 37분에 해당 서류를 8층 회의실에 있는 자신에게 최대한 빨리 가져다 줄 것을 요청하고 있다. 따라서 Choi 씨는 곧 Han 씨에게 원하는 서류를 가져다 줄 것임을 알 수 있으므로 정답은 (B)가 되겠다.

Miguel's 멕시코 레스토랑
우리의 20주년을 축하해주세요!

[176] 올해, Miguel's 멕시코 레스토랑이 Phoenix 지역에서의 영업 20주년을 기념합니다. 이를 영광스럽게 생각하고 단골손님들에게 감사를 표하기 위하여, Miguel's 에서는 이번 달 특별 할인행사를 개최합니다!

7월 동안 다음과 같이 명시된 날에 있는 할인행사를 이용하세요!

[177] • 7월 5일 – 전채와 주 요리 50% 할인!
[177] • 7월 10일부터 7월15일까지10달러 이상 구매하시는 분께 나쵸 한 그릇 무료!
• 7월 20일 – 주 요리에는 멕시코 맥주 두 병 무료!
[177] • 7월 30일 – 모든 손님들에게 타코 무료!

또한, 다음과 같은 환상적인 이벤트에 참여할 수 있는 기회를 놓치지 마세요.

[178] • 7월 3일 – "멕시코 모자 주변에서 춤을" – 기타리스트 Fernando Chavez의 라이브 음악
• 7월 8일 – 퀴즈의 밤 – 우승 상품: 멕시코 모자, 티셔츠 외 다수
[179] • 7월 16일 – 전통 의상의 밤 – 멋진 멕시코 의상을 입은 모든 분에게 상품수여
• 7월 21일 – 가라오케 경연대회 – 개인당 10달러 참가비: 1등은 100달러를 받습니다.
• 7월 28일 – 멕시코 문화의 밤 – 멕시코 시인 Maria Osolitos의 낭독

Miguel's 멕시코 레스토랑의 축제에 참여하세요.
140 Main 가 – HB 은행 반대편
www.miguelsmexican.com

어휘 honor 경의를 표하다, 존경을 표하다 loyal customer 단골고객 designate 명시하다 starter 에피타이저, 전채 fancy dress 민족 전통 의상, 무대의상 entry 입장 poet 시인

Miguel's Mexican Restaurant
Help us celebrate our 20th birthday!

[176] This year, Miguel's Mexican Restaurant is celebrating its twentieth year of serving the Phoenix community. To honor this event and to say thank you to all of our loyal customers, Miguel's is hosting a month of special promotions and events!

Take advantage of these great upcoming promotions at designated times throughout July:
[177] July 5 – 50% off all starters and main dishes!
[177] July 10 to July 15 – A free bowl of nachos with any order over $10!
July 20 – Receive two free Mexican beers with any main dish!
[177] July 30 – A free taco for every guest!

In addition, do not miss the chance to take part in these fantastic events:
[178] July 3 - Dance around the Mexican hat – Live music provided by guitarist Fernando Chavez
July 8 – Quiz night – Win great prizes: Mexican hats, T-shirts, and many more
[179] July 16 – Fancy dress evening – Prizes awarded to anyone in a fancy Mexican dress
July 21 – Karaoke contest – $10 entry per person: Winner will receive $100!
July 28 – Mexican culture evening – Readings from Mexican poet Maria Osolitos

Join the fiesta at Miguel's Mexican Restaurant.
140 Main Street – opposite the HB Bank
www.miguelsmexican.com

수신: Miguel Sanchez 〈miguelsanchez@miguelsmexican.com〉
발신: Tony Simpson 〈T.Simpson@yaho.com〉
날짜: 6월 29일
제목: 기념 행사

Miguel 씨께

저와 제 아내는 귀하 레스토랑 기념 축하파티에 관한 광고를 읽었습니다. Miguel's 여러분 축하합니다! 귀하의 레스토랑은 거대한 성공을 이뤘고 사람들이 그곳을 얼마나 좋아하는지 잘 알고 있습니다.

20년 전 레스토랑이 개업한 이래로 저희는 단골이었습니다. 저와 제 아내 Irene은 멕시코 음식을 정말 좋아하고, Miguel 레스토랑은 멕시코 밖에서 최고의 멕시코 음식을 선사한다고 생각합니다. 저희는 당연히 가능한 많은 행사에 참가할 것입니다. [179] 저는 특히 7월 16일에 있을 행사를 정말 기대하고 있습니다. 제일 재미있을 것 같네요!

To: Miguel Sanchez <miguelsanchez@miguelsmexican.com>
From: Tony Simpson <T.Simpson@yaho.com>
Date: June 29
Subject: Anniversary Event

Dear Miguel,

My wife and I read your advertisement for the birthday celebrations at your restaurant. Congratulations to everybody at Miguel's! The restaurant has been a huge success, and I know how much people love it.

We have been regulars at your restaurant ever since it opened twenty years ago. Both my wife Irene and I love Mexican cuisine, and we believe that Miguel's serves the best food outside Mexico. We will definitely try to attend as many events as possible. [179] I am especially looking forward to the one on July 16. It sounds like it will be great fun!

As you may remember,[180] I work for the local newspaper The Phoenix Express. Would it be okay to interview you for the paper sometime this week? I'm sure a picture of you and the article appearing in our publication would increase publicity for the great promotions and events that you are hosting. Please let me know when you are available, and I will stop by the restaurant.

Many thanks. Keep up the good work!

Tony Simpson

기억하실 수도 있겠는데, [180] 저는 지역 신문 The Phoenix Express에서 근무하고 있습니다. 이번 주쯤 신문에 실린 위한 인터뷰를 해도 괜찮을까요? 저는 귀하의 사진과 기사가 게재되면 준비하고 계신 대규모 할인행사와 이벤트에 대한 인지도를 높일 거라 확신합니다. 가능 여부를 말씀해 주시면 식당을 방문하도록 하겠습니다.

감사합니다. 지금처럼 계속 열심히 해주세요!

Tony Simpson

어휘 regular 단골손님 cuisine 요리(법) publication (정기)간행물, 출판물 publicity 평판, 홍보, 선전 stop by ~에 들리다 adjustment 조절, 조정

176

What is the restaurant announcing in the poster?

(A) Changes to its menu
(B) Adjustments to its opening times
(C) Its anniversary celebrations
(D) Its reopening of a restaurant

★★ 포스터의 주제

레스토랑이 포스터에서 언급하는 것은 무엇인가?
(A) 메뉴의 변경사항
(B) 영업 시작 시간 조정
(C) 기념일 맞이 축하 행사
(D) 레스토랑의 재개장

토익 분석

지문의 주제/목적은 단락 구분이 있는 경우 첫 번째 단락 초반 2-3문장에서 제시되는 경우가 대부분이다.

문제 해설

포스터의 첫 번째 단락 This year, Miguel's Mexican Restaurant is celebrating its twentieth year of serving the Phoenix community. To honor this event and to say thank you to all of our loyal customers, Miguel's is hosting a month of special promotions and events!를 통해 식당 20주년을 기념하며 한 달간의 특별 판촉 행사를 개최하는 것을 전달하고자 하는 것이 포스터에서 다루는 주된 내용임을 알 수 있다. 따라서 정답은 (C)가 되겠다.

177

Which of these promotions is NOT being offered in July?

(A) Free tacos
(B) Half-price starters and main dishes
(C) Free dessert
(D) Complimentary bowls of nachos

★ 세부사항

판촉행사 중 7월에 이뤄지는 것이 아닌 것은 무엇인가?
(A) 무료 타코
(B) 전채와 주요리 반 값
(C) 무료 후식
(D) 무료 나쵸

토익 분석

특정 정보가 일목요연하게 정리가 되어 있는 지문의 경우 선택지의 내용과 대조하며 풀이하도록 한다. 포스터에서 구체적인 혜택들이 제시되어 있으므로 이를 단순하게 선택지의 내용과 대조를 하면 수월하게 문제를 풀이할 수 있다.

문제 해설

구체적인 행사 내역에 대해 묻고 있으므로 포스터에 제시된 행사 내역을 살펴봐야 한다. 7월 행사에는 전채와 주요리 반 값, 무료 나쵸, 그리고 무료 타코를 제공하는 행사가 등장하고 있다. 하지만 모든 구매에 따른 무료 디저트 행사는 존재하지 않으므로 정답은 (C)가 적절하다.

178

★ 세부사항

Fernando Chavez가 식당에서 공연하는 날은 언제인가?
(A) 7월 3일
(B) 7월 8일
(C) 7월 16일
(D) 7월 21일

토익 분석

인명은 중요한 키워드이므로 해당 문제처럼 인명이 키워드로 언급되는 문제에서는 해당 인명이 제시되는 부분을 전후하여 단서를 파악하는 것이 효율적이다.

On which date will musician Fernando Chavez perform at the restaurant?

(A) July 3
(B) July 8
(C) July 16
(D) July 21

문제 해설

Fernando Chavez가 식당에서 공연하는 날짜에 대해 묻고 있으므로 포스터에서 Fernando Chavez란 인명이 등장하는 부분에 집중하도록 한다. 7월 이벤트의 목록을 보면 July 3-Dance around the Mexican hat – Live music provided by guitarist Fernando Chavez이라고 하여 7월 3일에 Fernando Chavez의 공연이 있음을 알리고 있다. 그러므로 정답은 (A)이다.

179

★★★ 두 지문 연계문제

이메일에 따르면, Tony Simpson 씨가 가장 기대하는 행사는 무엇인가?
(A) 퀴즈의 밤
(B) 전통 의상의 밤
(C) 음악 경연 대회
(D) 멕시코 문화의 저녁

토익 분석

• 해당 문제의 단서가 나와야 할 지문에서 단서가 불충분하게 제시된다면, 또는 문제에서 정답을 취합하기 위한 두 개의 정보가 서로 다른 지문에 위치하고 있음이 드러나는 경우 이는 두 지문 연계 문제라 할 수 있다.
• 한 지문에서 날짜/시간별 해당 정보가 제시되어 있는 경우 이를 토대로 하는 두 지문 연계 문제는 필히 출제되므로 제시되는 특정 날짜/시간을 두 지문 연계 문제를 풀이할 수 있는 결정적인 연결고리로서 활용하도록 한다.

According to the email, which event is Tony Simpson looking forward to?
(A) The quiz night
(B) The fancy dress evening
(C) The music contest
(D) The Mexican culture evening

문제 해설

Tony Simpson 씨는 이메일의 두 번째 단락 하단에서 I am especially looking forward to the one on July 16이라고 이야기하며 7월 16일에 있을 행사에 대한 기대가 크다는 사실을 직접적으로 밝히고 있다. 아울러 첫 번째 지문인 포스터에서 이벤트에 대한 목록을 살펴보면 July 16 – Fancy dress evening – Prizes awarded to anyone in a fancy Mexican dress이라고 언급하며 7월 16일에는 아름다운 멕시코 의복의 밤이란 이름의 행사가 예정되어 있음을 확인할 수 있다. 따라서 Tony Simpson 씨가 큰 기대를 걸고 있는 것은 바로 이 아름다운 멕시코 의복의 밤이란 행사임을 알 수 있으므로 정답은 (B)가 되겠다.

180

★ 유추

Tony Simpson 씨는 누구일 것 같은가?
(A) 식당 주인
(B) 음악가
(C) 의류 디자이너
(D) 언론인

토익 분석

인물 유추는 인물의 정체를 유추할 수 있는 관련 어휘나 표현을 파악하는 것이 관건이다.

Who most likely is Tony Simpson?

(A) A restaurant owner
(B) A musician
(C) A fashion designer
(D) A journalist

문제 해설

Tony Simpson 씨의 정체에 대한 유추 문제이므로 있으므로 Tony Simpson 씨가 작성한 이메일을 중심으로 Tony Simpson 씨의 정체를 가늠할 수 있을만한 관련 어휘나 표현에 집중해야 한다. Tony Simpson 씨는 이메일의 마지막 단락 초반에서 I work for the local newspaper The Phoenix Express라고 말하며 자신이 신문사에서 근무하고 있음을 밝힌 후 이어서 Would it be okay to interview you for the paper sometime this week?라며 이번 주에 인터뷰가 가능한지 여부를 묻고 있다. 따라서 이를 토대로 그는 지역 언론사에서 일하는 언론인임을 유추할 수 있으므로 정답은 (D)가 되겠다.

Questions 181-185 refer to the following memo and schedule.

To: Faulker and Pennyworth Accounting
From: Dina Wilks, General Manager
Subject: May Painting Plans
Date: April 25
Attachment: Office Packing and Moving Schedule

All Staff:

[181] We are all aware of the interior design changes that will begin in May. Many rooms will need to be emptied in order to accommodate painters, designers, and electricians. [182, 184] Staff members will need to pack up their personal items and office supplies by 6 P.M. the day BEFORE their scheduled move. PLEASE LEAVE YOUR DESKTOP COMPUTERS (the schedule is attached).

Three separate teams will be working simultaneously so that we experience the least amount of lost productivity, so more than one office will be moving at a time. [184] Note that rooms due for work on Monday, May 2 must be packed up and vacated by Friday afternoon, April 30.

Boxes and tape will be provided. Please do not lift a box that you cannot carry yourself —ask for help! Unfortunately for some, sharing offices can be a bit cramped. [185] You can use one of our conference rooms, copy rooms, or the employee lounge to work. Please make sure you have your files and laptops handy. [183] Telecommuting for your assigned moving day will be allowed, but please see your supervisor for permission.

Again, we apologize for the temporary inconvenience this may cause. Just know that when the entire project is complete, we will have a modern and innovative workplace that will facilitate our continued excellence.

Work ScheduleMay 2 to May 6

Monday, May 2 / Tuesday, May 3	Office 502 (Meeting Room) / Room 506 (Stephen Blass & Jarvis Embry)
Wednesday, May 4 / Thursday, May 5	Office 503 (Courtney Goodroad & Cynthia de la Cruz) / Office 507 (Meeting Room)
[184] Friday, May 6	Office 504 (Oliver Tran) / Office 508 (Yejin Hwang & Trisha Wang)

181-185 다음 회람과 일정표를 참조하시오.

수신: Faulker and Pennyworth 회계 법인
발신: Dina Wilks, 총무부장
제목: 5월의 도색 작업 계획
날짜: 4월 25일
첨부: 사무실의 짐 정리 및 이동 일정

전 직원 여러분,

[181] 우리 모두는 5월에 시작될 인테리어 디자인 변경 작업에 대해 알고 있습니다. 도색 작업자와 디자이너, 그리고 전기 기사들이 와서 작업을 할 수 있도록 많은 사무실들이 비어 있는 상태여야 합니다. [182, 184] 직원 여러분께서는 각자 예정된 이전일의 전날 오후 6시까지 개인물품 및 사무용품들을 옮길 수 있도록 해야 합니다. 여러분의 데스크톱 컴퓨터는 그대로 두시기 바랍니다 (관련 일정표 첨부).

생산성 손실을 최소화할 수 있도록 세 개로 분리된 팀들이 동시에 작업할 것이므로 한 번에 하나 이상의 사무실들이 옮겨질 것입니다. [184] 5월 2일, 월요일에 작업 예정인 모든 사무실들은 반드시 4월 30일, 금요일 오후까지 짐을 꾸려 비워야 한다는 점에 유의하시기 바랍니다.

상자와 테이프가 제공될 것입니다. 직접 옮기실 수 없는 상자는 들지 마시고 도움을 요청하십시오! 안타깝게도 일부 직원들께는, 사무실을 공유하는 것이 조금 비좁을 수 있습니다. [185] 우리 대회의실 중 한 곳이나 복사실, 또는 직원 휴게실들을 이용하셔도 됩니다. 여러분의 파일과 노트북 컴퓨터는 반드시 이용하시기 편리한 곳에 두시기 바랍니다. [183] 배정된 이전일에 대한 재택근무가 허용될 예정이지만, 소속 부서장으로부터 허가를 받으시기 바랍니다.

다시 한 번, 이번 작업으로 인해 초래되는 일시적인 불편함에 대해 사과를 드립니다. 모든 작업이 완료되면 우리 회사의 우수성을 지속시켜 줄 현대적이고 혁신적인 근무 환경을 갖게 된다는 점을 알아주시기 바랍니다.

작업 일정 5월 2일부터 6일까지

5월 2일, 월요일 / 5월 3일, 화요일	502호 (회의실) / 506호 (Stephen Blass 씨와 Jarvis Embry)
5월 4일, 수요일 / 5월 5일, 목요일	503호 (Courtney Goodroad 씨와 Cynthia de la Cruz씨) / 507호 (회의실)
[184] 5월 6일, 금요일	504호 (Oliver Tran씨) / 508호 (Yejin Hwang 씨와 Trisha Wang 씨)

어휘 packing 짐 꾸리기 accommodate ~을 수용하다 electrician 전기 기사 pack up (짐 등) ~을 꾸리다 move 이동, 움직임 attached 첨부된 separate 분리된, 별도의 note that ~임에 유의하다 due for ~할 예정인 vacate (건물 등) ~에서 나가다, ~을 비우다 oneself (부사적으로) 직접 cramped 비좁은 handy 이용하기 편한 곳에 있는, 가까운 곳에 있는 telecommuting 재택 근무 assigned 배정된, 할당된 supervisor 상사, 책임자 permission 허가, 허용 temporary 일시적인 inconvenience 불편함 cause ~을 야기하다

181

★★ 회람의 목적

회람이 직원들에게 전송된 이유는 무엇인가?
(A) 일정의 축소를 알리기 위해
(B) 사내 디자인 콘테스트를 알리기 위해
(C) 곧 있을 보수 공사를 전달하기 위해
(D) 컴퓨터 소프트웨어에 대한 최신 추가 사항을 설명하기 위해

토익 분석

회람도 여느 비즈니스 서신처럼 목적성이 뚜렷한 글이므로 회람 초반부에서 주제/목적부터 명확하게 밝히고 난 후 세부적인 내용으로 이어지게 된다. 따라서 회람의 주제/목적은 대부분 첫 번째 단락 초반 2-3문장에서 제시된다.

Why was the memo sent to employees?

(A) To announce cutbacks in schedules
(B) To announce a design contest in the office
(C) To alert them of upcoming renovations
(D) To explain recent additions to computer software

문제 해설

회람을 보낸 이유, 즉 회람의 목적에 대해 묻고 있으므로 회람 초반부에서 관련 정보를 파악해야 한다. 첫 지문 시작 부분에 We are all aware of the interior design changes that will begin in May라며 5월에 시작되는 인테리어 디자인 변경 작업을 언급한 후 이와 관련된 조치 및 일정 등을 공유하는 내용으로 지문이 구성되어 있으므로 회람의 목적은 곧 있을 인테리어 개조 공사에 대한 공지임을 알 수 있다. 따라서 정답은 (C)가 되겠다.

182

★★ 회사의 요청사항

직원들은 무엇을 하도록 지시받는가?
(A) 5월 2일과 6일 사이에 이틀 간의 유급 휴가를 떠난다.
(B) 고객과의 모든 약속에 대한 일정을 재조정하기 위해 연락을 취한다.
(C) 각자의 개인 물품과 용품들을 상자에 담는다.
(D) 온라인으로 각자의 연락처를 갱신한다.

토익 분석

요청/요구 사항을 묻는 문제가 마지막 문제가 아닌 두 번째 문제로 출제되는 경우 이에 대한 단서는 지문의 첫 번째 단락에서 제시된다.

What are employees instructed to do?

(A) Take two days of paid vacation between May 2 and May 6
(B) Call to reschedule any client appointments
(C) Box their own personal items and supplies
(D) Update their contact information online

문제 해설

회사에서 직원에게 요청하는 사항에 대해 묻고 있다. 첫 지문 시작 부분에 The staff members will need to pack up their personal items and office supplies라며 공사 작업과 관련해 직원들에게 개인 물품과 사무용품을 꾸려야 한다고 요청하는 내용이 제시되고 있다. 따라서 (C)가 정답이다.

183

★★★ 세부사항

영향을 받는 직원들은 어떠한 선택이 가능한가?
(A) 재택 근무가 가능하다.
(B) 스케줄을 조정한다.
(C) 추가 주차 공간이 제공될 것이다.
(D) 통근비가 환급된다.

토익 분석

특정 키워드가 없거나 있어도 지문에서 해당 키워드가 어떻게 유사표현으로 패러프레이징이 되었는지 파악하기가 어려운 경우, 또는 해당 키워드에 관한 내용이 지문 전반에 걸쳐 언급되는 상황에서 지문 전체의 내용을 토대로 진위/특정 세부정보를 묻는 문제의 경우, 선택지에 나온 내용을 먼저 파악한 후 선택지의 내용을 간단하게 정리하여 이를 키워드로 삼아 지문에서 해당 내용이 등장하는지 여부를 역으로 신속하게 파악하는 방식으로 문제를 풀이하는 것이 효율적이다. 이 때 선택지를 두 개씩 나눠 두 번에 걸쳐 지문에서의 해당 내용이 언급되고 있는지 여부를 확인하는 방식을 추천한다.
아울러 시간이 부족한 경우, 진위/세부사항/유추 내용을 묻는 문제들은 당연히 우선적으로 건너 뛰어야 할 문제 유형임을 잊지 않도록 한다.

What option is available to the affected employees?

(A) Telecommuting
(B) Schedule adjustment
(C) Additional parking
(D) Commuting fees refund

문제 해설

영향을 받는 직원들에게 선택이 가능한 것이 무엇인지 묻는 문제이므로 영향을 받는 직원이 어떠한 직원인지 파악한 후 지문에서 이들에게 주어진 선택사항에 대한 정보가 제시되는 부분을 빠르게 찾아가야 한다. 회람 초반부에서 We are all aware of the interior design changes that will begin in May라고 이야기하며 곧 있을 내부 인테리어 공사에 대해 공지하고 있다. 이어서 Many rooms will need to be emptied in order to accommodate painters, designers, and electricians라며 공사 기간 동안 작업자들이 작업을 할 수 있도록 사무실을 비워야 한다는 내용이 등장하고 있다. 따라서 이를 통해 영향을 받는 직원들은 작업이 이뤄질 수 있도록 사무실을 비워줘야 하는 직원들임을 알 수 있다. 아울러 첫 번째 지문의 세 번째 단락을 보면, Telecommuting for your assigned moving day will be allowed, but please see your supervisor for permission이라며 배정된 이동일에 재택 근무를 할 수 있으므로 이를 위해 소속 상사와 만나 논의해볼 것을 언급하고 있다. 따라서 (A)가 정답이다.

184

When should Ms. Hwang have her supplies boxed up?

(A) On May 5
(B) On May 6
(C) On May 7
(D) On May 8

★★★ 두 지문 연계 문제

Hwang 씨는 언제 자신의 짐을 꾸려야 하는가?
(A) 5월 5일
(B) 5월 6일
(C) 5월 7일
(D) 5월 8일

문제 해설

이동 작업 일정표인 두 번째 지문에서, Hwang 씨의 이름은 5월 6일 금요일에 쓰여 있다. 그런데 짐을 꾸리는 시점과 관련된 정보가 제시된 첫 번째 지문의 첫 번째 단락을 보면, The staff members will need to pack up their personal items and office supplies by 6 P.M. the day BEFORE their scheduled move라며 예정된 이동일 하루 전에 짐을 싸야 한다는 점을 알리고 있다. 두 번째 단락에서도 직원들에게 이에 대한 이해를 도모시키고자 Note that rooms due for work on Monday, May 2 must be packed up and vacated by Friday afternoon, April 30라며 5월 2일 작업 예정인 사무실에서 근무하는 직원들은 4월 30일 오후까지 짐을 꾸리고 사무실을 비워야 한다는 점을 밝히고 있다. 따라서 5월 6일에 작업이 예정된 사무실에서 근무하는 Hwang 씨는 5월 5일에 짐을 꾸려 사무실을 비워야 한다는 점을 알 수 있으므로 정답은 (A)가 되겠다. 단순히 작업 일정표만 보고 5월 6일을 정답으로 선택하는 경우가 발생할 수도 있다는 점에서 상당히 교묘한 형태의 두 지문 연계 문제라 할 수 있다.

토익 분석

한 지문에서 날짜/시간별 해당 정보가 제시되어 있는 경우 이를 토대로 하는 두 지문 연계 문제는 필히 출제되므로 제시되는 특정 날짜/시간을 두 지문 연계 문제를 풀이할 수 있는 결정적인 연결고리로서 활용하도록 한다.

185

What is suggested about workflow for affected employees?

(A) They can choose where they will be working.
(B) They are not required to leave their offices.
(C) They may not share offices with others.
(D) They must remain in the copy rooms.

★★★ 유추

영향을 받는 직원들의 업무 처리 과정에 관해 유추할 수 있는 것은 무엇인가?
(A) 어디서 일할 지를 결정할 수 있다.
(B) 사무실을 비우도록 요청받지는 않았다.
(C) 다른 사람들과 사무실 공유는 하지 않아도 된다.
(D) 반드시 복사실을 이용해야 한다.

문제 해설

영향을 받는 직원들은 내부 인테리어 공사로 인해 사무실에서 근무를 못하게 된 직원들을 지칭한다. 그러므로 사무실에서 근무하지 못하게 된 직원들이 다른 장소나 외부에서 근무하게 되는 상황에서 업무 처리와 관련된 정보가 제시되는 부분을 토대로 유추할 수 있는 내용을 파악해야 한다. 다른 장소나 외부에서 근무하게 되는 상황에 대해 다루는 부분은 첫 지문의 세 번째 단락이며 이 부분에서 You can use one of our conference rooms, copy rooms, or the employee lounge to work라며 기타 사용가능한 장소를 언급하고 있다. 따라서 장소 선택의 가능성을 유추할 수 있으므로 정답은 (A)가 되겠다.

토익 분석

유추 문제의 키워드가 지문 전반에 걸쳐 언급되고 있거나 키워드의 범위가 너무 넓어 키워드로서의 가치가 반감될 때는 선택지에 나온 내용을 먼저 파악한 후 이를 간단하게 정리하여 키워드로 삼아 선택지의 유추 내용이 가능한 근거가 지문에서 제시되는지 여부를 역으로 신속하게 파악하는 방식으로 문제를 풀이해야 한다.

186-190 다음 기사와 두 이메일을 참조하시오.

Crescent River의 개방 • City Magazine • 4월 호

작년, 시 당국자들은 Crescent River 혁신 프로젝트가 완료되어 강이 일반 대중들에게 공개되었다고 발표했습니다. 이 공개 시점 이후로 줄곧, 강과 그곳의 경치 좋은 산책로는 전국에서 찾아 오는 방문객들로 붐비는 곳이 되어 왔습니다.

그곳을 둘러싸고 있는 번잡한 도시와 [189] 대조되는 Crescent River는 녹색 식물과 많은 휴식 공간들로 가득합니다. 방문객들은(소풍 나온 가족들, 데이트하는 연인들, 놀이하는 아이들, 그리고 휴식 중인 직장인들) 모두 이 강이 제공하는 평온한 환경에 매료된 것처럼 보입니다.

하지만 이 프로젝트에는 몇몇 중요한 문제점들도 있었습니다. 첫째로, [186] 시에서 2억 달러가 넘는 비용이 소요되었습니다. 또한 Crescent River 복구 프로젝트에는 세심한 계획과 18개월이 넘게 지속된 강도 높은 공사를 필요로 했습니다. 이 기간 동안, 통근자들은 극심한 교통량과 늘어난 통근 시간으로 불편함을 겪어야 했습니다.

그 비용과 상관 없이, Crescent River는 많은 사람들로부터 엄청난 성공으로 여겨지고 있습니다. 한때 악취가 나고 더러워서 도시의 수치로 여겨진 이 강은 현재 가장 인기 있는 관광 명소들 중의 하나입니다. 시민들은 다가오는 여름을 고대하고 있는데, 강의 여러 지점에서 공공 수영장들이 개장할 것이기 때문입니다.

City Magazine에서는 독자들께서 Crescent River에서 겪으신 개인적인 경험들을 들어 보고자 합니다. Crescent River와 관련한 여러분만의 이야기를 저희에게 보내 주시면 가장 따뜻한 이야기들을 선정해 다음 호를 통해 공유할 것입니다. [188] 선정되신 분들께서는 상품권도 받게 되실 것입니다.

어휘 official 당국자, 관계자 announce that ~라고 발표하다 transformation 변경, 변형, 탈바꿈 the public 일반 대중 ever since ~한 이후로 계속 scenic 경치 좋은 walkway 산책로, 보도 crowded 붐비는 contrast with ~와 대조되다 bustling 번잡한, 북적대는 surround ~을 둘러싸다 be full of ~로 가득하다 greenery 녹색 식물 plenty of 많은 resting area 휴식 공간 on a break 휴식 중인 seem to do ~한 것처럼 보이다 attracted 매료된, 이끌린 setting 주변 환경 drawback 결점 for starters 가장 먼저, 우선 cost A B A에게 B의 비용이 들게 하다 restoration 복구, 복원 intensive 집중적인 last 지속되다 commuter 통근자 suffer from ~로 고통 받다 traffic volume 교통량 regardless of ~에 상관 없이 consider A B A를 B로 여기다 tremendous 엄청난, 막대한 once 한때 shame ~을 부끄럽게 만들다, 창피하게 하다 attraction 명소, 명물 look forward to ~을 고대하다 heartwarming 마음을 따뜻하게 하는 receive ~을 받다 as well ~도, 또한

Questions 186-190 refer to the following article and e-mails.

Opening of Crescent River • City Magazine • April Edition

Last year, city officials announced that the Crescent River transformation project was finished, and the river was open to the public. Ever since the opening, the river and its scenic walkway have been crowded with visitors from around the country.

[189] Contrasting with the bustling city that surrounds it, the Crescent River is full of greenery and resting areas. The visitors—picnicking families, couples on dates, playing children and workers on breaks — all seem to be attracted to the peaceful setting the river offers.

However, the project had some major drawbacks. For starters, [186] it cost the city over $200 million. Also, the restoration project of Crescent River required careful planning and intensive construction that lasted for over 18 months. During that period, commuters had to deal with high traffic volume and increased commuting time.

Regardless of its costs, the Crescent River is considered a tremendous success by many. The once smelly, dirty river that shamed the city is now one of its most popular tourist attractions. Citizens are now looking forward to the summer as there will be public pools opening in various parts of the river.

City Magazine would like to hear about our readers' personal experiences at Crescent River. Please send us your own Crescent River story, and [188] we will select the most heartwarming stories to be shared in our next edition. Winners will receive gift cards.

발신: carmellafischer@biznet.com
수신: editor@citymagazine.org
날짜: 4월 19일
제목: 제 이야기입니다

편집자께,

제가 어렸을 때, [187(A)] 저는 Crescent River 주변에서 수많은 시간들을 보내곤 했습니다. [187(B)] 제 집이 불과 5분 거리에 있었기 때문에 저는 항상 이 강으로 가서 물에서 놀면서 가재도 잡고 동네 친구들과 많은 시간을 보내곤 했

From: carmellafischer@biznet.com
To: editor@citymagazine.org
Date: April 19
Subject: My story

Dear editor,

When I was young, [187(A)] I would spend countless hours by Crescent River. [187(B)] My home was only five minutes away, so I would always go to the river to play in the water, catch crayfish, and hang out with the neighborhood kids. I got along with one in particular, Charlie. We became dear friends, and we met every single day. [187(C)] When I turned nine, my parents moved to the countryside and I lost touch with him. I didn't know that Crescent River had changed so much over the last twenty years until I returned to the city last year. Last month, I heard that the construction finished, so I decided to visit. As I was strolling along the walkway, someone called my name. I looked back and could not believe my eyes. It was Charlie, just twenty years older than when I last saw him. [189] Now we are engaged. I owe my love story to the Crescent River. I have attached a photo of us now and when we were nine years old.

Carmella Fischer

습니다. 저는 특히 Charlie라는 이름의 한 친구와 잘 어울렸습니다. 저희는 서로에게 소중한 친구가 되었으며, 매일같이 만났습니다. [187 (C)] 제가 9살이 되었을 때, 부모님께서 시골 지역으로 이사하셨기 때문에 저는 그 친구와 연락이 끊겼습니다. 제가 작년에 이 도시로 되돌아 오기 전까지 지난 20년 동안 Crescent River가 이렇게 많이 변했다는 것을 알지 못했습니다. 지난 달에, 저는 공사가 완료되었다는 말을 듣고 찾아가 보기로 결심했습니다. 산책로를 따라 거니는 동안, 누군가가 제 이름을 불렀습니다. 제가 뒤를 돌아 봤을 때 저는 제 눈을 믿을 수가 없었습니다. 바로 Charlie였는데 마지막으로 봤던 때에서 꼭 20년이 지난 모습이었거든요. [189] 현재 저희는 약혼한 상태입니다. 드라마 같은 저의 러브 스토리는 모두 Crescent River 덕분입니다. 현재의 저희 모습과 저희가 9살이었을 때의 사진들 1장씩 첨부해 드렸습니다.

Carmella Fischer

어휘 in one's youth 어렸을 때, 젊었을 때 countless 셀 수 없이 많은 crayfish 가재 hang out with ~와 시간을 보내다 neighborhood 동네, 이웃, 지역 get along with ~와 어울리다 in particular 특히 named ~라는 이름의 dear 소중한, 사랑하는 countryside 시골 지역 lose touch with 연락이 끊기다 return to ~로 되돌아 오다 stroll 거닐다, 산책하다 along (길 등) ~을 따라 look back 뒤돌아 보다 engaged 약혼한 owe A to B A가 B 덕분이다, B에게 A를 빚지고 있다 attach ~을 첨부하다

From: editor@citymagazine.org
To: carmellafischer@biznet.com
Date: April 23
Subject: Congratulations

Dear Carmella Fischer,

Thank you for sending your story to us. I was instantly hooked by it. It is such an incredible love story. I would like to share your tale with all our readers. Would it be alright if I added the two photos as well? I'm sure I can write a very interesting article about strange and wonderful ties, and it will get a lot of attention from our readers in the May issue. [188] Also, can you send me your address so that I can send you your gift card?

Congratulations on your engagement.

Sincerely,
Zack Cruse
Chief Editor

발신: editor@citymagazine.org
수신: carmellafischer@biznet.com
날짜: 4월 23일
제목: 축하합니다

Carmella Fischer 씨께,

귀하의 이야기를 저희에게 보내 주셔서 감사 드립니다. 저는 곧 귀하의 이야기에 빠져 들었습니다. 정말로 믿을 수 없고 꿈 같은 러브 스토리입니다. 저희 모든 독자들과 함께 귀하의 이야기를 공유하고자 합니다. 그 두 장의 사진들도 함께 넣어도 괜찮으신가요? 저는 제가 귀하의 기묘하고도 멋진 인연에 대한 흥미로운 기사를 작성할 자신이 있고, 이 기사는 저희 5월호 잡지에서 우리 독자로부터 많은 주목을 받게 될 겁니다. 또한, [188] 상품권을 받으실 주소를 보내 주시겠습니까?

약혼을 축하합니다.

안녕히 계십시오.
Zack Cruse
편집장

어휘 instantly 즉시, 즉각적으로 hooked 빠져든, 매료된 incredible 믿을 수 없는 share ~을 공유하다 Will it be alright if ~? ~해도 괜찮을까요? ties 인연 receive ~을 받다 contain ~을 포함하다 engagement 약혼

186

★★ 세부사항

기사에서, **Crescent River**에 관해 알 수 있는 내용은 무엇인가?
(A) 아직 일반 대중에게 개방되지 않았다.
(B) 복구 프로젝트에 2억 달러가 들었다.
(C) 공사가 20년 동안 지속되었다.
(D) 현재 공공 수영장이 있다.

토익 분석

특정 키워드가 없거나 있어도 지문에서 해당 키워드가 어떻게 유사표현으로 패러프레이징이 되었는지 파악하기가 어려운 경우, 또는 해당 키워드에 관한 내용이 지문 전반에 걸쳐 언급되는 상황에서 지문 전체의 내용을 토대로 진위/특정 세부정보를 묻는 문제의 경우, 선택지에 나온 내용을 먼저 파악한 후 선택지의 내용을 간단하게 정리하여 이를 키워드로 삼아 지문에서 해당 내용이 등장하는지 여부를 역으로 신속하게 파악하는 방식으로 문제를 풀이하는 것이 효율적이다. 이 때 선택지를 두 개씩 나눠 두 번에 걸쳐 지문에서의 해당 내용이 언급되고 있는지 여부를 확인하는 방식을 추천한다.

In the article, what is indicated about Crescent River?

(A) It is not yet open to the public.
(B) Its restoration project cost $200 million.
(C) Its construction lasted for 20 years.
(D) It currently has public pools.

문제 해설

Crescent River 프로젝트와 관련된 문제점들이 언급되어 있는 첫 지문의 세 번째 단락에서 it cost the city over $200 million라며 2억 달러의 비용이 들어간 사실이 언급되어 있다. 따라서 정답은 (B)가 되겠다.

187

★★★ 유추

Fischer 씨에 관해 암시된 내용이 아닌 것은 무엇인가?
(A) 어린 아이였을 때 강가에서 놀곤 했다.
(B) 강 근처에서 살았었다.
(C) 복구 프로젝트에 관여되어 있었다.
(D) 시골 지역에 살았었다.

토익 분석

특정인에 대한 유추 가능한 내용을 묻는 문제의 경우, 해당 인물의 정보가 언급되고 있는 내용을 파악하면서 이를 토대로 선택지의 내용을 대조하며 유추 가능한 내용이 담긴 선택지를 정답으로 택일하는 방식으로 문제를 풀이하는 방식이 효율적이다.

What is NOT implied about Ms. Fischer?

(A) She used to play by the river as a child.
(B) She used to live near the river.
(C) She was involved in the restoration project.
(D) She used to live in the countryside.

문제 해설

Fischer 씨가 자신의 이야기를 쓴 두 번째 지문에서, 초반부의 I used to spend countless hours by Crescent River 부분과 My home was only five minutes away 부분을 통해 (A)와 (B)의 내용을 확인할 수 있고, 중반부의 When I turned nine, my parents moved to the countryside 부분에서 시골에 살았던 경험이 언급된 (D)도 확인할 수 있다. 하지만 복구 프로젝트에 관여된 것을 보여주는 내용은 애당초 제시된 것이 없기 때문에 (C)가 정답이다.

188

두 지문 연계문제

Fisher 씨가 상품권을 받게 되는 이유는 무엇인가?
(A) 그녀는 Crescent 강 개장에 일조했다.
(B) 그녀는 사진 대회에서 수상했다.
(C) 그녀는 대기업들로부터 많은 광고를 유치했다.
(D) 그녀는 City Magazine에 의해 우수 사연으로 선정되었다.

토익 분석

• 삼중 지문의 두 지문 연계 문제는 대개 두 번째 문제와 네 번째 문제(2-4) 또는 세 번째 문제와 다섯 번째 문제(3-5)로 짝지어 출제되는 경향이 있다.
• 해당 문제의 단서가 나와야 할 지문에서 단서가 불충분하게 제시된다면, 이는 두 지문 연계 문제라 할 수 있다.
• 두 번째 혹은 세 번째 문제가 두 지문 연계 문제인 경우 주로 첫 번째 지문에서 문제풀이에 필요한 단서가 제시되며 네 번째 혹은 다섯 번째 문제가 두 지문 연계 문제인 경우 대개 마지막 세 번째 지문에 문제풀이에 필요한 연결고리로 활용할 수 있는 결정적인 단서가 포함되어 있다.

Why will Ms. Fisher most likely receive a gift certificate?

(A) She helped with the opening of Crescent River.
(B) She won an award at a photo competition.
(C) She attracted many advertisements from large corporations.
(D) She was chosen as a winner of the *City Magazine* contest.

문제 해설

상품권이 키워드인 문제이므로 우선적으로 지문에서 상품권, 즉 gift card나 이와 유사한 어휘가 제시되는 부분을 중심으로 관련 정보부터 파악해야 한다. Fisher 씨가 작성하여 발송한 이메일에서는 상품권에 대한 내용 자체가 언급된 바 없으며, 편집인이 Fisher 씨에게 받은 이메일 종료 직전에 can you send me your address so that I can send you your gift card? 라며 상품권을 발송할 수 있도록 주소를 알려줄 것을 우회적으로 요청하고 있다. 그리고 첫 번째 지문인 기사문 종료 직전 we will select the most heartwarming stories to be shared in our next edition. Winners will receive gift cards라며 Crescent River와 연관된 가장 따뜻한 이야기를 선정하여 상품권을 받게 될 것임을 공지하고 있다. 따라서 이를 취합하면 Fisher 씨의 사연이 City Magazine 사에 의해 선정되어 상품권을 받게 되는 것임을 알 수 있으므로 정답은 (D)가 되겠다.

189

In the article, the word "contrasting" in paragraph 2, line 1, in closest in meaning to

(A) differing
(B) monitoring
(C) comparing
(D) describing

문제 해설

Contrasting 뒤에 이어지는 내용을 보면, 분주한 도시의 모습(bustling city)과 대비되는 Crescent River 지역의 여유로운 모습이 쓰여 있다. 따라서 서로 다르고 대조적인 주변 환경을 설명하기 위해 contrasting이 사용되었다는 것을 알 수 있다. 그러므로 '다른'이라는 의미의 differing, 즉 (A)가 정답이다.

★★ 유사어

기사에서, 2번째 단락의 1번째 줄에 있는 단어 **"contrasting"**과 의미가 가장 가까운 어휘는 무엇인가?
(A) 다른
(B) 관찰하는
(C) 분석하는
(D) 묘사하는

토익 분석

유사어 문제는 해당 어휘가 포함된 문장을 비롯하여 그 전후 문장 내용을 파악한 후 해당 어휘와 유사한 의미를 지닌 어휘를 선택한다. 아울러 이중 지문 및 삼중 지문에서는 두 지문 연계 문제가 아니라 각각의 지문에서 단서가 명확하게 제시되는 문제들을 우선적으로 풀이하는 것이 바람직하므로 유사어 문제를 가장 먼저 풀이하는 것도 하나의 좋은 방법이다.

190

What is suggested about *City Magazine*?

(A) It was involved in the construction of Crescent River.
(B) It published an article on Crescent River one year ago.
(C) Its editor is getting engaged.
(D) It is a monthly magazine

문제 해설

City Magazine에 관해 암시되고 있는 내용에 대해 묻는 문제로 첫 번째 기사문 타이틀을 보면 City Magazine • April Edition이라며 4월호임을 밝히고 있다. 아울러 마지막 편집장의 이메일의 후반부를 보면 it will get a lot of attention from our readers in the May issue이라며 해당 기사는 5월호에서 독자들로부터 많은 관심을 받게 될 것임을 언급하고 있다. 따라서 이 두 가지 정보를 취합하면 City Magazine이 월간 잡지임을 유추할 수 있으므로 정답은 (D)가 되겠다.

★★★ 두 지문 연계문제

City Magazine에 관해 암시되고 있는 내용은 무엇인가?
(A) Crescent River 공사와 연관이 되어 있었다.
(B) 1년 전에 Crescent River에 관한 기사를 실었다.
(C) 편집자가 약혼을 한다.
(D) 월간 잡지이다.

토익 분석

• 유추 문제의 키워드가 혹은 키워드에 관한 내용이 지문 전반에 걸쳐 언급되고 있는 상태에서 적절한 유추 내용을 파악해야 한다면 선택지에 나온 내용을 먼저 파악한 후 선택지의 내용을 유추할 수 있는 근거가 지문에 제시되는지 여부를 역으로 확인하는 방식으로 문제를 풀이한다. 이 때 선택지를 두 개씩 나눠 두 번에 걸쳐 지문에서의 유추 근거가 제시되고 있는지 확인하는 방식을 추천한다

• 두 번째 혹은 세 번째 문제가 두 지문 연계 문제인 경우 주로 첫 번째 지문에서 문제풀이에 필요한 단서가 제시되며 네 번째 혹은 다섯 번째 문제가 두 지문 연계 문제인 경우 대개 마지막 세 번째 지문에 문제풀이에 필요한 연결고리로 활용할 수 있는 결정적인 단서가 포함되어 있다.

191-195 다음 일정표와 이메일, 그리고 편지를 참조하시오.

Austin 현대 미술관
예정된 전시회

날짜	전시회제목	행사설명
5월 7일-10월 5일	The Moon and Sea	뛰어난 이 그림 및 사진 수집품들은 [191] 여러 카리브해 국가들을 포함한 다양한 지역에서 온 작품들로, 여러 세기에 걸쳐 인류에 영향을 미친 달과 바다의 중요성을 묘사합니다.
5월 28일-10월 5일	Furniture is Art	우리는 가구가 도구에 불과하다고 생각하지만, 예술품이 되기에 충분합니다. 이 수집품들은 [191] 유럽 전역의 여러 독특한 골동품과 현대적인 가구들을 보여줍니다.
7월 3일-12월 18일	Dance: Art by Movement	조각품과 그림, 사진, 그리고 디지털 녹화 영상들을 통해, 이 전시회는 [191] 일부 아프리카 국가들의 공연예술을 묘사하고 있습니다.
7월 24일-8월 22일	The Photography of Animals	이 전시회는 [191] 전 세계의 다양한 야생동물을 촬영한 사진들을 모아서 보여줍니다.

입장권에 관한 더 많은 정보가 필요하신 분은, 저희 홈페이지를 방문하시거나 cedlecon@magob.org로 이메일을 보내주시기 바랍니다. [192] 모든 회원들께는 두 장의 무료 입장권을 제공해 드립니다. 회원이 되시려면, 멤버쉽 페이지를 방문하십시오.

어휘 scheduled 예정된 outstanding 뛰어난, 훌륭한 drawing 그림 photograph 사진 various 다양한 region 지역 including ~을 포함해 describe ~을 묘사하다 affect ~에 영향을 미치다 humankind 인류 tool 도구 suitable 적합한 an array of 여럿의, 다양한 antique 골동품 through ~을 통해 sculpture 조각품 feature ~을 특징으로 하다 performing art 공연 예술 fascinating 매혹적인 piece 작품 a variety of 다양한

Questions 191-195 refer to the following schedule, e-mail and letter.

Modern Art Gallery of Austin
Scheduled Exhibitions

Dates	Exhibition Titles	Descriptions
7 May-5 October	*The Moon and Sea*	This outstanding collection of drawings and photographs from various regions, [191] including several Caribbean nations, how the moon and the sea have inspired humankind for many centuries.
28 May-5 October	*Furniture is Art*	We think that furniture is just functional, but it is also artful. This collection shows an array of distinctive antiques and modern furniture [191] from across Europe.
3 July-18 December	*Dance: Art by Movement*	Through sculpture, paintings, photographs, and digital recordings, this exhibition portrays performing arts [191] from several African countries. .
24 July-22 August	*The Photography of Animals*	This exhibition is a collection of fascinating photographs of a variety of wild animals [191] in the world.

For more information about tickets, visit our Web site or send an e-mail to cedlecon@magob.org. [192] We will provide two free tickets to all members. To become a member, visit the membership page.

발신: Molly Hudson⟨mhudson@mason.inet⟩
수신: Sharon De Leon⟨Sharondl@maga.org⟩
제목: 입장권
날짜: 5월 1일

[192] 저는 Dance: Art by Movement 전시회에 대한 무료 입장권을 소유하고 있지만, 두 장의 입장권을 더 구입하고자 합니다. 제 신용카드 정보가 귀사의 데이터 베이스에 있으리라 생각합니다. 따라서, 제 신용카드로 비용을 처리하시고 우편으로 입장권을 보내주시겠습니까? [193] 저는 Furniture is Art를 관람하고 싶습니다. 이 멋진 전시회를 열어주신 것에 대해 감사드립니다.

Molly Hudson

어휘 complimentary 무료의 make a payment 비용을 지불하다 via ~을 통해 gorgeous 아주 멋진, 아주 좋은 exhibit 전시(회)

From: Molly Hudson<mhudson@mason.inet>
To: Sharon De Leon<Sharondl@maga.org>
Subject: Tickets
Date: May 1

[192] I have complimentary tickets for the *Dance:Art by Movement* exhibition, but I wish to purchase two more tickets. I'm sure my credit card information is in your database. So, could you make a payment with my credit card and send the tickets via mail? [193] I'd like to see *Furniture is Art,* although I'd be happy to see any of the others. Thank you for these gorgeous exhibits.

Molly Hudson

3 May

Molly Hudson
P.O Box N-123
NASSAU N.P

Dear Ms. Hudson,

Thank you for being as a patron of the Modern Art Gallery of Austin. [194] I regret to inform you that the exhibition you requested has been cancelled and replaced with *Indigenous Cultures of the Americas*.
I have enclosed the two additional tickets you paid for. These may be used for this new exhibit, which will [193] run in our gallery until 18 December. [195] Your JPax credit card has been charged $24.

Sincerely,
Sharon De Leon
Modern Art Gallery of Austin
Enclosures

5월 3일

Molly Hudson
우편 사물함 N-123
NASSAU N.P

Hudson 씨께,

Modern Art Gallery of Austin의 후원회원이 되어 주신 점에 대해 감사드립니다. [194] 귀하께서 기다리신 전시회가 취소되어 Indigenous Cultures of the Americas로 변경되었음을 알려드리게 되어 유감으로 생각합니다. 귀하께서 구매하신 두 장의 추가 입장권을 동봉해서 드렸습니다. 이는 새로운 전시회에 사용하실 수 있으며 12월 18일까지 저희 갤러리에서 [193] 진행될 예정입니다. [195] 귀하의 JPax 신용카드로 24달러의 비용이 청구되었습니다.

안녕히 계십시오.

Sharon De Leon
Austin현대 미술관
첨부

어휘 patron 고객, 손님, 후원자 regret to do ~해서 유감이다 inform A that A에게 ~라고 알리다 cancel ~을 취소하다 enclose ~을 동봉하다 additional 추가의 substitute ~을 대체하다 traveling 순회하는 charge A B A에게 B를 청구하다, 부과하다

191

According to the Web site, what do all of the exhibitions have in common?

(A) They include photographs.
(B) They include live performances.
(C) They feature works by artists from the Caribbean.
(D) They feature works from multiple countries.

문제 해설

모든 전시회의 공통점에 대해 묻는 세부사항 유형의 문제이다. 첫 번째 지문의 각 전시회 설명을 보면, from various regions, including several Caribbean nations, from across Europe, from several African countries, in the world와 같은 표현을 통해 다양한 국가에서 온 작품들이 전시된다는 것을 알 수 있다. 따라서 이와 같은 특징을 언급한 (D)가 정답이다.

★★ 세부사항

홈페이지에 따르면, 모든 전시회는 어떠한 공통점을 지니고 있는가?
(A) 사진들을 포함한다.
(B) 실황 공연을 포함한다.
(C) 카리브해 지역 출신 작가들의 작품을 특징으로 한다.
(D) 다양한 국가에서 온 작품들을 특징으로 한다.

토익 분석

특정 키워드가 없거나 있어도 해당 키워드에 관한 내용이 지문 전반에 걸쳐 언급되는 상황에서 지문 전체의 내용을 토대로 진위/특정 세부정보를 묻는 문제의 경우, 선택지에 나온 내용을 먼저 파악한 후 선택지의 내용을 간단하게 정리하여 이를 키워드로 삼아 지문에서 해당 내용이 등장하는지 여부를 역으로 신속하게 파악하는 방식으로 문제를 풀이하는 것이 효율적이다. 이 때 선택지를 두 개씩 나눠 두 번에 걸쳐 지문에서 해당 내용이 언급되고 있는지 여부를 확인하는 방식을 추천한다.

192

What is implied about Ms. Hudson?

(A) She is requesting a refund.
(B) She has a membership to the museum.
(C) She is a contemporary artist.
(D) She has already seen all of the exhibits.

문제 해설

첫 지문의 마지막에서 We will provide two free tickets to all members라며 회원들에게는 두 장의 무료 입장권을 제공한다는 사실을 언급하고 있다. 아울러 Hudson 씨가 쓴 이메일인 두 번째 지문 시작 부분에서 I have the complimentary tickets라며 무료 입장권을 갖고 있다는 점을 다루고 있다. 따라서 이를 통해 Hudson 씨는 박물관 회원임을 알 수 있다. 따라서 (B)가 정답이다.

★★★ 유추 / 두 지문 연계문제

Hudson 씨에 관해 암시하고 있는 내용은 무엇인가?
(A) 환불을 요청하고 있다.
(B) 해당 박물관의 멤버십이 있다.
(C) 현대 미술가이다.
(D) 이미 전시회들을 관람했다.

토익 분석

• 삼중 지문에 따른 문제에서 특정 대상/인물에 대한 세부정보를 묻거나, probably, most likely, imply, suggest를 대동하는 유추 문제는 두 지문 연계 문제일 가능성이 매우 높다.
• 해당 문제는 Hudson 씨가 작성한 이메일에서 제시된 내용만으로는 문제를 풀이할 수 있는 충분한 단서가 제시되지 않고 있으므로 두 지문 연계 문제라 할 수 있다.

193

★★★ 유사어

편지에서, 1번째 단락 4번째 줄의 단어 "run"과 의미가 가장 가까운 어휘는 무엇인가?

(A) 지속되다　　　　(B) 관리하다
(C) 이동하다　　　　(D) 덮다

토익 분석

유사어 문제는 해당 어휘가 포함된 문장을 비롯하여 그 전후 문장 내용을 파악한 후 해당 어휘와 유사한 의미를 지닌 어휘를 선택한다. 아울러 이중 지문 및 삼중 지문에서는 두 지문 연계 문제가 아니라 각각의 지문에서 단서가 명확하게 제시되는 문제들을 우선적으로 풀이하는 것이 바람직하므로 유사어 문제를 가장 먼저 풀이하는 것도 하나의 좋은 방법이다.

In the letter, the word "run" in paragraph 1, line 5, is closest in meaning to

(A) last　　　　　(B) manage
(C) move　　　　　(D) cover

문제 해설

주어진 문장 which will run in our gallery until 18 December에서 동사 run은 행사 등이 진행된다는 것을 뜻하므로 주어진 문장은 해당 전시회는 12월 18일까지 계속 전시회가 진행된다는 의미를 지니게 된다. 따라서 run의 유사어로는 '지속되다'란 뜻을 지닌 last가 적합하기 때문에 정답은 (A)가 되겠다.

194

★★★ 두 지문 연계문제

취소된 전시회는 무엇인가?

(A) Moon and Sea
(B) Furniture is Art
(C) Dance : art in movement
(D) The Photography of Animals

토익 분석

- 삼중 지문의 두 지문 연계 문제는 대개 두 번째 문제와 네 번째 문제(2-4) 또는 세 번째 문제와 다섯 번째 문제(3-5)로 짝지어 출제되는 경향이 있다
- 해당 문제의 단서가 나와야 할 지문에서 단서가 불충분하게 제시된다면, 또는 문제에서 정답을 취합하기 위한 두 개의 정보가 서로 다른 지문에 위치하고 있음이 드러나는 경우 이는 두 지문 연계 문제라 할 수 있다. 해당 문제도 전시회 이름과 함께 전시회가 소개되는 내용이 제시되는 부분에선 취소 여부를 알 수 없으므로 이는 두 지문 연계 문제임을 바로 파악할 수 있다.
- 두 번째 혹은 세 번째 문제가 두 지문 연계 문제인 경우 주로 첫 번째 지문에서 문제풀이에 필요한 단서가 제시되며 네 번째 혹은 다섯 번째 문제가 두 지문 연계 문제인 경우 대개 마지막 세 번째 지문에 문제풀이에 필요한 연결고리로 활용할 수 있는 결정적인 단서가 포함되어 있다

Which exhibit has been cancelled?

(A) Moon and Sea
(B) Furniture is Art
(C) Dance: Art in Movement
(D) The Photography of Animals

문제 해설

취소된 행사 정보는 Hudson 씨에게 보내는 이메일인 세 번째 지문에서 등장하고 있으며 I regret to inform you that the exhibition you requested has been cancelled and replaced with *Indigenous Cultures of the Americas*라며 Hudson씨가 기다려 온 전시회가 취소되었음을 언급하고 있다. 또한 두 번째 지문에서 Hudson 씨는 I'd like to see *Furniture is Art*라며 Furniture is Art의 관람을 기다려 왔다고 왔음을 알리고 있다. 따라서 두 가지 정보를 취합하면 Hudson 씨가 고대하던 *Furniture is Art*란 전시회가 취소되었음을 알 수 있으므로 정답은 (B)가 되겠다.

★★ 세부사항

De Leon 씨는 Hudson 씨를 위해 무엇을 했는가?
(A) 다가오는 행사의 목록을 우송했다.
(B) 전시회 날짜를 변경했다.
(C) 멤버십 가입 비용을 제해 주었다.
(D) 신용카드에 비용을 청구했다.

토익 분석

- 이중 지문/삼중 지문의 마지막 문제는 주로 마지막 세 번째 지문에서 단서가 제시된다.
- 특정 인물에 관련된 세부사항에 대해 묻는 경우 해당 인물이 작성한 지문을 중심으로 단서를 파악하는 것이 바람직하며 이 때 단서가 불충분하면 이는 두 지문 연계 문제라 할 수 있다. 특히 마지막 문제가 요청/요구/제안/권고 내용을 묻거나 다른 사람을 위해 무엇을 했는지 묻는 문제의 경우 해당 지문의 마지막 단락에서 단서를 파악하는 것이 효율적이다.

What did Ms. De Leon do for Ms. Hudson?

(A) Mailed a list of upcoming events
(B) Changed the date of an exhibition
(C) Waived a membership fee
(D) Charged her credit card

문제 해설

세 번째 지문의 마지막 부분에서 Your JPax credit card has been charged $24라며 De Leon 씨는 수신인인 Hudson 씨의 JPax 신용카드로 24달러의 비용이 청구되었음을 알리고 있다. 그러므로 정답은 (D)가 되겠다.

Question 196-200 refer to the following e-mails and the attachment.

To: Mary Benson; Ramina Taylor; James Porter
From: Tim Rolland
Date: June 12, 7:54 A.M.
Subject: Office Space
Attachment: Properties

Hi all,

[198] I thoroughly enjoyed our luncheon at Manke Grill last Monday. As an AHG Consultants employee, I am excited to be a part of the first branch in Alamo. [196] I look forward to giving advice to clients in Alamo about using information technology to help them with their startups.

I would appreciate it if you could give me your opinions about the type of office space that would be suitable. I have explored syeogain.ca to find well-conditioned ones that can fit our basic criteria and budget and have summarized the information to make a short list. Please read the attached document and let me know your opinion.

Tim Rolland
AHG Consultants

3874 Thunderland Hilltop

Open concept office/retail space in a well-developed rural area of Alamo with a lot of pedestrians. The building has a remarkable appearance and enough space for a signboard for your company use. High energy-efficient heating system will keep your winter expenditure low.

Monthly lease: $1,000

29485 Clearance Path

First-floor office. Elegantly decorated. Surrounded on-site parking with security fence. Located near Union Park, in the vicinity of the train station, 30 minutes from downtown. [197] Union Park's path is very popular with exercisers. Vodafone phone system is already installed for your use.

Monthly lease: $950

4991 Commercial Park Lot

Non-communal, one-story building. Equipped with furniture made by famous designers. Safe parking lot near the street and a discount for renters. Fast Internet access can be installed. Located west of the city, in the suburbs.

Monthly lease: $875

196-200 다음 두 이메일과 첨부 문서를 참조하시오.

수신: Mary Benson; Ramina Taylor; James Porter
발신: Tim Rolland
날짜: 6월 12일, 오후7:54
제목: 사무실공간
첨부: 건물들

안녕하세요, 여러분,

[198] 저는 지난 월요일에 Manke Grill에서 있었던 오찬이 대단히 즐거웠습니다. AHG Consultants의 직원으로서, 저는 우리 회사가 Alamo 지역에 개장한 첫 지사의 일원이 되어 기쁩니다. [196] 저는 Alamo에 있는 고객님들이 설립한 신생 기업의 경영에 도움을 줄 수 있는 정보 기술 활용에 대한 조언을 드리길 고대하고 있습니다.

여러분께서 적합할 것 같은 타입의 사무용 공간에 관한 의견을 제게 알려주시면 감사하겠습니다. 저는 우리의 기본 조건과 예산에 맞는 좋은 조건의 사무공간을 찾기 위해 Syeogain.ca를 검색했으며, 사무실에 대한 정보를 요약하여 간단히 최종 목록으로 작성했습니다. 첨부해드린 문서를 읽어보시고 제게 여러분의 의견을 알려주시기 바랍니다.

Tim Rolland,
AHG Consultants

어휘 thoroughly 완전하게, 철저하게, 철두철미하게 be excited to do ~해서 흥분되다, 들뜨다 branch 지사, 지점 effort 노력 give advice 조언하다 appreciate ~에 대해 감사하다 opinion 의견 suitable 적합한, 알맞은 explore ~을 검색하다, 둘러 보다 well-conditioned 좋은 조건의 fit ~에 적합하다, 알맞다 criteria 기준 budget 예산 attached 첨부된

3874 Thunderland Hilltop

보행자들이 많고 잘 개발된 시골 지역인 Alamo에 위치한 개방된 개념의 사무실/소매점 공간. 건물은 멋진 외관과 함께 회사가 사용할 수 있는 충분한 공간을 지니고 있음. 뛰어난 에너지 효율성을 지닌 난방시스템이 매년 지출 비용을 감소시켜줄 것.

월 임대료: 1,000달러

29485 Clearance Path

1층 사무실. 고급스럽게 장식되어있음. 보안용 담장으로 둘러싸인 구내 주차장. Union 공원 인근에 위치해있으며, 근처에 기차 역이 있고, 시내에서 30분 거리임. [197] Union 공원의 보행로는 운동하는 사람들에게 인기가 높음. Vodafone 전화 시스템 이용 가능.

월 임대료: 950달러

4991 Commercial Park Lot

공용이 아닌 단층 건물. 유명 디자이너들이 제작한 가구 구비. 거리 근처에 안전한 주차장이 있으며 세입자들에게는 주차비 할인 혜택 제공. 고속 인터넷 서비스 설치 가능. 도심 서쪽 지역, 외곽 지역에 위치함.

월 임대료: 875달러

[200] 1432 Timothy Street

4층에 위치한 사무실. 보안 시스템과 경비 직원이 포함한 지붕이 설치된 주차공간. [200] Alamo의 도심에 위치. 컬러 복사기 / 스캐너 / 프린터 / 팩스기와 같은 사무용 장비가 사용 가능. 최신 기술을 활용하여 보수된 화상 회의의 스튜디오와 무료 고속 무선 인터넷 구비.

월 임대로: 1,000달러

어휘 retail 소매 well-developed 잘 개발된 rural 시골의 pedestrian 보행자 remarkable 놀랄 만한 appearance 외관, 모습 signboard 간판 high energy-efficient 에너지 효율이 뛰어난 reduce ~을 감소시키다 expenditure 지출 비용 lease 임대(료) decorated 장식된 surrounded 둘러싸인 on-site 구내의, 현장의 parking 주차 (공간) located near ~ 근처에 위치한 in the vicinity of ~ 인근의 path 보행로, 산책로 popular with ~에게 인기 있는 exerciser 운동하는 사람 install ~을 설치하다 communal 공용의 equipped with ~가 갖춰진 renter 세입자, 임차인 access 이용, 접근 depending on ~에 따라, ~에 달려 있는 choice 선택 shopping district 쇼핑 구역 covered 지붕으로 덮인 garage 주차장 commercial zone 상업 지구 equipment 장비 video conferencing 화상 회의 renovated 개조된, 보수된 free 무료의

수신: Mary Benson; Tim Rolland; [199] Ramina Taylor
발신: James Porter
날짜: 6월 15일, 오후 4:39
제목: 회신: 사무실 공간

여러분께,

선택 범위를 좁혀 주셔서 감사합니다, Tim. [198] 지난 월요일의 회의가 매우 잘 진행되었다고 들었습니다. 저도 그곳에 있었다면 기뻤겠지만, Toronto로 출장을 가는 바람에 참석할 수가 없었습니다. 제 생각에 제가 이메일을 통해 의견을 전달해드리는 마지막 직원인 것 같습니다. 기다려 주신 점에 감사드립니다.

[199, 200] Ramina 씨, 저는 넓은 공간이 있는 사무실이 마음에 들지만, 시내 한복판에 위치하는 것이 더 바람직하다고 생각합니다. Alamo지역의 대중 교통 시스템을 잘 아시는 분이 계신가요? 우리가 통근을 위해 대중 교통을 이용해야 한다면 알아두는 것이 도움이 될 겁니다.

저는 또한 우리가 Alamo에서 열리는 기술 박람회에 참석해야 한다는 Tim 씨의 의견에 동의합니다. 다음 주말에 제가 머무를 집들을 살펴볼 겸 Alamo에서 열리는 기술 박람회를 방문할 예정입니다. 또한, 우리 AHG Consultants에서 근무한 적이 있었던 Alamo의 대표자와 함께 점심식사를 할 예정입니다. 전해드릴 소식이 생길 경우 여러분께 알려드리겠습니다.

James Porter
AHG Consultants

어휘 narrow down (선택 범위 등) ~을 좁히다 go well 잘 진행되다 provide ~을 제공하다 comment 의견 through ~을 통해 patience 인내, 참을성 would be better to ~하는 편이 낫다 be located ~에 위치하다 in the middle of ~의 중간에 위치하다 be familiar with ~을 잘 알다, ~에 익숙하다 public transit 대중 교통 helpful 도움이 되는 commute 통근하다 agree with ~에 동의하다 delegate 대표자 used to do (과거의 한 때) ~하곤 했다

---

[200] 1432 Timothy Street

Fourth-floor office suite. Covered garage for vehicles with security system and guards. [200] Located right in the heart of Alamo. Business equipment, including a color copier, a scanner, a printer and a fax machine ready for use. A video conferencing studio renovated with the latest technology and free high-speed wireless Internet.

Monthly lease: $1,000

To: Mary Benson; Tim Rolland; [199] Ramina Taylor
From: James Porter
Date: June 15, 4:39 P.M.
Subject: Re: Office Space

Dear all,

Thank you Tim for narrowing down the options for us. [198] I heard last Monday's meeting went very well. I would have loved to be there, but my trip to Toronto made it impossible. It looks like I am the latest person to provide comments through e-mail. Thank you for your patience.

[199, 200] Ramina, I like the office with a lot of space, but I feel it'd be better to be located in the middle of downtown. Is anyone familiar with Alamo public transit systems? It would be helpful to know if we will be using them to commute.

I also agree with Tim's opinion that we should attend the technology fair in Alamo. I'm going to visit it next weekend while I look at housing options. Also, I will be having lunch with an Alamo delegate who used to work for AHG Consultants. I will let you know when I have any news.

James Porter
AHG Consultants

196

Who most likely is Mr. Rolland?

(A) A technology expert
(B) A small business owner
(C) A conference organizer
(D) A real estate agent

★★ 유추

Rolland 씨는 누구일 것 같은가?
(A) 기술 전문가
(B) 중소 기업 소유주
(C) 회의 주최자
(D) 부동산 중개업체 직원

토익 분석

인물 유추는 인물의 정체를 유추할 수 있는 관련 어휘나 표현을 파악하는 것이 관건이다.

문제 해설

Rolland 씨의 정체를 묻는 문제이므로 Rolland 씨가 작성한 이메일에서 그의 정체를 유추할 수 있을만한 관련 어휘나 표현을 파악해야 한다. 첫 번째 지문인 이메일 첫 단락에서 Rolland 씨는 I look forward to giving advice to clients in Alamo about using information technology to help them with their startups 이라며 Alamo에 있는 고객님들이 설립한 신생 기업의 경영에 도움을 줄 수 있는 정보 기술 활용에 대해 조언할 수 있길 바란다고 이야기하고 있다. 따라서 Rolland 씨는 기술과 관련된 조언을 해 주는 일을 하는 사람임을 유추할 수 있으므로 정답은 (A)가 되겠다.

197

What is one property feature mentioned in the attachment?

(A) A break room for employees
(B) A popular fitness club
(C) An electricity bill paid by its owner
(D) A location close to exercise trail

★★ 세부사항

첨부 문서에서 언급된 한 건물의 특징은 무엇인가?
(A) 직원들을 위한 휴게실
(B) 인기 헬스 클럽
(C) 소유주에 의해 지불되는 전기세
(D) 운동에 적합한 공원로와 가까운 위치

토익 분석

특정 키워드가 없거나 있어도 지문에서 해당 키워드가 어떻게 유사표현으로 패러프레이징이 되었는지 파악하기가 어려운 경우, 또는 해당 키워드에 관한 내용이 지문 전반에 걸쳐 언급되는 상황에서 지문 전체의 내용을 토대로 진위/특정 세부정보를 묻는 문제의 경우, 선택지에 나온 내용을 먼저 파악한 후 선택지의 내용을 간단하게 정리하여 이를 키워드로 삼아 지문에서 해당 내용이 등장하는지 여부를 역으로 신속하게 파악하는 방식으로 문제를 풀이하는 것이 효율적이다. 이 때 선택지를 두 개씩 나눠 두 번에 걸쳐 지문에서의 해당 내용이 언급되고 있는지 여부를 확인하는 방식을 추천한다.

문제 해설

두 번째 지문의 두 번째 단락에서 Union Park's path is very popular with exercisers라며 Union Park의 보행로가 운동하는 사람들에게 매우 인기가 높다는 점을 전달하고 있다. 따라서 운동하기에 적합한 공원 보행로와 가까운 곳에 위치하고 있다는 점은 첨부 문서에 언급된 한 건물의 특징임을 파악할 수 있으므로 정답은 (D)가 되겠다.

198

What is suggested about Mr. Porter?

(A) He missed the gathering at Manke Grill.
(B) He is currently living in Alamo.
(C) He plans to attend a performance.
(D) He prefers not to use public transportation.

★★★ 두 지문 연계문제

Porter 씨에 관해 알 수 있는 것은 무엇인가?
(A) Manke Grill에서의 모임에 불참했다.
(B) 그는 현재 Alamo에서 거주하고 있다.
(C) 공연에 참석할 계획이다.
(D) 그는 대중 교통의 이용을 선호하지 않는다.

토익 분석

삼중 지문에 따른 문제에서 특정 대상/인물에 대한 세부 정보를 묻는 경우 두 지문 연계 문제일 가능성이 매우 높다.

문제 해설

마지막 지문인 Porter 씨의 이메일 첫 단락에서 I would have loved to be there, but my trip to Toronto made it impossible 이라며 월요일에 있었던 회의에 자신도 참석했었으면 좋았겠지만 토론토로 출장을 가는 바람에 궁극적으론 회의에 불참했음을 언급하고 있다. 그런데 Rolland 씨가 작성한 첫 번째 이메일의 초반 our luncheon at Manke Grill last Monday를 통해 월요일에 있었던 모임이 Manke Grill에서 열렸음을 알 수 있다. 그러므로 이 두 가지 정보를 취합하면 Porter 씨는 Manke Grill에서 열린 모임에 참석하지 못했음을 유추할 수 있으므로 정답은 (A)가 되겠다.

★★ 유추

Taylor 씨에 관해 가장 사실일 것 같은 내용은 무엇인가?
(A) 막 새로운 집으로 이사했다.
(B) 이전 고객을 만날 것이다.
(C) 자신의 동료 직원들에게 이메일을 보냈다.
(D) 과거에 Alamo에 거주한 적이 있었다.

토익 분석

특정인에 대한 유추 가능한 내용을 묻는 문제의 경우, 해당 인물과 관련된 정보가 언급되고 있는 내용을 파악한 후 이를 토대로 선택지의 내용을 대조하며 유추 가능한 내용이 담긴 선택지를 정답으로 택일하는 방식으로 문제를 풀이하는 방식이 효율적이다.

What most likely is true about Ms. Taylor?

(A) She just relocated to a new home.
(B) She will meet her former client.
(C) She sent an e-mail to her colleagues.
(D) She used to live in Alamo.

문제 해설

Porter 씨가 작성한 세 번째 지문인 이메일 중반부에서 Ramina, I like the office with a lot of space, but I feel it'd be better to be located in the middle of downtown이라며 Porter 씨는 Ramina 씨에게 넓은 공간이 있는 사무실이 마음에 들지만, 사무실은 시내 한복판에 위치하는 것이 바람직하다는 자신만의 의견을 제시하고 있다. 이를 통해 발신인인 Porter씨는 넓은 사무실을 선호하는 Ramina 씨와는 다른 의견을 피력하고 있는 상황이며 또한 이메일 수신인 명단을 통해 다른 동료 직원들과 각자의 의견을 서로 주고 받으며 공유했음을 유추할 수 있다. 그러므로 정답은 (C)가 되겠다.

200

★★★ 유추 / 두 지문 연계문제

Porter 씨는 어느 건물을 좋아할 것 같은가??
(A) 3874 Thunderland Hilltop
(B) 29485 Clearance Path
(C) 4991 Commercial Park Lot
(D) 1432 Timothy Street

토익 분석

• 두 번째 문제에서 네 번째 문제까지가 주로 두 지문 연계 문제가 출제되는 부분이다. 따라서 이 부분에서 해당 문제의 단서가 나와야 할 지문에 단서가 불충분하게 제시된다면 이는 두 지문 연계 문제라 할 수 있다.
• 삼중 지문의 두 지문 연계 문제는 대개 두 번째 문제와 네 번째 문제(2-4) 또는 세 번째 문제와 다섯 번째 문제(3-5)로 짝지어 출제되는 경향이 있다.

Which property does Mr. Porter most likely favor?

(A) 3874 Thunderland Hilltop
(B) 29485 Clearance Path
(C) 4991 Commercial Park Lot
(D) 1432 Timothy Street

문제 해설

건물 주소가 제시된 사무실 소개 내역은 두 번째 지문이지만 Porter 씨는 세 번째 지문인 이메일을 작성했다. 그러므로 이 문제는 두 지문 연계 문제임을 가늠할 수 있다. Porter 씨는 세 번째 지문인 이메일의 중간 단락에서 I like the office with a lot of space, but I feel it'd be better to be located in the middle of downtown이라며 사무실은 시내 한복판에 위치하는 것이 바람직하다는 자신의 의견을 제시하고 있다. 사무실의 특징이 소개되고 있는 두 번째 지문에서 도심에 위치한 사무실은 Located right in the heart of Alamo라고 소개되고 있는 1432 Timothy 가에 위치하고 있는 사무실임을 알 수 있다. 그러므로 정답은 (D)가 되겠다.

Answer Sheet

TOEIC Actual Test

응시일자 :

성명 / 한글 / 한자 / 영문

Listening Comprehension

Reading Comprehension

Answer Sheet

TOEIC Actual Test

응시일자 :

성명	한글	
	한자	
	영문	

Listening Comprehension

No.	ANSWER A B C D	No.	ANSWER A B C D	No.	ANSWER A B C D	No.	ANSWER A B C D	No.	ANSWER A B C D
1	a b c d	21	a b c d	41	a b c d	61	a b c d	81	a b c d
2	a b c d	22	a b c d	42	a b c d	62	a b c d	82	a b c d
3	a b c d	23	a b c d	43	a b c d	63	a b c d	83	a b c d
4	a b c d	24	a b c d	44	a b c d	64	a b c d	84	a b c d
5	a b c d	25	a b c d	45	a b c d	65	a b c d	85	a b c d
6	a b c d	26	a b c d	46	a b c d	66	a b c d	86	a b c d
7	a b c d	27	a b c d	47	a b c d	67	a b c d	87	a b c d
8	a b c d	28	a b c d	48	a b c d	68	a b c d	88	a b c d
9	a b c d	29	a b c d	49	a b c d	69	a b c d	89	a b c d
10	a b c d	30	a b c d	50	a b c d	70	a b c d	90	a b c d
11	a b c d	31	a b c d	51	a b c d	71	a b c d	91	a b c d
12	a b c d	32	a b c d	52	a b c d	72	a b c d	92	a b c d
13	a b c d	33	a b c d	53	a b c d	73	a b c d	93	a b c d
14	a b c d	34	a b c d	54	a b c d	74	a b c d	94	a b c d
15	a b c d	35	a b c d	55	a b c d	75	a b c d	95	a b c d
16	a b c d	36	a b c d	56	a b c d	76	a b c d	96	a b c d
17	a b c d	37	a b c d	57	a b c d	77	a b c d	97	a b c d
18	a b c d	38	a b c d	58	a b c d	78	a b c d	98	a b c d
19	a b c d	39	a b c d	59	a b c d	79	a b c d	99	a b c d
20	a b c d	40	a b c d	60	a b c d	80	a b c d	100	a b c d

Reading Comprehension

No.	ANSWER A B C D	No.	ANSWER A B C D	No.	ANSWER A B C D	No.	ANSWER A B C D	No.	ANSWER A B C D
101	a b c d	121	a b c d	141	a b c d	161	a b c d	181	a b c d
102	a b c d	122	a b c d	142	a b c d	162	a b c d	182	a b c d
103	a b c d	123	a b c d	143	a b c d	163	a b c d	183	a b c d
104	a b c d	124	a b c d	144	a b c d	164	a b c d	184	a b c d
105	a b c d	125	a b c d	145	a b c d	165	a b c d	185	a b c d
106	a b c d	126	a b c d	146	a b c d	166	a b c d	186	a b c d
107	a b c d	127	a b c d	147	a b c d	167	a b c d	187	a b c d
108	a b c d	128	a b c d	148	a b c d	168	a b c d	188	a b c d
109	a b c d	129	a b c d	149	a b c d	169	a b c d	189	a b c d
110	a b c d	130	a b c d	150	a b c d	170	a b c d	190	a b c d
111	a b c d	131	a b c d	151	a b c d	171	a b c d	191	a b c d
112	a b c d	132	a b c d	152	a b c d	172	a b c d	192	a b c d
113	a b c d	133	a b c d	153	a b c d	173	a b c d	193	a b c d
114	a b c d	134	a b c d	154	a b c d	174	a b c d	194	a b c d
115	a b c d	135	a b c d	155	a b c d	175	a b c d	195	a b c d
116	a b c d	136	a b c d	156	a b c d	176	a b c d	196	a b c d
117	a b c d	137	a b c d	157	a b c d	177	a b c d	197	a b c d
118	a b c d	138	a b c d	158	a b c d	178	a b c d	198	a b c d
119	a b c d	139	a b c d	159	a b c d	179	a b c d	199	a b c d
120	a b c d	140	a b c d	160	a b c d	180	a b c d	200	a b c d

Answer Sheet

TOEIC Actual Test

응시일자 :

성명	한글	
	한자	
	영문	

Listening Comprehension

No.	ANSWER				No.	ANSWER				No.	ANSWER				No.	ANSWER				No.	ANSWER			
	A	B	C	D		A	B	C	D		A	B	C	D		A	B	C	D		A	B	C	D
1	ⓐ	ⓑ	ⓒ	ⓓ	21	ⓐ	ⓑ	ⓒ	ⓓ	41	ⓐ	ⓑ	ⓒ	ⓓ	61	ⓐ	ⓑ	ⓒ	ⓓ	81	ⓐ	ⓑ	ⓒ	ⓓ
2	ⓐ	ⓑ	ⓒ	ⓓ	22	ⓐ	ⓑ	ⓒ	ⓓ	42	ⓐ	ⓑ	ⓒ	ⓓ	62	ⓐ	ⓑ	ⓒ	ⓓ	82	ⓐ	ⓑ	ⓒ	ⓓ
3	ⓐ	ⓑ	ⓒ	ⓓ	23	ⓐ	ⓑ	ⓒ	ⓓ	43	ⓐ	ⓑ	ⓒ	ⓓ	63	ⓐ	ⓑ	ⓒ	ⓓ	83	ⓐ	ⓑ	ⓒ	ⓓ
4	ⓐ	ⓑ	ⓒ	ⓓ	24	ⓐ	ⓑ	ⓒ	ⓓ	44	ⓐ	ⓑ	ⓒ	ⓓ	64	ⓐ	ⓑ	ⓒ	ⓓ	84	ⓐ	ⓑ	ⓒ	ⓓ
5	ⓐ	ⓑ	ⓒ	ⓓ	25	ⓐ	ⓑ	ⓒ	ⓓ	45	ⓐ	ⓑ	ⓒ	ⓓ	65	ⓐ	ⓑ	ⓒ	ⓓ	85	ⓐ	ⓑ	ⓒ	ⓓ
6	ⓐ	ⓑ	ⓒ	ⓓ	26	ⓐ	ⓑ	ⓒ	ⓓ	46	ⓐ	ⓑ	ⓒ	ⓓ	66	ⓐ	ⓑ	ⓒ	ⓓ	86	ⓐ	ⓑ	ⓒ	ⓓ
7	ⓐ	ⓑ	ⓒ	ⓓ	27	ⓐ	ⓑ	ⓒ	ⓓ	47	ⓐ	ⓑ	ⓒ	ⓓ	67	ⓐ	ⓑ	ⓒ	ⓓ	87	ⓐ	ⓑ	ⓒ	ⓓ
8	ⓐ	ⓑ	ⓒ	ⓓ	28	ⓐ	ⓑ	ⓒ	ⓓ	48	ⓐ	ⓑ	ⓒ	ⓓ	68	ⓐ	ⓑ	ⓒ	ⓓ	88	ⓐ	ⓑ	ⓒ	ⓓ
9	ⓐ	ⓑ	ⓒ	ⓓ	29	ⓐ	ⓑ	ⓒ	ⓓ	49	ⓐ	ⓑ	ⓒ	ⓓ	69	ⓐ	ⓑ	ⓒ	ⓓ	89	ⓐ	ⓑ	ⓒ	ⓓ
10	ⓐ	ⓑ	ⓒ	ⓓ	30	ⓐ	ⓑ	ⓒ	ⓓ	50	ⓐ	ⓑ	ⓒ	ⓓ	70	ⓐ	ⓑ	ⓒ	ⓓ	90	ⓐ	ⓑ	ⓒ	ⓓ
11	ⓐ	ⓑ	ⓒ	ⓓ	31	ⓐ	ⓑ	ⓒ	ⓓ	51	ⓐ	ⓑ	ⓒ	ⓓ	71	ⓐ	ⓑ	ⓒ	ⓓ	91	ⓐ	ⓑ	ⓒ	ⓓ
12	ⓐ	ⓑ	ⓒ	ⓓ	32	ⓐ	ⓑ	ⓒ	ⓓ	52	ⓐ	ⓑ	ⓒ	ⓓ	72	ⓐ	ⓑ	ⓒ	ⓓ	92	ⓐ	ⓑ	ⓒ	ⓓ
13	ⓐ	ⓑ	ⓒ	ⓓ	33	ⓐ	ⓑ	ⓒ	ⓓ	53	ⓐ	ⓑ	ⓒ	ⓓ	73	ⓐ	ⓑ	ⓒ	ⓓ	93	ⓐ	ⓑ	ⓒ	ⓓ
14	ⓐ	ⓑ	ⓒ	ⓓ	34	ⓐ	ⓑ	ⓒ	ⓓ	54	ⓐ	ⓑ	ⓒ	ⓓ	74	ⓐ	ⓑ	ⓒ	ⓓ	94	ⓐ	ⓑ	ⓒ	ⓓ
15	ⓐ	ⓑ	ⓒ	ⓓ	35	ⓐ	ⓑ	ⓒ	ⓓ	55	ⓐ	ⓑ	ⓒ	ⓓ	75	ⓐ	ⓑ	ⓒ	ⓓ	95	ⓐ	ⓑ	ⓒ	ⓓ
16	ⓐ	ⓑ	ⓒ	ⓓ	36	ⓐ	ⓑ	ⓒ	ⓓ	56	ⓐ	ⓑ	ⓒ	ⓓ	76	ⓐ	ⓑ	ⓒ	ⓓ	96	ⓐ	ⓑ	ⓒ	ⓓ
17	ⓐ	ⓑ	ⓒ	ⓓ	37	ⓐ	ⓑ	ⓒ	ⓓ	57	ⓐ	ⓑ	ⓒ	ⓓ	77	ⓐ	ⓑ	ⓒ	ⓓ	97	ⓐ	ⓑ	ⓒ	ⓓ
18	ⓐ	ⓑ	ⓒ	ⓓ	38	ⓐ	ⓑ	ⓒ	ⓓ	58	ⓐ	ⓑ	ⓒ	ⓓ	78	ⓐ	ⓑ	ⓒ	ⓓ	98	ⓐ	ⓑ	ⓒ	ⓓ
19	ⓐ	ⓑ	ⓒ	ⓓ	39	ⓐ	ⓑ	ⓒ	ⓓ	59	ⓐ	ⓑ	ⓒ	ⓓ	79	ⓐ	ⓑ	ⓒ	ⓓ	99	ⓐ	ⓑ	ⓒ	ⓓ
20	ⓐ	ⓑ	ⓒ	ⓓ	40	ⓐ	ⓑ	ⓒ	ⓓ	60	ⓐ	ⓑ	ⓒ	ⓓ	80	ⓐ	ⓑ	ⓒ	ⓓ	100	ⓐ	ⓑ	ⓒ	ⓓ

Reading Comprehension

No.	ANSWER				No.	ANSWER				No.	ANSWER				No.	ANSWER				No.	ANSWER			
	A	B	C	D		A	B	C	D		A	B	C	D		A	B	C	D		A	B	C	D
101	ⓐ	ⓑ	ⓒ	ⓓ	121	ⓐ	ⓑ	ⓒ	ⓓ	141	ⓐ	ⓑ	ⓒ	ⓓ	161	ⓐ	ⓑ	ⓒ	ⓓ	181	ⓐ	ⓑ	ⓒ	ⓓ
102	ⓐ	ⓑ	ⓒ	ⓓ	122	ⓐ	ⓑ	ⓒ	ⓓ	142	ⓐ	ⓑ	ⓒ	ⓓ	162	ⓐ	ⓑ	ⓒ	ⓓ	182	ⓐ	ⓑ	ⓒ	ⓓ
103	ⓐ	ⓑ	ⓒ	ⓓ	123	ⓐ	ⓑ	ⓒ	ⓓ	143	ⓐ	ⓑ	ⓒ	ⓓ	163	ⓐ	ⓑ	ⓒ	ⓓ	183	ⓐ	ⓑ	ⓒ	ⓓ
104	ⓐ	ⓑ	ⓒ	ⓓ	124	ⓐ	ⓑ	ⓒ	ⓓ	144	ⓐ	ⓑ	ⓒ	ⓓ	164	ⓐ	ⓑ	ⓒ	ⓓ	184	ⓐ	ⓑ	ⓒ	ⓓ
105	ⓐ	ⓑ	ⓒ	ⓓ	125	ⓐ	ⓑ	ⓒ	ⓓ	145	ⓐ	ⓑ	ⓒ	ⓓ	165	ⓐ	ⓑ	ⓒ	ⓓ	185	ⓐ	ⓑ	ⓒ	ⓓ
106	ⓐ	ⓑ	ⓒ	ⓓ	126	ⓐ	ⓑ	ⓒ	ⓓ	146	ⓐ	ⓑ	ⓒ	ⓓ	166	ⓐ	ⓑ	ⓒ	ⓓ	186	ⓐ	ⓑ	ⓒ	ⓓ
107	ⓐ	ⓑ	ⓒ	ⓓ	127	ⓐ	ⓑ	ⓒ	ⓓ	147	ⓐ	ⓑ	ⓒ	ⓓ	167	ⓐ	ⓑ	ⓒ	ⓓ	187	ⓐ	ⓑ	ⓒ	ⓓ
108	ⓐ	ⓑ	ⓒ	ⓓ	128	ⓐ	ⓑ	ⓒ	ⓓ	148	ⓐ	ⓑ	ⓒ	ⓓ	168	ⓐ	ⓑ	ⓒ	ⓓ	188	ⓐ	ⓑ	ⓒ	ⓓ
109	ⓐ	ⓑ	ⓒ	ⓓ	129	ⓐ	ⓑ	ⓒ	ⓓ	149	ⓐ	ⓑ	ⓒ	ⓓ	169	ⓐ	ⓑ	ⓒ	ⓓ	189	ⓐ	ⓑ	ⓒ	ⓓ
110	ⓐ	ⓑ	ⓒ	ⓓ	130	ⓐ	ⓑ	ⓒ	ⓓ	150	ⓐ	ⓑ	ⓒ	ⓓ	170	ⓐ	ⓑ	ⓒ	ⓓ	190	ⓐ	ⓑ	ⓒ	ⓓ
111	ⓐ	ⓑ	ⓒ	ⓓ	131	ⓐ	ⓑ	ⓒ	ⓓ	151	ⓐ	ⓑ	ⓒ	ⓓ	171	ⓐ	ⓑ	ⓒ	ⓓ	191	ⓐ	ⓑ	ⓒ	ⓓ
112	ⓐ	ⓑ	ⓒ	ⓓ	132	ⓐ	ⓑ	ⓒ	ⓓ	152	ⓐ	ⓑ	ⓒ	ⓓ	172	ⓐ	ⓑ	ⓒ	ⓓ	192	ⓐ	ⓑ	ⓒ	ⓓ
113	ⓐ	ⓑ	ⓒ	ⓓ	133	ⓐ	ⓑ	ⓒ	ⓓ	153	ⓐ	ⓑ	ⓒ	ⓓ	173	ⓐ	ⓑ	ⓒ	ⓓ	193	ⓐ	ⓑ	ⓒ	ⓓ
114	ⓐ	ⓑ	ⓒ	ⓓ	134	ⓐ	ⓑ	ⓒ	ⓓ	154	ⓐ	ⓑ	ⓒ	ⓓ	174	ⓐ	ⓑ	ⓒ	ⓓ	194	ⓐ	ⓑ	ⓒ	ⓓ
115	ⓐ	ⓑ	ⓒ	ⓓ	135	ⓐ	ⓑ	ⓒ	ⓓ	155	ⓐ	ⓑ	ⓒ	ⓓ	175	ⓐ	ⓑ	ⓒ	ⓓ	195	ⓐ	ⓑ	ⓒ	ⓓ
116	ⓐ	ⓑ	ⓒ	ⓓ	136	ⓐ	ⓑ	ⓒ	ⓓ	156	ⓐ	ⓑ	ⓒ	ⓓ	176	ⓐ	ⓑ	ⓒ	ⓓ	196	ⓐ	ⓑ	ⓒ	ⓓ
117	ⓐ	ⓑ	ⓒ	ⓓ	137	ⓐ	ⓑ	ⓒ	ⓓ	157	ⓐ	ⓑ	ⓒ	ⓓ	177	ⓐ	ⓑ	ⓒ	ⓓ	197	ⓐ	ⓑ	ⓒ	ⓓ
118	ⓐ	ⓑ	ⓒ	ⓓ	138	ⓐ	ⓑ	ⓒ	ⓓ	158	ⓐ	ⓑ	ⓒ	ⓓ	178	ⓐ	ⓑ	ⓒ	ⓓ	198	ⓐ	ⓑ	ⓒ	ⓓ
119	ⓐ	ⓑ	ⓒ	ⓓ	139	ⓐ	ⓑ	ⓒ	ⓓ	159	ⓐ	ⓑ	ⓒ	ⓓ	179	ⓐ	ⓑ	ⓒ	ⓓ	199	ⓐ	ⓑ	ⓒ	ⓓ
120	ⓐ	ⓑ	ⓒ	ⓓ	140	ⓐ	ⓑ	ⓒ	ⓓ	160	ⓐ	ⓑ	ⓒ	ⓓ	180	ⓐ	ⓑ	ⓒ	ⓓ	200	ⓐ	ⓑ	ⓒ	ⓓ

Answer Sheet

응시일자 :

TOEIC Actual Test

성명 | 한글
한자
영문

Listening Comprehension

No.	ANSWER	No.	ANSWER	No.	ANSWER	No.	ANSWER	No.	ANSWER
	A B C D		A B C D		A B C D		A B C D		A B C D
1		21		41		61		81	
2		22		42		62		82	
3		23		43		63		83	
4		24		44		64		84	
5		25		45		65		85	
6		26		46		66		86	
7		27		47		67		87	
8		28		48		68		88	
9		29		49		69		89	
10		30		50		70		90	
11		31		51		71		91	
12		32		52		72		92	
13		33		53		73		93	
14		34		54		74		94	
15		35		55		75		95	
16		36		56		76		96	
17		37		57		77		97	
18		38		58		78		98	
19		39		59		79		99	
20		40		60		80		100	

Reading Comprehension

No.	ANSWER	No.	ANSWER	No.	ANSWER	No.	ANSWER	No.	ANSWER
	A B C D		A B C D		A B C D		A B C D		A B C D
101		121		141		161		181	
102		122		142		162		182	
103		123		143		163		183	
104		124		144		164		184	
105		125		145		165		185	
106		126		146		166		186	
107		127		147		167		187	
108		128		148		168		188	
109		129		149		169		189	
110		130		150		170		190	
111		131		151		171		191	
112		132		152		172		192	
113		133		153		173		193	
114		134		154		174		194	
115		135		155		175		195	
116		136		156		176		196	
117		137		157		177		197	
118		138		158		178		198	
119		139		159		179		199	
120		140		160		180		200	

TOEIC Actual Test

성명 | 한글 / 한자 / 영문

응시일자 :

Listening Comprehension

No.	ANSWER (A B C D)	No.	ANSWER (A B C D)	No.	ANSWER (A B C D)	No.	ANSWER (A B C D)	No.	ANSWER (A B C D)
1	Ⓐ Ⓑ Ⓒ Ⓓ	21	Ⓐ Ⓑ Ⓒ Ⓓ	41	Ⓐ Ⓑ Ⓒ Ⓓ	61	Ⓐ Ⓑ Ⓒ Ⓓ	81	Ⓐ Ⓑ Ⓒ Ⓓ
2	Ⓐ Ⓑ Ⓒ Ⓓ	22	Ⓐ Ⓑ Ⓒ Ⓓ	42	Ⓐ Ⓑ Ⓒ Ⓓ	62	Ⓐ Ⓑ Ⓒ Ⓓ	82	Ⓐ Ⓑ Ⓒ Ⓓ
3	Ⓐ Ⓑ Ⓒ Ⓓ	23	Ⓐ Ⓑ Ⓒ Ⓓ	43	Ⓐ Ⓑ Ⓒ Ⓓ	63	Ⓐ Ⓑ Ⓒ Ⓓ	83	Ⓐ Ⓑ Ⓒ Ⓓ
4	Ⓐ Ⓑ Ⓒ Ⓓ	24	Ⓐ Ⓑ Ⓒ Ⓓ	44	Ⓐ Ⓑ Ⓒ Ⓓ	64	Ⓐ Ⓑ Ⓒ Ⓓ	84	Ⓐ Ⓑ Ⓒ Ⓓ
5	Ⓐ Ⓑ Ⓒ Ⓓ	25	Ⓐ Ⓑ Ⓒ Ⓓ	45	Ⓐ Ⓑ Ⓒ Ⓓ	65	Ⓐ Ⓑ Ⓒ Ⓓ	85	Ⓐ Ⓑ Ⓒ Ⓓ
6	Ⓐ Ⓑ Ⓒ Ⓓ	26	Ⓐ Ⓑ Ⓒ Ⓓ	46	Ⓐ Ⓑ Ⓒ Ⓓ	66	Ⓐ Ⓑ Ⓒ Ⓓ	86	Ⓐ Ⓑ Ⓒ Ⓓ
7	Ⓐ Ⓑ Ⓒ Ⓓ	27	Ⓐ Ⓑ Ⓒ Ⓓ	47	Ⓐ Ⓑ Ⓒ Ⓓ	67	Ⓐ Ⓑ Ⓒ Ⓓ	87	Ⓐ Ⓑ Ⓒ Ⓓ
8	Ⓐ Ⓑ Ⓒ Ⓓ	28	Ⓐ Ⓑ Ⓒ Ⓓ	48	Ⓐ Ⓑ Ⓒ Ⓓ	68	Ⓐ Ⓑ Ⓒ Ⓓ	88	Ⓐ Ⓑ Ⓒ Ⓓ
9	Ⓐ Ⓑ Ⓒ Ⓓ	29	Ⓐ Ⓑ Ⓒ Ⓓ	49	Ⓐ Ⓑ Ⓒ Ⓓ	69	Ⓐ Ⓑ Ⓒ Ⓓ	89	Ⓐ Ⓑ Ⓒ Ⓓ
10	Ⓐ Ⓑ Ⓒ Ⓓ	30	Ⓐ Ⓑ Ⓒ Ⓓ	50	Ⓐ Ⓑ Ⓒ Ⓓ	70	Ⓐ Ⓑ Ⓒ Ⓓ	90	Ⓐ Ⓑ Ⓒ Ⓓ
11	Ⓐ Ⓑ Ⓒ Ⓓ	31	Ⓐ Ⓑ Ⓒ Ⓓ	51	Ⓐ Ⓑ Ⓒ Ⓓ	71	Ⓐ Ⓑ Ⓒ Ⓓ	91	Ⓐ Ⓑ Ⓒ Ⓓ
12	Ⓐ Ⓑ Ⓒ Ⓓ	32	Ⓐ Ⓑ Ⓒ Ⓓ	52	Ⓐ Ⓑ Ⓒ Ⓓ	72	Ⓐ Ⓑ Ⓒ Ⓓ	92	Ⓐ Ⓑ Ⓒ Ⓓ
13	Ⓐ Ⓑ Ⓒ Ⓓ	33	Ⓐ Ⓑ Ⓒ Ⓓ	53	Ⓐ Ⓑ Ⓒ Ⓓ	73	Ⓐ Ⓑ Ⓒ Ⓓ	93	Ⓐ Ⓑ Ⓒ Ⓓ
14	Ⓐ Ⓑ Ⓒ Ⓓ	34	Ⓐ Ⓑ Ⓒ Ⓓ	54	Ⓐ Ⓑ Ⓒ Ⓓ	74	Ⓐ Ⓑ Ⓒ Ⓓ	94	Ⓐ Ⓑ Ⓒ Ⓓ
15	Ⓐ Ⓑ Ⓒ Ⓓ	35	Ⓐ Ⓑ Ⓒ Ⓓ	55	Ⓐ Ⓑ Ⓒ Ⓓ	75	Ⓐ Ⓑ Ⓒ Ⓓ	95	Ⓐ Ⓑ Ⓒ Ⓓ
16	Ⓐ Ⓑ Ⓒ Ⓓ	36	Ⓐ Ⓑ Ⓒ Ⓓ	56	Ⓐ Ⓑ Ⓒ Ⓓ	76	Ⓐ Ⓑ Ⓒ Ⓓ	96	Ⓐ Ⓑ Ⓒ Ⓓ
17	Ⓐ Ⓑ Ⓒ Ⓓ	37	Ⓐ Ⓑ Ⓒ Ⓓ	57	Ⓐ Ⓑ Ⓒ Ⓓ	77	Ⓐ Ⓑ Ⓒ Ⓓ	97	Ⓐ Ⓑ Ⓒ Ⓓ
18	Ⓐ Ⓑ Ⓒ Ⓓ	38	Ⓐ Ⓑ Ⓒ Ⓓ	58	Ⓐ Ⓑ Ⓒ Ⓓ	78	Ⓐ Ⓑ Ⓒ Ⓓ	98	Ⓐ Ⓑ Ⓒ Ⓓ
19	Ⓐ Ⓑ Ⓒ Ⓓ	39	Ⓐ Ⓑ Ⓒ Ⓓ	59	Ⓐ Ⓑ Ⓒ Ⓓ	79	Ⓐ Ⓑ Ⓒ Ⓓ	99	Ⓐ Ⓑ Ⓒ Ⓓ
20	Ⓐ Ⓑ Ⓒ Ⓓ	40	Ⓐ Ⓑ Ⓒ Ⓓ	60	Ⓐ Ⓑ Ⓒ Ⓓ	80	Ⓐ Ⓑ Ⓒ Ⓓ	100	Ⓐ Ⓑ Ⓒ Ⓓ

Reading Comprehension

No.	ANSWER (A B C D)	No.	ANSWER (A B C D)	No.	ANSWER (A B C D)	No.	ANSWER (A B C D)	No.	ANSWER (A B C D)
101	Ⓐ Ⓑ Ⓒ Ⓓ	121	Ⓐ Ⓑ Ⓒ Ⓓ	141	Ⓐ Ⓑ Ⓒ Ⓓ	161	Ⓐ Ⓑ Ⓒ Ⓓ	181	Ⓐ Ⓑ Ⓒ Ⓓ
102	Ⓐ Ⓑ Ⓒ Ⓓ	122	Ⓐ Ⓑ Ⓒ Ⓓ	142	Ⓐ Ⓑ Ⓒ Ⓓ	162	Ⓐ Ⓑ Ⓒ Ⓓ	182	Ⓐ Ⓑ Ⓒ Ⓓ
103	Ⓐ Ⓑ Ⓒ Ⓓ	123	Ⓐ Ⓑ Ⓒ Ⓓ	143	Ⓐ Ⓑ Ⓒ Ⓓ	163	Ⓐ Ⓑ Ⓒ Ⓓ	183	Ⓐ Ⓑ Ⓒ Ⓓ
104	Ⓐ Ⓑ Ⓒ Ⓓ	124	Ⓐ Ⓑ Ⓒ Ⓓ	144	Ⓐ Ⓑ Ⓒ Ⓓ	164	Ⓐ Ⓑ Ⓒ Ⓓ	184	Ⓐ Ⓑ Ⓒ Ⓓ
105	Ⓐ Ⓑ Ⓒ Ⓓ	125	Ⓐ Ⓑ Ⓒ Ⓓ	145	Ⓐ Ⓑ Ⓒ Ⓓ	165	Ⓐ Ⓑ Ⓒ Ⓓ	185	Ⓐ Ⓑ Ⓒ Ⓓ
106	Ⓐ Ⓑ Ⓒ Ⓓ	126	Ⓐ Ⓑ Ⓒ Ⓓ	146	Ⓐ Ⓑ Ⓒ Ⓓ	166	Ⓐ Ⓑ Ⓒ Ⓓ	186	Ⓐ Ⓑ Ⓒ Ⓓ
107	Ⓐ Ⓑ Ⓒ Ⓓ	127	Ⓐ Ⓑ Ⓒ Ⓓ	147	Ⓐ Ⓑ Ⓒ Ⓓ	167	Ⓐ Ⓑ Ⓒ Ⓓ	187	Ⓐ Ⓑ Ⓒ Ⓓ
108	Ⓐ Ⓑ Ⓒ Ⓓ	128	Ⓐ Ⓑ Ⓒ Ⓓ	148	Ⓐ Ⓑ Ⓒ Ⓓ	168	Ⓐ Ⓑ Ⓒ Ⓓ	188	Ⓐ Ⓑ Ⓒ Ⓓ
109	Ⓐ Ⓑ Ⓒ Ⓓ	129	Ⓐ Ⓑ Ⓒ Ⓓ	149	Ⓐ Ⓑ Ⓒ Ⓓ	169	Ⓐ Ⓑ Ⓒ Ⓓ	189	Ⓐ Ⓑ Ⓒ Ⓓ
110	Ⓐ Ⓑ Ⓒ Ⓓ	130	Ⓐ Ⓑ Ⓒ Ⓓ	150	Ⓐ Ⓑ Ⓒ Ⓓ	170	Ⓐ Ⓑ Ⓒ Ⓓ	190	Ⓐ Ⓑ Ⓒ Ⓓ
111	Ⓐ Ⓑ Ⓒ Ⓓ	131	Ⓐ Ⓑ Ⓒ Ⓓ	151	Ⓐ Ⓑ Ⓒ Ⓓ	171	Ⓐ Ⓑ Ⓒ Ⓓ	191	Ⓐ Ⓑ Ⓒ Ⓓ
112	Ⓐ Ⓑ Ⓒ Ⓓ	132	Ⓐ Ⓑ Ⓒ Ⓓ	152	Ⓐ Ⓑ Ⓒ Ⓓ	172	Ⓐ Ⓑ Ⓒ Ⓓ	192	Ⓐ Ⓑ Ⓒ Ⓓ
113	Ⓐ Ⓑ Ⓒ Ⓓ	133	Ⓐ Ⓑ Ⓒ Ⓓ	153	Ⓐ Ⓑ Ⓒ Ⓓ	173	Ⓐ Ⓑ Ⓒ Ⓓ	193	Ⓐ Ⓑ Ⓒ Ⓓ
114	Ⓐ Ⓑ Ⓒ Ⓓ	134	Ⓐ Ⓑ Ⓒ Ⓓ	154	Ⓐ Ⓑ Ⓒ Ⓓ	174	Ⓐ Ⓑ Ⓒ Ⓓ	194	Ⓐ Ⓑ Ⓒ Ⓓ
115	Ⓐ Ⓑ Ⓒ Ⓓ	135	Ⓐ Ⓑ Ⓒ Ⓓ	155	Ⓐ Ⓑ Ⓒ Ⓓ	175	Ⓐ Ⓑ Ⓒ Ⓓ	195	Ⓐ Ⓑ Ⓒ Ⓓ
116	Ⓐ Ⓑ Ⓒ Ⓓ	136	Ⓐ Ⓑ Ⓒ Ⓓ	156	Ⓐ Ⓑ Ⓒ Ⓓ	176	Ⓐ Ⓑ Ⓒ Ⓓ	196	Ⓐ Ⓑ Ⓒ Ⓓ
117	Ⓐ Ⓑ Ⓒ Ⓓ	137	Ⓐ Ⓑ Ⓒ Ⓓ	157	Ⓐ Ⓑ Ⓒ Ⓓ	177	Ⓐ Ⓑ Ⓒ Ⓓ	197	Ⓐ Ⓑ Ⓒ Ⓓ
118	Ⓐ Ⓑ Ⓒ Ⓓ	138	Ⓐ Ⓑ Ⓒ Ⓓ	158	Ⓐ Ⓑ Ⓒ Ⓓ	178	Ⓐ Ⓑ Ⓒ Ⓓ	198	Ⓐ Ⓑ Ⓒ Ⓓ
119	Ⓐ Ⓑ Ⓒ Ⓓ	139	Ⓐ Ⓑ Ⓒ Ⓓ	159	Ⓐ Ⓑ Ⓒ Ⓓ	179	Ⓐ Ⓑ Ⓒ Ⓓ	199	Ⓐ Ⓑ Ⓒ Ⓓ
120	Ⓐ Ⓑ Ⓒ Ⓓ	140	Ⓐ Ⓑ Ⓒ Ⓓ	160	Ⓐ Ⓑ Ⓒ Ⓓ	180	Ⓐ Ⓑ Ⓒ Ⓓ	200	Ⓐ Ⓑ Ⓒ Ⓓ